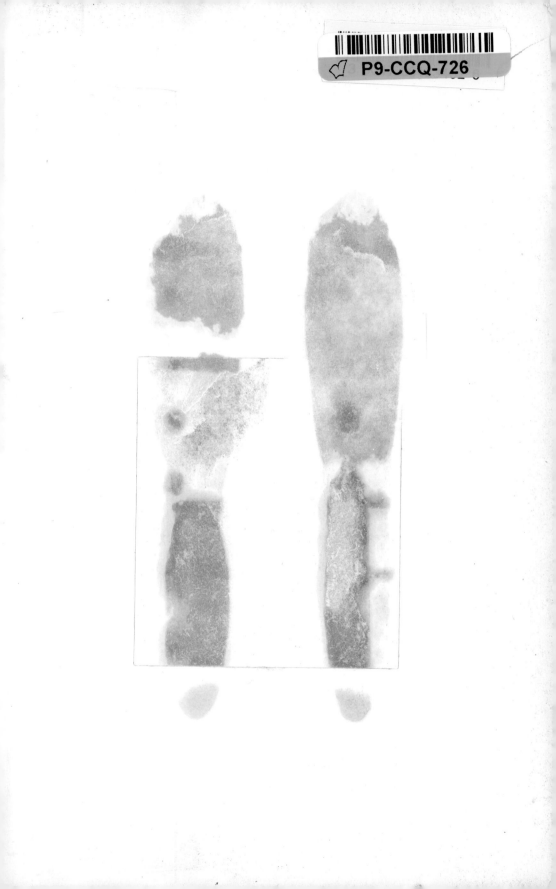

Forbidden Diary

American Women's Diary Series 2

PENELOPE FRANKLIN, *General Editor*

NATALIE CROUTER

Forbidden Diary

A Record of Wartime Internment, 1941–1945

Edited with an introduction by LYNN Z. BLOOM

With drawings by DAPHNE BIRD

Burt Franklin & Co.

Published by Burt Franklin & Company
235 East Forty-fourth Street
New York, New York 10017

Library of Congress Cataloging in Publication Data

Crouter, Natalie, 1898–
Forbidden diary.

(American women's diary series; 2)
1. World War, 1939–1945—Prisoners and prisons,
Japanese. 2. World War, 1939–1945—Personal
narratives, American. 3. Crouter, Natalie,
1898–   4. Prisoners of war—United States—
Biography. 5. Prisoners of war—Philippine
Islands—Baguio—Biography. 6. Baguio,
Philippines—Biography. I. Bloom, Lynn Z.,
1934–   II. Title. III. Series.
D805.J3C76   940.54'72'5209599   79-27116
ISBN 0-89102-105-1

Designed by Bernard Schleifer

Manufactured in the United States of America

About the American Women's Diary Series

The American Women's Diary Series is based on a simple, yet amazingly neglected, approach to the study of history—through the lives of individuals as recorded by themselves in the diary or journal.

Although professional historians regularly make use of diaries in their researches—and find in them one of their most useful sources of information about life in the past—relatively few of these journals have found their way into print. The majority of diaries that *have* been published are those of men, as are most of those preserved in libraries and archives. And yet, throughout this country's history women have kept diaries, and thousands of these records have been preserved.

The diary as a historical record has certain advantages over other first-person accounts. It is likely to contain details lost to the memory of the autobiographer. It is honest—sometimes in spite of itself—since it generally is not intended for an audience. And it communicates a sense of immediacy, of the process of everyday life, which is usually lost in a retrospective account.

We feel that the American Women's Diary Series fills a great need, both for feminists interested in women's past place in society and for students of American history searching for more than its standard version. We feel, too, the importance of making these works available to all women. For it is our belief that almost every woman can experience in their pages the shock (or the thrill) of recognition—the recognition that she has a feeling, an insight, or an experience in common with a woman who lived fifty or two hundred years ago.

Finally, we wish to emphasize that we have chosen to focus not on famous women, whose stories have been obscured by telling and retelling, but on the unknown women whose voices are yet fresh, and whose lives, upon examination, prove to be far from ordinary.

PENELOPE FRANKLIN
General Editor

Praise for The
American Women's Diary Series

A series of books everyone should know about.
—**Henry Kisor,** *Chicago Sun-Times*

The historical value of a series such as this is significant ... presents the unsung narratives of some remarkable women.
—**The** *Christian Science Monitor*

Franklin believes that an important part of history is 'knowing what one person felt at a certain time'.... As general editor she works for a 'unified editorial approach', avoiding the genteel deletions relatives are likely to make.... Reveals that women were not mute nonentities in American history.
—**Richard Lingeman,** *The New York Times Book Review*

A significant and exciting addition to the field of human studies.
—**Eve Merriam, author,** *Growing up Female in America*

A new and commendable approach to history.
—**Birmingham (Ala.)** *News*

The Series is not only unearthing forgotten manuscripts, it is also unearthing the hidden thoughts and feelings of women, frequently uttered nowhere but in these private 'letters' to the self.
—**Laurie Stone, book reviewer,** *The Village Voice*

It is a wonderful series and I will spread news of it.
—**Tillie Olsen**

The Series is a way of personalizing history, making it less abstract. These are lives that students can identify with and that give a true picture of everyday life.... These books will be eagerly awaited and widely used.
—**Leonore Hoffman,** *Modern Language Association*

A very impressive list.
—**Nancy F. Cott, author,** *The Bonds of Womanhood*

A meaningful contribution to the history of women.
—*Reprint Bulletin*

I congratulate you on this very inspiring undertaking.
—**Charlotte Painter, co-author,** *Revelations: Diaries of Women*

Contents

To Jerry, June, and Fred, Nellie McKim, Rokuro Tomibe, and all 500 internees.
And to Nida Bacani, an old family friend.

N.C.C.

To Mildred Zimmerman.
And to Dorothy Cline, cryptic chronicler of American Politics.

L.Z.B.

Acknowledgments

THROUGHOUT THE EDITING of this *Diary* and the writing of the introductory material, I have been indebted to Natalie Crouter and to June and Richard Wortman for friendship, information, hospitality, and continual cooperation. They have supplied most of the information for the biographical portrait of Natalie, and the numerous photographs. Frederick E. Crouter has thoughtfully supplied useful information. Daphne Bird has graciously permitted the reproduction of her watercolor illustrations of life in Camp Holmes and in Bilibid prison.

Retired U.S. Foreign Service Officer James J. Halsema (*Jim* in the *Diary*) has generously shared his extensive knowledge of Philippine history, politics, culture, and mores, and of World War II and its aftermath, as well as his own experiences in internment. These corroborate and supplement Natalie's account, as does information from his rare collection of published and unpublished materials on these subjects. Halsema's contributions to this edition of the *Diary* have been invaluable; Alice Halsema's hospitality during our work sessions has been both pleasant and elegant. The Reverend Carl Eschbach of Dayton and the Reverend Joseph Smith and Winifred Smith of Cleveland, Georgia, have furnished additional perspectives on, and verification of, the events recorded in the *Diary*. Dr. Martha Ozawa of Washington University, Saint Louis, has commented on the Japanese point of view and provided definitions and correct transliterations for many of the Japanese words in the text. Major Gary Turner of the U.S. Military Academy at West Point has used his expertise and the resources of the military library at Fort Eustis, Virginia, to interpret various points of military strategy.

I am grateful to the English departments of the College of William and Mary and the University of New Mexico for the services of the following people: Gerald B. Berdan for perceptive and thorough research assistance; Deborah Kiser for skillful editorial help; Gloria Hall, Nancy Staley, Kimberley S. Cross, and Lynn Mowry for extensive manuscript typing.

Floyd Stewart and Tom Franklin have contributed good advice, legal and practical. To Penelope Franklin I am particularly grateful for her vision of this American Women's Diary Series and for her editorial expertise in bringing it to fruition. My children, Bard and Laird, have enriched their lives and mine through vicarious sharing of these events and have enhanced my understanding of their implications as their ages have paralleled those of the Crouter children in the *Diary*. My husband, Martin Bloom, merits again and always my profound appreciation for his continuing sustenance—in my endeavors to re-create Natalie's life, as in the living of our lives together.

Introduction: Diarists, This Diarist, and Her Diary

CONFINED PERSONS ARE often prolific diarists. This has been true for centuries, as shown by the abundance of memoirs and journals of prisoners, whether in the Tower of London, concentration camps, or hidden residences, as in the case of Anne Frank. Such persons may be physically confined or restricted to a limited existence, physical or psychological, for protracted periods—because of illness, imprisonment, geographic isolation, or emergency conditions. They may be in a threatening, unfamiliar, or uncongenial environment where they have little if any control or freedom to pursue their customary activities. Enforced routine or exceptional leisure may allow them an unusual amount of time for reflection.

Natalie Crouter kept her *Diary* throughout World War II during her internment as a civilian captive of the Japanese. She used her journal partly to gain perspective, partly to analyse the organizational and human strengths and weaknesses of her unaccustomed life. She also wrote to ventilate her hopes, fears, anger, and righteous indignation. Above all, recognizing that this confinement was perhaps the most significant phenomenon of her lifetime and her family's life together, she wrote to leave a record for her children and, ultimately, for generations after them.

The importance of Natalie Crouter's *Diary* to her survival can be compared to the experience of psychologist Bruno Bettelheim, who clandestinely recorded the behavior of his fellow inmates in two German concentration camps in 1938–39. He explains:

> This study was a mechanism developed by the author *ad hoc* in order to retain some intellectual interests and thus be better equipped to endure life in the camp. His observing and collecting data was a particular type of defense, individually developed . . . to protect him against a disintegration of his personality. . . . His main problem during the time he spent in camp . . . was *to safeguard his ego in such a way, that if he should regain liberty, he would be approximately the same person he was when deprived of liberty.*[1]

Such efforts are a valuable means of maintaining a necessary sense of self, of being in touch with external reality, of recognizing a continuity of life within and beyond confinement. As Natalie herself acknowledged, "In some ways I live in a world of my own with these notes, which are an outlet, saving wear and tear on other people. Perhaps everyone should keep notes for a healthy mind." To write such a diary in confinement—particularly when record keeping is strictly forbidden and punishable by death, as it was in her case—is to exhibit a strong sense of one's own worth and of the validity of one's observations, even under stress. And it demonstrates the form of courage that Ernest Hemingway is said to have defined as "grace under pressure."

Natalie Crouter's life has been marked by privilege and privation, shelter and exposure, fragility and strength. In some significant respects it has been highly conventional. She has upheld many of the cultural expectations for an American woman of her class and time in the roles of dutiful daughter, single young woman, wife, mother, widow. Yet Natalie has never been bound rigidly to those roles. She has felt free to champion politically radical causes (some with potential reprisals dangerous to herself); to befriend people of a variety of backgrounds; and to travel to Europe, Africa, and the Orient, often alone.

The family heritages of Natalie and her husband embody quintessential features of the American character. Natalie derived considerable moral fiber and strength of will from her traditional, highly ethical, sometimes eccentrically independent Bostonian ancestors. Her maternal family, the Scotts, proudly identified their descent from Peregrine White, born aboard the *Mayflower* off Cape Cod in November, 1620. Her father's side claimed as kin General John Stark of the American Revolution. Her paternal grandfather sought Utopia on the South Atlantic island of Tristan da Cunha, but he found there a grim environment with inhabitants unexceptional rather than exotic, and returned to Boston, disillusioned, a year later.

Natalie's father, Frederick J. Stark, was a self-made man, a successful realtor who married Bertha Scott in 1876. Of quick wit and serene temperament, Bertha was ever active; even her quiet moments were occupied with knitting or sewing. Natalie, like Bertha, became a "dynamo in her own style, equally energetic but less practical than her mother."[2]

The Stark family shared an enormous red brick two-family house (staffed by a cook, a housemaid, and a laundress) in the Boston suburb of Dorchester with Frederick's brother John, his wife, and their three daughters. Natalie's own sisters, Mary Ethel and Marguerite (*Ethel* and *Muggs* in the *Diary*), were, respectively, eighteen and ten years her senior. Another child, Frederick, had died in infancy shortly before Natalie's birth on October 30, 1898. Her mourning parents had hoped for a second son, and Natalie's father soon nicknamed the child *Pete*, although she had been christened *Natalie Corona* after the heroine of a popular novel. The nickname became hers for life.

Natalie was born prematurely, with rickets, and almost died at birth. After the initial struggle, however, her childhood was relatively uneventful until she was nine. That year she had been sent to summer camp, and returned to Boston pale and thin. Although Natalie was feverish and complained of fatigue, her mother insisted that they walk home from the streetcar to save cab fare, as usual. The walk became one of the longest of Natalie's life, as she stumbled repeatedly. She finally arrived home delirious and collapsed. She had contracted polio, complicated by meningitis, and was to be critically ill for weeks.

Natalie attributes her survival to her mother's indefatigable care during the years that followed. Twice a week for a year, then once a week for the next two and a half years, the diminutive Bertha Stark pulled her daughter by coaster wagon to the streetcar and then took her to an osteopath in Boston for physical therapy, avant-garde treatment at the time. Through exercises and continual self-discipline, Natalie gradually regained her muscular strength, until she was left with only weakness and a slight limp in her left leg.

Natalie's handicap, minor though it was in the long run, helped ally her with the weak and the dependent. Her wearing of a brace, albeit briefly, forced her to identify with a conspicuous minority. These allegiances persisted throughout her life and contributed to her political radicalism, her defense of the weak, and her openness toward members of minority groups.

An eager student who loved to read—in an era when it was unfashionable for women to know too much—Natalie attended the Dorchester public schools through high school. She went on to obtain the equivalent of a finishing-school education at the Deverell School and at the Burnham School in North-ampton, Massachusetts, and then attended the Katherine Gibbs Secretarial School.

Despite this training, Natalie, as befitted a proper young lady of genteel background, was expected not to earn her own living but to marry a suitable young man who could support her. For some time she was indifferent to the idea of marriage. Life was comfortable at home; Boston was full of the cultural and political stimulation on which she thrived. She soon put her secretarial skills to use in the defense of Sacco and Vanzetti, the first of the radical causes she was to work for throughout her life.

In 1925, Natalie left her volunteer job to accompany her father on one of his periodic trips around the world. At the halfway point, Manila, Mr. Stark became seriously ill, and they were forced to stop for a time. It became Natalie's responsibility to reschedule the remainder of their trip and to adjust their tickets.

Natalie at twenty-seven was characteristically outspoken and quite capable of coping with emergencies. But her petite size (she weighed scarcely ninety-eight pounds and was five feet tall) made her seem more helpless than she was, and Jerry Crouter, an American whom she had met in the lobby of the hotel where she and her father were staying, offered to assist her with travel arrangements. Although trained as a lawyer, Jerry disliked legal work. He had enlisted in the Army and was delighted when he was sent to the Philippines, which he loved immediately. He had lived there since his discharge in 1918.

Erroll Edgerton Crouter (who had dropped his real name, taken from *Little Lord Fauntleroy,* and used a nickname inspired by Jack London's *Jerry of the Islands*) was the son of prototypical Westerners. Born on April 11, 1893, he had been reared in Greeley, Colorado. His father, Charles, was the son of a Canadian Tory sympathizer who had gone West to escape family problems. Charles had worked as a cattle driver on a ranch before becoming a pharmacist. Known for his friendliness and his honesty (traits that were also outstanding in his son), Crouter always honored all his obligations, even when a partner once cheated their customers and fled. He married Mabel Maltby, who had arrived with her family by covered wagon some years earlier. Throughout her life, she remained a "practical jokester with one helluva temper."[3]

Jerry's friends remember him as gentle, easy-going (though not always even-tempered), with "open, Western-style friendliness," in contrast with Natalie's feistiness and New England reticence. While waiting in Manila for Mr. Stark to recuperate, the pair enjoyed lively discussions of books and politics. These they continued by letter after Natalie's journey was resumed.

Two years later, the execution of Sacco and Vanzetti marked the defeat of the cause to which Natalie had devoted herself. She was at loose ends. Her outspokenness had antagonized a number of possible suitors, even those who sympathized with her views. Yet it was time she got married, she believed, if she did not want to end up like her sister Ethel, an erstwhile belle whose temperament had soured with age and spinsterhood. There was the tantalization of Natalie's correspondence with Jerry—vigorous, flirtatiously casual, and uncommitted. It was, in part, uncertainty about his affection for her that led Natalie halfway around the world again, this time by herself.

Instead of going directly to the Philippines, she went to China, where she visited some friends in Tientsin. Jerry came to see her there, and this time he proposed. Natalie accepted at once, and the couple went on a whirlwind sightseeing tour of Peking, conducted, she emphasized, with the utmost propriety. Upon returning to Tientsin they were married and immediately sailed for the Philippines.

The Crouters established their first home in Vigan, a tropical Spanish town where Jerry had been sent by his employer, a Hawaiian sugar planters' association. Jerry and Natalie found Vigan entirely to their liking. Jerry spent the days recruiting Filipino laborers to work in the sugar fields of Hawaii and also transmitted the wages they earned to their families in the Philippines. Natalie settled easily into the sheltered life expected of women of her class, although the Crouters made many friends among the Filipinos and Chinese, instead of restricting their social life to the very small British-American colony as custom dictated, at least among business people. Their daughter, June, was born in 1929, and a son, Frederick Edgerton (Bedie), in 1931. Although she had the aid of an *amah* (nursemaid), Natalie spent more time with her children than did most of her peers. She also taught English on a voluntary basis to Filipino nurses, and spent hours in Red Cross and other community service. She was not overly concerned with fashion; Jerry, according to June, "picked out Mother's clothes. He had a sense of good style and she didn't."

During this time the Crouters established the pattern of open communication that characterized their entire marriage, as the *Diary* makes apparent. Both Jerry and Natalie enjoyed vigorous arguments on political or intellectual issues. Discussions that began with calm seriousness often escalated to vehemence, as Natalie staunchly defended her radical principles against the ideas of her liberal husband—until Jerry usually exploded with laughter and defused the situation.

Despite her adventurous mind and spirit, Natalie was physically frail, and often suffered from illness and various allergies. When she or the children were ill, Jerry nursed them. June remembers that her mother "had sharp bones; it was angular when she held you. But Dad was enveloping, reassuring, and very comfortable. He was a nurturing, warm man who enjoyed caring for all of us, Natalie included."

When the Depression came and the demand for Filipino laborers in Hawaii ceased, the Crouters moved to Baguio, the Philippines' mountain-ringed summer capital, nearly a mile high. Jerry obtained a lease for a Shell gas station—an occupation that later led to the mistaken Japanese assumption that he was a "rich oil man." While an employee managed the station, Jerry opened an insurance agency that eventually prospered.

Although the Crouters had at times to choose between eating well and buying Chinese jade (they bought the jade), they were never without household help. Natalie supervised Ismael and Nida Bacani, the cook and *amah* who figure so prominently in the *Diary*. As was typical of servants in the Orient, the Bacanis and their relatives not only did all the domestic work, including the laundry and gardening, but also helped prepare part of Natalie's contributions to the Red Cross—linens, clothing, and bandages. With their two daughters, Eppie and Felie, and five to ten other relatives, the Bacanis lived in a room adjoining the Crouters' garage. According to Philippine standards, they were well paid and very well fed. Although the children played together, the Crouter children, like the other American children in Baguio, attended the Episcopalian-run Brent School,[4] while the Bacani girls went to native schools.[5]

In general, the Filipino population of the islands felt grateful and friendly to the American residents. The establishment of a system of native schools, including the University of the Philippines, and the American policy of employing Filipinos as local labor instead of importing Chinese as did colonists in other Oriental countries, were two main causes of this, as were the improvements in health facilities, water systems, and roads effected since the United States had wrested the Islands from Spain in 1898. And, as Philippine political scholar David J. Steinberg explains,

> Central to Filipino values has been the sense of debt felt by each individual to the network of people who surround and help him. No Filipino dares to ignore this social obligation, called *utang na loob* (an eternal debt of gratitude), for fear of being liable to the accusation of *walang hiya* (shamelessness). This code of behavior regulating social contact, which the West has all too often dismissed disparagingly as "concern for face," actually has fulfilled a fundamental human need. . . . the Filipino norm acknowledges the reciprocity of all human relations.[6]

Economic conditions in the Philippines improved dramatically after 1934, when the United States went off the gold standard. The price of gold rose, and mining activity increased dramatically in the Baguio vicinity. Miners and their families inundated the area; Jerry sold them insurance and bought and sold gold stocks. With one windfall he purchased for his wife a diamond bracelet, which, along with jade objects and ivory carvings bought during this time, eventually served as insurance against the privations the Crouters endured in internment. (Buried as war broke out to protect them from discovery by the Japanese or looters, these possessions were later sold by the Bacanis, who used the money to buy food for their starving former employers.)

During the late 1930s, Natalie became involved in several Chinese-relief efforts. She raised large sums of money for Madame Sun Yat-sen's program to aid Chinese orphans, earning Madame Sun's friendship in the process. At this time the Crouters also met China journalist and interpreter Edgar Snow, who had left that country in ill health and was recuperating in Baguio—a favorite resort spot for travelers to and from the Orient. The Crouters, ever on the lookout for interesting people, befriended Snow and his wife Lois, and made them feel so welcome that they stayed for nearly a year while Snow wrote *Battle for Asia*.

Through Snow the Crouters met Rewi Alley, who had recently established Indusco (Chinese Industrial Cooperatives) as a means of economic relief for Chinese Communists who were victims of the recent civil war in their country. Many had been living as fugitives, hiding from the forces of both Chiang Kai-shek and the Japanese. Indusco aimed to make them self-sustaining by teaching them to manufacture necessary products (such as shoe-making machinery) that they then sold to other revolutionaries. Natalie directed her organizational skills toward raising money for Indusco; the Baguio fundraising parties became prestigious social events. Because of the success of these activities, she later came to fear Japanese reprisals during her internment, but these fortunately did not materialize.

Natalie had a busy social life, enjoying bridge, mahjong, little theater, and parties accented by lavish decorations of local flowers. She spent much time entertaining international visitors, and also wrote the society column for the *Baguio Bulletin*. The Crouters' life, even during the Depression, was comfortable, convenient, relaxed.

Yet during this period the Crouters and their friends were well aware of world economic conditions, of the worsening political and military situation not just in Europe but also in Asia. The Philippines—with the large American air base at Clark Field and naval base at Cavite (both on Luzon), as well as other military installations throughout the Islands—were seen as vital in defending "air and sea lanes stretching from the northern Pacific through Southeast Asia and the Indian Ocean to the Middle East and Europe."[7] Because of the Philippines' strategic importance and their vulnerability, by the end of 1941 many families of American military personnel had been sent back to the States. The choice was not as clear-cut for other American civilians, many of whom had lived in the Philippines for decades and knew no other real "home." The current U.S. High Commissioner to the Philippine Islands, Francis B. Sayre, was advised by the State Department not to "give official notice that American civilians should leave the islands" and, if they asked about leaving, to "reply that no one at the time could foretell whether an attack would occur or, if so, when, and [to] leave it to each individual citizen to decide for himself."[8] This evasiveness was dictated by the State Department to buttress its foreign policy: if Americans fled the Philippines, the Filipinos would feel betrayed by their erstwhile protectors. So, in effect, the American citizens who remained in the Philippines became hostages to national policy—as Sayre said, "entrapped in the Philippines with no way of escape" once the war broke out.

The Crouters pondered the feasibility of Natalie and the children returning to Boston, but ultimately the family could not accept separation from one another and from the Philippines. Natalie and Jerry finally agreed that they should stay together in Baguio and take their chances.

The *Diary* that follows records the consequences of that choice. Natalie began it inadvertently on December 5, 1941, two days before the bombing of Pearl Harbor incited the United States' entry into World War II. It started as a routine letter to her mother, but it took on ominous overtones as people sought sanctuary in Baguio, away from the more strategic Philippine locations, such as Manila and Cavite, the naval base on Manila Bay. On December 8, while hearing a radio report of the attack on Pearl Harbor, the Crouters observed "seventeen big bombers in formation" that they took for American planes until, "as they passed almost opposite the house, we heard a long ripping sound like the tearing of a giant sheet and saw an enormous burst of smoke and earth near officers' quarters at Camp John Hay—the first bombing of the Philippines, before our eyes." The war had begun. The Japanese quickly occupied the area, and the Crouters were interned along with five hundred other British and American civilians. The letter home, never mailed, turned into a record that Natalie kept daily throughout her three and a half years of confinement.

Natalie wrote her journal in microscopic script on small scraps of paper—flaps of envelopes, margins of book pages, cut-up fragments of discarded records and ledgers. She hid them from the Japanese guards' inspections by wrapping them in square packets made from a cut-up plastic raincoat and concealing the packets under food supplies in a tall can, which in turn was secured in a bag woven by Igorot natives. At first she covered the packets with butter; after the Crouters ate the butter, the covering became brown sugar, then beans, then peanuts. Even as the *Diary* grew, written in faithfully every day and sometimes more often, "the bag was not heavy and was innocuous looking," Natalie explained. Throughout the war she carried the *Diary* whenever her barracks space was likely to be searched, particularly during roll call, when the Japanese were looking for hidden radios.

Natalie and her fellow internees had the advantage of being confined for most of the war in the relatively safe former Filipino Constabulary (national police) Camp Holmes, located in an idyllic mountain setting near Baguio. Its high altitude meant that the tropical climate was mild and healthful, not sweltering and conducive to disease as was sea-level Manila. Although space within the camp confines was at a premium, there was a central parade ground converted to various utilitarian purposes, with animal sheds, a school, a workshop—even a hot tub, originally constructed to aid therapy for a child with polio. And best of all, the camp stood near forest-covered hills, a source not only of wood supply, lovely tropical plants and flowers, but of solace and beauty.

At no time did the internees, while in camp, appear to be victims of the unmitigated hatred of "white devils" manifested so consistently in the Japanese press,[9] as in a Tokyo newspaper editorial of 1942: "To show [Europeans and Americans] mercy is to prolong the war. Their motto has been, 'Absolute unscrupulousness.' They have not cared what means they employed in their operations. An eye for an eye, a tooth for a tooth. Hesitation is uncalled for, and the wrongdoers must be wiped out."[10] The relatively mild treatment of the Camp Holmes internees may have been partly because they were civilians, partly because they were unthreatening in demeanor and small in number in comparison with the military forces. This was also, in part, due to the inadvertent good fortune that among them were two people who before the war had worked closely with the Japanese, and had established considerable understanding and rapport with them.

One of these was Arthur [a pseudonym], the internees' first elected Chairman of the Executive Committee. At the time war broke out he was the largest employer of Japanese in northern Luzon, managing lumber for the Benguet Consolidated Mining Company. This meant that he knew many Japanese living in the Baguio vicinity throughout the war and could obtain special favors for the camp by capitalizing on his prewar associations. He also used his executive authority to obtain some special privileges (such as a private room for himself, his wife and daughter in a barracks where the other women and children lived communally) and in so doing aroused egalitarian Natalie's continual ire. But on balance, Jim Halsema claims in contradiction to Natalie, the camp benefited considerably from Arthur's negotiations with his former employees.

The other person was Nellie McKim, missionary daughter of the Episcopal bishop of Japan. With a thorough understanding not only of Japanese and English but of the customs of both cultures, Miss McKim functioned as interpreter and diplomat. She was always treated with respect by the Japanese because of her aristocratic accent and vocabulary, acquired in the Peeresses' School, which obliged them to address her with reverence as "Honorable Aunt." She also conducted classes in Japanese so that the internees might begin to communicate more fully with the guards and gain a better understanding of Japanese culture.

The internees were doubly fortunate in being supervised, for part of the time, by such thoughtful men as Major Rokuro Tomibe, whose solicitude for the internees was reciprocated not only during the war, but afterward.[11] For instance, Tomibe was responsible for the safe arrival of the only large shipment of Red Cross food, clothing, and medicine that reached the internees. To prevent the shipment from being diverted to other camps or stolen by grafters and looters, Tomibe saw to it that the precious cargo was protected on its hazardous journey from the Manila docks to Camp Holmes. By the time the hardhearted, hardheaded Lieutenant Oura (who had formerly been a village chief in the back country of Honshu) arrived as camp Commandant in 1944, the internees had sufficient experience in dealing with the Japanese to enable them to get along with a minimum of friction.

Counterpointed against the *Diary*'s motif of Japanese-American relations are the interwoven themes of community organization and everyday life. The camp was highly structured, carefully organized. Some organization was, of course, necessary to keep five hundred inmates functioning as an integrated unit in a space limited for over two years by mutual agreement (a fence was not erected until May, 1944).[12] Yet with characteristic American efficiency, the internees imposed a great deal of structure upon themselves, for by organizing and managing their own work details—kitchen, waitressing, inside and outside sanitation, wood crew, hospital, school, and others—the camp's residents gained more control over their lives than would have been possible had the Japanese taken charge of assigning and enforcing duties.

Indeed, such thoroughgoing organization frequently provided the means for circumventing Japanese demands. The Japanese often made such severe rules as, in the beginning, "No schools for the children." But they quickly became lax in enforcing them, at least in part because, once the internees had reached a consensus, their collective behavior was so single-minded and insistent that in many cases, the Japanese simply acceded. So the internees set up an elementary school and a high school and even taught the "forbidden" courses—history and geography—switching to safer subjects when guards came within earshot.

The internees conducted their own affairs along roughly democratic, though sexist, lines. The Men's Committee, also known as the Executive Committee, was composed of representatives elected exclusively by the men. Subject only to the Japanese Commandant's veto, the Men's Committee established major camp policy. It determined allocation of communal money, facilities (such as buildings—subject to occasional Japanese takeovers), and supplies (such as firewood, and the clothing, food, and medicines contributed by the Red Cross and other sources).

For the first year and a half, if the women wanted their views to be known, they could only lobby privately or through the Women's Committee, composed exclusively of women. During this time the recommendations of the Women's Committee were merely advisory and had no binding force in general camp matters; the advantages of the Nineteenth Amendment remained strictly in the outside world. Natalie was particularly angered by this, as her continual railings in the *Diary* indicate, although many other women appear to have accepted their political subordination meekly. In April of 1943, the Men's Committee was finally pressured to poll the camp to determine whether the majority favored woman suffrage. They did, but the Men's Committee disregarded the vote and did not capitulate for two weeks. Even after the women could vote in general elections, however, the Executive Committee remained composed entirely of men. The women's lack of assertiveness in this matter may indicate the greater urgency of their other priorities, such as the necessity, despite depleted energy, of caring for active children without the help of their husbands or the servants to whom they were accustomed. It is nevertheless surprising, for as a group the women appear educated, articulate, and competent—quite capable of getting their own way.

The Men's and Women's Committees allocated jobs and work-related materials to the able-bodied adults and teenagers in their respective jurisdictions. Based on each individual's available time and strength, then actual work per week averaged between twelve and thirty hours, although during epidemics the hospital staff—ten doctors and thirty-two nurses who were medical missionaries—worked much longer. As far as possible, the jobs were assigned according to the skills available, along sex lines. Thus women were waitresses, babysitters, and laundresses; men cut wood and ran the machine shop; both sexes taught school. Unlike the practices in some other prison camps, routine services were provided to the community free of charge, except in the case of the unusually selfish dentist, who, because of his power in the Men's Committee, got away with charging fees for his services.

The Japanese occupiers, outside of camp, were attempting to enforce the concept of "Asia for the Asiatics." Yet they did not understand the collective impact on the Filipino population of *utang na loob*, enhanced by many warm prewar relationships between the Filipinos and their American employers, that exacerbated the differences between the Japanese and Filipino cultures. The Japanese, for instance, publicly humiliated the lower classes by beating and punishing them in public and even conducting public hangings—all of which were anathema to the Filipinos. In consequence, during the war many Filipinos were far more sympathetic to the Americans than to the Japanese. The presence of Americans in prison camps on Philippine soil served as a further stimulus to the loyalty of their Filipino friends, stiffening the natives' resistance to the Japanese government.[13]

In addition to extensive and effective guerrilla activity throughout the war there were continuing contributions of food and other necessities that Filipinos living on the outside sent to the internment camps. Until the Japanese prohibited the practice in 1944, the Bacanis did this for the Crouters on a regular basis. And "it was not by chance," says fellow internee Jim Halsema, "that a Filipino would be leading a cow along the road near Camp Holmes and sell it to the Japanese guards, when meat was not available in Baguio. The Filipinos knew that although the Japanese would keep half, the rest of the meat would go to the prisoners."[14]

For most of the war, except for three months at the beginning and again at the end, the Japanese provided the internees with the basic Japanese army ration, a peasant diet of low-quality food, consisting basically of vegetables and staples such as rice sweepings (spilled rice swept with stones and chaff), which the camp members had to pick over before using. The camp kitchen prepared three meals a day, using these rations supplemented by food paid for with communal funds, which became more and more scarce as the war ground on. Extra food and supplies were provided from friends outside or bought at the camp store—with money from the internees' prewar cash reserves or from sale of their possessions to outsiders. Profits from the store were pooled for communal purchases. Barter and payment in extra services, such as private ironing or cooking, were the internees' common media of exchange among themselves.

One's prewar social status was often irrelevant in camp, as a hierarchy arose based on a new set of values. The highest status was reserved for members of one of the several major cliques, to which the Crouters never belonged. Although Natalie was known as "Baguio's resident intellectual," her mental acuity gained her no power. The high status of some cliques was ensured by their control over necessary services or supplies. Thus in camp the cook and the kitchen crew, including waitresses and dishwashers, ranked among the elite because of their constant proximity to food, with its advantages of extra nourishment and opportunities for graft. The hospital staff maintained power through a combination of professional skill (and the gratitude it engendered), executive authority (some carried over from outside), and unity because they lived together in the hospital, away from the others. The continued high status of Arthur and Nellie McKim was ensured because of their familiarity with the Japanese. And some people became leaders because of a fortuitous combination of altruism, executive ability, and tireless energy—including the very diplomatic missionary Carl Eschbach and Father R. E. Sheridan, a Maryknoll priest who had voluntarily interned himself because he thought that the Catholic prisoners should have a priest.[15]

Not all the leaders were that selfless. A number gained power because of their ability to bully the weaker or to take advantage of the unsuspecting, as Natalie's continual denunciations of the abuse of privilege make clear. Characteriscially, she observes in her *Diary,* "When the purchases come in, a certain few gather in the store at night and choose what they want. What is left is sold at the store next day to the long clamoring line. Small orders of two or three cans are unimportant compared to Execs who want case lots."

Such disruptive elements were never completely quelled; the powerful tended to maintain their power and to protect their friends, primarily in such matters as extra allotments of goods or leftover food. On the other hand, there was considerable public pressure for fairness, which prevailed in the distribution of most of the communally purchased food, in meticulous administration of medicines and extra food to the sick and infirm, and in allocation of work and other community responsibilities, despite the few chronic shirkers. And, as the minutes of the meetings of the Men's and Women's Committees indicate, these governing bodies tried to be fair in assigning duties and responding to individual and group petitions.

Depending on the temperament and mood of the incumbent Commandant, the Japanese sometimes threatened, sometimes enforced instant reprisals for violations of their rules. "The mistake of one is the mistake of all" was the reiterated motto, a threat more at the beginning of the war, when captors and captives were still getting used to one another, than later, after patterns of living and communication had been established. Yet at the most serious violation, when two internees escaped, Tomibe was in charge and the reprisals were far milder than could have been expected. Although the men who had slept in the barracks near the escapees were taken to the Baguio jail and tortured by the Military Police, they were saved from death and returned to camp as a result of Tomibe's insistence that "These are my prisoners, not yours, and you cannot kill them without proof of a crime."[16] During the entire war, only one person from Camp Holmes died as a result of Japanese maltreatment: Rufus Grey was tortured to death, outside of camp, for alleged espionage.[17]

Despite the enforcement of separate quarters for men and women, after the first few months families ate and enjoyed recreation together. Leisure activities ranged from lectures on geology, geography, or great books to team sports and talent shows—with some of the internees' own confiscated goods returned to them by the Japanese guards as "prizes." A favorite adult pastime was bridge—occasionally with Japanese as partners, although Natalie once noted her fear of being misunderstood or of playing badly as "cold steel across my throat." Parties became frequent in 1943 when fear of currency devaluation stampeded the camp into a period of frenzied eating and mer-rymaking—of which Natalie noted her disapproval.

Although five hundred was a relatively small population as prison camps go, space was the most precious commodity next to food. The rooms were carefully measured; in Natalie's barracks in Camp Holmes every adult was allotted a space thirty-three inches wide, and Natalie was aggrieved because her space was three inches less than this. Such conditions contributed, even in a time of international holocaust, to many of the bickerings, antagonisms, and internecine smolderings that caused fire and smoke throughout the camp's life.

Family cohabitation was one such abrasive issue. For the first two years of the war, the Japanese decreed that the men and older boys would live segregated from the women, older girls, and small children; but by early 1944 they expressed a willingness to let family members live together, leaving the final decision to an internees' vote. Surprisingly, a substantial number of the camp's residents resisted the "family unit," as it came to be called. Principal advocates of segregation were a group of married Episcopalian missionaries, who raised alarmed cries about the imminence of a population explosion if husbands and wives lived together. (In unwitting corroboration of this view, June had made her paper doll "a lovely bridal gown and four maternity dresses—'in case they are stuck in Concentration Camp.' ")

In desperation over the delays, a number of families finally began to burrow dugouts beneath the buildings, to be together in quiet and isolation. Gradually the individual barracks adopted the family unit, but a number of dissenters held out, thus preventing their quarters from forming family cu-bicles, until December of 1944 when the Japanese forced a change in housing arrangements.

The missionaries' perspective, however, was more counterbalanced by the emotional closeness among other families, far stronger than it might have been in peacetime, when they would have spent less time together because of jobs, community activities, and servants caring for the children.

Psychological strains took their toll on the internees. There was a continual undercurrent of stress with the guards—the lower echelons were as deprived as their prisoners, and as homesick. There was the isolation, paradoxically, in the midst of constant overcrowding. There was the separation of families, both within the camp and from relatives outside, at home and abroad. Celibacy was imposed for three years; many independent decisions were preempted either by the Japanese or by committees of internees who established the rules. Communication with native Filipinos and other nearby residents was restricted. Internees received no mail from outside or Red Cross packages during the first two and a half years of the war. Medicines, dental materials, and most other commodities were in short and erratic supply. And always there were confinement, regimentation, and crowding, which made animosities overt.

There were also myriad physical problems, many of which were related to inadequate diets. Loss of energy, susceptibility to dysentery and other infections, and low tolerance of physical and emotional stress were common. By the time the captives were liberated, in February of 1945, they—as well as their captors—were suffering from severe malnutrition. Yet, despite chronic dietary deficiencies and related physical problems, the camp death rate had been significantly lower than that of the average noncaptive population in a three-year period. Besides the murdered Rufus Grey, only twelve internees died during the war—either from afflictions related to old age or from the effects of prewar illnesses.

One explanation for this striking phenomenon is that the integrity of the captives' individual personalities was not destroyed. The internees did not lapse into passivity or childlike dependence on their captors; they were never ''brainwashed.'' Indeed, the resourcefulness and ingenuity they had exhibited in their prewar occupations—as missionaries (members of twenty-two sects were in camp), business people, and mining engineers—enabled them to adapt well to new conditions and to prevail over them as fully as possible. The internees maintained a strong, life-preserving sense of their identities, and their solidarity as members of functioning, purposeful groups, despite individual disagreements. Although there were emotional fluctuations, the prevailing mood among most of the internees was resigned and determined optimism, as evidenced by the wild rumors of imminent deliverance by General MacArthur's forces that circulated during the early weeks of 1942, when the Allies actually were losing disastrously in the Pacific. Even when this optimism was tempered by infiltrations of actual news from the internees' clandestine radio,[18] their collective morale remained relatively high—perhaps because they usually focused on camp affairs, over which they had some control, rather than on the desperate world situation.

Unlike many prisoners, Natalie was able to see her captors as human beings with merits as well as faults, as people subject to the same deprivations and hardships of war as their captives, rather than as mere propaganda stereotypes. Fortunately for her mental health at the time, and for the reader now, her perspective was remarkably free of bitterness and vindictiveness.

This *Diary* is a narrative not of horror and torture but of courage—grace and ingenuity and democracy and levelheadedness—under the pressures of privation, confinement, uncertainty, and frustration. Because Natalie was *there*—mentally, physically, emotionally—the *Diary* lives, full of the wonder and pain and beauty of her life, even in wartime. It is an intricate rendering of family life, of a social microcosm, of feuds among allies and friendships among enemies, of birth and growth and maturity and death, accompanied by the obligato of the bombs literally bursting in air. Natalie Crouter's *Diary*

is a song of selfhood, of sanity in a mad world. It is a significant document—social, historical, and human—painstakingly rendered for the sake of
those past and present and yet to come.

The Genesis and Editorial Principles
of This Edition

In 1968, Natalie Crouter heard me address a national convention of the
Women's International League for Peace and Freedom. I spoke about the
trial of Dr. Benjamin Spock for conspiracy to encourage draft evasion, which
I had been attending in preparation for my biography of the defendant.[19] She
evidently sensed a responsive spirit, although she did not know until later
that I had grown up in New Hampshire, only sixty miles from her beloved
Boston, and that I had experience in editing as well as in writing.

Several weeks later, after dinner at her daughter June's (which Natalie
had discreetly arranged), she described the project to me and stated that if
I could do right by Dr. Spock, she thought I could do right by her. Would
I edit her *Diary* and help her find a publisher?

It is particulary difficult, as the writers of personal works—letters, diaries,
and autobiographies—know, to expose the manifold facets of one's private
selves to public scrutiny. Exposure leaves authors of personal writings vul-
nerable to others' analyses, judgments, and possible ridicule, and can be
threatening or frightening. So the benefits of publication—in this case, the
chance to communicate to others the complexity of her unusual war
years—had to outweigh a sacrifice of the sympathy and privacy obtainable
from the diarist's original, exclusive audience: herself and her family. After
twenty-four years, Natalie was willing to take this chance.

In order to make the mammoth record of these experiences accessible to
readers whose patience and time do not permit perusal of its entire five
thousand pages, I have cut the *Diary* to less than 10 percent of its original
volume. Yet I have tried to retain the *Diary*'s major themes and its author's
perspective. Through careful selection I have attempted to convey the diarist's
continual sense of the significance of life in internment, as well as her fluc-
tuating states of mind and body.

The *Diary*'s chronological organization has the advantages of immediacy
and of letting the reader see events, relationships, and characters develop,
mature, and die. Yet the diary format also has the intrinsic disadvantages of
redundancy and lack of topical organization. I have eliminated considerable
repetition. This included many passages written for personal ventilation that
emit more heat than light, Natalie's continual discourses on community spirit
and unselfishness, and her numerous descriptions of scenery. The constantly
hungry writer itemized every scrap of food she consumed during her entire

incarceration; the Crouters seem to have eaten camotes and beans or rice for at least 2,500 of the 3,785 meals originally mentioned in the *Diary*. What was monotonous and repetitive for them need not be imposed on the *Diary*'s readers. For comparable reasons I have also eliminated many of the detailed minutes of the Men's and Women's Committee meetings.

I have not used ellipses to indicate omissions; the large number necessary would have rendered the *Diary* unreadable. Grammar, punctuation, and spelling have been silently corrected, but other changes and additions have been indicated with brackets. Natalie translated most of the Japanese words in the original text of the *Diary,* and these translations remain in context. Where Natalie did not translate the Japanese, I have, with the aid of Martha Ozawa of Washington University, supplied the meanings, either in brackets in the text or in the notes, which appear at the end of the text. Place names not identified in context may be located on the maps that follow.

In her original manuscript Natalie disguised the names of a number of internees, and in accordance with her wish, these pseudonyms have been retained. Other people she identified by their actual names or camp nicknames. For example, Denki, Japanese for electric light, was the nickname of the camp's electrician.

With the help of James J. Halsema—for many years an officer of the U.S. Information Agency, Major Gary Turner of the U.S. Military Academy at West Point, and research assistant Gerald Berdan, I have tried to check the accuracy of the rumors and speculations about world events, especially war news, that were rampant in camp and often recorded in Natalie's *Diary*. A considerable portion are correct in essence if not always in specific details. If the information is correct, it is not noted; discrepancies between report and fact are explained in notes.

I have been able to verify many of the facts reported in the *Diary* through other eyewitnesses to these events. Jim Halsema's commentary, buttressed by his extensive library on the South Pacific and World War II and his own manuscript diary of 1944, has been invaluable, and he has supplied information for many notes. Conversations with the Reverend Carl Eschbach of Dayton, Ohio, and with the Reverend Joseph Smith, formerly of the Christian Theological Seminary, Indianapolis, and his wife, Winnie (Jo and Winnie in the *Diary*), validate many details of Natalie's account, as does a brief memoir by former Commandant Rokuro Tomibe.[20] A number of the facts and many of the interpretive aspects of Natalie's narrative are corroborated in another memoir, *God's Arm's Around Us,* by William R. Moule, published by Vantage Press in 1960.

LYNN Z. BLOOM

Williamsburg, Virginia
December, 1979

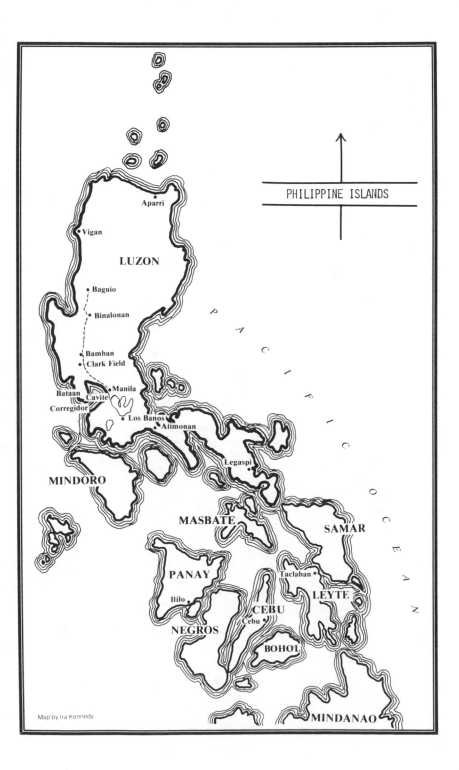

PHILIPPINE ISLANDS

LUZON

Aparri

Vigan

Baguio

Binalonan

Bamban
Clark Field

Bataan
Corregidor
Cavite
Manila

Los Banos
Atimonan

Legaspi

MINDORO

MASBATE

SAMAR

PANAY

Taclaban

Ililo

CEBU

LEYTE

Cebu

NEGROS

BOHOL

MINDANAO

P A C I F I C   O C E A N

Map by Ira Kennedy

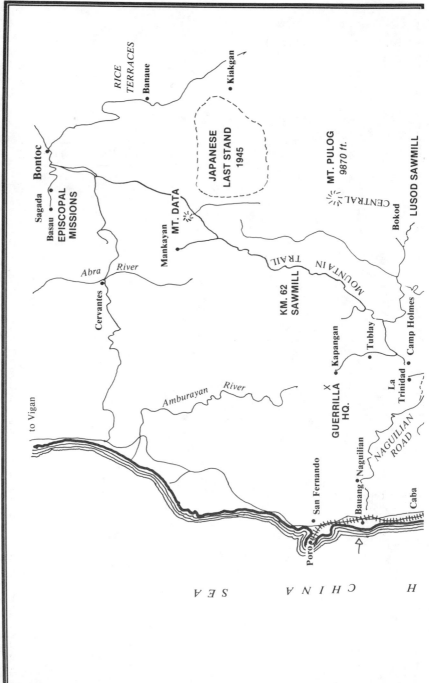

RICE TERRACES

Banaue

Kiakgan

JAPANESE LAST STAND 1945

MT. PULOG 9870 ft.

Bontoc

Sagada
Basau EPISCOPAL
MISSIONS

Mankayan MT. DATA

CENTRAL

LUSOD SAWMILL

Bokod

Abra River

Cervantes

MOUNTAIN TRAIL

KM. 62 SAWMILL

Kapangan

Tublay

Camp Holmes

Amburayan River

GUERRILLA X HQ.

La Trinidad

NAGUILIAN ROAD

to Vigan

San Fernando

Naguilian

Poro Bauang

Caba

CHINA SEA

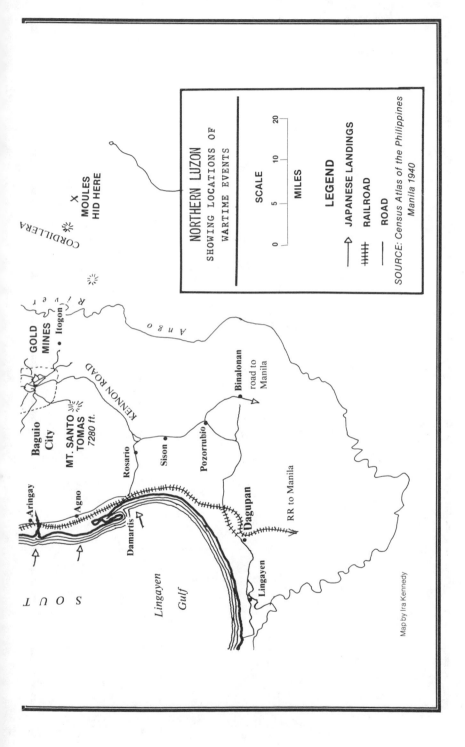

NORTHERN LUZON

SHOWING LOCATIONS OF
WARTIME EVENTS

SCALE

0   5   10   20

MILES

LEGEND

↑ JAPANESE LANDINGS

╫╫╫ RAILROAD

—— ROAD

SOURCE: Census Atlas of the Philippines
Manila 1940

CORDILLERA

MOULES
HID HERE
X

GOLD
MINES

Itogon

Anso River

Baguio
City

MT. SANTO
TOMAS
7280 ft.

KENNON ROAD

Rosario

Sison

Pozorrubio

Binalonan

road to
Manila

Aringay

Agno

Damartis

Dagupan

Lingayen

RR to Manila

Lingayen
Gulf

SOUTH

Map by Ira Kennedy

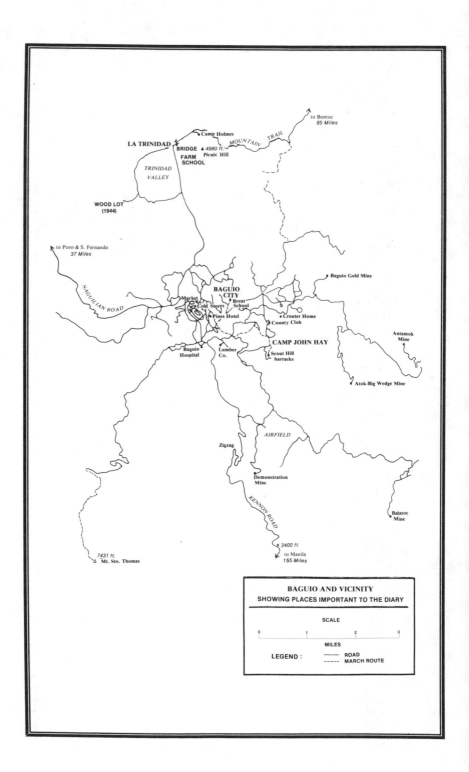

to Bontoc
85 Miles

Camp Holmes

LA TRINIDAD

MOUNTAIN TRAIL

BRIDGE   ▲ 4980 ft.
FARM   Picnic Hill
SCHOOL

*TRINIDAD
VALLEY*

WOOD LOT
(1944)

to Poro & S. Fernando
37 Miles

Baguio Gold Mine

NAGUILIAN ROAD

**BAGUIO
CITY**

Market   Brent
        Cold Stores School
        Pines Hotel   Crouter Home
                             County Club

Antamok
Mine

Baguio
Hospital

Lumber
Co.

CAMP JOHN HAY

Scout Hill
barracks

Atok-Big Wedge Mine

AIRFIELD

Zigzag

Demonstration
Mine

KENNON ROAD

Balatoc
Mine

7431 ft.
△ Mt. Sto. Thomas

2400 ft.
to Manila
155 Miles

BAGUIO AND VICINITY

SHOWING PLACES IMPORTANT TO THE DIARY

SCALE

0   1   2   3

MILES

LEGEND : ———— ROAD
          ----- MARCH ROUTE

1941

November 28, 1941. Today I bought materials for eighteen triangle bandages to use in First Aid class. I rode to Mansion House pool on my wheel [bicycle], then read ''Berlin Diary'' which depressed no end as people out here are just as sure nothing will happen (that the Japanese will back down), as they were sure in Europe before each country fell.

I sent P120[1] raised through selling Christmas cards to the Manila treasurer for Chinese Industrial Cooperatives.[2] We had dinner at Bev's and Jo's. He drew me out as to what I thought was going to happen but became irritable when I answered that very soon life would not be carried on as usual in Manila. He didn't want to face it but was worried himself. We went to watch the Game crowd at the Baguio Army-Navy Club. It was significant that no Navy or Clark Field [Air Force] boys were there. Lorna W. has just lost her brother in North Sea action.

November 30, 1941. Sunday morning we tried for hours to keep alive our kitten Pippy and the big yellow cat. We had been treating them for three days with a medicine dropper. While I was warming Pippy with my hands, he died. I wept. He was such a crazy, joyous kitten. I couldn't believe life would leave so fast. We were sad as we buried him before the children arrived from Sunday School. We continued to work over Tiger though he was dying. It was so hard for him to breathe that I couldn't stand it. We called the veterinary again to put him to sleep. This was two in one day and we felt weary, working against death and getting nowhere. The children cried bitterly so we went to ride to help them forget. June wailed, ''Mummie, I can't bear it. Aren't we ever going to see Pippy dance about the garden any more?''

In the night a noise awakened me and I flashed the light on Bedie's bed. There were sounds in the kitchen, as if our remaining Persian cat might be poking about. Next morning Nida greeted us with the news that thieves had cut the screen, come in the kitchen window and stolen oranges, eggs, sugar jar, tea, ketchup, cereals and a dish full of cheese whose Chinese cover we found in the yard. The police came to check but found no fingerprints, for later we discovered two socks in the road which they had used to cover their hands.

December 1, 1941. I brought sheet material from the Red Cross for Nida and the lavandera [laundress] to sew. They have made three dozen sheets, two dozen surgical coats, and the same number of angel gowns in two weeks. Nida has hemmed triangles, sewed up Treasure bags for Christmas to fill with gifts for sick soldiers in the hospitals. We have worked a long time to prepare for what might happen.

I received a Christmas card from Mme. Sun, signed Soong Ching Ling.[3] Nehru had written her from prison that he was more interested in Indusco than anything he had heard of in a long time and thought there were lessons in it for India.

Later in the evening we heard Romulo's speech to Young Philippines over the radio. He said to remember we were only sixteen million—that this was a small number in the large picture we were about to enter—with 400 million Chinese, 70 million Japanese, and other nationalities.[4]

December 4, 1941. There were 102 present at the Tuesday Club meeting at Mrs. Sayre's. Many signed up for a first-aid course to begin on January 6. Everyone enlisted to help on Treasure bags for soldiers. We made warm Christmas coats for Igorot[5] babies so they won't die from "wind on the chest" as they call pneumonia.

December 6, 1941. We worked for the Red Cross. The American School came up from Manila to play Brent School in basketball. There was much esprit de corps and yelling on both sides. All were invited to the Tuesday Club box supper in the pavilion at the country club in the evening. The affair was a huge success as to money and crowd. P460 alone was raised on auction of baskets. The seventy young people from the schools made it colorful and gay with pretty dresses and dancing. A few enlisted men came and some Navy and Clark Field boys. The children were all eyes at their first big party. The club never looked so well. There were large boxes filled with banana trees and tree ferns. In between, there were tall white vases filled with flaming poinsettias. At one end of the hall hung a row of woolen coats made by the women's club for the Igorots.

December 7, 1941. All week I've maintained something would pop on the 7th but could give no reason except a 7 in my tea leaves which is no reason at all.

Carl came over to ride with us around Baguio taking colored pictures which Jerry is giving him as a present to show in the States. We stopped at the caddy house at Camp John Hay for a peaceful Coca-Cola. Mrs. Dudley had come up from Cavite with another civilian wife and child, thinking Baguio was safer in case of attack.

December 8, 1941. After the children left for school, we turned on the radio about 8:15—and heard of the attack on Pearl Harbor. While listening, we heard planes and went out as usual to see them. Almost over the house, quite high, came seventeen big bombers in formation. We could see them plainly and thought they were American. I remarked, "Well, we probably won't be standing here looking up at planes like this much longer." As they passed almost opposite the house, we heard a long ripping sound like the tearing of a giant sheet and saw an enormous burst of smoke and earth near officers' quarters at Camp John Hay—the first bombing of the Philippines before our eyes. Huge billows of smoke and dust covered the Post as we looked. No one said a word. We turned to each other, speechless. At last Jerry said, hoarsely, "My God, those are Japanese planes." The smoke rolled up and the smell of powder reached us. We could hear screaming and men yelling orders. Suddenly we all ran into the house. The planes passed out of sight over the mines and mountain ridge.

Our knees were shaky. We kept staring at each other, wondering if we could believe what our eyes had seen. Jerry had to go to the office so I went along. We told Nida to take all the family into the stone rain-drainage ditch and to lie flat there if any more planes came. I showed her how to pack the Celadon dishes—very old Sung Dynasty Chinese plates. We packed them in between pillows, and then stacked my files and Indusco books together.

As we drove to town, we could see that no one knew what had happened. On Session Road [the main street] everyone was strolling casually, looking into windows, going in and out of stores. Japanese storekeepers stood unconcerned in doorways. We had had no answer from dialing the Post so did not go over. We met Betty Lander pushing her son in his carriage down in market square. She smiled as we stopped to speak, saying, "You don't need to tell me; I heard the news about Hawaii." I said, "You'd better take the baby home at once. Those were Japanese planes. We saw them bomb the Post." She uttered a "My God!" and turned running toward home.

We still couldn't realize it and didn't fully take it in for an hour. Everything seemed so quiet and peaceful. I kept saying, "You don't suppose we are mistaken—we'd better not tell people till we know more—it's a bad rumor to start." Jerry stormed that he knew a bombing when he saw it and that was that.

We met a radioman from the Post. He was all out of breath and his eyes fairly stuck from his head. He started to tell us but we said we had seen it. He gave us some dreadful details. We started to town again but halfway [there] saw the Filipino children streaming from the public school, so we turned back. There was a sound of distant bombing and at last the air-raid siren—one hour after the first bombing.

This was a lone plane laying eggs beyond the Post. Two bombs landed beside a house killing a man and a young Filipino servant girl, blowing out windows and shingles. It was so near other homes that many mothers, children and babies went up the Mountain Trail to stay with friends. Those of us remaining are building bomb shelters right now.

At Brent, school was dismissed. We went home and stayed there. It has been blackout ever since and we are glad we were prepared. Whenever we hear the throb of motors we rush out to the stone-lined ditch—no telling whose plane it is. Though the sirens are working, we hear the planes long before. I took down all the wall pictures and stowed them in the closet. Nida is wonderful. She keeps working every minute, but is very grim. When we told her the planes had dropped leaflets along the Ilocos coast telling the Filipinos that the Japanese were bringing their independence, she was eloquently silent.[6]

Jerry has contracted for two miners to put in a tunnel for air-raid shelter. It is built into the bank behind the garage, well-timbered and safe. Meanwhile we pile into the stone ditch. The children are calm, though the third day June said her stomach felt like a lot of fingers working in and out. We sleep in our clothes, as we rest better when ready to dash out into the night.

December 12, 1941. It is now Dec. 12 and we've all had hot baths—an event! We listen to the radio and reports seem organized, coordinated, so it is more reassuring. There was an announcement that Davao, Tarlac and Clark Field were bombed later in the morning after Baguio.[7]

There are seven living in our garage quarters now. Nida's cousin brought his pregnant wife the second morning. We are learning "Gung Ho" or "Work Together," fast. In between cooking and dishwashing, the women sew on surgical coats, hospital gowns, and cut out material. The children make beds, sweep, run errands and get covered with mud. We feel better when busy. We took a walk at sunset—so peaceful and beautiful. We looked at another dugout and came home feeling better about ours. We go to bed early in blackout, rise early too. We are tired at night. No mail or papers all week. It is well we have stocked up on rice, bouillon cubes and canned goods calculated to last four months.

Watching the Filipino reaction in general we see what must have happened in France. Many have streamed up from the lowlands to Baguio—and about the same number have streamed down. Some miners start walking to remote mountain homes, while lowlanders wanting jobs replace them. With most, it is the desire to get to the "home" province. All the servants in bombed sections here left immediately. For two days, families trekked past the house carrying white-wrapped bundles of belongings. Dozens of buses from the mines go by crammed with passengers, loaded on top with baggage until the truck almost rolls over. Ismael said the lowland barrios [native villages] are like ghost towns. He did not even look up his own family, sure they had taken to the hills. There is high praise for Filipino defenders of Dagupan. If the Japanese think they will be a pushover because they will side with Orientals, they are due for a shock.[8]

December 13, 1941. There was a bad raid on Manila this week but so far the Japanese seem to have kept to military objectives like the Air Fields and Cavite. I do not know how soon I can send letters to Mother but am putting it down while it is still fresh in the mind.

Today the radio mentions attacks on Apparri, Vigan, San Fernando, Zambales and Legaspi. It seems to be still invasion phase. We hope to hear of our attack, not just defense.

We have filled all kinds of bottles, as well as one of the bathtubs, full of water in case service is interrupted, though so far only one bombing here. I packed up most of my valuable jewels for the deposit box at the bank. Nida works like a little demon and keeps the three other women going for the Red Cross. I mend and put away laundry, trying to keep a kind of routine. A long line of trucks and buses went by the house from the mines, with drawn curtains [transporting dynamite].

December 14, 1941. The Post was just bombed. No deaths, one injured. We could see six bombers going into the clouds. We have had so many alarms we have cut meals to a minimum, eating Filipino chow with the servants and like it. It is rice with a mixture of vegetables and meat, garlic or onion. For sweet we have candy from a large bag full, which I bought after the first raid. Housekeeping is simple—each uses a dish and a fork. We eat down in the garage near the shelter entrance as it is too tiring to run up and down. I think we will like simplicity even after peace comes. There are twenty using our shelter now—12 Filipinos, four Americans, two British and two French.

The Blacks' baby is beginning to talk and calls the shelter "Auntie Pete's Black Hole," so we have named it that, like a night club back in the States.

Rice is now rationed. Business is disorganized, the mines shutting down. The military, civilians and Red Cross seem to be coordinating though none of them were too good for three days. Twelve alarms yesterday, only four today. I brought the last two bolts of material home and sent a dozen cut gowns to Balatoc mine residents to be sewed. At the Red Cross room I gathered all the Christmas bags together. There are fifty filled, forty empty and ready for gifts.

Session Road is a different place, few people on the street, only army cars, trucks and gasoline wagons. All the Chinese stores have boards over plate-glass windows. They are only open half the time. Still no mail, no newspapers from Manila. Carl brought a several days' old *Bulletin* which we devoured. It listed Filipinos killed in Pasay and American homes burned. We are a headquarters. People drop in to see the shelter, give and take news.

December 15, 1941. I went to town with Jerry to hunt for bread but there was none so we'll get along on rice and hotcakes now and then. Flour cannot be bought at the moment.

Carl has organized a "spotting system" for siren signals on approaching planes, with about ten American men from the Chinese Language School which has closed with others by government order. In the middle of the night when it grew cold I thought of those men and phoned Carl in the morning who said they surely would like mufflers and warm socks if we had any. So I gave out wool to the British women to make socks and Balaclavas (head and neckpiece combined). They are expert knitters, have completed all their own projects and were only too glad to work.

It is astonishing how quickly one adjusts to circumstances. I don't mind being downtown in a raid half as much as I did. On the way home [from town], Jerry and I had to duck into a culvert. We could hear the roar of planes clearly overhead.

Jerry is now head of coordinating the phone system of alarms.

Another astounding thing is how fast time goes. It doesn't seem a week since the first bombing. Actual living is simple for we have dispensed with doilies and other formalities. Meals are easy to cook, but it takes longer to do anything and transportation is so shot that everything is difficult.

While I was waiting at the Shell Station, one of the Filipino boys brought me an exquisite Magnolia bloom, its fragrance appreciated a thousand times more after hiding behind stone pillars with eighteen planes overhead.

We have a light in our shelter now. One more cross-section, the "raise" to give ventilation and a rear exit—then it will be complete. Jerry will be relieved to have the emergency outlet ready.

There are many stories flying around—one good tale about some Igorot mountaineers bringing in Japanese trussed up in nets like animals. Tough on the captives.

December 16, 1941. Bedie has a cough and temperature. Both children have terrific appetites. They mustn't work so hard at the dugout for it doubles their hunger.

Our phone rings all day, and we ourselves keep contact with many people like Mrs. Saleeby and Helen who are alone. I go to the Red Cross nearly every day. The knitting progresses, so the men on the hilltop will not be cold. For two days we have been almost free from alarms. Ismael and the miners stand watching the planes sail by, their nerves accustomed too quickly!

December 18, 1941. As I was finishing coffee at lunch, trying to get some kind of news from the radio except "everything is under control," I heard a car stop and someone running down the stone steps. It was "Blondie" Barker, an American engineer at the mines. He came in the door, took my hand and said, "I've come to say good-bye, Pete." He was smiling a little but so serious and deeply moved that he was breathless.

I faltered "Good-bye? Where are you going?" and hung on to his hand. He answered, fiercely proud, "To Corregidor. I'm going to fight for my country."

For the first time, it came home to me that the radio was only stalling, though underneath had been that feeling of France falling again as the street was still a trek of natives carrying bundles out—anywhere.

I suggested a cup of coffee but Blondie said Mike was waiting in the car and they must go at once. We said so little and looked so much. He was to be in charge of some mine-tunnel workers. I went to the porch for a last handshake and waved to them as they leaned out the window, the car sliding slowly down Outlook Drive. Like a host of others, they looked really happy to be doing something, not waiting, but into action at last. They looked awfully young and serious as young people do. I called "We'll be seeing you!" and so it goes now. Every day brings changes and we live one day at a time. Only four days ago when he drank beer with us on the shelter roof, we didn't know it would be our last visit together—for some months, at least.

Dr. Abellerra said all his patients went to the mountains after the first attack and he had almost no calls. Now his patients are flocking back and he hasn't a quiet moment, there are so many calls. As in an earthquake, people instinctively feel they must go somewhere. Those who went far up the trail have returned in order not to be cut off from food if the roads are blown, so they would have been better off "to stay put" in the first place. Jerry asked if I would like to take the children up the Baguio Mountain Trail to a less exposed place and I said definitely No and I still think this was right. It was really panicky to move at all. We will try to send Mother a cable from our dugout at Christmas. We have a turkey on ice at the Cold Store and will share it with some holiday guests even if it is our last big splurge.

One of our English friends decided to while away hours between alarms by having a permanent wave. Those in the hotel shelter say it was a wonderful sight to see her appear with her hair standing up like a Gorgon's head each time the siren went off. At the market one sees Igorots with bolo knives on the hip or a lowlander with huge crossbow and arrows, ready to carve anything that bails out. I can't help thinking of the mothers and wives back in Japan who will never know what happened to their men in the Philippine attack. It is not being soft—just that women's roles are always the same, anywhere.

This is bringing out the best—and the worst—in people, and we truly see of what stuff each acquaintance is made. It is interesting—when we have time to think about it or talk it over in the evening in blackout. Kalinga province has declared its independent war on the Japanese and is out in force, with bolos, back to primitive defense and loyalty to the land. There is personal courage and stamina, people plugging along heroically in everyday habits that require strength of will just to stick to the hourly grind.

December 22, 1941. Among the vegetables in the returning Cold Store truck yesterday were three big cases of Red Cross supplies! We are now busy making bath towels, and hand towels, surgical coats and hospital gowns, sheets and slings.

Yesterday while several of us were unpacking, with the chairman, at the Red Cross, Jerry came saying, "Come on, Pete, let's go kiss our livelihood good-bye." We drove four kilometers down the trail to a point over a valley where we watched the Shell oil and gasoline tanks burn.[9] Of course, no one buys insurance and there was our last way of earning a living pouring out in thick black smoke. We continue to live a day at a time.

One of the main roads may be blown up this afternoon by our defense. When the second one goes, we will be cut off except for Igorots who can carry food on their backs to us. We have not touched our reserve yet.

At five in the morning, a man telephoned that the word was being passed around that anyone desiring to go to Manila must be down the trail by seven as the road would then be closed to all unnecessary traffic. We sat up in the dark and debated for half an hour. Finally, Jerry called back to the man that we had decided to stay and he replied that he and a lot of other people felt the same way. However, many left within half an hour—several mining camps fled wholesale. It is Hobson's Choice anyway. I do not care to join in what I consider panic flight. A trip to Manila now could develop into ghastly terror—we might run into a stampede of refugees, a mass of moving army or even enemy formations. We might have a head-on collision and undergo strafing from enemy planes as we lay injured for hours. No, we'll take what comes, here. If all the Americans flee, it will be very bad for the morale of the Filipinos and Chinese up here.

I packed all the silver in the little wool bags in which it came as wedding gifts. I also packed a suitcase with changes of clothes for either warm or cold weather.

The planes are busy elsewhere. We heard at noon over official radio that eighty ships were in the Gulf of Lingayen. All morning we heard booming, which was not thunder or dynamite.

By Christmas we may be all divided into concentration camps for men and women. I tell Nida she must be prepared to take care even of Japanese wounded, for wounded are the same anywhere, but she makes a wry face. All the people of our small group of houses stayed on. It is a salvation to keep busy on Red Cross work while we wait for—what?

In Manila we hear people live twenty-two in a house formerly occupied by one small family. Smiths have seventeen at their place, with a shelter made of packing cases and sand bags.

It is no use being afraid, whatever comes. A critical time like this brings out the stamina—or lack of it—in everyone.

We went to bed with no sign of vegetables growing in our garden and in the morning there were two rows of beans half an inch high. They push up the dirt like steamrollers and it does me good to watch them steam ahead, climbing the poles, obeying nature, quite regardless of the mess man is making nearby. We have two huge red lilies in the front garden.

We wonder if America is going to help us. Much of this is the fault of

Congressmen who would do nothing, balked all suggestions about Guam. It is hard to believe in this quietness that men are dying in mud and heat and agony at the foot of the trail. Now I must get to work and finish the bags for the boys in the hospital.

The cable we sent to Mother the day after the bombing was just returned as no cable code address is allowed through. Blitzkrieg is over and bombing less but invasion is the danger now. We still feel the line will hold and help will come, but we are very small in the large plan so perhaps we are wrong.[10]

It is late afternoon and the neighbors were all having tea with us when the siren sounded. One plane dive-bombed the Post right in front of us. It dropped two or three lots and we could hear the thuds. Our shelter was bedlam with so many small children.

December 23, 1941. It is six in the morning and we are packed, ready to join with other Americans at Teachers Camp or Pines Hotel. Ostensibly we are an open city.[11] Nida is taking over our house with her family. The children are good and very calm. We may be binding up Japanese wounds by this time tomorrow. We have given the children their gifts in the cold light of five o'clock two days ahead of time. They are sweet and patient. We'll be all right.

December 26, 1941. We have lived a lifetime in the three days since I last wrote. I guess it was three days. I'm not sure. Since we were awakened at 2:30 one morning to be told it was the last chance to get to Manila before roads closed, the telephone has been ringing every five minutes, telling us facts, rumors, facts, rumors—and denials. I couldn't begin to put down all we heard and had denied.

The blowing of Naguilian and Zig Zag [Kennon] trails down from our mountains was loud and clear and near, and then came the sound of Balatoc mine oil tanks going up in smoke which hung over the valley all morning. The sound of guns from Lingayen was clear—and not to be denied.

We finally settled on joining the Americans at Brent School in a sort of voluntary concentration so we would be all together. It was a terrible day. There was panic in the air, in the trees, and in the ground!

When it came to leaving home and good-bye to Nida, I said "We'll be seeing you," and started to leave the kitchen. There was silence behind me and I was too near the breaking point to turn around, but I did. Nida looked so bowed down that I went back and put my arms around her. We both burst into tears and she clung to me sobbing, "Oh Mrs. Crouter, I don't want you to go away or anything to happen to you. I have been so happy with you all these years. I don't want to lose June and Bedie!" We kissed and comforted each other like sisters till I finally broke away and ran out to the car still in a flood of weeping.

At Brent there were a number of air attacks and the trek down the steep bank to their shelter was too exhausting so we found a smaller hole to crouch in. Later we merely stepped outside our sixth grade room to crouch by a tree trunk on the thickly wooded slope. We had brought mattresses and blankets, several cases of food, and two sacks of rice among other things.

We had divided our rice and tinned goods with our servants. Nida and the other women all ran down to stay near an Igorot barrio, as they are terrified of the Japanese, but Ismael and another boy have stayed faithfully by the house. We told them to take down our name off the tree and move into the house. There are 17 of them now, still working on Red Cross materials! A tiny stray kitten appeared, mewing, so we fed it.

We spent the night on mattresses on the floor at the school, devoured by mosquitoes, children crying and adults wondering in wakeful hours how soon the enemy would arrive.

In the morning we went home for breakfast, stayed for lunch and tea out by the garage. It was heavenly to have one more day of respite *at home*, away from tired mothers with howling babies.

The less said about the town officials the better. The day of the panic they all left town, returning the following day. There was looting of Japanese stores but the Police Chief finally checked it even though the police were missing. We were near the scene and the humming of the mob was not pleasant to hear. They ran off with sacks of flour and sugar over shoulders and boxes under the arm.

Christmas morning still no enemy had appeared. We opened our packages in the damp dawn on the floor. Jerry gave me slacks and a white sweater. The children had slacks, blouses and jackets. We came home again at noon and had turkey down at Bacanis', marred by two alarms which left us breathless from tearing up the hill to the shelter.

I finished packing up twenty-eight hospital bags and gave them out to American and Filipino soldiers at the hospital on Christmas day during raids. It was worth all the effort to see their faces light up. One boy, in a group of about eighteen with malaria and wounds in a crowded ward, called as I was leaving to ask if I could get them each a toothbrush and toothpaste. I promised to try. Jerry drove me to a Chinese store between raids and I made the purchases. The Chinese in the stores were pleased that we had not left Baguio with so many others. When I handed the bundle to the nurse to give out to each one, the boy who had made the request turned to the others with a triumphant sweep of his arm, calling, "There, what did I tell you? See? The Red Cross can do anything!"

December 27, 1941. We are at home again for at least half a day. Only enough eggs for the children's breakfast but we opened codfish and scrapple, orange juice and coffee. We had a good night's sleep at Brent. Church and Jerry each did a share of two-hour guard duty and watching the phone during the night. At two or three in the morning Christmas night at Brent we had heard the long shrieking of a siren and thought the Japanese had arrived as it was to be the signal to congregate. It was so cold we put on shoes and heavy coats over sweaters. Report over the phone said it was a garage on fire and we went outside to see the fierce glare in the sky. It was soon under control, fortunately. We crawled back to sleep with coats on under thick blankets. Four nights on the floor now and we are no longer lame.

Yesterday we spent the day at home with the children, having our last big feast of the turkey we would have had Christmas, with candied sweet camotes [yams] and Swiss peas and beans mixed as a final treat. We eat supper at school with the big group. I haven't had my clothes off since December 7th at night as I sleep better if ready to move anywhere anytime. We've all had sponge baths or quick showers in between alarms and sirens.

Planes are beautiful always in the air. They look so free and move without effort. One machine-gunned the Post yesterday.

In the evening we heard a tremendous roar from many throats in the valley back of Brent and feared rioters coming our way. We listened, frightened, then heard faint ''Banzai'' on the wind. It was the Japanese soldiers releasing their interned civilians in the school on Trinidad Road. What fierce joy it was.

The Japanese Army took over. They woke us at 11:30 P.M. and kept us standing in one small crowded room until 2:30 A.M. checking off each one over and over. Finally they herded us all onto the second story where we all slept on the wooden floor all night. Mrs. Saleeby was allowed a mattress because of her age. About a dozen of us put our heads on it all around her, our bodies stemming out like rays of the sun. Many did not have blankets and it was a fire trap. [The Japanese officers] came about every half hour with heavy clumping boots and sharp staccato talk, would look in, stare at us like zoo animals, then go away. A machine gun was trained on us at the front door.

December 28, 1941. Moving from one room to another all day as they kept bringing more people in. Finally to another dorm on the first floor. Very little to eat except something cold out of a can. They finally let me go downstairs to get something out of my bag. They cut the thick fire escape rope right in front of our eyes and this left us no way to get out except by the one stairs. Several people lighted primus stoves and I was terrified for fear they would upset. The fire hazards and no food laid me out. I saw a number of men break down and weep because of the hunger of the children. The invaders kept shoving us about which prevented our organizing and they would not permit us to go downstairs to get our belongings. They took all our flashlights, our big bag of chocolate candy and P200 from under Jerry's pillow the first night. The whole night was a bad dream of stamping feet, clanking bayonets and guttural orders.

December 29, 1941. Weak on mattress. Got up to wash then collapsed. Seemed to have no middle and my head felt queer. They called us all onto the tennis court and told us that if we did what we were told that the Japanese soldier was kind. We must give up all guns or tell where any were hidden. They had already taken all scissors, nail files and pointed objects the night before. They seemed as frightened as we. They divided the men into one group, children and older women into another, and younger women into a third, and told us we were to walk in these groups to Camp John Hay. We were to carry blankets or what baggage we could. What we left behind *might* be taken by truck afterward. The children cried, afraid we would be kept separated. Mukibo, a Harvard graduate, with perfect English and cold, suave manner, was in charge. I wanted to walk but couldn't navigate very well and Jerry got a place for me in one of the cars taking a few elders and sick who could not walk. Those who walked started after a lunch of watery soup with two small cubes of meat in it. We left many things behind as the men were staggering under double loads. Our car passed them halfway to the Post and they looked weary and bedraggled. In the night, the water gave out. One of the Japanese had threatened us with no water. Said they went without it for several days and we would have to go without too. We had previously interned them in the same barracks.

December 30, 1941. No water till 11. Then mostly given to the children. Jerry says he fought Enid until he got a half a cup for me. I was able to walk and felt better. No chow till 10:30. Another brief meal at 3. No water again in the night. They finally brought in a few tanks.

December 31, 1941. No water till nearly noon. Bad head. The toilets have been stopped up and overflowing because of no flushing. We used the latrines dug by our men in relays, with their stomachs sticking to their backbones from hunger and thirst. Oatmeal, buns and cocoa about 9:30. The Japanese took our pictures. Rice and pork fat at 3 tasted very good. We have pooled all the canned goods brought in. Bedie sick with cramps in A.M. I had sinus headache in the night. Awful lying on the floor with people pounding by constantly on the boards. The lights came on at last.

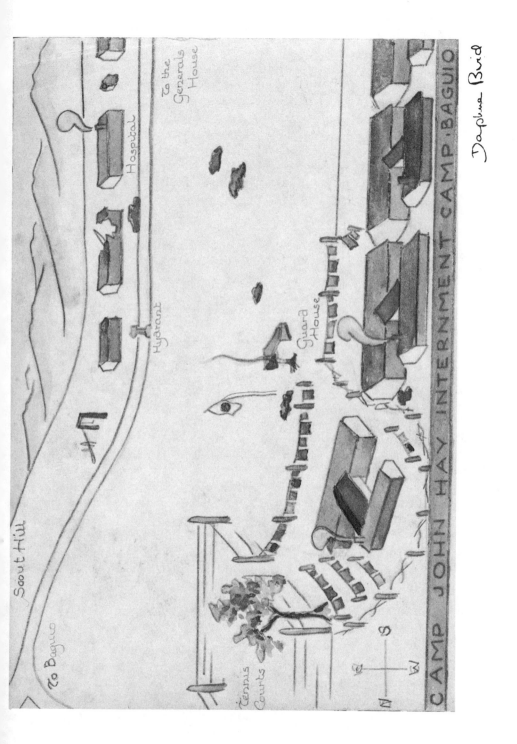

CAMP JOHN HAY INTERNMENT CAMP·BAGUIO

Daphne Bird

1942

January 2, 1942. Dysentery broke out during the night. Three cases, children. Back to regular toilets, cleaning everything with lye, etc. I bathed the kids. Killed millions of flies. Then took names of 127 who had dysentery shots. Five more cases in the night and one screamed for hours.

January 3, 1942. Killed flies and washed clothes. The Japanese took our safety deposit box keys. They made Carl do the collecting and when I asked him if we couldn't hold out he shook his head. The rage and feeling of helplessness was ghastly.

January 4, 1942. Washed clothes. Three more cases. The men moved into the next barracks building, relieving the terribly crowded conditions of over 500 in a building intended for maximum of 250. Jerry was taken to town to open up his office safe but it had been blown and jammed. We were all lined up on the tennis court inside the high wire for roll call names and numbers. Inspection in the middle of the night. A Bombay Indian and an American Indian were brought into internment together.

Two meals a day, cooked by our men organized into a kitchen staff—the first organizing by us allowed by the enemy.

January 6, 1942. Ismael brought fresh laundry, slacks and my gray wool dress! How wonderful to see him from a distance. He called out that the family and Fuzzy the cat were all right. Lysoled all floors. I was in charge of three sections. Tired.

January 12, 1942. Lucy hid her jewels under a rock where Mrs. Wilson had hidden hers previously, but not noticing it. When Lucy retrieved hers later she took all and was horrified at finding others with hers later but was afraid to say anything for fear it would get back to the Japanese. Mrs. Wilson went on the rampage, wanted to know who stole her heirlooms and was going to yell about it whether the Japanese heard or not. Someone finally untangled it but it gave us our first real laugh in weeks.

January 14, 1942. Streetlights on for first time in six weeks. A quiet night as there was no clump, clump of army boots, mostly local gentry guarding us.

January 16, 1942. A Japanese soldier appeared with an armful of antlers looted from the American General's house.

January 17, 1942. Fruit for breakfast! Japanese schoolchildren came en masse with good wishes and candy boxes for us. Their faces pressed against the wire to view the bears. Their teachers took their pictures in a group, with soldiers behind them and Americans in the far rear. The Japanese children are on a holiday, picking flowers. They marched off with two teachers after cheering their soldiers.

January 22, 1942. In the list of work details put on bulletin board by Committee, Jerry is down as Outside Sanitation, I am down as Inside Sanitation—both meaning garbage disposal.

January 23, 1942. We had lemon pie—a gift from some Japanese.

January 24, 1942. I was not well but rested on mat after working on beans and carrots. Many children throwing up and crying in the night. No garbage collected by Japanese for six days. Missionaries queried five at a time all day. Total of 30 dysentery cases in all. We are ravenous for sweet. Bucayo sent tasted wonderful.

January 26, 1942. Fourth week anniversary.

January 27, 1942. Nakamura is proud of his camp organization and we had many bowls of flowers for the inspection, but the officer only looked in at the men's section, lined up the guards for salute and took his plump self away, in *our* car with a star on the front and a special license.

January 28, 1942. Jerry and his garbage salad marvelous! Made from pieces of lettuce cut off leaves thrown out.

The lootenants told a good story of a guard wanting to get in a house to capture something they fancied. He handed his gun to one of our men to take care of, climbed in a window, gathered up the object and came out to retrieve his gun which was still there!

January 30, 1942. The missionaries were called onto the court where an announcement was read that they were to be packed to go out at two! It does not matter whether they want to go or not. No choice. Terrible flurry and flutter. Where and how will they live? Is it because our water is getting short?

And will we also be let out to cope with a new world? A mad rush of packing.

Isobel took castor oil and plans to go to hospital for arrival of her baby. We had pea soup, camotes and meat topped with tomato, plus carrots, banana and taffy. A big day. Full for once. Isobel's pains began amid the general excitement, but the Japanese said she must wait until morning. Arrangements were made to have the car come back ready to take her to hospital in the night with Dr. Bruce and one of the nurses. 125 missionaries and the 25 British Indians departed, including about 20 different faiths. They were taken to the Baguio Hotel and left amid confusion of heaped baggage and howling children and told they could go home! Lt. Mukibo of Harvard was in charge again and very efficient! We watched them all depart over the hill into freedom.

I heard the first baby cry at 1:30—a three hour travail. A son! Seven pounds and all's well. I took a peek at the infant in the silver drawer from Brent School made into a receiving crib.

January 31, 1942. When I told Isobel she was like a heroine of drama, her baby the first American born in Igorot Barracks Concentration Camp, she could only say, "Oh my mother will have a fit!" I guess she is right, but what a story! Headlines—"Japanese Imperial Command tries to stop birth, says wait till morning!" Everyone wants him called John Hay Scott which it doubtless will be even though he is *named* Richard Hawkins. We went in to see Isobel and celebrated with peppermint sticks while watching the baby learn to drink.

Notes jotted in late January, 1942

Igorot Scout quarters where we live are three long barracks on a dry sandy parade ground full of bomb holes from the first attack. The roofs are covered with shrapnel holes. Our building was made to house a maximum of one hundred and eighty. Before the men moved, there were four hundred and fifty. The women and children number about three hundred and fifty.

There are bare rafters, shelves around the windows, nails for hanging clothes, and lines down the middle for laundry drying. We all sleep on mattresses on the floor, surrounded by bags. We have pillows and blankets but no sheets. Washing the floors every morning helps to lay the dust.

It is absurd how many are trying to live as though they were still at home, with satin nightgowns, hair curlers, cold cream, lipstick, eyelash brushing every morning. There is no privacy of any sort and at least one baby crying all the time, usually a maelstrom of sound combining wails and tramping feet. Irritations crop up, expand or diminish according to the lack of sleep or hunger or ill health.

The bombed quarters across the street, with the kitchen chimney at an angle and the walls going three ways, are a symbol of the world at present.

Babies are being given baths in buckets painted bright red and marked "Fire." It is most adorably effective. Ministers of the gospel are pulling a pushcart full of wood or mattresses or kettles. One of them wears an army hat always jaunty above a faded blue army coat.

The army thinks that candy or cakes given to the children can compensate for losses or our present status. Sugar is desired by both soldiers and internees.

At three we heard that all the missionaries were returning and on the heels of the rumor, in they drove! Poor, hungry, exhausted people.

February 1, 1942. Every night we meet on Peg's mat with our children, for a snack and songs. Five officers trooped in about nine. The guard tried to tiptoe in his heavy boots at night. Jerry brought two tiny white potatoes for June and me.

February 3, 1942. Our fifteenth wedding anniversary. Jerry came early on the back porch where we meet as he carries out the garbage cans and thus has an excuse if caught talking to me. He brought sugar he had boiled down from dark and dirty cakes. Later he brought a box of candy he had secured with great difficulty from town and said he would knock my block off if I gave any out! Also brought a piece of celery and two infinitesimal tomatoes. Just like a picnic box. The kids started school again.

Some of the improvisations for the delivery of baby John Hay:—A silver drawer was the crib, a piece of unfolded gauze as tiny mosquito net, a bath towel cut into wash cloths, a flannel nightgown from the army post infirmary cut into two shirts and two bands, the ether cone—a tea strainer with cotton in it. The nurse warms the bedpan by sitting on it before giving it to the patient.

Volley ball on the enclosed tennis court on the men's half of it brings everyone out after supper. Lines are drawn—red on the men's side, white on the women's; a wide gulf between is marked "Keep off." We have to yell all our conversations and grousings. These lines were painted the day the missionaries returned.

February 5, 1942. I was up at two and saw the guard covering small [sleeping] Diana. A seven course meal of bean soup, meat loaf (too hot with peppers), baked camote, pan de sal [salt bread], rhubarb and banana, and eggplant with tomato.

February 6, 1942. Peg washed my hair in a fire bucket. Mrs. Dawson would have set it in waves, but the straight-back effect plaited into a pigtail every morning by June seems more suited to the simple life we live on a mattress surrounded by bags of leather and paper. June has knitted a red and blue tie for my pigtail, which has been dressed this way ever since we entered camp. June says I look young and like a little girl in my round-neck Christmas sweater. My state of mind has no time for waves, rouge, or lipstick. I cannot read or play cards when I am living this hard and I do feel it is a real experience, not a drop of which should be wasted or missed.

The berries from an unknown giver were consumed. It is a job to wash them without too much gazing and we hate to eat in front of people who have no extras. Everyone who has anything eats behind the hand, or bent down over it.

Our camp is lucky to have the beauty of pines, blue sky, clouds, and mountains. We could not be detained in a lovelier place. I have not been conscious of being a prisoner yet, do not notice the barbed wire, fence or guards, bayonets or guns. Even the machine gun trained on us for two days, covered with canvas, made little impression. For a while it was touch and go, so I no doubt should have had more fear and perhaps did, subconsciously. Most of us can walk on the path right at a soldier coming forward with bayonet held out and remain unmoved. Are we too tired or have we had too much taken away to be bothered by small things? Have nothing left to worry about, only to be concerned for our lives? Perhaps being stripped of possessions clears out worry, makes for peace of mind. It may be only simple living from one meal to another that makes us adjust. We don't do much head work.

February 7, 1942. It costs each about P8 a month for food here and the Committee[1] uses somewhat less than P100 a day.

One Japanese ex-miner said to an engineer, ''Sir, the Japanese are leaving and I would like to work for you again and can I borrow five pesos?''[2]

February 9, 1942. A bag came from Ismael with loaf of bread and two tins of jam we had left as their portion! We were thrilled. Nearly two months since we tasted bread. We shared with Scotts, two pieces each. June talked about home and Ann listened and said, ''I want to go home! Let's go back to Brent!'' Poor child, she has moved so many times lately that she cannot remember any nearer home than Brent.

Many in panic, and bag packing, due to rumors. One child cried, said he was frightened. His mother asked what he was afraid of and he wailed, ''Rumors!''

February 10, 1942. Japanese radio claims Singapore landing and taking Tengah Airport, also bombing Sumatra. This was almost eclipsed by the furor of four pies made in the kitchen. Jerry brought me some marrow he dug out of a bone at great pains.

February 11, 1942. Bedie's 11th birthday. I whispered a song to him with kisses. He received a bag with 12 pan de sal with ''Happy Birthday from Ismael and Nida.'' He cried, ''Oh Mummie, they are both alive!''

A ration of radish at noon—Jerry's idea since we have no meal given us then and something has to be done with the heap of radishes given us. Bedie had a fabulous party with *five* other boys in the backyard trench with contribution of food from two mothers. Enid and Nakamura are on the rampage over flies and dysentery.

The Inside Kitchen Group will never live down the pies, coffee, pancakes and extras, more particularly the attitude and atmosphere that developed, glowering everyone away from the kitchen, even others who worked in there.[3]

February 13, 1942. The dentist's hours are three to four, his dental chair is an Epsom Salt tin, his fillings are temporary, only guaranteed as far as the gate.

The Women's Committee is surely amusing. They don't really want suggestions. The nicknames for them are not bad, the Dragon being one. The chairman lines us up to clap the cook just as the Japanese line up for applause. Peggy spoke a word for the toilet cleaners, who were given real claps.

One man says this camp has given his daughter the equivalent of a college education. She has always had everything but now she has learned to carry heavy trays, wait on table, wash floors as well as sleep on one, wash clothes, tend babies and mend—as well as to go hungry, feel thirst, to know fear, to give and take with many. One has to keep a certain detachment or the small things get one down. Otherwise, it is a play, a book, a great drama, history—where one can learn to take a part.

Nakamura says we will be shipped home in two weeks. He oozes relief at the thought.

February 14, 1942. Some of the children's valentines were very bright. June's to Mrs. Macabee, "a dish cloth dripping with love for you"—to Daddy, "A garbage can full of hearts for you." All were typical of our trades in here. There are fifteen now in our tiny hospital. When clearing out the bombed building, they found two toilets unflushed and completely full, probably the source of our dysentery, with a few carriers.

February 15, 1942. Junkin baby born in cottage hospital at 5:30, starting at midnight. What are these babies—Japanese subjects, citizens? It is Chinese New Year today also. Lee's amah washed all her clothes for it last night. The Women's Committee listed working hours credited to each internee. With care of two Scott children plus supervision of sections, cans and rags, I'm down at five hours a day, thirty-five a week. Bessie, a nurse, is down as seventy hours. Della, mending clothes, is 48 or 50 hours. Peg with many [family] duties is 23 hours. These are typical; many unfair estimates.[4]

One of the funniest rumors is of a Japanese telling the Chinese group they would soon be out because there were so many of them running around that they couldn't all be interned at once and had to take turns. We saw two Chinese beaten as looters.

Phil's beautiful fur skin on his bed is the most out-of-place item in camp, but he is lucky to save it and there is no other spot to place it. My beaver collar coat covers us at night and the silver fox fur is in the duffel bag.

The men sent us berries as a Valentine, figuring eight to each if properly doled out. We had three each with our breakfast fruit. Are we to have the balance in dessert for supper? I should say not. The large shortcake was for the kitchen and dining room crew and some of the Committee. No wonder the Dragon resents entrance into her domain and rates 84 hours a week.

Now, all hands clap loudly for that delicious shortcake which we did not get! The berries, the flour, etc. were spoiling of course! That poor, over-worked cooking staff—we see now why "no one can take its place." We seem to be nicely fixed, with a Fascist group inside as well as outside the wire.

February 16, 1942. With loud pounding, Nakamura and the guards waked us in the darkness, tacking a huge sign on the tree in front of barracks—headed by "NEWS" in big black and red letters, "Singapore FELL on Feb. 15 at 7:50 P.M."

At roll call, we were given a number to sew on ourselves. I can now write to mother and sign it "Your loving daughter No. 87" if and when we are allowed to write. Neither can I be shot for looting, being identified as a camp member. I sewed 88 on June and 89 on Bedie's sweater.

Leung Nang and other Chinese were ordered to dig a hole out front; a tall thin pine stripped of branches was brought to it, and Dr. Dean stamped and pounded the base in. From the guardhouse came forth a white cloth with large Rising Sun which was tied to the top of the tree post. Nakamura, Sergeant and six privates lined up, took off bayonets from sheath at waist, put on gun, faced left and back twice, Sergeant in front, Nakamura in line, all shouting three times what sounded like "tag" as the flag was pulled to the top.

Men and women can join on the tennis court till 7 but must talk only family affairs, nothing about "soldiers."

February 18, 1942. High school began this morning here.

We were allowed half an hour on the court at 6:30. Can take husband's arm if we walk fast, but no "cohabiting" on mattresses or blankets on court (this means merely sitting together)! We were warned not to talk together before the hour.

February 19, 1942. I went on the rampage and jacked up people about Lysoling and rolling up mattresses every day as ordered. We are military now and must be all alike, no exceptions.

What a *small* life it is, so bounded and detailed by checking and numbering. The floor space is being measured now to see how much each occupies.

FEBRUARY 15
NOW YOU MAY REALISE THE ORIENT IS FOR THE ASCIATICS
FALL OF SINGAPORE

My back aches every night now. Being in the middle, it is hard to turn over, with three of us sleeping on a three-quarter mattress.

February 20, 1942. Jerry was on the rampage over the 12 five-pound cans we had turned in—milk enough for three months for four of us. They won't give even a can of it back and it is not being used just for babies and children. A few favorites get it in coffee every morning.

We hear that about 20 to 25 thousand were wiped out by Corregidor guns.

We are allowed no commingling for two nights because of infractions of rules.

The girls now get autographs on handkerchiefs which they then embroider in black as souvenir of internment. They clamored for Nakamura's the day he was to leave until he must have felt like a movie actor.

We recall Mukibo's talk to us the first night. "This is war. The Japanese Imperial Army is in command and you must obey. If a gun is found, not turned over, you will all be held responsible. The mistake of one is the mistake of all (this over and over for two days). If one tries to escape, five will be shot." Later we were told that five men and five women had been chosen for this out of our group.

February 22, 1942. There is to be no more cocoa or sugar. There is some but the Japanese won't sell it to us. Looting has emptied many places in town. Lysol almost gone, no more. We hear the Red Cross is almost defunct in Manila, supplies looted. Will we all be let out to remove the Japanese responsibility of starving us, when *our* funds which feed us are gone? Everyone thinks and talks about it.

Nakamura and his family are now being fed by our camp as they had been receiving nothing.

British Consular girls received letters about their transfer, maybe to England. People began to come and look at their space and shelves "as though we were already dead!"

February 23, 1942. Nakamura also chafes at the inactivity. His home at the mine is looted and gone. It is war, he says. His wife has only the clothes on her back. The Japanese Association is now taking care of his family, he *says*.

February 24, 1942. A package from Ismael with olives, chicken spread, from our own stores, plus Bedie's and Jerry's shorts!

June made herself a sunsuit out of a Red Cross triangle bandage!

The one time I was crimson and furious was when they took the safety deposit key where the very old jade pin, the black opals, the pearl and other pieces were, all listed conveniently. I swore I would get back the jade if it took thirty years of tracking down. Perhaps they only want cash or securities. I still have three pieces elsewhere—the diamond bracelet, the Peking jade engagement ring and Grandmother's diamond ring. I left my checkbook on the bed in plain sight where it was passed over completely. This small detail may keep us alive for weeks someday. We still know nothing of our house and the ancient Chinese Celadon plates which is the most that matters of our possessions.

February 25, 1942. Several people still smile as they remember how I held a vase of sweet peas in Brent office the night we were taken over and they crammed us into the stifling little room. When the soldiers were ripping up the telephone wire, they upset the vase and I took it and buried my face in the cool freshness of the flowers. Later I took it upstairs and put it on the mantel over our heads. The Capital Bazaar man[5] thought I was insulting the Japanese—that I didn't like the air they brought, so he would not let me have my typewriter the next day nor for weeks afterward when it stayed on the table on the porch. Finally one day he saw Virginia looking at it and said to her, "Is that yours? Do you want it?" and she took it gladly and gave it to me quietly later. I have never dared to use it. He had put a vase of flowers next to it on the porch saying perhaps that would make the air better. So do we misunderstand each other.

28 days of our funds left—then what?

Missionaries heard in a note from Manila that "Uncle Sam is just around the corner."[6] We hope so. Ruth feels we'll all be out in a week. We all started guessing how it would happen and nearly all feel "They" will melt away in the night.

Lola, a refugee from Hitler, said the camps in Europe were far worse than this one. Many members would be taken out at night, and after horrible sounds of torture, they would never be seen again nor would any one know what happened to them. As for stopping the school,[7] she says we must understand they do not want our children to learn or us to enjoy anything. They like to see us wash clothes and floors and do hard work. She says that a Japanese officer told a woman on the outside that a year and a half ago he was in Munich, so they have studied directly and learned more than the goose step there.

February 26, 1942. There are many thoughtful acts here—stronger arms doing the personal washing for older or weaker people; sharing of food packages with those who get none. Many Filipinos outside are sending in their native homemade products as gifts which taste so good—bucayo, peanut candy, oranges from trees in their yard, Sinnoman (gooey cake of coconut juice and cassava flour) which is wrapped in banana leaves.

We can get along *without* much better than a month ago. We accept *every* day, without looking ahead, better than we did then.

We hear that eight Chinese refused to give themselves up so the Japanese set fire to the Dainty Bakery where they were entrenched.

February 27, 1942. I still marvel at what food craving does to individuals. The strangest acquaintances—not really friendships—spring up. One who gets gifts or purchases attracts one or two others who have none, often odd combinations. In normal times they would not see each other. Lack of food changes people generally, makes insidious inroads in many directions of the personality.

A charming baby basket was left on Ronnie's bed and she knelt in delight before it, almost as though the baby were there. It is a market tampipi [woven basket] with stiff frills of white curtain material (donated and freshly laundered), a pink bow on the outside and arched bamboo at each end holding the draped mosquito net, so dainty and sweet, as pretty as from Best's in New York! Ronnie and other expectant mothers have received small sweaters and booties knit with yarn on hand or brought in from the outside, little dresses and gowns made from all sorts of odd material. Dozens of women had a hand in the cutting, sewing, washing, pressing.

The porch at evening sing was quiet and peaceful, no fires in the distance for the first time, and the moon was high. The campfire at the guardhouse was picturesque, with five guards and Nakamura sitting in silhouette against the blaze. I would like a color block print of it by Ito.

We had competition in our porch songs as the young people were all out under the moon singing and dancing. The small children gazed with enjoyment, around the fringe. June cried with homesickness and craves milk. This is hard for parents to bear.

February 28, 1942. Nakamura at the Committee meeting burst forth profanely that we would not need the bomb holes in our roof mended for the rains as we would probably not be here then—that *they* might instead, as the Japanese did not seem to be doing so well lately in some respects!

The Gilberts, Marshalls, Carolines, are now ours with the Navy cleaning up as it goes.[8] Filipinos are not allowed to talk to Americans any more. There may be restrictions of food gifts coming in to us.

A poster in town tells of Filipinos ordered back to work, that Americans have destroyed their fields and burnt their cane and they must get back to it. This could be guerrilla destruction. It is Union Now for all allies in the Far East, large and small, Americans, British, Dutch, Filipino, Chinese, Burman.

March 1, 1942. A petition requesting the kitchen to cut down on the red pepper and chili in food brought out an odd reaction. "Are we going to pay them, now that we start dictating to them?" An interesting attitude! The women cooks resent any criticism or suggestion. We hope the men are less sensitive as that peppery flavor is hard to take and petition is our only recourse, if we are still democratic, which I sometimes doubt.

The Japanese sent in three cases of milk and some candy for American children. Valdez and Arvisu wrote that the Filipino women want to make diapers for the American babies. We certainly found out our friends among the Filipinos. Many stuck by and sent gifts even with little themselves but they know what real need is. It is better being inside where one can lose oneself and not bow. The outside is more difficult in many ways.

Rumors are bread for the spirit to feed upon. Even the weak and unbelievable ones keep the flame alive. I prefer them to skepticism or pessimism which may also be only half true. A delicious one—that 75,000 Australians landed in the Philippine Islands—simply can't be true.

March 2, 1942. Our first irritations are less. We do not notice the lack of privacy quite so much, nor the constant tramp of feet and crying. Second irritations have cropped up however. We hope we never have to see this face again, or hear that particular whine, or that ineffectual discipline.

John Hay came to his space today and his tiny cry is like having a baby in our own family, we share his presence so completely. His wail is soft, pitiful, trembly. We also enjoy watching Ah Yi, the only Chinese allowed on our side, taking care of young Lee since his doctor-mother is so busy. She is a universal amah, with fine motherly face.

Natures that withdraw take more of a beating in internment than those who adjust or melt into the group. Becoming sociable or a democrat, if one is not inclined that way, is a lesson that takes long learning.

After all, Singapore did fall, and so did Manila, so this time all prides are down, we are in it together, British and American.

We had "common" time at six but the men are restless and uneasy under public chats. It is unsatisfactory with khaki eyes on one and constant walking required; sitting together is too intimate by Japanese standards.

If we were Outside, we would take news for granted. Here, the men especially, have become hopeless. They work hard, to forget, all day, and refuse to believe anything.

March 3, 1942. We look like Ellis Island émigrés every morning with wooden boxes, market bags, duffel bags, pillows and typewriter piled up on three mattresses so we can put a sea of soapy water around them. I take pride in doing the floor with petty thoroughness.

Someone told me last night that Davis had said it would have been his duty to escape and rejoin had he not known that five of our men and five women had been chosen for shooting at the first escape.

I listened to Daddy while he gave an eloquent talk on camp life to Bedie who is in a bad rut of doing nothing. He told him he himself not only paid out a small amount of cash to feed us every week but contributed hours of work and effort as well. The money was not enough. Bedie must do his share or he would be looked on as among those boys who ate extra and did nothing to earn it. He must do garden detail every other day and help shell peanuts in between those days. He must not feel *we* got nothing from the garden because it was for the future and perhaps even American soldiers would need it and eat from it.

One has to live *Inside* for two months to know how really good fresh coconut and strawberries taste. A few guns and barbs can give Inside and Outside a new meaning too. Inside we have a hard time believing anything can happen Outside but we learn to value simple things. We look at the full moon without the aid of an Old Fashioned or the comforts of a club porch. We see the sunrise. With our heads on the floor, reverberations reach us which would never find us at home. Perception is sharpened when other facilities are removed.

March 4, 1942. Two Japanese landings have been made in Java, defeat all over the Philippines for the Americans, the road to Manila wide open and in Pampanga is wide, horrible devastation and stench.

The Army, the Navy, the Intelligence, the Samurai with the beautiful old swords, they do not give, they take and take, even from their own people here. How many sacrifices have the *people* made for these Big Swords that they may come into towns like this and not even feed the families of their guards and helpers?

A big surprise of a package and letter from Nida! The first word from home! They have all been living [in our house] since January 6th. What a thrill to get this word! It was tucked in with two cans of Nestlé milk and some consommé. We felt as though we had heard from the whole world.

One of the guards played tennis with several of our men.

March 5, 1942. It is hard to credit some with real work in here when they look continually crisp and spotless. This is the basis for some class prejudice outside. Even Bedie asked how Della could always have those exact creases in her slacks every day in here.

When "shifts" had been instituted in the kitchen, the new assistants were all "friends" of the group and no "hold" was relaxed. It is work everyone wants because of the food rewards connected with it and privileges shown, such as a private back room. No matter how hard they work on hands and knees, the general opinion is against them due to graft. The woman chairman is severe, dogmatic, takes no criticism or suggestion, is high-handed, no one will stand up to her (with one or two exceptions) but she is not as unpopular because she does *mix* and tries to be just by her own standards and is a tireless worker. She has her own room but does not stay in it all day and has tackled many problems.

March 6, 1942. Peg has permission to sketch scenes from the hospital area any time she wishes. The freedom almost unnerves her. She sketched all morning there.

We rally various sources in defense, to protect our hopes from cancellation. We weigh this and that, figure half of this is right, part of that one exaggerated. It is a world of rumor where the invader constantly batters at the gates of Hope in a thousand small insidious ways.

Annoyances are inevitable in such close proximity and scarcity. One woman who usually loves children hopes not to see any for months after she gets out. Communism or socialism will fail if they disregard privacy. Crowding does not produce efficiency and economy. It wastes too much energy and does not make allowance for relaxation and rest. Men can have barracks if they want them—but give them the children and changing diapers on the floor, lifting constantly, cry, cry, cry, and they'll change it in a hurry. If it is to be *close* communal living in the future, I'll join a real revolution.

Tokyo radio says they have never interned or held any prisoners in occupied countries!

One girl says she has had a swell time with her baby in here. She would only have seen her about once a month if at home with an amah.[9]

Three of the young were discussing one family which has much to eat so that they have no appetite left for camp meals, when Barb jumped in with a vehement, "When I see her spread ketchup on her cocktail sausages, I could kill her!" Did the poor always feel like this toward the rich who had what they could not buy? Our watching and scrutiny is constant. The incident epitomizes some general feelings.

March 8, 1942. One lady is very depressed, says nothing will be done about the Philippine Islands, that we will be left for the "duration" until conclusions are reached in other places more important. Since we do not know and can take our choice it is preferable to enjoy continuous analysis, the mind occupied with darting about, watching and learning.

There is some discussion as to whether it is Saturday or Sunday since every day is alike in here. It helps to keep notes like this and I won't have to recapitulate to Mother, only type, which I've never quite dared to do here as it takes up too much space and notice from the guards. I only hope to get out with these notes as the days fade from memory very quickly and would be almost impossible to recall. Rings of growth for all of us as if we were trees.

We are not starving but we thoroughly crave *accustomed* food. There is a definite unbalance to our diet besides the fact of only two meals a day. We lack enough proteins, sugar and fat. The children have rice, syrup and a drink of hot water for breakfast; adults the same, plus weak coffee without milk or sugar. Strawberry jam in a piece of bread for lunch but no soup or tea. A radish for the adults and a piece of O'Racca candy for the children. Gifts from the outside have satisfied my cravings for the moment but I'm still mad for a 24-hour soak in hot water, in a tub, solitary and alone—no fire buckets, no three others splashing cold shower in the small enclosure, all standing on one leg to dress.

March 9, 1942. The Chinese babies get no milk, only rice gruel with vegetable juice added, and they thrive on it. None of them are sick, which is more than can be said about our children. Our resistance is soft compared to that of the Oriental but their mortality rate as a whole is high, not just in camp. Perhaps it is a buildup in immunity. They are receiving the usual diet, do not have to make the adjustments that we have to make.

Bedie brought sweet peas, bell flowers, purple larkspur, yellow cosmos, phlox and Queen Anne's lace from the garden, a lovely combination of colors.

March 10, 1942. Roof repairers interrupted baby naps and were routed by an irate mother. So it goes, individual versus communal activity!

Geraniums have given way to lettuce around our barracks. The small boys plant with terrifying energy. June says, "Mummie, I don't care for dolls any more. They are tame after taking care of a baby."

Two sheets of typed news came in someone's bag and Nakamura is furious. He cut open many loaves of bread to find more notes but there were none.

There is a story which has just reached feminine ears from the men's side—of Winslow who has started a small store at his space where he sells bucayo for fifty cents that usually is priced at twenty-five, a sandwich at twenty cents in the same ratio. The Japanese found his wife outside, buying quantities on credit, and traced it back to him. Two gallants (not husbands) continue late talks on the back porch with romantic looking Juliets. Sooner or later we all suffer from such infringements of rules; they deny us common hour or impose other restrictions because of one or two—"the mistake of one is the mistake of all." Even the young fry linger and carry on a romantic attachment or two. Love, like news, will find a way.

March 11, 1942. Mrs. Henderson asked for some books sent in weeks ago and they only just arrived at this bad time. The whole stack is to be burned, 25 pounds worth, says Jerry. This is the order: "No messages, orders, or writing of any kind is to go out from the camp from now on. If any message of any kind is sent out, the penalty will be that no further packages will be allowed into camp. This order affects the whole camp and not individuals."

Jerry nearly fell off the railing when I put on lipstick and rouge for the first time in camp, to see how it looks with a pigtail.

Delicious roast pork, gravy with rice, pepper soup and one of the Chef's[10] "creative" salads chopped fine.

It is now said that someone wrote out "Send us food. We are starving." Nakamura found it and was sore as he was "called" on it by the Intelligence.

March 12, 1942. Grandma just initiated me into the mysteries of quilting. She has six kinds to work on in here with her, having sent out for it in time. One is known as the Bulgarian Whirligig, another is the Ocean Wave, two Windmills (large and small cuts), a Nine-Patch, and the Ship Pattern. I tell her it is enough for a lifetime. She replies placidly, "Oh yes, I'll do vegetables half a day, quilting half a day, then I'll be plenty satisfied till we get out which will be soon if our Navy is in Manila Bay. Pa sets the 15th for the day."[11] Her serene confidence jacks me up and I don't need any more rumors. She sounded so sensible, I wish that pessimists could have heard. She has also completed her rag rug, sewed in long thin lengths then knitted on big wooden needles. It is circular, with purple strips and gay red Japanese designs. Someone said, "The Japanese admit their surprise at the way American women can work. They didn't think we could and find us pretty good."

Peg said as we looked at the porch rail from her mat, "This makes me think of East Side New York from a fire escape. Bedding hanging out all windows and over railings, children everywhere yelling, no place to get away from it, caught and held by it." How true, yet we always feel there is escape from it sometime ahead, whereas many of those tenement dwellers are dulled by malnutrition which has no hope of ending, caught by low wages with little hope of changing, no cheerful future or much background behind them. There, they have greasy smells, not pine-scented air and clear skies without soot or smoke.

March 14, 1942. The Filipinos are cooperating with the Japanese in some cases but there must be a vast silent mass who are not. Now that we are forbidden to write or talk to them, the Japanese will say that we have forgotten them. But Art winked at our buyers today and Nang and Chan smiled broadly from the pushcart on the road.

March 15, 1942. Many people are shelling peanuts on the front porch. June dreamed there was a big party at the club and all the women were presented with a box of Kotex. No wonder, it is an important topic, and every shelf has a box!

Nakamura has a fine combination of profanity learned from his American superintendent at the mine. It makes his character even more colorful and picturesque. There is something forthright about him, a directness which is American rather than Japanese.

March 16, 1942. It is interesting to watch the war of nerves' effect on different ones. Some want to be square and play ball, others have a dash of the devil and get away with all they can.

Two Japanese soldiers are playing baseball with the Americans on the court. When they miss three times, they roar with laughter. It is all very fraternal.

About 3:30 the outside world came over the hill—a car with the Red Cross flag on the front, waving proudly—not that infernal, eternal Rising Sun! Philippine Red Cross was printed on the door of a blue car, not the eternal army brown. How breathless we felt, looking at it, with Dr. Devenicia inside. It was also full of supplies—cod liver oil, medicines, milk, fruit juices, blue and pink wool, cloth to make pajamas and other things. The doctors and some of the Committee sat down with Dr. Devenicia. They were joined promptly by the Japanese in the persons of Nakamura, Nagatomi in khaki cap and long khaki pants, and the Rising Studio man that we call Joe Philadelphia who arrived in beautiful jodhpurs on a motorcycle. They talked two hours and unloaded the car while the gong rang and we ate supper. I seemed to realize for the first time how many months since we said good-bye to home and Nida and Ismael and their children and all the friendly Filipino faces we used to see. I want to see them again! Does this coming of the Red Cross mean anything for us, an opening wedge for more? I shall cry if I go on. I must go and dress up, put on a white sweater, forget how long I stood gazing at that blue car and the symbol of international good will. It tightens the throat, that sign of somebody giving a damn as to what happened to us. At least six women have told me that they went back to the mattress and wept after seeing the Red Cross flag, a banner of hope from beyond.

In the evening, "Life Behind Barbed Wire" was so good that we laughed immoderately at ourselves, which was good for all of us. The play was in seven scenes. The first was "nighttime" with internees falling over sleeping figures, babies crying and all the rest of our hectic sleep hours. Next came "the dining room," the Smoker's seat near the toilet, scratching of heads over menus by the kitchen staff, groups trying on Tuesday Club gowns in the dining room, another smoker scene with the guard insisting on proper container for ashes. Frankie made a good Arthur calling for cups and knives and "what is this—a clip joint or a concentration camp!" Mary Dyer brought an avalanche of applause singing several songs, dressed in her Christmas Eve gown for the first time. How glamorous and odd an evening gown looks in here! "Cleanin' Day" and the camp theme song "Mañana" were sung by the group, shaking the rafters.

The audience sat on tables, benches and boxes. Nakamura and the guards want to see the show so there will be a second performance. It was a much-needed outlet for our emotions.

March 17, 1942. The climax after the play was dramatic. Nakamura and the guards came through with arms full of embroidered pieces. They called for the cast of the Players in the dining room and gave each one a gift which turned out to be tablecloths, napkins, handkerchiefs, delicate piña pieces—all from Doreen Garwick's wedding chest at the Club. This brought mixed emotions to everyone and all of them returned their pieces to Doreen. It is one way of getting loot returned. The guards really liked the play and wanted to give something in appreciation so took what was at hand at the guardhouse. It may be their idea of humor, too. To us, it was the last straw for it brought so many memories of the past.

Ronnie started giving birth to her St. Patrick's Day baby that night.

March 19, 1942. The rumors are on again, everyone glad to swallow them after a long dry spell. Mrs. Mainz says, "They can say what they like about our wild rumors but we were a lot happier when we had them. We were up and we were down, but now we are down all the time and it's awful having nothing." So I told her the latest crop.

I often think of Romulo's speech—how the people of Indo-China were made paupers before his very eyes and he hoped his own people could be spared but feared they would not be. Now they have reduced us to it, first looting the homes, then taking the safety box keys to remove money, securities, jewels, bank and checkbooks, insurance papers, finally our cash in the camp. Nagatomi says no Red Cross help. We must live entirely on friends and charity and Japanese Army support.

We are getting more primitive every day with the men in thick beards and tanned bodies without shirts, hauling like horses or trucks. It is man power in here.

I remember what a woman said of the fierce typhoon which wrecked their mine—"You save and accumulate for years and suddenly, like a great hand, something reaches down and wipes it all away and you can't lift a finger to stop it." Now it is our turn to feel like that.

June looked wistful and sad sitting by herself, looking into the distance. When I put an arm on her shoulder, she broke, cried without warning. Homesick again.

I'm feeling very low and it takes the form of quarreling with Jerry who just goes away and leaves me when I grouse, so I have to recover.

March 21, 1942. Martha received a baby basket trimmed with ruffles by her Filipino girl on the outside. Little did we think we would be using so many of the Red Cross garments ourselves when we made adult and baby clothes. I remember their advertisement for the drive—"Will it ever happen to You?" And here it is!

March 23, 1942. Inez, a lovely Igorot girl, sent a large tin of delicious native coffee for the camp through me. I will not turn it over to the kitchen but have made arrangements to serve a pot of coffee to different groups every day, until all have had a cup. First the toilet-workers, next the towel-washers, then the women vegetable cutters, the porch groups, the British girls who get no packages, and so on.

We all live a day at a time much better than two weeks ago. Life is accepted with the daily routine gone through with less hope, less irritation about tomorrow. We have learned a little about how to wait. There is still debate on how long it will be and there are many schools of MacArthur strategy. "Any day now" we say each morning, and do not feel worse when many days pass in saying this. There is always a bit of news, a new baby, someone sick, someone coming home from the hospital, a fall down the stairs, a new flag raised, a change of guard or the Chinese and Japanese playing doubles tennis together. The High Command cannot keep these little items of living from us and we can still hear the drone of planes and feel a glorious day.

March 28, 1942. The funeral of Sally's premature baby took place this morning. The men made the casket, the women lined it with satin taken from pieces of a slip, the baby was covered with a blanket knitted by his mother. Twelve were allowed to walk and carry it the two miles to the cemetery on Balatoc Road. Nakamura brought flowers from the garden and these were made into sprays and set pieces. Enid was thoughtful and helped much but she had no time to attend to camp needs—rows over soap requisition and mosquito nets. She should delegate some of her responsibilities to others instead of wearing herself threadbare trying to hold it all tightly in her own hands.

It is odd how we feel about spaces. Each one hangs on to his allotted spot like grim death. We haven't moved an inch from our 34 inches in three months. It seems to be a "home" feeling. We talked about adjusting ourselves after we get out. One young person said we would adjust as easily as we had in here. I could not admit it was easy. It took me weeks to get used to the clamor and constant tramping. After three months very little bothers me except being cut off from communication and expression of thanks. This assumes vast proportions at present. Is it the only vestige left of my past? Must I discard this also? What is left of my former self? Jerry says I must curb my old desire to thank people. Why must I? Why should even my husband have to tell me this? Appreciation is one of the most glowing forms of life. We cannot let all the flames go out in us even though Churchill did say the lights were going out one by one everywhere. June wept, homesick, "When, oh when, Mother?" I answer it may be tomorrow and she wails, "but when it isn't then, I am so disappointed." I can only reply, "Any day may be the day. We hear nothing and we do not know how near it may be. We must simply wake each morning ready. It will come as sure as the sun rises in the morning." Perhaps I do not feel as sure as I speak, always.

March 29, 1942. One day when the three American soldiers were locked up and received no coffee, some of our men fed it to them through a small hole in the wall, with a rubber tube and an enema bag.

March 30, 1942. Nakamura gave the girl garden detail a talk on useless American women yesterday. He must have been watching some of the women in here for many of them spend hours on their makeup. It seems very out-of-place, poor taste, if not vapid. I for one cannot keep on looking like the Queen of Sheba while emptying garbage. One of the girls who waits on the table can be seen curling her eyelashes at 4 A.M.

Most of all the Japanese abhor buying milk for babies and think our women are no good at all because they cannot or won't nurse their children. They feel that no woman should enjoy herself without her child, therefore a baby should never be left on the bed or in another person's care while the mother commingles. A guard tried to get Mrs. C. to take Penny to the court. He took Donald away from the girl who was taking care of him, out to his mother on the court. He is probably a simple, hard-working peasant whose wife takes her baby into the field with her when she works or into the park on Sunday, on her back. Naturally they think we don't do anything but attend to makeup from what they have observed of white women in the Orient. To them we are just a bunch of "organizers" getting someone to do our work for us.

Nakamura wonders why we all wear slacks—only coolies wear slacks in the Orient.

April 1, 1942. I never expected to sleep so long without sheets, on a plain mattress. But we must not forget—This is War! Mosquito nets look so queer at night. Some are square, some oblong, some peaked, some round, others just little face veils. In the dusk it looks like a cobweb city of fantastic shapes.

No one can know unless he's been in it what it is like to live in a vacuum, of no news, no messages, no reliable information, except what is poured out for the dull mind, to depress the spirit, until everything becomes automatic, as though one were a robot or five years old. We can eat, wash, carry garbage, live on charity, but we must not think with our own minds.

One waitress said while giving out the buns, "Wasn't the cook grand to make these for us?" It is camp material, camp cooking, but they always have to be kissing the cook or patting her on the back, as though it were a personal affair. No one pats the towel-washers, the toilet-workers, who get up just as early, work just as hard, with less reward. No one pats me for carrying garbage or washing floor cloths. I would think they were crazy if they did. It is our job and we don't expect constant praise. Many of us are tired of the sickly sentimental, ingratiating attitude on the part of the kitchen crew. The buns were swell and I said so but no fawning, thank you. The flour was mixed with cornmeal to make it go around.

Someone remarked that she did not miss a bed as much as she missed chairs. Then only did I realize we had no chairs but sit on the mattress, on the floor, or on the front steps. Recently some benches have made an appearance.

April 2, 1942. Jim has an Authentic.[12] Russia is not in the war in any way but is getting tons of American supplies which come faster. Russia is no further in Germany than when we were out, is just holding them. Americans and Chinese have invaded Thailand. MacArthur has gone to Australia which now has air supremacy in South Pacific and they are to start a tremendous drive up from there. The Navy is busy clearing the seas over here. Fifty-four planes raided Corregidor and twelve were brought down. Cebu capital has much activity. Davao is a Japanese naval base but we have a big army somewhere in Mindanao. Wake and Guam facilities were destroyed by the Americans, have not been retaken by them.[13]

April 3, 1942. Good Friday. Young Florey weighing seven pounds came into a war-torn world at 5:40 A.M. His father is in a Japanese jail in town and his mother in Concentration Camp. A Chinese woman in breech birth had a daughter half an hour later. She had not even told anyone she was in labor.

An Easter service of prayers and songs, but no address, with Nakamura present, will be allowed tomorrow. It is the first service since we came into camp, and very important to all the church groups.

April 5, 1942. Easter Sunday. I could not help thinking during the service how much stronger people look in their own element. The preachers looked, sounded and seemed better as they assumed their former roles. Intellectuals and ministers find this life hard. They are not used to washing floors and working with their hands. Brains, minds, are not wanted in here except to receive propaganda. Practical people adjust the best.

It was a beautiful sunrise service, with many attending and all standing, no chairs. There was reading from Luke and John and the Acts, and a fine Men's Chorus. Mary sang, with violin accompaniment "I Know That My Redeemer Liveth." With all of us gathered in a triangle, the sun bringing out the pine fragrance and covering us with light, there was inspiration. I thought of Mums as we sang "The Day of Resurrection" and "Christ the Lord Is Risen Today." All types, kinds and groups were represented. Many men came with their families; McCann who had almost died was there, the Jamaica Negro,[14] the anthropologist, diverse missionary beliefs. Bedie put his head on my lap and cried afterward. First he said it was because there were no Easter eggs but later admitted there was a dachshund at the guard-house and they kicked it away. He wanted to go home and see Lallie. I told him it was spring and he must cheer up (though I nearly cried with him). He mustn't be of little faith for he might receive an Easter egg. He said no one could get enough for all the children. At breakfast there were white garden lilies on the tables, green pine boughs, and phlox—and Easter eggs! Bedie was sure there would be enough only for the babies—but they all received them and ate them too. How many days the senders must have worked to prepare them, thinking of us. We hustled to put on name tags, hid our sugar and even the eggs when the guards came through. One never knows! The children are smiling again.

June has an onion sprouting in a little can. We talked about how dry it had looked, withered, yet that spark of life was there to come forth under proper conditions into lovely green points. I told her that everyone was like that and some day people would understand; there would be no more prisons, only hospitals or schools to correct abnormalities; society would try to correct unhealthy surroundings and malnutrition which warped people and covered their spark of life. As we went arm in arm to breakfast, she said, "Mummie, I just learned an awful lot. I never thought about people that way before. It's nice." Whether it is religions, idealism, socialism, art or some other creative expression, it must go with the bread. For those who have not been able to develop inner resources there must be outside help to draw forth their green shoots of hope and courage.

Everyone is covering strawberry baskets with flowers, putting on ribbon ties, for Easter hats. Camp is growing more and more hilarious over it. There is noisy laughter at Nora who wears a branch on which is a paper bird; at Rae in a wide dark cloak, with onions hanging from her ears as earrings, the long green sprouts on her head. All have gathered on the porch to look and laugh until this is an uproar. It makes me uneasy. They are carrying it too far and will pay for it later. Some others agree that it is too gay and noisy, foolish during war and concentration. The Japanese temper is getting shorter.

April 7, 1942. There are no cars traveling about; several of the streetlights are out but the dark is restful. It seems queer to have been within sight of our home for three months yet unable to go there.

Anyone who has any privacy here is fiercely envied, even the mothers in the crowded back room. Anyone who finds it, hangs on to it like death. It has become a craving, like a tangible possession, almost a new commodity, a fight to hold even a crumb of it.

As in the Army, most of the rumors spread in the latrine.

This is a universal experience. It interests me chiefly from the point of view of communal living, watching the benefits and the irritations, considering how the friction could be resolved or worked out differently. It is a forced situation, not the perfect setting for an experiment, but that is always so in life.

April 8, 1942. Wallie went to the bank with the Japanese, to the private safety deposit boxes for the *first time*. They only opened one or two where they knew there was money, took out P7,000 for us and the Chinese to live on for a month. Before this, only the bank's own funds were taken, in deposit in their name, not out of personal funds. Perhaps my jade and opals are still there when I thought them gone three months ago with the keys. It is better to think that all has been taken, once the mind has adjusted to it. Then if something is left, it is like new.

I never expected to sew up tears in paper market bags in order to make them last. I pick out cloth from the trash can for Grandma's quilt, and cardboard boxes to make fly-swatters. Renée watched the cans go into the incinerator one day—six for us, one less than full for the Chinese. That is about the ratio for America and China as to waste.

One of the nurses said as a Chinese baby was born "Oh, I'm afraid it's a Chinese baby!" Her mind had been working with an American mother and even the Chinese women laughed.

April 10, 1942. Hammering was heard in the middle of the night. I wondered who had the temerity. At 6:30 Izzy came to tell that the wrapping paper sign in grand lettering on the tree says "Bataan Fell! Finally with unconditional surrender on April 9, at 7 P.M. Now let us realize the Orient for the Orientals."

Bedie pulled a good one, talking with two other boys about what they would do when they got out. One was going to join the Army, one the Navy, but Bedie said, "Well, I'm going to commit murder and adultery." He does feel savage and sinful, poor kid!

April 11, 1942. A vegetarian who has been allowed two tins of milk a day is now having this cut off due to shortage. She went direct to Nakamura about it, saying it was against her religion to eat meat, so Arthur blew up on religion again. There should have been no special privilege from the beginning in this emergency. The Seventh Day Adventists and their no-pork rule should have been suspended. Instead they have consumed all the cheese, macaroni, spaghetti etc. Now there is none left. Even the people who brought in cheese had none of it due to this religious rule. Managers always complain they cannot find enough people to take responsibility. There are too many who cheat or give privilege or take it. Everyone wants to be the exception. It can be worked out, I'm convinced, from observation in here.

April 12, 1942. Some shoe soles have been made for the children out of old pieces of rubber fire hose nailed onto the shoe. Another rubber sole was wired on.

The purple Jacaranda tree has two lovely blooms beside the guardhouse.

Daphne brought practically no clothes when she was ordered from the Club. She has only slacks and a sweater, but whenever I watch her walk, I see her gowned all in black velvet, white neck and arms, red gold hair, head set regally as now, with that erect carriage sweeping into some British Colonial ballroom, to be in great demand, disdainful yet liking it.[15]

People change when they change elements. We may like a steamer acquaintance, see him constantly, yet when New York or London is reached, each melts back into a former environment, seems another person, not so interesting often. Some people here who were enjoyable outside under pleasant conditions are not so interesting in this bedrock environment of camp and they will not seem so again outside perhaps. Is it fair to judge by these trying standards? Not many can take it well, this war of nerves. On the other hand, everyone is doing better than one might expect generally.

I never felt more like crying than when June bumped into my shoulder—breaking her glasses in a new place for the third time. She put them away, came back and wept in my lap. We hated the Japanese and wanted to go home. She must wear them for it is important.

April 13, 1942. I gave June's glasses to Jerry and he raged as I hoped he wouldn't, being upset myself. I have saved some paper for typing and he wants it to make into cigarette papers. Everything I have saved goes like this—someone else gets it or it goes up in flame. It all seems futile. I guess I'll start using everything. I gave Jerry some sheets of paper and left him as he often leaves me when annoyed. I just can't talk today.

Bedie traded his dented bullet for two pieces of fudge with a boy going to Manila. He had refused to trade it with his sister at any price for weeks. I made him give a taste of the fudge to his sister who always shares with him. Later the small child went by with the bullet polished and hung as a pendant around the neck. I feel it should have been June's. But what is it but a piece of destruction anyway! Why does everyone covet such souvenirs, hunt for them and trade and hang them like a jewel on the breast? The children are not the only ones. It keeps them busy, shining the small cases which hold the pointed objects of death.

The Committee has made an anti-dog ruling which upsets many. There were only two stray dogs and many have enjoyed them. It was only scraps and old bones that were given to them. The wellsprings of our affection have been crushed and dried enough by Nagatomi and his crowd without this unnecessary ruling by our own. The Japanese would have let the dogs stay.

April 14, 1942. A truck drove in with Florey and Loddigs who have been in jail for questioning, unheard of for three months. Grey was not with them. They looked well in spite of pallor and they say that thanks to murderers and other prisoners who shared outside chow, they managed to get along.

Late in the evening a high-ranking group of officers came through the barracks. They said it was the best-run camp in the Islands, congratulated Nakamura and asked for the names of the Committee. Does this make the Committee good Nazis? They liked their reception by the mob, said we were so clean and courteous. Clean and courteous, after all these months.

April 15, 1942. Someone asked one camp member to help out with vegetables. She was furious, says she has two children to look after. She is too good to do hard work. However, her older daughter helps her in everything, even the washing. Like many others they wash too often and as many clothes as they would have washed at home. It can't be done here with so many shortages—soap, water, pails. There are about forty mothers who do no communal work, simply look after their children. If many more of our workers leave camp,[16] these others will have to help cut vegetables or they won't get any.

April 16, 1942. Jerry brought June a bullet, shined and with a welded ring to hang it by. She literally jumped for joy and now has a pendant of destruction on her chest. Bedie is very put out and wants one.

April 17, 1942. All we think about is Freedom and Food.

April 18, 1942. All prejudices are exaggerated in here. We are under klieg lights. People's traits are emphasized a thousand times where there is no privacy, no possibility of concealment under social graces. Everything is known.

June is reading, so concentrated that she almost forgets her baby tending. She is proud of giving her first bath to Susan. Jerry brought some ginger fudge, which is delicious. He made a ginger syrup with something else very secret in it. Says it is his patent stomach tonic. It is potent, zippy, practically alcoholic. We've had much fun over it.

There are those who still get outside orders but they grow smaller. Mr. Shultz still sells eggs, beef sandwiches and other things sent in by his wife, and some still seem to be able to purchase. We receive about three packages a month from Miss Ramos, Jerry's Filipina secretary, which is luxury while it lasts.

I feel strongly that work details should be in shifts, with no one exempted except for illness, age and lack of strength. No one should be allowed to perform the "nice" jobs all of the time. The distasteful ones should be shared. So-called menial work would lose some of its menial quality and distastefulness if everyone had to take a hand.

We all have the "Nazi look"—over the shoulder, when talking together, to see who might be listening.

April 19, 1942. A four-motor Flying Fortress went over to the north, steady and beautiful, the first we have seen from this camp. Some of course saw red circles under the wings. There is always an argument but it was a thrill.[17]

A life like this could be interesting if the group had similar ideals and tried to work them out in living together. There could be a comradeship more bearable than this one of assorted persons. A few can still joke about the work they are doing, the daily job, though most of them have lost all sense of humor.

April 20, 1942. Isobel is all upset over the rumor that the officers are considering moving us to Camp Holmes. Ray says they were talking it over and have been to inspect it and we might as well start packing. Nakamura told the garden workers to pick all the vegetables as we would be moving day after tomorrow to Trinidad Valley. In no time the news traveled up and down with the fury of a storm. Knots of people gathered chattering into terrific clamor; babies, taking on the nervous atmosphere, cried as in the early days. Nakamura is still saying the Japanese are angry because five hundred civilians were killed in Davao and that we are not good to the Japanese in the States.

The children are getting a liberal education on babies. They hang around different ones at bathing and feeding times, seeing them at different stages of development. Many of them help the young mothers, carry the bottles, change the panties, assist those who are learning to walk.

I had a long talk with Jane about flower arrangement, which she studied for a year in Japan. The full course is seven years. It depressed me; it showed such passion for detail. I asked if it was art or religion with them and she said both, nearer the latter. But it started in the Army! It is an outlet, sublimation for the soldiers.

April 21, 1942. Our men went off in the bus early to clean up Camp Holmes. They say that new barracks were built for the Filipino trainees but we do not know what it is like except for a glorious view, a nice garden and yard for the children, a tennis court and ball diamond. We are busy repacking, moving stuff from paper bags to suitcases and duffel bag. Shoes are in a furoshiki [carrying cloth]. Whenever we become too settled or comfortable, we are jolted out of it by the old technique. This time we are a little harder to terrorize and beat down.

The Camp Hay *News* tells of the trip made by special crew to prepare living quarters for about 800 people, including 300 Chinese. Camp Holmes is on the Bontoc Trail through high mountains. It commands a tremendous view up the range and down to the China Sea.

"There are three main barracks, two of them regular army cadre buildings two stories high. Upstairs are sleeping quarters while downstairs are kitchen, mess and smaller rooms. The sleeping space is 29.5 by 138 feet, including a room at the south end. Already a number of double-deck bunks have been fitted into spaces. It will be crowded. There will not be much space for baggage or personal belongings but the buildings are new and consequently dry.

"The men will sleep in a one-story barracks with front porch and separate mess room. Today was spent in a continuous round of cleaning out dust, dirt and debris; washing down floors, moving in double bunks, moving out surplus furniture, getting water running, and surveying the general situation. Each crew, American and Chinese, went to work with a will. Crews were subdivided under their regular detail chiefs, with the chairman and liaison officer in charge.

"Expedition scenes: the Chef glumly surveying his new cooking apparatus—a Filipino style tile and concrete oven with two huge iron cauldrons atop the fire. Each has a large cover lifted by pulley . . . the experience of riding in a bus, forgotten after all these weeks . . . Familiar scenes in a changed atmosphere . . . passing the garden crew on their way back from pulling up the last edible things in the garden which was completely planted in beans and corn. . . ."

April 22, 1942. Bedie is graduating to the men's side and will help his Dad with vegetables.

April 23, 1942. The trucks came so thick and fast that it took only five hours to move the 800. The Japanese wanted to move their soldiers right in as we left.

At Camp John Hay the barbed wire was cut and we walked right out the front. When I stepped through to attend to my group, I did not even have time to realize I was out in the world! We drove out through the back of the Post and all along the way it seemed a ghost city. We passed no cars, only Igorots carrying or pushing loads. We waved to each other, they breaking into delighted grins or looking utterly astounded. Session Road was boarded up but many Filipinos were out to see us, waving, holding up two fingers into a V. No sound, only waving. Any other time we would have all shouted, cheered. The market was crowded, the street lined to see us go by. It was good to see many familiar Filipino faces after nothing but Nipponese eyes. Their pressure was there but the Filipinos showed they were glad to see us. Many were crying. All the Igorots looked friendly. We were much moved to be out riding in a bus. Is it a forerunner to Mañana at last?

Lt. Mukibo, who is always in evidence in a crisis, says that mothers and babies cannot have the cottage, after they moved into it, so they all piled out again, worn and threadbare, babies crying. The gardens are dry, full of weeds, covered with filing papers, brown dry piles of pine, file cabinets and drawers strewn about and several iron safes blown open. It is so desolate, this destruction. Pictures in frames, letters, possessions all over the yard, showing quick departure of soldiers and looting afterward by Japanese and Filipinos. There is plenty of space outdoors for us to wander about, down by the hospital building and in several groves overlooking the road. It is a welcome change outdoors, with space for the children to run and play, swings and courts. June with others found precious typing paper on the field. Even I "looted" a good typewriter ribbon on the dry hot parade ground. It was unwound so I rolled it up to stow away.

A resumé of news somehow came in, about Australian and U.S. planes pounding Timor, New Guinea, New Britain. Destruction of docks and shipping, with several Japanese cruisers sunk. U.S. bombers from Australia using advance base in Mindanao bombed Davao, Cebu, Manila and Batangas. Bataan has fallen but Corregidor still fighting off heavy bombing attacks and shelling from Big Japanese guns. Successful raids by our guerrillas in Mindanao and Northern Luzon. Planes from U.S. carrier raided Japanese cities. We continue building up strong force in Australia. Russia still holds initiative. Lubeck in Germany bombed more heavily than Coventry. Future prospects good but it will *take time*. Burn this when it has been digested! All this seems to have been tossed into someone's lap in the truck en route to Camp Holmes.[18]

April 24, 1942. We have a gasoline tin cut down, with wooden binding and handles around the top, to use for laundry and bath water. Enid announced at breakfast the rules about using water. No shower baths, only bucket baths. No laundry or baths at all for a day or two until we see how much water there is or unless it rains. June caught rainwater in our can today. We'll bathe in it and catch another for laundry tomorrow if it rains. It is cold but fresh.

We all eat in two sittings in one mess room. The men do all the cooking, serving, and waiting as in the first days at Camp Hay. We can really be proud of the way everyone has adjusted in this new complete shakedown. Everyone is living out of a bag, no shelves, no comforts at all.The bunks aren't bad except that bedbugs appeared this morning. There is no gasoline, no kerosene or bug powder so we'll have to pour boiling water down the cracks or else scratch.

The garbage detail went back to Camp John Hay, found the wagon, and pulled it over here on foot. They rolled into our grounds with a grinning guard riding on top. There are 300 Japanese at the Post [Camp John Hay] already and 5,000 arriving!

Jim heard that our captured troops at Bataan were made to walk barefoot to San Fernando, Pampanga, without water or food.[19] This the Japanese will have to pay for some day. They claim 50,000 prisoners.

These barracks are light, airy, built on the tropic style with sliding shell-paned windows, much pleasanter than the buildings we left behind. We have been fortunate in our mountain views and scenery.

April 26, 1942. Violent quarrels have developed over space, often a matter of three inches only, but it rages back and forth. It takes just about six hours to call it home. The same people have strung up individual lights and other things just as they had at the Post. Thirty-six inches marked off; then two can sleep and stow all their belongings there.

April 27, 1942. There is rebellion in camp though it may die. After we had clear soup and cold corn mush, many of us saw the In Group in their alley eating plates full of rhubarb.

Grandma has a budding night-blooming cereus.

Ted brought a wood stove which has been installed outdoors for all the women to do private puttering, cooking fudge, roasting peanuts; and lucky ones who have market orders are scrambling eggs.

April 28, 1942. Nakamura says tomorrow is the Emperor's Birthday and we could celebrate by having a minstrel show, with "Life Behind Barbed Wire" presented again, in the mess hall. We hope we'll get bananas by then.

April 29, 1942. Our view of the gulf, glimpses of mountain along sheer ridge, the wooded mountain in back of our buildings, is a scene and setting which would cost much money at a summer resort in New England. It is beautiful here and I love it. We watch the men felling trees on the slope beyond the window.

And so we honored the Emperor's Birthday against a beautiful backdrop with many hopes in our hearts. The Japanese take this day more seriously than we do Washington's Birthday. It is not only patriotism, but religion and history—the past generations to them. Nakamura and all the guards attended the performance given at their order. There is something hearty and friendly about Nakamura that one can't help liking. He tries very hard to make things go. He appreciates our entertainment efforts with much gusto.

There is a petition to the General Committee which reads: "We, the undersigned, feeling that a group of six or eight of our servers and kitchen workers are neither expectant mothers or nursing babies, invalids or over-worked, object to their consuming special foods meant for the children, and other items from the camp stores. In order to eliminate waste and to insure distribution of leftovers and extras *equally* in the camp we recommend that a detail of three or four persons of integrity including the head of Special Diet section be appointed to work with the serving committee on such a project so that no one group consistently benefits thereby."

The guards are greatly interested in Jerry's size—215 pounds—and height [6 feet 2½ inches].

I tried to get more signatures [on the petition] and was disgusted with women. They talk, gripe, criticize, but won't *do* anything about it. Perhaps men are the same. All are scared of any possible unpleasantness in such close quarters.

April 30, 1942. In the valley near us are fine bananas, papaya, pineapples, calamansits (limes)—and we do not need to buy even native coffee in town for it is near us—but the Japanese won't let us buy out here. It must come from the market where they can tax, put the squeeze on the stalls as well as on us, catching it both ways. They say we must live on our 21¢ a day per person, not a 39¢ average. This is what the soldier is allowed per day. They won't listen to argument even though it is our own money from the bank. We are prisoners, we must find out what it is like to suffer and run down. They tell us we are lucky we are not being bombed as is Japan.

Another couple has been caught commingling and the guards are on the prowl. One guard said to Mr. Brown, "You married?" The answer being in the affirmative, the guard said "Okay. You go up visit wife. I no care. Nakamura say no. But I no tell!" The wife in this case was in America, but Japanese or American, we are brothers and sisters under the skin and the guard was entirely sympathetic from his own experience.

May 2, 1942. A wild night. Young Peter upset a water pitcher in his sleep. It soaked nearby mattresses and dripped through to others downstairs whose owners came up to raise heck. In the dawn, we heard glorious liquid bird notes on the wooded slopes behind barracks. I have never heard so many in these islands before.

We watched the Chinese funeral. Two long lines of men stood out under the drizzle of rain, a few women huddled under the roof of the shed nearby. One man read from a book, then there were the final hammer blows on each nail. The coffin was carried to the cart to be pulled by ten or twelve men.

On it was placed a wooden cross, a Christian burial, with a wreath of green leaves, yellow flowers and a bunch of Everlasting. All the men fell in, walking behind the cart, the women and children last. Many of them were outstanding in looks, dignity and strength. They went past the boundary, down the hill, out of sight. They soon returned so were not allowed to travel far. The man-drawn cart is the one used to haul firewood, trash, everything—just like ours. It was the first burial service in this camp.

Across the wire Jerry reports a three-pronged drive in Europe, Americans and British already in Occupied France.[20] Imagine the thrill of those people! We know what it would mean. Churchill made a speech saying the war would be finished by 1943. If we were in the beginning of a Far East drive this might encourage us. Churchill making a speech—how far away it all seems to us who have been shut away for five months. News, radio, newspapers—can there really be such things, not just an underground of rumors?

May 3, 1942. Someone sent out a note with some cash, handed over the fence to the wife of one of our company men who came by at an arranged time dressed as an old Igorot woman with basket held by strap across the forehead. Another group has arranged to have news put under a stone. Thus do we keep contact.

I washed some extra floor sections that needed it. Everyone kept asking why, offering to share it on certain days. This was why I did it.[21]

May 4, 1942. The doctors look worried. Many more children are sick. They say that in January the men had bad "trots," the women had only a few sick ones. In February the women had it on their side. In March everyone had a touch of it. In April 90% [of the camp was] down with it. All were much sicker than before. The percentage of infection from cuts and scratches has increased alarmingly. All this shows lowered resistance and the chance of fatalities in another month's epidemic would be increased. We lack chiefly Vitamin B for resistance. We have no citrus fruits, no milk or eggs or butter, only unpolished rice in the diet. Our family is fortunate in having the yeast tablets, two a day even yet. We have liverbraun in reserve. Garlic too and peanut butter help.[22]

There is a certain amount of hazing going on among the boys and I'm sick to death of it. Mrs. Larson, whose son is still going through it, blew up to me. The men won't do anything, just say the boys must learn to take it, so the bullies keep right on, picking on the smaller guy. There's enough to take in here without that, with idle boys turning into bullies, destroying shoestrings where there are none to replace them, twisting arms and tying up little kids with ropes. It is what the Japanese are doing to helpless people in a bigger way.

May 5, 1942. A Chinese was reported missing *before* roll call by his own people. There is general consternation. He was soon brought in by the guard and from all over camp we watched him slapped, knocked down, kicked, stepped on, hands tied at last and bound to a tree where water was poured over him. In an hour he was untied and he fell. He was pulled up by his tied hands, the same process repeated again, beating with sticks and the butt of a gun. All the guards took a turn at it. It was a demonstration of how nice the Orient for Orientals could be. Whenever he passed out, the bucket of water was doused all over him again. He is still there, an example to the rest of us. Rage was in my heart and on my crimson face. The little mustached guard whom we like took his turn with the rest at knocking down, kicking with hobnail boots. Our men say the Chinese is crazy. He seems almost normal in here—he did what we all want to do—walked out the gate. He put a stick over his shoulder and walked past the guards after dark, looking like one with a gun. It is said he was homesick, not crazy, just wanted to see his woman. The whole world is crazy, symbolized in that poor figure sitting on the ground, soaking wet, covered with mud, stepped on.

May 6, 1942. Dr. Lee refused to write a letter to the Major, her husband, asking him to surrender. She said it would do no good for he would not be influenced in the least by it but would go on as he saw fit, regardless.[23]

Nakamura still says we waste too much; we don't eat the vegetable tops and many things that the Chinese and Japanese use. One of our staff told him we weren't used to eating some of those things so could not use them. At that, we have learned to eat a number of new items.

May 7, 1942. The New Order in Asia and the Nazis count on and succeed in using malnutrition and fear which weakens will to resist. A certain number of people may want to get out of here badly enough to cooperate in various ways eventually. They use weakness everywhere as their best weapon.

Editor Jim says in Camp Holmes *News*, "We wonder whether someday we won't be at a loss as to how to act when meeting a woman who is not behind a wire fence."

Rice-picking brings young and old, all kinds together. Each member is supposed to do a daily plate at least. Several remarked they had been thinking a lot about prisons and prison reform lately and would be more interested in it in the future. The boys are going over the corn at one table, very noisy and smart. The girls start singing "The Lights of Home," drifting into other songs softly. It made working pleasanter. Mrs. Hay, who has a great deal of social responsibility, said it was good for all of us to contribute to the camp work for it helped us to keep a dignity which she feared we might lose as our clothes became more shoddy, our pride less.

The staccato voice on Tokyo radio which depresses and eats into us like acid, reports, "Manila and Corregidor fallen after 72 hours of pounding from land, sea and air." Corregidor, the Rock, the Impregnable, which would last a year, with supplies for even longer and all the bank funds removed to there!

A package from Miss Ramos—bananas, pineapple, and two loaves of white rice bread! It is a lighthouse in [a] storm.

May 9, 1942. The brown Intelligence car full of Swords came to question Leung Nang. Rumor reports him saying that the Chinese in the hills are worn out, with many skin diseases from malnutrition, so they are anxious to come in. They are too weak to walk and ask that trucks be sent for them. There are about 200 though one rumor said 1,000.[24] 500 Americans are reported scattered in the hills.

One or two people have gone to the hospital in a long [emotional] nose dive over Corregidor.

May 10, 1942. Jerry is planning to learn a new trade, starting at the bottom again, which is not bad adjustment at middle age. I'm proud of him.

A sign at the guardhouse does not call it "surrender," merely says that "Corregidor was completely occupied." They claim they came in from three sides. Many are being very sentimental, super-patriotic, trying to minimize the defeat. There was a torchlight celebration procession in town.

The Chinese teachers are to be released to stay in Whitmarsh apartments, Carl the guarantor.[25] The Chinese are urged to open stores, start business going again, everything back to normal, for Japan, not for America. We see now what occupation is like, how it went in China. Starvation, weakness, fear, terror. One must live. When the Chinese come in from the hills, they will be only one version of thousands of groups in occupied territory all over the world. All of them are to go out together, even those who have been interned. They must all sign a paper.[26] Mrs. Hall says Mukibo must have been badly treated in America for he has a large inferiority complex. It makes him forget his education and attempt to give us the same complex. We should learn something from this but will we?

At four the Chinese began to straggle in, and were still coming at six-thirty, in about six groups totalling around one hundred. Lilian Lim, the trim, stylish sophisticate, is another person in blue denim trousers, much like the rest of us. Her old mother with blue cap wound about her head was serene as ever, sitting on the ground by the guardhouse. Helen and Lilian waved at us, and Lilian pointed to her drawn cheeks calling out, "No more rouge," showing empty hands. In every direction, bundles and suitcases were opened, contents poured out on the ground,—the picture of ourselves as we came in.

A guard who had been practicing car driving on the parade ground drove off it too fast, crashing into the Rising Sun flagpole, bending it half over. An audible chuckle, almost a cheer, rose from our side of camp. We hope it is an omen!

May 11, 1942. Jerry thinks we should not put any one down as a sponsor for it might get them into trouble.[27] He is right. We'd be wiser to wait for deliverance.

May 12, 1942. Grandma has a new color for her quilts—concentration gray.

There will be about 100 Chinese remaining until houses can be found for them to occupy. Nang's family of nine had to go to a new one as his is "occupied." All those who have been driving trucks, delivery wagons or cars, this morning returned to the old pole system of transportation. Such a collection of round packs, flat packs, boxes, looted army trunks, burlap sacks, tied mattresses and red blankets holding all belongings—everything swinging from shoulder poles. One fellow carried out the gray cat yowling inside a burlap sack. Down the hill they trekked, checked off in line, on the march with what they have salvaged, a replica of thousands in occupied countries in the Orient. Will we look like them soon, refugees all? One truckload of heavy baggage was taken, the rest went by hand or shoulder, head or bent back, suitcases swinging at a jog-trot. Rich and poor, educated and ignorant, young and old, they are all walking out the same way. I watch the procession as an older woman totters along on diminutive "lily" bound feet, followed by the distinguished looking language teacher from Peking in long olive-green gown, her hair coiled in braids above a lovely face. They are going in the truck with others piled on top of the baggage, a Shanghai amah lonely and weeping in a group of Cantonese, a husky peasant woman with bandana on her head, Leung Nang with his wife and seven children—the littlest one in a suit with red sailor collar. All the men are walking. Everyone is equal today. Sometime we may see the Big Swords on a level with their guards and peasants. The Chinese barracks are silent, the murmur of departure stilled. Nang waves as the truck turns down the hill out of sight.

Jerry says he has been hammering away at the idea of giving the children aged five to twelve more food for months. They are the ones who have taken a beating, with no milk at all since February.

May 13, 1942. The old guards let the garbage detail go on a shopping spree before they departed, knowing full well that the new [guards] will be tough for a while. In our better moments, they liked us and we liked them when not under pressure from above. The gold tooth boy, the huge fellow with big teeth in an enormous grin—all are gone. The new ones seem small in stature by comparison. Two cars of officers, one looking like the High Command, came on a tour of inspection of all the buildings. As he left the grounds, he said to a group of internees, "I am sorry you stay here. Sometime good-bye."

May 15, 1942. One of the guards held Donald in his lap, talking to him. Every time he tried to put Donald back into the playpen, baby arms twined around his neck, refused to let go. The guard finally pointed to his gun resting on the floor, indicating he must go on guard and the mother must rescue him. Another mother finally took Donald, who hung on protesting to the last.

May 16, 1942. The Japanese watch who works and who doesn't. They watched Larson washing clothes, asked if he was married. Upon an affirmative answer, they pointed to the washing, saying "Japanese woman." Even if one does work he is watched. It is interesting to hear oneself criticized as a *nation*, compared with a feudalistic setup. Their women do the work all right—there is no equality there.

Every time the news is bad for Japan, the guards tighten up, crack down. The new [guards] were jumpy and disagreeable because they were sent to guard us instead of sailing for Japan as promised.

Maud saw a poster in the guardhouse headed "Peace regained," picturing a happy Filipino family rejoicing at being under Japanese rule at last.

May 18, 1942. We talk about what it will feel like to eat off of something besides a tin spoon; to sit at a polished table with a cloth on it; not to swing our knees over a bench before dining; to use something besides thick cup or enamel plate; to have water in glasses and dessert on a plate again. We will have no manners for a while, will reach across the table, bolt our meal, talk—if at all—with mouths full.

May 19, 1942. The children are digging into the hill bank, Bedie coming in gloriously dirty. The birds are singing with full throats on the hill.

We have seen the newly issued Japanese government one peso bill, so the currency is being established, the Sun still rising, even if the flagpole is badly bent.

Miss Lewis says that the first week we were interned we all wanted to get out. Now many want to stay in, to keep on being regimented, have a free hospital, afraid to go into the unknown.

May 20, 1942. Isobel at her mat is learning from Bessie the correct proportions of camote and meat bone to stew into a strained substitute for milk for her two babies when the meager supply of milk gives out. Coconut milk, made by squeezing the white meat, is also a substitute.

Some hate dependence fiercely. It is like breathing to me, the realization of one's dependence on another. It is more fully realized in here but the Indusco cooperatives prepared me for it. It would be no shock, no strain, to go home to work for my servants. I know they would share what little they have but Jerry hates to ask them. It really hurts him. First it is our turn to share, then it is theirs. What difference does it make? It did not hurt their pride, why should it hurt ours? We are all friends in adversity or in the future. We are all alike. War makes paupers of everyone. We have a little, we have friends, which is more than have millions of men with hungry children, who live on the verge of starvation from one day to another, clutching each morning to keep from going under.

June is making paper doll dresses, with a lovely bridal gown and four maternity dresses "in case they are stuck in Concentration Camp."

May 21, 1942. Nakamura told Jerry that our Filipino servants had volunteered to take care of us if and when we got out. It takes courage and faithfulness to come forward in these times to stand back of denuded Americans. Bless them, I knew they would come through, though not quite so staunchly before we even got out. We have never known just this kind of anticipation, waiting to see them all. What a homecoming it will be, even if our things are gone. Our sponsors satisfy my sense of fitness.

Jerry came to the talking fence looking sheepish and pleased at once, perhaps it could be termed rueful. He said they asked him about a sponsor so he told them we had written down none because we had none. "Then who are Nida and Ismael?" asked Nakamura. Jerry answered, "Our cook and his wife, the amah who has been with us for eleven years." "I have a letter signed with those names guaranteeing your support in their house if and when you get out," Nakamura told him. Jerry told him they couldn't possibly do it but Nakamura said he would fix up our application. I know that Jerry was deeply moved for he couldn't talk much but he said, "I don't ever want to hear anyone say again in my presence that Filipinos have no loyalty." He remarked that his secretary was supporting him in Concentration, his domestic staff taking care of him on the Outside. I shouted, "Silly, that's the new order in Asia, not the Japanese order, but the cooperative one of working together, the real thing."

You at home cannot know, without five months like ours behind us, how wonderful was the glow, the warmth of all this. We had cast aside the idea of naming our servants or Miss Ramos or Carl because it might mean trouble for them with the authorities, let alone the financial strain. To have them volunteer was tremendous. We can imagine them planning, talking it over, putting the words down on paper, committing themselves irrevocably to any future whim or accusation of the invader. Do the Japanese know the bonds they are forming? A new basis is growing like coral under the sea of invasion. Americans and Filipinos can thank the Japanese eventually for new character, new ties, formed in adversity, more lasting than any built during prosperity or gold boom. It is beyond the price of all possessions which war may have stripped from us.

May 23, 1942. Another lovely day. Someone shared a cup of tea with me, another a mango. Nakamura seems to be busy hunting up sponsors even for those he doesn't like. There are a number of people sick again, with worn-out nerves due to the long-drawn-out release red tape, in which the Japanese wallow. It amuses me to watch husky Nakamura tramping about with lists, checking in and checking out the Chinese, marketing, ordering, somehow keeping a fragmentary sense of humor. He planks down his shiny boots in a sturdy, upright manner, though he can be as nasty as anyone at times.

The most depressed members of camp are the Jewish women who feel hopeless about rescue. They say it will take years. They have seen so much, so long, in Europe, that they have lost the recuperative power of hope. Driven from pillar to post, each haven of refuge turning into a fallen bastion through blindness and stupidity, who can blame them if they now see nothing ahead, their courage undermined. They are an example of what Nazi propaganda can do in time by repetition. One of the German doctors said when he was brought into camp, "Oh, then it is for the duration." He knew all the signs but we still do not believe him.

This morning I told a woman at breakfast what a wonderful mother I had. How she pushed me in a carriage in summer, dragged me on a sled in winter through deep snow, to the electric car, on a twenty-five-minute walk to take me in town twice a week for a treatment for my paralyzed leg after polio. If I walk well today, have any strength or courage, it is due to a cheerful pioneer who is never daunted by anything. June listened, absorbed, suddenly cried out, "Mummie, you are just like your mother, always cheerful!" My daughter appreciates her mother as I appreciate mine. It was comforting to hear her spontaneous outburst.

June is drawing paper doll clothes in the dining room. The fresh Sergeant stops to watch it. He takes the pencil, draws kimonos showing the men's short sleeve, the girl's sleeve which is shorter than that of a wife. In three lines he drew Fujisan with a cloud in front of it. Later we asked him to draw it on another sheet and he drew it with exactly the same cloud. He wrote Japanese words in *English* letters to the tune of "Auld Lang Syne," then another Japanese song, finally the words of the national anthem which he called a march. He showed great distress because the American women wear pants. "Men, boys, yes. Japanese women, no!" He also dislikes the way we push and pull doors for he gave a graceful pantomime of Japanese women kneeling, sliding the door slowly, quietly, instead of an energetic pull, push. As I watched him working hard over his pencil drawing, I noted U.S. buttons on his American army coat which being too long had been cut off at the bottom by scissors or a knife (perhaps the bayonet). The soldier is age 26. How old was the American boy?

May 25, 1942. June is agog over the Museum of Natural History—a white glass cabinet which now holds branches with leaves, on which cling slugs and huge bristling worms which later will become butterflies. Some of them have turquoise and pink spikes on them, others have evil eyes in startling black and white. There are all kinds rooting in the earth or chewing the green leaves, which fascinates the children.

A bag from Inez came with four mangoes and six handsome biscuits. We fell upon them. How faithful she has been, this young Spanish-Igorot girl who is head of the 100 Igorot women who helped send funds to Indusco. It will be a pleasure to see her serene eyes under coronet braids when we can tell her how high she kept our spirits.

From Camp Holmes *News*: "Every crew on the campus thinks the other crews don't do any work; the Committee thinks none of them do any work; the rest of the camp thinks the Committee is loafing; actually, they're all right and wrong. A lot of work does get done here despite all insinuations. If it didn't, we'd all be in a bad way." And this—"It's getting so that even when a piece of news is true, someone has to start a counter rumor just to keep things confused."

May 26, 1942. Our chairman has announced that school will be allowed to start tomorrow for the grades. After [five] months we have church and school again.

Bataan and Corregidor may go down in history annals as heroic but the final details of it here are anything but pleasant to hear. We do not see the glory, only the defeat, the helplessness.

May 27, 1942. Jerry has seen the new release blanks we must sign, said he didn't want to sign them, to be a prisoner in our own home, seeing and talking with no one. Sponsors have to market for us, etc.

A guard just marched toward the guardhouse with a gun over one shoulder, a long vivid green banana leaf over the other.

I'm getting a reputation for keeping as well as anyone in camp. People come to ask me how I eat my garlic. Part of my health is because I don't feel down, find much to be amused at every day. Morale is highly important as good Nazis know. Otherwise, it is rice, bananas, peanut butter, garlic and yeast tablets which do the trick. I'm practically a test case on garlic as an intestinal antiseptic.

Jerry hears that 17 planes were in the first Tokyo raid led by Major Doolittle who received a cross for it.[28] He and I had a terrific battle against the gloom at the talking fence. He asks me—when has he been wrong, Singapore, Dutch Indies, all the way to New Guinea, including Bataan and Corregidor? Hadn't he been right about everything, our staying in camp long etc.? I told him not to get a swelled head, that he had thought Japan would back down and not fight, with which I had not agreed, and that I had prophesied a British, American, Russian combine two and a half years ago when everyone told me I was crazy and didn't know what I was talking about. The battle at the fence was good for us. I need it after seeing women all day. Jerry forecasts a long stay in here, says we'll be lucky if we get out by the end of the year. I say he is crazy—a lot can happen quickly. He says our forces will have to come back here to clear up, while I say they will bomb Japan and use the Navy, clearing up here through negotiation.So we keep our wits sharp.

The young American soldier-driver said that everything but trucks were destroyed in Bataan and they had expected to be transported in those, but they were made to take the long Bataan march, all stragglers hit on the head or bayoneted. This hits the pit of our stomach. Those left are fairly tough and how they must hate. How can one ask for mercy for the Japanese at the end?

Jerry sends me a small jar of some Basi (rice liquor) which wafts me into the golden past after two swallows. Wonderful what a little alcohol can do if you haven't had any for months. I doubtless look pink-cheeked, for all is rosy as Basi takes me back to Laoag and Vigan days, no babies howling or anything.

Nakamura bows so easily, so perfectly, from the waist, when a General leaves. There is no bend of the head, knees or back—all straight lines but no stiffness, the same way the women sink to their knees. When we do it, it is awkward, absurd, not part of us.

Thick fog around us thinned before it reached the top of the ridge so that branches and tree trunks were like shadows through a veil. It was a Japanese print, a lovely one.

As I went up the stairs for the night I passed a woman sitting on a wooden chest, her face in her hands, sobbing bitterly.

May 29, 1942. At 7:30 a.m. Dr. Lee, a man and a woman went out on release with their bags piled high on the truck. The two women departing today were extremes; [Dr. Lee] firm, cheerful, head as high as when she came in, her very posture an inspiration, though she is expecting a baby and her husband is out with the fighting forces or imprisoned by now; the other, bent, unsteady, morale crushed by the fall of Corregidor, her hands shaking, lips quivering, eyes dark with tragic emotion—she is what any of us can become overnight if we give in. There are fifteen or twenty in camp who are close to the border of this state. It is one way of escape, to collapse. As time goes on it will not be easy to resist it. All the activity of moving, even the quarrels, the slaps, are better than tears, bent or broken spirits.

Nakamura brought 25 bars of soap and cut down on the vegetables. We hear that Vancouver and Seattle were bombed!

The Japanese have always killed their own sick, weak and wounded who could not keep up, as they did to ours in [the] Bataan march.

June 1, 1942. The Pampered have a fine setup, in a long room all windows on one side, only two double bunks, the rest beds; a corner sitting room which they say is being reserved for one of their number who is working at the hospital. She will never come back up here. Everyone is making cracks at them so they are upset and want sympathy which they don't get. The rest of us call the room the Country Club. I believe the men have one too. When a woman Committee member from that room tries to tell others not to cut their beds down into singles, she has no comeback when they ask why not?—nearly all the beds in that room have been cut down. Once privilege creeps in it is hard to stop it or control other requests. Members of a committee should fall over backward in keeping level with the majority. They should have less privilege than any one.

June 2, 1942. Jerry was up at five, making coconut-cocoa candy, in memory of a scorching hot week thirteen years ago.[29] Instantly I was back in Vigan waiting, panting for breath in the heat, driving to Pandan or Santa Catalina for sea air from the hill on the golf course, with early rains making everything steamy. Those beaches where we used to swim in tropic warmth, lie on the long sands in the sun afterward—beaches where the Japanese made their first landings, pouring in waves over the same roads we traveled—we could visualize it all as the planes went over our heads en route to Vigan while we crouched in a stone ditch. There Filipino troops made their first valiant stand against the waves of troops pouring ashore, in that section where June was born on June 11th, the middle of Hot Season.

'Tis said that Corregidor has been bombed as never before by our planes; that Cologne, Germany, has been laid waste.

Franz says if anyone writes the life of concentrees in Baguio they must chronicle how the men built the latrines in the backyard against time, staggering under each load and shovelful, resting every ten minutes from exhaustion due to no food or water. That was the week of terror and travail. How blessed the rain falling now! We all have palm leaf rain capes.

We had from 600 to 800 calories a day the first week at Camp Hay. Then the doctors joined with the Committee to work out a menu that gave us a minimum of 1,600, sometimes 1,800, which is what it should be.

June 3, 1942. Camp has settled into a routine, almost a contentment, just enough of that divine discontent to keep it from being dull, static. Most of the troubles were aired like blankets on the wire.

As they talked about the future at corn-picking, I was pleased to discover that I live almost completely in the present—forgetting past possessions, grasping a new kind of life, certain of something worthwhile ahead. Months ago I stopped worrying about home for it is useless. It does mean a lot to have the family here. For those who are separated, the mind cannot be at ease. Uncertainty is torture. This camp is an experiment. Observing it each day gives me a lively, unbroken interest, a serenity which I do not realize until others complain so bitterly. Reconstruction outside would be equally absorbing.

Germany is launching an offensive in Russia, trying to encircle Leningrad.

June 4, 1942. Individual work averages higher than before. A few still stall around but must feel their unpopularity. It has become of general interest that each one accomplishes something. People have less chance to fool themselves or others with so many telling the truth. Each gives according to his ability and strength—from the eminent pathologist, skilled surgeons, expert chef, shop specialist, artist with machine tools, ax wielder, down to the corn and rice-pickers, mop wringers, garbage collectors and staunch toilet-workers, not to mention the mothers with endless tasks. To be sure, each hopes to be released, but there is fun and good humor along the way. We makeshift in countless ways to accomplish wonders out of nothing. How much could be done if expert planners, proper methods, modern tools were put to work on it.

Conversation discusses how eager the doctors are to give their services so that their skill will not become rusty. They want to keep alive mentally. Mining engineers, teachers, missionaries, businessmen, all feel in a backwater. We note that the men are glad to work in the shop, the kitchen, on the hill, until they are dead tired, because it keeps the mind occupied, the hands from idleness that would drive them all crazy. The women scrub, wash enormous stacks of clothes, putter over cooking. Work is the great healer, the strong motive power which keeps us normal.

During the trouble over starting school, Arthur asked why arithmetic alone could not be taught—what harm was there in a book of problems, figures.[30] The reply was that there is a problem in the book asking if so much of a certain product were grown in Manchuria now, how much could be grown if the Japanese were no longer there (or some similar phrasing). This may be a translation in the Nipponese mind. At any rate, it is a good excuse. With the new Command, we have permit for school, religious service, use of the Chinese barracks, several releases and prospect of more.

Four men are studying Ilocano [a Filipino] dialect, under Grandpa. Maud is sprouting mongo beans, which contain enzymes, for camp consumption.

June 5, 1942. Two men brought a table over from the shop this morning. Enid asked them to carry a second one but they looked ''set'' as though further effort along those lines was not their detail. When she suggested that a couple of the garbage crew could help, they plainly showed their horror at such encroachment. It recalls the unions—paperhangers who must not touch a brick or board, stage workers who must only move sets without touching a curtain rope. Good old rugged American individualism! Each crew sticks to its own detail with all the tenacity of the caterpillars on green leaves in the white cabinet.

With rumors of a new General in town, some hope that Mukibo might be removed but he is only a symptom, an indication of a condition. There would be another like him. He is an infinitesimal part of a system, a state of mind, something out of gear in the universe.

We all become mellow on the morrow. Flanders Fields grow dim—and so will Vigan, Singapore, Bataan. The Japanese hate democracy, but they are handing it to us never-the-less and for this I make a deep bow of thanks to the Emperor (no tongue in the cheek). Pick up your mop and your garbage can—we'll show you democracy and make you like it. Perhaps you would rather be scalded by steam from the big caldron in the kitchen as the Chef was this morning while cooking for 500—five hundred British, American, Spanish and mestizos all poured in here together.

June 6, 1942. Everyone is buying bakia (wooden clogs) to cope with the puddles and mud. We make an Oriental clatter now. One bearded male is buying a pair for the Russian girl who stitched a mosquito net for him out of material wangled from town via the tienda and the garbage detail.

Tokyo paper quote: "Minister Tojo made it clear that it is for the purpose of defeating the Anglo-American ambition of dominating the world, of emancipating East Asia from exploitation and of realizing the grand idea of establishing a new world order that Japan is waging the present war at hazard of her own existence. . . . The desertion by General MacArthur of his forces during critical Philippine battle is probably the smallest and cheapest publicity stunt."

For the children in here this education is something that cannot be bought. It is the one seed that can grow in all the death, horror and destruction. Mopping, sweeping, washing their own clothes, climbing the hill with older or younger boys to take food to the lumberjacks, holding sheet iron to help the men lift it to nail on the new runway—here is education with a communal flavor. It can be taken in through the pores, providing the parents guide the child into it. There is one family which is trying to be impervious to camp life. They receive packages from their home through servants several times a week. It provides a normal diet including milk and eggs, dresses made up from new materials, everything as nearly like home as possible in this situation. Yet three of them are not well; they live only to escape from this experience; the girls do no work—not even their own washing or sweeping; their mother ill, struggling to do more than her share and spoiling them in the process. Their boys have learned through contact with other boys, have grown and expanded in six months but the girls are static, withdrawn, untouched by camp life. Near them is a family of about the same size who share duties. The girls are self-reliant, sturdy, not ill or withdrawn or difficult.

June 9, 1942. Up at three to find out what the noise and talking was about. Almost half the camp were violently sick with ptomaine symptoms.

A supply truck is here, driven by a tall blonde American boy—the set of his head so fresh and young, the way he walks, his height and blondness so American. There he is—the result of our underestimation of the enemy, our overconfidence, our ignorance of the driving power behind Japan, our weakness and neglect of vital points, drinking, dancing, gambling, not only here but back to Senators, Representatives, all of you isolated in peace and security while the rest of the world boiled. Now this boy from Nebraska is a prisoner, driving a captured American truck for the aggressor. You, too, are in it with us, worrying about relatives or friends unheard of for months, learning the uncomfortable uncertain feeling of blackout, not quite so confident as yesterday, even as we. Someone has given the boy a cup of tea, some sweets. He says he is on kitchen detail. He was formerly air corps. The children crowd around him in hero-worship. He represents so much to us—more than you can know. We worry over these boys, even as you do who cannot see what they are enduring.

June 10, 1942. Nakamura has bought a flock of live chickens for the hospital. He keeps right on going, with American ideas of time and efficiency.

June 11, 1942. In Sumatra, on our vacation there, there was what we called "the Dutch Bottle System" in the hotel bathroom. It was a row of bottles full of water which was used instead of toilet paper. One simply poured the water down the back into the toilet. We made the remark that the System had arrived here, for sure, as there is no more toilet paper. Every family is told to look after itself. *We* have cut into small squares the charred papers of forms for physical examination for Reservists which June rescued from bonfires when we first came here.

In our imagination, any rescue is accompanied by cans of milk and toilet paper.

June was thrilled with a bag from Nida containing a bouquet of tiger lilies, gladioli and Benguet lilies from our terraced garden. There were four eggs from Nida's own chickens, a bag of cookies which June shared like pieces of birthday cake with six different families, and two pineapples, plus a sweater which I had bought for Joan's birthday and three pairs of socks for me. So there *is* something left in the house. Over and over, June said, "I want to go home, I want to go home." She always weeps when we hear from Nida. There was a gardenia from our bush, with the flowers. Miss Ramos sent bread, four mangoes, and a jar of jam. Marie and Betty gave June candy and canned meat. The four of us had a picnic out by the wire on a little seat built around the fir tree. With the half loaf of bread we had saved, Daddy made canned corned beef sandwiches with sliced fresh onion and salt. We had three each. Daddy had another present—a bottle of wild honey which we poured on some bread.

Health posters have been designed and tacked up in the main hall. "A Specimen in Time Saves Nine" is one. Daphne and some of the younger girls are making them.

The picnic was our first real gorge—we'll remember June's 13th birthday.

June 12, 1942. Coming out from breakfast I asked Kink what he was guarding and he answered, "Three plates containing mongo beans, black beans, and black-eyed peas which are to be made into baby's milk, but I don't believe it." He was surprised when I said the Chinese babies thrived on this all the time they were in here, having practically none of the genuine article.

Yamamoto [a guard] in the evening brought one of his charcoal sketches to Virginia—a village street of little shops and houses at the foot of high mountains. He explained with his hands that it was like the tienda and barrio below us, only in Japan. It is done with feeling and ability by this Yokohama dock worker now guarding prisoners after slaughter in Bataan. We can see of what he is capable if the best, not the worst, is brought out. He was still breathing fire when he arrived, is now most eager to talk, to learn, to express himself in charcoal—"pencil no good"—he does not understand our word charcoal.

June 13, 1942. Bedie has come in all hushed and thrilled over a snail crawling on his palm. The tiny horns are feeling the way, the perfect shell adjusts itself on the middle of the slithery back. It hunches along slowly, nibbling a blade of grass.

Jerry has lost 34 pounds in six months, from 212 to 178.

Jane said that being Outside was like being in a drama. She laughed when I said it was the same being Inside.

June 14, 1942. As the truck came back from market we all piled down to wait for package call-out. Who should step out of the car but Mukibo himself, young, thinned down, smooth as ever, the first time he has come any nearer than the guardhouse to us. All the children were called and Lt. Mukibo, Special Section, Imperial Army, gave each a handful of candy—colored gumdrops and chocolate caramels and nougats called "Good Pomposity" on the wrapping. Mukibo smiled that constrained, secret, little smile, bowing to the children, looking very kind and good. He is an attractive looking person (unusually white teeth under black mustache) but he seems cold. Old Mrs. Watson was introduced so that she could talk about getting out. Some others pushed in like old friends. The group of seventeen "chosen" were called. After their conference, twenty-six in another group asked to be heard, soon signed their release. Three other families signed. There was constant flutter, discussion of all the pros and cons at the wire. In contrast to his mien with the children, he said coolly to a British mother wanting to take her small infant to join the father in Manila—"Your country and my country are at war. You cannot expect me to be interested in doing for your comfort." In my own mind I do him a certain justice. Always do I remind myself that we are in the center of slaughter, suffering and destruction; always do others tend to forget it. There is constant complaint of discomfort when there might be agony and death.

June 15, 1942. I went into the dormitory to see the first wall built between mattresses. It reminded me of Robert Frost's poem about our building walls between us. This one is of heavy wire on wood frame, completely enclosing the measured space allotted. It looks utterly ridiculous.

June 16, 1942. Some of the young girls are imitating the various whistle calls of husbands to wives in camp. One remarked, "I used to call my horse the way these men call their wives." This gave me a long chuckle. Jerry has a cricket chirp to signal me to the wire. One man sounds like a mourning dove. The cadences are many.

Fabian says "Each one enjoys the small graft of his line." Jerry always said his graft was the use of the peanut grinder (plus a bone to gnaw now and then) but anyone can use the grinder for there was a big time with it in the kitchen during Sunday communal hour. Vinnie said the only job she couldn't find any graft in was mine. There doesn't seem much left in garbage and no one wants to carry it so there can't be any percentage. As for pails and mops, they are their own reward if I use the fresh clean water and keep the mops from getting slimy which is my bête noir.

A reconditioned Socony tin weaves and bends when carried half full of cold water (no hot water ever). We are lucky to have any water.

Mrs. Estrich had handcuffs clipped on because she took a knife engaged in slicing bread and went after one who was eating a fried egg sandwich "in front of people who have nothing."

During supper of pork, green beans, cabbage and tomato, the three big trucks arrived loaded with Sagada and Bontoc mission people. Nuns in their dark robes and high stiff headdresses, [several] Fathers and their families, including six children badly sunburned, the priests in long robes and high collars, came through the fog to the front of the barracks. All was disorder as they piled out. Mattresses, bags and boxes were open for inspection all over the ground as Nakamura and Hayakawa poked into every crevice. They have only been interned three weeks, listened to the radio every day till then. They did not know they were coming here until five last evening when the trucks drove in. They will have to sleep in the middle aisle on the floor tonight until the others go to Manila tomorrow.

We are told that Walter Cushing is one of the demon guerrillas, a leader in Abra near his mine. He hid out all kinds of Constabulary[31] material and organized from the beginning. The Filipinos maintain he has killed 500 Japanese himself and that he can't die! These are the ones who warm my heart, fill me with hope. The bulk of the guerrillas are still out, harrying, rushing in to destroy, dispersing quickly without loss, always gaining a rifle or two and some food. They are the type of leaders with spirit that the Japanese most want to catch for they keep the flame burning. They go up one side of the mountain, down the other, in and out, driving the enemy mad, building ties of courage, admiration and common experience with the Filipinos, part of the new fraternity, new students in democracy, educated by war. One American admitted to the Japanese that the Mission had helped to feed Cushing's men which is why they were brought in here.

The newcomers thought us terribly crowded. The nine nuns were crammed into the small quarters in the end room where five people moved out to give them room and a curtain was hung for privacy when their headdress is removed for the night.

The new campers are like a yardstick for us. We can see how far we have come in six months. We are used to being crowded, used to noise and a thousand other things.

June 17, 1942. Garbage has a graft! It is the tale of an old army coat. I picked it out of the garbage can where it was cast by one of those departing, a coat looted from Camp Hay cottages. There seemed to be months of wear left in it in spite of mends, patches and holes, so I gave it to John Morgan to trade from the garbage wagon. He first asked if anyone wanted it on the men's side. When he returned from the detail, he handed me three bunches of bananas in payment from an old Igorot sitting by the roadside who welcomed the coat. It is now giving warmth and pleasure instead of being at the bottom of an ash heap.

One of the mission group had talked to one of the officers left on Corregidor recently and he said the Rock was as flat as a pancake. All the months of engineering, boring down into the earth, gone as though it had never been at all. The last twenty-four hours of firing was so terrific that they couldn't make it known they wanted to surrender. Then 2,100 enemy stormed the island, only six hundred reaching it to capture it. This is paying dearly, but the loss is even dearer. The officer says that the holding of Corregidor and Bataan saved Australia by concentrating the Japanese here until reinforcements could be poured into the Antipodes.[32]

So we lift our eyes to far horizons hoping that something better may come out of it all. These are not bad thoughts for the 17th of June, the Battle of Bunker Hill, from a New England rebel in the Far East waiting to see the whites of some more eyes.

June 18, 1942. We get it from both sides but still try to strike a balance, to find the germ of truth in between. They are still dishing out glory stories about MacArthur. Well, we've finally been told that it is Europe first and we can be thankful for that much frankness. We don't want to be told it is all the fault of that man Roosevelt either, for he has been trying to show what was on the horizon for the last four years. Before the curtain fell on the Orient, even the U.S. Press was not leading the public, was shortsighted and bound up in internal problems. All of you were too secure on your continent until the Pearl Harbor attack jolted the country out of its rut. We must thank the Japanese for our own unity.

As we fried our supper, the Country Club group with its two new members, cooked, before our eyes and nose, huge round pancakes, devouring one apiece then taking a tower of extras back somewhere to eat at leisure. June was almost beside herself. Later we were fortified by Daddy who made two eggs feed four by combining them into French toast. We stood at the kitchen cage with Daddy on the other side, but it is one of those moments which is balm to the spirit, christening our new frying pan made goodness-knows-what fashion by Daddy at the shop. A frying pan makes us almost independent. We *possess* a frying pan! You cannot know what it means. We ate fried rice out of an apricot can. Jerry grinned when I told him I had an inch-high binge of Basi from someone which made me feel like Planter's Punch and the ruins of old Panama.

June 19, 1942. Daphne who does beautiful artistic lettering and drawings on birth certificates is making a sketchbook. It is said she has done drawings for *Vogue*.

One of the minor miracles of this war will occur if I learn to cook. Last night I made some good fried camotes for supper and the children lapped it up. Today I'm juggling with calamansit skins left from a tea party which will make a strong jam of lime flavor which I crave.

Jerry is desperately tired every night but is in better condition than he was before the exercise. There is a peach and gold sky, with pearl and deep blue and light blue clouds. One can hear rain in the trees on the hill before it reaches camp.

June 21, 1942. Jane made an exquisite iris flower arrangement for church. We listened to the great words of the Sermon on the Mount, as simple and magnificent as in those times but taking on new meaning as we sat on a similar hill to listen. The inner light and beauty of it survives through the years.

Men's Committee notes: "Attention is called to the prohibition of commingling. When officers visited camp recently several couples were sitting together in front of the buildings and made no effort to separate during the visit, which brought forth warning from the guard. . . . Cafeteria style will be introduced at the morning meal of the 22nd. Please ask only for the quantity to be consumed as seconds may be obtained. Food supply is based on daily money value and saving in any one article will enable a larger quantity of another or purchase of additional to improve the Mess and add to the health, contentment, of all. There will be a change of serving order—the women first, then the children, the men last. . . . High school opening is discussed."

A London paper wrapping some of the market things was dated 1939 with an article in it entitled "Garden Party Year." It was the last one of those for London as the war hit them the next month. It seems like another century—that day we arrived at Calamba sugar estate near Manila, with headlines blaring the invasion of Poland and over the radio came "England is at war with Germany."

Truth is better at all costs, rather than the damage to faith and belief which is the aftermath of propaganda. All writers must be groaning over censorship and rainbow stories. No clouds are allowed. It must be all light, no shade.

June 22, 1942. There are many tales to be discarded but they all give an atmosphere that we live in, the color of war. Manila letters are full of food obsessions, Work Details, operations, sickness, friends, like our life here. The experience of this camp, this family is similar to camps and families all over the world, a universal chronicle of war life. Many camps are worse, some are better, but all are bound together by common trials, work, fear, hope, hunger and losses.

June 23, 1942. I started work in the wrong mood, sick of mops, my hand hurts across the knuckles like a bruise from wringing. I'm tired of garbage and washing out three cans every morning. Tomorrow I will see the dignity of labor again but today it's off! I'm weary of watching families go by with hot coffee and cocoa, hot brown toast, scrambled eggs. Many still have a complete appetizing meal. June gasped with horror when she saw the whites of several hard-boiled eggs in the garbage. This has happened several times from a group that eats only the yolks, throwing the rest away instead of giving it to someone who would like it. Thoughtless, criminal waste! I know what the Chinese think as they gather food to sustain them under the garbage shoot of big vessels in Shanghai and Hong Kong harbors. It used to depress me to watch them. Now it depresses me to see the waste in cans.

The Japanese have the courage which comes with economic scarcity and pressure. We need to realize what this means. America might try two meals a day for a month, cutting off some of the necessities, not just luxuries. If you watch other people consume it or throw it around carelessly, when you can't give it to your own children, then you know how it feels, and the feeling accumulates. You don't blame any one person, you are very general about it, but you want to go on the move. It is the quite simple beginning of revolutionary stirring. There is a deep stirring everywhere of these millions who want to go on the move. Even in this place we have seen what food obsession can do to ethics and the veneer of civilization in a few months.

We have eaten our rice with syrup, coffee and banana; which we have had every morning for six months without much variation. June says it tastes good. She is a great comfort, steady, enthusiastic and on her toes, absorbing, losing nothing, working, learning, and liking it. She asked one if they would give her the egg whites instead of throwing them away and they said they would be glad to do it. Today they gave her a quarter cup of cocoa they couldn't finish which they were on the way to throwing out. She loved it, with no false pride, only enjoyment. The others have so much that they had not thought of their action being waste.

We had a morning of surprises. First, a package from Inez of bananas, sliced fried camote and jack fruit with the seeds taken out ready to eat. What a lovely girl to remember us with one whole meal every week. It feeds our mind too. Carl sent us a dozen mangoes which we fell upon with ravenous joy. There was a heavy bag from steady, smiling Nicolas of the station pump—two huge hands of bananas, nine avocados which are nectar, two papaya for which we longed. In two days three Filipino and two American friends have sent thoughts in concrete form.

June 24, 1942. Jerry has worked too hard at times for the camp with not enough [food] to compensate for the continued drain on the system. He looked at me this morning and exclaimed, ''You look like a million!'' It is strange that I, the weaker, continue to gain and escape the camp illness, while he the stronger, should lose thirty-four pounds and contract ailments. We are each doing more physical work than customary, both get the benefit of bananas, peanut butter and yeast tablets. Can it be the garlic?

One of the ironies is that after spending years subduing the tribes, trying

to educate them away from barbarous headhunting, our own men now encourage this primitive instinct and the gathering of all the tribes so that both
peoples may survive against a new invader.

Camp milk is composed of mongo beans, black beans, sugar, coconut
milk, vegetable water and calcium hydroxide.

I almost wept when two loaded bags came in from Nida and Miss Ramos.
Nida sent a can of chicken-pork adobo from home—it still carried the scent
of Outlook Drive kitchen and past feasts. How good, how rich, the spiced
fat juice! She included sugar, a can of cocoa, chocolate cookies, a long bar
of laundry soap, a spool of thread and safety pins! A magic bag that seemed
to read our minds.

One young mother sits every day upon a bedspread which was once a
beautiful Chinese tablecloth from the High Commissioner's, looted and reaching her by many hands and devious routes. It should be stowed away, not
used for such a purpose for it is too delicate for camp wear. I wonder how
many eyes and hands became tired in the making of it, embroidering in poor
light, ill-nourished but fashioning beauty in order to keep alive one more
week—for the cloth to fall into enemy hands. It is odd that in this place
instead of despising and complaining about the invaders, I should be more
troubled about our own waste and defection.

June 25, 1942. June asks a hundred questions at night after lights are out,
athirst for knowledge. She has the inquiring mind that must dig down to the
roots. She will suffer, but she will live and feel. It is a joy to watch her mind
awaken and unfold. Her eyes leap, her whole being seems to come forward
to draw out all that one can tell her about the subject under discussion.

June 26, 1942. Grandma says that one of the Sagada [mission] women said
she had never seen such a spirit as there was in this camp, that it was apparent
the minute they came in the gate. Everyone was going about with a job to
do and getting it done, busy, organized, accomplishing much while looking
cheerful and not downhearted as they expected us to be.

June 27, 1942. There are rumblings of revolution in the diet kitchen. The
Russian cook is very stubborn. The new milk and pureed vegetables for
babies take much time but must be done. Today is a day when everyone is
fed up with camp life and of knowing nothing of the outside world. We wish
we did not have to see this one or that one again, or to take orders from this
one or to have to appeal to that one to get anything done.

June 28, 1942. Rumor now says that Nakamura is being promoted to Tarlac
prison camp where our Army is located. He is gratified but still asks for a
recommendation from our Committee, which delights us. Prisoners whose
words count for nothing, asked to say a good word for their overlord. He

feels that the Sunday Chorus singing was a farewell in his honor. Often he has sat on the woodpile listening to the men as they practice. He is the strict disciplinarian, with a weakness for song, flower arrangement, and color. Many like him, some do not.

June 29, 1942. There was a glorious orange, cloud-piled sunset and another refraction and diffraction rainbow above it, a real glory with huge light rays going up into the arc of the sky. Afterwards we gathered in a welcome at Betty's home base where the new baby cry sounds and we watched a full moon rise over the black ridge.

June 30, 1942. Up early to watch Nakamura's last roll call but Hayakawa took it. He is younger, a more sensitive type, better educated but not as mature. As Nakamura went by on his last round through the barracks saying good-bye, with sleeves rolled up over his elbows, his force and vitality stood out. He seemed sorry to go for he has watched over our trials and tried to straighten out some of the tangled months. We could search far to find one more equable in such an emergency of war and hate. Before he departed he grumbled to someone about wanting to get the women some clothes before he left town.

The wind is cold but the sun warms it. Last night the Sergeant went about giving bananas to the children—his good-bye gifts. The tough guards are leaving—the fire-breathers from Bataan—now tame and friendly.

One of the real stories in here is of the accumulated friction between the doctors, two in particular. Each has temperament, both are strained by the war of nerves. In this week of crisis and fight for life by one, the two have been brought close together, both acknowledging the debt to skill and medicine which all men owe, each remembering their differences, but losing them when joined in the common fight against death.[33] It was a terrible week, a battle in every sense, but they won. The nurses move in and out, always there to hear the whispered word of patient or doctor. The hospital staff has done heroic duty in six months of complicated ruling. With emergencies, simplified methods of sterilization, washing and other techniques, they have safely delivered babies, tended mothers, major and minor operations, severe accidents, without loss of life during all the stress and strain. There has been drama down there even in the long process of research for bean milk.

The truck comes in with Nakamura, his white teeth in a wide smile, on the front seat which is piled with shoes, hats, evening gowns, and coats—"odds and ends from somewhere" they are called.

The gowns are a strange collection for us to carry in piled over our arms. They are not practical for camp wear, even for dressing gowns or housecoats, for the material is too elegant to be worn before the eyes of soldier guards who are curious. The gowns bring the past before us. Their appearance aroused mixed sensations like the night after the play when the wedding linen was given to the players. There before us in smooth, shining black satin, diamond shoulder straps, silver lamé, suave cut, shape and design, the last word in style before bombs—we have not seen such beauty of line for six months and it mixed oddly with the barracks mops in kerosene tins, garbage tins, and waitresses. That pile of rich material coming into our isolation and severe war atmosphere makes the other life seem very distant. French-heeled slippers, delicate cut-velvet, expensive cloth fashioned into coats soft to touch. The gowns are marked "A.Q."—Paris, London and American models of the First Lady of the Philippines.[34] Some announce "original model," many have scarcely been tried on, not really worn. They were being looted, rescued and sent here, another gift from Nakamura. It is a farewell gesture from one who had only loot to give us.

The sequins and other gorgeousness will be packed away, a sound decision by the Committee because of the impractical material.

We hear how the natives adore Cushing, his tireless effort to do anything possible to obstruct enemy occupation; there one hour, gone the next, with only a small band but powerful in harassing. These are the torchbearers, keeping up Philippine morale, with constant energy, beyond self, during the difficult months of waiting for America. They feel he cannot die, cannot be captured. He is a leader against hopeless odds, losing battles but always just out of reach.

July 1, 1942. Last night we heard much singing at the guardhouse to the tune of "Auld Lang Syne." This was a farewell party to which some of our men were invited, enjoying the family-style sukiyaki, singing with the departing guards. They really liked each other. The guards told someone that they had had the best time of their lives in here with us. The pity of it—that our enemies should tell us this—that prisoners in a prison camp had given them more fun and friendliness than they had ever had before. How it lights up the poverty, the barrenness of their past, the severity of their lives, a mere struggle to exist, no time for years of pleasure such as we have all known. This place that most members hate or merely endure for a brief spell—in this place they had the time of their lives. They came from the hell of Bataan and we seemed like heaven. They go back to a hell in China—anywhere but the peace of home. No wonder they hate to leave, look back on the two months here as a wondrous interlude. So American and Japanese men in the Philippines sang "Auld Lang Syne," just boys again, sorry for the mess we are mixed in together, forgetting it in an all too short evening before "historical necessity" called again toward some tragic fate, today liking us, tomorrow hating us.

In the evening Roy Barton, anthropologist, author of books and articles, gave a brief lecture on his subject, the beginnings of human culture, the super-organic level. It was wonderful to listen again, to absorb twenty minutes of someone's research and knowledge, back into a world where one is allowed to learn, not suppressed.

Manila has been searched for insulin (four people here need it). It used to be P2.50 a bottle, now P18 when it can be found at all. Only thirteen bottles were found in the city. It is a nice problem of ethics for the doctors if the total is turned over to them, but it will surely be divided into four. Sugar has trebled. It is well that Jerry stocked up for typhoons, and that Nida sent us a kilo. We try to conserve it in case we go home.

July 2, 1942. Gradually we have church, grade school, high school, lost clothes returned, other clothes given to us, lectures, singing, singing together while the guards look in the window smiling and listening. How vast a difference to February!

There are food riots in Baguio over sky-high prices. Flour has leaped up to fifty pesos a sack because there is hoarding and profiteering.

July 4, 1942. As soon as June fed Susan and swallowed her own breakfast, she joined Dad and Bedie in the backyard. I waved good-bye, watching them go through the shop to climb the side of the hill, hidden by the trees and bushes. June must have been breathless in two ways as she had her first glimpse over the other side when they came out in the clear space at the top. She ran back to look down on camp before going on. I watched them from the window as they walked along the skyline, Jerry naked to the waist, June in light blue blouse, Bedie in dark shirt, silhouetted against the blue heaven. This is the first holiday they have been together on an adventure. They are going into the wet, ferny, jungle forest in the canyon near the palisades covered with growth above camp. It will take them two hours and is a secret because it might start an exodus of junglers. The mystery adds to the enjoyment. Every year Jerry has driven us to watch the parade, returning to his golf at the Club where we usually wound up for the annual orange juice and special sandwich. This year, nothing artificial, a completely natural celebration of back to nature, tramping together, becoming really acquainted in the woods where Daddy fells trees with other men on workdays. We are lifting our eyes to the hills now. No silver cup to play for this year. The stakes are more desperate.

June comes in alight. She says it was like a meadow on top, so quiet that they all sat down and just listened to the lovely birds and looked at the Cathedral in Baguio. She kept saying over and over, "It's just as though there wasn't any such thing as a concentration camp." They found wild strawberries too difficult to carry down. They saw dripping stalactites in a limestone cave, sat on a wet log listening to more silence! They brought home saline [pitch] wood, and each male carried a leech bite oozing thick, dark blood. June was scraped by a fuzzy caterpillar. Bedie is greatly interested in the powers of a small, slithery leech inching its way, waving its head to locate a juicy spot. He simply must tell me about it. They are thirsty, hungry and happy. "Just the three of us, no one else, but we kept wishing you were there," says June.

Someone whispered that an American flag was being made with red, white and blue pieces which came in with some clothes. It will be hidden until Mañana comes but it will be ready and we will feel we had a part in it.

I dressed up for supper which was a stew, with green beans and cucumber. We toasted Freedom, with two inches of Basi.

Phil Whitmarsh gave one of his best talks on African wild animals. The weekly lectures are greatly enjoyed.

Later, whispering in the Baby Section upstairs, we listened to the handful of men who had celebrated too thoroughly with Basi, whooping, throwing things, bellowing, arguing about Australia. What a young roughhouse, like our small boys! Some were long in quieting down and it was remarked there might be no more packages because of the outburst.

July 5, 1942. As far as I can see, the men have the same problems as the women, the same grumblings, criticism of the Committee. They are minus the care of children and babies, they lack certain types of pettiness and they do clear up their problems by action, not just talk. The woodcutters refused to help with cesspool digging on Sunday, their one day off. Others have not labored at all but they are hard to track to their hiding place and the Committee is loath to tackle unpleasant ones. There are some who just can't be moved toward work so certain [people] are depended on as usual. The Committee finally took shovels and dug in as an example, much to the general joy.

July 6, 1942. Many are wearing clothes that were given away months ago to the Igorot rummage sale now returned to us again. Those Igorot women have stood by us in many ways.

Peg stood up for the mothers and general public when the indignant Committee wanted the names of any one who complained about food distribution. Then she was appointed to look into the question. She has integrity and is democratic. She sifts all the vexing questions, settling some quietly, taking others to the Committee if necessary. Many reach her motherly care, and her normal, instinctive reaction calms some stories while they are only in the ripple stage. She has a feeling for what is right and fair, a balance which weighs the petty and important equally well. Though she is busy making a dress and knitted night socks for her eldest daughter's birthday, she is never too busy to help any appeal, always thoughtful, capable.

July 8, 1942. Jerry fried out some pork and he gave me some of the crisp remains. It tasted so good and I was so hungry for it that I cried over it and couldn't talk. He fried up some rice with the grease and June and I ate it with our fingers, out of a bowl. Jerry understood how I felt emotionally wrought up over that meat with real flavor, for he says they feel the same way on the hill at noon—the stomach runs out to meet the food and all the juices start flowing.

Only the mountains are untouched by invasion. We went out beyond to stand before the most glorious free view, more sweeping than others in camp. Clouds trailed into each valley and indentation, piled in huge heaps like snow. It was beautiful, quiet and detached. Six Igorot women with full baskets on their backs came down a narrow trail toward home, then a boy and a carabao. Rice paddies are full of water like glass, already planted. Some are just turned dark earth. The Igorots and Japanese go on normally, only the Americans do not.

July 9, 1942. I had a session with Bedie over geography homework. He missed the games, howled and wept, was spanked. He has broken one pencil at the eraser end, there are no books or paper, only lectures and memory to rely upon so there is only the mind for reference. He hates to work. I will have to buy paper and notebook somehow. The unsettled conditions make it difficult for the less studious to apply themselves.

July 10, 1942. Bedie snuggled up sideways and whispered he is sorry about yesterday and is going to do better. Perhaps my steam was not wasted. Missing the races probably turned the trick. He could hear it but could not join it because his work was not done. It is a respite for me, this sign of understanding. It is wonderful to see him melt after toughness and bluster. I told him to forget points, credits, just to drink in all he could through his mind and ears, without books or paper, in a new way. If he can take his mind off credits, being unsettled or changed about won't disturb him in this unstable existence. Like the Chinese stream of migration of refugees, we carry our knowledge and learning with us. When books and paper are looted, burned, we must turn to oral teaching.

Here is the leaflet dropped by the plane in vicinity of Camp Holmes July 9.

"SURRENDER YOURSELVES BY JULY 31, 1942

"The time limit set for surrendering with the respective treatment to be recorded to the surrenderers as prisoners of war was previously proclaimed as the 30th of June last; but the contents of the previous proclamation did not properly reach the knowledge of everybody concerned, and as a result there are still some persons who have not taken advantage of the chance to surrender within the prescribed time limit, and are still continuing their futile resistance to the Japanese Imperial forces, and it is very much regrettable and sympathy-worthy not only for such remnants in particular, but also for the people of the Philippines in general, that they still remain obstructing the sound development of the Philippines.

"Considering the above mentioned circumstances, the Commander in Chief of the Imperial Japanese forces has consented to allow a special privilege to these remnants, and those who will surrender on or before the 31st of July 1942 will be treated as prisoners of war in accordance with International Laws in time of war. . . ."

Adult classes in Japanese three times a week are starting and I think I will sign in.

July 11, 1942. A bag from Nida with raw pork chops, mangoes, toothpaste, chowchow pickle and pineapple. That girl is inspired. How do they manage to live? June, all agog, leaps in with news that one of our feminine members stole a whole can of Purico[35] and her husband put her over his knee and spanked her, then tossed her onto Col. Vega's lap.

Dr. Skerl [a geologist] lectured on geology. On his clock chart our own age showed in seconds, not even minutes, and a broad sense of time and space was imparted to us again.

July 12, 1942. In some ways I live in a world of my own with these notes which are an outlet, saving wear and tear on other people. Perhaps everyone should keep notes for a healthy mind.

Instead of church in the barrack room, I went to visit the shop. A list of the things which they have manufactured and which are important to our existence are:

A buffer put on an emery wheel to polish metal or stone is made of a piece of fire hose and the grit is residue from a wet grindstone. They also looted some jeweler's rouge. They showed me some fossilized coral made into a heart, a spade, a diamond and club joined to a pin made from silver award plates picked up at Camp Hay. The power grinder is of an old unknown motor mounted on a Ford generator, bearings and armature. A watch chain with charms in grey and white stone and a V for Victory was also made from two plates which had "marksmanship" engraved on them, also "bayonets." The emery wheel was found at the Post. The solder holder is made out of part of an electric-light fixture. The portable grinder and buffer are made from a windshield-drying motor from an automobile. The pistol grip on it is a piece of carabao horn. The forge is made out of rock and motor from an electric fan, cemented with mud. A charcoal burner has been constructed from the base of an old road roller, with an army field safe for a door, a base of rocks and dirt. Various minor tools are fashioned from firing pins, sights of rifles—cape chisels, punches and awls. Twist drills are made out of coil springs to drill anything from rock to steel.

A knife blade is from a ball-bearing cup, the hilt a plate from a National

Cash Register, the handle of leather disks from cartridge pouches, the end knob from a rifle-cleaning rod. They have an alcohol torch made from two rifle oil cans soldered together. Soldering, plumbing and electrical supplies were fortunately found at Camp John Hay. Their work bench was a serving counter at the Constabulary mess hall here at Camp Holmes.

Camp carpenters are Dunne, and Bart Rice, who remodeled the kitchen and barracks, put up shelves, made wooden beds and other necessities. The blacksmith has made hammers, knives, frying pans, repaired axes and even made some new axes at the forge. He made a hose for the gardeners, works continuously and is most accommodating to camp members. Out in back of the shop there is a still made of an old fire extinguisher for the pressure cooker, the firebox a gasoline drum, the end of a steel reel for plate, some copper tubing, and a gasoline tin for the cooling system. All material and equipment was found or looted from Camp Hay and Camp Holmes after it had been looted first by Filipinos and the Japanese Army.

The shop was started by those with mechanical ability, for communal, not private use, by Ward and Fabian with help from the looting parsons and the wood crew. Many camp members have private tool collections and no communal spirit. The experts say that the most ingenious contrivance is the hand corn-grinder attached to the meat grinder which has given service for six months, grinding coffee, cornmeal, bean and rice flour. Twenty-eight frying pans have been made at the forge so far. The most useful machine for the shop is the electric grinder. They have everything in stock from worn-out light bulbs to old inner tubes.

Sy Stone has completed an army belt with sections holding bolo, toma-hawk, carrying-pouch and first aid kit. Eric, the blacksmith, has wooden shoes with an old leather boot top for half the foot to slip under in front. They presented me with a handmade stone button which I watched them form and my name was placed on a steel mirror with an electric writer composed of a wooden handle, small coil and nail point. The gasoline supply and the oil is a credit to the looting wood crew at the Army Post. The blacksmith does some excellent cooking on the forge also. Fabian has repaired a set of false teeth with sealing and a soldering iron on the lower plate. Even a sewer pump was made though not used as yet. Nakamura permitted the men to bring all tools and supplies from Camp Hay to this camp, and the guards took all tools from the Chinese for the use of the shop.

Carl says the outside is having the same food that we have—rice, native products and rice flour substitute for wheat—but the big difference is in the home-cooked flavor and the variety which we cannot have with 500.

July 13, 1942. June has gained a pound, now 84.

One hears all kinds of strange information in this camp. I have been told seriously that at least four or five individuals here have three or four wives in various sections, not all in one spot of course. One man is writing his thesis for a Ph.D. in here, another is writing a book on the Islands which is being typed as it goes, a third has [written] part of his autobiography.

The high school has about twelve subjects—Latin, German, French, Spanish, Japanese, English, Algebra, Geometry, Trigonometry, General Science, Biology, Reading, Chemistry.

I took my first lesson in Japanese! The light on the blackboard was awful and the noise from children overhead was simply terrific so it is studying under difficulties. It is estimated that out of fifty attending Japanese class, about forty will stick.

July 15, 1942. Nakamura came to see the new baby, so proud it was a boy, before Dr. Lee was even out from under ether. Her neck, shoulders and arms ached from nerves and she wanted someone to massage them. Nakamura stayed an hour granting the request, with his powerful shoulders, arms and hands relieving her ache and pouring strength into her. She says she will never forget the strength of those fingers. He went to Manila to find work, returning in a few days, quiet, subdued and silent. No job, no house, no place for his family, nothing paid to him while he worked at camp. Dr. Lee told him to go to her house if he wants to and can get permission. She has a permit to live Outside for two years. We see how the New Order treats its own people. In giving out supplies from the spoils, rumor says that prominent names were put on paper slips into a hat, drawn out. Hayakawa drew Heacock's supplies, Nagatomi the Pines Hotel, which is running full blast with a cabaret—a Filipino band leader whose wife is the dancer (she used to sell in a Session Road store), all forced to earn a living any way they can. So it was the old way after all, not a new way—as simple as pulling it out of the hat. No attempt to give the people anything. The spoils go to the upper locals.

News from several sources in resume: On April 18, Tokyo, Yokohama, Osaka, and Nagoya were bombed in manufacturing centers by thirteen U.S. bombers. At Midway 27 ships sunk or damaged. Coral Sea the same. Japanese lost 270 planes on sunk carriers, the U.S. only four ships. The Solomons occupied by Japanese. They lost 254 planes in a week here.[36] The Philippine Islands is a member of the United Nations (28 in all now).

'Tis said the prisoners at the Post get dreadful treatment. They wash clothes, hang them out to dry, then the clothes are taken away. They are seen at market in burlap sarongs, enormous holes in ragged shirts, tags and tatters, thin, worn, noses running, faces dirty. They probably have no soap or rags to use. They are allowed to go to market to show how we have lost power and face out here. But it may have the opposite effect.

July 16, 1942. The four of us drank some rich cocoa made by Jerry, standing on each side of the serving counter. After the children left, Jerry and I talked over gossip and news, still with the counter between us. We had some laughs over this crazy, amazing camp. A cosy time together, with the typhoon rain and wind outside. Toward morning I was awake for hours, feeling empty.

July 17, 1942. With my hair down and streaming, Jerry called and I went out in the gusts and more streams to drink half a cup of coffee. He told me the news—and a fit day for it too, with leaden skies, depression, noise of storm, rain in sheets, everyone scurrying to keep dry. His big brown eyes were serious, his face gray, as he whispered, "Sy Stone has gone over the hill. He's in my group and they may hold me responsible. We just missed him, don't know when he left. We don't know who they might take away so I'll send the liverbraun and some things over to you now." It is the first breakaway—Sy of the black beard, perpetual grouch, cracking disparaging remarks on busy workers, muttering discontent for months, but not talking to anyone of his plan for a getaway. He did make the belt at the shop, to carry things around the waist. God knows what it will mean for us. Jerry says the pressure will be tough and he is right.

I did not see Jerry till noon when we all felt better after full stomachs. He sent nothing over so I concluded there was a calm. The guard staff here took it equably enough and by noon it seeped around that the Intelligence had found us such model prisoners that no action would be taken this time but if it happened again punishment would be drastic. There is more behind it than model prisoners, probably weakness in town. Four months ago they would have acted at once.

One choice space-spot is no longer the envy of all because it has developed a stream of spray in the storm.

During the move from one dorm to another, three families fought in boisterous quarrel to stay in the spaces where they were located. Now they are covered with spray and cold wind in the very spot they chose and they clamor for protection. Another case who moved heaven and earth to go Outside is now lonely out there, not allowed to lift a finger to keep busy where she is staying. She would probably adore to be back in the companionship of rice picking or vegetable cutting, anything to keep occupied with work and friends to help pass the long hours. Life is full here, a constant stream of flowing energy and comradeship. Everyone says it is lonely Outside.

July 18, 1942. It is still typhoon and fine guerrilla weather. No washing on the lines, no mopping, more time to talk, to read, to study till it clears.

Supplies and foodstuffs are coming in. A good deal of it is loot from empty houses. Nothing like paying double for our own stuff, but at that it's better than being hungry.

July 19, 1942. Hayakawa told someone he hoped no more would escape for we are a model camp and first on the list to be exchanged to the U.S.

July 20, 1942. Cute bamboo hobby horses were made at the shop of bamboo slats suspended from one end into a springboard effect. The little kids adore them.

July 21, 1942. The Japanese have raised our monthly amount. 460 of us are now fed for thirty centavos a day apiece, covering everything. We are allowed 4,500 pesos a month. Nine pesos a month per person.

My Japanese language lessons get thicker and thicker. No wonder they take themselves so seriously and go on sacred invasions. The tone is even, monotonous, and the complicated indirections fascinate me. It seems quaint, much of it, and there is much bowing and feudalistic attitude, out of touch with present reality.

July 22, 1942. I dreamed of being shown two exquisite violins carved from ivory. I did not handle or touch them but the one who had brought them dropped one and it smashed into a thousand pieces. I was down on my knees picking up the little fragments of ivory, bits of jade and carnelian, feeling responsible for the breakage as though I had dropped it—a symbol of the beauty scattered everywhere, coming out of soldiers' pockets, held only by ignorant, careless hands. My mind is trying to pick up and piece together what is left of the present and past life, to carry on in some shape into the future. I told the one who had dropped the ivory that though I had not touched the piece, I was as responsible as she was and so was everyone. I kept reiterating "We are all to blame."

I missed the first Amateur Night. Jim Halsema was announcer for Major Bozo hour, with Concentration Rice the sponsor—"in seven different flavors—burnt, coconut, caramel, perspiration, cockroaches, fish, and syrup." Carol sang hillbilly songs and yodeled; little Francie sang "Smile Awhile," each winning first and second prizes which are said to be a ride on the garbage wagon to Trinidad. Rae recited her concentration version of the poem about the tropics ending "Oh, how I want to go home!" Mr. Perry fluted and Alice and Gerry sang in spite of an attack of stage fright. There is a new theme song with words and music by Marvin Dirks, "Have you tried rice? It's the best food in all of the land." This brought thunderous applause and cheering no end, with the evening a howling success.

July 24, 1942. We heard of an Igorot who played Fifth Column, betraying a group of Chinese hiding in a mission dugout, and many other betrayals by him—even his father willing for USAFFE [U.S. Armed Forces, Far East] to shoot him, but an Igorot doing it would precipitate tribal war. This man is a perfect example of Fifth Column taking advantage of our weaknesses, betraying his own people as well as the Chinese, sold out to the Japanese and traveling with them to give away his knowledge of native haunts. It would be interesting to find out why he turned against everyone, married as he is to a half-American mestiza.

July 26, 1942. Jerry spent the whole morning frying sweet camotes for his women folk. We ate a whole watering can full which is what they soaked in. He also made fudge and a fluffy omelet from the first eggs we've had in weeks. We simply hung over them. Bedie was torn between food and a new guerrilla game the boys are playing on the back slope. It is out of bounds but the guards don't seem to mind the youngsters up there and what a thrill for them, in the haunts of real guerrillas.

Somebody outside hears broadcasts every week in Tagalog, Ilocano, Visayan, even Ibanag,[37] from the U.S. to encourage the Philippine Islands. Within three days a happening here is told at home, showing contact by radio, both receiving and sending.

July 28, 1942. We became possessors of a Figure 9 teapot made from an oatmeal can at the shop.

I floundered, gurgling, in Japanese class, clicking now and then. After supper, at the bunk I saw the bag from home sent through Nida and Carl with our three raincoats, Jerry's two shoes, an umbrella, towels, four enamel plates and four tin spoons. No one in America can know what huge proportion it assumes in our eyes—the plates and spoons taking us out of a long waiting line for dishes, with the tin teapot making us independent of borrowing, as did the frying pan. It puts us in the luxury bracket. These everyday things are more exciting even than our fine raincoats salvaged from the past. We marked them with name on precious adhesive tape.

In a Red Cross box from Nida, sewed in our garage all through air raids by faithful Filipina women, there are 17 bath towels cut from a bolt, 35 hemmed hand towels, 2 surgical coats, 8 angel gowns, 8 cut gowns plus one third of a bolt of uncut material for the same thing. There is one full bolt (50 yards) of linen toweling, 9 spools of white thread which are worth their weight in gold right now, a pair of scissors, 6 packages of bias tape and a roll of cotton tape. Last week's note did the trick. The sewing machine carried out by truck during the bombing also came in the same way. It is a small amount in the total of Red Cross relief at home and out here—but it seems great to us in our need after the headquarters has been looted. Again we think of that last appeal for funds before the war—"It may happen to *YOU*. You may benefit from Red Cross help." This little pile of last supplies sent from Manila during invasion days appearing almost miraculously in Concentration Camp gave me more thrill than seeing my own possessions for it means more to 500.

The Committee presented me with four hand towels and the scissors, as the Japanese had taken all of my cutting or pointed materials, so I feel rich and was too stimulated to sleep, awake for hours recalling hectic days when things were salvaged in our Zephyr car which is now part of the Imperial Army. After the Red Cross supplies had been settled, Peg said she had more for me. First she gave me a whole container of pencil leads from Nida. Then she put into my hands the two velvet cases of miniatures of June and Bedie, given to us by their godfather one Christmas years ago. These pieces of beauty came from our house, from the past, things we had forgotten, not even asked for.

July 29, 1942. A gorgeous day—Peg and I climbed until we reached the first ridge where the men have cleared out many trees. We could see the limestone palisade of the next ridge blocking our view of town. We sat down on the straw pillow and drew a long breath, filling our lungs with clear air, the sounds of camp far behind and the buildings only in panorama. Beyond us spread shade after shade of blue from dark crevices and valleys to light along the ridges, an enormous range of strength which made us exclaim, "There is the Philippines!"—the "mountains of Northern Luzon" which I read about years ago in primary school geography, never thinking we would be imprisoned in the heart of them, with their beauty unrolling before us from dawn to sunset for eight months.

An Igorot boy came up the twisted trail. He smiled shyly, ready to pass by, but Peg, all out now for adventure, beckoned him over. He squatted native fashion near us and we talked. He pointed where he lived, overlooking some rice paddies, across from the camp. He said he had come by arrangement to see one of our men up there, and carried messages to some of the native wives for them. About news he called it "our side." He said Roosevelt had told them not to be discouraged for we could retake any time and would "come like many birds."

It was so simple, so sweet to hear him, that confidence and surety that we used to have before it was shaken. He brought it to life again, standing there, the wind blowing around the three of us—the Igorot boy barefoot, in ragged blue denim shorts.

Yesterday came tragic confirmation, expected but hoped against for months, of the death of one of our number by shocking violence on March 15—Rufus Grey at the hands of the Intelligence Special Service of the Japanese Imperial Army. The cause was third degree questioning and torture, with sadists at work.[38] Hayakawa had been impressed to find out and brought the information to the Committee and the young wife and small child this evening. No one envies him the telling of it. What was feared when the others were returned without him is now known.

Jerry brought me a "jerky stew" with distinctly individual flavor among the delicious small white potatoes, celery and beans. It was a rare taste, out by the water tank under the runway, with Jerry all eyes while I devoured with greedy gulps, whispering about the hill. What fun, what tastes in snatches here and there in odd settings. Peg still laughs at the speed with which I went up the mountainside—like one of the slant-eyed goats scenting adventure, no puffing, no stopping for breath as once I would. This is from carrying heavy cans!

I talked with a pessimist who always doubts all rumors. She is always of little faith, feels man is completely selfish; she emanates futility, insists that the Japanese do things in cycles with no reason behind any action. I think there is often a reason behind even a small item. My mind jumps to the contrast of her and the boy on the hill—his serenity and confidence, with fresh clear wind blowing, the quiet untroubled pleasure of his smile. And I knew what Ruth meant when she said she felt she could do anything outside and began to feel crushed down when she came back. The boy is the simplest, purest freedom, able to come and go on the paths of the hill. But he is watched and may be caught. We do not need to climb the hill. The mind can travel there without feet. I shall go back to that spot some day but I will feel the wind numerous times before I do. Freedom is a state of mind like many other things as prisoners occasionally find out. Prison should be a school, like war, for education and guidance, not dark confinement. We must make it so for the future, clearing debris from warped minds.

July 30, 1942. The various romances are flourishing the only way they can in concentration—stilted, public, leading to no actual courtship, but tender devotion in conversation and looks, with food preparation ending in twosome parties under pine trees or iron-roofed runways.

Mrs. James has her prison number etched on bamboo section by an electric needle, making a striking brooch for the future.

July 31, 1942. Mr. Frost is making an ersatz coffee by parching cornmeal. We sampled it and it is as good as most submarine varieties.

Jerry said casually, "Of course you've heard the truck story." But I had not. Twelve [Japanese] went up the road "going like a bat out of hell" around a curve—where there wasn't any road. They all piled off and the seven trucks we saw going up loaded with troops were going to [find the bodies of] those others. Asked if the road went out by rains or guerrillas, Jerry grinned, "Your guess is as good as mine." The mothers and wives of those in trucks will be weeping as mothers of our men in the States. Everywhere women are waiting and weeping.

A second store is set up at one end of the barracks. Capitalism crops up in our midst in the form of middlemen. The nipa [palm-thatched] store tried to sell bread for 85 centavos when the cost price was 60 centavos. People refused to buy it when the garbage detail started a mild purchasing [revolt] again and revealed the high prices. One lot of bread was returned unsold from our store to the tienda and the woman who had worked hours baking it wept because of people needing it for food and it was left to spoil because someone wanted to profit.

August 1, 1942. Sylvia and Maud have made two charming moss gardens with gray tree bark, tiny gray and red lichen, ferns, soft green grasses, ground pine and an ice plant.

August 2, 1942. After breakfast, I casually remarked I felt like climbing the hill and Jerry said, "All right, let's!" We stowed away half our breakfast rice for noon and I started off with June, Bedie and Geoff up the steep log shute in full view of the guards. Jerry went up from back of the shop with sack and ax for chopping fire timber. The children kept holding back for me to catch up until finally I told them I was a goat and could go anywhere. They looked so surprised. At the top, June said, "Why Mama, I've never seen you like this. What is the matter with you? You look like a little girl."

The ferns, berries, grass and general contour reminded me of our yearly trek to the real woods at Squantum[39] when I was June's age and we gathered valley lilies in wet places. I loved it and now the children will have similar woodsy memory of the pasture, hilltop and cool glen. We scrambled on wet leaves and twigs down into a humid jungle spot where overhanging limestone showed stalactites, wild white orchids which we left untouched, exquisite lacy-thin ground pine like ferns which we gathered for Sylvia's garden, purple berries close to huge thick tropic leaves, all sorts of rich growth which only dark cool places know. Then back again, clambering over the limestone pile which Peg and I had seen a week ago. There were long steep views through V-shaped crevices in which bushes nestled with white star flowers and berries. Across the meadow were two cows and a bull who stared at us so we veered slightly away! The children felt very important showing with great pride just where they went and what they saw on the 4th. Only a month ago and now I have been to the top too, never expecting it in Concentration.

We came back to sit near a baby pine clothed in new green and we gazed down at camp in a new proportion—perhaps the true one—three long barracks, the small low barber shop, the ugly shaped hospital building which looms large but is so cut up inside that it is really small, the Baby Cottage, the almost hidden school, the log cabin guardhouse, the shop near the pig and goat pens, the long nipa sheds. Sounds rise distinct. The gong in slow, mournful beats for church, gathers the congregation with pillows under arm and hymnbooks in hand from all directions on the slope opposite the hospital. They look very small, the little band, each with his individual problems and important difficulties to adjust. "When morning gilds the skies, my heart with rapture cries" floats up as clear as bells from the mixed choir and seems lovelier than we ever heard it. We look down on the bowl of the valley, with the small congregation in the center, the mountains rising on all sides around it, clouds heavy, resting evenly on the range which makes a perfect rim to the cup. We cannot penetrate to the sea for a cloud mist is drifting slowly in. We hear Grandpa's voice in Scripture reading, can hum the second hymn and catch the benediction. Then we know that the memorial service for Rufus

Grey has begun, following the regular service. The people stand, there are prayers and Scripture "to give comfort and sympathy from all to the strong hearts left behind." Marion Grey stands bravely in the group, her long months of uncertainty, agonizing doubt, at last ended. She knows he has not suffered since March. Whatever her tortured mind may have imagined, it is far in the past, and if she could have been on the rim of the hill instead of in the valley she would have heard the song rising to the heavens, to the Creator, even to Rufus who is beyond all mortal suffering now, far from the cruelty of man to man. "Lead, Kindly Light"—how sad it is, written from the depths of some troubled soul. I could not have borne it without weeping down below, but on the hill it was so clear, full of sun through mist, cloud banks shot with blue sky over mountain ranges.

Jerry left us with his wood sack loaded on his back. We watched him going down the trail, stripped to the waist, in shorts, brown from the sun, bent under his load "just like an Igorot," said June. We sat on there in the warmth while a plane went loud but unseen through clouds overhead and the congregation filed back to barracks. June wanted to talk about the beginnings of life, babies, creation, so we lay on the grass another half hour and discussed it simply, directly. It was a perfect time and place to absorb it. We talked about children growing from the primitive, savage stage, under parental care, to school, when they left home to move into community life.

The U.S. is getting too much news from the Philippine Islands, too quickly, too accurately. The Japanese are trying to track down the communication lines.

It seems there are numerous petting parties going on, which accounts for the guards flashing about at night in odd corners of camp. They are lenient about [daylight] commingling but in this setup there isn't much use stirring up the emotions beyond a certain point. Of course it is a strain on the sex instinct to be so near and yet so far!

August 3, 1942. "The use of Nippongo [Japanese] and Tagalog language for official purposes was prescribed, thus initiating gradual elimination of English from official use in the P.I."—Camp *News*.

I bemoan that more than fifty trees have been cut down on the hill—one alone had 86 rings. They are on a reservation and would never have been cut at all except for invasion and our need to feed 8 stoves—barracks, hospital and special diet. The 86-year-old pine has stood under Spanish, American, Filipino and Japanese rule—which finally stopped its growth.

August 4, 1942. I never expected to enjoy myself so much, on two meals a day, without any sheets, in an army bunk crowded in with my daughter who has become a real pal in close-corner association.

Someone hailed me yesterday, "Hello, here comes the Charwoman," as I hove into sight with full can and a mop. Charwoman and proud of it. I do it the best I know how, which might not win me any prize if stacked up against experts. Still it is something to do it and like it when you start from dumb. We have been a lot better off than in a rigid, brutal regime of German prison camp—under white people.

A washboard has been manufactured at the shop to replace the broken one. The ridges are made with smooth bamboo and on the back is printed "Danger, use for washing only."

Bedie came in with a flour-sack bag [from Nida] containing many of Jerry's shirts, my wool turquoise skirt, odds and ends from the closet, camphor chests and drawers, and my two new pair of shoes in black and tan. It showed more was saved than we expected through faithfulness and loyalty. Another sack came with Jerry's brown sweater and more shirts so that he has the main part of his wardrobe and all his shoes.

Later Peg whispered to me that when she and another were outside that afternoon, Carl said to them, "Do you want to see some shoes? Twenty-five pairs?" He opened a closet door and there was civilization jumbled in together—blue and gold, white and red—Pete's shoes, he said. Peg said she thought of me in concentration and how little I seemed to care for clothes, and she shouted with laughter over the pile of the past, with contrast to the present. I told her that Jerry bought most of them and he grinned wryly, remarking that out of the 25, I wore about three pairs over and over—the broken-in, comfy ones! She said that after being on the hill all morning, far removed so to speak, it was drastic contrast to look at the muddle of gay shoes and slippers. All these things our servants had brought over bit by bit in unobtrusive paper bags for weeks at a time to this place of safekeeping with Carl.

After the evening lecture came the fashion show with the parade of Concentration Modes, Inc. Much curtain material was in evidence. Della Inc. made up two denim work suit models for the hospital staff that were very snappy.

August 6, 1942. We had a package from Miss Ramos with a pineapple pie at which we gazed and gazed. There were sausages, lemons, and candy. Daddy came to eat the pie with us on the front porch, with sub-coffee (grounds used more than twice) with milk. We gave the children each a full glass of milk, their second in eight months. Jerry opened a can. It was fish dinner so he opened a chicken and noodle soup. We had mashed sayute [soft, pulpy green vegetable] and Jerry experimented with mashed gabi [potato-like root vegetable] which he made into little cakes and fried. It tasted like Irish potato cakes, a swell discovery.

August 7, 1942. June, wanting to know all about death as we dove under the warm blankets, kept me wide awake for hours. The questions she can ask at night! I told her that death was often relief, release from extreme suffering, like unconsciousness or sleep—one of Nature's ways; that many religions had different ideas as to what happened after death but that none could be sure; that like the future, perhaps it was best for us not to know. She was upset and said she wasn't going to be able to sleep so we talked it out again. She wanted to know why people feared death so much and I explained we were like children, merely afraid of what we did not know, that its seeming finality bothered us but that we did not need to feel final about it. Finally I turned her mind to other things and she talked about home, giggled, laughed—and was asleep. I lay awake, thinking with amusement of Jerry and his lemon candy into which he poured cup after cup of precious sugar, boiled and boiled, beat and beat, pulled and pulled, telling me, "Stick around! My morale is getting lower and lower." Precious supplies and an afternoon of labor made him desperate. It is hard to cut or chew, must be sucked. One of his few failures in culinary experiments!

August 8, 1942. News by word of mouth that 125,000 were killed in Düsseldorf raids, 50,000 injured, and America and Britain have delivered an ultimatum to Germany that all her cities will be bombed like this if she does not stop war now.[40] A dreadful, horrible world.

In here our common lives are so close that illness, a fight for one life, touches and saddens us all. It is still incredible that in eight months death has only struck one [adult], and then from the outside.

Dr. Dean went to town for special instruments in a deluge of rain, and about 10 P.M. he operated on Paul Thorson's brain to relieve the terrible attacks that became so severe that four men had to hold the patient. They found much fluid and inserted a drain, finishing about 1 A.M. It is called a tumor but I have not heard many facts. Everyone felt quiet and depressed. Rain and more rain.

August 9, 1942. Sunday School classes begin today and religious lectures are being organized by some of the ministers under the head of "Religion and Life." A number of the younger missionaries, feeling a radically changed world, would like to discuss the place and position of missions after the war, drawing into closer touch with economics to give a well-fed body as foundation for feeding the spirit. It helps to know that there are some stirrings of progressive thought.

We had twelve inches of rain in one day, 26 during the storm of 78 hours.

August 10, 1942. It is strange to feel no longer shorn after having accepted the loss of everything. We learn bit by bit that the house was practically untouched and the treasures are in a safe place.

Ghandi is in prison and India in revolt. The drive into Russia is deep and the southern General tells his troops to hold, retreat no further. It is very critical. Are the British going to continue their old regime in India or be forced into a new program? They will never give in afterward so the Indians want it now.

August 11, 1942. Before Japanese lesson, Jerry and I sat on the bank in the lovely evening, the hills fresh after rain, peaceful after storm. Paul Thorson was conscious and asked for Father Gowan about four. At eight he died, in coma, peacefully, after the storm of dreadful attacks. Everyone is walking about silent, husbands and wives holding hands, moving closer as the first one passes from our midst. We think of the days at Brent when Paul arose to the emergency, helped to organize the meals, bringing sausages and other things from the store to keep us from dropping with exhaustion. Genial, hearty, he has been missed since he became ill. The camp car is driving up to take him to town tonight. It is a tragic place for grief, nowhere to hide it.

It is increasingly obvious in here that those who do their share of the community work, no matter how distasteful it is, are the happiest and best adjusted in camp. The unhappiest are the ones who won't face their tasks, twist and turn away with all kinds of reasons and excuses, working only for themselves, doing their own washing, their own extra cooking, puttering about in a narrow circle, feeling abused and ill-treated. There must be a balance between personal and community duties. It must increasingly be a community solution because those who are maladjusted become community burdens.

August 12, 1942. I seem to be absorbing something from Japanese class though I'm not exactly clear as to what. It is helping me to understand my enemy, giving me an atmosphere, the shades and color of his background. An enemy can teach more than a friend who may spare the truth. While I feel completely submerged by the language at the moment, there is pleasure in listening to the words and phrases which gradually assume a form and feeling, a sense, though still imperfect and dimly grasped.

August 13, 1942. It is election day for our men. It still surprises me that the chairman doesn't want the women to vote or have any kind of election. The General Committee appointed our group and will continue to appoint them but we can write in any ideas we may have for the Men's Suggestion Box. He thinks any other way would end in a "mess" and the Japanese don't consider women people anyway so it is all one piece. Perhaps there never will be any official democracy in here except for the men.

Jerry and I listened to Jim Bozeman tell of the week of panic on his hilltop, the junction of wire and the end of the road for army, miners, and civilians. What a picture, in his salty telling of it!—the blowing of Balatoc [refinery] tanks with no warning at 2 A.M. one morning, with the mighty roar followed by red glare, men pouring up from the tunnels, families dragging

children, babies and possessions up the mountainsides; Americans in a group
of lighted cars almost ambushed by Filipino and American guard posts until
they heard English spoken; phone bells ringing constantly, asking questions
no one could answer; the Filipinos wanting to go home to the lowlands, piling
down the steep sides with their families, reaching another ridge where they
could go no further, able to see all the troops pouring in and against each
other, fighting far below; all marooned on the ridge, compelled to watch the
battle, with little food, only two springs of water at distant spots, he sending
them water by tramline; babies born right there in sight of battle, people
dying from age, strain, exposure and exhaustion. "Pitiful," he said, "pitiful"—with his eyes back there looking at it.

August 15, 1942. Jerry's cricket call brought me out for coffee at quarter
to seven where we watched the loading of the truck with bags and mattresses
and later bid Grandma good luck. Grandpa was torn between wanting to go
and wanting to stay with his classes and his reelection. He knows action will
be zero outside. Grandma has her desires, longed for during six months, and
I hope it won't be ashes in her hands. With drastic restrictions on passes and
moving about, life Outside is not pleasant.

At five a car arrived full of Japanese, with Arthur.[41] The Japanese figure
we are giving information to the guerrillas as well as getting it from them.

August 16, 1942. There are some good stories. One on the men's election,
during the preliminaries. One man said he had made 42 frying pans and
polled only 8 votes—there was no justice! Another said he had made 48
coffeepots and had been given only 8 cups of coffee in return. "That's
nothing," retorted Dave. "I've made 200 beds—"

August 17, 1942. The truck came in with stacks of plates and cups for which
we had implored weeks and months ago. A little package of birdseed came
in for the canary who is dipping in all over, joyous at seeing real bird food
again! We will do the same when we are relieved from rice.

About four when I was dunking mops, I heard my name called loudly
and Arthur said I was wanted at the guardhouse. With all the investigations
going on, my heart did flip-flops. I hung up the mop, tossed the can to Bedie
who wanted to go to the guardhouse with me. Arthur came along and I asked
if Jerry were sent for too and he replied, "Nope, just you." I said maybe
our sponsors were about to get us out and he laughed grimly and said not
a chance. "It's a package for you." It was less than a week since we had
one from Inez so I could not imagine who it might be from. The guard
pronounced my name and looked me over, then in front of Arthur and Miss
Spencer who was there to interpret, he portentously cut the string and we
craned forward—to behold a bunch of bananas on top of a covered luscious
pie with grated coconut on top. The sergeant repeated, "A pie, a pie," then

handed me the package. It was such an anticlimax that I wanted to shriek with laughter and flushed crimson trying not to do so. I was allowed to depart with the pie. Inez actually came to the guardhouse with two other girls and Arthur tried to impress on them that it was dangerous and they must not come again but send [food] by the regular routine in the truck.[42] Anyone knowing or contacting Igorots, even by pie only, is suspect and on a blacklist in these times of guerrilla suspicion. She had never written a word to me and I had never tried to thank her. People were hanging out of windows and watching from the front porch as I came back, calling out "What was it?" and it sounded so absurd to say a pie. It was such a surprise to receive a gift through the guardhouse, pleasant ending to what might have been different.

August 18, 1942. The Women's Committee report with the paragraph by Enid shows growth during 8 months. Though the paragraph doesn't cover everything and is partly a noble defense of the serving crew who are again under fire, it nevertheless attempts to outline the attitude of the leader and the problems confronting committee members, and it succeeds in spite of gaps and defense mechanisms. Many of the women have had little political experience but they are getting it right now. In the conversations on nominees, there is little acrimony, nothing very personal, but a steady, quiet desire for change. Nearly forty names are up on the sheet. Everyone seems to have a mental platform worked out without rancor.

August 19, 1942. At two o'clock two truckloads of trunks and bags were brought in by the Army Intelligence. It was dumped on the ground by the guardhouse. Sylvia and Daphne found three out of their four trunks, some still locked and intact. They recovered most of their belongings, after hearing two weeks ago that it had all been shipped away. It was all mixed up, several people's things in another person's trunk, clothes, films and snapshots all jumbled in together. There were boxes of Kotex and piles of unclaimed clothes which finally reached the community chest in Enid's room. At the last the guards opened some unclaimed boxes and told those standing by to take what they wanted. This was the signal for a mad scramble, rush, pull, haul, not to mention maul. There doesn't seem to be a human being that won't respond to the call of loot. Why anyone wants other people's belongings or a piece of loot as souvenir is beyond me. Even the best ones grab and laugh, and how funny the guards thought it. They too can see no one is immune. The reason no one could do anything about regulating it was because the Gestapo brought it in with the attitude that it was their property, not ours, and they were distributing it to people who needed clothes and shoes, were not the least concerned that the rightful owner receive it. Most people were able to find their own shoes and match up all but a few. It was all depressing to watch, especially when rain began to fall on ostrich feathers and silks and fur coats. One usually quiet women grabbed a Chinese coat and pulled hard to get it away from a man who kept insisting it was his own as indeed it proved to be. Her whole face was changed as she screwed it up in anger and possessive sharpness. Her hair became disheveled and streaming, her eyes shrewd, her voice edged. One box from Brent uncovered many luncheon sets, and baby garments of the Richardsons. Maud fished out her kimono. Those who found their own things went to bed very happy, surrounded with goods. One poor European couple, refugees several times, had some of their clothes snatched out from under their nose. These were later located through the community chest. Jerry was not on the scene but he came out of it with a blue-green tweed coat presented to him because he and it were both very large. I still think the real owner will come up to him on the street some day.

August 20, 1942. It was a sensation to cast a ballot,[43] to be considered people again. The chairman's excuse that the Japanese kept us from voting was rather thin.

Manila *Tribune*, August 16, headlines were "All India Rises," and much print was devoted to arrests and trouble, including meeting in Manila by Indians who closed all their stores in protest, condemned the British and made resolutions.

August 21, 1942. One man was reprimanded by Arthur and the guard for being in the women's barracks. So many take advantage of leniency that it is more overdone every day and we may end up with no more commingling again. As it is, couples can play bridge in the evening and there is pleasant mingling in the dining room. Why some men have to be smart and brag about how much they get away with is just another one of the human mysteries.

Last night the guards came in to all sections to check lights and outlets. All this is really checking up for a radio.

On the way back from the cook house one of the election committee congratulated me on my election [to the Women's Committee], so I was a dark horse. Hazel of Australia is the highest. Ellen who has worked hard on diet staff is second and Ruth who battles with toilet cleaning is third, Enid fourth. Baby House has a representative and Peg is still on. It represents a big change, with only two of the original committee still on. It is a fair slice of camp, though the hospital is not represented.

August 22, 1942. I went to Jane's flower arrangement class on the front porch. She is happy because Hayakawa brought in one of her lovely bowls with pale green glaze, two flower holders and her teaching books. The class watched her arrange two gray leaf branches, some cosmos and lilies with grasses and sharp leaves. She explained the positions and symbols. I enjoyed it and shall try to attend each Saturday, but art, self-expression in delicacy and beauty seem very remote from this situation. We are so deep in the center of battle that such a study seems as fragile as an exquisite glass globe tossed from one to another. But even here we try to escape, seek loveliness, form and balance. This class will give us another view of our enemy, his idea of release, a bit of his character and nationality, his search for something beyond every day. While we listened and watched, the choir practiced hymns very audibly in the shed, familiar songs floating sweetly across the parade ground. Before they gathered, a portable organ, violin and other voices had practiced. The hum of school and various camp work buzzed in every direction.

The camp and Committee now run the store, no more private enterprise or high prices. The revolution is on, though democratic and peaceful. Arthur reported that the Nipponese authorities had directed that such a store be operated by and under the immediate control of the General Committee. It was moved and carried that it be operated on a nonprofit basis, for cash only.

August 24, 1942. Many clothes sent in by Nida are covered with drops of candle wax showing they must get things out at night by this light only.

My feeling that the Fifth Column is our own weakness, of which the enemy makes the most, is stronger than ever. There is one couple who seems not to realize how much they give away in conversation with a man who deliberately cultivates them, draws them out skillfully, humbly, pretending ignorance, promising friendship and service as he winds his way in.

The Women's Committee from six till seven-thirty was a revelation. The author of *The Women*[44] would have written about it with a pen dipped in irony. They all want to hang on to the kitchen job as though life depended on it. May, her voice dripping with tears, her face long and woebegone, told how the children would be upset if Auntie Dee or Auntie Muriel were changed for another. Her motion, which was *not* seconded, was full of veiled threats, showing clearly the line of politics, privilege and bucking we would run into, if we attempt to change the detail. I was elected Secretary. We are supposed to be frightened of this long trail of opposition opening up ahead. When I asked if the Chef would go on strike, merely because a Work Detail was changed, they laughed it off but it had been hinted before I even put it into words. I mentioned the general criticism, which they pooh-poohed. I even quoted two of them as saying in my hearing that anyone connected with the kitchen would be a fool if he didn't get all he could out of it. I was willing to concede it if the detail was changed often enough so that the gravy was spread in order to make better feeling, goodwill and to clear the air of the whole matter. May gave up the veiled threats finally and resorted to sob stuff, running the whole gamut of tricks which took me back to days spent in Boston City Hall listening to the political wheels go round, and to the Sacco-Vanzetti trial where smoothness and suavity scarcely veiled the clash of class and privilege versus attempts to change, and other horrible complications which resulted in the execution of two men and showed me life that is still vivid as this camp will be to the end of my life.

August 25, 1942. Immediately after breakfast, May came to ask if I would take over Frankie's place as waitress and I accepted instantly. I didn't know how long I could stand up under heavy trays but we can carry by plates so it is all right.

Nida sent us popcorn, sugar, cocoa, Kotex, a can of corned beef and one of sardines, and some of my socks and hankies from home. We continue to marvel at each package.

The Boy of the Hill[45] is at the guardhouse, hands handcuffed behind his back, leaning forward on the chair as though it hurt him to have them tied that way. He was caught for the third time carrying bundles of wood down the hill. [The Japanese] are watching the hill now. I would like to go up but will not.

No irons, hot plates or lights are to be used in daytime. Current consumption went up like mad. The men have many electrical gadgets and the hospital is worst of all. Americans are extravagant and badly spoiled.

During the last storm the Nippon flag blew down and has never been put up again. Will the regime change like this, without our realizing it, and we won't believe it?

August 26, 1942. The Igorot Boy of the Hill was released last night with a warning to get no more branches or wood on our reservation.

August 27, 1942. I wish I could put Daphne Bird's wit on paper when she comments on various camp antics but it's the lift of her brows, the quirk of her mouth, the thin voice which gives an ironic twist to whatever she says, crowned by the reddish glint of her hair. She has Irish spirit, lightning dart of humor. She is half conservative, half radical and one never knows which will prevail but the expression of it is always laughable.

August 28, 1942. I made an excursion to the hospital. The first call was on Dr. Hall, who showed me his laboratory lamp heater made of a coffee can, two spikes, a piece of bamboo bridging and an alcohol lamp. The alcohol lamp is made of a medicine bottle with wick through a corkscrew top. His staining tray is made of a little glass dish found in a scrap heap plus the top of an inkwell to support the slide in the center. An incubator is made of a pasteboard box with electric lamp suspended inside by a long cord, and a clinical thermometer. The temperature is regulated by lengthening or shortening the cord and keeping tabs on the temperature by watching the thermometer.

Going upstairs I must have arrived too soon for I came across a chicken being defeathered and cleaned on the operating table,[46] well out of sight instead of in the kitchen across the hall. However, another staff member rallied enough to show me a bedpan holder made into a rubber-glove rack, the surgeon's headlight made from an auto spotlight, a hot plate fashioned from a stove at Camp Hay, two medicine cabinets from a china cabinet and a bookcase, a filing case to store sterile goods, an inkwell holding thermometers, an old filing cabinet holding instruments, a trunk tray holding small clothes for new infants, two bookcases stored with sheets and linen. After being sterilized in the autoclave, instruments have to be dried in the stove oven. Old bottles are used for the patients' drinking water jars, a tire patch mends rubber gloves, country club tablecloths are turned into sheets and pillowcases. The Colonel's bed is on two wooden boxes to make it as high as a surgical bed. Thick chair-cushions are used to raise the patients in bed. Rain is used instead of distilled water, for sterile solutions and boiling instruments, as there is too much chemical in the spring water, which covers the instruments with powder. Many surgical tables, jars and other supplies came from Notre Dame hospital so that improvising was unnecessary. There are five patients, none very serious.

August 29, 1942. I stopped writing because I felt drained and fed up with human beings. The constant furtiveness in camp, the low ebb of ethics, the general atmosphere of shrugging shoulders, camp riddled with petty graft—it had me down for a few hours. How they can all be so swell and so rotten within a short space of time is incalculable and I give up. I like them and despise them all at once.

August 30, 1942. I went up the hill briefly with the children. There the mind opens out and releases the spirit to the mountains, all the cobwebs and dust of the week are brushed away, the terrific struggle of humanity taking its proper place in the perspective of nature.

Jerry and I had an evening discussion in which he gave a noble defense of the hard, unselfish work of the shop men, woodcutters and a number of other good workers. It did me good to hear him and he is right. It is only now and then that glaring defects overshadow the steady cooperation and integrity of half the members. He did admit the small privileges which many try to hang on to which grow large when added together and leads into a complex web of defensive loyalty and battle. Anyone who tries to straighten it out, to make or keep rules, finds himself the butt of wisecracks, stings and criticism. It is why many Committee members won't enforce rules and say nothing can be done to unravel or clear up difficulties, why they get discouraged and give up. They just can't take it, especially when it comes from friends. Committee members should be above it, impartial, ignoring barbs.

September 1, 1942. We scorned black bean soup and fell upon Nida's and Ismael's fresh-made empanadas [meat pies fried in deep fat]. She read my mind in sending two bars of soap. There was a large jar of coffee, 2 cans of jam and cigarettes for Jerry. It made us all feel cheerful. Miss Ramos sent another pineapple pie and muffins shaped like hearts, clubs and diamonds, a can of corned beef, one of Vienna sausage, a bag of cookies, and bag of lansones [white, grape-like fruit]. We will make them last as long as possible.

Most people are not influenced much by ethics in this situation. They rationalize if ethics get in the way of a desire. Even idealists justify themselves with "When I see everyone else taking, grabbing, getting away with this or that, it makes me angry and I take what I can too. It's terrible what goes on." Thus another and another are added to the list. The slang expression still holds—"It isn't what you do, it's what you get caught doing"—getting caught is considered dumb, not the act itself which is wrong.

The men talk over Dr. Dean's value to camp, how he was not only useful as a surgeon but that he got things done because he is a go-getter, has drive, power and daring which inspire confidence. Like others, he has made errors and the petty graft at the hospital was equal to any. It is too bad that errors of this sort accompany outstanding service but it often happens and one cannot blink it. He recovered much for camp but he overdid provision of food and privacy for his helpers.[47]

September 2, 1942. One of our most unhappy and nervous camp members fainted last night and today put her head down on the wash bucket as though considering it again but decided to weep instead. Her face was very red, not weak or white. It looked more like anger at having to carry a bucket of water to a table to wash like the rest of us when she prefers to stay at the sink. When the monitor asked her to do it, she began to wail about her health and anemia, finally crying into the pail and taking it back where she wanted it, like a spoiled child. I heard one of the doctors telling another childlike wife today that her health and nerves would be all right if she had an amah to look after her children and a lavandera to wash her clothes. He talked to her quietly about psychoneurosis and told her to face the fact that she was doing a lot of things she didn't like to do and was trying to get out of it by the excuse of illness. She giggled with embarrassment and said she got so tired! Who doesn't?

Some think that the community store is the best thing that has happened to camp. Even eggs are now on a sales list so that everyone who can or wants to buy a dozen can have the order filled sooner or later in turn. Criticism is dying down as it is run smoothly and fairly. Sales should have been semi-rationed like this long ago.

I scold myself for being too impatient and critical. Half of me is projected into the future and I keep forgetting that nearly 100% of the camp are living in the past, not even in the present, dreaming of boom days in hopes they will come again. It is still Family Culture, not Community Culture. But we continue learning under protest and force of war. It is Transition Culture with a vengeance.

September 4, 1942. Several women were talking over what they had learned in here. One said she had learned to stand on her own feet and say No. Another said she had learned to lie and cheat and steal. Still another had learned things she hadn't expected.

September 6, 1942. Jerry, June and I finished camp duties and glided up the hill. From the top we heard the beating of a ganza [gong], the faint voices and chant from an Igorot cañao [feast] in one of the distant barrios. We were level with the range across the valley and could see a lovely inaccessible village with green rice paddies up on the mountain side. We want to go up there sometime. June said we would come again when we were free but we probably wouldn't have any more fun than we had as prisoners. She is right.

We saw two trees with ivory blooms, looking like Nara, its beauty in the mass, not in individual blossoms. There were luxuriant tree ferns, shining holly leaves, and orchids on moss-covered trunks in one canyon. We stayed until the last minute, scrambling down the steep sides with wobbly knees. It was like Red Hill at Squam, New Hampshire. June wanted to know what summer camp was like and we told her it was not unlike this camp only no one had to stay and life was more comfortable, less tense. I arrived back just in time to wash up for waitressing, tired from double exertion but a healthy, happy tiredness.

September 7, 1942. The rumors came out into the open after skulking all day. Tokyo bombed. Formosa invaded by U.S. soldiers (probably just bombed) and all forces called back to Japan to quell the revolution. Premier Tojo has committed suicide.[48]

September 8, 1942. A package from Nida with ten sausages, a dozen cucumbers, one can of lychee tea (worth at least P8.50 now), a jar of mayonnaise and can of pepper, sweet-scented soap, Jerry's shaving cream—all perfectly miraculous.

Stalingrad defenses are in fierce fighting. Rumor says if Stalingrad can hold out three weeks more the Germans will collapse because of losing 65,000 a day.[49]

September 12, 1942. One doctor, in talking of the camp situation, said he had seen far worse conditions of diet than this in the center of cities in America, and in homes of far worse sanitation, crowdedness, darkness and dirt. He has seen babies born on a mattress with several children sleeping with the mother, five other people living in that same one room. We are favored compared to some slum homes of families caught in an economic rut, in poverty and ignorance. The waste here still bothers me.

September 13, 1942. Wilma Morgan is now sorry she has a stout wood and wire fence around her space, as everyone else is spreading out due to the departures.[50] She is nailed down, limited, and the barracks and camp are chuckling quietly about it. There is no room for that important factor of growth behind a wall.

We had a last evening in Peg's space as she was busy with packing to go Outside. We will miss her deep nature and friendship.

September 14, 1942. A party for 40 guests last night, serving 100 pieces of chocolate cake with egg-white icing, fried mush-cake canapés of corned beef or sardines, with hard-boiled eggs. Poor taste is hardly the term for such affairs when any number of families cannot give their children even one egg a week and no milk at all—to give eggs to forty guests seems a sacrilege or sin of some kind! Women who look down in the mouth all week, caring for children and working hard, dress in their best and scintillate at the prospect of a gay time. Fruit punch was termed by others as a cocktail and everyone had a large time. Though it is glaring in here, it is probably no worse than ostentatious parties in the world outside when people in rags look in the window, starving, envying, hating those who can throw away on guests what the onlooker cannot give a hungry child. It is not unusual in the present, only in the projected future which is in here where such lavish entertainment stands out as thoughtless, shallow, shortsighted and stupid under the circumstances. It is a microscopic view of a larger picture of dislocation in the world.

From the Men's Committee report: "In order to teach the young people the actual mechanics of civics, Mr. Blake and Father Gowan are appointed as supervisors and instructors in such work. It is desired to encourage the young people to form a government of their own for the control of their actions and behavior in camp. Parents must encourage and lend active support. All can share in the good results obtained as well as the responsibility attendant."

September 15, 1942. Bedie, worn out with the week, is nauseated. I am only thankful I have been with them both, not separated by an ocean and continent at this impressionable stage of their lives.[51]

September 17, 1942. Jim Blake gave me a taste of what he calls Dumbrau Cordial which made me very sharp in Japanese class. It took me out of the "slough of despond"!

Tokyo rages over our inhuman treatment of internees in America, moving them from camp to camp, making a seventy-year-old man work, kicking a thirteen-year-old boy in the stomach etc. It sounds like our complaints.

June is learning Lincoln's Gettysburg Address. Its simplicity, directness and understatement sound well today. No dramatics, only simple truth.

September 18, 1942. Some are chuckling over the rapidly developing Lovers Lane in the alley.

September 19, 1942. Ten months is a long time to be away from home without cause. This day of flowing water and wind makes one long for a fireplace and a cosy couch, quiet dryness and peace.

Sylvia had a delightful party of 18 guests. The table was decorated with cellophane Christmas papers and pink lining in coconut shell plates of candy, ferns and red leaves at each end. Bread with margarine and raspberry jam "like home," cocoa-peanut cookies looking very "Outside" but made on our own tiny stove, chocolate fudge and bean-milk fudge with the consistency of Divinity, tea with milk and sugar (milk P1 a can, formerly 18 or 28 centavos)—all made by the hostess on the small stove. It was topped by delicious white sponge cake with chocolate frosting made by Emil in the kitchen at night and truly a feast. Tex gave a toast about friends and we all enjoyed ourselves but I cannot get over the feeling it is out of place during war and scarcity. These parties are numerous now, a form of escape needed in the cycle following departures and during a windy downpour. It is dreary, the coldest, most penetrating weather yet.

September 20, 1942. We made light, tasty hotcakes from soured coconut milk. I spent most of the day under a blanket trying to get warm. What a Quiet Hour it was! Two groups reading aloud in each corner, one intoning several acts of *Romeo and Juliet* in young, monotonous voices. Two younger children banged in and out, singing and stomping. And always the rain and wet feet with every trip between dormitories. I will never forget [these] past ten days. It has been ten years.

No news or rumor for two days. [A secret radio] was dismantled which is good, as it was nearer and nearer to being closed in. But its [absence] means a vacuum.

September 22, 1942. Near the end of Japanese class, two new soldiers came running by the door with bayonets almost cutting each other. They stopped, startled to hear their own tongue, looking very young and alarmed. They were on their way to the road, with none of our guards to guide them. With no "dozo" [please] in their speech at all, peremptory tones sounding like angry commands to prisoners, they asked Miss McKim the way to the road. She turned to us and we pointed back and down the stone steps. There were others running about with bayonets ahead of them, breathing fast like the days after Bataan. They were defending their lives and looked it, every inch. The trucks were still in blackness and the last thing we saw in fading light was a file of twenty soldiers climbing the rise in back of camp.

September 23, 1942. Men's Committee minutes in part, for September 20: "From the number of complaints received by the Committee, the store is not meeting the expectation of many members. With a view to rectifying this, the Executive Committee will meet with storekeepers and discuss ways and means of increasing quantity of articles to be carried, especially fruits. . . . At present the women are allowed only fifteen minutes to eat their meals. This is not sufficient time for proper mastication of the food served, therefore 20 minutes will be allowed hereafter. . . . After the bathroom is scrubbed and cleaned in the morning, no one should walk across the floor with shoes on as this soils the floor and endangers everyone bathing. The washing of shoes, boots, night pots, etc. in the bathroom also endangers the feet of everyone bathing. These articles should properly be washed at one of the outside faucets or along the open drain in back. The hose may be used when necessary. Some have been observed washing night pots in the troughs where we wash our faces and clean our teeth; a very unsanitary practice to say the least. . . . The unloading of the food truck is often done in a haphazard manner, many bananas being mashed beyond the edible stage and thus lost to the Mess. This is often the result of too much hurry to get at private packages coming in. Pending selection of a man to take charge, the officer of the day will take charge. One Librarian now in charge, Mrs. Lorna Vail.''

Some of these are delicious understatements.

We went to Father Gowan's lecture, about his various school experiences in the Philippine mountains and China. He is witty and vigorous, so there were roars of laughter. ''Information Please'' was fun afterward. I sat on the front bench alone, sending Jerry home to warmth and sleep after a final cup of tea in the kitchen. Upstairs later the rumor gang talked about Japanese jitters and how we get plenty of attention after a period of none. They talked of how much will be different after the war, with many changes everywhere. Yet there are some here who still live in the past isolation and think they can go back to the old ways, not seeing that breakup will be greater than the last war.

September 24, 1942. There was a glorious full moon, calm and bright as the song says, and we talked awhile out front facing the circle rising through clouds. The crisp air smelled sweet and fresh. I played checkers with June then both children sat on the empty bunk outside with me, covered with moon glory. Everyone said we looked like an evicted family. At 9:15 there were shots beyond the hill. A truck came down the curve and it may have been backfiring—but the lights were put out immediately in the guardhouse, showing their jumpy nerves. The Sergeant came with gun and bayonet, helmet on head, walking out back. The guards put on helmets and the phone there rang twice. We went to sleep to the tramp of hobnails.

September 25, 1942. We hear there was a strike at the pig pen. It is Mr. Meyer who has risen in the world since his store made him a plutocrat at our expense. He refuses to feed the animals and there is other friction. A committee member who was once a banker was seen carrying the chow pail out.

Mr. Meyer has the only white-painted baby crib in camp. He turned down the first screened crib made at the shop as not satisfactory.

June is writing scenes and learning parts for a play on Priscilla Standish and Alden. Bedie is busy noting errors on campus to report at meeting of students' committee. He is police of sorts. I advised him to report errors, omitting names, which can be corrected by a general rule.

There are many rumors floating about of guerrilla supplies received by submarine, also that many have gone to the lowlands and are trekking up the mountain trail with packs on backs or heads, in handkerchief bundles or in trundle carts. When people start to move slowly from a trickle to a larger volume, there is something in the wind and it passes from one to another.

June is elected secretary on the students' committee, Bedie a member. The young girls are now reading aloud in *Gone with the Wind*, steeped in romance! The latest good story is that since the last baby arrived, those from now on will be considered illegitimate!

September 26, 1942. Jerry's disposition is certainly not normal. He has no appetite or pep, looks thin, just pushes around and has no hope of any American approach or deliverance. It is low ebb morale in camp right now anyway. But he is no comfort to us or himself unless immersed in cards [poker] where he forgets the present world of inaction.

September 27, 1942. Jerry brought sub-coffee, fried mush and pomolo [grapefruit-like citrus fruit] in sugar for early breakfast. I tied my hair in the back, unbraided, which seems to make me look younger, with Sunday lipstick. I had to do something to take off that ten-year aging feeling of the past fortnight. It has been the worst time in camp as to morale.

The new Nipponese rules are—

By Order of Nipponese Guard.

Any place on the hillside is *out of bounds* except for members of the wood crew *actually working*.

WOMEN are not allowed on the hill at any time.

WOMEN are not allowed at the pig pen.

After lights out (9:30), every one must be in their bunks in the barracks, with following exceptions:

1. Night kitchen crew.
2. Early morning kitchen crew.
3. Those using the bathrooms.

No loitering—or *smoking of cigarettes behind the barracks or on the stairs after lights out.*

No commingling (after lights out).

No one, except those on duty or on definite business, allowed at *the Hospital* after lights out.

Offenders will be punished. (Japanese Seal)

One can get plenty of atmosphere from just reading posted rules. We haven't had a set like this for months. A gay party in the kitchen last night after hours was caught by the guards, though some of the women tried to dash upstairs. And our barracks was singing and dancing jitterbug furiously up to lights out. Everyone is moonstruck—then they always clamp down.

Bedie seemed homesick so we sat on the porch talking till he finally had a cry which snapped the tension. He said Daddy had a boil now and had had so many things the matter with him since Brent—"Remember that first day when we were all so hungry and Daddy gave you and June and Tish and me the last crackers, and when we tried to make him take some he almost cried and said, 'Don't be damn fools.' " So Bedie remembers it all too—funny little boy who never seems to be taking in such things. This evening it all piled up on him and he was feeling full of omissions and sins. We held hands tight and the tears washed away some of the sins. He went on to say the men were all cross now, swearing terribly even over the littlest thing, growling all the time. He is right. They all have restlessness, nerves and hopeless feelings. This no-contact business is specially hard on the men whose families are Outside and Bedie is surrounded by them. No wonder he wants to come over here out of the gloom. He says they play poker all day and evening, even on Sunday, and have no time for us any more. He got it all off his chest which I suppose is what the men do at poker with nervous energy more and more pent up. And now the new rules, the blight of Mukibo whose mind is like frost where it turns. He lectured the Sergeant who takes it out on us to show he is effective after all. We are like poor insects, all caught in the same net, controlled locally at least by a bigoted, disappointed man. Somewhere in his life some woman must have turned the ice on Mukibo. Perhaps he is just reverting from Harvard education back to feudalism. He seems to be having an attack of nerves and nastiness too.

September 28, 1942. It is rainy, cloudy, but feels as though fog was lifting. June is not well, no pep, always tired. We are always cut down on food the end of the month as money runs short, and we feel it. Dr. Hall says he has felt hungry for four days and so have I. Jerry is gaunt and grey in the face, shows the effect of cut diet. We get less meat. I simply cannot load up on rice, gabi or camote for too much starch fills my mouth with canker. The diet seems to make us acid.

We hear that Major Lee died of malaria and malnutrition at Cabanatuan, where 2,000 officers are in prison camp, badly fed.

I went down to see Dr. Hall. He cheered me as usual but says Jerry must watch his temperature for pulmonary reasons. Jerry looks and acts sick, his disposition impossible. I have three children on my hands! With his glasses gone, he says there is nothing to do but poker for he won't pick rice, says he has done enough for this damn camp. He still burns over the milk and the rest of the supplies he turned in.[52] Three fourths of his malady is morale and I cannot help him or reach him.

My theory of cut-down food is confirmed, for Hayakawa only spent P82 yesterday. He says no pork, very few vegetables, little fruit. He bought only 50 kilos instead of 100 camotes as usual. Very little meat. The Committee is worried about the increasing cuts in food but Hayakawa squirms out of it. With mashed camote and okra soup for lunch we made cinnamon pie out of the first and put onions in the second and managed to eat quite a lot.

The Committee meeting was mostly about no newspapers left to use as toilet paper, and baths should be finished before 9:30 at night. We put an appeal on the board to stop wasting paper and to give in all the available sheets.

Whenever Hayakawa and the Sergeant are raked over the coals, they have to pass it on to us and show results. There will be sewing machine rules soon as the last needle has been bent on too heavy material. We had some laughs out of this as one sewer was termed ''tough on machines'' and the tension having been meddled with was referred to the present general atmosphere. Our smoking rule is being ignored and the men say go ahead and enforce it but the men are the chief offenders in the Baby Dorm, and are Committee members at that. So it goes—no cooperation, until the dictators in the guard-house crack down.

Bedie waited an hour for me outside the meeting, slid his hand into mine and we played some cards and then read Bible chapters. He likes to hear familiar passages and is proud of recognizing certain majestic lines. The Sermon on the Mount is always serene and comforting. He went back to the gloomy, masculine side quite happy. Fabian made him a swell pocket knife from an old piece of steel and Daddy made him a leather cover after Bedie had fit it into a bamboo sheath. I have reached him in some way and we are close now. He too has been through deep waters the last few weeks. We all have growing pains.

September 29, 1942. One of the guards asked one of the men on an early walk, ''Can I get you a woman?'' Why are men so filthy? This one was trying to pick up some cash but the enemy would like to undermine that way too.

This is the strongest typhoon yet, a wild one, and all the windows closed in our room. The young girls have come in to play jack-stones, read stories aloud, and the younger fry are roughhousing on the upper bunks. There are about 25 in this small room with no air, the sewing machine running, with me typing letters for people and trying to study Japanese. I finally went out on the porch to work and get air. Vivian admitted she was nearly crazy with the bedlam. But where can the young fry go?

October 1, 1942. Mrs. Davidson heard singing of "God Bless America" in town, said it was very touching and they switch quickly to the Japanese national anthem if given signal of approaching steps.

We hear that 100,000 Japanese were killed in Bataan[53] and they were so furious over this cost that they have treated all Bataan prisoners worse than any, even than Corregidor prisoners. They would not let doctors take First Aid kits to prison camp, so it is not only starvation, no medicine, neglect, but *deliberate* neglect. The men can only lie there suffering, praying for the end to come. This is awful to hear when one sits not far away but helpless. We all want the Japanese officers to suffer for it. But that is not the end. The road leads back not only to feudal minds with modern weapons (deep, dark depths, these) but to American Senators, Representatives and those who cared so little that their neglect made money and comfort from selling scrap iron and other supplies to Japan during five years of China's war. Finally the iron and neglect came down on our own boys, men we knew well, in Bataan. We dodged our own metal from the skies and were taken by an energetic enemy because we valued money and what it would buy.

October 2, 1942. Jerry and I talked about food. He says Cushing was caught in a surprise attack while eating at the table and was shot on the spot. This must mean betrayal by a collaborator. It is the end of a leader and a life of adventure by one who was not afraid. We hope betrayers and informers will find their own kind in the end on the road they have chosen. It is sad to hear of such courage trapped, not dying in a last fight with an even chance. His work was well done and he held out long.

October 3, 1942. Tokyo reported an attack on Missouri. Miss McKim said, "But Mr. Hayakawa, that is in the middle of the U.S., very far inland." And he replied quite seriously, "Yes, I know."

October 4, 1942. Jerry came over to the porch but holds his head in his hands, sags all over and has no spark, no desire to talk or even think. With most of the men poker is the only thing that makes the hours pass from dreariness to cheer, keeps them from thinking. They cannot wait to get back to it, to lose themselves, like a drug or an enchantress. Of course the missionary men do not play. June and I walked in the starlight.

Jerry feels so hopeless about the present. Sabrina confided she was having a bad "down spell," felt we might all die in here. This is typical. Everyone needs inspiration and cheering—no one can *give* it. And it isn't believed when offered. They laugh or look down when I try to be cheerful. It is a constant spiritual struggle to keep above it, to believe that America will return sometime.

I like to read the Bible's mighty lines, feel closer to the flaming quality of Jesus than ever before. He was a true revolutionary, crying against injustice and hypocrisy. Right now I am sick of religions in every direction that I could yell. At the bunk, on the grass bank, on the porch, Bible reading in every direction, until I could throw it off the cliff. Church here, church there, Sunday School and Sunday classes all afternoon, with the main room given over to hymns and prayers in the evening. An entire day given over to it and if one doesn't attend, well-meaning people want to know why and what can they do about it. They feel personally responsible. If they only felt this way about changing the world economic setup we would get something done in a hurry and the soul would take care of itself in the process. I'm going out to preach free-thinking if some of the persistent ones don't leave me and my children alone. We don't want to be organized. We want to read and interpret the Bible in our own way, not have someone dish it up for us.

October 5, 1942. I know exactly how a man would feel who threw a rock through a plate-glass window. It would gain him attention, give shock to the populace—but his pent-up grievances would be too many to express and the judge would not admit the long list of details burning small holes in his brain. He would get thirty days for raising his hand—a month in which all the grievances would pile up again. This diary is a safety valve! It is a rock through the window!

Cushing's body was brought in wrapped only in banana leaves. The enemy took all his papers and identification. Hundreds braved the wrath of the Japanese to come see his body and when he was buried some stayed long, until the Japanese left, then buried his body deeper, not a shallow grave that dogs could dig up.

The Japanese main drive is "Resistance is futile. The U.S. will not come or help. Do not hope or resist further. It is useless. Give up resistance," over and over in a dozen different ways.

October 6, 1942. A wonderful bag from Nida with roast leg of goat, hearts of artichoke, can of asparagus, jar of mayonnaise, two bags of lemon and cigarettes. We had a feast at noon.

Japanese class after watching a noisy ball game. The season is on, with men and children serious and intent on practice. June is out with her eyeglass guards looking very professional. The scene is intriguing, with all the guards joining the spectators as well as practice, giving an international, democratic coloring. While we drank Jerry's cocoa, we were entertained watching three of the guards trying to learn Indian wrestle with hand and arm on the counter with our bigger boys.

October 7, 1942. Marvin's new chorus of 22 members gave a program of 9 new songs, *Tannhäuser* being most impressive.

October 11, 1942. Communal responsibility has solved an invalid's problems. Sickness preventing her from earning a livelihood, her food, laundry, quarters and medical care are all shared in here. The bereaved family likewise shared with all and the mother was not cast forth to be the breadwinner. She is studying shorthand in every spare moment in this breathing space of communal protection to her, two children, and sick mother.

October 14, 15, 1942. Awake at 3:30 by the sound of a shot, then more. It sounded below the barracks on the road. Many more shots, up to forty or fifty. From the hill came more gentle "pings" said to be pistols. Everyone was awake. From the window we saw Hayakawa and the guard and Miss McKim come out the barracks door. She told us all to put on dark coats and go to center barracks. We dressed and I gathered emergency rations into a bag and put on heavy coat. June was a great help but we shivered with cold and nerves. My precious bag [with the diary] went astray but I found it under Marie's bed. What a relief! June came up with hot coffee and said Jerry was down there so I went down. He had coffee, sugar and the margarine which I used very promptly as a cover [for the diary pages]. He was feeling ill with fever. Fortunately we were allowed down the back stairs to the toilets which were crowded with nervous people and no paper on hand. Then three of us rested on Isobel's bed. At 6:30 we were allowed to go back to our barracks. From an upper window we saw a truck of soldiers arrive. Others saw flashes from the guardhouse which put out lights after the boom at 1:15. Rumors flew thick and fast. Haykawa had said Trinidad Bridge was out but this was denied at first. The soldiers were divided into three parties which climbed the hill, going along the ridge, but came back shortly. It was a truly warlike scene, more than any we have had since our men left and planes ceased. A second truck with three Americans came with chow for the Japanese, a third one on the road below. All left but one with three officers and party.[54]

A lone plane flew over Naguilian way mid morning. Garbage wagon allowed only to the gate but the bus went off for our food. Children fraternized with soldiers, who always seem to like them. Breakfast as usual and routine mops and garbage and waitressing. The sewing machine is going and everyone busy in the kitchen and veg room. All feel tired after traipsing around with bullets whizzing through the air in the darkness. I'll never forget how Ruth sat up in bed in the dark saying, "Well, they certainly sound like shots to me," as the fifth one sang through the air—as though someone had told her it was a rumor!

One girl implored everyone not to wake her baby during the height of the shooting while all of us were pouring into the unlighted upper story. We fell over one group relaxing in the aisle. Hayakawa admitted our morale was very good because we "know they were friends." Miss McKim said no, it was because we were Americans, but there is some justice to his conclusion.

[During the skirmish] Hayakawa and the guards mixed with us behind the counter for coffee in the small hours.

By chewing on my front teeth I can enjoy one peanut at a time. A number of New England habits have been invaluable in this parsimonious and pioneer existence, habits I didn't have to acquire. Kidded about them in the past, now they are normal.

Several are showing symptoms of lack of Vitamin B—pains in the hands, numbness of hands and arms as though they had gone to sleep. The doctors give tiki-tiki [vitamin B extract, made from rice hulls]. Massage may help but it is chiefly dietary.

October 17, 1942. Now there is said to be a battle going on down in the valley below, machine guns and pounders and fighting. It can be seen from the hospital. It may be just ruthless mopping up of a village. Thunder and guns, which is which; we had both today. By dinner time, it had become landings and battle in Lingayen Gulf. While they fight and die in the valley within our sight, flower arrangement class adjusts bouquets exquisitely on the porch and the choir practices in the nipa shed.

Some of us discussed the bird calls at night. We never can tell the real one from what might be the guerrilla call and we hear them often.

October 18, 1942. Our community store keeps a waiting list on selling and closely follows it on everything. This infuriates those who crave preference and were getting plenty. There are three men selling privately—if customers want to pay. The hamburgers that they sell are smaller yet higher in price. So there is crabbing about both capitalist and cooperative sales as there is in the world.

After supper, drama, scandal, made its entrance. Mattresses were seen going to the guardhouse and the word went around that one of the venturesome, young married couples had been caught out of bounds *and* commingling, both major offenses at the moment. Both were found by a guard at the high school house where they said they went to get out of the rain, holding hands, maybe more.

Miss McKim went to the guardhouse, a relative went there, a missionary and both of our liaison men. There was a huge flurry and much stewing. After several hours of talk, scolding from the guards, pleas from Miss McKim whose tact, diplomacy and comprehension of Japanese intricacy is above reproach—it was decided the culprits were to remain in a small room at the guardhouse for 24 hours, without any mattresses, only blankets and a pillow, to sleep on the floor with a guard between.

Everyone is whispering sympathetically (having the same desire to be normal). A crazy world, the center of the great psychosis, war! Our people worked till ten trying to abate the penalty. The humble centers of the storm were finally permitted to return to their separate barracks after that.

A new light was on toward the pig pen and someone asked, "Aren't the pigs allowed to commingle either?'' Apparently only the goats can be normal in a war-torn world.

The Committee was asked if the goats couldn't be kept off the parade ground as the small children are using their droppings for marbles.

October 19, 1942. Miss McKim says the commingling affair background is a feud at the guardhouse. Hayakawa had very little to say and the Sergeant would not even appear, being outranked as Military Police by the Private of the Regular Army who is nicknamed the Baboon by us and who was insistent, running the whole show. The other privates did not approve. However, one of them gave the jailed couple peanuts, tobacco and a bunch of bananas, besides talking to them at great length, which must have been interesting considering the language handicaps.

The Baboon while talking with Miss McKim kept looking at one of the august committee members. In Japanese, which the member could not understand, the Baboon kept saying, "He'd do it too if he could," Miss McKim replying, "Oh no, I'm sure not!"—but the Baboon looked wise, reiterating positively, "Oh yes, he would!" He is a farmer, all crude simple peasant. You can't fool *him* on the elementals, for nature is on his side.

When young Derham saw Betty's baby in the white-painted, pink-lined crib made into a go-cart on effective solid wood wheels made by the father, he said, "Oh, a little garbage detail!"

October 20, 1942. Jerry got me some of the hottest bath water I can remember in camp. It was wonderful. I put up my big towel as curtain and took my time in the corner.

October 21, 1942. I spent the morning with a hot water bag on my swollen face,[55] viewing the funeral services in brief glimpses from the window. It is our first service in camp and brings sorrow and death very near.[56] Till ten, everyone was working for it, bringing flowers to make wreaths, and all the simple things that must be done at the last. The choir songs and Mr. Roberts' words of service floated down, past the long file of people ranged the length of the mesa-like bank of the hill. Mrs. Poulson is wearing Aurora Quezon's black dress.

October 22, 1942. No package has come from our house for over ten days. There is almost an ominous silence as trenches are dug. There is a feeling of waiting for something. It is different from three months ago. The guards are doubled, now 18, and they feel better about it. They now haven't enough pots to cook with in the guardhouse, nor facilities, so they bring rice to be cooked with ours. Their meat is supplied from our beef and they point out what they want, no bones included. They ask for and get enough meat for 18 individuals which is reasonable but in amount is what we feed 64 people. They are meat starved and trying to make up for it.

October 23, 1942. There was real excitement for us when a bag arrived from Nida. We don't know how much it means until we go nearly two weeks without it. Now we know they are standing by, able to gather and deliver a bag. How do they manage to pay for it, and how can we ever repay them! She sent laundry and Lissar soap, a kilo of coffee, a bag of cakes, a kilo of sugar, a bag of tomatoes and a bunch of bananas.

October 25, 1942. The chairmen are having a bad time placing the [nuns] in the would-be schoolroom into other quarters. Several have been told off in the process, spaces measured, meetings held, and everyone dissatisfied. One of the Sisters said that every place had been suggested for them except the pig pen and perhaps they weren't good enough for that. The latest spot is the barber shop, which may be it.

October 26, 1942. The guards get less than we do, God help them.

October 27, 1942. Little Robbie is making progress in re-learning to walk after encephalitis. He is fortunate to have a good masseuse who makes him use his legs pushing himself in go-cart. She manipulates him in water and sun bath on clear mornings, is very constant and devoted.

The doctors are forced to turn dentist and pull teeth that need it.[57]

The guards were upset when a couple of the small children stopped going down to see them because parents were tired of going after them. The visits are on again and the guards happy.

Jerry is better and works hard for us, spends hours on tripe preparation, which is one way of showing affection, which is limited in this camp.

October 28, 1942. The children are the largest age-group here.

> 121 between one and ten years.
> 53 in the teens.
> 106 between 21 and 30.
> 115 between 31 and 40.
> 77 from 41 to 50.
> 59 between 51 and 60.
> 44 between 61 and 70.
> 10 between 71 and 80.
>   1 over 80.

532 has been the maximum concentration number this year. There were 505 in February, and it gradually declined to 457 in August.[58] Of the total, there are 272 males, 315 females, 83 boys, 91 girls or a total of 174 under 21 years of age. This is from Camp Holmes *News*.

No 2 Barracks on Tuesday. Children Cleaning

October 30, 1942. Jerry worked all yesterday morning after Bedie shucked peanuts to present me with a two-pound tin of rich nut fudge for my birthday at breakfast.

Big surprise on the truck sent me into a final daze—from Peg, Leonora, Carl, Grandma and Grandpa, Harriet and the children. There was a big box holding a chocolate cake, a roll of toilet paper, a can of milk. There was a big bag from Nida with fragrant roast chicken garnished with tomatoes, cucumbers, pepper and onion; three big grapefruit, small oranges, cocoa and a bag of cookies. Happy Birthday was written on the bags. It was a lovely day in spite of rain. But I wish I could get some word to Mums in Boston.

Back to my small evening celebration at a table at the end of the veg room. There were five wood crew, 1 assistant cook, Isobel and self. Small but delightful crowd.

June and Bedie had their first big glass of milk in six months—a whole can between them. The quips and repartee were immense after long abstinence. We hummed, then sang, "God Bless America" with another party which was a huge departure [from the norm] for prisoners. I cut my cake into twenty pieces to share with people who had been good to us.

October 31, 1942. The school principal admits [camp] has been a wonderful experience if only from an educational point of view. She says one could write a thesis on the Camp Holmes school year—getting along with only one or two books which had to be passed around in turns of study, no ink, scraps of filing sheets for paper, limited pencils, no song books or piano, classes held in the bedlam of the dining room with kitchen-pan-din and cook's yells, baby-scraping and banging from above, not to mention the alley sounds, the nearby toilet, having to meet on the porch, nipa hut or garden when the room was being scrubbed, dashing in and out of rain; noise, confusion, every kind of obstacle—but all overcome.

The results showed in the program at 2:30. The room was decorated with pine greens, black and orange cutouts of black cats, witches and punkins. The stage was two dining tables put together, with a backdrop of two black boards. June's Puritan costume was a dressing gown of black belonging to Mrs. Moore (which was formerly Miguel's cassock at Brent School) with wide paper cuffs, a kerchief made from dimity curtains and a cap of some other material, borrowed shoes, and a small black paper bow. Miles Standish and John Alden wore similarly inspired costumes. June was Priscilla in the play of the courtship. They did it very well and when one Puritan said, "Oh, now I suppose we'll all be scalped," we all laughed because it sounded like our own situation and rumors. The kindergarten and first grade songs and recitations showed teachers' hard work and pupils' ability to learn in [chaos]. Bedie in his long trousers, scrubbed clean by himself, took part in a question group which ended with the final history quotation "America is waiting for you." We almost wept—for we are waiting for America.

November 1, 1942. A huge branch, wreath-shaped, covered with orchids was brought by the wood crew from the hill to hang on our porch-wall. A crooked one, covered with live holly, has dark green shining leaves against gray lichen. Jane has made up single orchid plants in coconut shell baskets packed with moss.

Later we heard of transport convoy we attacked, sinking many, crippling 58. A big battle for both sides, all at Guadalcanal, to hold that dot on the map. Our troops have turned up in Libya and Egypt—are they all over Africa? In this experience we do not feel alien, American, but a part of the Philippines going through war and invasion. We are small but we are not alone. It will not be us that they rescue, but the Philippines, China and the Far East. The men are going through another savage period of suspense, believing nothing hopeful, sore and cynical—"another year or two in here"—"no major battle won by us yet."

I went to sleep with the Hong Kong plight and the gloomy report of Guadalcanal ringing through my head, but other bells rang with it and I could not swallow the full bitter dose so began to leaven it with as much common sense as I could muster. We need a sign, an outward sign, for many are beaten down spiritually. We have reached such a point in humility that there is even talk of the Allies losing the war.

November 2, 1942. At least we have pure air, none of the stench of prison cells or festering corridors, no rats or lack of sun or light. How important they are—sun, light and air. No darkness, except in some minds. There is green grass with cows and goats nibbling it!

November 3, 1942. Jerry brought tripe and coffee. A large pig dug out of her pen and tore all over camp looking for a mate. She burst into the men's dorm and tried to crash the kitchen which was a riot. There is much laughter as it is a symbol of camp repressions.

I watched a brief, interesting ceremony at the guardhouse. Hayakawa and three guards faced the Rising Sun, he bowing deep and low, the others presenting arms in honor of the Shogunate ending—the Restoration of the Meiji—holiday of Meiji-setsu, commemorating the first Emperor of modern Japan.

Quotation from the daily *News* of camp: "Good old Camp Holmes, the place whose motto is Every Man for Himself and Best Things for Those Who can Grab the Most."

Dr. Hall insists that whether boiled or not, the watercress is contaminated when it comes in and reaches any one who handles it so he says it should be kept out as he fears it as source of River Fever. He hasn't found the bug but is worried about our two fever cases.

Stalingrad attack has been given up and the Germans are retreating. Eisenhower is top General of our forces in Europe.[59]

November 4, 1942. Jerry combined tripe, garlic and scrambled eggs—simply scrumptious. We ate in the tiny cook-shed, punctuated by two full-sized rifle shots and the nasty rip of machine guns. Our nerves have come a long way from Camp Hay for we sat undisturbed, saying it was target practice on the emplacement below.

November 5, 1942. A bale of toilet paper came at last, paid for out of our food money. But it is here!

November 6, 1942. There is an Authentic of big victory in Egypt—Rommel in flight and ten thousand Germans captured. Over a million Allied troops and supplies there.[60]

November 7, 1942. There is bad news from town—seven missionaries have been in jail for a week; Carl, Art, Father Barter and four others.[61] Grandma and the women with her must be in a state of mind. No one has heard from them in that time.

November 8, 1942. There is a new Men's Work Detail list. It takes 25 men [to procure wood] from the time the tree is felled until three in the kitchen wood crew split it. There are 3 pig and 2 goat tenders and 2 storekeepers. There are 23 dish wipers and washers, 11 teachers, 9 shopmen, 6 for barracks cleaning, 13 on toilet guard.

All the children are outgrowing or wearing out shoes and no one can get any so they go barefoot or wear wooden clogs.

In *town jail* there is rice *only*, twice a day; 2 glasses of water *only*, a day, for either drinking or washing; the toilet pail is *in* the cell and air very bad; no sunlight, only vent holes in the ceiling which is also low. Sanitation and atmosphere is very bad.

November 9, 1942. Iron bars were removed by the shop men from our windows. We now feel light and free. Ruth suggested it and we wonder why we didn't think of requesting it before, it makes such a difference.

If I devised a prayer these days it would be "Dear God, let me communicate with my people."

November 10, 1942. The children like the new school room and organization. As I pass by with mop and pail, I see them getting an active education. It is worth much hardship. I am still content that we stayed here though the months have added lines, gray hairs, and taken a tooth.

At Japanese class we had primers [tokuhon] and started to learn our first characters of Kata Kana.[62] Am I now at sea! In an open boat and no supplies! It is fun, a whole new world. At this rate, life begins at forty-three. We learn by sight and association, by repetition and habit, just as the first grade learns English.

November 12, 1942. The guards told Miss McKim the missionaries were coming back in this afternoon. Peg's family drove in on the 6th truck about 7 P.M.—with the seven men direct from jail, with 12 days beard, thin and unkempt because they were given drinking water only. Everyone stood around to gaze at them.

November 13, 1942. At breakfast we heard that 17 Sisters were coming in. The first load came at 9:30 and all beds are shoved close to the wall to get 25 in our dorm, 40 in Baby Dorm and 50 in men's dorm.

November 14, 1942. There are about 172 new [people], many who have never been interned before. There was a big row over the private fence space but it was finally taken down and thrown out, much to the owner's fury.

But it was one of those evenings on a peak—rest after turmoil, the air soft, the sky tender and song rising to it. We were all together after ten months—almost as we came in except for those now in Manila, and despite hard words during settlements and tension of the day, we felt joined and united, almost mellow.

We who have lived in defeat all these months know many kinds of bitter depths, and how wonderful even the smallest rise, the slightest hill can be. We even understand our enemy, which is one of the last things one learns.

November 15, 1942. There is a new battle in the Solomons, about 500 ships (300 transports and 200 convoys), the biggest armada in history.[63]

November 16, 1942. A big poster in town says:

(November 5, 1942)

TO THE PEOPLE OF BAGUIO

A beautiful and peaceful city of Baguio. Shops and stores wide open and the passers in the streets are increasing and inhabitants are happily engaged in their work. Baguio is a city above the clouds of trouble.

Such a city of Baguio recently an important bridge on the Benguet Road has been blasted and causing a food shortage. Destroying water tanks and waterworks and other bridges in the vicinity of Baguio. Worst incident was the attacting of peaceful civilians on October 25, 1942. In Benguet Road, Mr. Goncales, Judge Regalo and three women who fortunately escaped narrowly from the bullets of the USAFFE. The people of Baguio are terrorized with fear and the rumors of attack of Baguio.

The Japanese Army who are protecting the people of Baguio are concerned with this matter. Those USAFFE who are giving trouble and fear to the public of Baguio are not only the enemies of the Japanese Imperial Army but also your bitter enemy. So don't you come to think that leaving this trouble in the hands of the Japanese Army alone is unfair? Why don't you cooperate with the Japanese Army—you have nothing to lose by making Baguio a peaceful city in the whole Archipelago like before?

It is a pity there are many "SKUNKS" of USAFFE in the city, and it is much to our regret that there are still believing in American Propaganda such as coming to your aid.

Think thoughtfully for a moment. Did you not hear and see the Japanese Army in operation? Did you not hear the mighty Japanese Airforce and Navy which never lost a single battle?

You, inhabitants of Baguio judge well and cooperate with the Japanese Imperial Army together with to make this famous Baguio a progressive City.

Signed,

THE COMMANDER IN CHIEF OF THE IMPERIAL JAPANESE ARMY, of NORTHERN DIVISION of LUZON.

End of poster.

With 104 new members, we total exactly 500 today.

November 17, 1942. The Chinese, Filipinos and Igorots will make history of their own. There are still stories from Manila and the lowlands. One tale says that when the U.S. comes back in, the Japanese plan to gather in one huge building and surrender only to Americans. Their Army will retire to Corregidor and surrender by flag to our Army. They know only too well how the Orientals will feel toward them.

November 18, 1942. Camp *News* says: "For less than what many of us spent on cigarettes in a day we are having three meals and doing hard work on them. Veg represent half or 17.5 centavos of our daily individual food allowance. Meat, 25.73% or 9¢. Rice 12% or 4.2¢; while the two non-food items out of the daily 35¢ apiece are medical supplies at 8.57% or 3¢, and electricity 3.7% or 1.3¢."

Camp Minutes: "1. All privately owned goats shall be turned into the camp herd, under care of a goatkeeper; all the milk is to be equally divided between camp and the private owners. The appointed goatkeeper shall have complete charge, determining those to be kept for milking purpose and those to be disposed of, subject to approval of the General Committee. All privately owned chickens may be kept by present owners until the end of the present month, after which time all chickens shall be placed in a flock under a duly appointed poultryman. All eggs from combined flock shall belong to camp, the individual retaining ownership of the fowl. Live chickens may be brought into camp for slaughter but no waste food of any nature shall be taken to feed them, except by consent of the Keeper of Livestock. The General Committee may purchase up to, not more than, fifty hens to add to the community-owned chickens. These shall be kept for eggs which shall be used for dietary purposes determined by the doctors. 'Pop' Carberry is appointed supervisor of livestock and may have any needed assistants."

November 20, 1942. When I remarked there was nothing like learning to be a good waitress and charwoman after forty, Jerry growled, "How about learning how to tackle a saw and clean tripe after fifty?" We are younger in some ways, older in others.

November 21, 1942. During Special Diet serving, 8 booted officers including a real live General, inspected camp with a bodyguard of 8 soldiers with bayonets. These last pressed their faces against the screen to watch the children eat, smiling and laughing. They are so curious, so interested, that often I feel sad for them, fury mixed with sympathy and understanding of their plight, their fate being to fight us when they feel friendly. I can see how their minds worked with the reasons they were given, and for many common soldiers I feel pity and respect. It is terrible involvement for us all, so many killed in our defeat, so many more to die in theirs. We cannot go back or stop, only go on remorselessly. The soldiers chatted happily in their own tongue with Miss McKim. Their faces light up when she speaks. It is someone who is not a blank to them.

Camp Holmes *News*, Saturday, November 21: "The Camp Holmes High School will make its own bid for recognition in the world. Of its unique features there is no doubt. What other school for instance, can boast of an Alger story in reverse—from dean of a university college to janitor of a high school, C. Heflin is now on the way up again, having been made proctor, with certain disciplinary supervision added to his duties as building super-intendent."

The Faculty Minutes say, "presented the purpose of school which is, to serve the camp young people as a school of the highest scholastic standards possible, a school entirely independent of Brent School or any other, existing on its own merits alone and giving credit as the Camp Holmes Concentration High School for all work satisfactorily completed. The school year is six marking periods of 30 school days each, the first to end on December 24. As all regular high school students, 23 in number, have been excused from camp work-details, it was voted that all be present at school building from 9 to 12 and 1:30 to 3:30. Study hall is required of all those whose general average falls below 85. There is no study in the camp dining room. A course in music is required by all regular students except those excused by Mr. Davenport."

November 23, 1942. A seven-foot python was killed in gory battle at the hospital.

The purchase of chickens from camp members is a necessary concession to a transition stage from private property to community life and makes confiscation easier.

November 24, 1942. In here we are constantly surrounded and pressed by nearly 30 different religious sects, each one thinking it has the correct form. I can take my heart and mind with me anywhere without forms, and shall teach my children to do the same in case they are imprisoned, denied or repressed. They shall learn not to be slaves to a candle service, to kneeling, bowing and bells. If they want it, all right, but they must be able to get along without it if necessary. They can learn to feel creation, their own way of prayer within, when it is needed, so that they do not interfere with others, can always be considerate and adjust. They shall be open-minded, subject to constant growth and do their own thinking, not take what is handed to them. I asked June why she stopped Sunday Class and she tells me, "I don't know exactly. I liked it at first, then the teacher got into the Prophecies and I had to take the Bible word for word. I just couldn't, and you said I didn't have to take all of it literally so I stopped going."

Hayakawa says we can have no more soap—only ashes. It is fine for dish towels and aprons. They use ashes in Japan. Countless vexations! Also reported to our merriment was the attempted theft of a light bulb in the schoolroom at night, foiled by one en route to the toilet seeing it and saying, "Naughty, naughty." There was another tale of a garlic snitcher swallowing a whole mouthful of it rather than admit having it.

The Camp *News* reports that those most consistently sticking to their detail are the cook staff. There is one good reason why.

November 25, 1942. There is a minor riot over decorating the mess hall for the holiday. Some are furious because they were not asked first, others because they think the British should not be included on an American celebration, so there are even international complications as Nationalism dies hard even in this jumble.

Evening gathering reported 50 thousand Germans captured by the Russians at Stalingrad and Roosevelt says the tide has turned.[64]

In a Thanksgiving bag from Nida and Ismael was a roast chicken and eggs for Mrs. Wyllie from her boy Melanio after all these months. She could hardly speak, almost wept. "They are alive," she said as we all say each week when a bag comes. It is a message of life, our only communication, even more than the food to eat.

November 26, 1942. In order to make room for newcomers, the sacred precincts have been invaded. The last bastion of camp may fall. Arthur is moved to the men's barracks after 11 months of family life in a private room. Enid and daughter are squeezed up with stacks of camp supplies. Dr. Dean had one of his good brain waves![65]

Camp had a huge Thanksgiving dinner of home-raised pork, rich gravy for our rice, baked squash, a minute dab of precious green peas in mint (yes, really), candied camotes, fresh pechay [greens], papaya salad, coffee and two shortbread cookies which were works of art for camp.

The whole dorm finally moved an inch or two to make room for the new people and Enid is learning firsthand at last, to everyone's delight, what it is to be surrounded and shoved, pushed about and squeezed. We are tough now, like the "lower classes" who want the "uppers" to know what they go through, live with—or without. Arthur is cooperative and good-natured about it but we all chuckled as he stood below the window last night calling to his mate like all the rest of us, to stick her head out so he could speak to her.

November 27, 1942. Enid began to stew at once for a separate door—and got it the first thing this morning. Also Arthur is back with her again, because the Japanese looked for him last night and couldn't find him so he must move back, the women must have a protector!

November 28, 1942. The first lecture on architecture starts today, beginning with Gothic. Joan T. is starting dancing classes on the tennis courts.

Father Gowan says that in ten years we will look back with nostalgia on Camp Holmes comradeship and experience. He was greeted with roars as he enlarged on this but he is right. We will talk about it the rest of our lives, laugh over the battles and the mistakes.

November 29, 1942. A type of rugged camp humor; one man raved about marriage and his love for his wife which grows with the years like a flower. Another tough customer asks, ''Yes, and how are you managing to keep the flower watered in these times?''

A guard went off with a bayonet in a car. An hour later, without any warning of newcomers, it returned and spewed out five forlorn, gaunt, possessionless Americans. They had been living in the hills eleven months, all from Itogon mine, comfortable and well-fed until November 17 when they were betrayed (at P100 a head) and the soldiers walked in without warning. Our crowd gathered around them and they were fed as faces pressed against every screen and closed in on every mouthful, talking and asking avidly. Young, sensitive, Filipino Dr. Biason had been with them, his pretty, dainty American wife who was a nurse, and his sister. The last two were shot in the abdomen, he was not allowed to go near them and his wife was still alive when he was led away, beaten, head held in tub of water—all that sadists can think up to do. The two women were cremated that night. The others, elderly Mr. and Mrs. Perles, Ted and Ruth and a child younger than June were made to go without any mats, blankets or belongings, walking fifteen miles on empty stomachs, he tied up for four hours, in jail eleven days in a room 8 × 3 feet. Thirty-one prisoners [had] two bowls of rice and two glasses of water a day. The Japanese told them that thirteen others were captured and that most of us had gone to the States and they would probably go too. In Baguio they were questioned closely about Mrs. Kluge—the Japanese want her for hostage against her husband. The price on him is high, but she is the one they want to locate for they can reach a man by capturing his love. Dr. Biason is said to be in Baguio released, his child with him, a bullet through her middle but she is alive. He wanted to die, he felt so responsible. They tried to pry much information from him, to make him pay for his loyalty to Americans. These newcomers say that people everywhere are terrified of the invader for villages are burned, people beaten and tied up, tortured. It is the old, old story, repeated endlessly.

November 30, 1942. The new people tell of every inch of ground being dug up, passports and cash found, all taken; houses ransacked and things confiscated, the houses then burned to the ground with all their possessions in them.

December 4, 1942. During lunch, after several days buildup of watching and trailing Mr. Menzies, the guards beat him. They found a five gallon can and 4 bottles of gin cached in the grass near the cottages. They stopped all the work and said nothing more could be taken from the cottages for building until the owner of the gin confessed. A guard, Miss Shore and our liaison man were seen with Mr. Menzies who claimed he knew nothing of it, wished it was his. An hour later, from our windows, we watched him standing at the guardhouse, taking it. About eight guards standing around him, before our eyes, two beat him with bamboo sticks—legs, back, head, anywhere it fell. He tried to shield an infected swollen thumb and a boil on his head. Finally they closed in, made him lie on the ground, beat him with army belts, a golf club, baseball bats, anything at hand, until he was unconscious. His screams at the last were horrible to hear. It was degrading to see, nauseating to witness, and the children watched. He was taken to the hospital and no bones were broken. He had been warned two days ago.

All [aspects] of alcoholic consumption seem to be entering into the picture, including a still. But there was a note with [Menzies'] cache and this is the chief reason—outside contact, guerrillas. He was questioned about notes. Rumor has it the guards took their bats and bamboo sticks and beat up on the tienda woman but this we did not see.

December 5, 1942. Regarding commingling—1. Husbands and wives may walk together on Sundays, from morning until 7 P.M. On weekdays after supper until 7:30 P.M. 2. Couples are not to be together at any time off the parade ground or away from the barracks. 3. Girls and boys are to walk to school separately. 4. Special meals may continue as usual on the parade ground and porches, not in other places (such as women's dorm, nursery, etc.). 5. Evening recreation in the dining room may continue according to the following regulations; Mon., Thurs., Sat., up until 9 P.M. Sun., Tues., Wed. and Fri. up until 8 P.M. *Offenders* will be punished.

Hayakawa and four guards went to the hospital at noon to see Menzies, one carrying a baseball bat with a black tassel on it. The four returned shortly in single file along the bank. I shall never be able to look at a bat with equanimity again. Young Hansen was asked about kissing his wife often in public, so they watch all this too. There are sex cycles, pent up energy released every so often, all the abnormality of war reaching a peak and exploding regularly.

December 6, 1942. I finally found out that "musume" is the word for daughter in Japanese so that Jerry could explain if caught talking to June.

December 7, 1942. It is interesting to note that many now argue against anyone charging for tripe or effort for camp—a new feeling that each must give his service to camp like the doctors, cooks, nurses etc. The idea is actually beginning to take. We must all give service of some kind without gain or return. But squeeze and favors die hard and still go on in milder form.

December 9, 1942. Betty and Daphne are working on Christmas gifts for all of the children, wrapping up finished stuffed animals, puzzles, doll caps etc.

Two rumors: one that Roosevelt has said nothing could be done about the Philippine Islands for two years. Another that the Americans in Africa have met with a setback. Fine for our morale!

December 12, 1942. History is known at school as biography due to stringencies.

December 13, 1942. Daphne hopes the Americans don't come in before Christmas because she wants all plans of gifts and decorations and out-door tree carried out so we can all see it. She is the only one so far who doesn't want the Americans to come in at once. She is British, working hard, teaching drawing, making posters and signs, all sorts of Christmas things for camp. She and Viola have left British isolation behind them more than anyone in camp this past year. They have many new friends, do camp work cheerfully and have changed a lot. We have all changed but theirs is more striking because they seemed so reserved and aloof at first. The wood crew are bringing down a large tree for which Daphne and her helpers have plans. Daphne has drawn and colored tall red paper candles to set against the pine branches in the dining room.

I wore my brown coat with beaver collar and Dr. Dean said, "Where did you get that? Whose is it?" This is the usual query and typical of camp now. I haven't worn it so it hardly seems reasonable that I own it, bringing it in in my duffel bag rumpled into a ball with the silver fox fur.

Camp *News* of December 10: "Matters of public and private concern at the present juncture include such diverse affairs as wondering what to give one's wife, children or husband for Christmas or how to get the materials to make it; how to obtain by hook or crook, salt, between now and the promised Saturday; how long this all will continue; and chiefly how to keep out of the chill winds which nightly sweep down from some close proximity to the Arctic to penetrate the bones of each and every one of us."

December 14, 1942. It is a constant struggle to get spoons enough to set the table, bowls in line, to keep track of tins or soap. Once a thing is set down and left, it is never there after sixty seconds. Pails disappear like magic, onion tops are snatched up, the mental process apparently being that it is not wanted and in the discard. It is a wild life of fighting to hold your own, to keep the little you have and not do others' work way beyond your share.

December 15, 1942. Dr. Skerl is growing yeast for those needing Vitamin B. Jerry, whose ankles have long been swollen, has been much helped by it. Many with this symptom are on the verge of beriberi or pellagra. Mrs. Tangen brought in the start of yeast. One thing leads to another—she advertised on the board to sell starts to those who are cooking.

The *News* for December 14 says, "This was one of the 'no' mornings; no syrup, no salt, no coffee, at times no spoons, no plates; one of those days upon which a person, after a suitable wait in line, is served and sits down to contemplate the pleasure of eating soft rice, completely flavorless, with a fork, seasoning the mixture with what passes for a banana—the kind of a day one realizes, if he hasn't already done so, where he is and why."

Camp Holmes School was formerly the goat pen.

Jerry is fixing up a new garden plot for Bedie's Christmas, with earth from the hill. Bedie has developed vast enthusiasm for it under great difficulties. Jerry will make a bamboo trowel for him. We will give June some desired notebooks for school at 15¢ apiece. Our cheapest Christmas but everyone looking forward to it with delight instead of gloom. Some are carving buttons out of coconut and bamboo, some painting them. Doll spreads, beds out of boxes, are being sewed or fashioned.

December 16, 1942. The men are on the rampage over private clothes lines. One had his laundry moved, promptly put it back when he found it and sat by it all morning till it dried. There is a battle over our lines too. It is fascinating to see a form of socialism working out before our eyes—the bitter resentment over private lines, the fury of hard workers over those who do nothing for camp.

Hayakawa admits he does not want to drive out from Baguio after dark. It must be tough to wonder each night if your head will be on in the morning.

While hunting for drapes for the Christmas pageant, a P10 bill fell out from one of my undies, stowed there during our search-times of 11 months ago. Talk about coming across the Bank of England!

A large boar arrived in the back seat of Hayakawa's car. Soon there may be piglets. It is borrowed, not bought—a trial marriage at the pig pen.

All must indicate their preference for Work Detail. All adult classes must register whether athletic, academic, aesthetic, or religious.

December 18, 1942. Only occasionally do we let ourselves think of two grandmothers in America, how they are faring in health and finance. This way could lie madness. Even Jerry admitted he had to stop his thoughts for he had worried one night until one.

December 19, 1942. One girl wonders why we have a Women's Committee—why not let two represent us on the Men's Committee. Jerry protests it is good for us to learn to run ourselves and be educated in equal suffrage.

Bedie is keen over his Cow Detail. He chose it as against practicing Christmas songs, said it was much more important.

We enjoyed hearing Carl tell how many trips Jaime made with bags to get all my gowns and shoes and undies over to his house, not to mention the tense day they wrapped up the Red Cross sewing machine and rolled that over disguised under a blanket. It was a dangerous trip for he could have been accused of looting.

December 20, 1942. Phil Whitmarsh showed some of his photographs rescued from the maw of invasion and talked on photography. Tex recited O. Henry's "Gift of the Magi." Rae told the story of the first Christmas. Dorothy, dressed in pinafore and a huge hairbow, recited *The Night Before Christmas*. Sid imitated Harry Lauder and Al Jolson in songs. The women's quartette was good.

December 21, 1942. Hazel went to town and had a grand time buying 2 oranges apiece for 150 children, 2 sacks of peanuts, more than a thousand pieces of candy and about 300 cookies. She said cloth materials are sky-high, saw young Filipino boys in uniform goose-stepping at drill, passed a white woman and child who pointed to her saying, "Oh Mama, look, there's a real lady, a white lady," in wartime Baguio.

December 22, 1942. Jim Bozeman brought me lovely wild white roses and another white flower from the hill. Oh how I want to go up there and see them blooming. The wild red Canterbury Bells from Jerry and the white delicate blooms grace our tiny corner for Christmas.

The Evangelical Church people sent in 33 chickens and 130 pomolos for camp's Christmas. Carl has been busy with the pushcart full of feathered squawks and fruit. It is a deeply moving time for us all, for we are touched by so many expressions of deep ties outside. It is our second Christmas in disorder. Last year was a dash to the dugout and mouthfuls on the fly as sirens wailed, planes roared overhead dropping bombs.

December 23, 1942. The truck is coming in crammed with extra bags, bundles and boxes, tied even in tiers on the top. I'm tired from the strenuous three days and haven't found the Christmas spirit. I want to hear from home—real give and take, communication again with all it means. I want to say "Oh, that looks like a Marine!" That is all I want, except the top of the hill. I'll get none of it, so back to mop and pail. Work is satisfying and so is this meager sheet of expression.

December 24, 1942. Jim and his wood crew brought all the greens and flowers down the hill, looking festive and sheepish as they came in well loaded. Daphne justified all the championship of her (though it cost many votes) for she and her crew made a bower of the dining room. At the counter end was an arch of pines with green and red festoons, dripping with silver bells and colored shining balls. Along the windows at intervals were huge pine wreaths, with red paper bows at the base of Daphne's tall painted cardboard candle of silver with red or gold flame set in the center. In between at the upright post hung the branches of red digitalis bells or big clusters of white flowers with buds like wax orange blossoms set in dark green leaves. At the other end, from the arch, was a small tree simply trimmed with streamers and a few ornaments. Near the door on a long box with white sheet on it were arranged Santa and his reindeer, trees, animals to entrance the children. The holiday is really here. Outside, Daphne's red hair hovers over the trimming of the tree, topped by a glittering, shimmering Christmas fairy according to English custom, dressed for the occasion by Viola. It is truly an international camp. In every direction there is trimming and decorating as people fix up their own small trees, wreaths and space.

The truck made two trips loaded today. Jerry brought me a beautiful spray of mountain holly, dark shining leaves and yellow whorls of delicate flower. He said it was from him to me because it reminded him of me. I said, "Oh, shining and full of thorns!" and we both grinned. He never gives me a real compliment without a sting in the tail and we always laugh over it. He brought another red bell spray and another white one with waxy ends. I spent an hour or two wrapping up the few gifts in saved paper and string.

On Nida's last sugar bag was a string marked, "Boston Gardening Co., Waban, Mass."—from Nida at our house, from Mums in Boston last year. There is at least some string left in our home. With what mixed emotions I saw it, so often kidded about my New England string-saving propensity.

Miss Chou's cookies, candies and chocolate were given to all the children at noon so there was a riot at the table, excited whoops over the decorations and surprises.

Meanwhile, just to remind us where we are and why, traffic roars up the trail below us, trucks geared and loaded for war as we sing Peace on Earth, goodwill toward men.

The afternoon program was excellent, guided by Phyllis Goodenough's genius. The tiny ones sang their Christmas songs first, halting and a bit off at times, laughable, adorable, embarrassed and twisting skirts and pants. The act from *Little Women* was full of poverty and hard times—many lines suitable for our own situation and how we too have worked to overcome it. The Dutch Christmas scene was a big chuckle with Janie in cap, wide skirt and wooden shoes, Jim Bill in wide pantaloons and difficult clogs bringing down the house by balking all the way across the stage. Crachit's Christmas dinner was awfully good with Derek as Scrooge. All the children in camp sang Chritmas carols on the stage at the end. Many parts were well done, clever costumes made of nothing. It was a well-drilled triumph.

We took our rice and vegetable onto the parade ground with Scotts and

Mac who helped us eat a succulent roast pork. Jerry made strong coffee and candied camote, opened our can of cranberry jelly long-saved. Jim joined us en route to another party. So we had our private feast on Christmas Eve. Special diets did not linger over their rice so I could get away from waitressing early.

At seven, we sat together on the bank, looking down on the simple manger of bamboo frame covered with pine boughs. The choir sang in the distance, drawing nearer, then the paper star lantern glowed, shone upon Mary [June] sitting quietly beside the cradle where a soft blue light illuminated the spot where the baby lay. June looked serene and graceful. She said afterward, "Oh Mother, I felt so Holy!" She had the humble, gentle spirit for it. The choir stopped beside the manger and while they sang the familiar hymns and carols, Wise Men and Shepherds came bearing gifts of gold, frankincense and myrrh to lay at the feet of the baby. A young lamb, bleating and kicking its heels, gave reality to the scene in the dusk. Everyone sitting on the grass watching was very still until the choir faded into the distance. Many admitted they wept all through the beauty and peace, simplicity of the pageant. It couldn't have been more impressive anywhere, with the natural background and the strength of our situation bringing it home forcibly. "There was no room at the Inn."

A moon came up silver full over a cloud bank which sent rainbow halo above its rising. A bright star shone near it.

We talked outside afterward as the tables were being set for tomorrow in the common room. Again we were being guarded by six or eight Filipino boys whose heavy shoes tramped on the gravel every hour during the night. Everyone talked, slow to settle down, keyed up with emotion. I was desperately, unutterably, unbearably, homesick and felt I could not bear it if Nida and the children came next day.

December 25, 1942. At five the choir woke us singing "Midnight Clear," "Herald Angels," "Holy Night," "Joy to the World" and other hymns. It was beautiful to lie listening in the dark. Jerry called us for coffee at the counter at six and Peg gave us coffee cake to go with it. We opened our gifts in the gray dawn outside, with the moon setting huge before us and the star clearer than ever.

Daddy loved his homemade tie and the red muffler from the suitcase. O'Neils in Manila sent him cigarettes and me a first-aid kit of Band-Aids. They sent Bedie a striped shirt and June two pairs of socks and toilet soap. There was laundry soap for all of us. We gave June two copy books and Betty painted a paper doll with dresses and gave her squares to sew into a quilt. We gave Bedie parsley, carrot and celery seeds and a bamboo trowel made by Jerry for his garden to grow things we can all enjoy. We gave him some crayons too. They are simple things, but useful, desired. We were rewarded for our sewing by Jerry's delighted laugh when he saw the tie.

He said he would go to 6:30 Anglican Communion with us if we wanted to go so we all stood in back of the crowded schoolroom for a baptism and a second Mass. It was richly decorated with dark massed pine boughs hung from the rafters and back of the altar a deep red curtain hung in folds against which white candles blazed and several scarlet poinsettia stood out sharply. The ritual was High Catholic, with chanting all through the service. Jerry whispered, "It sounds pagan," which it did. It is pageantry, steeped in art and beauty. I have come to prefer my religion unwrapped, deep and still, far in the heart.

Breakfast was a rush of noise and excitement. The candles centered the tables with long red streamers holding gilt and silver balls—simplicity the keynote. Marvin beamed when he thrust his gift of cookies at us labeled, "Merry Christmas to my waitress." I treasure this. We had cocoa with milk and sugar, coffee, fried egg and bacon and banana bread. June said, "It's too good to be true!" about a breakfast we used to have every day. It was a treat after only rice and water for a week. On the way out the door, June received two oranges, peanuts, cookies and candies. I was to choose a gift and picked a piece of Igorot cloth.

We went to see Dr. Hall who read us his poem on an atheist's thoughts at Christmas. It was very fine. He said the pageant touched him to speechlessness.

We four went to Carl's service at ten and his short sermon was as sincere and big as he himself, not narrow or bigoted, but including everyone. The weather was brilliant, the terraces full of reflected water, the mountains lovely blue.

The guards did let Santa come in. He appeared with a black-clad nimble figure which is a Filipino custom we had never seen before, strolling in from behind the shop. Santa with white beard and mustache was the real thing. The children all let go in one loud squeal and started running across the parade ground to meet him. It was a charming sight. He unloaded his pack from his back with a crowd surging around him near the tree. For the very young, it was the climax of a perfect day, for he brought adorable handmade dolls of all sorts, cloth books, doll beds painted blue or yellow, stuffed ducks, horses and frilled clowns. There were 150 gifts of every description, satisfying and the product of hard work at the shop, Daphne's art, and the women who sewed for weeks. With a sigh of relief at completion, the shop closed down for the day before going back to Committee work tomorrow. It was Fabian's first day off in six months. The shop and kitchen deserve medals.

During breakfast we were treated to another goose-step drill.

At 11 the Filipino relatives and friends began to arrive to visit until five. The High Command had said all could come but Nagatomi said No, not Americans, only Filipinos. [Some] came in a special bus. Jim and Mac were beaming, new men, happy with their families to eat on the green with them. Mac was seeing his 20 months old baby for the first time in a year and Jim meeting his 8 months old infant for the first time. All were required to stay by the guardhouse on the other side of the road and we were not allowed to cross the line. But Jim brought Martha over to shake hands and she was a neat, bright and smiling Igorot girl, in a snappy blue dress, keen and alive looking.[66]

For lunch we had good tomato soup and gabi and papaya from camp—and a bag from the Bacanis! They did not come and we are relieved as we feared it might get them into trouble. Nida had made a dress for June who promptly put it on, then wept down my neck. Eppie and Felie knitted a string washcloth apiece for the children so we know Nida is keeping us in their memories though we must be almost myths after a year. We could not even talk we were so deeply moved.

Jerry produced mistletoe without any berries and kissed his wife, the chairman and the ex-chairman in the dining room. It was a sensation.

June was delighted with the gift of a sewing basket containing thread from camp. She made me a Christmas card with a touchingly appropriate verse copied inside.

Nakamura came at noon looking fat, husky and pleased to give marshmallows to each child. All propaganda aside, there is no doubt that the Japanese like children.

We rolled out of the dining room after a huge dinner of fried rice, roast pork, fresh green peas, bright yellow squash, candied camotes, real coffee and steamed pudding with sauce. The soldiers and gun came in again at meal time and there was a camouflaged truck full of troops on the road.

Something was gone from the day in spite of everything. It is a spirit I usually catch, never miss, yet this year I cannot shake off a depression and sadness. It must be "home" that is lacking. I am just plain ordinary homesick as the children have been so often. It is the first time it has made inroads upon me and I must face it to dissipate it. But I'm glad Christmas is over. I want to spend it at home with the family, or on the hill, not lost in the crowd which presses in day after day. The crowd is for every day, not Christmas. It is always with us, making our spirits soar one day, breaking our hearts the next. Even Christ had to go to the Mount to get away from it, ponder all it taught him about men and living.

We have had a beautiful Christmas—the pageant, the climax and the row of good meals next in importance, with the glittering tree and decorations over it all. But many say they are glad it is over, admit weeping at the pageant or during early carols. It is a load on the emotions and we need to come back to earth after high attainment.

The children are asleep clutching dolls, horses, clowns, thoroughly happy. It was fun to see the mothers pinning up their stockings the night before. The guards tramped about every 15 minutes, turned lights on beds all through the night, but I slept soundly.

December 26, 1942. Many are sick with gastric trots and Dr. Hall must be swamped with specimen cans. We can't take the rich food.

The gifts that touched me most were the children's two cards, Nida's children knitting washcloths and Nida sewing clothes for us, and Marvin's mother who has two young babies taking time to bake cookies so that her small son could share and know the spirit of giving to his waitresses. Bedie drew Lallie and Fluffy on the cover, with the sentiment inside showing we all felt alike—"Remember the cat and dog, from Bedie Crouter." On another page he wrote "To Mommy, I am going to work as hard and well as I can so that I will pass into 7th grade." There was a star on it too. He was more homesick than June.

December 27, 1942. The Russian girl says it was the best Christmas in six years for her because she has usually been lonely and this time she was in the middle of friends. Communal effort and feeling does pay, but we need much education in it still.

An excerpt from Vargas'[67] speech on December 8. "We are Orientals and as Filipinos can not but cooperate with Japan *without any mental reservation* in the achievement of her historic mission . . . Side by side with the Manchurians, the Burmese, the Indonesians and the Malays, we acclaim the Rising Sun of Japan which lights the dawn of Asia. Hand in hand, shoulder to shoulder, with all our Oriental brothers, from the northernmost plains to the farthest southern islands, we are ready to build a new Asia for Asians, a new Philippines for Filipinos, under leadership of Japan, guardian and protector of the Orient and of intolerable Anglo-Saxon interference in the Orient."

December 28, 1942. O'Dowd, who is worth thousands, was brought in by the Japanese without any baggage of any kind, looking like a gypsy or tramp. He was unrecognizable. He told of men in the jail having to crouch, not allowed to stretch legs out, for if they did their legs were beaten with broomsticks, his included. He said Leung Shank[68] died quietly outside, with his family, still in hiding. He voiced the general feeling of many old-timers, and Filipinos, that America had let the Philippines down. They feel bitter over the young untrained boys who were so terribly slaughtered in the first week because of our "strategic" withdrawals.

December 29, 1942. We went to see Dr. Hall whose report on Bedie[69] indicates drastic treatment before he really gets run down, so we laid plans.

December 30, 1942. I still resent those four approaches from different religious groups trying to get hold of my children. They are sincere and devout but their persistence implies that I lack intelligence and their own way is superior to mine which they think is negative. How they would resent it if I tried to draw their children out of the circle of their home guidance and thought. They are all for bending the twig to their belief—why not allow me my feeling for freedom and open mind?

December 31, 1942. One man leaving another said, ''I must go now and take care of my wife's baby,'' adding quickly and very seriously, ''Of course it's mine too.''

This must be an offshoot of the baby-tending and washing for dancing lessons. These seem to have stopped. One woman doing her payment in washing said I ought to be doing it too for she saw my daughter in one of the classes. I said that was easy to settle. June would have to stop going. I don't mind doing June's washing so she has time from study to help care for Susan who is one of three but I'll be darned if I will wash and tend for another baby, an only child, which has become a racket. Mrs. Carson squeezes calamansit juice 2 hours every day which helps to benefit the teacher's baby but her child can't attend the classes because Mrs. Carson has not time to pay in labor for dancing.

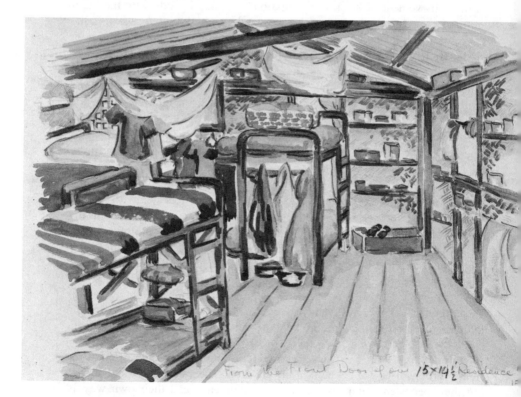

1943

January 1, 1943. Bedie brought early coffee to the window as Daddy whipped up hotcakes from ground parched rice, rice flour, mashed banana and camote, a triumph of ingenuity to start the new year. Camp gave us a fried egg, real coffee and pomolo cocktail! It is a vast diversion from soft rice, hot water and a miserable banana.

We are permitted to commingle, as if it were Sunday, all day.

A New Year is here, and we hope again, as we hoped all of 1942, but we are still concentrated, our teeth crumbling, our bodies lacking Vitamin B, still lacking toilet paper and using septic tanks for 517 which were intended for 250. As Dr. Hall says, this camp has 18th-century sanitation.

The guards were presented with punkin pie, as they hovered over its preparation the night before, greatly interested and sniffing at each spice box, looking into all ingredients. Introduction to American Indian food!

January 2, 1943. The Termite Man, who tootles as well as mends gadgets, turned magician and delighted the children with many tricks. The high point was Betsy coming out of a box where she hadn't been present, and hypnotizing Buck to take needles in his neck and spikes on his tongue, not to mention being suspended on chair backs from head to feet.

Women's Committee Minutes; "We are aware that Barracks No. 1 houses women who have willingly put in many hours at camp duties. We hope with a new work schedule to balance the camp work so that every woman who is able will want to do her part. With friction between barracks, worry and comment over how little 'Mrs. Jones' does, and how much we do, harmonious working conditions are impossible. With cooperation from everyone, what little work we have can be made enjoyable.

"It is our sincere hope that during the first four months of 1943, the women may work more harmoniously together, with each one who is able doing a fair amount of the work, and no one undertaking so many duties that she develops a martyr complex as a result." Regina Washburn, Secretary.

I sat in the common room waiting for Jerry to make cocoa after checkers. All around were couples, pitiful couples hungry for each other and kept apart by war and hate and evil minds. Young couples deeply in love, married only a year or two, some with one baby and wanting another; sitting together, a few gazing drowned into each other's eyes, not daring to touch; others holding hands, quietly, patiently, smiling a little; some flirting openly, with sparkling eyes and speech; some trying to read Bible chapters and not succeeding too well in the uproar. The crowd broke up early, drifting off, away from provocation, wanting to be normal yet helplessly channeled into abnormality, thwarted, repressed, treated like children or idiots. All the suppressions of war were in the atmosphere of that room. They will all want to pen up the invader, make him know the torture of denial, going without normal instinctive satisfactions. This is only one form, for many are built up for revenge. That living body dragged along the road before it was beaten to death, one of their own countrywomen who was married to an American—force, sadism, unmentionable primitive depths and experiences must have been built up in the enemy who does this. Will we want to do the same? Can there be no end to it, no outgrowing?

January 4, 1943. Hunting for her children in the fog after dark, Mary ran into many couples merged and silent, and she finally retired from the scene in embarrassment. The moon was not full but fog contains romantic elements. It is a gentle curtain of nature, soft, intangible and kind to lost souls.

January 5, 1943. June and Bedie had excellent reports ending December 23d. She averaged 87 and he 82, which is a major miracle. His attitude is better. She is steady, gains weight, keeps her health and plugs along, with her Dad's practicality and adjustability to quick changes. She is more equable than Bedie. He is slow but gets there, and will have personality as unique in its way as hers. Whether it is dancing, piano lessons or studies, her teachers have always remarked on her perfect coordination. Concentration is an important factor in it. Bedie has not developed this to the same extent, so far.

January 6, 1943. It infuriates me that so many are grateful to Enid personally because she has given them things in here. She gives out camp materials with the personal flavor including all the Red Cross stuff I handed over to her as being in charge of the Secondhand Department. She has clung to its folds ever since she came in, given grudgingly, making people cringe with her ungraciousness, under that fierce personal touch which makes those in need of charity bow humbly in thanks. I have never liked personal charity and will be glad when an impersonal means of rehabilitation like Indusco can supplant the old, vain, selfish kind. One cannot make people see that the gifts were from camp. They write in letters "Enid has been wonderful to us." She uses the department for her own ends.

January 7, 1943. One who really envies another who walks by, says, "There goes that dirty commingler."

It is encouraging that so far in a year of defeat and adversity I haven't laid off work one single time of mopping or serving, have only had to take to bed with a toothache or headache. After the hot water–rice breakfast, so so dull, without syrup or bean milk, a banana I couldn't eat—I hate to have to admit that stark simplicity has agreed with me on the whole. I feel more alive than in years, perhaps due to reaching a philosophical age.

January 9, 1943. [Tokyo] reports that Roosevelt called in 33 editors for conference then threw some, including Henry Luce, into jail. They say that *Time* has yelled that Stalin is one of the great men of modern times and it has also asked questions about the Solomon campaign which Roosevelt doesn't like, hence the jail term. However twisted, it tells us news.[1]

Miss McDonald, being in a mixed foursome, asked the guards how about it—could one eat with a man to whom one was not married? At 9:15 in our dorm of single women, the announcement was made that one not married could eat on the parade ground with a man or boy friend, but that all, including the husbands and wives, must make a definite business of eating and on no account to look romantic, for the guards (with their binoculars) are watching and they know all the romantic ones, including those married. This shook me to the foundations of laughter till long after lights out. How can one turn on and off that spigot which releases the romantic look?

January 10, 1943. Wilma and Carol announced their engagement, after quite a romance. He has given her a ring made of stone at the shop. Every one is agog over this camp affair.

The Japanese report that Mrs. Roosevelt was voted the most unpopular woman in the U.S.

We wish Miss McKim had been at Camp Hay to translate some of the terror which comes from an unknown language. Not being able to understand a language is a great handicap.

January 11, 1943. From a lab report—"During 1942 there were 65 primary cases of bacillary dysentery and 2 of amoebic, 28 of the former type relapsed. Gastrointestinal disturbances including food poisoning amounted to almost two apiece for each member, with 982 recorded cases during the year. Of the total, 2,554 were stool examinations; 330 urinalyses; 162 blood studies; 41 miscellaneous; and 26 were various exams in the Chinese camp."

There are no heroes in this camp, only human beings with weaknesses and possibilities.

January 12, 1943. In bed last night, June asked questions about the universe, God and how it all started, including the Garden of Eden, Christ and great men. We talked for some time and she wanted to know how one knew a great man. We spoke of several she had met and whether they were great or not. Then we discussed vision and farsightedness. She asked if there was any one great in here and I thought not but she said, "You are, Mama. Didn't you see the war coming even to the day?" With a chuckle, I assured her it took more than that kind of prophecy to make one great but she still insisted. There is nothing like having one's daughter so confident and trusting as one struggles hand in hand with her through the morass of war, learning together in the same school.

It is cold, windy, and I was up at 3:30 to give water to June. She clung to me for warmth, shaking the bed with a chill, while I fought my headache. Later her fever broke into a sweat and we slept.[2] At least the night is quiet, no thumping or jolting of the bed and floor as people trek in and out. The toughest part of being sick in here are those constant assaults on an aching head.

January 13, 1943. June had a second chill so I gave her aspirin. She was a little delirious, clawing the air and talking school problems. It was a long night. But Peg says Wake is in our hands at last.[3]

January 14, 1943. The Committee is working hard to put dental equipment across, as teeth are a serious problem.

One of the goats was found dead, [accidentally] hung on a barbed wire fence.

January 15, 1943. At five minutes to two we were gonged and yelled at to assemble for roll call and took our little stools along to sit for one hour and forty minutes. My emergency bag [with notes] was handy. Four groups were checked by Hayakawa, two guards and Wallie, each with a stack of list papers. We went forward slowly in a row of five each, then were checked back as to nationality. The men took only a short time due to everyday check, but the whole business was in process till four, with babies fussing, boys tearing around, chatter, laughter, grumbling and no school in session. All morning there were wild rumors about the reason for roll call, showing how little we trust our enemy—1, that we were being checked in order to be sent to Manila like all other camps, because our firewood was getting short; 2, that there would be a search for canned goods or almost anything from money to notations; 3, that Sy would be brought in, tortured, then killed in some manner before us as an example to any who might have thought of escape.[4] Any of these things could have happened, but none did. Everyone felt tired, let down, after the strain of it was over, it is so long-drawn-out.

January 16, 1943. Dr. Hall examines the yeast regularly and reports it a remarkably pure culture. It supplies Vitamin B complex, lack of which causes pellagra and beriberi. Doctors say a lot of people here have mild cases of beriberi and don't know it.

Camp gave us syrup for rice and real coffee after several blank days. Mac delighted the children with soda pop in several flavors.

Dr. Skerl makes enough yeast for 172 who now receive it every day.

Art talked on Igorot superstitions, ghosts, spirits and magic, with many appealing tales. Their best spirit is one that "will catch" children if they get too near him. They bury a ragged blanket with the dead so that the spirits will not want to steal a good one, especially with little children who cannot defend themselves. [Art's] affection for them, his understanding of their simplicity, their way of thought, their pitiful little gestures in the face of death (not unlike our own), their groping explanation of things beyond them; his comprehension touched with quiet, gentle humor was enjoyable and restful as well as instructive. One felt he knew these Igorots well because he liked and respected them, admired and sympathized with their struggles.

January 17, 1943. After I made June comfortable [in her bed,] Jerry and I sat on hospital point for nearly an hour. The rice terraces were full of water reflecting blue sky, the range of powder blue towering over them and the long ridge, burnt brown, winding into the valley like a dragon's tail. In the middle were several squares of brilliant green seed beds. It was quiet, a heavenly stillness and majesty—far from the day-after-day noise in our room where June's headache and dizziness strives for relief as the dispensary talk goes on and on over the wall, the sewing machine vibrates by the hour, eleven young people shake the room and bed as they bound in and out thoughtlessly full of life, forgetting Sally and June who are ill. Every hour as I pour liquids into June, it follows that I must walk past eleven bunks and side aisles, down seven wooden steps, along a cement walk, down eleven more steps, to empty the rusty can into the toilet. A cold wind blows but she makes a first shaky trip down there. Daddy makes an omelet with three duck eggs, and some good banana hotcakes which June relishes. Caring for her, I miss half an hour of the forum with Don Zimmerman on pacifism. If one takes a stand, can one stay out of the fray—unless one is "concentrated"?

January 18, 1943. Freda had a letter from her sister and mother in England addressed to "prisoner of war" without postmark, 6½ months en route from England and So. Africa. She broke down and wept, as we all will when we hear.

An ad on the store says certain canned goods are for sale, such as chili con carne, Libbys etc. When I asked if we were to buy back some of our own things from the storeroom, Jerry said it was bought Outside. But I was right for the *News* says, "Cans that may seem very familiar to you are appearing on the store shelves as the kitchen seeks to raise enough money for purchase of a grain grinder from sales of odds and ends of tinned food which were donated to the camp larder in our early days at Camp Hay." That peculiar use of "donated" adds salt to our wound! The *News* also says,

"Appreciate paper while still available. Banana leaves may be here sooner than you think."

January 20, 1943. An interesting report on the board is the "Audit of December books of camp store, showing sales of P3,263.43 for the month, more than P6 a person. Of this amount the majority was for purchasing food items. P43.80 of store profits went to buy milk for babies, and for chickens for the community poultry yard. . . . We still get supplies of sugar, vegetable fats, coffee, tobacco, eggs, which in most countries today, some or all, are severely rationed."

I heard someone say who came in recently, "What I mind most is the terrible waste of time!" Are we wasting it or are we learning something, much as we hate the method and manner? The American and mestiza groups in general get along very well. Many are friends who would not have known each other before.

January 22, 1943. I dreamed of being dressed in blue satin, black velvet picture hat and white furs, not to mention the latest hairdo. But I woke up quite the reverse, doubled into a ball with the cold.

From the *News*: "Heard at the Store: Lady to Salesman, 'Give me a dozen cooking bananas. I want to make an apple pie.' His amiable retort, 'Yes, they make much better apple pies than squash does.' "

The new guard is a big husky, handsome type. He was in Manchuria, Bataan, Corregidor and Samar. He speaks English, talks with Paul Sagada, whom he knew before, and walks about fraternizing with families and girls. He is 27 and has military bearing, with fine chest and shoulder carriage. He admits he is an A-class man in physique and is proud of it. Clothes make a big difference—he has a swanky American khaki shirt and trousers, as well as boots. The three guards who left were patched, ragged and seedy. One told Miss McKim that she had the whole barracks to talk to, they had no one. They are bored, lonely, homesick, inactive, and we won't be friendly, can't fraternize because of too much suspicion. So they watch, poke about, make petty rules in irritation and release of their attitude.

January 25, 1943. There are 500 of us in crowded space and undernourishment, and only two deaths in 13 months.

One said, "My group always cooperates. They are always willing to do anything I suggest or say."

June has her first case, on one of the older boys, and we hope her future judgment is as good.

January 26, 1943. After worrying all day for fear I would have the usual course like the last three nights of chills and fever, I slept all night from nine to six as completely out of this world of discomfort and trouble as anyone could be. Like the carved motto on our mantelpiece in Boston, "I have had many troubles in my life and most of them have never happened." It is not as true in here as in Boston however.

We are all grateful to the Mansells for their communal spirit in giving hundreds of sulfa tablets to camp which had been intended for mission use in the heart of Africa.

I might have been happier in here if I had not started these notes, thereby projecting myself into the future, far ahead of any possibilities in this camp. But even the criticism, defeats and battles have been grist for the mill so there is nothing to regret.

January 27, 1943. The dentist's wife worries because he has brought in some of his cache. "What will we live on afterward?" she asks. That is what all of us want to know about ourselves. Another one told him he should charge for the materials though not for time and labor. The answer was that this idea has been turned down, evidently by the Committee, so it must have been broached. Dr. Dyer has tried to keep things as near communal as possible since he arrived. He helped formulate rules about no medical fees, no charging accounts to the future in this connection, and he brought in a stack of supplies at once without any withholding. Though he does not believe in the communal idea, he saw that it was the only way to survive in here and he has stood strongly for it. He thinks it applies only in here on the whole.

Jerry is worrying about the toilet paper shortage again and I remind him we still have the Field Manual. That is no good says he, but I assure him it is signed by MacArthur and must be good.

January 28, 1943. Dorothy brought me a Special Diet plate this noon—red hot graft whisked out past authority. I'm up to my chin in it this noon and so wobbly and sore that I don't give a damn. It tasted good but I would rather get along on regular chow and save friction and face. Jerry thought the doctor was putting me on Special but I guess I'm not sick enough or special enough to rate it and I am not anxious to attain jaundice privileges so I hope I escape that. That would be zero diet. If I can just stay undistinguished, I'll be grateful.

The goat chow pail is carried out full of garbage, with cerise bougainvillea flowers carelessly strewn across the top from party decorations. June says even the cow manure is used on the garden after collection every day by Mr. Porter.

The chair, drill and dental supplies were at a convent where they serviced 50 people. When they protested at the dentist taking them from the fifty, he said, "But I need them for 500 and you owe me that much on them anyway." First he had to convince Hayakawa to let him go out to procure it, to overcome the disgrace to Japan of the terrible condition of our teeth.

January 29, 1943. The most miraculous bag yet from Nida! Jerry says she read *his* mind this time. I made him come over so I could see his face when he pulled things out. Three bottles from our home shelves—curry powder, chili powder and Parmesan cheese, all more than half full. This means so much in his cooking, [for] flavor and appetizing taste. His face was an open grin with inner light coming through all the cracks. He rolled his eyes, smacked his lips and stowed a bottle in every pocket. All this, after 13 months of invasion and looting outside. There was a precious package of white beans and a bundle of beefsteak! All the makings of a curry or chili dish! He took all this, leaving with me fresh-made doughnuts, two huge homemade corn-balls, a two-pound tin of butter and 8 luscious semi-ripe tomatoes which are too high for us to buy. We are going to celebrate on a rug in the sun out front where no guard can stop us.

There is news of a big conference in Morocco, with Churchill, Roosevelt and many leaders there.[5]

Fukihara is the name of the new Sergeant. The first thing he asked on arrival was—are there any women here? If there are the kind who would go to the guardhouse, he will find out beyond a doubt. The men say that these three guards are the ones who do the beating-up at jail. Sy and others who have seen the inside of jail know them. It is why the former guards warned us they would be tough. When Col. Hata came yesterday, Fukihara strode up to join him after a salute, then walked up the road by his side, an equality most unusual for a private or acting sergeant. What is more, he got away with it. Is this a sample of the much-vaunted new fraternity between soldiers and officers in the Japanese Army? It pushed Hayakawa into the background.

I've felt light-headed, sort of fuzzy, all day, not dizzy, just goofy. Jerry says there can be no more egg, only coffee, for breakfast and we must eat camp chow now. He appeared later with a large tin of tobacco, just bought, to pour syrup on it from our bottle. Cigarettes or tobacco have been constant through all this stringency, but not eggs. That is the world all over! It is like cutting off three or four pesos from the servants' gifts at Christmas then going out and spending all the amount saved on several bottles of liquor. Most economizing is like this. He had the whole evening free last night and was near the hot water but he couldn't be bothered getting cocoa. This is not like him for he is usually more than willing. I was too fuzzy to care.

Bedie has been in to rest near me for a long talk. I am glad I did not send them home apart from us. This experience will change their whole lives and characters, give them a firsthand understanding of poverty, want, oppression and the terror of brute force. If they are able to take it, it means more than safety and luxury in America away from us.

January 30, 1943. It must be near the end, for Japan is promising inde-pendence very soon to the Philippine Islands and within a year to Burma.

We drank cocoa at the counter until my legs were tired from standing so I skipped the program of Heflin on Chautauqua, Tex and her players, and the Dirks singers. Marvin is making singers out of hundreds who might never have known music intimately without Concentration.

January 31, 1943. It is John Hay's first birthday and we gave him June's painting book and four teaspoons of malted milk.

At a second Medical Committee meeting it was passed that anyone who wants yeast should be provided with it. When Dr. Lee returned from town her request had been granted that the Japanese give us two sacks of sugar extra a month for yeast requirements.

One of the most astounding happenings of Concentration came off when Ritchie pulled the covers from Ray's bed this morning and disclosed Hayakawa sound asleep in it. No one knew he was there or when he came in or who had said what during the time. Why should Hayakawa pick that bed or why should it be shared with the enemy without saying a word? Someone said Hayakawa was afraid of the new guards and didn't want to sleep at the guardhouse and had been going to town at night. Are they so tough they consider picking on a sensitive student type with their coarse, brutal vitality? There he had been all night, sleeping with his prisoners. We wonder how often he has tried it. Another version says it was the night the Sergeant had a girl on his hands so Hayakawa had to give up his room. That and the yeast are causing plenty of ferment. Hayakawa went to school with one or two of the men in here.

February 1, 1943. We are studying "The Three Little Pigs" in Japanese class!

February 2, 1943. Jerry made a Parmesan cheese omelet with the things from home and four eggs, with rice flour to give it body. A taste of cheese after 13 months—it is the one thing everyone craves! When we get out we want a huge kitchen where we can sit and eat, a beautiful bathroom, two bedrooms, and a small library, and that's all! We make plans to enlarge our home kitchen, spreading it all over the place. June is obsessed with it and Peg laughs at all of us.

February 3, 1943. Jerry produced a grand mixture of baby kernel corn, sausage meat and green peppers which were my birthday gifts from Mac and Jim and we ate our anniversary dinner at noon—a far cry from the ceremony performed in Tientsin by the army chaplain sixteen years ago.

February 4, 1943. Bacillary [dysentery] reached into the upper dorm last night and took Penny to the hospital. Four men have had it but it is the first case in that dorm. We are busy killing flies as Dr. Hall mourns over the many cases of chronic colitis which many will take out of here. Mary already has it.

An open trench latrine is being dug this morning in back of the Convent buildings. If one of the Sisters contracts dysentery, the flies will do the rest. There are already six cases since yesterday morning. Dr. Hall worked at the microscope till 11 last night and was worn out. He says he doesn't know why he cares, for no one else seems to worry much about it. They have given the serum but the youngest has a temperature of 105 and another one of 102. Mr. Downs had eaten fresh strawberries which is one way to get it. I warn the children to keep their hands extra clean and fingers out of mouths.

Up in the dorm Peg looked panicky and small beds were being carried out fast to the hospital for each has to take his own with him. Now it is John Hay's. Seven positive since yesterday morning and no comfort to Dr. Hall to say "I told you so."

These flies are vicious, biting through a sweater.

The upper dorm is being Lysoled from head to foot, side to side, floor, beds, shelves and all. Beds are pushed down one end, space wide open, mattresses and blankets on lines and racks outside, crying babies parked and dumped on irate fathers.

The doctor, Miss McKim and the Sergeant with his white notebook went to the guardhouse at noon. They need serum and Lysol. Camp is subdued, nervous. Miss Whit fell and broke her hip so was taken to town hospital.

February 6, 1943. The eight babies make a new and eloquent chorus of their own at the hospital as parents are not allowed to visit and there is a strict no visitor rule, so the patients are lonely, hungry, sad, deserted. Donald has adopted Mr. Davis and won't leave his bed, which must be fine for the old man.

I switched from margarine to a sugar pack [to hide] my notes.

Everyone works with a feeling of waiting and suspense—"who will be next in dysentery?" 21 since the first case. Our table still has none out with dysentery and we watch flies like hawks. We dip hands in Lysol before serving.

Everyone stopped walking to look up at a thin crescent moon with brilliant Venus close to one tip as it set luminous over the ridge.

February 7, 1943. There was a forum on labor with Arthur speaking for the employer, asking plaintively what was the wage index for contentment among labor. What is it for all human beings? What is it for Arthur and his family and other people in here? These extras come fairly high, Arthur, and labor is just another group of people. I had to leave to attend a meeting on how to prevent the spread of dysentery. Dr. Lee tried to impress us with the seriousness of it. During the details connected with toilet precautions one mother made a classic remark—"My Potty is cleaner than some people's dishes." Her child is in the hospital.

Vargas in the *Tribune* Independence number emphasized early attainment of Independence now depends on full understanding of the Filipino people of the three-point program. A-B-C of the new order: Act, Build, Collaborate. The communiqué read to Filipino leaders at the Manila Hotel follows. "In order that Independence can be granted Filipinos should strive, firstly, to eradicate all entanglements and connections with past regime [guerrillas]; secondly, to initiate ways and means of bringing about economic self-sufficiency; thirdly, to work for the speedy reorientation of the people both spiritually and mentally [Go Japanese in a big way]." They are told it is up to the Filipinos themselves who must eradicate the remnants of America and bandits. Outside of a few bands of recalcitrant elements which continue to exist, most are happily collaborating. "It must indeed be a matter of chagrin that Philippine Independence is being realized at later date than Burma Independence. To us it is also a matter of regret and disappointment."

Many people are making rough drafts of house plans. There is a regular epidemic of it. One is planning sunken gardens to dine in. They are living in the past with not much eye to the future. It all sounds leisurely and abundant which I don't see how the world can be after such an exhausting war. There will be much to do and much to be *shared*.

Some interesting hospital facts from the *News*. There are 18 on the staff, which is more than the number of patients they usually have. It mentions the Director-Surgeon, the Biologist, the Chief Nurse Ruby, five nurses, Orderly Bob, kitchen staff of three, Sewing Head, [two] laundry helpers, the wood man, and the Janitor. Three of the staff also teach school. During the year, 256 patients have been hospitalized, nearly half the camp. Wallie holds the record as repeater—five times—making 278 counting all repeaters. Dozens were treated as outpatients for first aid, medication and minor surgey in both hospital and dispensary so probably everyone has had some kind of medical service.

The mortality rate is low. Average expectancy under normal conditions for an equal number of people over our period of internment is 7. We have had three deaths (one an infant who expired following premature birth). Through planning and cooperation of doctors and cooks, special diets have been provided for invalids, sick, and children. 68 cases between August 7 and January 7, compared to 154 in previous six months, 36 in past month. Health is probably best in much-feared rainy season even if drop in number of internees is included. Despite lack of soap and disinfectants, no cross-infections have occurred at hospital. Nurses and doctors are constantly exposed to infection, realize the dangers of it and take corresponding measures.

There are screen doors on the bathroom today, which could have been there weeks ago.

February 9, 1943. I lost a safety pin which is like gold these days.

Arthur insists that the four Swords[6] were Intelligence and not Medical and no one can tell him any different. He blew the whistle at tournament and made the announcement that no one was to go to the guardhouse to hear radio as the guards want no contacts during the epidemic. They are afraid of us! This is an order from the Swords. There will be no more fruit or veg for sale at the store, as outside sellers are not allowed in. No bags may be sent out, though they may come in. We are pests! A specimen is to be taken from each, the cellophane containers provided by the Japanese Army Hospital. In response to Dr. Dyer's request for castor oil and magnesia—the first came immediately in large quantities; also serum will arrive today. The specimens will go out in groups. 27,000 died at Capas.[7] 5,800 have been released recently and will carry some germs to their homes. The Army doesn't want this repeated. Diana makes number 29.

Notice on the Board says, "The Japanese authorities have ordered that all members of the camp be innoculated with triple vaccine (cholera, typhoid, dysentery) and vaccinated against smallpox."

Dr. Dyer is bristling like a fire horse these days. A potty with a specimen was brought in and was placed in the middle of the floor where all the Swords and doctors gathered around it, the Swords making weighty cluckings in their throats and nodding. The word "carrier" was introduced and this seems to be why they want specimens from everyone. There was some indecision about their going upstairs where one can hardly step between beds. The Sergeant was against it but finally they all went up. The two Swords were a medical captain and a lieutenant. Miss McKim notes that the drains down by the guardhouse are in need of cleaning and thick with flies. The Swords said the upper dorm was very "mechakucha" which means higgledy-piggledy! Miss McKim replied, "But of course—there are so many—it has to be."

In Japanese class we learned the polite phrases for making calls and serving tea.

February 11, 1943. Bedie's 12th birthday and his gift was two fried eggs for breakfast. It is Kigen-setsu or Japanese Empire Day so there were Banzais and bows to the East at the guardhouse.

Miss McKim asked the Swords when we would be released, saying, "We are 'akite shimamasu' [becoming bored]." They looked a bit startled and said, oh, before very long, which of course means less than nothing.

Ten planes roared over in the same formation as December 8, this time for Empire Day. There is a fresh new Rising Sun flag posted at the guardhouse.

June sent a specimen in at 8 and was again upset at 10. She ate the rice but didn't feel like the cakes. As we came in from lunch, we met Dr. Dyer looking for us to say that June had dysentery. Poor kid, she had a rotten time and poor diet for weeks. I dug her out of school and she wept. Jerry carried down his pad and I gave up the double blanket for the hospital bed. Greys loaned me a blanket and a pillow. We saw Junie settled amid all the other wailers. Dr. Hall says it is a light case.

This dysentery does make things bleak, but twelve years ago was harder, with caesarian with local anesthetic, without benefit of ether, able to follow it all with my ears. It was easier than the one with ether at that. Mums, you were in Vigan then and a horrible day it was for you of waiting, finally shown a little blue baby boy. His heart is all right now.[8] We haven't seen each other for twelve years and it is a good thing we didn't know it would be that long, with all this silence of prison included. Parting was hard enough as it was, with Baby June trying to cheer me up at the lonely table when Jerry went down to see you off. Now we are all in Japanese hands and the waiting is longer than that day twelve years ago.

This experience is not unusual but something universal which is happening to us; our child is everyone's child—we are every parent, helpless and dependent on many others for food and medicine and care.

Enid was down on her hands and knees helping to scrub the toilet in the dysentery campaign. Afterward she went out and rightly told four women bridge players in the nipa shack at 10 A.M. what she thought of them—some with babies at the hospital for whom half a dozen women are doing nursing, cleaning, washing sheets, and other labor. These mothers think they have time for bridge in the middle of an epidemic when rice pickers and veg cutters are short because of added duties. Some have had time for two big parties too.

February 12, 1943. The *News* reports that a new navigation class is starting, three days a week, and no knowledge of trigonometry is necessary. This seems the ultimate in futility in Concentration but of course we can "see the sea."

Diana and Marie had the most severe cases of all 35, each having serum *twice* to pull through. One woman has a child with "trots" for four days unreported. This is the day's scandal.

February 13, 1943. Other results are—square boxes looking very Japanese outside each entrance door, with Lysoled cloth in each one on which we must wipe our feet before entering. If we do not obey this (the Sergeant says we do *not* obey rules and that is why we lost the war), then Mrs. Larson is to bring any offender to the guardhouse where *they* will beat us over the head and make us obey. Also we must keep cleaner barracks. A lot of this is put on by the Sergeant to impress officers but some of it is all too true.

One saw a man all trussed up brought out on the road by soldiers. He pointed out a truck driver who was given the "works," then trussed up and both thrown in a truck, taken back to town. All of which points backward and forward to torture, sickens me again of the war, makes me say, "The dirty b's—God strike them!'' and other strong phrases. I'm no lady anymore. I'm sick of it, I said again—sick of war and men who make it, putting all their ingenuity into torture and killing, instead of construction and health. I'm sick of hearing people say it is Fate or God's Will—when God gave us eyes to see and brains which we don't use to improve the world, which we concentrate on bridge and other aimless pursuits. God's Will—it is men and women, you and I who are to blame, some of us not even caring to look and learn through this suffering; we always blame someone else.

Bedie came in smoky, bare-chested, and happy from a morning on the hill cutting a tree and helping the wood crew. He feels he is a full-fledged member and wants a knife of his own. He has joined the wood-carving class.

February 14, 1943. I dreamed of being at a big tea in a large stone house on Marlborough Street or Beacon. There was gleaming silver, steaming samovars, satins shining and taffetas rustling, subdued lights and restrained murmur of conversation—very Boston. All were turning to stare at me with that frigid look which all good Bostonians can turn on at times. I suddenly realized that I was dressed in Concentration brown slacks and purple sweater combination, not to mention rundown shoes. I kept saying over and over, "I'm only trying to find the way out. I'm just trying to find a door."

February 15, 1943. The gutters are rivers of white, the grass has drifts of it—lime, to kill the baby flies growing by thousands in mud puddles under laundry tables etc. The men have been working for days with drainage and cesspool problems.

Occasionally I hear that horrible radio voice from Tokyo—clipped, monotonous, monstrous and dripping with propaganda, the tones of which can depress unutterably in three minutes.

When June left for the hospital, it dawned on Jerry that we had only one pillow between us (and that not ours) for we had lost six pillows with covers as well as several mattresses brought into internment. He acquired a mattress cover for us and no questions asked. I wish this was all over for I hate this "borrowing" business myself even though plenty was "borrowed" from us the first weeks. It is no wonder I feel culture is thin.

February 16, 1943. Daphne has made effective posters. Raised hands captioned, "Clean nails, Better nails." "Foil Flies—Fit lid with CARE" near garbage can. "Fly Trap" showing disheveled man in bed, with flies hovering over opened papaya, cups etc. "Shut the Door" for veg room doors. "Fruit workers, clean table before and after work" which Daphne says won't be put up because it is too offensive for sensitive fruit workers. "Cover food" put in the men's dorm.

There was a very complicated strike by the rice pickers yesterday. They objected to picking rice in order for it to be ground up for flour to sell in the store. The men who grind it by hand work sometimes seven hours a day at it and the proceeds of its sale go to buy community extras in the kitchen. The men were furious and went in to pick for four or five hours (while some of the women involved were out playing bridge). The women said that the commercial cookers were the only ones who bought the flour and they thought these ought to help pick it. However, some of the complainers are the biggest buyers and constant cookers. But the wood crew is muttering and they threaten no more wood for private stoves. Strike is a game more than one group can play.

News says Kiev and Rostov have fallen, Kharkov hard pressed. Rabaul Harbor smashed to pieces is the result of the last blitzkrieg.[9]

February 17, 1943. June came home! We went down to carry up her bedding after getting Bedie a pot of hot tea, tucking him into his own bed. June bounded out of the hospital all aglow saying, "I've gained two pounds and a half!" It speaks well for rice and bananas, milk and an egg a day. She lost three pounds on her jaundice diet.

Peg says that every day there comes a low moment when she stands on the edge looking deep down and wondering how she can go on. Our family is together, but her [husband] is missing.

Concentration seems especially hard for older ones. Fourteen months shut in like this when one is over fifty seems a real waste, and it is a loss to those in the medical or engineering professions, though there could be plenty of research. They feel out of touch with [current] developments.

June says they used Dr. Hall's reports as toilet paper at the hospital and some of it made very interesting reading. We ourselves use school paper with French, Japanese characters and history, and arithmetic on them, as well as pages from D. H. Lawrence's *Women in Love*, to read in fragments while we wait.

It is more than a year since Singapore fell. The Sergeant strode about bragging of it. Miss McKim says the guards abhor the independent manner of American women—their walk, their slacks, the way they talk to men as equals. They like meek, subservient, bowing, scraping, adoring, timid women. Feudal man!

O'Dowd says he was shocked at how many of us had changed in a year, showing the strain of events in our faces and carriage. He said Jerry and I had changed the least of any and thought I looked better in some respects. This must be soft soap!

February 18, 1943. During waitressing, the coupé came tearing in crammed with two bearded American men, a small boy and three guards, but no woman. It was Jack, son of the elder Pearsons in here, with their grandson. He buried his wife at Itogon mine two days ago after a heartbreaking time. She was diabetic but they had a two-year supply of insulin. They had to hide in the bush for ten days with nothing to eat but rice and milk. This diet did not fit with her condition and she developed intestinal stoppage with dreadful nausea. They decided to give themselves up so came in but were held at Itogon barrio jail for three days where she was violently ill and died after acute suffering, a frail girl always. The husband watched helpless and imprisoned, not able to lift a finger. The other man was Wick from Itogon whom the Japanese suspected of being USAFFE and guerrilla but he denied it.

February 19, 1943. A large bottle of chlorine solution cracked by someone on the dispensary floor leaked slowly under the door over our floor all night. There was complete sanitation under our bed and around us by morning—a solution that would have bleached all the camp clothes for three weeks. It is a major loss in these times.

The shop has made horseshoes and pitching is the latest craze down there, interfering with work.

February 20, 1943. Miss Miller says, "Talk about class lines! I've never seen so many as in this small community." I was interested that someone else noticed it too. It is group within group, room within room. Only two or three have any race prejudice, however, and they conceal it better than at first for it is not popular. One of the well-liked families in here is a mixed marriage family. On the whole if one is a troublemaker or not liked, it doesn't matter what nationality or race she is.

It is odd what being in here, thrown against people all at once en masse, does to us. Outside, charm counts for a good deal; in here if you have charm but no stamina, you become less. Attitude toward work, willingness to carry a fair share of the load cheerfully, weighs infinitely more than charm and sophistication, though brains, wit and humor count as much as ever.

February 21, 1943. Men's Committee Minutes: "Rev. Ellis will consult with whatever experts there are in camp with a view to ascertaining the possibilities of a garden, if undertaken on a large scale, and will report results. . . . The kindergarten is officially sanctioned as a camp project. Mrs. Ross will have charge of the class which will be housed in a tent to be set up for the purpose."

Children's posters are on the dining room walls. "Don't Bite Your Nails."—"Send Your Specimen on Time."—"Don't drink Tap Water."—"Swat him Now. Swat Flies."—"Don't let the Tap Drip."—"Cover all Food!"—"Don't Chew your Toys."—"Invite us more often (picturing a mop, broom, soap etc.)"—"Clean Ditches, less Flies." A toothbrush in a glass, "Cover it." All had original and different crayon drawings.

February 22, 1943. Washington's Birthday and a strong cold wind. The table is loaded with outgoing bags. Store opened with baskets of luscious pink tomatoes, shiny green peppers, bunches of onions and yellow bananas. A long queue waited hours, going away loaded like a native market. Welcome extras! John says we use 1,500 bananas a day in the dining room, 37,000 a month, ¾ million a year (you check it!).

Some members have lost their upright carriage in this year. Shoulders aren't back and head high the way they used to be. Is it shoddy clothes that make one feel slack, or poor diet, or less of spirit and morale? It may be a combination. Many shuffle along in clacking shoes, neck stuck forward. Perhaps it is loss of an old pride which has not been replaced by a new one in a new kind of life. Carrying cans has made my shoulders more square than before. My chin feels higher too.

Dr. Skerl made the statement that this is one of the happiest years he has ever known, full of busy days, with time to read a book now and then and to make at least one or two acquaintances. It was greeted with incredulous laughter and boos. Yet he is nearer right than the scoffers for he is getting a good deal out of the experience by putting a lot into it. He and his wife are among the hardest workers in camp.

February 23, 1943. Miss McKim is smart and tactful. She often [settles problems] quietly, taking considerable time, and no one knowing just where or how she stands on it. Her Japanese upbringing and knowledge contribute to her diplomacy. Her serenity, patience, and enigmatic quality seem part of an Oriental background.

February 24, 1943. We have a wonderful bag from Nida and Ismael. There is a huge watermelon (we plan to pickle some rind), a kilo of fresh green peas—so beautiful to look at!—two rolls of chocolate and a huge bag of cookies. Two days ago there were 58 kilos of meat for us, today 75 kilos. It is a slim amount for 500. We are on a regular Filipino diet.

Miss McKim and Miss Sara portrayed a charming tea-call ceremony on top of the table in the veg room. They sank into the part so beautifully. We all tried and ended in gales of laughter but it was good practice. They sang a Japanese children's song and another gay little tune. The two women are very different from each other.

The Work Detail sheets are causing a big stir. One column shows hours promised, another in blue the hours done, in red the hours not completed but *due* camp. This is pinning it down and a good way to do it too.

February 25, 1943. I found out how to strip the inside tough lining from the pea-pod, removing the crisp green part to cook. It takes hours so no wonder the veg workers rebelled. The time is not worth it in result unless one is hungry enough for green vegetable, unsatisfied on a diet of rice. I definitely am hungry for it so it was worth the labor as it must be to coolie families who haunt the garbage chutes of large steamers, shouting and scrambling like mad to pick up the fresh orange peel, the thick veg peelings, half-rotted tomatoes, melon skins and other luxuries which come tumbling into the sea water in great harbors. Coolie families, houseboat inmates, never buy any of these in all their lives, but they can catch, salvage, wash and cook portions, peels and skins to make a tasty, nourishing addition to a bowl of rice with a small dash of fish or meat. It is well worth their time and effort, and is more than millions of half-starved inlanders ever contact. Thousands can live on what we throw away. Come and learn it in Concentration! Nida would chuckle if she could help me with these pea-pods for she could see how far that Japanese cash is going, that cash which they earn. She comes from a family of 12 herself. What a narrow margin they live on compared to most Americans. Yesterday the peas were so sweet, so succulent, I could have cried over them, and today the pods are as tender and fresh green. No one knows what it means to want green who hasn't had that special craving after going without.

I asked the assistant cook what they used to make the cream in the creamed onion soup. Without a smile, he said, "Gabi."

I am rather confused over Japanese politeness and tea ceremony in comparison with the Sergeant offering to slap any woman who wouldn't dip her feet into the door box. Like us, their nature is capable of contradictions but they could cut down on the bows when they are in the slapping phase. We are still laughing over our practice tea ceremony. Diminutive Miss Sara sinks into the part well. Miss McKim is more animated but gets into the spirit of Japanese womanhood easily, gracefully, without effort, as to the manner born. The rest of us were awkward in baggy slacks, hole-y stockings or short wool skirts quite unlike the gentle, clinging, enfolding kimono. We bobbed instead of bowing, undoubled our legs for respite, forgot to slide the pillow forward in trying to concentrate on strange phrases and actions in coordination—all on top of the narrow table covered with rice dust from the day's picking. Miss Young is so serious and gawky, Mrs. Watherace so Scotch in accent even in her Japanese, Mrs. Nance doubled up with forgetfulness and chuckles, Miss Greaves so intent that it threw her off when I supplied a cue word too soon and she couldn't get off the track.

February 27, 1943. Today, the Banana Machine, which is a picture, plan and execution of our state of mind, a masterpiece by Fabian at the shop, appeared before our astonished eyes. It is on a heavy base and curved holder, a series of grooves to hold bananas which can be turned and rolled out as each person comes by in line. It is a commentary on our system that time, ingenuity and scarce materials should be needed to go into this squirrel cage and whirligig. It is a result of everyone wanting the best banana and of the dysentery outbreak which made it necessary to wash bananas and to keep many hands from pawing over them to procure the best one. The Banana

Detail was formed and after it an old-timer swore volubly at Mrs. Watson when she tendered a not-perfect banana, then burst into tears and fled. Later on another man took one handed to him, looked at it and dashed it onto the cement floor, stamping all over it until the ground was slithery and traffic in the dinner line had to be stopped for cleaning. This is the state of mind from which the Banana Machine was born, out of necessity for coping with problems of equal distribution and for appeasing irate members. It is a constant daily grind to appease this one or that, this group or that—then it begins all over again. One can't have the best, or the worst, all the time. There must be division. So now at the door we have a Robot rolling out a banana apiece to each member. You take what comes up in the groove and you can swear all you like, stamp all you like—the Robot remains blank. You can take it and like it—or go tell the guards what rotten, small, squashy or hard green banana you happened to receive, and see how far it gets you.

February 28, 1943. Waitresses have become expert in mashing calcium tablets for small boys to eat disguised in rice; in squashing peas and peeling camotes for post-dysenterics, coaxing food into recalcitrant youngsters, or into those who would rather talk; keeping track of bananas which somehow switch about or disappear; remembering who wants hard or soft or small rice, with or without sugar; keeping in mind who doesn't eat potato, those who don't eat at night, those who bring spoons of their own or special dishes, those who put yeast in a cup—and the Banana Machine cannot help us at all!

Men's Committee Minutes again: "The Garden Committee [concluded] that because of lack of tools and seeds it would not be practicable to enlarge the area now being tended, but that every assistance possible be given Larry and his crew [so] they may continue the work in hand, with the hope that in the near future they will be able to add to our food supply considerably. Arrangements will be made to supply all available waste water for use of the gardeners. . . . The present stock of silverware has again dropped to where it is almost impossible to serve meals."

The Chef is in a bad mood. He gave one and a half stuffed cabbage rolls to the men, which miscalculation deprived 35 women of the main food dish, many of whom had worked hard all afternoon preparing the vegetables. They were naturally empty and irate. The Chef apologized personally to many but some won't let it die.

March 1, 1943. For toilet paper, the Jan. 25 [Manila] *Tribune*, two sheets apiece. It headlines, "Guerrillas futile. Resistance useless," but under "1 million enemy lives lost in first year of war" it says, "Imperial troops in Malay, the East Indies and Philippine Islands are maintaining a careful watch over their respective areas against any enemy attempts to launch a counter-offensive." This is the most important item for us for months. They admit they expect it, while denying it.

March 3, 1943. There are increasing problems of wood supply and rationing.

March 5, 1943. The Sergeant knocked down Larry at the garden. There are various versions. The Sergeant is adamant in talk with Larry, Dr. Dyer, Miss McKim, and liaison. Sergeant says he does not trust Americans anymore. The Sergeant says they want no camp news to go out, either about food or dysentery or what we don't like. It looks as though information might be leaking to the U.S. somehow.

We listened to Roy Barton on Russian folk songs, with a program of folk music of several countries. Ruth Zimmerman was lovely in a white satin embroidered Chinese gown, singing a lullaby and hymn in Chinese. Gerry was a pretty Mexican and Alice a vivacious Filipina. Mrs. Taylor sang a French song charmingly. The quartette gave "Turkey in the Straw" in such a rousing manner that two women did a square dance outside the window.

March 7, 1943. Wisecrack of camp—Dr. Shaffer has a hernia because o' the great strain of trying to balance diets.

Daphne Bird tore out of the dining room to grab a missive from Arthur then tore back to Miss McKim to get the long Japanese script translated into words saying her man was alive and well.

March 8, 1943. Fabian has put more than hand-skill into the Banana Machine. He has worked democracy into it, a glimpse of possible future management; cold fact, technical accuracy, with true justice and balance between the large and small banana, the fresh or the bruised, the ripe and the unripe, all of which must be the lot of every one at one time or another if some are not to receive the hand-picked always while others get the poor ones, with no privilege at all. The Banana Machine does away with favoritism, privilege, graft, politics, personal touch and hurt feelings. It is dispensation unseen, equal distribution, no one "in the know." It cannot be used by committee members to gather votes—at least until someone sits up nights working out a plan to beat the game. We need more and better Banana Machines! They are great fun, with just that element of chance in the grooves to make dispensation and division exciting and mysterious. Will we draw a fat, long yellow one, fresh and unbruised today? No, it's the green, hard one. Ah, but tomorrow! That may be *our* day! It is bound to come, the lucky groove, under the law of averages.

Looking at my jade ring, Grandmother's diamond, and the diamond bracelet of boom days tied casually in corners of my handkerchief in my slack pocket makes me realize how far we have come, what a long fifteen months it has been, how deeply we have learned.

March 9, 1943. It is a joy to see how well the cloistered nuns have adjusted to the maelstrom. Not all the religious people have done as well but children complicate life in any case. After convent life, this must be an exciting, vivid storybook, a chance to be acutely active after long quiet years of prayer.

There is rain, blessed rain, after threatening for days. It is a hard one and at it all evening, filling the tanks and the spring and enough to wash away some of the garbage dump, drowning flies and their eggs. And there is piping hot water for sponge baths.

March 10, 1943. Very early an Igorot woman was brought in, in a bad condition of labor. It was a cross-presentation, with one tiny arm protruding all night and no further progress. Dr. Dyer picked her up in his arms and carried her upstairs. The baby was born dead, registering one Igorot infant stillborn at Camp Holmes. Her people carried her out again on a stretcher after it was over. Poor soul, all that night in agony for nothing. Perhaps she has a large family and it was only one more problem. It is still hard to have nothing to show for all that pain.

I shall always remember sitting in the camp lab, talking of life and Concentration with Dr. Hall—the majestic mountain view from the window and the surrounding odors of dysentery specimens in contrast.

Fabian has invented four different kinds of fly-swatters—the first of wire which snapped and broke without supports; the second of cardboard sewed bamboo stick with string. These lasted two days at the rate of 200 flies a day when I used them, then they bent and cracked. Finally he has produced a shredded bamboo brush effect which works, stands up under cracks and can be washed. Also leather ones made of old and hoarded pouches found here and confiscated by Japanese soldiers. They are now punched with holes and attached to a stick.

March 11, 1943. Many admit feeling the effects of the improper diet—fatigue after a short amount of work, only staying power for two or three hours, many afflicted with indigestion and intestinal trouble.

March 12, 1943. I had expected more progress in camp with the sum of education and intelligence in here.

Carl and Art and some others who came in four months ago gave new heart and impetus toward a new attitude which shows up when compared to eight months ago. It seems a slow growth however. Ignorant, simple peasants couldn't be any slower. It may be partly psychological reaction to loss of home and property, from complete uprooting and readjustment. But it all points to something wrong with educational methods, a need for new conditioning on the subject of living and working together.

March 13, 1943. Both committees staged a raid for tableware which raised a big storm. In our dorm at one space, Dr. Dyer turned boxes upside down on the bed, disclosing a complete set of plates and silver for four, including cups. With only two to provide for, the lady said lightly, "Well, it was fun as long as I could get away with it." By far the most was found in the cook's section and the Committee had fun checking each other's spaces.

There are no new cases, which helps the hospital. Peg heard she had a package and went to the guardhouse where she saw it on the desk near Hayakawa who merely looked through her, saying coldly, "It was a mistake" and would not give it to her. Some day he needs his face slapped.

March 14, 1943. The birds sang from one hill to another and across the trees in the garden, filtering through the songs of the choir with notes of natural beauty. The sun warmed my back and shoulders, and the 23 different sects scattered in the congregation on the grass looked united, [even] if they were not.

Mac and Jim Bozeman shared boiled beans and tomato, pimento-rice-and chicken with us at noon, and Jerry made hotcakes to go with sun-cooked jam. I slept two hours afterward like a stuffed bird, replete and somnolent.

I had heard Bedie say if Daddy was willing he'd shave his hair anyway, ignoring my pleas. He came over later, grinning delightedly, with towel coat over his head. Unsuspecting I said, "What have you done? Washed your hair?" He merely lifted the towel coat. Horrible, nauseating—that awful gray mist on a shaved scalp. A jail color. I told him to get out and he did. It is his disregard, his thoughtlessness, deliberate going against my request that hurts. Jerry laughed as usual until I said I will cut off my hair which I have grown only to please his desire. I've been wanting to cut it for months. He stops laughing, has nothing to say. It hits home as no other thing would. We may be prisoners but we don't need to look like convicts, I tell them. It was the last straw, a betrayal of confidence. I swore, made the air blue.

We sat on the corner of the road eating our supper when a khaki car drove in with two Americans, the woman leaning forward to smile as she recognized Jerry. It was the Greers of Mt. Data and Klondyke. They said they had been well off in a swell place but it was betrayed by a native. There is not only money in betrayal, but now fear, threat of actual reprisal in burned villages for even one who is accused of harboring, protecting or helping an American. The pressure is terrific. These two were far north of Bontoc. It was a five-day tough walk in, then 21 days sleeping on a guardhouse floor. They had four blankets but two were taken from them. Their house was burned in front of them while he was bound and tied to a tree, she permitted to salvage what she could. They were accused of having guns and hiding them for guerrillas. Later they took the coat of her suit, the trouser part of her pajamas, leaving her only the skirt, just to annoy and irritate. They are masters of detail and smallness. She is still smiling and jolly, fairly rotund though she has lost 100 pounds! They said it was heaven to get here. After the month of capture, even hell would be heaven. I remarked that it was better to be together, protected as a unit, and he answered, "Yes. We know what a hunted animal feels like." This is the year 1943 of Civilization.

March 15, 1943. Jerry tells me the most startling headline of the month. Arthur and Jim Bozeman were called to the guardhouse by the Intelligence man from town, and a smooth, casual proposition was put to them during questions and talk. It seems there is no activity, nothing doing, the guerrillas hiding out, so it is better that all Americans come in like Greers. They want the Crosses, and Arthur, and Jim to go get them peacefully with the promise of internment here and practically no questions asked. They will accompany an officer and another American to Kapangan where the last-named two will stay as mutual hostages. Then Arthur and Jim are to strike out on a hunt to ask and locate Kesslers. The alternative is—the Japanese will track down Kesslers and kill them both without quarter. It seems Kessler has maps they must have. His head may be full of information too. What screws they could put on to open him up and get it! Of course they want him alive and healthy and there is nothing like a good friend as bait in the trap. It is a chance to play hero of a sort, although they have not any choice but to accept and will be given various inducements to soften the rigors of the game. One may visit his family, the other will achieve results in seeing many of us released. What a nasty spot for Arthur and Jim because they were in the same company and knew the man, Arthur an old friend who has worried about the couple. He cannot believe they will be well-protected and cared for if they surrender.

March 17, 1943. Three Americans in khaki stand among a dozen or 15 Filipino soldiers who are smiling secretly, quietly, with packs and guns around and between them. None have any choice but to go on this miserable manhunt, this quest which is typical of occupied countries and total war where all are helpless, no one free to be decent, straight, loyal or honorable. By contrast, the air, sun and sky are glorious. It is a day of beauty.

We all feel lead in the stomach, hate in the heart, bitter dismay at our helplessness.

Kessler's information may be complete, just what they want. His capture might mean death and torture to many, maybe the end of direct or indirect contact outside. He might be an important link, and the "lights are going out, one by one." Our morale is so low that we look for the best and trust the enemy promises in a game of war where *all* is fair, even lies. It is not the comfort and health of Kessler alone, but how much depends on his being free.

March 18, 1943. One newcomer to camp says she won't do any cooking in that private kitchen—the struggle there is awful and it is seven deep around the stove. Otherwise she thinks camp is fine.

At noon Bedie came into the dining room while I was serving, carrying below a wide smile and shaved head a heavenly spray of huge white orchids with three sprays of pale yellow ones giving off delicate perfume, from the trees at home. We have forgotten orchids—delicacy—beauty of that sort. It almost undermined me. They came in a bag from Nida and Ismael, with pork chops, 3 baskets of berries, a bag of crisp luscious doughnuts and many pink tomatoes. What a feast for mental and physical hunger! We felt refreshed, renewed, replete, after eating at noon. I never expected to eat such chunks of pure fat, but the chop was consumed except for the bone. Jerry fried them in a pan with sliced tomatoes which he also put into a delectable fried rice for which we yearned. Flavor is so important to us. With good camp soup and a tantalizing spoonful of fried cabbage from the kitchen also, we topped it all with coffee and sank our teeth into a doughnut. I felt like moving mountains afterward.

I took the orchids into the dorms, the veg room and the kitchen, and everyone responded instantly to their beauty, exclaiming with faces alight with pleasure. To think they came from home, not the hilltop!

Pertinent extract from meeting of the General Committee: "The Committee admits again that nothing which it does will please all. It does ask the support of the camp in its efforts to do what seems best for the greatest number. Idle criticisms can sap the camp morale as certainly as idle rumors. Individual activity promoted with more zeal than responsibility can reduce camp life to dissension and anarchy. The Committee alone can assume responsibility for the internal management of this community; it requests every member of Camp Holmes to respect the orderly processes by which this responsibility is sustained."

It is the feud come to a head, with both sides given a hearing at separate meetings, and good to get it into the open.

March 19, 1943. A typed notice on the Board: "*In Memorium. Deceased*—The spirit of Liberty as expressed in Women's Suffrage. If the Women's Committee being duly elected by the women of the camp is only functioning through the forebearance of the General Committee, then why not bring us Women's Suffrage that we women may have a voice in choosing our General Committee?" Signed, Women's Committee.

Another piece on the Board: "Do you like a taste of garlic in your stew? Do you like tomatoes in the gravy or eggs for breakfast sometimes? How about banana bread for lunch with cinnamon in it? If you do, there is a way we can all have these occasionally. The Big Boss in the kitchen says it takes an average 135 lbs. of rice for breakfast, 110 for dinner and 50 for children, gravy, croquettes, bread, etc. daily. If, in addition to this, we can have enough hand-picked rice for the grinding room to produce an extra 30 or 40 lbs. of rice flour daily, this can be placed in the store and sold to camp for personal baking. *But* the proceeds from sale of that flour go into kitchen account and the kitchen gets onions, tomatoes, Purico, sugar, eggs, garlic, pepper, fruit for the children, spices, etc. in exchange. At present market prices—20¢ for a head of garlic, 60¢ a kilo for peppers—our friends in the guardhouse *will not buy* these articles for us. But the camp store is able to get them as occasion arises and often more cheaply. . . . Let's pick that little extra rice every day—put in all the time you have promised and more!'' Signed, the Women's Committee, approved by the Chef.

The Religious Committee has met twice on whether to present a four or five act Passion Play in Holy Week. There seems to be doubt and hesitation as to whether it could be put over properly or is wise to even try it. The chief worry among all the religious representatives seems to be on having one of our own number represent Christ. We live so close to defects rather than virtues that it is hard to rise above.

March 20, 1943. The truck drove in with Filipino soldiers and guns and our three men from the manhunt.

[Arthur and Jim Bozeman] had been told by Hayakawa at 6:30 that they were going to Baguio—but when the truck came they had to prepare for a trip and the truck curved into the opposite direction, straight to Kapangan. When they reached Kapangan it was already known that they were coming, for an old woman apologized for a wash basin saying she had nothing at hand as they took everything away when they heard, expecting the Nipponese also. At two stops men were sent out to various barrios asking for news of Kessler and his whereabouts. In every case, no one knew him, of him or about him. No one knew anybody, or anything. It was the blank wall of non-cooperation in full view. With no Nipponese, only the Constabulary boys with them, they were fed royally—chicken Adobo, pink rice, eggs three times a day—and how they ate! They linger over telling of every mouthful. The second thing they dwelt on was the beauty of the valley—hot and rich with growth—animals, fruit, vegetables and newly built terraces up a spur of the mountain, steep and sheer. Everything was dripping with sprays, some a foot long, of lavender or red orchids. To hear these tough lumbermen rave about the orchids in the midst of food and war talk was delightful. The Igorots have been more loyal than we ever dreamed they would be. There is no news—but it still travels somehow. They "knew you were coming." It gets through fast.

They listened to the Bataan panorama again, this time through Filipino eyes. "We were not beaten, not licked, not defeated. Our spirit was strong to hold—but first the ammunition, then the food gave out. Then they cut off the water supply. This was strictly rationed. Finally orders came we must surrender, and even then many did not, broke away and are still free—waiting." Dysentery and malaria struck them down like flies; five or six thousand died in a day. The sick were carried out of barracks to a field, left in the sun, no one going near except carriers of stretchers. If they recovered, they crawled out themselves, the rest remained where they died. The same story that Leung told, about complete neglect at first, acting as though the Japanese figured it was cholera and untouchable; then there was care under Filipino doctors who gave it only when paid—one had to have money. Finally it was all turned over to the American Army doctors who were prisoners and still in charge, but they were allowed in too late and the worst was over. One day of the four days they were out, they met 70 Japanese soldiers returning from a search for guerrillas who had recently killed Bruner, the Nazi. Dozens were sure he was a headquarters of some kind, including radio. This four-day trip of our men with the Filipino Constabulary hinges on the capture and death of Bruner for they are looking for the guerrillas who did it, apparently suspecting Dangwa[10] with possible assistance of Kessler. It is implied that Dangwa and Kessler are far from that valley. When it became evident that no one would know anything, that there was little danger of contact, our three men relaxed and enjoyed the trip. They would like to go on further and be gone longer. This could lead to a slipup somehow and they shouldn't tempt Fate. They were quite the heroes when they returned and they tell the tale well in their own ways.

The moon is nearly full, and Mrs. Burch has broken a bottle over the head of her husband and has beaten her child twice this evening. She has also delivered a long tirade to Mrs. Bell in a breathless, breaking voice because the latter told her she was tired after a hard day's work and she should not punish a child in such weariness. It is the end of a perfect day—yelling, beating, crying.

March 21, 1943. I went to Peg's art class and it was a surprise to see how she took on a new personality—voice, facial expression and manner—a different Peg from the practical vegetable worker with strong hands, cold efficiency and determined eyes. In art she is emotional, looks soft and glowing with a diffused light of deep feeling and happiness.

Jerry's leg is yielding to treatment of powdered sulfa in the open infection. He is off wood crew, with foot in the air.

Fabian has achieved another triumph. Now he has carved two front teeth out of an animal bone and the dentist has fitted them onto Delphine's plate where the missing [teeth] have marred her looks for months. Others want their gaps mended so Fabian's spare time will be bone-whittling for beauty's sake.

Since Hayakawa's trip to Manila the guardhouse has left us very much to ourselves. Many couples are now seen in a stranglehold, kissing each other goodnight. This visible sign of affection intrigues June very much, since she has not seen it during her formative years.

I'm reading *Darkness at Noon* by Arthur Koestler and find it interesting from a prisoner's point of view. It is well written and some of it was no doubt experienced but there is an obscure false note which I cannot analyze. I think it rings of propaganda.

March 22, 1943. Rolls of toilet paper came in—66 sheets apiece!

March 23, 1943. A boyfriend has surprised June with a sudden presentation of a beautifully made leather-link bracelet with her name carved on a small aluminum link. She was excited and amazed.

June came in weeping over *The Man Without a Country*. It is especially poignant to one kept away from home.

One woman takes her rice from the server each meal even though she throws it out—because it is her right to have it. A strange conception of rights.

March 24, 1943. Yesterday Inez surprised us with a bag of bananas and a bottle of grape juice. This morning there was excitement over Nida's and Ismael's bag with sausage, chocolati, cookies, two melons, colored candies and four cakes of soap. On the list it said, "Homemade sausage, Fuzzy has four kittens." So our wild-eyed Persian is still going strong.

Jerry tells me I am much easier to live with right now and I say he is immeasurably so, which is part of the reason. The other part is that I keep a lot to myself.

An unpleasant development is one with light fingers, bad habits from past hardship, who was seen by at least ten women stuffing green peas into her blouse in the veg room. It cut down the supply for soup so much that a howl came from the kitchen and it had to be tackled directly.

The most amusing battle of the year in here is between George age 72 and Walter age 74. Walter's wife says he was "protecting his wood." George was infuriated because his cleaned area was spoiled. He is like a demon housekeeper about it. They brandished wood and broomhandles at each other, drew off for attack as with guns or swords. George spun Walter around and pushed him with a knee-kick so that he landed in the gutter with a cut requiring one stitch.

March 25, 1943. Men's Committee Minutes, March 25: "Mr. Greer is hereby appointed as Camp Pharmacist and is authorized to set up a camp pharmacy in the present location until more adequate space becomes available. The playing with or use of bows and arrows by children is prohibited as there is great danger to other children.

"To facilitate handling the many diversified community jobs, the utility and shop activities are divided under the following section heads:

"Fabian—Shop Foreman
Ray—Electrical
Willis—All carpentry and utility
    jobs

Jess—Plumbing
Erich—Blacksmith
Eric—Record of projects and
    progress made.

"That another of the small houses be built to relieve the congestion in No. 3 barracks. . . . All people are requested to refrain from singing, loud talking or other unnecessary noises near the grade school building in the evening during study hour. . . . The grade school building is not to be used for social purposes, including eating meals. . . . Mr. Watson is, in addition to his other duties, appointed custodian of the Kindergarten Tent.''

Daddy and Bedie gave a popcorn party to Richie and Herbie one evening and Bedie was in a dither over entertaining a real live guerrilla. He melted the butter and helped in a thrilled state of mind.

March 26, 1943. Jerry's leg is better. He feels the most striking thing about the hospital situation is the preference given staff convenience over patient welfare. He says a move would break up the last country club atmosphere and thinks that spreading them through three barracks would improve their morale by giving them new outlook and more people to talk with at meals and other times. It would take congestion off of hospital toilets and the kitchen there, where they do so much private cooking. He says they admit their compactness and desire to stay that way by mentioning they don't want to spread out. Furthermore, they admit it would benefit patients by saying that the spaces would be immediately filled.

March 27, 1943. Dr. Hall spoke on dysentery as a symptom-complex and a protein condition. Dr. Bergamini delighted everyone with a lecture on Egyptian architecture, his visit to the Sphinx, pyramids and Temple of Karnak. Jack Veroff sang "Bloody War" but Nakamura changed words from the Verboten version. Just as Sid told him to shoot the works—no guard was near—one clattered up. However it did not register and there was laughter to relieve it. Marion Gammell sang "The Way You Look Tonight" and "Let's Fall in Love" in her effortless, unaffected manner which is very effective! The songs made a tremendous hit. Jerry went to thank her for he had suggested them. I am afraid it stirred gray ashes into flame and sentiment. Jerry pulled my pigtail romantically as we sat on the bench with Bedie between us. A brilliant star hung over the hill above silhouettes of dark pines against pastel sunset sky. The ridge rising to the hilltop was like a rich block-print of the mountain in northern China on our wall.

March 28, 1943. Jerry and I shucked peanuts, talking on hospital point. Many couples were sunbathing there. The rice terraces were filled with thick green grain hiding the water. The season is advancing, showing the length of our abnormal life without permissible sign of affection. The guards are lax just now but one hesitates to stir desire even by the holding of hands when affection is near the surface after being unleashed. Young romance is in every direction though only awkward, embarrassed, unformed expression.

March 29, 1943. An armored truck drove in—with Mr. and Mrs. Moule and three children all under six, one a baby born in the hills outside. They came on a horrible trip from Bayumbang and all five have malaria. He is thin, pale, hollow-eyed and gaunt, unshaven, with great tears in his shirt. He looked hunted. They were fed and given a place to lie down.

March 30, 1943. Memo: "The Women's Committee wishes to bring before the General Committee of the camp the question of Universal Suffrage and a joint committee of both men and women to govern this camp."

Four ducks waddled impertinently past the guardhouse, flicking tails, en route from pen to pond. Another delightful scene was husky Wick shepherding the two Moule children at the playground—from guerrilla to nursery in two months.

Due to lice in the jail, the Moule parents decided to shave the heads of their three children so the little wayfarers have lost their lovely curls and look forlorn. Everyone is being wonderful to them for they are bewildered by crowds of white people after seeing only Igorots for a year. With their exhausted mother in the hospital, they have several substitutes and their Dad hovers over them.

We heard how the Moules were hunted from place to place, losing more possessions with each flight. Two Filipinos were shot to death because they would not reveal where Moules were, a third was wounded but managed to crawl over to warn them the Japanese were coming. The Filipino doctor who had been treating them did not dare to come near any more and they became so ill with malaria that they only got up from bed to cook and feed the children. They were barely able to crawl around. They moved 18 times in one month and at last were so low in food that he butchered a cow with a penknife. It was six days from the time they were captured until they reached camp. He has fever every night and both are anemic and exhausted. Their relief at getting the children and themselves in here is immeasurable, though up to four months ago they were all right.

March 31, 1943. Excerpt from letter of Dr. Lee to the Committee; "I beg of you to think of the camp as a whole and to think of the mothers who walk up and down the windy street or huddle in the corner of a cold toilet room for hours at a time during the night with half-sick children so that a hundred other mothers and babies can get a little rest. If there were a room in the hospital with light and available hot water etc., many illnesses could be avoided. You should decide before the new house opposite the barracks is filled up."

Sign on the Bulletin Board: "Playground for children under three will begin today at 8:30 to 10:30 every day except Sunday. Older children are welcomed unless they interfere with play of babies. Do your camp work knowing your baby is playing happily.'' Signed by E. Mather, the Super-intendent. This is real progress!

Committee Minutes: "That universal suffrage be adopted for the Camp in the election of members of the General Committee: Motion was lost in voting that Election of General Committee be continued in form as at present—passed by unanimous vote.''

Jerry is starting accounting two nights a week as an opportunity to prepare for the future. He has needed it before.

The library has moved into the little gasoline hut, with the barber shop!

April 1, 1943. The six Brent students are joining their parents in Manila as adults, no longer children. We could watch them change in here. Three are left forlornly behind, with no word from parents in Surigao. They were all so excited they nearly exploded. Many who rose to wave farewell were excited too, as there is a sort of intoxication about seeing anyone depart for the unknown.

The Women's Committee petition follows: "Because the right to vote was granted to the women of our representative homelands, the United States, Britain and her Dominions and the Philippine Islands, after plebiscite on the question had been taken, WE, THE UNDERSIGNED, believe that here in Camp Holmes, the question is too large a one for an executive committee to decide without reference to the wishes of the existing electorate . . .

"WE, THEREFORE, respectfully petition the General Committee to conduct a plebiscite on the question of Women's Suffrage as soon as can be arranged. By 'women's suffrage' we mean that women should have the right to vote for the entire membership of the General Committee just as the men do at the present time. We request that this plebiscite be held prior to the forthcoming committee elections, so that in the case of a favorable vote on the subject, the women may be given a chance to vote in said forthcoming elections.''

April 2, 1943. Fabian has hung a miniature barber pole created by the shop for its new quarters. It is six inches long and gave us all a laugh.

Jerry seems more like himself than for 15 months, his sociable, gregarious instinct awakening. He asked Moule and Wick for cocoa at 7:30 and it was an interesting evening of conversation. Wick relates his experiences without embellishment, compact but vivid. The tales are as colorful as any I've heard in here. We asked Wick if he himself was sold out by Filipinos and he ruefully answered, "No, I ran right into the Japanese myself. I had been warned they were coming and I was cutting across to get away along a riverbank with two Igorots when the Japanese came up behind us and started shooting before we even saw them. The Igorot threw my gun away but they found it and they asked potent questions about the Japanese ammunition belt found on me which I said I had purchased from a Filipino as a Bataan souvenir.'' He was in Binalonan jail 21 days, ''given the works'' twice. They found his commission and passport with Ted's stuff so they knew all they needed. The Japanese did not provide meals but left it to the natives who fed him well. As to third degree methods, he said mostly they used the broad belt for striking, not sticks or bats; also the water cure—forced drinking or head held under water, then they prodded the full stomach and belly with bayonets or sticks, sometimes kicking or jumping onto it. When this is done a number die, of course. He says they have tortured Filipinos dreadfully and about one in ten die under it. He was with the Japanese on trips to several towns where they rake in about 25 men *and* women for questioning and torture as reprisal for any kind of guerrilla occurence. He says the Igorots have been terrorized and many cowed, but hordes of lowlanders were so badly treated they don't care any more and will risk anything. The Socialist group in Pampanga and about 7 districts are loyal and waiting, with cached discarded weapons, some even now in action. They are anti-Japanese, more pro-Filipino than pro-American but they helped him.

Both Wick and Bill tell of many banditos at large, roving about merely to pillage.

April 3, 1943. Thinking of the destruction of monuments of the past, buildings full of history in London that are demolished, now only ghosts, which I had hoped to see and now never will be able, I could find consolation only in G. B. Shaw's sentence in *Caesar and Cleopatra*—''Would you destroy the past?—Aye, and build the future on its ruins!'' This is what is ahead for all of us.

April 4, 1943. The turkey gobbler is trailing his feathers and blowing himself red, all over camp. He is another pet for the children. Someone stole six eggs, leaving only one under the Mother Turkey which was a dirty trick to the hen as well as to the owner.

Camp Holmes *News*: ''Men's fashions, considerably more original and practical than those displayed in *Esquire*, are being created atop the hills behind camp as members of the wood crew seek to reduce washing to a minimum and increase area of exposed skin to maximum while they toil to bring firewood over the mountain. Loin cloths and G-strings, once exclusively worn by Igorots in this area, are extremely popular, varying from plain white to a vivid-hued number of native materials which once graced a country club dresser, but which now gives to its bronzed but hardly brown-hued wearer an air of Hollywood aboriginality, as he nimbly brings forest giants crashing to the ground. Most impressive is the gentleman, rumored to have clerical connections, who stalks magnificently about, bearded like a prophet of old, wearing a felt campaign hat, a loincloth, sandals, and not much else. It's easier to wash and to renew skin than cloth these days.''

It could be said truly that the Japanese have fed war prisoners and housed them according to their own standard for average living—which is not very high. In here, we are probably fed better than their own privates and their families back home. We are accustomed to higher standards and *not* accustomed to high starch diet. This is of small matter to they who have countless more pressing matters to attend. We are as inconsiderate about their standard and about the malnutrition of a large class of our own people, thinking it is not our affair but the government's or the welfare society to whom we give money and then forget about it.

After Ray and Hayakawa drove in from Manila, first we heard that Santo Tomas itself is a far better camp than this, fine buildings etc. But it is overcrowded and the weather is HOT!

April 5, 1943. All day there was talk of Manila everywhere—how their breakfast is like ours but they get no lunch from camp, only what they buy for themselves privately. For dinner they had two hamburgers, a piece of squash, and one other item, no rice at all. Wow, said we, rice may not be good in such large quantity but it does fill up the hole. They have no eggs at all, vegetables very scarce and beef the only meat, while we get only pork. Ray says there is no sugarcane growing in the fields, that Manila is badly damaged and the beggars on the streets are so many that one hardly dares to go out.

April 7, 1943. Women's Committee [Minutes]: "On days when no rice needs to be picked, the pickers are asked to *put in their regular time* on veg work. Also the pickers are notified that if they do not record their hours or if they record illegibly, *no credit can be given for their time.* . . . People are reminded that no one is allowed to pick over or handle bananas in the dining room but must *take bananas as they come* from the machine."

The Men's Minutes are full of revealing information too. "Prior to the war, meat was imported into the Islands—now no meat is imported and there is a shortage all over the Islands. To prevent the extinction of animals, slaughtering is carefully guarded within each district. The people of Baguio are not receiving one-tenth the quantity of meat that is being consumed within the camp. The keeping of livestock at camp is encouraged and we will be assisted wherever possible. No alkalines are being manufactured in the islands. Factories are being constructed and soap will be manufactured later on.

"A petition signed by five members and endorsed by 64 others, asking that the General Committee authorize a poll of the camp electorate on the subject of women suffrage, was read and thoroughly discussed. It was decided to hold two polls: one of the men of voting age of camp and one of the women on the identical question: 'Do you favor women's suffrage for the election of the General Committee of the camp?' "

I listen to all the male objections that my father's conservative friends used to voice and that my mother's timid, ladylike elders put forward, shocked at the modern ones who had to earn a living and who knew firsthand what they had to fight against.

Japanese Mr. Nakano brought in a piano and set it up in the dining room! Wild excitement, especially among the children. June cannot wait to play on it.

At Japanese class the peanut crusher was at work, almost drowning us out, until it was moved to the doorway. It is on the principle of two large pieces of wood sliding back and forth, not quite against each other, crushing the shells fed from above which drop down with the peanuts to a shelf below, from there swept into a box or basket to be handpicked. Another product from Fabian!

April 8, 1943. I went about calling for voters [in the poll] as the hour grew late. Seven men and twelve women did not vote. At 11 o'clock we counted. First the women's—109 Yes (56.7%)—No 83 (43.3%). Then the Men's—72 Yes (45.8%)—No 85 (54.2%) with 11 men "blank." These total 181 Yes and 168 No in all.

The ballots were full of exclamation points, underlines, *darkened or large print*, and one wrote, *"No, a thousand times no!"* One Colonel says women always make trouble. Here speaks the South and the Military. The Camp *News* had a paragraph beginning, "The [General Committee] election will proceed as before," which shows how the Committee voted, ignoring and thumbing its nose at the feminine vote.[11]

April 9, 1943. One woman with eyes still blazing said, "It will be fine for some of these fathers to tell their sons later how they refused equal suffrage—in a Concentration Camp of all places!" Another revealed that someone had told her not to vote at all and if she did to make it No.

Jerry who is back at work again to his great content brought me lovely sprays of fragile flowers, bud and berry the color of honeydew melon from the hill. It is charming against the fresh green of young lettuce grown by Bedie. We always feel something is missing when no bag comes from the Bacanis. I worry, without this contact.

Arthur was allowed to go to Benguet mine to bring back medicines, axe handles, soap, and the needed tools. He learned from the Nipponese themselves that Kanmori and Mukibo are back in Japan. The first has one million pesos worth of loot for himself, was tried and given life imprisonment; the second was court-martialed for looting and conduct in Baguio, sentence unrevealed. They will get no mercy from their own.

April 10, 1943. Miss McKim called out that something is coming and we must be clean inside and outside barracks. I thought she said, "Big Apple," but it turned out to be "Rear Admiral"! So we mopped with vigor and bustled about.

Jerry kids me about my jade which is probably in Japan by now. All right—I'll get it if I search all the rest of my life, unless it is sunk to the bottom of the ocean. I think we will get that jade pin back. It had been worn at the court of the Empress Dowager by the Chinese lady who sold it. The opals, the pearl, the gold, not so important. The jade is different. It has history, symbolism as well as rare beauty; China itself.

The new piano made all the difference in the world when Sue and Gerry sang. Mr. Fildey's variations on "Annie Laurie" were received with shouts while a guard looked on enjoying the children's yells of delight but not quite understanding why we laughed. The guards like to watch the babies and often pull some of them in small carts. Why must this horror continue—hundreds killed when a bomb devastates a whole acre; women, children and men dying together in a bloody mass of total war, and young guards of prisoners really yearning to play with babies, not to kill them. It is a mad world and we are all crazy that we let it come to this—two terrible wars in one generation.

April 11, 1943. It is Jerry's 52nd birthday and we opened a precious can of scrapple to eat with ranch scrambled eggs—our first in weeks. We all kissed Daddy warmly—a big event in Concentration and more dangerous than it sounds!

How happy we were to see the bag from Bacanis with sprays of two kinds of white orchids from home and "Happy Birthday to Mr. Crouter" tucked in with succulent fried chicken which we consumed at lunch. There were cupcakes, papaya, a roll of chocolati and a can of butter. How glad we are to be in contact again and amazed at their remembering the birthday. We took some hotcakes and a piece of chicken to Dr. Hall.

Our new arrivals, the three Griffiths and Miss Tavener, from the mountains, were held two weeks before coming here and were told to send out for their household goods, which they had dispersed with Igorot friends. These were sent in—then confiscated as property of the Army because they had hidden out so long. Even the rings were taken off their fingers, wedding ring included. Mr. Griffiths was tied to the wall with a rope around his waist. We feel worn out with fury and disturbance.

April 12, 1943. The returns are up with Carl four votes ahead of the Hero. Dr. Skerl is third and Art is fourth. It is another index of political intelligence, with a man of Skerl's capacities halfway down the list. Denki is in the running again. We hope Carl will be chairman but Denki may get it again. He can stand on his own merits.

Jerry brought me a beautiful branch of smooth olive green leaves with waxy red berries on scarlet stems. On the smaller branches was pale green and dark hoar moss. We hung it near the orchids' whiteness and the crimson shades with green made lovely contrast. There is always something shining in camp.

The Japanese tell of Nagatomi in jail with heavy leg irons and an iron bar across his back, forbidden to see his wife and two children. Those poor souls are incommunicado now even as he made us, only they are worse off. The Japanese say they are allowed to see him only once a week. He took all the Camp Hay money of ours for himself, plus 25,000 Benguet account and some other amounts they can't locate. His cousin and Mukibo have the rest.

I hear Jerry go into the dispensary saying he has been a damn fool and wants his leg treated again. I groan and go in—to see a small stream of blood from the gash made by a stick which snapped directly into the healing wound and "hurt like the devil."

At last I have Upton Sinclair's *Boston* from the Library, about the Sacco-Vanzetti case in which many familiar names appear.

April 13, 1943. The women are tired of having their faces pushed in by the Men's Minutes! We have all been told off. It is bad for morale of the women.

April 14, 1943. From Camp Holmes *News*: "Bean milk has become a recognized and much demanded product since its introduction some months ago. Based on a product manufactured in China as a cheap milk substitute, the local "milk" contains mongo beans and coconut milk (instead of soybeans), rice flour, sugar and vegetable water (formula varies occasionally)."

April 15, 1943. Jerry is making a bench by hand, cut, sawed and shaped from a piece of log brought down the hill on his bare back. It is for my birthday in October and he spends hours at the shop.

Mr. Matsumoto, head of the Japanese Ohta plantation in Mindanao, came to camp chiefly to see Peg, an old friend. He had talked with her husband on Davao Street only two weeks ago and said he was fat and well. He had been given hard treatment (road work) at the beginning but was all right now, though 300 were living far out in a cabaret building with no running water or any conveniences but none had died and there was little sickness. There were 80 planters, gold mining people and the Del Monte group there. The harsh treatment was because the same kind had been given to the Japanese during their internment after war broke out, he said. He could hardly believe that Peg had had no word of her husband nor been able to send word in all this time.

April 16, 1943. Dr. Dyer has posted a notice on a yellow sheet on the Board: "A case of probably acute anterior poliomyelitis (infantile paralysis) has developed in camp. He is isolated at the camp hospital. Strict isolation for all contacts of this case is considered impractical by a majority of the medical committee, with the facilities available in this camp. Polio is not as contagious as is commonly thought. There is no reason for undue apprehension. The camp personnel are urged to report cases of colds, fever etc. promptly to a member of the medical staff.'' Signed, The Medical Committee. The patient is Bill Moule.

It takes me back to 1907, polio, leg aches that can never be described, delirium, consultations, nurses and more delirium, braces, casts and treatments. Pray God my children don't have to go through it.

We enjoyed Nida's tomatoes after the lecture. Gene and Jim Tebiz read their excellent papers on ''The Development of the Atomic Theory and the Modern Conception of the Structure of Matter.'' It was exciting, stirring and somewhat connected with Dr. Hall's course on cell structure. We had some laughs over Gene's saying the energy possibilities in uranium were dangerous. He envisaged some of these and other scientific developments that might be ahead. It was peering into the future which left us a little breathless. I could not begin to grasp it all.

April 17, 1943. Last night two guards were drunk, friendly, foolish and giggling. One finally disappeared and there was a hunt for him. He was found gently resting in the gutter. It was loss of face for the guardhouse and today they landed in more trouble through H.Q. in town finding a note inside a seam of a Catholic Sister's bag. It was only a sad note of condolence but someone must have known enough to look for it in town. They threw it back here at once and no bags were given out after inspection.

Late we took coffee down to Dr. Hall and he mentioned how Dr. Lee and he had suggested at the last Medical Committee meeting isolation of all newcomers from the hills and lowlands, for a period of time and test. They were given all kinds of reasons why this couldn't be done and no action was taken.

A military car containing Virginia and Johnnie McCall arrived. As I went past, Hall told me, ''Have you heard the news? They are going to quarantine, isolate, all new internees.'' Whoops, it is beginning to resolve! Polio showed up and started a melting, cracking process.

Morale is still bad among the women since the minutes so flatly printed our position of unimportance. We all knew we were secondary, subsidiary, but to have it put down and the vote on suffrage so twisted and turned was devastating. Many see no use in a Women's Committee and want it dissolved with the men running everything. I plead that we must manage our own work details, offer our own ideas on sanitation, and I maintain this last Committee has done excellent work in both ways even though they did have internal friction which they managed to conceal until recently.

April 18, 1943. There is a yellow sheet on the Bulletin Board. ''April 17. There has occurred today another infraction of the strict regulation imposed on us by the Japanese authorities that there shall be absolutely no notes passed out of this camp except through official channels. The General Committee has met and imposed the following punishments on the violator of this regulation: 1. She will work on veg detail three hours each day for two weeks. 2. She is not allowed to receive packages from outside for two weeks. 3. Library privileges are withdrawn for two weeks. 4. She is not allowed to attend camp entertainments for two weeks. 5. Store privileges will be withheld for two weeks. The Japanese authorities have indicated they consider these punishments too moderate, and that should such offenses occur in future, they will be inclined to take matters into their own hands. The General Committee is cognizant of the fact that legitimate channels for correspondence with the outside, have, in the past, been disappointing and unsatisfactory. They are at present in process of negotiations which they hope will lead to much improved facilities. Pending conclusion of these arrangements, the personnel of the camp is urged to bear with us. The General Committee.''

It is Palm Sunday with many carrying green palm branches home from church.

Jerry has the new bench finished and it is a beauty. We are proud of [it]. It is like starting home, as we can picture it in front of the fireplace, with maybe a second one. Even June began to talk about her own bedroom which we promised long ago she could have ''after the war.'' It finally came and now we are waiting for ''after.''

Marj Moule has had a rough road from the time she took to the hills with her unborn child, up to now when her husband has polio, her children have dysentery and she has malaria.

April 19, 1943. Dr. Skerl asks for all peanut shells to be saved as he is chemically making alkali for soap from them. Fabian's grinder is always in action.

I found a school paper of Bedie's signed ''Fred'' [his real name] which intrigued me. I watched him start with a heavy pitcher among three other boys up the hill and he looks taller, more responsible, proud of his job, almost out of the careless puppy stage, advancing a little, and I take heart. June goes in leaps and bounds, Bedie slow and unperceivable, but he is moving and not always sideways!

Miss McKim says that what she wants is a mixed men and women committee which is interesting to me. I could not fathom how she felt as I had not talked with her but when I congratulated her on the stand she took on maintaining a Women's Committee, she told me in one sentence. She readily agreed with me, however, that the men at present were in no frame of mind for the mixed committee.

(The following from the Japanese): ''As your life is not a detective novel, of course, you must not intend to communicate with outsiders without being examined, don't have interest in trying your chance. If you continue doing such unlawful acts, we have to become more strict which you would not prefer and it is just the same on our side.'' Marvelous, marvelous!

April 20, 1943. Two cars full of officers came during roll call. The stocky, plump, jolly one examined Dr. Hall's centrifuge closely, said something to the other officers, and they all laughed. Before the arrival of these officers, all the doctors were called to the guardhouse for a talk by and with Mr. Nakano who has many ideas and seems to have more power than Hayakawa. They were there half an hour with Miss McKim translating. He told them they were not taking good care of us and that was why we had dysentery, not because of overcrowding. We might not be used to overcrowding but this had nothing to do with the case. He suggested that if they had done all they should we would not have had the epidemic—and there is enough element of truth in this to make it thoroughly unpalatable. He also managed to convey that we were not ill but neurotic. The Japanese will do as they think. There is only one fact—we can't win in here—it will always be their way. We can only leaven it a little by constant pushing. Dr. Lee spoke up about poor diet and malnutrition making us susceptible, and said that after one attack of dysentery the susceptibility increased, and that flies, close contact and dirt were contributory. According to Japanese standards, we are well off on space, food, light and comfort. The dietitian asks for more beef and chicken and is told to make out the food lists a week ahead and they will see what they can do on buying. Nakano comes from Japan and knows war stringency. He practically tells the doctors to call off feuds and politics and get down to business. Dean has been put in his place quietly by the enemy and some others have been told to stop playacting and dramatizing too.

April 21, 1943. At the request of the Japanese Military Authorities, the Committee has composed the following letter to all American and British civilians at liberty in Northern Luzon: ''At the request of the Japanese Military Authorities, we, the duly elected General Committee of Camp Holmes Concentration Camp, La Trinidad, Benguet, where over 500 American and British civilians are interned under Japanese auspices, send you the following message . . . We have been interned since Dec. 27, 1941. Our treatment, on the whole, is considerate and fair, and we do not suffer unnecessary indignities. Our health is good and we receive adequate food. . . . We believe that we are better off in the Concentration Camp than we would be on the outside living surreptitiously. This opinion is corroborated by the experience of several families who have given themselves up and arrived here in recent weeks. The Japanese authorities have assured us that any of you, surrendering to their military authorities, will not be harshly treated, and will be brought to this camp for internment with us. Sincerely, (Signed by all members of the Committee.)''

April 22, 1943. Jerry, who is the only graduate lawyer in camp, isn't even considered but this would be a wifely objection. We are told about law, government and housing by a bunch of doctors, but if Jerry tried to tell them something about medicine they would laugh. If you want to know anything in here, ask the doctor, whether it is Japanese psychology or how to influence people. He will tell you and show you. He is his own worst enemy. Dean is to be head of Clinical Pathology and the dentist is to take over branches of Law. The new plan is below. [See following page.]

We went in the evening to the lower gardens, which were an ideal setting for the Passion Play. The drops of rain ceased, the clouds slowly lifted in the west and the stars came out one by one from the passing mist. In the damp, cool air, fireflies flickered in the dark pines, darted through the moist bushes. All the camp sat on the terraced bank in hushed silence waiting for the world's most real drama to begin. It was a living presentation, perfect in production of picture, costumes, lighting, emphasis and beauty. First there was the Scripture reading by a man with an electric torch standing in the dark. Then the choir sounded in the distance on the road. The dark curtain of light was lifted by a spotlight centered on the long white table of the Lord's Supper, with Christ and his twelve disciples, clothed in the flowing garments of that day, dark beards, gray beards, flowing locks and thoughtful serious faces looking toward the Leader. He passed the bread and the cup and they did not understand. The lights went out.

We waited, watching the fireflies gently glowing here and there. Again the darkness sprang into light and the Garden of Gethsemane was before us, with Peter asleep during the hour of watch and Christ kneeling with head bowed on his hands at the gray rock. The rock was real, a part of our own sunken garden. The soldiers and crowd came with spears and torches and took the Leader away as none protested after Judas' betrayal. The darkness fell, lifting again on the court scene with Pilate saying that the man was innocent and the mob clamoring over and over again, "He stirs up the people. He stirs up the people!" Pilate washes his hands in the basin and turns Christ over instead of Barabas while the mob cries loudly that it will be responsible. Never have I seen the revolutionary emphasis placed upon the Christ teaching so accurately and truly as in this scene.

The final scene was of three crosses on the hill, with the seven words, as Mary kneeled at the feet of her son. The suppliant was promised Paradise today as the mob howled that he could save others but not himself. The slight rise of ground in the garden was again ideal for the crosses to stand out above the gray rocks and the jeering crowd below. It was reverently presented, nothing out of key, scenes of human suffering significant yet humble, chosen and drawn together in verse, costume, personalities, makeup and emphasis by a director who has insight into the heart of it as well as training for pageantry.

Imperial Japanese Military Administration Office

Camp Administrator
General Committee
Executive Committee

Interpreter
Housing
Liaison
General Inspection
Censorship

Census
Group Assignment
Work Details
Information
Bulletins

Finance[12]	Health	Recreation Education	Judicial	Kitchen Dining Room	Utilities Miscellaneous	House and Grounds	Religious	Women's Committee
Budget	Hospital	Kindergarten	Justice of the Peace	Menus	Shop and Repair	Dorm heads	Worship Service	Sanitation
Store	Dispensary	Grade School	Police	Commissary	Electricity	Garden	Union	Kitchens
Camp	Pharmacy	High School	Jail	Diet Preparation	Water	Grounds	Anglican	Housing
Purchasing	Dentist	Adult Education	Codific	Grinding	Fuel	Barber	Roman Catholic	Work Details
Audits	Diets	Forum	Court of Appeal	Serving	Shoe Repair	Packages	Seventh Day Adventists	
	Sanitation	Library		Dishwashing		Sanitation	Lutheran	
	Inspection	Playground		Vegetables		Garbage Disposal	Religious Classes	
	Livestock	Athletics		Fruit				
	Nursery	Entertainment		Rice				
	Clinical			Butchering				
	Laboratory			Night Cleaning				

Now we know why so many men were growing beards, black, red and gray.

During all the scenes, trucks rolled noisily by on the road just below the garden, the guardhouse lights and radio were strong and loud, and two Japanese civilians from town crouched down in front of the silent audience to take pictures, the camera clicking in our ears for the first time in many months. Smith's dramatic, yet humble and self-effacing Christ was the key to the whole presentation. There is high praise for the director, his wife Winnie.

April 23, 1943. News that trickles in has all come to sound alike to me, for so long we have heard it.

Jim Bozeman is doing a good business in Gogo—an inner, lacy bark which is fine for washing hair, hands or body in place of soap.

Dr. Hall held the door open for us when we went down there, [was] excited as a small boy because he had heard the list of ten for Manila had come in approved and he was on it. He said he had missed the companionship of his wife more than he ever dared admit but now realizes as he is about to join her.

April 24, 1943. After many delays the 13 who were to go out to live in Baguio went off on the truck piled high with their belongings.

Since I told Regina that I was keeping notes which I would use in any way I liked if I left out names, Enid begins to have qualms and Regina thinks it is dastardly—shades of Somerset Maugham and hundreds of really good writers who collect material. There were no qualms until now. How many times have reporters been attacked for their wretched habit of relating both sides, events as they happened. If people would live and act as though all of it were to be printed and bound into a chronicle for the future to read we might not have quite so much to write about. Or if they lived as though today were the last, tomorrow too late for the good deed—would they be models or grabbing all in one last clutch? It is better to live as you would want your children to read it, I think.

There was confirmation of six by the Episcopalians at evening service under green boughs before white altar cloth and pure lilies on slender green stems amid tall candles waving flames.

The Mass Meeting—with the women suddenly given the vote when it had been subtly denied them in order to produce certain results. Now in order to produce other results, it is granted with wide gesture.[13]

Yesterday there was a great abundance of chop suey, with much left over. Tomorrow the children's menu reads "fricazeed chicken" for lunch and we have tons of beautiful cabbage heads which heretofore have been taken for the Japanese Army. It is time that the Committee put on pressure for this, after long inertia. Pressure at the guardhouse must be delicate, not too bullish nor too constant, yet kept before them to show our need without antagonizing.

April 25, 1943. I was awakened by the Episcopalian early Communion singing "Christ the Lord is Risen Today" which took me back to Mother in a pew at St. Stephens, her reverent, penitent little head bent over like one of the world's worst sinners. June and I dressed in the dark as the song continued, then went with Bedie to hospital point for the sunrise service of hymns, scripture and prayer. We faced the mountainous backbone of the Philippines like a Japanese print of layers of blue mist. Valleys appeared under clouds, veils drifting across five or six different ranges from low ones near and below, to distant piles towering and far. It was a soft, gentle picture, with the strength of the hills under it. We sang "Christ the Lord Is Risen Today, Allelujah" while on the road just beneath us Igorot men, women and children with heavy baskets held by headband to the back trudged in to market, and trucks loaded with Japanese soldiers and baskets of vegetables for their meals rumbled up the trail. Heavy clouds hung over the East but as we sang, the sun came through underneath, in long shafts of light that rose in the valley near velvet green rice terraces and shot up over the ridge. We have beauty at every turn and this we found more surely during the pageant and the sunrise service. Heaven is at our back door.

I went again to church in the sunken garden to hear Alan's sermon and to sing one of Mother's favorite triumphant hymns—"The Strife Is O'er, the Battle Done, the Victory of Life Is Won." Tears came and I wondered if Mother was standing up under the long strain and wait which is a dreadful test of endurance for one over 85. Two silver planes went high over us during the services.

We all had an extra special breakfast of bucaco cereal which is like millet. Also four delicious hot cakes apiece straight from the griddle in the kitchen, with a cup of coffee and a peanut butter sandwich—a combination and sufficiency we have not had since Christmas and a treat beyond words. At noon we had Spanish rice, a large section of cabbage and more bread. For dinner, we had spiced hamburgers with tomato sauce and bread and butter pickles. It was a Feast Day and Spring Festival. We opened Herm's milk for our cereal and coffee—oh how luscious! And we consumed their gift of canned sausage meat at lunch. It was really too many good things at once, but we like doing it that way after long food boredom.

April 26, 1943. In the month of May there will be kids born to mother goats every two and a half days according to the number of expectant mothers in the herd!

Fabian has finished another infinitesimal, beautiful, rivet job on June's glasses and she is radiant to have them on after a morning of listening in school. I left another mop pail at the shop to be tarred on the bottom to stop the leak. There is no more solder.

Dining room scene: Waitresses hustling to and fro with dishes, colliding with fond parents, doctors and a line trying to procure lunch ahead of anyone else. Beyond is the kitchen full of steam from the cauldrons and dishwashing and cookstove, men moving to and fro naked to the waist, stirring, grinding, staggering under heavy loaded kettles, mixing, washing and wiping. No restaurant could be more hectic than Camp Holmes behind the counter. Easter Sunday was no holiday at all for the cooks who not only made bucaco but 1,200 hot cakes and Spanish rice on top of that, plus hamburgers for 400 odd at dinner. There are many constant workers who plug along without any notice or credit or committee honors to give them a vote of confidence. Guerrilla Wick carries in market loads from the truck, vegetable loads from storage to the veg room, kitchen loads, and also does grinding and stirring with the big ladle at the stove. Gene is a chemist, teacher, server, dishwasher. Carl and Art are logrollers on the hill all day. Skerl rushes about with yeast mixture or peanut shells for soap base. He says he has netted 2 pounds of peanuts from 60 pounds of discarded shells, incidentally.

The piano is pouring forth notes under fingers long out of practice. One player is artist and scientist combined.

Hayakawa is sick with stomach trouble. Nakano is sick and they must have a picture of his lungs. Not only *we* wear them out, but their own factions tear them asunder. The man in uniform is to replace them, though it is not definite as yet. Hayakawa tells Miss McKim that this man has spent 11 years in America, knows Americans well and speaks excellent English. He considers us military prisoners and will be very strict. Miss McKim meets the officer named Kira and in conversation remarks that he must have been in America. He inquires why and she answers because of his accent and excellent English. He says he will have to change his accent, speak Japanese. He listens closely, watches her intently as she talks with other officials, then asks straight at her, "What were you doing in Japan? What was your profession, your work?" The daughter of the Bishop of Tokyo was born there and speaks the language with precision and beauty. Has she now become a spy, which all missionaries are considered to be by Japanese? We begin to wonder if this new regime will hold a Mukibo for us, with the circle becoming complete, back into the stern military phase with all the petty persecution and nervous energy released upon our heads as we sit helpless and take it.

There is a rice machine now installed in the veg room. Into a wide tin mouth, one pours the white grains down a long tin chute in which there are three stages of sieves. These also cast off the dust into two small side pockets, so that little grains of stone and other hard objects are gleaned out in one performance, the gray powder dust in another. It makes rice picking much simpler and easier. These principles are worked out at the shop by clever hands with inventive minds like Fabian and Irwin.

The Medical Committee met in the afternoon and Dr. Mather [told them] he could perform long hours of labor, but he could not cope with the friction

and pressure in the fight for correct sanitary standards. His health was sufficient to carry on his work but not against constant opposition to the basic
essentials of what should be done to minimize dysentery and therefore his
own labor. They presented him with new plans for sanitation, inspection, etc.
They hoped he would alter his decision but he said it was unalterable as he
had written in his resignation, for he could not work with the Committee to
which the entire camp had given a very recent vote of confidence. Most of
the new plans were his and Dr. Lee's recommendations for months past which
had been ignored or turned down and were now adopted. He withdrew and
the questions then poured upon Dr. Lee. She had to depart to feed her baby
but they had more to ask and waited for her return. Much was aired, cleared
and exchanged. It began to resolve and it is a pity that it did not come to a
head sooner.

Dr. Hall thanked me in a deeply moved voice for the great friendship we
had shown him and which he appreciated more than he could say. We can
never express to him our gratitude for the health, time and energy he has
given to our camp and our children, the long evenings of conversation which
took us far away from camp pressure and politics, often into the realms of
science and the future and which made us almost happy.

April 27, 1943. In conversation at breakfast one of the Sisters told me what
a Filipino doctor and another who escaped told about Tarlac Military camp.
More died there than at Bataan. For months they carried out from 54 to 200
a day. No soap, no razors, terrible sores under the beard growth all over the
face, and no treatment for it. No plates or cups or spoons—they were given
a ration of rice *in their hand*, sometimes too hot to hold and they had to drop
it, or they were so starving that they clutched two handfuls and were beaten
on the head and all of it knocked out of their hands. Filipino doctors tried
to smuggle in coconut shells for containers but nothing was allowed. The
deaths were from neglect and starvation and all this was broadcast in the
States at the time with a sending set still working here. It is too terrible for
us to contemplate right now. I shall never again complain of cups or spoons
after hearing this. What does anything matter in the face of such suffering—and
why do waitresses fight for place, Enid and Dean for power, all dominating
and unkind. This heavenly setting, beauty all around us—and nothing but
wrangling.

April 28, 1943. It is great business seeing people tread as though they might
be written up some day. They are considerate, wistful, polite, treading softly
and gently and not nearly so much trouble.

A Sister tells me of going out to the toilet at midnight, seeing a guard
crouched in the bushes [secretly] watching the hospital. One man remarked
that this would be an all-night session as it was bridge game night at the
hospital. This is what June complained about as well as old Mr. Ezekiel, and

others who wanted to leave the hospital, not because of crying babies who slept at night but because of staff parties below, much laughter and voices heard plainly until late hours.[14]

April 29, 1943. This is the Emperor's Birthday. Six guards and the Administrator lined up to face the Rising Sun with a hand salute instead of musket presentation this time.

May 1, 1943. Everyone likes the guerrilla and when one woman asked who is this Wick the answer given was, "When you see a husky staggering under a load, either mattress and blankets to the hospital, veg baskets on a pole, large tins steaming from the kitchen, or any kind of bulk belonging to someone, that's Wick; willing, generous with his strength, always looking for an outlet for his energy, glad to do anything to help and friendly to all who need it whether for camp or individual, a solid figure of a man." He is one of camp's hardest and most smiling workers.

Bedie confides shyly he has a girl, an Alice in Wonderland blonde. Many have spring fever.

In Japanese class Miss McKim gave the definition of Ronin—meaning a great deal in connection with the 47 retainers who committed hara-kiri after wandering till they avenged the death of the lord. This idea of loyalty, sacrifice to the point of suicide, has become a part of their religion and national life, even though Ronin have degenerated into gangsters used against the people.[15]

May 3, 1943. The ball game was a riot, what little I saw of it, and Wick seems to be developing into a genuine hero. He made base once on his stomach and chest with outstretched arms, and saved the day for the Hillbillies [team] in a grand finale by sliding into home, feet first on his back.

May 4, 1943. Two companies of Japanese soldiers walked down the mountain trail singing a Japanese marching song. The hills resound to strange unfamiliar echoes.

Jerry bends over and kisses me before God and everyone. One of those sudden, happy events in such a time. Like other couples, we wonder if we will ever be married again! There is so little opportunity to express affection in a mob, unless one has a Latin temperament! We are cursed Anglo-Saxons! What is the use stirring banked embers until one is free?

Dr. Hall had a wonderful malaria cell slide waiting for us. We could see the malaria devouring the blood corpuscle.

May 6, 1943. Confidential booklet entitled, "New Order. Short Essays Edited by Propaganda Corps of Japanese Imperial Forces": "The greatest single weakness of Philippine economy under American rule lies in this fact; that under the American system these Islands lost her economic independence and her power of self-support and what was formerly a healthy, self-supporting country was transformed into a helpless parasitic existence, completely dependent on the U.S. for supplies for the daily needs of life; became a colonial plantation for production of specific raw materials for American factories and the monopolistic market for manufactured articles. Now it is one of the fundamental tenets of political science that any semblance of independence can be maintained only when a country possesses a minimum degree of self-sufficiency. Before political independence can be enjoyed by a people, their agrarian and manufacturing industries must be organized into one compact and working unit and developed to a certain stage of efficiency through the sympathetic cooperation or direct technical assistance of some advanced country which is sponsoring this infant country's independence.'' Of course this substitutes Japan, but there is enough truth in it for us to heed afterward. It quotes on captures—''Sumatra surrender March 27—a total of 3,100 allied soldiers including 30 RAF aviators under a Lt. Col. were captured . . . Lexington and Yorktown sunk May 5–10 . . . Hermes sunk April 9. Kiska and Attu on June 8 in Aleutians. June 21, daring attack on military installations on Vancouver Island . . . June 22, a sub off Oregon staged a daring cannon attack on U.S. military installations near Forbrown and Westport near mouth of Columbia River . . . June 4 and 6 destroyed 21 aircraft and large part of important enemy facilities at Dutch Harbor . . .'' It lists:

Jan. 2—Fall of Manila	Apr. 9—Fall of Bataan
Feb. 15— " Singapore	Apr. 10—Occupied Cebu
Mar. 8— " Rangoon	May 7—Fall of Corregidor
Mar. 16—Occupied Mindoro	June 7—Landing in Aleutians[16]

May 7, 1943. Holiday for the Fall of Corregidor. I washed clothes and mended. Jerry brought ferns and orange berries and a pink orchid from the hill.

Men's Committee Minutes: ''The Pharmacy has been set up in the operating room of the hospital and all stock of drugs turned over to the Pharmacist. The Chair stated the operating room seemed the most suitable place because running water and a hot plate were convenient when needed in preparation of prescriptions. In joining these two departments it is possible to share the limited amount of equipment necessary to both Pharmacy and Operating Room . . . The Executive Committee now censors all correspondence going out of camp, before it is turned over to the camp administrator. Denki asked that a mailbox be made and set up near entrance to dining room for deposit of all outgoing notes. Those posted before three will go on the following morning, after three will be held till next day . . . We are fortunate in getting the approval of the authorities for controlling our own finances.

The Chef as Purchasing Agent had made three trips to Baguio and we have, even at this early date, seen the benefits to be derived from such an arrangement.''

Jerry is still chuckling over an episode in the shop. He was sharpening his small knife on the small whetstone when he was suddenly confronted with a long blade headed into his stomach and held by an Oriental hand. He looked up, into the smiling face of a guard who was proudly comparing the *size* of his knife with Jerry's. Later Jerry saw the same soldier turning the grindstone for Jim Bozeman to sharpen his murderous looking knife! In a short while, he looked again at the same picture reversed—Jim turning the grindstone while the soldier sharpened his long blade with a bone handle. We laughed as we recalled how they took nail scissors, nail files, everything sharp or pointed from us that long night at Brent.

May 8, 1943. Nida sent us a wonderful bag just as we were running low on sugar and coffee. She put in a big sack of pulverized coffee, the native kind which I love, two kilos of white and shining prewar sugar, a huge papaya, a bag of fluted cookies, a Peter's tin of pulverized chocolate.

Committee Minutes: "On motion carried it was decided to set aside a definite area for a cemetery. The House and Grounds department is to arrange for fencing and upkeep. . . . Kenneth Jorgenson has accepted the responsibility of getting the teenage boys interested in nature study. He plans to make trips up the hill and about camp so that they may study bird and plant life. Permission for these trips will be requested.''

During lecture time Jerry and I sat outside where the fog parted to let shine a thin silver crescent and two stars, then closed in till only the dark pine and two dim lights on each side stood out, the nearby guardhouse looking as misty and romantic as a teahouse in a Japanese painting.

May 9, 1943. I slept late then we all had our Sunday special meal of scrambled eggs and fried pineapple slices as well as hotcakes in which Wick joined us. Wick is as shy as Bedie who kept darting delighted and thrilled side glances at his idol. But they all unbent over a quantity of hotcakes with tomato preserve. It was a pleasant breakfast in the little smoky cookhouse with Jerry Aladdin at the clay stove. The children were all aflutter and had made a surprise corsage for me of white lily and bougainvillea of cerise color since it was Mother's Day.

Jerry washed clothes with Gogo bark and a bamboo plunger while I studied Kata Kana,[17] then we sat on hospital point looking at emerald and moss agate for half an hour.

May 12, 1943. Camp sights: Larry on the lower bank back of Dorm 2 gathering up for his garden all the onion roots cut off from onions cooked in the private stove kitchen. He assembled a large boxful. His garden has produced wonders for all of us. Skerl goes by with two huge sacks of peanut shells over his shoulder, en route to make soap. The garbage wagon rumbles by full of children on a squealing joyride, with Green running up to put on young Chuck who refuses to bend his legs and sit down. Green's worried scowl as he tries to manuever the plump little limbs into relaxing is delightful. They love to ride this old wagon.

A group conversation on the hill started casually enough and worked up to a fine pitch of razzing over the graft of the kitchen and hospital at Camp John Hay—how the girls gained weight on "rice and bananas" at the cottage hospital, how Dean kept supplies under his bed, alcohol was used in vast quantity for drinks with many cans of fruit juice. There was also kidding about the cans of fruit which were used by a few because "there wasn't enough for everyone." Some of us could have consumed our *own* supplies in this case instead of watching others steal it from the storeroom. The strawberry shortcakes, the cherry pies, the dozens of cans of milk opened for the kitchen staff alone—all these memories arose yesterday as alive and vivid as ever for they will never die and never be lived down.

May 13, 1943. Committee Minutes: "All exposed hot water tanks must be lagged (covered) in order to conserve heat and firewood. Denki was asked to investigate the possibility of supplying a more suitable gong for meals since the present one cannot be heard in Dorm 1. Mae asked that light bulb and chairs or benches be placed in ironing room so that children might be taken there at night. This was referred to Utility Department. . . . The question of supplying more substantial breakfast for those who do heavy work was discussed. The Chef said he was aware of this need and would do what he could to take care of it. . . . Motion carried that the Utility department be asked to look into the feasibility of changing or extending present shelter passageways for rainy season, any changes to be governed by their decisions. . . . Dr. Skerl's motion carried that a committee be appointed to investigate feasibility of creating a Welfare or Social Service department for distributing of clothing or any financial aid that might be forthcoming in the future."

In talking with Dr. Hall and Jerry, who did not go up the hill, [Hall] mentioned that during missionary questioning they were asked over and over who was the oil man who had done so much for China. When they returned they warned Jerry to be ready to go any time. Then Rufus died and the questioning stopped abruptly. Jerry said he fully realized he might be in for a damn good beating if not more, and possibly me, too. We had heard the talk about the wealthy oil man they were looking for but never connected it with Jerry either in wealth or oil.[18] When I wrote many months ago of the debt many might owe to Rufus Grey,[19] I had no thought we might be included particularly, until today. Now I can see it. How strange that by someone we

did not know at all, a turn of tragic circumstances, we may have been spared
months of mental and physical suffering, possibly even death, yet not realize
it until now—long afterward. It still seems odd that they did not discover the
matter in some other ways for we long expected to be questioned as Hayakawa
and Nagatomi knew it. Something seems to have watched over us.

One girl who was trying to get something mended by her husband, failing,
says that next time she is concentrated it will be with a sweetheart, not a
husband. This seems to be an indication on who gets things done around
here.

May 14, 1943. Jerry and I went to see Mrs. Barz. She looks well and her
personality is softer, not as sharp and acid as before this experience. She has
changed quite a lot for the better. Jerry asked where the ringlet-haired baby
was born and she said, "In a dynamite bodega near Dyaka mine, Dr. Biason
attending." Their first child in nine years of marriage was born in the center
of war. When her husband was asked to go on a hunt[20] she requested to come
in to camp to get better food.

Jerry is kidding me because he shaved off his mustache two weeks ago
and I never noticed till someone remarked on it today. Then I exclaimed that
I thought he looked different, sort of gray. He showed me the difference by
kissing me, scandalous conduct for Concentration.

Camp Holmes Judicial Code
Effective May 8, 1943
Procedure

The camp, through its constituted authorities, or any private individual,
    may bring charges against any other individual in camp in accordance
    with the following procedure:—

1. Complaints shall be made in writing and handed in to camp office.
2. Complaints will then be handed over by camp office to Chief of
   Police for determination of merit.
3. Should Chief of Police decide, upon due investigation, that the complaint is justified, he will submit same to Justice of Peace whose turn
   it is to try the case. The three Justices shall serve in rotation.
4. The Justice of Peace will then instruct the Chief of Police to summon
   the accused, the complainant, and witnesses, if any, and proceed to
   try the case at a time to be determined by Justice.
5. Once the complaint shall have reached the trial court, it may not be
   withdrawn by complainant.
6. Cases shall be handled by the Justices with least practicable delay.
7. Should the accused be found guilty, the Justice shall instruct the
   Chief of Police to see that specified sentence is carried out.

8. Should the guilty party be dissatisfied with decision of Justice, he may at once appeal the case to a Court of Appeals consisting of all three Justices.

9. Should an appeal be made, sentence shall not be carried out till after the decision of Appellate Court has been rendered.

10. Court of Appeals may sustain, reject or alter in any way the original decision of the Justice of Peace. Sentence shall then be carried out under supervision of Chief of Police.

Rules, Regulations and Offenses

Infractions of the following rules and regulations of the camp shall be considered within the jurisdiction of the Judicial Department.

1. The selling, purchasing, or drinking of alcoholic beverages is prohibited in camp outside of the guardhouse.
   Penalty—3 to 4 days in jail.

2. All messages, letters and other communications intended for those outside camp must be sent out through regularly constituted channels.
   Penalty—5 to 15 days in jail.

3. No one is allowed out of bounds (including the veg garden below drainage ditch leading from septic tank and the wood hill) without the express permission of Japanese authorities.
   Penalty—1 to 5 days in jail.

4. Men are not allowed in women's quarters, nor are women allowed in men's quarters, except for a valid reason and then only by special permission of a member of Executive Committee, the head of dorm concerned, or in the case of sickness, permission of the doctor in attendance upon the case.
   Penalty—3 hours hard labor to 5 days in jail.

5. All persons must be in barracks (which include the toilets and bathrooms) by 9:30 P.M.—with the exception of those who have assigned duties elsewhere.
   Penalty—2 to 10 hours hard labor.

6. All persons under age of 18 are required to retire at 9:30 P.M., the time of the official "lights out."
   Penalty—2 to 5 hours "woodpile."

7. All individuals must observe the regulations regarding "lights on" and "lights off" established by the Japanese authorities.
   Penalty—1 to 5 hours hard labor.

8. The use of electrical appliances of over 750 watts constitutes a grave danger and is therefore absolutely prohibited.

Penalty—temporary or permanent confiscation.

9. The use of private hot plates and other electric appliances is prohibited between the hours of 6:30 and 9:30 P.M. and they may be used between the hours of 9:30 P.M. and 6:30 A.M. only in cases of necessity.

Penalty—temporary or permanent confiscation.

10. Smoking in bed is discouraged at all times and during the "lights out" period at night it is absolutely prohibited.

Penalty—1 to 3 days in jail.

11. As a matter of courtesy men are instructed to stand at attention whenever an officer of the Imperial Nipponese Armed Forces passes near their vicinity while on an inspection tour of camp.

Offenses

Anyone who commits any of the following offenses shall also come under the jurisdiction of Judicial Department.

1. Refusal to perform camp duties to which one has been assigned by proper authority.

Penalty—1 to 5 days in jail and/or 5 to 20 hours hard labor.

2. Persistent neglect or shirking in performance of camp duties.

Penalty—1 to 3 days in jail and/or 5 to 10 hours hard labor.

3. Theft of personal property.

Penalty—Restoration and 1 to 10 days in jail.

4. Willful and wanton destruction of property.

Penalty—Restoration where possible and/or suitable punishment by the parents. Parents will be held responsible for such offenses committed by their children.

5. Appropriation of articles recognized by the camp authorities as camp property, at time of publication of this code.

Penalty—5 hours hard labor to 1 day in jail.

6. Infractions of local regulations (such as those governing the kitchen, dining room, bathrooms, dorms, etc.) which have been set up and duly published by authority of General Committee.

Penalty—at discretion of court.

7. Conduct prejudicial to good order and camp discipline.

Penalty—at discretion of court.

General Rules

1. The penalties specified in the above code are to be considered the

normal punishments. In the case of repeated offenses or offenses of an aggravated nature, the Justices shall have the right to impose sentences at their discretion according to the gravity of the case.

2. In the case of jail sentences these shall be understood to include the restrictions of diet, unless advised against by the Medical Committee.

3. Sentences consisting of hard labor shall be carried out in addition to and outside of the time of the regular camp details of the person sentenced.

4. In case of misappropriation of property, public or private, search warrants shall be issued by any one of the Justices of Peace at request of Chief of Police. Searches must be conducted in the presence of the accused, the complainant and one or more representatives of the police force.

5. Records of the cases tried shall be kept on file at camp office.

May 15, 1943. Bedie has grown very tall in here—his striped pajamas are almost up to his knees. Someone said he enjoyed seeing how much care and time Jerry devoted to Bedie for they seemed wonderful pals. This is a reward for Jerry who has struggled hard to become acquainted with his son, to guide and train him a little in this difficult [time]. They had less companionship before the war.

The Sergeant has remarked that once he thought Japan would win but now it looked as though America would. When Miss McKim asked him why, he said we had many more planes. She asked if Japan couldn't make them too and he replied, "Not as fast as America." He also told the Americans that America would come to retake these islands some day, that it would cost a lot in life and money but that America would succeed—and that meanwhile Dean could make the sick well and the rest of the men could play softball. This is priceless. He said it was very boring to take care of camp, so monotonous, nothing happened. It was apparent they would welcome a happening of any kind, even infractions by us so they could take action. We are bored alike, welcoming rumors whether good or pessimistic, just so we can chew them to pieces and have something, anything, to put our teeth into.

May 16, 1943. From the May 1st, Manila *Tribune*, front-page story headed, "Aliens Assured Good Treatment":—"The General Committee of enemy aliens interned at Camp Holmes Concentration Camp in Trinidad, Benguet, recently sent an open letter to Americans and British at large in North Luzon urging them to surrender as they are assured of good treatment by the Military Authorities." Following a list of the committee members, the letter, recently published in Committee Minutes, was quoted in part without change of wording. And some of them heard it go by radio to Australia! We are now *in* the propaganda machine to get guerrillas to surrender.

May 17, 1943. Jerry admits he will miss Bedie terribly if he moves out into the Boys' Cottage. Bedie feels the same way and may decide not to leave. He is subdued and worried over Herbie not coming back from the trip out.[21]

Many women are stewing and rationalizing over the new work demands. It makes me tired. They find so many reasons for not working, twisting and turning this way and that.

I felt almost sick after supper over the whole business of the Committee letter which is now famous. The letter was the price of our new political setup and control of finances. Of course we should have had these by right. Arthur wanted control and his position was weakened as he was maneuvered into writing the letter. Now he says we had no choice but were forced to do it. It is too bad they negotiated, for it seems hardly worth it though perhaps it may be in the long run. Jerry thinks it was poor judgment, ill-advised. Art is sick about the way it was garbled, twisted and misquoted, but he had been afraid of that all along. The [Executive Committee was] told that any member who refused to sign it could not remain on the Committee and it looked harmless enough so most of them signed.[22] It turned into an Oriental maneuver. According to the *News* only five names were broadcast the first night—three doctors and two reverends. Only titles seem to be impressive and doctors particularly useful as to food being "adequate." This seems to have been the "important, secret negotiations" hinted at during election time, the reason why the Committee must be kept in. There can be no dickering, no bartering, no bargaining in occupied territory. The only way is to deal openly and directly or take what they hand out. One can be outmaneuvered so easily. The price was not worth it. It was too tricky and dangerous and has weakened our position all around.

May 18, 1943. Talk, hammer and pound is all about Swing or Hang these days. We are not monkeys or criminals—just putting beds up in the air suspended from the ceiling. There are 17 in this dorm, which now resembles a Pullman car with uppers and lowers.

May 20, 1943. The shop has over 50 or 75 orders for wooden clogs which were arranged on shelves in all stages of carving down to the big log measured off in sections. Souvenirs are the latest thing. Daphne is selling her campsite sketch, colored, for 75¢ each with any requested additions. Jerry is carving an oval tray by hand for June's birthday. She will treasure it.

Eight went to town in a coupé. Dean brought money back; Wengel went in on his own loan matter—not for camp as a whole but for several chosen ones; Arthur for tooth X-ray; and others. They usually have drinks and transact business of their own as well as for camp. Being on a committee helps one wangle oneself around while doing the general good.

There are classes in French, Spanish, German, Greek, Latin, Japanese, Ilocano, Tagalog and English in camp now.

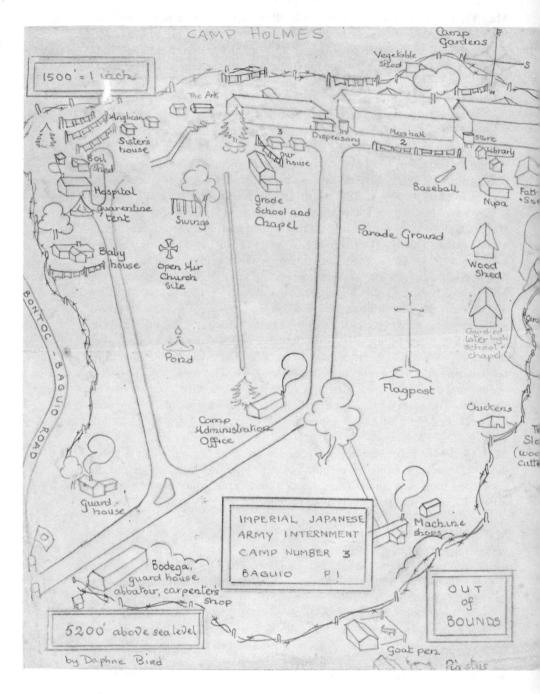

May 22, 1943. Wick and McCuish arrived looking very fit.

I keep thinking of Vanzetti in that awful Charles Street jail for seven years before he was electrocuted. That horrible suspense and waste of a good mind! I think of those other prisoners on Ellis Island in dead of winter without bedding or blankets in a room with no heat and broken windowpanes. This is paradise compared to the treatment of political prisoners in our country and other countries.

Jerry says Wick and McCuish walked two days then were held five days in Itogon jail. They say they should have danced to pay for their fried chicken and roast pork. Two men on a manhunt, jazzing for Igorots is a typical paradox of war life.

May 23, 1943. We played checkers, interrupted by Bedie's inability at arithmetic. Jerry scares him when he tries to help him.

May 24, 1943. Jerry came to oil my shoes so I sat out front with him while he did it.

Wick says MacArthur has done very little so far, even in New Guinea, and the Solomons are not all ours yet, contrary to rumors.[23] He wouldn't mind going to Manila as we could wear less clothing. Jerry agreed, and I almost exploded, they were so serious. Both of them wear only khaki shorts all day long at work here and Jerry up on the hill wears only fundoshi [G-string], so I am still wondering what they would take off.

The boy Palmer, American driver for the Japanese, survived the march from Bataan, saw men die, shot or bayoneted right and left. It was 120 miles of walking in bare feet, no food one day and no water one day. How any survived it and what happened afterward is a miracle for it was not by intention of the Japanese that they survived. No wonder Palmer is unafraid after that.

May 25, 1943. Dr. Skerl is now the last word in our family. June is entranced with General Science under him, tells me about rock layers in Grand Canyon and is busy feeding flies to poliwogs found in glutinous mass in pond-eggs biding their time.

I slept after lunch but still feel great lack of energy. I wish we could have more extras, eggs more often, but our cash must be stretched and we can't afford it. Rice flour is getting scarce and skyrocketing in price. Rice in town is rationed.

June has another gift from her boyfriend—a penny shined smooth and set in polished wood square engraved, "June. Baguio. Camp Holmes." She is amazed and pleased, doesn't quite understand it!

May 26, 1943. A basketball game in thick fog was wild and amusing.

Bedie was homesick again, drawing pictures of the house, the dog and cat. Jerry brought some pink wild oleanders from the hill.

May 27, 1943. Thousands of wounded have been brought up to Baguio which is now the Rest and Recreation Center for the Imperial Army as it was once for Americans.

Women's Minutes of the 24th: "All women of camp have been approached in regard to Community work. On the whole, the response was very satisfactory and the Committee appreciates the cooperation of the women in this respect. Report for the 'committee on used clothing.' Several requests were fulfilled by substantially patching the owner's present garments or by suggesting various trades of garments. Brent curtains and theatrical costumes furnished no small part of the raw materials needed to fulfill some of the requests. Except for a box of high-heeled pumps (No. 9 and up) and three boxes of clothing to Dr. Lee, no old clothing has been received by the camp from friends on the outside since Christmas. Our supply of these materials is almost exhausted. . . . However, donations of old clothing by camp members continue to enable us to fulfill many requests. These old things patched or remodelled produce startling results. We are not forgetting the great amount of private mending, sewing, and giving of clothes which help to fill necessary gaps of the camp. But if you have anything you do not want, please give it to us, we'll have a use for it. Other requests will be fulfilled as material and time permit."

Here is a *News* quote of Jim Halsema in one of his best moments: "Perhaps the principal intramural pleasure here is giving or being invited to parties. Almost any excuse is enough to find an occasion, but one must find the ingredients and place with difficulty. We have been given this outline. Who to ask?—1. The person who gave you an extra (rotten) banana at Camp Hay when you were hungry. 2. Someone who works in the kitchen. 3. People who have lived far enough away in dorms to still be friends. 4. Those who refrain from excessive argumentation on subjects theological, political or otherwise. 5. Someone who does you a good turn occasionally, like minding the baby. 6. Mrs. So and So because she has such good chow at *her* parties. When?—1. After children are asleep. 2. Not on Bridge Tournament or Jap Class or Camp Entertainment night. 3. After a fairly filling camp dinner. Where?—on benches 'looted' outside if clear; in the dining room if it rains and you get there in time to reserve space; elsewhere if you can manage."

Miss McKim says the Japanese Colonel told her he became "natsukashii" [nostalgic] when she talked in Japanese to him. They call her "Obasan" [Honorable Aunt] when they want her to come and converse!

Ray has put in an electric light at last for our corner after a year of darkness. It is marvelous, brilliant, exciting!

Our 18th month starts today and we wonder if it will go on into two years. I could howl at thought of being stuck here with some of these people another six months.

May 28, 1943. I mopped half the porch in addition to regular work. Mary

Tengren is not keen to do mopping and prefers to work at the playground. I may have to divide the porch work. No one wants to even share my job, get wet shoes and muddy pants. I can see it is something out of this world to mind it as little as I do.

The guards saw Eric and his wife eating together at the shop. They asked if it were husband and wife and they said yes. Guard said, "All right, eat together if husband and wife. Sleep together—husband and wife make baby, not all right. Soldier cannot do it now. No one can." A delightfully simple explanation of how they all feel. When Miss McKim was told the above tale about making baby, she said with a gay laugh and raised eyebrow voice, "Ah, but the trouble is the Japanese soldier can and does!"

May 29, 1943. We had large kidney beans baked for supper and they were so good. A guard came in to the men's cook house where I was sitting eating from the plate on my lap with Bedie standing behind me. Jerry was cooking fresh mushrooms combined with a can of celery soup. The guard stood with his feet planted apart in front of me, looking me all over, I looking back straight into his eye and smiling, not moving an inch. He smiled, and departed. After supper there was a ball game and a piano concert in the evening. At the rice table, Scott and Miss Lucy, Dr. Hall and Skerl, Jerry and I sat on the table talking past, present and future over a wide range. The two scientists wondered if research had stopped everywhere due to concentration of world's energies on war, limitations by governments such as Germany, lack of financial support for it etc. The stars were out, the evening was soft and cool.

May 30, 1943. I called on Mrs. Morris through her window. Both her children are malaria suspects. They were held 39 days at Asingan, her husband tied with a rope at his waist and made to lie on a wooden platform most of the time like an animal. The heat was bad, the food awful and there were no conveniences.

Patches on slacks, skirts, blouses and shirts are Concentration style—vivid, no attempt to disguise or to match color or material. They are downright obvious, poor, and proud of it.

Grandpa in jail gets only *one cup* of water a *day* to drink *and* wash in. This is the same regime the others had and they got dehydrated, constipated and very depressed.

June 1, 1943. Two of the guards are thrilled over the piano and three times yesterday they brought Japanese songs for Fildey to play so they could sing.

Moules tell of going into one barrio on their travels and asking the Igorots if they minded their staying. With their usual hospitality, the Igorots assured them no, pointed out the best house (also vacant) for them to settle in and helped them to occupy it. However, the next morning, Moules woke up to silence and found themselves the only ones in town. The entire village could not take the risk yet did not want to refuse, so they moved out en masse. Moules of course soon moved on.

June 2, 1943. Two guards, curious, invaded our toilet and baths and caught one with bloomers down. There is a furor over it in our dorm and complaint lodged at guardhouse by our Committee.

During Japanese class, the biggest event of the week in our barracks was catching the Theosophist violently ill and whisking her off to the hospital against protests, on a stretcher. She has been a problem for several weeks to the toilet cleaners and yesterday was awfully nauseated as well as involuntary. The toilet staff worked a couple of hours cleaning up and so did Mae, who scrubbed her space after the bed left. The lady's religious scruples may have been a source of infection to camp for some time. Dean brought a can, Nurse Rosa got a specimen and without waiting for report the patient was taken off. They are having a time with her—she won't take medicine, won't use the bed pan, won't eat.

June 3, 1943. The *News* says that 27% of our members are under 18, 64 boys and 73 girls; 167 men and 204 women over 18.

From the *News*: "More than 21 long tons of food were consumed by Camp Holmes members during May, according to statistics compiled by Frank Knight. Total cost P7,606.43 for 508 members was brought in, in addition to bought food at the store and private packages. 21,781 kilos of food of which 2,261 kilos represented meat etc. costing P2,411.65 (659.5 kilos of beef at 73¢, 1,413 kilos of pork at P1.05, 65 kilos of fish at P1.65, plus 3,300 eggs at 10¢ each and three kilos of liver at P7). We ate 2,343.5 kilos of camotes, 288 kilos of Baguio potatoes, 1,265 kilos of tomatoes. With a new purchasing policy, okra declined to 8 kilos, cincomas to 45 kilos. We ate 2,100 kilos of papaya, 1,320 kilos of Hubbard squash, 335 kilos of salt, 55 sacks of rice. Some of the many items. 'The kitchen through its sale of yeast bread, rice flour, cassava flour, and grinding services to individuals of camp has been able to add bucaco, camotes, green onions, bananas, coffee, vinegar, tomatoes, garlic, spices, papaya and baking soda to our food consumption' says a recent Committee report. Coffee, vinegar, spices and soda were items unobtainable except through the store."

June 5, 1943. Men's Committee: "The Chair reported that since a good many new internees had arrived in camp a request was made for permission to get additional mattresses. Camp Administrator said that many people were sleeping on two or more mattresses or pads. He conducted an inspection through men's barracks where numerous double pads and mattresses were pointed out (17 in all it is said). The General Committee has decided to make a list of individuals sleeping on more than one mat or pad and to take such mattresses for new internees, by lot, when necessary.''

Bedie got in a jam again with young Walter over a knife and the mother was naturally on the warpath. She called on Jerry and they went off to search. Bedie became scared and fibbed as he usually does when scared and was soon in up to his neck. It kept Jerry busy and interrupted the evening. The knife was finally found by Bedie in the middle of corn silk in his pocket. His latest fad is corn tassel cigarettes. He feels very tough and devilish but was sent to bed early under a cloud. He hasn't gained weight since we came in 18 months ago, is still 75 and growing tall. He needs eggs and milk but we cannot give them to him. June on the other hand is blooming, full of pep, gaining, eats anything, yells her head off at baseball and plays it violently. She is dating two different [boys]. One gave her flowers on the hill yesterday from where she and Bedie returned loaded with green branches, pink, lavender and yellow flowers. They also had a huge rock for General Science which clutters up our small corner.

We talked with Barz who says he had eggplant and other veg while out in the mountains, dried seaweed and dried cabbage in the lowlands the same as Japanese soldiers, and for two days he had nothing at all. They sent him out alone to look for Americans in one section, giving him money to buy food from the natives. He never met a soul and there was nothing planted or growing. He had been told not to come back for three days and he didn't dare go in any sooner, so he just didn't eat until he arrived back. We asked if he tried grass and he said no.

June 6, 1943. In conversation with Foster, he says the enemy slaughtered a whole village of 80—men, women and children—and it was horrible. They were accused of knowing where some Americans were and would not tell, so they were killed as an example to others. The villagers had been giving him food and he felt so badly about it that he decided to give up. Both men were in San Fernando jail for 15 days with about 80 Filipinos. They were given plenty of rice and could *buy* anything they wanted if they had money which was not taken from them. The worst feature was having the water shut off several times a day. When it was on, the Filipinos rushed for drink and bath, and about the time the Americans would get there, off would go the water. They were finally able to keep a can filled, also some small cooking pots they had. Jail members are always cut down on water. It is a Nazi-Japanese specialty. One Japanese captain yelled and bellowed and jumped around, gesticulating all the time he was questioning him, trying to get information. He was real Gestapo. I asked how long this went on and he said four hours straight. The Filipinos peeked in the windows and it was partly to impress them. We hope after the war all this Nazi and Gestapo stuff will be thrown into a dust heap. It is degrading not only for prisoners but for the men in charge. Many of them are sadists to start with.

Churchill promised offensive action in the Pacific *now*. I asked how soon is now and Foster said it had already started in the Celebes which is taken over. Much bombing first.

Tokyo last night reported that the Papal delegate said after seeing prison camps all over Japan that the "prisoners were being well treated according to the custom of the country." Exactly!

June 7, 1943. Jerry is feeling rotten, and has no energy at all. He and Jim are worried that they may have gallbladder trouble. Really it is just gaps in our diet which are beginning to catch up with us. Many are losing weight. I am down to 92, plus blood pressure of 88. We will just have to stick it till Roosevelt-Churchill and the Marines come through.

Foster says one of the worst lacks among the mountain people is salt.

June played cards with one date while the other one glowered. It is his turn tonight. She delights me with her natural manner. She thinks they try to date too far ahead and she wants to keep some evenings undated, just to herself. She is becoming wise already.

June 8, 1943. Jerry made elegant fried rice and bought a luscious pineapple which we ate with wind and mist and cold rain blowing into our faces in the cook-shed while Donald Duck splashed and reveled and scudded his yellow bill in the mud for bugs. Then he quacked and waved his wings in satisfaction. We all grinned, enjoying him.

June 9, 1943. The Japanese Army has taken over the pork from now on and there is very little beef, so tomorrow we are meatless. All is strict ration. More and more we feel the pinch of war, discover what Europe and China and Japan are going through as the blockade tightens and the enemy presses harder and scarcity grows. Jim in the *News* says that patched and worn clothing demonstrates the passage of time better than anything else, even the babies creeping and walking. Some outfits are very seedy but we are all alike in this, all equal. My sweater elbows are darned over and over.

June 10, 1943. No meat for Friday supper and this is only the start of short rations due to none in the market, so we are to have beans, onions, tomato and green pepper stew. We are fatless, meatless, sugarless, almost soapless and paperless and recipes are needed for such conditions!

June 11, 1943. This is June's 14th birthday and we woke early and talked of that day she was born. She asked me and I told her all about it as we are able to talk freely since she has grown up in here. Daddy and Bedie called us to the front porch for coffee for all of us with bread made by Uncle Church Scott, spread with peanut butter. Daddy presented his beautiful hand-carved tray and June was delighted with the smooth satin-finished grain of the wood.

Bedie brought forth the chocolate cream bars which he had the excitement of purchasing at the store with 5¢ of his own plus Dad's additional. This shows the state of then and now better than anything could. The first year of internment Jerry bought Whitman's chocolates in a box. It was still available and we had what we thought was enough in the budget to buy it. This year—no sugar—only 10¢ bars now costing 27¢ apiece, which is the price of two eggs which are now 12½ cents each, and we feeling 27¢ an exorbitant amount to put into a birthday gift.

Isobel gives June a pretty handkerchief; Church gives her a can of guava jelly; Carl comes with a mango and a boyfriend brings three budded orchids arranged and growing in a wooden case ready to hang up, which they proceed to do on the front porch. She is smiling and embarrassed.

There are three bags for June! Six mangoes and a pencil sharpener from Mrs. Saleeby; a beautiful frosted cake from Grandma and Grandpa with a pink towel and matching washcloth and a small tin of candy. It was exciting. Daddy turned hotcakes faster than any cook at Childs, in the men's cook house at noon for June, Bedie and Peg's three children.

After supper and my waitressing, we hustled to catch a place for June's small celebration of six guests for homemade cocoa with bean milk, Nida's sponge cakes and a coconut shell full of roasted peanuts. June invited two boys and a girl, Bedie invited his little blonde of the moment, and they all had fun at checkers. It was their first real party, as all others have been family affairs.

June 12, 1943. It was drizzly all day so no hill for June. A boyfriend made her a lovely coconut shell pin with her name burnt on it. Bedie did not screw up his courage to invite the blonde until late afternoon but finally walked up to it, wiggling and giggling. It is his first real date. Pat picked a bouquet of flowers from Camp Hay seed in his garden for June. She loved the flame and white balsam and soft, vivid nasturtiums. We put them on the supper table and we christened the tray. Bedie gave June his map of camp which we have pinned on the wall.

Bedie gave Peter a bloody mouth because he called him S.O.B., and Bedie said it was calling me names! He takes it as a very personal insult.

Men's Committee Minutes from camp store subcommittee: "Prepared lists for priority in the right to make purchases. Where the supply of any commodity is definitely inadequate to demand, it should continue to be the store's policy to ration such commodities from priority lists managed by the store. In the unlikely event of the store's obtaining sugar for sale, it is your committee's recommendation that this be made available in rations divided equally among the whole of the camp personnel." Three plans of rationing rice flour and other rationable commodities were presented by the subcommittee.

One of camp's little cherubs with his own particular share of hell upset his mother's cupboard with a resounding crash during breakfast. Every mother looked up with a face of anguish from her rice eating. The small boy's own parent was the last to realize it. It was a catastrophe—not a thing saved. Egg, glasses of newly made syrup, flour, broken cups and glasses, lids from tins emptied of contents—all in a sticky, brown, yolky, albumen, doughy, ground glass mess under the fallen cupboard.

Two women heard from No. 1 of Shell in Manila that both their husbands are alive and well, interned and gardening together in Hong Kong. This was so thrilling they could not speak of it without moist eyes, and more cash came to them as well, after months of scraping and privation.

At Anthropology Dr. Barton talked of the primitive herd and how we had relapsed into its ways in here—space friction, group battles, propinquity and neighborliness making friends (Jerry said this applied to the men's side more than the women's side and Barton looked quizzically at me), mission against nonmission; the early struggle for leadership, then attempts to hold privilege or to get more. He wants to hold a seminar and hear us go at it on data from observation in here. It was a lively lecture while a short typhoon roared, rattled and pounded on the roof and windows.

Barz told of their three moves outside when they gradually lost everything, carrying a small baby and all the baggage into various hideouts, which was very strenuous. He told of Dr. Biason being badly beaten up because he would not tell where Barzes were hiding. He said he would have been spared all of it if he had told but showed great courage and loyalty. His wife had died from seven bullets—nothing could have pulled her through. She was able to talk to her husband as she was dying, not unconscious at all. I can see her pretty, flower-like face, so gentle, and his so finely sensitive bending near her—then undergoing all that torture after she died. He couldn't have cared much about living for a while and must have been almost beyond suffering at that stage. Barz had urged her to come with the child and the sister to his hideout, but she wanted to wait for her husband to return. By then it was too late. They were surrounded and the jittery, frightened soldiers raked the bushes all around with rapid fire twenty or thirty times. Only the child escaped, by a fraction, grazed by a bullet. The two women hiding had no chance. Barz went back some time afterward to find the bodies but could not locate them. Faithfulness to his company group and standing by his friends who needed a doctor cost the Barzes an unbearable price, but he shows priceless qualities which are not wasted or unappreciated.

Bedie had June ask his girl to sit with him at the program but she was negative. However she came and sat by him after all and when I said, "Oh you didn't have your handful of peanuts that you wanted for her," Bedie replied, matter of fact, and very shy, "Oh it didn't matter. She's loose the same as I am and can't eat any." Concentration romance!

June 13, 1943. Tokyo announced the surrender of the Italian fortified island after weeks of pounding by our planes. We also heard of Düsseldorf obliterated by a thousand planes a day for three days—of which only 100 out of 3,000 failed to return.

June 14, 1943. June and I chuckled in bed over me trying to flirt with Daddy for three days but he just looks sad and growls. She giggled and told me to try someone else. This from my 14 year old daughter. Such ancient wisdom. I told her I didn't dare for Daddy would explode and then camp would have a real scandal. This sent her into fits of laughter and we finally told Daddy who grinned sheepishly but enjoyed it. By fair means or foul, we will have him relaxed and maybe he can enjoy life into the bargain.

Sylvia gave a party to celebrate hearing her husband was alive and she and her daughter able to dream dreams and build air castles again.

June 15, 1943. Kira was in our midst last night playing bridge with Gene and Fildeys. We will have to watch our conversation as Kira could be sitting just behind one in a wool jacket looking like an internee.

June 16, 1943. I studied Kata Kana and fell asleep just before supper. Meals are so dull. Beans nearly every day in place of meat juice. At Japanese class we learned that Kira said, "If the Americans invade and retake the islands, then you will soon be out and I will be in, in your place." He also says he is only "existing" now.

The *News* says, "Life continues its eventless, meatless, baseballless, sugarless, flourless, matchless, milkless, margarineless, comfortless, meaningless course, but we are all going strong."

June 17, 1943. Jerry made good soup from rice to which Mac added a huge No. 1 quality broken egg. As a surprise and for no reason at all, I bought four cakes from Edna made with cassava flour and banana and peanuts. They were delicious to us. We sat in the tiny cook house after the children left, in a pouring rain, wind blowing mist on us as I huddled in my raincoat, discussing loudly in order to hear each other over the elements, gesticulating and talking about Napoleon's character and whether men or events counted the most. Crazy as ever, we must have made a funny picture there, in the storm. I think we have had as much fun in this respect as anyone in camp. My old polio hip creaked, due to damp and cold, making me limp.

Baguio potatoes Lyonnaise for supper and were they tasty! We also were given an uncooked egg apiece. Jerry added four to these and made a yummy omelet with onions. We ate a little of the beans with some raw garlic, then threw out the rest. They are known as gas berries. But for a change we felt as though we had had a real meal. No place to dry, there is no place to sit and talk that isn't crowded or overheard.

June 19, 1943. Big American convoy in the Solomons near Guadalcanal.

I found fifty cents but turned it in and the owner was found so there was no chance to go on a wild fling.

"Committee wishes to remind members of camp that outgoing notes to Baguio are now being delivered through courtesy of the Camp Administrator. We have not always enjoyed this privilege. *Please* make your messages brief."

Rules on electric lights have been posted, giving us half an hour extra on dark rainy days, if we get permission from member of Executive Committee.

June 20, 1943. Jerry produced good coffee at noon and June and I kissed him in honor of Father's Day out in the smoky cook-shed.

Mrs. Coulter who often blows her top was at it all morning from one end of the backyard to the other. She had been disregarding dorm rules and was told that a warrant might be issued if it was not stopped. She broadcast a long gamut of opinion on the hospital staff, their freedom, their parties, commingling and privileges. There was enough truth through it all to make it difficult to combat and it gave camp some quiet chuckles.

Jerry made fried eggs and hotcakes for supper, and Dr. Hall, Mac, Jim Bozeman, our kids, Carlos, Curtis and I were all crowded into the cook-shed surrounded by pouring rain and having a huge laugh at Donald Duck throwing joy into the air from his puddle. Many fond observers, young and old, like his quack, white feathers, yellow bill and tiny curled tail which he flicks about amusingly. He now belongs to Jim, who plans to eat him. We all groan and kid him about eating our darling pet. Sitting on my small bench, the surrounding males made a curtain to hide me from the guards. We had lots of fun and oh! the taste of fried eggs!

In the fried rice at supper there was 5 pounds of pork for 500. It is the first meat for days and we whooped when we found a small piece. June laughed when I told her how gloomy my Dad became as Mums became more cheerful. She says it is like Daddy and me.

Fabian showed us the set of aluminum teeth he had carved to replace his broken set. He says they are smoother than the other set though they still need polishing down. At least they grind food and fill in a depression!

June 21, 1943. Mrs. Larson and Mrs. Junkin went to town with suitcases for two nights, to take bismuth and X-rays in connection with gallbladder trouble. Bob brought us a message from Ismael at the hospital, hastily scratched on paper. "Dear Mr. and Mrs. C. Everything is all right. Nida is in the hospital, operated on with appendectomy this afternoon. Much love to all. Ismael." How near it brought them and how upset and excited they must be. It was exciting to receive it.

June 22, 1943. The classic of Mrs. Coulter's tirade was when she said, "We were only doing what every respectable happily married couple does." Which points up the absurdities and contradictions of our situation. Here the freedom has gone to the unmarried or those without mates at hand. The rest of us get along apart somehow, very irate now and then! It is sabbatical year with a vengeance for most couples.

Manila *Tribune* quote of June 19: "The so-called big offensive so loudly publicized by Anglo-Americans is nothing but a fool's dream. It is your privilege and duty to collaborate actively, unreservedly and spontaneously with Nippon." A quote from Vargas at Manila Hotel: "In our deepest hour of despair and abandonment, Providence sent Japan to protect— enlighten—uplift—and bestow liberty."

June 23, 1943. One of the most pretentious couples in camp, who can't wash their own laundry, were recently very broke, now in borrowed funds are throwing a party for 90 guests. We hand it to them for the worst taste, the most asinine judgment, the most obvious play at politics, the poorest sports and greatest lack of community spirit.

I get many compliments on June. She is the kind of a daughter I wanted—natural, direct, sweet and spontaneous. I only hope she stays so.

Jerry couldn't eat the supper beans so had an egg. He is down in weight to 166, the first time so low since he was 17. He lost 9 pounds in 3 days in this last spell of sickness but report says it is not dysentery. I hate to see him hollow-eyed and gaunt but there is nothing to be done.

June 24, 1943. Junie has been going through her own particular brand of hell for about a week. Three girls and one lad have ganged up against her, make withering cracks, write Spanish epithets applied to her on her school desk, walk away when she sits near or freeze conversation when she comes. A desire for leadership and control is mixed up with it. Two of them are spoiled brats, the other at the cranky stage. They will all get over it but meanwhile it is putting iron into her soul or constitution. She has a good time laughing at games but they seem to resent this and try to destroy any pleasure, especially the one who does not want her to date any other. It will all pass but it seems unnecessary and very long to her.

June 25, 1943. Last night June kept talking after lights out about how she was going to fix up her room when she got home. I told her that things might be there and they might not so she must be prepared. In the morning she said, "Mummie, if all our things are gone then I can go and buy new things for myself. Always before this, people have sent me all of my dresses and clothes. Now I can choose my own, can't I?" I promised her she could. When I told Jerry he said, "Hm, she has grown up." He is right.

After supper the heavens fell around us and our world, as we have known it, crashed. We were walking on the road, smiling at the picture of Wick surrounded by a bevy of adoring little girls, he grinning in deepest embarrassment. Miss Gabriel came to call me to talk with Mrs. Larson, who had a bag from Nida and some things to tell me that she did not want to forget. We left Daddy waiting and went inside to look at the bag—green straw slippers from the closet, 5 fresh eggs from her hens, 8 fresh-cooked doughnuts, a gorgeous yellow bunch of bananas, green corn which she knows I love, and peanuts, with some little cakes for Alans from Corazon. Mrs. Larson thrust a ten-peso bill into my hand from them also. She told me at once that she had seen Nida's appendix at the hospital and it was in terrible condition. Someone told her that Nida was a very sick person. At this I mentally sank to the floor as the earth rocked and the rest of what she told me passed over like a tidal wave after earthquake—a huge wash of bad news without point or meaning after the first crack from the bat. Nida had told her that the Japanese had driven up to our house in a huge truck the day before yesterday and had cleaned it out—all my books, magazines—everything was gone except the piano and the stove. Ismael and the children stood by unable to lift a finger. He had sent the message Monday that everything was all right and he was standing by. On Wednesday it was all wrong and the past wiped out, to build a new future on the ruins. We could at least go home to sleep on our own floors. She was very anxious to have me know that they had saved all the things I most valued and that were irreplaceable—our ivories, the wooden box with my [Japanese] snap-books and the children's baby books, my collection of Bibles (this puzzled me but I soon grasped in the fog that it must be my Chinese Indusco books), the silver, etc. Also my big typewriter. All that we have left we owe to them. Mrs. Larson says Nida worries about my children's shoes, rubbers, would like to buy rubber boots but they are P10 a pair. She almost cried because she couldn't send June a birthday package, felt worse about this than the pain which came inside that day. She told how upset she was when they found all June's dresses had been taken in the night by looting natives who had dropped three in their hurry. It breaks my heart—it is more than I can bear now—this pure love and unselfishness from a Filipina who is seriously ill, thinking only of us, worrying about our things and our comfort. The contrast to what is going on and being given out by our own in here is too much. I hold on but for the second time something dies within and yet is born anew. It hurts enormously, yet it is too rare and exquisite to be borne. I go down and down under it, with roaring in my ears, bowed under the simplicity of being completely shorn, yet bestowed with the greatest and deepest of gifts at the same moment, humble before the affection, devotion and selfless loyalty of a Filipina who lies on a hospital bed "looking so young and pretty and weak." I would give many things to go in and be with her now. For the first time, at last,

I feel in prison, as though rows and rows of thick steel bars were holding me from her who needs help and friendship and return of the same depth of affection and understanding. I want to fly to her, to give her eggs, milk, and rest, all, everything to make her well. And we can do nothing. When June heard about her dresses, she looked up at me and said, "Oh, Mummie, now I can buy my own"—recalling our conversation in a flash, and it meant only this to her, no regret for loss at all. How blissful. But she cried over Nida and wanted to spend all we had to make her well.

We went out to Jerry and told him to be ready for bad news but first told him about the house then about Nida. He said I looked like the man whose car had burned when the garage caught fire from the house after his wife had run away with the salesman. He swore softly, helplessly, going over out loud all that had gone and what we must do if we could for Nida. Bedie came into the dining room and there in all the crowd, just as Daddy had heard it, I told him, minimizing Nida's health. He slowly took it in, put his head down on my lap and I let him cry quietly for a while until he raised his head and said in a smothered voice, looking straight ahead, "God damn the Japs." I told him the Japanese could not be blamed for Nida's illness, no one could. Right away he began to plan what we would do for her, how we would earn and spend for her. Each one in turn looked only toward this—the passage of possessions only the huge wave after a major earthquake. Nida is our family, our sister, our mother, her children are ours and we are welded together now for all time. She is the Philippines to which we are bound indissolubly by old and new ties. She represents their loyalty, all they have suffered, yet still stands, smiling and holding out her hands with gifts beyond purchase or price, rare and lovely bonds.

We sat in the dining room—gave up Bert's lecture on ant-free house construction, tried to play checkers and at last gave up. Jerry made hot cocoa which we drank with Nida's doughnuts. June had a white orchid fresh from the hill in her hair and her cheeks were pink as she played a game with a companion. I wept later after she went to sleep and was awake many hours, hearing two big booms at mightnight and another one later.

June 26, 1943. I wept all through breakfast when June said, "Oh, it will be fun, Mummie, going home and starting all over with nothing"—she went on and on, planning with the spirit that will count and the youth which will carry it, while I felt old, so old, for the first time. It would have been all she said—exciting, joyous fun, working together if only Nida was not under a shadow of being seriously ill. This I can hardly face. Perhaps it will not be as bad as we think. I will catch hold and go on soon with some courage. We may never again get so much bad news all at once. Our own house vacant will be heaven after barracks and bedlam.

Jerry says that from now on he feels like Jim—it is his personal war!

Bedie came home from ranging after flowers on the hill, looked at me reproachfully and said, "Mummie, you've been crying all morning!" Inside and out, he was right.

In Dr. Barton's class we discussed why certain races seemed to dominate at certain periods. I could see only dimly with my rocking mind but it pulled me along and started me ticking again. I was done in after two hours, my teeth aching and my head pounding, but I relaxed and slept after supper. My stomach feels well shot, like lead or rocks or a blob of iron. I am punch drunk but beginning to breathe again.

I slept soundly but woke feeling as though I had not slept at all.

June 27, 1943. In the shop, Denki showed us the new wood lathe they have recently completed over a long period of time from odds and ends of wood blocks made into the wheel, and various pieces of metal, machinery and a motor contrived into this great piece of utility. The recent craze is to carve chessmen on it from soft yellow holly branch on the hill, matched with darker wood. Smooth and well turned, they will make a fine souvenir set. Denki was rounding off a child's top for Francie's birthday. Ray had found green paint and black and was finishing an army trunk-locker in style. Fabian called me in to give me something—making two pairs of leather shoestrings before my eyes, with a sharp knife cutting round and round a piece of worn-out shoe leather, fining it down under a strip of wood, with the knife's edge held at the right place. Eric rolled a cigarette for me from his simple but useful little roller of paper pasted on a stick. He says they have made more than 160 bakia since April. There is no more metal for frying pans but over sixty were made. Sonny was making a metal cross as a gift. It is always a busy place.

Dr. Hall says not to feel final or sad about Nida as a typical gangrenous appendix is often called serious which it is not.

My mind dwells fleetingly upon possessions lost—Victrola records from 30 to 35 years ago in Boston; the antique Spanish table with heavily carved base ends, polished for days by Jerry; the one-piece Narra table made from a long slab to our design; the 8 carved chairs which we saw in the logs and watched for weeks as they were carved near Vigan; the Spanish couches; our wedding gifts—a Tiffany silver bowl like a calla lily whose flannel case now holds the checker marbles in here; the bronze god we packed by hand all the way from Peking fifteen years ago (he will probably go into a fighting weapon of some sort to kill our own men); the cloisonné bowl which was our first wedding gift as we left Peking; the willowware set so old and lovely; the colored green, lavender, pale orange, and pink European wineglasses bought from refugees as we are now; the Chinese china dogs which once brought us good luck in boom days—now all gone, not only boom products of jade and opal, but accumulation and gathering of thirty years including books of all kinds from psychology, English literature, university courses in drama,

Chinese and Japanese life, to the Webbs on Soviet Russia. We stand wiped out.

It is loot on a national scale, done by upper classes of officers, planned and coldly executed. This is not ignorant pillage under passion, or poverty seeing a chance to possess. It is done in the most calculating, degraded spirit by people holding themselves fit to govern and calling themselves a superior race, acting as low as any vandal of dark ages or as a racketeer from Chicago and the depths of the slums. The New Order, the Chosen People, the Rising Sun, performing exactly as ages of warriors have done before them. People are all alike.

From Manila paper: "The Japanese Neighborhood Associations [in Japan] have been grouped with 2,500 district associations. At this time when prime commodity supply is not sufficient, the markets have already ceased to be profit-making organs. Their function now is to make fair distribution of commodities. The telephone service is operated by the Ministry of Communications, the electric light and streetcars and buses by the Municipality. As Tokyo henceforth will become the center of the Greater East Asia Co-Prosperity Sphere, we presume that our relations with Manila will be closer."

June 28, 1943. 2,000 planes every other day are bombing Germany. The Germans are said to have asked Switzerland to harbor their women and children. Tokyo tells of Antwerp bombed terribly.

June 29, 1943. My head aches on one side and the veins stand out on my forehead. I feel and look like an old hag in spite of some relief from Ephedrine. I understand that line from *Lost Horizon* better now—of the little Manchu who left Shangri-la looking like eternal youth and when seen after buffeting the sleet and snow and storms of the world, frozen to death, "she was old, most old of anyone he had ever seen." Spiritually, it can come overnight and more than once when a lovely dream dies. We are only a part of the rocking world, taking the impacts in our various ways and sections. As Jerry says, no one gives any sympathy over losses—and no one expects it—because all are in the same boat and can merely exchange stories. It is universal, a world process, a tremendous shattering of values as well as possessions and materials.

Bedie was indulging in hate for the Japanese as we watched Jerry carve a new tray to replace our one lost at home, carved by other hands in a southern island prison. Jerry stopped him, saying, "Don't turn into a Japan-hater like some of these people. Blame the right things, don't storm at the wrong ones." Then we talk about the soldier-artist Yamamoto who had the best time of his life, the most friendly time, in this camp which to us is the lowest we have ever attained. We try to imagine how little he must have had, how starved his life, how wretched his diet, and we remember how eager he was to be friends and impart what he knew and loved in his own country which he thought was better than ours though it had given him little materially. We talked of the generally poor diet of the Japanese people which is apparent in their eyes, their teeth, their carriage and stature. And we hope for a better life for most of them who have known no more than Yamamoto.

Ray, with Kira, stopped us and asked if we would play bridge. Jerry said yes, but—. And Kira smiled cynically, a little despairingly, as though he had had excuses before. Jerry said he had an accounting class but didn't mind passing it up if we could get other players. I knew quite well I was left out of their thoughts but I said, "I'll play—" and I offered to get Sylvia. They agreed and she said she would enjoy it. Jerry went to get the blanket and cards and some tea and it turned into an unexpected, amazing and amusing evening which my perverse brain thoroughly enjoyed. Jerry poured the tea remarking casually that it came from a tea-taster American friend in Formosa and Kira said, "It must be good then." Almost on top of that, when I told him I was apt to be erratic in playing at times, he threw out coldly and tensely, "I may as well say that I have absolutely no sense of humor," which quite unnerved me as I had drawn him as a partner. It was cold steel across my throat! I didn't hear Sylvia bid a heart (it sounded like "pass" with her English *a*) and when he bid two clubs I took it for slam indication and went two no trump showing a bust. Realizing something was wrong, after three no trump, I left him in four clubs and we went down six tricks! That's all! Oh that cold steel! But from then on we got along fine. I didn't get my throat slit and he does have a sense of humor for he made slight responses to repartee and knows how to smile. He plays his hands perfectly and knows bidding, plays an excellent game in fact. The tin cups were hot and he found it hard to drink so let the tea become too cold. On the second round I asked if I could add some hot to it and he looked all around then poured the cold tea *under the table* and held his cup out for a small portion more. Sylvia couldn't help smiling and others at the long table lifted their feet. Perhaps he doesn't like tea, was being polite in some way. It may have been too strong or else we started off wrong. However, it staggered us to see a whole cup of our precious Formosa tea go under the table. Jerry asked him for a light and when he pulled out his matchbox, Jerry said, "Oh don't waste a match! Let me use the end of your cigarette" (in true Concentration economy and horror of waste). It didn't work so he got the match after all. Kira said he hadn't played for three years and Jerry asked where he had played then. He answered tersely, "Japan." Later, I inquired if many people liked bridge in Japan and he replied, "Nobody at all" so that settled that one. In the beginning, Jerry asked if he used Culbertson system of bidding and he said he knew nothing about it and played very badly. We soon demonstrated that to be evasive and unfounded, Oriental understatement or what you will. I looked at him straight and asked, "You like bridge very much, don't you?" and he nodded, deprecatingly, humbly polite, true to tradition. We dealt a hand at five minutes to nine and I said, "Wouldn't it be too bad if we found a slam just in time for lights out!'' He smiled and looked as though he would see the hand through. One had to watch every remark and he was no doubt doing the same. Once, watching June playing cribbage near us, Jerry growled without thinking, ''If we ever get out of this darned place I will have a cribbage partner now'' and this passed without comment. Daphne playing with three others just behind us discussed loudly that she couldn't tell Japanese and Filipinos apart. Her partner said he could but she reiterated ''not after all my years out here.'' Jerry made frantic eye and mouth motions at her until I almost burst with laughter inside but this passed too without comment. We weren't bad when we found our stride. Kira said he would like to play again sometime and I promised to be well-behaved next time and he laughed. He is lonely—well educated and out of his element in this mess. We wonder if he is trying to pick up information from conversations or just hungry for bridge and companionship? His English is very good, often slangy, except that ''club'' sounded slightly like ''crub'' as they have trouble with *l*. It was fun to make him smile and show a little humor in spite of his determination not to. No one can play bridge with me and not show a little. My sense of humor was at its height in such a setting, with a Big Sword at the throat. Even the Intelligence, cold and tense, couldn't squelch it. Kira is attractive and not dull.

June 30, 1943. There is Bill's story of being in a room with 40 or 50 Filipino prisoners, a space so small that only one half of them could sleep at once while the others stood. The man next to him was very sick and he presumes now that it was polio. We wonder if that poor fellow lived or died. Being sick in here seems bad enough, but in that jail, crowded, neglected—awful.

Another woman blew the works wide open to stem off the Committee and Judiciary. She is fighting for SEX and is pulling all the stops she can. She told someone what she had seen on a snooping trip of her own to the hospital. She names husbands and wives who were in bed together, and others down there not with their own wives. There was one room with a spring bed and mattress, two rooms with four couples in each with the doors shut tight. One room was playing bridge, the other not. She herself refuses to obey commingling rules when the hospital staff, including the chairman, and the Baby House are exempt. She says the rules must cover all or none. She really has something on this score.

Women's Committee Minutes: *''Do Not Wait for a Public Call for Workers.* Please record accurately and honestly the actual hours worked each day. . . . Endeavor to feel a sense of responsibility for getting the needed work done, not merely for putting in a certain amount of time. More time is required on some days than on others, but if each does her share the burden will not be heavy for anyone. TO ALL WOMEN WHO ARE WILLING TO HELP IN AN EMERGENCY. An announcement in the dining room or barracks or a public call for veg workers indicates an urgent need not only for regular veg workers but for volunteers from among those whose details are not heavy or any others who can respond in an emergency to help prepare the veg in order that beans may not be delayed. The above requests apply in principle to other details. Please observe!''

The *News* says the total rain for June was 23.4 inches—five more than average and 10% of year's precipitation. It rained 25 out of 30 days.

July 2, 1943. We had a grand bag from Nida—two hands of cooking bananas, four avocados, 2 bars of Luto soap [strong brown laundry soap], 4 packages of cigarettes, a package of cookies, and a bag of candies. Bedie took it in when it came and rushed over with his voice thrilled, calling me. We wonder how Nida is, whether she is home and we fret over every day that passes without our being able to do something.

There is much impetigo in camp which is spreading rapidly. It is unappetizing to see so much Gentian Violet or salve spread over people's chins.

Camp Fever
by June Crouter

I must go back to Camp Holmes again,
To the flies, and the rice, and the beans
And all I ask is a five foot square
There to dream my little dreams.

The wind can howl and mosquitoes bite
And the rain come thick and fast
But I'll lie in bed and dream my dreams
Of the future and the past.

Dr. Skerl told me his father had managed a cooperative in England. He said bluntly that Americans are too individualistic, which is quite true. What we most need to learn is cooperation.

July 3, 1943. Jerry went up the hill with the wood crew and June and Bedie went with the young fry under a guide. It does not matter any more—my hill is inside at last.

From the *News*: "Missionaries and families are the largest group here. Of 506 people at present in camp, 50 men, 87 women and 53 children, a total of 190—are listed in this group. Mines and lumbermen [are] 65, 40 children, wives and employees (female) numbering 40—for a total of 145. Business, retired and miscellaneous professional men number 43, with 34 females (wives and employees) and 28 children totaling 105. Camp has 38 women and girls without families or husbands here. In education group are 19 persons.''

Five different landings in the Solomons and fighting in the mountains of Dutch New Guinea.

July 4, 1943. We had specially good noon meal—onion and potato soup, gingerbread, veg salad with vinegar dressing and fruit salad of papaya and banana.

Jerry brought me a white orchid and Mac brought a branch of long green leaves with beautiful orange seed pods.

June and I find we do not have such gnawing hunger, such desire for almost anything to eat, since we have been getting some eggs. It must be protein lack that bothers us. But now that we have a little cash,[24] eggs are sky-high.

While Jerry took a long sleep I went to the Handicraft Exhibit until he joined me. It is unique. It combined county fair, arts and crafts, shop and garden and artistry, showing the things people can do with little to work with but a mind, some patience and plenty of time. The enemy should have seen this display before writing an article on American love of luxury, idleness and softness. We have some of that too, but so have they in the upper brackets. Before listing the most striking things, I will quote from the *News*: "Attended by a capacity crowd, dressed in their Sunday best (most of them, anyway) who stood patiently in line to enter. . . . Bereft of worldly goods, faced by both scarcity and high prices of all necessities and lack of money to buy them, internees have proved during 18 months that worn adage "Necessity is mother of invention." Ranging from boondoggling to chemical lab . . . it combined country fair and Early Development Room of Patent Office . . . with few tools and little material, men, women and children have created for use and enjoyment."

The line was continuous and the crowd kept moving past Dr. Skerl and others appointed to see there was no snitching or looting! At the door, outside, was a handsome white rooster with red and blue ribbon tied to his leg. He was raised from a Camp Holmes egg, inside the barbed wire, by O'Dowd, Jake and Bea who are proud of it. The guard gazed with much amusement at ribbons on the leg. Just inside the door was a tall stalk and tassel of corn at whose base were two large green pumpkins and some gabi raised by Larry on the green land below. On the wall near the door were some fine crayon and ink drawings of flowers. One of hibiscus, by our son, which was discovered by Jerry, astounded and thrilled us to think he could accomplish this unsuspected artistry.

There was a Camp Holmes sampler by Sue Burnett; baby books designed, drawn and painted exquisitely by Daphne Bird; baby bedspreads with the names of all the camp-born babies embroidered on them; Daphne's colored map of camp; a chessboard set beautifully fashioned in the natural shape of the piece of wood which was like the bow and stern of a boat, by Fabian; a tree-fern vase carved into beautiful relief of its own design by Jane Gilbert;

Jerry's satiny tray and his iron prong potholder; an eggcup carved as thin as china or a shell from wood by Dr. Skerl; Dick Patterson's dirigible with tiny motors; the Camp Holmes *Snooper* newspaper by the 8th grade; a sextant by Phil Whitmarsh and Lofsted; suede and leather baby shoes by Mrs. Morris and 3 men; Chinese checker game on a cloth sampler by Jessie Junkin; painstakingly fashioned dolls made and dressed out of scraps of cloth by Lucy Scott, Sylvia Harrison, Miss Sims and Miss Ashcroft; a Japanese doll which pleased the guard; a child's cart by Cam Gray; many sweaters of varied color and stitches by many hands; five or six months of a calendar, with paintings or drawings at the top. (The guard stood long entranced before Sylvia's pastel of a crimson hibiscus. He brought another guard to see it, then went back for two more. All stood gazing and loving it, wanted one to take to Japan as a souvenir. How even those who have known little but poverty turn to beauty and appreciate a lovely expression of it. They move and respond to it as to the sun—these fellows who are half-starved for beauty as well as food and may not live to reach their own country again.) Two watercolors of Florey as a goatherd in his canvas-strip raincoat, standing against a pine in Igorot pose which was very striking; lipstick made of beeswax from native honey and a dye; handmade dresses with handmade coconut or stone buttons; tools—bow, saw, needles (from fence wire), wooden drills of bamboo; coconut boxes with lids by Junkin; a huge ringed slice of tree-fern trunk made into a table of irregular shape, bound with brass; a handsome Swedish-style pocketknife with fine beveled edge and beautifully wrought handle by Lerberg (it is composed of an airplane strut, carabao horn, ramrod, copper wire, sewer pipe and pouch fastener); a soupbone crochet hook for his wife by Palmer, and the braided rug made with it by his wife; very effective high school lab material by Markert, Hungerford, and Thompson—a densitometer, sound transmission apparatus, an A-C-D-C converter, a still; a small wire eggbeater by Junkin; knitting needles; the prize aluminum false teeth by Fabian, with assistance from the dentist; vinegar made of pineapple, sugar and water, and sauerkraut, in bottles, by Erich Lenze; mint, onion and potatoes by Derek from his garden; Carol's and Wilma's garden produced squash, pumpkin, corn, onions, green beans, potatoes, strawberries, tomato and mint; the shop from its endless products submitted a bread pan, fluted round and shallow tins of varied size, hammer, saw, grapple hook, ax, ink, a frying pan, coconut scraper and bakia; they should have submitted the wooden press for making gallons of coconut milk. Jim Thompson's totem pole, hand-carved, was there with his explanatory remarks—"Very rare totem pole, found in ruins of Camp Holmes, date about A.D. 1943. Believed to have been used by prehistoric totem cult; top figure is thought to represent the lamentations of the cult for their square-headedness for getting in such a mess; the central figure symbolizing their national sickness (pigheadedness); the bottom figure represents the ultimate condition of these people—the rice belly.''

The exhibit was remarkable, covering all phases of camp life, with emphasis on the private and personal, rather than the communal and camp affairs.

July 5, 1943. There was a marvelous bag from Nida with half a pound of white sugar (very precious now), coffee which is also high and rare, a tin full of heavenly aromatic fresh-cooked pork Adobo (from our pig, they wrote on the list), half a can of molasses, two heads of lettuce, 12 ears of corn, two avocados, a kilo of camotes and some crisp young cucumbers. What an outlay! With it were nearly a dozen boxes and bottles of our spices, taken off the kitchen shelf before the invasion of Baguio. There was also a clean pack of cards but not from our drawer. We christened it at bridge with Winnie and Jo under very dim lights, so we finally argued about the Managerial Revolution instead and drank delicious hot limeade and Win's cookies which were very "short" with peanut butter.

The big happening of the day during breakfast was in an argument over P25 between the tranquil domestic Encinas of the night before. June met her after breakfast, covered with blood all over the front, holding her nose and being helped to the dispensary where they could do nothing and sent her to the hospital for repair of a broken nose. It seems her devoted husband told her as he stood below the window that if she didn't do what he said she would be sorry. She talked back and forth from above and the next thing anyone knew he was stalking up the stairs with a hammer in his hand, into forbidden territory without permission, struck her twice in the middle of her face (whether with hammer or fist is not clear), left her on the floor where she dropped without a sound of pain or protest of any kind, and marched off saying, "Maybe that will teach you not to lie to me." Her face was swollen beyond recognition, black around the eyes, and she was nauseated all night. He has pleaded guilty and no witnesses were called. Rumor says his wife asked that he be charged and tried. He had a reputation for getting into fights on the Outside.

June gave a succinct account of the trial—"All over in about ten minutes. Lombardi was the judge, King the recorder, the prisoner pleading guilty to two charges—entering barracks without a permit and assault and battery on wife. He was given a chance to make a statement without any questions but would say nothing. The sentence was 20 days in jail, 10 of these on restricted diet. He seemed penitent and subdued, and Lombardi acted regretful in imposing the sentence." The sentence starts immediately—but there is no jail! It is not yet ready. Of all things—a judicial code and court, a trial, but no jail.

After all—I have not put down what a great day this was. I was told there was big news among the men but they would not tell and would especially keep it from the Women's side. Out by the red water tank with Jerry, this information was divulged to me. It is what we have waited to hear and must not reveal until the Nipponese give out that they know it and tell it their way.

Europe invaded from two spots—Italy and northern France, with barges and men pouring in. It is the greatest naval feat the world has ever known, ferrying two millon men across the Atlantic with loss of only 235 in a barge accident. Two million men in Australia are *moving north* and four million more in America moving west.[25] Three of us grin and move away from each other lest our smiles and excitement be contagious, our pores give it out.

July 7, 1943. Miss McKim, no longer a chairman, is also relieved of interpreting as Kira has taken over this function, accompanying all the officer visitations at camp. It means we know less of what takes place.

Out in the cook house Ward came around the corner and asked if I would be interested in an envelope addressed to me from Grandpa containing ten P10 bills, the receipt marked under his name with the word "Nida." How wonderful it all seems, with our positions reversed in the Biblical manner, the master supported by the servant in more than one way. I signed the envelope as receipt and kept the slip itself with her name on it. I counted the bills so that Ward could witness that I could not charge Mr. Hayakawa, who brought it, with cheating us! If they help us, they can feel it is good security and investment. Jerry was floored, for all his anxiety is relieved. I could weep over it but I don't. Last week we were far down, trying to raise funds by selling our powdered milk to buy a sky-high egg now and then. This week we are almost wealthy with funds from several directions. It always seems strange that there is either famine or feast, that threads fed out months apart should be drawn together all in the same week. We must never forget what it is like to have no help, for this is the condition of thousands, millions all over the world.

July 8, 1943. The typhoon passes and sun comes out pale but visible. I write to Nida, aching to say more, "The Adobo and everything this week was perfect. We are sending the tin back in the bag. So many thanks. Do not send any rubbers or boots. The children do not need any as we have bakia made at the shop from logs. These are fine in mud and rain and they like them. Only get well for we want you to be better every day. It is all we need. The [playing] cards were most welcome. Again our love, especially June and Bedie." This is probably the epitome of restraint.

From the *News*: "Each Tuesday evening a little group gathers in a room at the hospital to discuss current camp problems. Although for the most part men with considerable experience (executive), their paths were divergent before the war, and they were interested in managing gold mines, schools, missions, hospital, doctoring, preaching. . . . Now they are united in an effort to do the best they can for the community of more than 500 individuals here."

Minutes: "Motion carried that the request that [milk] goats be moved to bodega [for their health and protection] was denied. . . . Dean presented problem of marked increase in present food prices as compared to those of a month ago, and pointed out the fact that our allowance is at present inadequate to cover this increase. . . . Motion carried, the Executive Committee will write a letter to Imperial Japanese Military Administration urging increase in our present daily allowance. . . . The Chair read a copy of a letter which had been sent to Imperial Military Authorities, requesting a stove of sufficient capacity for our baking needs. . . . A petition presented from residents of Barracks No. 2 requesting that a change be made in the Camp Code which would allow men to visit [their families] in Barracks No. 2 at certain specified hours during rainy season. . . . Head of Judicial Department presented report from Chief of Police listing men who had visited in Barracks 2 from June 26–28, with and without permission. It was his recommendation that no action be taken against these persons, as in many cases it was the first report of offense. . . . Mr. Hayakawa stated that they had made a rule regarding men visiting in women's dorm and that under no circumstances would it be permitted except for valid reasons. . . ."

This place is indeed the other side of the looking glass where years of saving go for naught, bank and homes are scattered to the four winds, and only those things which are eternal are still with us—the sun, the wind, rain, earth scent, devotion and faithfulness, forms of self-expression in kindness, consideration, or learning and writing. The devotion of our servants is like an adventure, with the inarticulate contact carried on in bags and envelopes.

We sat in the warmth of cloudy sun on the wash table near the cook house and talked about the reversal of all things and how we were seeing truths from the Bible in life, that the first shall be last and the servant shall be ahead of the master, the master glad to wait on the servant, when all shall be equal and inherit the earth. It is not new to me but to Jerry it is new for he was not as well acquainted with those who served us. He is just realizing that they are part of the family and that we are all in the same boat for once and for all. It is so interesting, so touching, how they have carried on and come through.

At noon Wick was a picturesque sight standing on a bench to work the coconut press in the middle of frantic activity in the steaming kitchen. His strong back, legs and arms pushing down, muscles standing out, rounded and smooth as they pound and press the white meat which gives body and flavor to our soups and other foods.

One of the old-timers has failed much in the last six months. His mind is going. He goes in to eat, takes only a little, then becomes hungry and eats from the garbage cans. He doesn't wash or shave, is careless about the toilet. This old fellow needs constant looking after and hospital care. Art has tried to get Committee action but they only leave it up to head of the Medical Committee, who evades it. His staff does not like a chronic case, of course.

July 9, 1943. At breakfast, the news of P7,000 was out and all day everyone was talking over ideas on distribution.[26]

It will do a lot of good even if the Welfare Committee does have headaches from its distribution. They know by now who is really at low ebb, who gets money from Manila or Baguio. All is fairly well regulated and will work out for the best on the whole as the Welfare Committee is a good one.

Well, we have cash on hand now—and can't spend it! There were no eggs in the store, no grease to fry rice or onions—except at sky-high prices, everything soaring—sugar, fat, soap, if one can get them. The reason for all this is outside—fall in currency value. Everyone wants to get rid of Japanese bills. No one wants to sell anything, particularly and especially if it brings in Japanese bills. They will lend because it means security and good interest in the future and helps to get rid of Japanese currency. The tide has swung and American notes bring high value, Japanese going down and down. It is a sure sign of change and coming events.

Sally and Jess asked us for coffee served in their new streamlined pot made from the curve of a sax horn, and cookies and tarts served from a hand-beaten plate from another part of the same instrument.

July 10, 1943. Women's Minutes: "Please bring mending before holes are too big. . . . Sanitation Committee reports that on the whole people are much more careful to cover food and garbage. . . . All folks [should] discontinue the throwing of garbage and water from dorm windows."

The *News* says—"Rising food prices combined with a shortage of some food items due to the advent of rainy season have been responsible for decrease of approximately 25% in daily caloric total of camp meals, according to dietician Dr. Shaffer."

Jerry and Scott have pooled on a Manila *Tribune* subscription and will divide it for toilet paper. One headline shows that the guerrillas are still resisting on Hainan Island. Another article proves that the Solomons are only a pin point in a vast front where Japan has won all the victories from Alaska in a southern circle to Singapore. They devote columns to showing their unity, our disunity of strikes, discontent with Roosevelt and the war, food shortage, etc.

July 11, 1943. The small fry have passed from soap bubbles which was restricted because of no soap—to jack-stones, and now to handmade light wood propellers used like planes.

Father Gowan gave an evening sermon in which he seems to have shot the works again—among which was that if he had not been a Christian before he came in here, he would not become one from the example set by many of them. He is a brilliant speaker.

July 12, 1943. The visiting Japanese nurses stood watching the male cooks in the kitchen and when the baked camotes left from lunch were given out to them, they disappeared like magic. The party seemed very hungry. The men ate their share first, the girls getting what was left. This seems to be customary. By their standards, it is excellent chow, and the new form and variety of cooking tasted fresh and delicious to them. To us it is just one more starch which we can't face, a monotonous everyday item. One girl asked, "Can't they ever go out of here?" and Hayakawa answered, "Oh yes, under guards." This is not strictly true, of course, for only the Executive Committee, the sick and the garbage crew can go out with guards. The question interested me—it shows imagination, her mind figuring what our situation might be like, comparing and thinking.

Carl came with the cash for my check and he says the rest of Nida's amount is coming in today, though we wanted them to get it for their own needs chiefly, but nothing can be done about it. They feel that way and wanted to send it. It means less worry and we can make it last, but losing everything has changed my values and I am in a queer state of new clarity. I suppose Nida and Ismael feel aghast at seeing everything stripped from us, knowing that they are used to less but we are not. Even the thought of us reduced to bakia instead of rubber boots doubtless disturbed them. Nothing that we can say will show that their health means more to us. We worry about them and they worry about us, which is good for both of us, for it takes us out of ourselves. I lie in the dark, with others asleep, thinking about money and possessions, how one has it one day and the next does not have it, and how often due to conditions it will purchase only a little and means nothing without health or love behind it. Yet if one is sick and one has money—what a difference it makes in comfort and recovery. How vital, yet unimportant. It means everything, yet nothing without the proper value. As a symbol, with the meaning destroyed, it is useless.

I scolded Jerry and crabbed because he had bought no extras and we were hungry. He finally overcame his horror at high prices and worry about the duration of these conditions, also the habit of spending little for so many troubled months (one does lose the capacity to spend), and he bought bananas, a pineapple, and an infinitesimal papaya at top prices which hurt but he shot the works.

July 13, 1943. Statistics from the *News:* "Our population represents only 7.8% of the total population of American, British, Dutch and other nationals registered with Japanese authorities in the P.I. [Estimated 6,508 total.] Santo Tomas has 3,686. 534 are interned in outside institutions or other places; 144 on conditional release for health and other reasons and 488 in religious groups permanently released. Los Baños has 799. Baguio is third in size, Davao 4th with 250 internees. Iloilo is smallest with 96. These were compiled in order to effect equable distribution of the two relief funds of P50,000 and P46,994.08 received by Santo Tomas Camp on May 28 and June 20."

Twice the Executive Committee has been to town to shop. They have four new goats, are negotiating for four cows, and found a case and a half of milk. They would like to collect a six months' milk supply. They went into all the drug stores and took what they wanted from shelves, asking the price afterward which often was plenty, in some cases no higher than a year ago. Some stocks were marked "For the Japanese Army only."

By new standards, we are rich, very rich, and do not need to apply for relief. It is the third time I have signed for P100. Nida's family and Grandfather's legacy by check on the bank at home are keeping us going during inflation and concentration. It is a combination of past and future which pleases me.

Today I learned that for a month at Camp Hay five Chinese were kept in irons.

July 14, 1943. The latest craze among the young is green bows and arrows, giving a distinctly Robin Hood atmosphere to the grounds.

Two things I am sick to death of hearing handed out from all kinds of people—"Well, you're a fool if you don't take everything you can get away with"—this in connection with the waitress job and I retort as I close the door behind me, "I don't agree with this. It is what is the matter with camp, the camp sickness, lack of standards and ethics." The other saying is "Well, everyone does it and I might as well get my share. Why shouldn't I?" This is how rackets start out in the world too. Both sayings are symptoms of lowered mental and moral tone induced by war and looting. I will take no part or have none of it. It is a tough time to live through and stand firm. One is looked upon as a fool and a sap and one ceases to care about such names.

July 16, 1943. June came asking to look into the suitcase for a dress to wear at the school exercises—"something to look older, Mummie, for I'm going into high school." It suddenly dawned on me that it was a big day, graduation and growing up. All her [dresses] had been looted except a few, yet she did not mind. So we took out of the paper bag where it had been folded away my white challis dress with gold leather buttons and gold belt. [June] tried it on and the style and fit were perfect, only the hem had to be hurriedly taken up. Then we hired an iron and pressed out 18 months of wrinkles.

I sent word to Jerry at the shop that he must be sure to attend his daughter's graduation, and he embarrassed her greatly by telling all the men at the shop that his daughter was graduating and was he proud! We wouldn't tell him what she was going to wear and it was fun to see his wide grin and hear his exclamation when she stepped onto the platform to receive her certificate and to sing, looking almost sophisticated in the trim style, with a dozen tiny white orchid flowers nestling in one fold of her dark hair. [My] tan shoes were on her feet—"our communal clothes."

After Carol, Katie, Evelyn and June received their Concentration diplomas signed by Dean and Principal Cordie, dated July 19, 1943, they took off their finery and June could hardly be recognized as Quince giving the Prologue to *Midsummer Night's Dream* play of Pyramus and Thisbe. Carol and Sonny brought down the house as the lovers but all did exceedingly well. It was good to hear Shakespeare lines again. They were well memorized. Four other little girls did a perfect piece of memory work in an act of history review. They wound up with a resumé of what they would like to eat upon release which struck a chord in the audience. Father Gowan compared this school to the Little Red Schoolhouse of olden times, with shortage of books and paper and chalk, poor blackboards, dim light, and rain roaring on the roof to drown voices. He said the teachers had all these handicaps, and that even more than usual a class depended on the teacher being a shining light, though she was better off than most of us because she was in her own element and knowing that she was really making progress by feeding young minds.

July 17, 1943. Old John was taken to the hospital at last, so endeth that battle. His bed was in dreadful shape.

July 20, 1943. Jerry skipped accounting as he was weary and lame from new labor—milking the coconut cow with Wick and Ritchie. He has joined the

July 1943

Servics!

Food line - Rice + stew if lucky for supper

bronze torso brigade and likes it. Two scrape out the meat and the other one presses it. Last week when I saw a new naked sun-browned back muscling about at the stove-end of the kitchen, I couldn't figure who it was, and behold, 'twas mine own family. It is fun to watch all the kitchen workers moving about in the steam as one sees them in perspective from the center of the room. They pull kettle covers from giant cauldrons, hoist huge ladles, stir and poke and shove, grind, mix, lift big stacks of dishes and kettles, and have a good time joking with each other. Scott always has a casual air and good natured grin no matter what the pressure of work. Jerry also helps Doug with his peanut and coffee grinding. He puts in five or six hours quite often, and so does Pat who is wood chopping and piling in the hut. Carl plugs along at the tough job of seeing that all work details function.

Enid's autocracy seems to have been undermined by democratic methods, which does not displease me. She brings someone with her to make the list of articles sewed on the machine in our room. And miracle of miracles, revolution indeed, after many efforts to pry loose and give out some shelved materials in her room for nearly 18 months—at last Mary has given out two items to each woman. It will help out during rains when nothing dries. Enid was keeping it for bandages in time of battle in the future, even though Hayakawa had said he could bring in more of it. Even my New England instinct for saving doesn't carry me that far. It is good to see a committee functioning at welfare, not just an individual who couldn't manage it all. Now it is organized into a tactful system. Some of the men deserve credit for keeping at this until it was worked out and formed properly. It took months of patient insistence, against obstinate, stubborn will and fight. Dysentery is with us again strong.

The *News* says that on July 18 there had been 20.76 inches of rain. "Resourceful and inventive cooks have created a new recipe book in here, developing knowledge of strange materials as they go along. Rice and cassava flour, native chocolate, peanut butter shortening, bean milk, panocha [dark sugar] syrup, native fruits, have been the subject of continuous experimentation for many months, and perhaps at the price of many a ruined dish and a few stomachs, are now no longer the mysteries which they first presented to menu-managers. . . . So successful have some cooks become that they can create complete meals from local ingredients which would not find detractors under ordinary conditions, meals which use different ingredients but which adhere to national tastes. No wonder food is the most popular subject at any meeting. Seven pounds of meat in the corn chowder—we are all now close to being vegetarians. . . . We have leisure time aplenty but it seldom coincides with the time of day when study is possible. There are camp jobs to do in the morning, and washing clothes, minding Junior and a hundred and one other things. Few books, little light. Adult education classes are numerous but there is little time for outside study. . . . Things are quiet, residents fighting off mildew and boredom and busy keeping dry—no mean task when confronted by Baguio-scale rains, no umbrellas, leaky raincoats and shoes which in the normal process would have been in the garbage can months ago."

July 21, 1943. Bougainville bombed. Today rumor says we are taking Rabaul and New Britain.[27]

Rome bombed so Tokyo knows what to expect and is railing about it. Hitler is conferring with Mussolini in Italy over changed situation due to invasion of Sicily.

June went to a school party dressed as Heidi.

July 22, 1943. Still typhoon, wind, sheets of rain, mud, slosh, floors won't dry, feet wet, icy.

A bag from Home, real Home, and Bacanis cheering us no end on a dreary day of one typhoon on top of another. There was coffee, homemade chocolati, cigarettes, three avocados, fifty cookies and a dozen green corn.

At four when June was making syrup, eating hotcakes, reading and knitting happily in the warm kitchen, Dr. Viola called me to say [June] had dysentery and must go to the hospital. I could have cried. Her face fell but she quickly said, "Oh I can help Susan and knit and it won't be as bad as before, 'cause I know all about it now." Jerry was terribly upset and went off in the deluge with canvas pack of mattress and blankets on his shoulders. He will sleep on slats tonight and I will be less one blanket and pillow. How I miss Junie.

We are all steadily running downhill on the diet; there are new sick cases for the first time with dysentery each week, many repeats.

July 23, 1943. The 800 are still at Los Baños and Reggie wrote a long note about it all, telling us to bring shelves, tins, everything we could carry if we came down. Life down there is not as primitive nor as communal as here. We are ahead of them in many respects. They have no hill for firewood and have to buy their own which is high. Each cooks on a clay stove privately, near his own shack which is built on a registered plot else is illegal. They have no community store but private selling. Buck earns P1.50 a day and a big steak delivering store orders. They write that social life is dull and monotonous in Manila camp since the 800 males left for Los Baños. They have boiling or ice water on tap all the time, but a long carry. They have more facilities, less initiative, and less necessity for ingenious contrivance. Yet the heat means constant washing and their diet is no better, often not as good as ours as to variety and vegetables. They have beans every noon. Stay up there if you can, says Reggie, especially with a baby or child.

I got soaked going to and from the hospital but June is very cheerful and takes full care of Susie. They were both tucked in June's bed while she read to Susie. Susan watched her unpack when she arrived and said, "Junie, where is your potty? You forgot to bring your potty.'' June loves her devotedly, like a little sister. No wonder the staff said she was a Godsend when she arrived, but to me it is a bitter pill that she is there. She was glad to see me with the soap and other things.

I went to tea with Carlotta at the hospital in the little center room, cosy and warm, with double-decker bed, shelves for all her belongings, a hibachi made from Socony can and wire netting, hot coffee warming on it, and a coffee cake served on nice china plates with cups, all of which used to be in the camp kitchen but were snaked off for hospital staff use like many other things. The hero sees that they get what they need no matter what it is, if at all possible. We joked and laughed in the old manner of sophisticated patter, far from barracks noise and the roar of the storm. They live in a different world down there and don't know what we go through—and what is more they don't care. They are friendly, intimate, one large family, with wisecracks and fun and parties, lights on all night if they wish and on during the day at any dark hour. It is a world all its own. Our conversation injected some of the barracks difficulties and troubles but it is only funny to them though they could see it was a long way to the toilet in the rain and the wind. Peg told of Annarae upsetting her foot-bath water while Peg was hoping to get a siesta—of the howl that went up from the kitchen below and the mopping up that she had to do. I told of washing my hands, all ready to go to tea, falling on muddy steps and having to go back and wash them all over again. We had a gay and pleasant hour in this Bohemian hideaway, but I came home in savage mood, thinking of June upstairs and how she wouldn't be there if things were run right and dysentery under other control.

July 24, 1943. I patched my raincoat most of the morning and typed. The two lectures were called off as rain is too heavy on the roof. I mopped and got soaked as usual. We are conditioned to wet and cold by now, a good thing or we would catch pneumonia. Mums and Ethel in their sheltered life at home would die if they could see what I'm in. They would be shocked at things which no longer seem a hardship to us but easy.

Two soldiers came and looked in our door, stood in the doorway looking toward my space, talking. I caught the words ''Kirei desu,'' and wondered what in the world they could see in this room to call beautiful, with wet towels, clothes and raincoats draped everywhere on wire. They left smiling, and Coila said, ''They were looking at you.'' Having no illusions about my looks, in Concentration Camp at least, I answered, ''Not me. They said something was pretty,'' and then I remembered the vivid furoshiki I had packed long ago and dug out of the suitcase two days ago to hang up on the net as a gay, bright spot of colors which only the Japanese could combine—orange base with yellow lines and lavender and pink and white bird. How those soldiers loved it. No wonder they gazed and talked. It is only a cheap square such as they use to tie bundles but it was a splash of artistic color, a piece of home to both of us.

We went in to hear Private Gibbons sing old British war songs in an A.E.F. cap and uniform. She made us homesick for the last war, yes, verily. All the songs sung with a vaudeville dash and a rippling touch on the keys.

July 25, 1943. When I go to see June at the hospital, there is always the little troop of 8 or 10 small children, their insides all shot, going back time after time for treatment, crowding around the stairs, asking wistfully or eagerly or wailingly for parents. They are isolated and on soft diet till their lacerated insides can take something else.

July 27, 1943. Every morning Jerry brings us a baked banana piping hot.

I spent all morning in the kitchen boiling down syrup and lemon for breakfast rice. There were more than half a dozen busybodies in there, shoving tins about, pushing them back and usurping space as soon as someone's dish is boiling, peeking in to see if this or that needs to be on such a good spot. If one leaves, her can is removed or moved promptly. It is a constant fight for place and rights. There are pots full of steam puddings, steam bread, cobblers, pie filling, piecrust, small new potatoes, hot water to make tea, soup of pork and vegetable; messes frying—of onion (fresh green tops cut up), pork and sliced potato or tomato sauce if one is lucky enough to have it; green beans boiling in round butter tins, all kinds and shapes of coffeepots, fried rice with sliced sausage meat and onions, big plantains bursting open and oozing juice, one luscious pan of fried brown chicken.

July 28, 1943. Bedie has really been off his feed for some time and is afraid to eat fats. I hope this camp doesn't turn out a fine bunch of hypochondriacs for the future. Everyone is worrying about diet, what they can, what they can't eat.

July 29, 1943. Dr. Viola reports Bedie on the verge of sprue,[28] with a case of diarrhea. He wants blood tests tomorrow. This cast us down a long way. If it is true, it will cost us plenty in eggs and red beef from the one who sells it—it is hard to get and none too good. Bedie is feeling important, glad to be noticed and to come in for his share of eggs with June. He acts loving and cuddly. I have soaking feet from downpour and mops. Sqush, sqush, in shoes, and slacks drenched. It is so cold.

The *News* says, "Ten day storm with 71 inches of water."

From news on the Board . . . Announcement made today says, "A small group of philanthropic gentlemen, having nothing but a spirit of helpfulness with which to be philanthropic, have expressed willingness to repair, mend or construct any necessary personal articles which cannot be handled by the shop because of lack of time. The gentlemen, who wish to remain unknown, will do this work in their spare time. They are on regular camp duty schedules and the work they do is not to conflict with any of their regular details or of those details that offer regular service to internees. Don't bring anything. Address a note to 'Fix It Shop' and drop in mailbox.''

A year ago four adventurous comminglers had what may have been the first mixed game of bridge in the dining room, forerunner of hundreds of others.

July 31, 1943. At Anthropology Barton spoke of economic mating—the man with cash plus the woman who could cook, the companion of tea or coffeepot. He was apt and amusing.

August 1, 1943. Jane and I practiced Japanese. Pork salted in the lowlands was put in our chop suey tonight. There was also ginger cake with frosting for all of us to help celebrate the Chef's birthday. The Kitchen and Hospital are still the Elite, the arbiters of Concentration-style parties, the ones who entertain as a group, have fried chicken and other such, all loyal and rallied around the proper center. I can see that the Moppers Union lacks something—chiefly the desire of a leader to rally others around, not to mention the fund to buy supplies for retainers. Two children are enough to worry over. I am content with work and keeping busy. The weather, diets, and sickness are heavy burden but parties do not relieve it for me. I prefer small conversational foursomes.

Parties, parties, indeed it is true. In spite of poor camp meals and low calories, no one is hungry. Inflation is in the air. Spend, spend, spend. Buy all you can, for tomorrow those Japanese Government pesos won't be worth anything. Get rid of them. You will never need the eggs more than now either. It is not a bad philosophy at the present.

Art said he never could understand why those of us who headed Indusco in Baguio hadn't all been grilled about it, particularly me. He said when he was grilled as a prisoner in jail for guerrilla contacts, they asked if he knew the oilman and he said casually that he had bought gas of him. They asked if he knew the one who made the radio speech for cooperatives and did he hear it—to which he answered no. This set me up no end—no one here heard it, no one knew about it actually, it was quite unimportant, unnoticed, unheard—but the Japanese knew about it well enough; it was important enough for that even though they only read about it in the paper afterward, which pleases me and carried me down to posterity with that little drop in the bucket which pricked them. My work in that was finished. I hope the snowball is now being rolled by others so that it grows larger. Art laughed hard when I told him this set me up no end. I told him about tearing up my article and burning it in small scraps with matches in the Brent fireplace only a few hours before the enemy came in, of tearing up the Christmas card with Soong Ching Ling's [Mme. Sun's] signature and throwing it casually in the waste-basket with other scraps as Nagatomi and his crowd came through the door to search our bags and take our cash and bankbooks.

August 3, 1943. Tokyo tells of terrific fighting in Sicily.

August 4, 1943. June says the little kids stomp about saying "God damn" over and over. Buddy on potty remarks, "I hope God will give me a good specimen today," and small Heather admonishes, "Sh! You mustn't say that, it's a bad word." There seems to be slight confusion, but Buddy really voices the Dysentery Prayer.

August 5, 1943. Bill Moule is out in the yard on crutches now, with his wife and three children around him, happy to be together in the bleak sun. There are patches of blue sky which is heavenly to see. It is a lift to our frayed nerves. Everyone is tired and cranky from cold, mold, mud, wet, and dull food.

It is the first sun in 20 days, says the *News*. Everyone is washing.

Helen suggested a tea and cake party for Miss McKim at Nippongo class. We all fell in with enthusiasm and Esther came with a tray to collect tea, sugar, egg, syrup, flour, spice, shortening etc. Helen baked and frosted a beautiful affair and Mrs. Wright drew clever place-cards with our names in Kata Kana and Japanese phonetics along with the characters, from the tokohon [lesson book]—"Oni, Saru, Inu, Kiji, Mōmōtaru, Obasan, Ojiisan."[29] Miss McKim came in looking disgusted to see another table spread for a party, knowing she would have to teach over the din of it and thinking some of us had a nerve to be helping at class time—when we all shouted, "O medette Gozaimasu"[30] and burst into laughter. She was overcome with surprise and pleasure. Everything tasted good and it was warming. The conversation was about Japan and she gave two wonderful imitations of Japanese English.

August 6, 1943. Jerry made a marvelous rice soup with curry, sausage, pork, onions and peanut butter.

Carl received a cable but the message, from his wife last May, was delivered verbally through a Japanese friend in Manila who came to his house. So this cable message has been at Manila headquarters since May, undelivered like hundreds of others, from six to eight months. How cruel, heartless, cold, to hold up these messages. There is nothing too small, no way too petty, for [the Japanese] to show the depths of their hate of us.

For the moment, the great experiment is over. We no longer know what it is to feel hungry and thirsty and poor. The various pangs are forgotten already in the orgy of cakes and parties. Gone are those tough and terrible days, as inflation is here and everyone [is] glad or anxious to loan, while borrowers spend recklessly on scarce and overpriced meat, eggs, flour, brown sugar balls and shortening. Triple price is nothing. We shoot our wad mostly on eggs and cooking bananas for the children, trying to build them up on the limited things they can eat and that we can procure. To me, the terrible days are still only yesterday and I see people too clearly as they are, not as I want them to be or as they could be. I am weary with the petty struggle in here, money and loans intensifying it. I am still trying to see both sides and hear all versions, when sometimes I am sick of both.

August 7, 1943. Mrs. Encina is on the rampage. First, he put welts and scratches on the children and when she went to him in fury about it, he hit her on the head with the same stick of wood. It is presumably over cash and accounts. She trailed him to the veg room with Arthur right beside her, but too quick for any stopping she caught up a knife and flung it at her man, just missing him because he ducked in time as a woman yelled, "Look out!" Now Mrs. Encina is looking for the one who frustrated her!

August 8, 1943. We collared Bedie at the goat pen pool, took pole and wire and started up the hill. It was sunny and warm, yet cool on the skin and so heavenly to go upward away from drab barrack buildings and the 500, to breathe new air and be able to hear even a leaf fall, to exclaim over the green blanket of a wide expanse of weeds! Bedie was grouchy and did not half appreciate the trip for he wanted to stay and swim in the pool. I call him Buttonface because his lower lip needs to be buttoned in. It has become a bad habit over some years, this pouting, sulking look.

The distant pile of mountains, the clouds—soft piled or drifting, the ferns, dewey grass pastures, cool dusky dells that we crawled along past muddy spots rooted up by pigs, the large garage and barrack buildings camouflaged and showing in Trinidad Valley, a few wild berries to pick and taste in delicious coolness—it was all something rare to take in with every sense. June talked joyously and leaped ahead as Bedie lagged behind. We saw slender white orchids, green and gray berries, and picked up a yellow holly wood branch for our carry-pole. Far down the other side we found the huge tree stump and many sawed logs wet with rain and waiting to be carried. We set off climbing the hill back to camp, swinging the logs like pole coolies and earning our permits to climb as members of the wood crew or log rollers. Bedie and I hand-carried, but when he and June took turns with Daddy on the big log it was a shoulder carry. My fingers swelled and blistered a little, my nose burnt red, we all burned in the sun. On top we rested several times in grass wet with dew and shaded by one or two of the few pines left standing. All the big ones are gone, only stumps everywhere, and long trails where they have fallen or been rolled along and down. The bush and saplings are beaten down in many places. It was a perfect day and I drank enough view and blue atmosphere and distance to last a long time. But June thought I wanted some of her bottled water when I expressed the desire to sit and drink. We could watch the planes [Japanese bombers] until they were tiny specks melting into the clouds.

Russia expects German surrender on that front within two weeks, after tremendous pounding and defeat. They say Eisenhower has gone to the Near East, Montgomery in charge in Italy. Hamburg is no more, flattened like Cologne, and we have warned Berlin to get women and children out for that city comes next. The pace becomes terrific in Europe, and out here too, as intensification of propaganda shows every day. Shelters are being built all over Baguio, machine guns trained on every plane that goes over.

Crossing the dewy, quiet pasture on the hill where peace itself was tangible, it was impossible to imagine we were in the center of war, carnage and death in numbers never known before. It was queer to look toward our home and realize it was only a shell with all the personal touches removed except for the small loyal family—and that we could not go to it, held prisoners almost in sight of it for two years.

It becomes plain that every Tuesday when the purchases come in, a certain few gather in the store at night and choose what they want from the lot. What is left is sold at the store next day to the long clamoring line. Small orders of two or three cans are unimportant compared to Execs who want case lots. The auditor has resigned from the store, giving no reason. Something brews.

August 10, 1943. Stag surprise parties by wives for husbands on birthdays are the rage now, mostly for kitchen crews who are therefore stuffed all the time. Wick says it has been one after another for ten days. He likes it!

Parties, parties, everywhere one looks. It grows more hectic, and futile. We gave Scotts a cup of coffee and some honey brittle at 10 for their anniversary, but he was overfull of coffee and pie from the stag surprise party for the 19 kitchen crew which his wife gave for him. The oven is crammed with the roast pig which Enid and Arthur are spreading before the grade and high school teachers tonight. There is more point to these two affairs. However, next week is election so other parties continue.

The *News* says that camp has gone out of the goat business and sold them to the goat tenders. Milk supplies from three other sources are now adequate for months to come.

From the *Tribune* toilet paper we get news and learn of new fronts, buried in long columns.

August 11, 1943. I have heard of "Eat, drink and be merry, for tomorrow we die" and the "After me, the deluge" spirit, but I never expected to see it concretely expressed before my eyes, and all on borrowed money. No one has earned in here for two years, and it is all Japanese currency at that. But the answer is that it helps morale. Never mind the digestion.

August 12, 1943. High school grads are learning a new song by Father Gowan, not like the usual Alma Mater. It expresses this thought—"We hope it won't be long before there's nothing left of her (our Alma Mater)."

"The Women's Committee referred the question of the swimming pool for younger boys to the General Committee. . . . It was the opinion of the majority of the members that the problems presented by a swimming pool could be answered with adequate safety and sanitary supervision. Motion made and seconded that the swim pool be allowed subject to proper chlorination by the Sanitary Inspector, a fence that will keep the smaller children away from the pool, and supervision by Father Burke. This motion passed on conditional stipulation that the regulations laid down by the Counsellor are observed by the children."

There is a baby mouse funeral up on the lower hill in the bomb-practice hole, complete with bamboo cross, hibiscus flowers, and the children singing hymns.

August 13, 1943. Jim Bozeman says anyone with any integrity can borrow any amount, even a million in town without any interest, just the security of knowing they will get good money later.

August 15, 1943. Many trunks poured out costumes for the play [Thornton Wilder's *Our Town*], even to a delicate white organdy Princess style for the bride, who also found a half-portion veil and looked most charmingly ingenuous. There were several mispronunciations of New Hampshire words but no one but a crusty old New Englander would notice. I had the feeling after it was over, that our time too had switched into the future and back again, and that we had lost everything and seen the world crash, had died with it and been born again into a different one. And when we went out under the clear sky and cold moon, I had the illusion that it was snowing. The play put over the New England atmosphere that well.

August 16, 1943. While we watch Wilder's play without any permit from the author, U.S. bombers annihilate Berlin and a B.B.C. broadcast tells frankly of plans to lay waste a path 250 miles wide by 300 long in the Ruhr.

August 17, 1943. From Jim in Camp Holmes *News*. "Dear Mr. Wilder, Last night our high school presented the three acts of your play *Our Town*. We didn't get your permission, I'm sorry to say, but it really would be a little difficult to do now and I know you will excuse us. You see we are in a Concentration Camp up in the Benguet Mountains of Luzon Island in the Philippines. We have been without our freedom for nearly twenty months now. Most of us haven't had any mail in that time and none of us have been able to send any. Besides, we wouldn't have very much to pay you with except maybe a hand of bananas and lately they haven't been any too easy to come by, the way prices are going up. So perhaps you will be satisfied with our thanks. Sometimes we don't get along too well with each other here; we've been together too long without an opportunity to see other people, but there's a lot of cooperation and help, and a lot of people who know how to do things in this camp. They used the mess hall tables put together for a stage, benches for seats, army blankets for curtains, borrowing light bulbs and stringing up extra lighting wire for the occasion. The costumes were fine—some of the girls even had 1904 style shirtwaists. The parts were so well played that you'd have thought they were real almost. You wanted to show people a thousand years from now how the people in Grover's Corners really lived 'growing up, marrying, doctoring, living and dying.' Well, we're not living in 2900. We're in 1943 but it's fine to know that's about the way our own people are; living in a Concentration Camp all these months sometimes makes us wonder if any one still lives a normal life any more. And *Our Town* is good medicine for that. We had a good time last night. We depend on ourselves for entertainment these days, you know, and it's not very often we have anything quite so worthwhile as your play. Even sitting on a hard bench for two hours wasn't difficult then. We had permission to have the lights on after 9:30. After we got out of the dining hall we looked at the moonlight lighting up the mountains and the pine trees around here and it didn't seem quite so hard to wait. Let us know if you want those bananas, Mr. Wilder, and thanks from Camp Holmes."

I stood in line for duck eggs so missed part of Lady Gregory's *Spreading the News*, which was done in brisk comedy and most gorgeous Irish shawls of colored-square worsted afghans recruited from camp owners. On the table-stage there followed the [high school] graduation exercises. Dean as chairman and commencement speaker looked as though he thought oratory was not his forte, acted boyish and casual as one of the students, in his gray suit with long trousers and hair slicked down. [He] spoke briefly after the presentation of the ten graduates—five in each year—who marched in to the strains of "Toreador." The girls looked lovely in newly knit sweaters and white skirts, with corsages on their shoulders and carrying a sheaf of white lilies, callas, and gladiolas on their arms—a touch that would have been impossible last year, but now due to much cash and the Chef going out to purchase, it was his thoughtful gesture to bring flowers from the market. Dean noted that "some of us have not stood still in camp" and told them how lucky they had been to continue their line and conclude their education while others "marked time."

Father Gowan then spoke, saying, "You have escaped education by gadgets . . . more than made up for handicaps . . . have learned that life is not a game but work." He spoke of the eager spirit of the students, their fine response and the giving of the teachers. He referred to the diplomas tied with a ball and chain made at the shop by Denki and Fabian—"these the symbols of imprisonment which should remind of lessons learned from loss of liberty."

He adjured them never to forget what hate could do—and distortion of truth. There was no Salutory or Valedictory or Prophecies, but they sang several groups of songs. Shafe gave out the diploma rolls with chains, Art made the closing prayer as Fildey had given the opening one. It was a suitable program, as brief, simple and pointed as the two years of excellent schooling which has taught them more than other years when we all dressed in our most stylish best and sat on the Brent hillside listening. At these exercises today we were dressed in all kinds of clothes—shorts, slacks, khaki, wool, and patches. Following is the first verse of their Alma Mater song—

> We sing our Alma Mater
> We hope it won't be long
> Till there is nothing left of her
> Except this fleeting song
> And History o'er her emptied halls
> Will knell a last ding dong.

Jerry's back does not improve at all and it is tough on his disposition. I am discouraged. He has had a bad experience in here not only with his back but general health which hasn't been as good as mine, and the political setup has pushed down talents he might have used for benefit of all. It was a bad start, with all our case goods confiscated yet not equally distributed and our own children getting no benefit from the milk. Jerry lost all his pet things one by one—car, camera, roll of pesos, radio, golf clubs.

Many are using cloth rags as toilet paper now, washing them in the disinfectant solution which doesn't seem quite right. It should be kept for hand-dipping. Lenore says she is using pages of her recipe book compiled at much pains in Camp Hay and now going down the drain. Ruth carrying a heavy can of laundry water looked at me laughing and said, "I guess I'm the No. 2 Coolie of camp, aren't I? I know who Number 1 Coolie is!" And that is what I don't mind being—No. 1 Coolie carrying three cans of water every morning, sloshing it later with mop and thinking "char" thoughts, interspersed with mental flashes of a waitress.

August 18, 1943. On August 17, thanks to Japanese permission, I sent my first letter to Mother and signed it "Your devoted daughter, No. 87."

Bedie is down in weight from 76 to 74, back to his weight of two years ago. I feel anxious about it and want him to lay off his adored but strenuous swims for a week while we feed him. He gets double eggs and must start to gain.

August 19, 1943. The *News* says, "Standing in line is Camp Holmes' chief occupation. Rumor says some individuals spend all their time in queues except when asleep. Unless one is willing to devote from two to three hours to waiting, there isn't much to be bought. The reason is "seller's market" conditions now existing; many people with adequate means seeking to purchase a limited quantity of goods.

After supper Dean brought the word that Dr. Hall, Dr. Lee and her children, Betsy M. and Delphine were all leaving for Manila on Saturday at 7.

August 20, 1943. A mad, wild, hectic day, typing letters all day long with the air crackling with typewriters, people letting out emotions, packing, and tea parties for the two young girls. Dr. Lee pierced 8 to 10 ears for earrings at the last minute. Oh, thy name is Vanity even in Concentration! By five I was tired and almost ready to weep after looking into the heart of camp in the letters. I typed 32 in all. There were so many longings held down for so long, a reaching out for contacts, aching to hear from home from someone who cares. Between the lines there was courage, restraint, yet the throbbing was there.

August 21, 1943. The day before departures Bedie was completely examined by Dr. Lee. His lungs and heart are okay but he needs to eat every two hours and to drink much more liquid though he can relax on the fat-free diet. We decided to give him two eggs a day and keep him out of the cold, strenuous pool for a week. He promised—and today first whack went into the pool but did not lie about it at any rate. Bed for him all day in punishment and no play program tonight.

Highlights which make up a cross-section or a composite of the "heart" of camp, from what I remember of many letters home. "Am still not very thin. . . . As far as we are financially able, we purchase extras. . . . I am a vegetable worker. In leisure time I study New Testament Greek. . . . For beauty, this is an ideal spot. . . . Am I an Aunt? When you write be sure to tell me about more nieces and nephews. (Many missionary letters said this.) . . . Someday, someday, it will all be behind us! . . . "One listed classes in Chinese, Japanese, Latin, Greek, German, Spanish, French, English, Ilocano, Tagalog, accounting, higher mathematics, architecture and Japanese flower arrangement. One missionary, the only one to strike this note of a changed world, said, "I feel I have had a small share with you in this changed world. I realize I shall not return and find things as I left it." . . . "I have a pan made from part of a safe and a brooch with my name and number made from a loudspeaker. . . . Lack of proteins and chairs gives us round shoulders, and lots of rice gives us round tummies. We line up for meals, store and even the toilet. . . . Only a very few possessions with us. All else is gone. Someday we will have a great family reunion though and so we try to look forward. I am so thankful my husband is with me. . . . It has been so long it now seems incredible that we may write. We are soon entering our third year. . . . There are three sittings at meals. All have community work to do every day. Fortunately no censorship on thoughts and those go out to you often. . . .'' (Many who used to drink much now speak of improved health and far better condition in spite of hardships. They do *not* mention that it is lack of stimulants, or that regular hours of sleep and meals and outdoor life with hard work help to keep us in condition during unaccustomed rigors. We have poor beds, no chairs, no bathtubs, no fireplaces, no warmth of any kind.) Another wrote, ''I have certainly learned a lot about cooking with coconuts and rice flour and other native products.'' ''Fourteen babies born, almost two years old now. . . . Three men died, one 83 years old. We live an active, hurried, crowded life. . . . Wear bakia which are heavy, clumsy, noisy, wooden sandals carved for us by our men. . . . I live with many women. Before sickness Lorenzo lived with many men. . . . A milk substitute is made from black beans and green leaves. . . . One sent me a cake of soap, six ounces of margarine and handful of limes—a gift of much greater sacrifice than you can imagine.'' Most of the letters show hidden appreciation and remembrance of even the smallest details. The most tragic note was by a young missionary trying to convey indirectly what had happened to Rufus Grey—''. . . Marion and her son who looks like Rufus as I remember him. She has done a superb job of looking after the baby alone.'' One writes, ''On the whole our treatment has been fair and considerate,'' but it seems better left unsaid when one thinks of Grey and Kluge and Shevlin among others.

August 23, 1943. Dr. Shaffer came to say that Bedie's temperature was over 103 and he'd better go to the hospital.

Art told a terrific story of a Bataan prisoner toiling along the road, staggering under a heavy pack as cargo for the Japanese, only six miles from Bontoc. The man dropped by the road to rest, the prisoners and enemy going on. An Igorot boy crept out, told him to come and he would hide him and take care of him but the man said no, he was responsible to his men for he was a Sergeant—if he left, ten of them would be killed for the Japanese had said so. It is the old hostage story, from Europe. We damn the rotten minds that thought it up, however long ago.

August 24, 1943. Father Gowan is scratching his head over store problems. Sugar sold at the store today a pound per person at about twenty times what it sold for last year. We paid P1.75 a lb. for brown sugar which used to cost us 15 centavos a kilo. Hope was answered, for 5,000 eggs came in and every one could have a dozen if they had the cash.

August 25, 1943. There are many rumors about repatriation—the British, old people, and sick people. There is much buzzing about it. The repatriation consular official who came up with Miss Rodgers was treated wonderfully in the U.S. Concentration. He lived at a fine hotel in Ashville. He is now high in the Intelligence here and says we should be better treated and he will do everything he can. He was one of two officers coming out this afternoon, going all over the barracks and grounds. He asked Hayakawa questions about Miss McKim, and Hayakawa who has been avoiding and rather ignoring her for about six months—"shiran kao" as she calls it (a not-knowing face)—finally had to face it and her and give information. He is especially this way when officers are around and evidently fears what she may say or give away, as she knows both sides and the languages. She told us this incident in Japanese most amusingly.

August 27, 1943. We discuss how people are still loyal only to a group—at the group stage everywhere, whether it is religious group, work group, room group, social set or what not. They fight and stand by the group, not camp or the town or the city or the nation or the world.

August 28, 1943. Everyone goes around quoting 1940 *Time* and other magazines, as though it meant anything now. It drives me wild. I hope the world has changed a little since then.

August 29, 1943. It is sad to see all the big trees hacked down around camp. It destroys the beauty of the place and regrowth will take fifty years.

I find myself looking forward to Nida's bag each week and becoming anxious if it is late one day. It is our only message from the outer world.

We had black bean stew—a poor supper. I played practice bridge with June, Katie and Bootsie, and as we smelled cinnamon rolls, bacon and other supper treats near us, we became more and more famished. I felt exhausted as I did last night and June said the meal had not been enough for her either. Jerry had promised us a surprise at 8 and just as I was going home to bed he appeared with a beautiful gold and white fried egg for each of us, a slice of bacon and bread soaked in the grease, and hot coffee. How we fell upon it. In ten or fifteen minutes as my system began to react from the empty to the full feeling, my face became pink from the warmth of the coffee and the satisfaction of the food. It seems foolish for it to mean so much, but it does. I can only think of those who did not have any and perhaps could smell the fragrance of it as we had only a few minutes before.

August 31, 1943. Women's Minutes for the 30th. "Persons washing dishes at the hot water sinks are asked to conserve hot water by not leaving the tap open while washing each separate dish. Sunday, the Committee asks all members of the Veg Detail to come to work early so that those who wish to go to church may see the work finished in time. The Committee greatly appreciates the spotless condition in which it found the school building today."

September 2, 1943. I had another funny dream, of Bunny trying to talk to me but it sounded like a foreign language and I said, "It's no use. I can't understand. It can't get through."

Advanced courses for high school grads and genuinely interested adults willing to take full term. Accounts, Analytical Geometry and Calculus, Anatomy, Advanced Chemistry and Physics, Advanced French, Advanced Music, English Poetry, General Psychology, Shorthand and Geology.

September 4, 1943. Lucy and Harry presented their satire on "Our Camp" and it was a riot. It was full of wonderful lines straight from camp life and scenes that made us rock back and forth. The last scene was lined up as a cemetery—only it was those who were released, with Winnie saying, "Settle down. Settle down. You'll soon get used to it," monotonously. Paul was Jim Halsema saying, "You won't want to go back in—they will borrow everything you take with you!" It being 1949 "the Baby House still had babies." There was an epitome of camp cynicism when one asked what the people were waiting for in the cemetery so silently and the answer was, "Oh they must be waiting for the Great Offensive."

September 6, 1943. It was Open House from three to four, with tea and mint, lemon and a cookie.

Glimpse of a Sister on her knees—from the back she looked devout, in prayer; but from the front she could be seen extracting meat from coconut by pressing it on a scraper.

More Flashes from Letters Home—"Cleaning rice consists of picking out stones, worms and other debris one would not want to eat. My Cathedral friends may like to know that I make the altar bread using two electric irons for the purpose."

September 7, 1943. We were in the veg room, with the young party on one side. The girls were all dressed in formals. They were like gay butterflies, with hibiscus in their hair. There was much laughter and squealing and cheers. They had a good time, poor kids, for they are so confined here in the years when they should be having fun. I remember in the last war, all the boys leaving, farewell parties, knitting of socks and sweaters, writing letters to France, with some returned marked "Missing." Now these young ones are going through it and prisoners besides, conforming to Japanese ideas of propriety. It is too bad the girls have to do all the inviting, get up all the parties. Most of the boys have received money and could return some of the favors they accept by buying cakes and brewing their own coffee. If they did it in a joint party it would be easy and the girls would be thrilled. I wonder if women always take the initiative in wartime? In the end, what a man really wants he goes out after, when his mind is made up.

September 8, 1943. Rumor says Canton, Hong Kong and Formosa were bombed.[31] Philippine Independence and attendant embarrassment for us is accelerated. Independence will doubtless be given at the last possible moment before invasion [by the U.S.].

June is shocked to find young S. knows how to play poker. I tell her it is like any game, one can gamble or not in connection with it. She sees sweethearts kissing goodnight and thinks the affair very serious, then is shocked when they break up after awhile.

September 9, 1943. Edna rushed into the barracks panting, calling out two words—"Italy surrendered!" Instantly the subdued, murmuring excitement broke into cheers, down the barracks with a swirl, a roar, like the forest fire or the tidal wave or a storm wind. Even the little children knew something momentous had occurred, and cheered. The people listening at the guardhouse were silent, just looking at each other. The first point of the Axis is broken, the effective triangle has lost a corner. When Sonny went in to the men with the news, Jerry growled, "Are you trying to pull our leg again?" Everyone is buzzing, laughing, speculating, keyed up, feeling almost free. Later Dean said to Hayakawa, "First Italy, then Germany by first of the year. Maybe Japan a year from now, Hayakawa?" He answered, "And then you won't be interned any more." Yesterday someone was talking with a guard and mentioned they would be glad to get out. He asked, "Don't you like it here?" and when they replied "No," he said, "Neither do we."

September 10, 1943. Jerry looks well, all the men do, in a coat of brown tan and a G-string.

September 11, 1943. Dr. Viola asked for another specimen and in half an hour confirmed the suspicion that Bedie had dysentery. I was so discouraged that it was like a void.

September 13, 1943. June started high school and likes being in with the older group. She is thrilled to be able to join the choir. She takes Biology, Ancient History, and French.

I shifted our sugar yesterday, replacing its wetness with white beans (covering my notes). First it was butter, then peanuts, but we had to eat both. What a hash these notes will be.

Carl says they are taking up the matter of getting some people's clothes which were dumped in a room at the Intelligence and when they mentioned this Omura said, "Oh, the Intelligence? Keep away from them as much as you can." Even he sees the red tape and futility and difficulty.

September 14, 1943. From the *News*: "This morning (the 14th) the camp lost a man who had guided its course for the past year, making many friends, some enemies, in his capacity as Chairman of the General Committee and head of camp hospital. When war broke he was chief of the town hospital and mine medical service with headquarters at the laboratory in town, having arrived from China in the fall of 1941 to assume the post. A few weeks after internment began, he organized a hospital at Camp Hay, secured its equipment and supplies under difficult circumstances. When elected Chairman last year, he worked continuously for more privileges to be granted to us; made the Committee a recognized body for self-rule (within limits) of the camp; began and maintained relations with outside authorities which have resulted in establishment of a camp organized on the lines of Santo Tomas. Vigorous, outspoken, bold, Dean accomplished much. His services have been requested to organize and maintain a medical service at Los Baños.'' He left camp at 7:30 in the brown Chevrolet driven by Mr. Hayakawa and accompanied by Mr. Umezu who will go with him to Manila. We will miss him.

September 16, 1943. I would like to be married and in a home again for a while!

September 17, 1943. Both grade and high school started on Sept. 13 and there were 15 high students, 13 others of about school age and a great many adults enrolled in school. Father Gowan stated they now offer 31 courses and have a staff of 22 teachers.

There is a steady stream of people with sore mouth going through the dispensary. They make such awful sounds when throats and gums are painted that I haven't been able to take myself in there with my own mouth and throat full of cankers. They say it is an acid condition and is dietary.

The Japanese have taken the entire radio to town. They will probably remove the short wave. Apparently they don't want the guards to hear anything either. So, no more Tokyo, only Manila and the Philippine Islands.[32]

September 18, 1943. As we waited in the dispensary this morning, Jerry talked of starting again from scratch. First we buy pots and pans for the kitchen says he, peering around at me. No more great collecting of any kind for me, say I—no more thirty-year accumulation for men's stupidity to crunch over. But if Nida saved my book list I shall buy the ones I want, say I. Not with my cash, growls he. Oh no, say I, with U.S. government repatriation cash from Japan; at which Dr. Mather snorts cynically and says, "If and when, try and get it."

September 19, 1943. The wind is sending torrents in horizontal slant. It is a driving cold tempest in typhoon cycle. This is second year wet season to live through. All of it is like last year, telling us the second season is closing, a third about to start in December. October is the end of rains, the promised great offensive in Burma.

We discussed wires and radio being taken up all over the Islands, 20 thousand Japanese being concentrated in Lingayen, the propaganda being directed to Filipino and Japanese soldiers over American radio telling them they will be protected by us when they return to Japan and not to fear surrender. So this is the reason for changes in radio.

Bob was so amusing in his description of sleeping next to Mrs. MacIntosh on mats at Camp Hay, "with Donald clutching and crawling over him all night." In the morning he found that Mrs. MacIntosh had pinned their mosquito net to his trousers and he had to wake her in order to get up and dress!

September 20, 1943. At breakfast Helen Mann said she had learned two most important things in here—first that if you worked hard enough and kept at it, you could get *anything* you wanted (to which I added that often by that time you didn't want it any longer, having progressed to something else, to which she agreed with laughter). Second, she said never throw anything away, no matter what or how little, for you always want it desperately when it is discarded.

Jerry opened our last can of powdered milk for Bedie, who is thin and pale enough to be considered emergency. June and I each rated a glass which was indescribably good. It gave the illusion of being all cream. Such taste! One a day would clear up our troubles. We sat reading and drinking, Jerry having milk in his coffee. Bedie had his in an eggnog. June raved over it for an hour afterward. Bless their hearts—some day they may have enough.

There was news of capturing Salerno and of revolt of the Jugo-Slavs and the Czechs. I said I thought Wick was one of the most amusing, entertaining people in camp. It is his simplicity, the little boy quality in such a husky figure. Jerry has it too, an engaging freshness. They are particularly amusing together.

September 21, 1943. Wind but sun all morning, spits of rain later. I wore skin off with much washing.

September 22, 1943. There is a warning to keep the children away from grounds around the shop due to Japanese target practice—and how. They used several kinds, including machine guns.

The *News* says, "A carved squash sailing on a sea of spinach to a pile of rice marked Goa provided the centerpiece for the kitchen and dining room crews' farewell for Bill Portrude, who is going on the repatriation ship from Manila for the U.S."

Women's Minutes: "The Sewing Committee cannot undertake to outfit people for the lowlands. Also please do as much of your own mending as possible before asking the Sewing Committee to work for you. . . . A full-length mosquito net will undoubtedly be necessary for any one going to the lowlands. The Work Committee has tried to be fair; to study each individual case before assigning the number of work hours. For example, single women are asked to put in more hours than those with children, while the time assigned to mothers varies according to number and ages of the children. Also each case is considered from the point of view of the health of the individual. If anyone feels she. has been assigned more hours than she is able to give, she has but to come to the head of the Work Committee and talk over the matter to make the necessary adjustments. The Women's Committee has decided that hereafter; 1. The names of all those failing to put in the number of hours assigned, without the approval of the Work Committee, will be posted weekly and those women asked to come before the Women's Committee to state their case. 2. All those who feel that they are physically unable either to do any camp work, or that their hours should be reduced, must present a note signed by one of the camp physicians to the head of the Work Detail.''

September 23, 1943. For the first time there is not a single dysentery case in the hospital.

Men's Minutes: ''The Executive Committee was asked to attempt to purchase adhesive tape, to investigate soybean milk preparation (said to be available in Manila), and to purchase for the hospital utensils for sterilizing and medical glasses.''

September 24, 1943. The old poker gang is at it again day and night. It only takes fresh cash to start it up. This time Jerry takes no notice.

Note on the Board: ''Shortage of paper makes it impossible for us to supply standard forms for notes to Manila. If you have your own paper, please use it. Cut it to size of form below. Notes of odd size and incorrect form may not reach destination. No one is allowed out of bounds without the express permission of the Japanese authorities.'' The Japanese are watching us again as they haven't for 8 months.

September 25, 1943. Mr. Bontorp made us a table! We are now as independent as when we obtained a saucepan! The table is installed on the porch. Dr. Hall left us three boards and Mr. B. found one more and Jerry had legs from an old stool.

Miss Simpkins talked to Kira about release on account of her health. It was a long story. He said, ''You shouldn't have come to the Philippines.'' And she retorted, ''You'd have been better off if you hadn't come out here too but stayed in California.'' He smiled.

Still no news at all and we hear Jim has been asked by Hayakawa to omit his news analysis.

There is a third story of why no fruit. The Sergeant's lady friend went away and he asked Mrs. Fruit Seller to get him another but Mrs. Fruit Seller would take no part in the transaction. Therefore he ordered no more sale. So we are cut off extras! Perhaps life is like this—a man's whim or a sexual appetite depriving people of food. No eggs, no onions, no bananas or papayas come in the gate. Our money burns in our pockets and the food we need to get rid of acid or sore mouth is withheld. It takes so long to eat when the mouth smarts and burns and nerves grow tighter. I think pain is easier to bear than a sore mouth. It is like a steady drop, drop, drop of water wearing one down. I try rhubarb and soda internally as well as soda gargle. But I am not fit to live with, cross and weary and old!

September 26, 1943. A girl gave two big bunches of bananas to the garbage crew as they passed the bridge, and the guards took them all away from them.

Hughie and some other children were taken outside on a truck ride. He went by his own home but when his mother asked him where they went and what he saw, he answered, "Oh, we went passed some houses and a village." He didn't know his own home and village. He came to camp when he was four and two years have passed.

A guard came through our barracks with a gun and bayonet, swaying down the aisle, polite and genial, bowing and saying "Sa," but obviously under the influence.

There were five or six parties, one of about fifty guests for a husband's birthday. A guard with his nose pressed against the wire watched the party all evening and wanted to know what we were celebrating. Carl had a party in the ironing room with games and much glee behind a rug curtain. The Sergeant went in and sat in a corner, watching the whole time. When Hay akawa is away, the guards will play.

One went in to visit with Ray, was given a piece of cake and seemed rather hopeless. He said he left his wife expecting a baby, with three children already, in Japan. All his money goes to her, he has none for extras. If he is taken prisoner, his family will get no money at all. If he deserts, they get no money. If he deserts but kills self before captured, his wife gets pay. In Bataan, the Japanese soldiers who had been taken prisoners by the Americans were shot in front of their comrades' eyes when they were recaptured after the surrender of Bataan by the Americans. So there is no way out for them except death. They must die fighting, and if defeat comes all must die.

The soldiers flatten their noses against the window, watching parties which to them must look as glittering and luxurious as 5th Avenue windows to us. Steaming coffee, frosted cakes—big round chocolate-iced ones—bread spread with potted meat, dishes of peanut candy or salted nuts. These things are not for them—only death and the paycheck going to one's family. No extras, not even food as good as ours for the common soldier. They went off to fight, hoping to get some extras at the end of it, and now it looks dark and dubious. No wonder they drink when the cat's away, peer into windows or sit in corners watching our life which is joy and gaiety compared to their lot. Poor devils—most of them never had anything and have nothing to look

forward to except fighting and dying. I hope someday they will get cooperatives and a square meal a day even if no extra frills. It means nothing to
them when our fruit and eggs are cut off for they know camp gives us more
than they get.

September 27, 1943. We drink "submarine coffee" (made from the dregs
of a first boiling). Hayakawa saw [the repatriation ship] sail for Goa. Bill
Portrude found *deck* space as the ship was very crowded. They say it was
a small freight boat for about 100 passengers, carrying over 1,500. We think
of them all steaming toward home, packed in like sardines, and we are half
envious, half not.

Mrs. Saleeby stops to talk on Work Details and why shouldn't mothers
do their share of camp work. That is the big camp issue right now, with some
changes, some mothers back at teaching, and some still full of fine reasons
and excuses as to why they have no time to help on veg and rice. The juice
is squeezed for their children, the food is cooked and served with waitress
attendants, dishes are washed, the children cared for in school and playground,
yet they have not time, except for private cooking. There is the rub—private
cooking. If they have time for pies, cakes, cookies, muffins, and other
luxuries and extras, then they have time for 1½ hours of camp work. Too
many are dodging.

September 28, 1943. Sardinia and Corsica are admittedly occupied by the
Allies in the *Tribune*.

September 29, 1943. Ray yelled through the dorm, "Everyone get ready,
be ready, for inspection at 10:30. Generals Nagasaki and Sato are both
coming!" And me in the middle of cookies, flour on the unmopped floor,
eggs and spices all over the bed, the aisle and porch to be done in line of
duty. But the oven was ready for my turn! And two Japanese Generals have
to fall into my lap! I said the heck with them—they are always late—and I
went ahead with my first camp cookies. The Generals came fifteen minutes
ahead of time and the baking was a mad whirl of error. Lenore helped me
so that it came out with only one pan spoiled and I have a whole can of
cookies. We worked frantically, without a turner, only knives, crumbs in
every direction which we swept up and saved for a pudding.

September 30, 1943. Kiev has fallen, says rumor.[33]

A gorgeous bag from Nida with about 2 lbs. of peanut-sugar candy, six
eggs, cigarettes and matches, cucumbers, chicos, a pomolo and a kilo of
white sugar on the very bottom. We ate the fried eggs at noon.

"Medical cases. *Eye cases*: There is a man available at Baguio General
Hospital who can make eye examination and prescribe for glasses. Through
Santo Tomas the lenses can be ground from these prescriptions at a cost from

P35 up, depending on correction etc. This charge is for the lens only. We have received no information regarding charge for frames. *Diabetics*: Wally is to investigate the possibility of having blood sugars done for diabetics in town.''

October 2, 1943. Jerry milked and strained a coconut and we let it set from 3 till 6. Then I took off the cream and shook it for 3 or 4 minutes in a glass jar—and we had butter. I worked it over, pressing out the whey and putting in salt. We had a half cup full from one coconut, and the thin milk for breakfast. Our first churning was great fun.

The kids now have a pole-vault space near the hospital. Stilts have also been made, and baseball is on.

October 3, 1943. Bedie has been in a stew for days over his pin—getting safety pins to solder on, filing, breaking and refiling more metal to make the pin part of the ivory oblong carved with initials and painted in black. It is all he can think about or talk about. After many errors it is finally ready and presented to the young lady. She writes him two notes, one to say thank you and the other saying, "Bedie, why did you give me the pin and go away? Why not stay and talk a little bit?"

The young group who played Post Office are becoming more and more "select" and aggressive about it. They have a circle of about four now, with one or two chaperone couples. They have three or four parties a week and this evening the entertainment was a treasure hunt in which they tore about noisily like five year olds, hunting for a camote, or Carl's autograph which proved difficult as he was at a coffee party and had to be tracked down. They dumped all his books on the bed after finding one with his signature. Naturally he did not appreciate the mess.

October 4, 1943. Miss McKim gave Nippongo class a repetition of her talk to the Psychology class on the Japanese mind. She used [the] Durants' *History of Civilization* [*The Story of Civilization*] as a reference. Miss McKim said one must study their historical background to understand them, their legend of origin and the Emperor's divinity etc. She mentioned three stages: 1. Classical Buddhist. 2. Tokugawa Shogunate—the most peaceful era. 3. 1850 modern Japan, in which they have imitated the West and tried to absorb and pass our civilization. They are born of earthquakes (over 4,000 islands). Their poetry, most of nature, suppresses rather than expresses emotion. They transform creatively what they absorb in imitation. Most of their art and language is from China and Korea. Shinto is the Way of the Gods—the domestic cult of family and ancestors, communal cult of clan ancestors, and finally of state ancestors. Buddhism in 522 filled the religious needs of the people and the political needs of the state. It taught piety, peacefulness and obedience, to be content with a simple lot. Christianity came in 1549 with St. Francis

Xavier. The Shoguns (military) suspected political intrigue and in 1614 ordered all converts to depart or renounce the faith and it was outlawed for 200 years. Perry came in 1853 with 560 men in 4 ships. There were the Shoguns, the Daimyo and the Samurai. Making a sword was serious, prayerful business. It must have temper, soul etc. Miss McKim termed their chief traits—industriousness, frugality—they are used to hard work and no luxuries; great pride of race, very quick to sense superiority and resent it; not creative thinkers but very practical and can accomplish much. One of the great causes of the war is racial even more than economic. They feel they have been looked down on and snubbed and that they are really equal. School plays a large part—practically owns the child. Its propaganda is far-reaching—individual thinking is almost nil. Earthquakes and the battling of natural elements has produced in them infinite patience; courage and bravery, ruthlessness and determination, from the Samurai Code. Every soldier is a gentleman and every gentleman is a soldier. Bushido, their code, calls for courage, asceticism and self-control. The family is the real source of social order, with the father omnipotent.

Japan drank in everything she could from the West. From 1924 on, she became more strict in schools and propaganda, more national and anti-foreign.

October 5, 1943. Rainy season is about to end. Days are lovely, with less and less rain, but still fog, clouds, mist.

The medical staff and work heads are put to it to whittle down the rationalizing of those who try to get out of work.

There is another tale of the hospital. The nurses had a meeting and voted to wash down the cobwebs and walls etc., designating Bob and Fern to do it. They muttered a bit but started, soon finding it a very large job. They asked help from the nurses and the super answered, "Oh but we are all graduate nurses" (then quickly, thinking better of it and how it sounded in here) "but we will be glad to help." And they did.

October 6, 1943. The *Tribune* says in letter box, "Yes, it is correct that now there are to be no sharp points on kitchen implements." Back to those days again!

I would have liked to have seen two grandmothers' faces at hearing Marj say in typical camp lingo, "Well, June, where did you get that lovely gardenia in your hair? You must have a boyfriend on the garbage detail!" It is accurate too. Only the garbage crew can catch gardenias from a wayside garden bush. Garbage pays!

October 7, 1943. Medical Minutes: "There is great scarcity of drugs and all medical supplies. We will probably have to depend on our present supply for the duration. . . . An appeal is hereby made to camp to contribute old cloth and rags suitable for bandages to the Medical Committee, to be left at dispensary. Each post-dysentery patient wishing to return to Work Detail connected with food will be considered by the Medical Committee and passed or rejected on individual findings by said committee.''

A supply of sugar came in today, was passed by a guard but caught the eye of Hayakawa, who ordered it sent back to the sellers who can sell us no more.

October 9, 1943. The *Tribune* arrives with headlines of independence on the 14th.[34]

October 10, 1943. "To all Guerrillas. M.P. Chief Sends Impassioned Appeal.'' "Upon my word of honor, I guarantee you one hundred per cent that your life and the lives of all your followers will be spared and safeguarded if you lay down your arms and present yourselves to the garrison commander in your locality, the chief of the Military Police unit in your vicinity, the Provincial Governor or the Municipal Mayor. . . . I swear to God that I will be true to my word and pledge.'' Addressed to all guerrillas, this pledge was made by Col. A. Nagahama, chief of Japanese Military Police, in an open letter published in the *Tribune* last Friday, and transmitted to the guerrillas in their mountain hideouts. Bearing the salutation, "My dear friends" and the complimentary ending, "Your friend and brother,'' Col. Nagahama's letter stresses that the Military Police do not ask the guerrillas to surrender but to present themselves to the authorities and be "welcomed back home.'' "In the name of reason,'' Col. Nagahama appeals in the letter, "I ask you to open your eyes and see for yourselves the true facts and conditions now existing in the Philippines. When you turned guerrillas you claimed that you did so because you believed you were fighting to preserve the independence that America promised to give your Philippines and which you thought Japan would make forever impossible. Whether that cause is just or not, it has become obsolete because the very thing you said you are fighting for is now in the hands of your people, including yourselves.'' He closes the message "with a prayer to God that He may enlighten you so that you make the right decision.''

After dreaming of traffic at home, I wonder how we will all get along in it after being cooped up two years on a parade ground. Our children won't know how to cope with a jangle of cars, carts and people at all. And what diverse occupations I carry out here in a day—mopping, carrying water, wringing mops, waitressing, typing, making cookies, churning butter, setting cheese, patching pants, studying Japanese characters, listening to anthropology and cooperatives, not to mention copying minutes and writing up items on democracy every day. Whew! But this versatility makes for confusion and dizziness now and then. This life is endurable, not so bad, if one looks at it right. . . . If only one could hear from home. Yesterday I remembered Mao Tse Tung saying, "Somewhere along the line I lost myself," and I know now what he means.

October 12, 1943. Hayakawa called Miss McKim to the guardhouse last evening, said he heard we were betting on when the Americans would come in, asked her when would they? She said she did not know or what the guesses were and asked what he thought. He answered, "Never." He always goes stiff like this.

October 13, 1943. Inez sent a bag with two packages of Bucayo and 14 gorgeous orange persimmons. The persimmons and oranges from Nida, with vivid colors highlighted, make a striking spot on our tray-table, backed by Jerry's carved tray and dark polished coconut shell dishes.

The women of Camp Holmes are carrying in whole or in part responsibility for the following departments of service for the welfare of the camp:

1. *Children*
   Baby House (baby food, sterilizing etc.)
   Games (evening in dining room)
   Playground
   Study Hall
   Teaching (kindergarten, grades and high school)

2. *Clothing* (sewing, knitting and mending)

3. *Food Preparation and Serving*
   Baking, bean milk, serving, camote cahoy
   Diets (special menus)
   Fruit preparation
   Kitchen laundry
   Rice picking
   Serving and waiting on table (special diets and children)
   Vegetable preparation

4. *Medical*
   Dispensary
   Hospital (nursing, kitchen and laundry)
   Massage

5. *Health and Sanitation*
   Bathrooms
   Cleaning and sanitation
   Swatting flies

Marj Moule was in bed with malaria attack yesterday and Johnnie Moule was carried down on a stretcher with the same. Bedie puts on his swim suit and goes into Bill's warm pool twice a week. He loves it and is *so* clean!

The Big Ape guard is our latest laugh and annoyance. He constantly barges about in a consuming curiosity. The guard wanted his undies and belt sewed, so he parked himself in the lower room. Martha finally gave him a threaded needle. She then ducked out to take a bath and did not return. He sat on her bed and sewed for over an hour, taking scissors off the hook and being much at home. In the evening he was definitely "high" and sat himself down at a table with the "elite"—a party with a lace tablecloth, pink and white lily decorations, sandwiches and a huge rich, white-frosted cake. This big fellow will never be any nearer rich Americans or be any more convinced of our rolling wealth. He has picked up a lot of Tagalog and English and is not dumb at all, but his looks are wonderful. He shows huge teeth with vast gold outlay and a cavern of a guffaw which would swallow one whole. His head slants back and his jaw squares forward—the most terrible squares and angles. He is another peasant type, full of ideas and unquenchable spirits. He annoyed Miss McKim at bridge, pushing, shoving and telling her to come. She told him Mr. Hayakawa did not allow us to do such things as laundry for them, and he replied that Hayakawa was only a civilian while he was M.P. Irritated, and finding it impossible to play bridge with the guard sprawled across the table, she went to Hayakawa and repeated the conversation, knowing well that it would be enough. At once the Sergeant came and called him to go on duty. He went to the hospital and asked Dr. Shaffer if his wife was there with him. Dr. Shaffer replied that he was alone there and that she was up in the barracks. Big Ape gleefully opened his huge mouth, laid flat hands against his face telling Shaffer to get his wife thusly, then put hands over his eyes saying he would not see or tell. The good old primitive guards—what would we do without their advent every so often! Miss McKim is always a match for them.

October 14, 1943. A number of camp members are miserable with the pre-sprue mouths.

They took the Big Ape off to the guardhouse away from his joyous watching of our card games which are against the law in Japan and disturb him. He had time to sit on Rachael's bed, using her manicure set to cut his nails! She fled in fear of being asked to do it for him. The guards are all jittery and the guardhouse and camp were blacked out again. War is in the air once more. It is the natives they fear—and no wonder, for they have taken away the bolos from all Igorots who went to town to celebrate and had not returned these knives. Igorots can't live without the bolo to hack bamboo and coconut and banana. The Igorots have been holding meetings about Independence—they don't want it—which is why the tanks have been whizzing back and forth with impressive noise and mounted machine guns.

October 15, 1943. Five silver bombers swung over and back in a C effect. Natives going by smiled sheepishly and when asked if they had Independence one answered, "Well, somewhat." Another, asked if he was now free and independent, said with a grin, "Independent but not free."

The *Tribune* this morning says that the new Independent Philippines will not declare war on the U.S. because the J.M.A. [Japanese Military Authority] will have charge of all military affairs and will take care of that, while the new government will take charge of internal affairs.

Jim Bozeman died suddenly about 1:30 and we are all very sad. It was coronary thrombosis and the terrific attack lasted only fifteen minutes. Jerry came to supper with his eyes huge and mournful. He said the swift, acute spasms had been terrible to see. Jerry said brokenly, "He was such an ornery son of a gun. I liked him a lot." I nodded and we didn't say any more. There will be no more wild arguments in the cook house.

When they told me that Jim's arm had pained him in the morning I remembered my own arm and rushed to the dispensary to have my heart listened to! It is okay but I am to get tiki-tiki which is for beriberi or lack of B-1.

It was startling to see Dr. Shaffer leaping over the hibiscus hedge to run toward the hospital after Jim's tragic attack. One lady hearing the news said (characteristically) with her face pinched with distress, "Oh, there goes our foursome." Jim's wife Martha came in at once and Jim was carried from the hospital covered with a black cloth to the shop where the coffin was made for him. When it was placed in the military car which came, Martha threw herself upon it, weeping. All Jim's things were taken off in the car. It is as though he had gone Outside again.

We just can't believe Jim has gone. He was 47, from Colorado Springs, coming to Corregidor in 1920 in the Army. He has four sons and two daughters, according to the *News*. Because his family was Outside, he is taken out for Catholic burial service, not another grave on the hill.

October 16, 1943. Jerry dreamed he was dying and he gasped out to Bedie, "You must try to finish everything that you start. Don't leave things unfinished."

For several days we have had the treat of beautiful first-class pure white rice. It seems Primco could not supply us at the moment so we had to take from the General's bodega when we ran out of rice. Thus do we definitely discover why it takes 51 to pick over the 3d or 4th class stuff we have eaten for 2 years. Why should Wanda Gallagher, who has had eggs, milk, white potatoes, everything that cash could buy all along—have the same mouth condition, acid, cankers, that I have who have been deficient in the above?

Her family have all had acute dysentery, some have lost much weight and been in hospital a number of times—while I have kept fairly well.

October 17, 1943. Conversation scrap overheard—"Oh the war and this place didn't make him a heel. He's always been one." I heard a group of missionaries, all male, discussing Camp Hay tough days and saying, "I wasn't only surprised at what some people did in hunger and extremity. I was surprised and horrified at what I felt like doing and did myself by way of self-preservation and in desperation."

October 18, 1943. The various couples at Baby House have each built their own little nook of terraced tea-garden, out on the rocks filled in with dirt then moss covered, with a board table and canvas to sit on. It is all cosy and charming on this point jutting out above the road.

October 19, 1943. There is a can with printing on it in black paint saying "Soap Factory. Dump coconut meat refuse here for soap." At last all the milk and butter-press refuse is to be used. The coconut grinder is finally anchored in Mac's shack where all may use it.

Poor old Mr. Watson has begun to crack since his release was delayed. He got up in the night, went out and did not return. They found him weeping at the foot of the hill, a bottle cap in his hand, saying he had a ticket to Manila and was trying to find the way to the train.

October 20, 1943. When Hayakawa asked Miss McKim when the Americans were coming in, both he and Umezu remarked at the same time apropos of nothing that they were both ready to die, expected to—"it is fate" said Umezu.

October 22, 1943. Committee Reports: Internees are asked not to use tap water for drinking or brushing teeth. It is *unsafe at any time* but particularly so during the coming dry season. . . . The Women's Committee has requested an inspection of all camp children for head lice. . . . Complaint was received that plants and flowers placed on the graves at the cemetery are being destroyed.

If Europe cracks, the Orient will get a body blow. It won't be long then.

October 23, 1943. The choir of 42, augmented at times by 30 from the high school choir, gave a program of 17 numbers. The majestic strains of sacred, classical and Negro spiritual music by a group painstakingly trained for weeks floated out and surrounded us.

October 24, 1943. At Vespers each Sunday hymns are sung according to a different tradition each week. Great Masters, Catholic, Lutheran, Anglican, Calvin, Reformed, Wesleyan Revivals, New Day, Thanksgiving, Advent, Advancing Kingdom, International Brotherhood, Glorious Day and Life's Dedication.

I cut off the cookies and arranged 150 on 6 tins. This way it goes smooth and quick and they are the best kind to make in here. They cooked in less than half an hour. I shall call them Bed Cookies however for they were not only mixed on the bed but when I went to borrow Florence's cookie sheets she said, "There they are, under the baby's bed." Jerry made bucayo and chocolate candy. He also made butter and cheese, but new coconuts bring small return. The wonder of butter's appearance never fails. Now it is liquid—then suddenly it is sweet thick butter or curdy cheese. It is like a miracle and always fun.

October 25, 1943. Dr. Shaffer called Jerry over, asked him if he felt strong and gave him a large envelope. Jerry nearly fell over when he looked inside, brought it to me asking if my heart could take it. Enclosed was P500 "loan from Nida for the Crouters." What a surprise and thrill it was. Jerry said we would buy all the eggs we could get and feed the kids every time they said they were hungry or empty. Jerry says he is going to cook a dinner for Nida all by his own hands. We call it the New Order in Asia.

October 26, 1943. We had some friends for tea and pudding and Jerry talked and talked, wound up, but did not touch on the real matter till they left. I could tell he was jubilant, elated. He told me it was true—4 or 5 landings in British North Borneo, and 200,000 in Celebes where we had taken a big airfield from which our planes were reconnoitering Davao and Mindanao generally.[35] People [Outside] have been given until the end of the month to turn in radios for shortwave checkup and emasculation, then the Military would go after them, and the owners, and take both into custody.

October 28, 1943. Committee Reports: "Twice the amount of money originally earmarked for medical supplies has been spent. Our present supply of drugs is all that we can plan on for the duration—unless additional relief funds are received and even then the drugs may be unobtainable. Cooperation on the part of doctors and patients is absolutely necessary. The Pharmacy is operating to protect and carefully dispense our supply of drugs. When the supply is gone there may be no more here or in Baguio. If you now request medicines that you might well do without, you may be depriving a person who is seriously in need of that drug from having the advantage of it at a later date. Those persons who regularly take certain medicines might wisely arrange through camp store to purchase a supply for their future use."

October 29, 1943. While I was waitressing, Bedie came in with his head bent over, both hands clasped on his head. He cried, "Come to the dispensary with me, Mummie." It was bedlam with lunch noise at its height. I turned over to Dorothy and went off with blood on my apron and hands. Bedie was a sight—blood all over his head, face, neck and shirt, a scalp wound running true to form. He couldn't see through it and was scared and so was John whose rock he had intercepted as they threw pine cones. All the kids crowded around the dispensary door, such a gratifying audience when Bedie got hold enough to feel heroic. Walter cut the matted hair and June produced Dr. Viola and Daddy and we all trooped to the hospital for two stitches.

We talked about camp being well organized and run now, as frictionless as could be expected. We spoke of the better atmosphere now, the hospital run like a hospital, still parties but less of a pleasure palace, with responsibility spread among all the doctors on the Medical Committee, acting together with each having a chance to work.

October 30, 1943. My birthday, a happy day full of genuine pleasure and surprises. Jerry and Bedie brought camp bucaco cereal, coffee and grapefruit over to the porch and we had powdered milk on the cereal—oh so good. Jerry presented me with two beautifully polished coconut shells with hinged square covers put on by artistic Bill Junkin. They were full of Frances Gowan's cream fudge with peanuts, a great luxury made with some of our saved cocoa. Jerry also gave me a jar of guava jelly. June made by herself a jar of coconut butter which I crave. Bedie had polished smooth a copper cent on which Mr. Bonnemort had engraved my name and Caroll Dickey had soldered on a safety pin. Everything was done by hand, lovingly scraped and worked over for weeks, months. They have whispered, giggled and twittered for days as things neared completion.

June mopped the porch and I proceeded with routine too. At noon there was a heavy bag with birthday greetings from the Bacanis. In it was a tin full of cookies and a roll of chocolate with a poem from Grandma and Grandpa. And three bulbs of garlic from Marie! Bacanis' was topped with a three layer sponge cake with creamy frosting. There were 8 tomatoes, 4 cigs, a bag of white sugar, a kilo of young potatoes and one of brilliant fresh green peas, 18 bananas and a large papaya. This makes several meals and treats all in one bag. How deeply touched and appreciative we were. Jerry cooked over an open fire on the point back of the hospital and Baby House. The cloud mist came and went, disclosing a glasslike rice terrace full of water, rich greens and harvest yellows, ridges of blue. Jerry produced his usual masterpiece for our appetites which were whetted by the wood smoke. It was one can of corned beef and eight duck eggs—he grinned sheepishly, hardly daring to say, "Do you want to know how much this dish for four cost at present prices? I groaned and demanded that he tell us. "Six pesos!" he was triumphant, proud and despairing all at once. Then we went to Dr. Bruci's lecture on the Ifugaos [an Igorot Tribe].

The dining room was trimmed for Halloween and Harvest. Palm calapias (raincoats) made wonderful cornstalks stacked together. There were cheery, leering jack-o'-lanterns, a lantern scarecrow, a witch on a broom, bats on the screen, yellow sunflowers and lighted punkins on the tables. The lanterns were lighted and the shutters closed, making it crowded and noisy and very fiesta. Fildey played the piano and the children pressed in fascinated to see all the goblins.

November 1, 1943. The six men who were put in jail a year ago celebrated their freedom with a juicy breakfast in the sunken gardens. Peg made their rice into round balls as they wanted it, symbol of the form it was served to them when it was tossed through a hole in the door to each one who caught it in hands unwashed for two weeks. If they didn't catch it, they did not eat. Only rice eaten out of their hands, no other food, no utensils or cups or plates, barely enough water to drink, in all their stay. They went two nights without blankets in very cold weather. Johnson was the hardest hit and never quite recovered from it. He is now seriously ill internally. It was a terrible experience. Carl was questioned the third day and asked a local Japanese he knew if they could have blankets. He looked surprised, produced from a pile all six at once. They had been there all the time. It was no mistake, simply deliberate.[36]

November 2, 1943. Roxy went to the hospital on a stretcher with a rapid heart. There are quite a few heart cases, a number of bad chronic colitis and a good many beriberi with swollen legs, eyes and ankles. Nora who has flu, high fever, collapsed in the aisle after the long trip down to the bathroom. It is a tough jaunt when one is sick. She passed out cold. Now the young group makes a long line of callers and flowers for her.

There was a third costume party at the hospital within a week, this time the 15 single girls. One girl borrowed a dress from each guest and wore all 15 and kept taking one off [at a time]. With a mask on no one could guess who she was and with each layer it waxed more hilarious.

November 3, 1943. Jerry is reading De Kruif on pellagra and talking with the doctors on the similarity of our three-meal diet to what was fed those who wound up with sore tongue and mouth, aching hands and arms, upset stomachs. Scurvy, sprue, pellagra and beriberi—all those deficiency troubles—with many bordering on it in here, including myself. Yeast is good for it.

November 4, 1943. A beautiful golden day. I took materials up to Kathie for her to make a lemon pie. She earns a little cash this way. Then I typed to Grandma, and made lemonade and toast for Bedie and me. We are on a citrus campaign to fend off pellagra, which Jerry is sure we verge on. I have

a thoroughly sore tongue again and a fine cough. My hands are so sore from
strong soap that I cannot wash.

November 5, 1943. Jerry and Skerl are going to make calcium from lime
and vinegar, maybe from the rocks about here or from eggshells. Jerry has
ordered liver for me. I become tired easily.

There are rehearsals for *Pocohontas* every day. For a year we got along
without any piano, now it is going all day long for play or chorus or choir
or dance class or practice. Programs are more ambitious than they were.

November 6, 1943. Helga says she is "no longer cooking for love." [Ian]
asked for his frying pan back and she says that is grounds for divorce in here
so far as she's concerned. He wanted pancakes and she could not do it so
he got someone else to cook for him. These were brought to him, turned
upside down on the ground in a spill, picked up, brushed off and presented
eggs, cakes and all right before his eyes. He will probably go back to Helga's
cooking but she says this economic arrangement and cooking amid all the
inconvenience, without an incentive behind it, is a dog's life. Economic
mating is definitely not enough! There must be love, interest, companionship
behind it—or else all sorts of conveniences to keep the work going.

I was all in and sent June to ask Jerry for hot coffee. He was too busy
but promised very shortly a supper that would revive me and it did, but
slowly. Oh that piece of liver and what I could compare it to! And bacon fat
which I crave. Cassava and peanut butter fritters also. We had three small
pieces of fried meat from camp. Bedie, explaining an exciting baseball match,
upset his plate on June's clean floor, just missing my lap. It was one of those
days. It is doubtless the shot,[37] with other things added up, but I haven't been
so nearly sunk since Camp Hay days. Jerry has bought 8 ampules at P2 each
of calcium and glucose for me to take once a week. The total is about P20
in all but it is better to take it this way than by eggshell or rocks! Intravenous
won't be pleasant but life doesn't hold easiness or pleasure these years, except
for sun and scenery which is perfect. My mouth, tongue and throat are sore
all the time, the teeth feel acid.

From camp *News*: "Lt. Gen. Shigemori, Commander of Imperial Japanese
Army in the Philippines, was born in Fukuoka prefect, Japan. He graduated
from Military Academy and Military Staff College, took part in the Siberian
Expedition of 1919; studied in England in 1922; has held positions as Military
Attaché in India, Commander of conscription section of War Ministry, Com-
mander of an Army Corps in Mongolia and Acting Inspector General of
Military Education. Transferred to his present post from a position in the
south in May, this year."

The kids had a grand time making up for *Pocohontas*, daubing on red
mud to make Indian complexion. Dirks' operetta was very good. The songs
went well and there were many Indian blankets, thanks to Winnie who went

through the dorms. Heap feathers, bows and arrows, knives, axes, squaws, war whoops and feminine yells were impressively realistic. It was good to hear the *Tannhäuser* "Pilgrim's Chorus" again. In after years we will always associate it with Concentration even if we hear it on a magnificent orchestra or by a mighty chorus.

Arthur talked with us during coffee. He looks badly. His eyes take on a wild look as he talks about his phobia—missionaries and Mukibo. He told of Mukibo's smooth promises of how his house would not be looted, nothing touched, and the girls allowed to stay and protect. Then how these same Japanese were almost immediately leaders of looting the house, sending the girls away, burning the stuff. He thought it was all set because he had employed Japanese, had been kind to them, saw they were fed when the Filipinos neglected them after the bombing. He found it counted for nothing. Even the honor of his position in here is gone. He told of that night in town jail when Ruiz, an Igorot from the valley beyond us, was beaten within his sight and hearing until not one spot on his back was untouched and he was then thrown downstairs before Arthur's eyes into the jail room with him and Ritchie. He could have taken a beating himself better than enduring the sight and sound of this torture, which of course the Japanese knew.

Betty said Nida had made a long call on her mother, Marie. She looks fine and is well, only worries about us, what we need, how we are getting on. She said our big table, the Chinese porcelain lions, the Amorsollo paintings were gone, also the modern blue dishes set, but not the old willowware or the big cocktail glasses. How this thrilled Jerry! We wonder if she had taken them out ahead of invasion. She said an American driver was with the truck and he begged for the magazines so she gave them all and also a lot of [our] books to go to our soldiers at Camp Hay. This makes me feel better.

Men's Minutes: "Dr. Esquivel presented camp with a small supply of medicines, gauze and thermometers. He also gave us ten bottles of the vaccine and as only two additional are needed to complete the series of shots, the doctors will start injections at once. Felix presented us with an electric vibrator for use in camp hospital. Incoming internees will be isolated at hospital for a period of two weeks."

November 7, 1943. Carl came to say the General would arrive before twelve. As a concession to him I swept the porch and our space. Tables and chairs were set out under a tree near the guardhouse. About noon Carl, Walter, Miss McKim and some Japanese officers assembled there waiting and several guards stood to attention. As we served special diets they arrived in five shining cars, not much fanfare or deploying as formerly. Kira San, slim in his white uniform, was there with his sword. Two Intelligence men appeared, one of whom was Carl's questioner in jail. The irony of it—Carl who was once treasurer of Indusco entertaining a Japanese General at cocoa. Besides Lt. Gen. Kuroda who is highest in command in the Islands (he is slight, elderly, modest appearing, with graying clipped mustache), there was Maj. Gen. Araki and Maj. Gen. Nagasaki of Northern Luzon command, and staff officers. Much braid and many swords. They said they would not embarrass us by going through our quarters (very polite and considerate) but they did go through the kitchen, dining room and hospital. Gen. Kuroda spoke good English and was very courteous. They all showed willingness to converse on many matters. They noted that Manila buildings were better, but the climate and other things were better here. One General asked why the men did not live with their families—the Japanese had lived with theirs in the U.S. and babies were born on the *Gripsholm* and the *Teia Maru* repatriation ships, and more due! We have been asking this same question for two years. Our Committee enjoyed the visit. Miss McKim said it was great fun.

In the afternoon, Kira San, looking young and sensitive and homesick, stood watching the American women cooking on the tiny stove in the private kitchen. He accepted with a bow Hazel's cookie offering. He likes American food. He watched the ball game before going off in a swank car. Even the Sergeant looks lonely as he walks around in the dusk singing low a Japanese song, or holding an American child by the hand, or carrying Karen who clasps her arms around his neck. He has five children at home.

Last year we did not see the *Tribune* or know when the relief ship came in or receive our share of it except to buy it. This year they can't pull the wool over our eyes. We expect letters and packages for Christmas. We put two and two together from the radio. Tomibe seems to be taking hold so that we are not forgotten any longer.

Pete Moros tells his daughter, "Don't eat the food, I tell you. It's poison! We are all being poisoned! Moldy, wormy and full of toxins. Poison!" But he is several years behind, for it is not poisons which are catching up with us more every day but deficiency in vitamins, calcium and proteins, as Dr. Skerl says. It is under-nutrition, not bad nutrition; some of it due to war scarcity alone.

November 8, 1943. Missionaries are really too idealistic and sincere to mess into political scraps. They try to see the best in everyone and make the best of a situation, instead of seeing a man as he is (who may let them down eventually) or of admitting that food is poor, criticizing it and trying to produce a change.

November 9, 1943. The *News*: "Women's Committee astonished to learn that busy rice pickers, perhaps bored with their task, had attempted to *read* and sort rice, corn, or beans from the rocks, weevils, dust, straw, etc. with which 1943 versions are associated. The ladies let it be known they don't think the two occupations can be combined. . . . Attention is also drawn to the fact that those who have time to go on picnics up the hill frequently are behind in work requirements. Those exempted from Work Details because of ill-health also seem able to climb hillside in some cases, a camp officer pointed out.''

November 10, 1943. I rushed about getting tins and materials to cook peanut butter cookies to get protein into Bedie. They mix dry and I almost put too much peanut butter. Coila loaned me a board, helped to roll and slice. I borrowed the same tin sheets. Baking period only lasts 15 minutes so all had to be ready at the right time. By the time I washed the utensils and returned the tins it was 11. I tore over to see if the store was open, bought two pounds of onions, 6 small oranges, 3 large oranges, a big bottle of vanilla, and received a 4 pound ration of sugar. The load is too much and takes two trips. Then it is time to waitress. No time to fix Bedie's juice and bread—he has to grab a handful of peanuts at recess. There is flour in every direction so it has to be mopped. June and I made fried rice with bacon, sliced sausage and onion. There is cool papaya salad from camp, squash soup and a ration of peanut butter. After I finish community mopping and copy news from the board, I am tired. It is constant grind and going, little done.

November 11, 1943. Enid, meeting me at the hot water faucet, asked me to come and sew a star on the flag! I went up after lunch and buttonholed a star second from the top in the right-hand corner. Only then did I realize it was Armistice Day and this was why the flag was hauled out of hiding after more than a year stowed away. A guard watched from afar and began strolling our way. Enid kept on the alert but he did not come in. I only hope every camp member who is American has a stitch in it. It all seems fairly futile right now, with Independence and all the rest going on outside, but perhaps it does help morale. It takes more than that to whoop up mine.

November 12, 1943. The supply of fresh milk from town has stopped.

November 13, 1943. Some people have aged fast in here for varying reasons. Some look better because of the regular routine, outdoor life, and lack of dissipations. Some have changed only a little. Most of us look tacky all together, except for a few who make new sweaters and matching headbands and whose jobs allow them to keep immaculate. Many more speak of increased pressure upon the bladder, control more difficult from gas pressure from too much starch. Lady Lorna makes puddles and does not mop up so her neighbors complain, hence the talk of moving her.

November 15, 1943. The *Tribune* is full of repatriate[38] accounts of our terrible morals. There is shortage of gas and tires and transport, so people move in near factories and jobs so there is housing and apartment shortage. This could easily be true. There is a coal strike; people are eating horsemeat.
　　Watching development of characters in here has been interesting. Miss

McKim's latent powers have come out. When I was on the Committee with her she listened, said little, took no sides, and I am sure she thought I was the chief troublemaker. Now she is a leader in camp plans and duties, shows strong social sense in work detail adjustments and for the community. She is always the diplomat, very tactful. It *was* important when we fought to put her on the Committee.

November 16, 1943. June went "Outside" at two, about new glasses, for the first time in two years. She was thrilled. I watched her go—her first car ride in 24 months. She said she felt curve sick, and when she returned she was homesick and tired.

November 17, 1943. Rice is strictly rationed. This will cramp private cooking, cutting down on rice flour, puddings and fried rice. There is no sugar so yeast is about to stop. Swollen legs and wrists, numb hands, dizziness, lassitude at unexpected moments—these are the order of the day for many. If we could lie around, read and rest a lot, we could face it better, but many have to do hard work and the sudden spells of feeling "all-gone" hit at various times. Jerry admits it too. I have one day full of energy, the next with spells of extreme fatigue and exhaustion. Often we feel full, satisfied, unable to eat more, but weak. Liver is $5 a kilo. Someone says there is a sort of famine on and we probably feel it less than anyone, in here. Rice shortage is indicative. The Japanese do not officially face that their money is no good and all good money driven out.

Yeast will be continued for medicinal [purposes] only—not for private dough making where much has been diverted.

November 18, 1943. Jerry brought a round flat tin to put on our frame for a table. We moved it into the corner, switched nails, hung up bags, putting a lot on the walls which had been on the floor, and we look shipshape generally. The polished coconut shells, green tangerines, yellow bananas, pink tomatoes, orange persimmons, yellow oranges and a bright green cup are in gleaming array. I almost enjoy this mad little corner. It is a crazy mélange, tacky with old boards, bags, papers, nails with tin cups hanging next to shoes on the wall, sweaters, dresses, and shelves above, a five gallon wash tin and suitcases beyond, bottles, odd pans and pieces of wood and mop rags ready in a pile for use, but it is our home for two years—where we sleep, dream, wash, dry clothes, become sick and well, shell peas, mix material for cooking, hull peanuts, squeeze limes and all the rest. A bottle of Indian curry powder came in the last bag from Nida!

How blessed for our morale to see the sun.

November 19, 1943. Important notice on the Board: "By Order of the Military Police, internees are prohibited from going *outside the fences* at camp hospital and camp school, and from loitering *on or near Rock Wall* which borders sunken garden on the north. The purpose of this order is to prevent contact with persons passing along the road, a practice to which they seriously object. Compliance with this order will doubtless avoid misunderstandings and possible trouble with local Military Police.'' This is an understatement.

There is no sweet in the children's juice and it is so sour! No sugar or syrup for their rice. Today was the lowest caloric day all year and the Food Committee is stretching like elastic to keep it up. For three or four days no camotes could be bought, whether because Igorots have bought them up due to rice scarcity or did not bring them in to sell because of same or did not dig up during typhoon weather. Everything is tight and even drinking water must be hoarded from now on. We were lucky to get extra rain so late. The General Committee arranged for our yeast after all. It looks as though the Philippine Government is responsible for no sugar, no soap, no lard, no cloth ration during two months.

November 22, 1943. I have had three low days and no time or energy to write but will try to piece out.

The evening audience to hear Carl who had gone to Manila [on an inspection tour] for a week and stayed 11 days was eager for all it could get, noisy, emotional, bursting into roars of laughter over various foods mentioned, held it breath and let go heartily after being long pent-up in rain and wind and newsless days. Carl told of Los Baños and Col. Urabe in charge, of how it had been prepared for seven thousand and more—yet when the General saw it, he condemned it at once, saying it was unfit. Dirt floors, no plumbing or sanitation. It can't take more than a thousand. 200 women will be moved there soon, including wives who will be allowed to live with their husbands in small independent quarters. Several couples wish to marry and Tokyo has been asked permission but has not answered yet. He told us of the Teia Maru unloading 40 tons of private mail, mostly packages, Red Cross and private supplies for civilian and military prisoners. There are individual kits, medical supplies, shoe repair equipment (most of our shoes are too far gone) and recreational apparatus. Carl saw many friends, dined with them on juicy steaks and conversation. He told of discussions on closer relations between the camps and of uniform rules. Los Baños is a sort of experiment on families living together. There is a big military camp close by, with officers and soldiers coming and going all the time which brings forth much protest and criticism of a civilian internment camp so close to a military zone. They discussed (1) Exchange of supplies between camps and have half formed a plan to use Mt. Data truck from here once a month. (2) Exchange of internees between camps. Nine are to go down and 6 come up here, joining husband and wife. They are reluctant to take many there because they are so crowded and are told that 260 Davao group will arrive by the end of the month. The audience let out a full-throated roar when Carl told of butter, Klim [powdered milk], Spam, cheese and Chesterfields in some of the [Red Cross] Christmas kits. 11,933 cases were unloaded and carefully guarded on the pier until moved into warehouses where they were sealed by the Swiss Consul representative, the Japanese Military Administration and Santo Tomas officials. It is guarded *on the outside* by Nipponese guards. There is food, clothing, tobacco, medical and recreational supplies. It all sounded too good to be true and we couldn't contain ourselves.

Carl said Santo Tomas was like a Big City. (Privately both he and Ray said it was Big Business, everyone trying to make money off the next one; just one little business racket after another. There is no free service or communal exchange of labor—all is for profit and plenty of it.) Carl said publicly that he was glad to get "home" to the small town where we had our troubles but we all pitched in and helped each other on a service basis. He said the attitude and atmosphere is so much better here and he thought we had chosen the better and more democratic way. Carl says there are some U.S. letters so we still hope that when the censors are through we will get one. Bert and Jo have been supported by José, their chauffeur, as we have been supported by Nida and Ismael. He fed them for six months after Bert landed in camp with only 23 pesos and could get no money. Bev says many would not have pulled through as well or with belongings saved if it were not for the mass loyalty of most of the servants in Manila. Their standing by the Americans is one of the great stories of the war. This and Carl's gladness to be back at Camp Holmes again stand out above everything else. They all say our food is better here so God help the others! Children of teen age are better off there, for all up to 15 get an egg and a glass of milk for supper. This meal would make a whale of a difference to June and Bedie, Curt and Eloise. But they don't get it. We are likely to stay on in the mountains as Carl scotched the hardy rumor of any move to Los Baños for us. There was an irregularity about our not getting Christmas kits last year but no one can say what, who or where, though parts of the kits were sold on Manila streets. This year there is more order and there has been too much publicity about the supply ship and its contents for us not to get something. We should get cloth rations too. Neglected sheep is no name for us. The Forgotten Man is nearer.

I didn't do much all day and slept two hours in the afternoon. The triple injection hits me the second or third day, making me groggy and heavy. We are glad they are over but it was good to get them.

A cute bunch of kids trek down and later on come back from the playground with pails, cans, spoons, in sunbonnets, hats and overalls of all description. They are usually wet and muddy at the end but very happy unless wailing from a miniature battle.

I did not get my "moppu" done ahead of my shot at 10:30. I thought of my dream afterward for the shot sent me haywire. It was the first time it happened and I hope I never have to repeat such an experience. The doctor had trouble hitting the vein and pushed about, finally hitting it. Blood poured into the syringe. He took it out quickly saying he was sorry but would have to try the other arm. This time it went in well and I felt the usual warmth and bitter mouth and throat instantly all over. The intensity increased until I finally said, "Everything is going black." He had it all in by then and was holding my pulse. The nurse held spirits of ammonia on cotton under my nose. I concentrated my gaze, staring intently, trying to hold on. The grass beyond the window, the desk, everything, went white, pure white, but I could still see outlines. I mentioned this and he motioned her to give me a glass of water with ammonia spirits. I gulped it down but only half-conscious of motion or moving. The sensations at this stage were terrific. My whole system felt out of control, a most hideous feeling when one is hanging on to the thread of consciousness. A roaring in the ears, bells ringing in the head, a rushing all through the body, a terrific ebb and flow, all one's forces gathered and pushed this way and that in some tremendous sway of power. Color like a kaleidoscope not only in the sight but within one. Then a horrible sweet and sickening nausea. I think the doctor heard me say, "I feel so sick now," for he said, "Come and lie down on your bed." Both took an arm and led me out of the dispensary into my space on the other side of the wall. Carl saw me and told Peg I looked awful, that he didn't think I would be able to come for coffee this evening. But I walked in and by the time I lay down I could see clearly again. I rested, my mind empty of thought and the sickish feeling slowly passing but a little of it remaining until night. The doctor came to see how I reacted and I asked him what in the world happened, what went wrong, when it had not been like that the other two times. He said he was afraid that the blood in the syringe would coagulate so he had given it to me a little faster, not as slowly as usual, and I couldn't absorb it. He said now and then one shot in a series would act that way and the patient would pass out completely. They had expected I would when they saw it start but the nurse said that by intense concentration one can hold on and keep from going, which is what I did.

Gen. Nagasaki came an hour late to say good-bye before leaving for Mindanao. The General admitted lateness, shaking his head over his watch. He shook hands with each American, bowed to each Japanese, and as he stepped into his car, after a brief survey, he saluted each in turn including all the Americans. He told Miss McKim in Nippongo to tell us good-bye and to take care of ourselves, she returning the same figure of speech.

November 23, 1943. Jerry came for the lemon squeezer as he was going to make an orange cake, wanted a half cup of juice to put with 4 cups of cassava flour etc. He looked at me sideways, thinking of his three tries at bread, and said, "If we can't have bread, let us eat cake," bringing Marie Antoinette, French tumbrils and revolution right into our midst. What a time he had baking it, after it was mixed. Hordes of women mowed him down to make their cookies—seven trying to cook thousands of cookies! He finally let his cake wait till the bedlam was over at 9:30 and he stayed on till 10, baking.

November 24, 1943. As for Harry Barz, he seems to have made a real hit. A Japanese soldier back here as guard asked about him and his family at once, brought cookies to the little son. He was at the jail when they were held there, fell for the baby and greatly admires Harry. Another soldier who went on the manhunt with Harry that time when he went five days without food, came back especially to ask how he was and called him a fine man. Though there is no common bond of language, there is respect and appreciation of a real man, admiration, even affection. There are enemies but when they stand face to face and go through a common experience together, they know a man when they see one, without any words. And they do not forget. Friends have been made on both sides in spite of tragic barriers of cruelty and suffering.

June enjoyed another foursome. She does not like to be monopolized by one date; with life so close in here it is not easy to arrange with tact. She is in a dreamy daze and left her toothbrush, towel and my sweater in various spots where I rescued them. She loves music and gets 100 in all the tone tests of the advanced class.

A newborn baby was brought in by a neighbor with six children clustering around her. They wanted hospital treatment for the infant. [The Igorot women] age young and have internal troubles. The one who lost an infant last year now has another one, living, this time.

November 25, 1943. There was a wonderful home bag which touched us deeply. All four of us were waiting when the truck came in. Chicken salad—the bowl covered with fresh washed young lettuce leaves and scarlet radishes with green leaves! In it were new potatoes, green peas, diced carrots and celery, made carefully and like our springtime salad of old. There was half a jar of rich real mayonnaise made with olive oil. As Bedie ate, he remarked, "So that is what chicken tastes like." Also in the bag were six oranges, ½ kilo of sugar, and half a loaf of fruit cake with citron and dates in it like a real pound cake. Bedie was too full to eat dessert at noon and June was still full from last night's ham fat, but she managed to wind up with cake. Camp gave us beef broth with chopped parsley floating in the fat; camote, rice bread and fruit salad.

The childrens' Thanksgiving serving was at 4 in a gay dining room. On the table were candles set in tall reeds of bamboo holders resting on blocks with round tin slits to catch the wax drips. There were turkeys made of fluted newspaper painted black, with red head and body cut flat, resting on chopping blocks of wood with green leaves about it, for centerpieces at each table. In the center was a cloth stuffed turkey painted brown, with frills on each leg, ready for roasting; bamboo candles at one end and a heap of fruit arranged by artistic hands (Viola, Daphne and Helen Mann); at the other end a gorgeous heap of vegetables. In between these two harvest piles were two enormous pumpkin pies with fluted brown crust edge; plates heaped with cookies and dishes of quivering jelly. Squashes, peas, carrots, camotes, garlic, onions; papaya, oranges, pineapple, guayabáno [or ''soursop,'' a tropical fruit], waxy acorns, bananas—all the natural wealth of the Philippines was there, with some American additions. At the other end of the room was a fireplace made of tin painted red and divided into bricks by strips of newspaper. There was an iron grate holding logs above which was the mantelpiece—a huge log on which was carved in beautiful old letters ''Learn to Labor and to Wait.'' It is a camp creed and the best that has been given us about what we are learning in here. The room was a huge success, with everyone loving it and chirking up.

June and I went to Union Church service at ten, held inside because of gentle rain. Patton's sermon was fine, taking the place of Collier who was in the hospital. There is a minimum of patients now and a comparatively long spell without dysentery for which we can be thankful. We can give thanks for many things.

Dinner gave us one of our own pigs, with beef, made into hamburgers, delicious gravy, fresh peas, mashed white potatoes (in which the coconut milk unfortunately had gone sour since 3 A.M. but we ate it with gusto, having looked forward to real mashed potato all day), tomato-onion-cucumber salad, and spicy pumpkin pie with coffee. The dining room was so jammed with comminglers that it almost stopped the works. It would never do for everyday eating routine. Miss McKim made a heartfelt speech of thanks to the Kitchen and all those who worked hard to decorate and serve. The Chef responded with his cheery grin. If one stopped to think of home or the past, the eyes filled with tears, so one did not stop.

Jerry bought my Christmas gift—an P8 cerise and pale blue pair of sandals with ribbon bows tied around the ankles. I enjoy them lustily for the colors are lovely with my turquoise skirt. The shoes are soft and comfortable with thick heels, feel like lounge slippers.

The most pungent tale of camp life recently—Mrs. Polombo coughed her false teeth into the toilet. The first question every one asks after hearing it is, ''What did she use to sterilize them?''

Small Robert put his hand into Carl's and confided as they walked along, ''I'm going to be on the garbage crew when I grow up.''

Manila camp has not heard of Sub. 1, 2 and 3 coffee or tea. They do not use their grounds again. In an article in the American Weekly, Feb. 16, 1941, I read that 70 years ago in the seige of Paris they made first, second and third class tea in restaurants. The first was fresh, the others were leaves dried and used again.

Doris says that when she came into our Harvest dining room and the warmth struck her at the door, the dim light, closed shutters, noise, color, friendly gaiety reminded her of cafés in Europe and she instinctively looked for a waiter! It was like German Rathskellers.

June had a big argument with one of her boyfriends. He has firm religious convictions and she refuses to be pinned down, says anyone has a right to believe whatever he likes. He stormed, "Then you don't believe in Christ. What have you to live for?" She would not admit such a point and said she did not care to talk about her beliefs and that she wanted to work for humanity as a nurse or a doctor which she thought would give her something to live for. I was proud of her open mind and tolerance. Her expressions were original and she has done her own thinking. It surprised me to see how serene and content she was and how far she had gone on her own road.

November 26, 1943. None of us were greatly interested in the peanut butter stew but I liked the vegetables in it.

The Chef sent one of the large pies and a big can of cookies to the 12 American soldiers [imprisoned] at Camp Hay.

November 27, 1943. Medical Committee notes: "Most of the glasses obtained at Santo Tomas are on an exchange basis, so that the chances of getting eyeglasses are better and cheaper if the old glasses are sent down with the new prescription. Dr. Welles presented a new plan for the distribution of milk, soybean milk, and an egg to children under 2½ years. Attention of camp is called to the rule that *dogs are not to be fed in camp*. Their presence here may expose camp to rabies."

Contents of a sample Invalid Package from the Red Cross packages.

10 assorted cigarette pkgs.	1 whole milk, 1 lb. tin
8 bouillon powder in bag	1 salmon, 7¼ oz. tin
12 ascorbic acid tablets in bag	1 canned meat—Prem or party
2 emergency rations "D" pkgs.	loaf, 12 oz.
1 Domino sugar, ¼ lbs. pkgs.	3 preserved butter, Army spread
1 prunes, dried, 1 lb. pkg.	3¾ oz.
2 Swan soap bars	3 corned pork loaf, U.S.A. field
1 Rose Mill Paté, 6 oz. tins	ration, 3¾ oz.
2 Kup Kafay, 4 oz. tins	2 chopped ham and eggs, 3¾ lb.
1 corned beef, 12 oz. tin	tins
1 Kraft cheese, ½ lb. pkg.	1 grape jam, Grapelade, 6 oz.

Men's Committee. "The Chair reported that he had brought with him from Manila an additional Relief Fund of P4,000."

Bananas are 5¢ apiece and rationed to 2 per person today. They are scarce, due to rice shortage and natives eating bananas instead, according to rumor.

Tonight there is consternation. No more cooking in the kitchen except the bread-making three nights a week. The cookie makers are furious. It is not more than 10 or 12 in all who abuse it, yet wood consumption has shot up. Less than 10% benefit from it.

November 28, 1943. I intended to hear Carl's paper at the seminar but took Bedie's specimen to the lab first. Dr. Viola asked me to sit down while he examined it at once as he already had three cases of bacillary of the explosive type, high fever and very sick. Smitty had a heart attack from the severity of it. Dr. Viola is upset and worried. He let me look at the slide then said to bring Bedie down in about 15 minutes, as soon as a bed could be arranged. Bang—here it is again. When I took Bedie's soap and towel down to him he turned his face to the wall and wept. I could not comfort him without being contaminated. But I soon had him smiling and later he was very cheered by his and Geoff's girls calling from below the window.

After reading his paper at the seminar, Carl entered the hospital as bacillary patient also!

Miss Lucy and some of the older people who are not strong are failing visibly. These last months are tougher. Yesterday the flies seemed to start again.

November 29, 1943. The Igorots report great suffering outside—scarcity, privation and hardship.

November 30, 1943. Jerry and I sat together studying Spanish and Japanese. We had Peg for coffee and she is exhausted. It was her first day at the extra labor of serving; she made custards for her two patients and wrote a letter to her husband who she expects is arriving in Manila from Davao. She hopes he will be sent up here for it is easier for one to come up than for four to go down. She refuses to face the fact that we must cut down on firewood consumption, puts it off still further by volunteering to serve in replacement for a new wood crew. Controlled economy comes hard and people fight against it, twisting and turning, anything but face it.

December 1, 1943. My head still bothers me. I woke telling June that I was going to bake my last batch of cookies in here today. I feel that scarcity and restriction will come faster as the days go on. At breakfast we learned there would be no high school today so June said she would help with the cookies. We also learned from a very grumpy kitchen staff that the Japanese were not only taking over the school building but had ordered strict rice, corn, peanut and other items rationed. The kitchen is ordered to give out no rice in between meals. We are to receive just so much each time and if we want to fry it will have to carry out what we don't eat at each meal.

Later I saw Dr. Viola who looks worried and has Mrs. Kessler down as number 15. I heard one ask Dr. Viola if it really was dysentery and he answered, "Yes—there is no question at all about Carl's having it." I stuck in, "And Bedie?" Yes, Bedie had it definitely too. I remarked that I had just had three people in the dining room tell me it wasn't dysentery at all, just food poisoning. Viola answered that dysentery wasn't the whole picture, it was complicated by spoiled meat in the beginning and other things which didn't make it any easier for him. Mrs. Sobeck asked me at noon how Bedie was and I said he was home but too soon in my estimation if he had really had dysentery which I was convinced he had had.

Eloise Luzon is the parent of a 6½ pound girl born Outside, but manufactured in camp! It is our first married scandal. What a time to have a baby, and proud of the fact. It is underweight. No wonder the mother was jolly and rotund, waddling about. It is the last thing I would want now. When she went to the hospital it was said to be dysentery. One asks, "What will they do with the specimen?" and the reply is, "Put it in the silver drawer as they did little John Hay!"

The proud father says, "Wouldn't you like to know how we managed it? I told you we could make anything at the shop and now I've proved it." Jerry says the infant is not illegitimate but illicit!

When the Committee asks for a raise [in camp allocations], the [Japanese] authorities tell them that we get the best there is now, preference in buying through the Army etc. By their standards and present conditions outside, we are well off. The store was bought out of everything today.

The Medical Committee has *accepted* Dr. Viola's resignation and all has been cleared for him to leave for Los Baños.

December 2, 1943. No high school till further notice. The students moved all the school material out of the building over to the bodega. The four guards, the Camp Administrator and his seven staff and Hayakawa will live at the school building, and the office of Camp Administrator and Committee will be at the old guardhouse. For us, a respite from binoculars, but they will now be trained on the hospital.

The Minutes of Christmas Committee are up. Winnie was put in charge of coordinating various Christmas programs. Camp will be canvassed to find those who would like to volunteer to make presents for the tree. A Christmas fund will be established for those who prefer to contribute money toward purchase of presents for the children. A list of books and other gifts which may be ordered from Manila will be posted, with prices. Anyone willing to lend Christmas decorations will please get in touch with Hazel. The Committee welcomes and is glad to consider feasability of any suggestions that individuals may have toward making the season a happy one.

Doug has been ailing for some time, last week flu and diarrhea. Today his mattress and he went to the hospital. Della tells me he worked too hard with not enough chow and had finally cracked. Carl was worn out before dysentery hit him, and she said Dr. Shaffer was working so hard he would crack if he wasn't careful. Quite true, except that Doug has had plenty of extra cooking and parties on borrowed money. He has slacked off the last two months. They have all pushed themselves too hard for the wrong thing. There is so much cake and cookie baking to keep up morale that there are not enough workers for veg and rice, and the men are wearing themselves out to get wood for fancy stuff when in the end it is wasteful on both labor and supply. They should *control* the cooking. I bake about once a month, twice at most, rationing carefully. Some of them bake double recipes every other day and gobble it up in 24 hours.

It is the same with the hospital problem. They begin at the wrong end. The building should be cleared for patients only, except in one room for men where the doctor, a male nurse, and Barrett could stay on to be present for emergencies. The hospital could be divided up into sections for acute and convalescent dysentery cases, a third place for permanent cases, a fourth for heart and nervous cases as it is now. Instead of this, the dysentery patients are sent back after one good specimen when Dr. Hall's ironclad rule was three in a row of clear ones. This is why Bedie and others came home the third day, with each one a carrier spreading in various barracks. All because 10 or 14 women want to live close to their work and other privileges in the happy home.

December 3, 1943. While we ate lunch, Dr. Benedetti who had been put in charge of the lab came to tell us he was sorry but Bedie had to go back to the hospital, admitting quite frankly that he had been allowed to go home too soon because of overcrowding. Jerry said, looking grim, "This brings us back to the old argument—why not take out some of the staff and make room for more patients?" "I'm afraid it isn't as simple as that, considerably more complicated," was his retort. And being utterly sick at heart we stopped there. Poor old Bedie looked sick at heart too when we called him. Soon Jerry was going down bent under the mattress, blankets, discouragement and soreness. Bedie is sicker this time, feels rotten and nauseated. He waved his hand from the window and faded back to bed. It means he has to go on the starvation diet and take the purgative all over again. Carl feels wretched and is back on liquid first-day diet again.

After mops I threw myself on the bed feeling I could blow into a thousand pieces. I tried to read D. H. Lawrence and fell asleep. I awoke feeling clear and refreshed—which is dynamite!

Back in the barracks late, a swell story broke which came from the dining room. It was said that the Japanese had asked for some of our men to go out and rebuild the bridge destroyed by the storm on the Kennon Road. Walter had answered by all means No and the Japanese had said all right—no bridge, no packages or transfers. The Red Cross packages were supposed to be at Damortis waiting. Was this red hot! Edna said why shouldn't our men help open the road and at once a chorus of feminine horror proclaimed it would open the way to all kinds of pressure for our men to do other things outside.

There was a half hour of pro and con chatter. It was something to sleep on but Bedie's sickish fade-out haunted me.

December 4, 1943. We now receive 150 grams each of rice a day. At the start of the war Manila ration was 200 for well people, 350 for sick or weak, considered a minimum. The present sack is moldy, very bad, so we'll all be glad when it is gone.

It was originally the request of the Japanese that our men construct the guardhouse and school at the bodega at P1 a day, and Walter for the Executive Committee answered No because we needed every available man on present details. He also said it would not do because it might lead to outside work.

I remember a conversation some years ago in which I said I would not pick up and go to the States to get away from what I knew was coming. I said Nida and her family and thousands of others like them in these islands could not leave. They had to stay and take it and why should all of us leave when it was our home. I remember Eddie's surprised and puzzled look as he said, "Why, she feels responsible for it." I feel more than ever that if everyone felt responsible, as each one indeed is, for these terrible events then the sequence would not come about and we would all be spared the results. Again we find it in here. No one feels or wishes to be responsible.

I certainly never expected to see a hospital run chiefly to benefit the staff for two years. They have kept to one course, one attitude for two years and it hasn't worked. But they won't try the other course. Like the cows of India, the staff is too sacred to move. Every time there is a space in the barracks after a release, someone else is moved in in a hurry, but not from the staff. It is no joke to me and will never be commonplace. But I am just a common everyday reformer, a poor fool who won't accept the inevitable and tries to stop the deluge. I am a Queen Canute holding up a hand to stop the sea, just as I hoped Indusco would hold the fighting line in China, as it could have done if given full support in time. Fools, fools, but it starts in Manchuria, then Ethiopia, then the Ebro, till it covers the world and even German women and children beg for time to bury their dead. It goes on in fury to the usual end which is not victory for anyone.

Dr. Shaffer admitted the pressure had sent Bedie home too soon and said they were preparing to take care of 8 more patients, with flooring being laid in the tent. Jerry did not ask whether patients or staff would go into it, but the guess is easy. It was patients who occupied the tent before until even Japanese medical officers noticed and called them down about it, said a cottage should be vacated. Then they stopped putting patients into the tent. It is a disgrace to treat patients like this, but no one seems to think so. They all take it meekly except Mrs. Crouter who has decided the only way to get anything in here is to raise hell. The hospital is still full of staff, no chlorine solution is put out, nothing has changed, and I am about to lose all my friends and I don't care. The Pilgrim and Puritan concentrated in the mountains of Northern Luzon is blowing [into] pieces.

December 6, 1943. Helen Kessler told us about her illness and says the hospital organization now is so much better, cleaner, beds made up every morning shipshape, baths given, nets hung up for patients every night (which was not done before, a year ago), rounds made by the head nurse as routine to inquire if anything is needed, the general tone improved. But the crowded condition is a disgrace. We heard from her and the one involved that when Mrs. Kessler was scheduled to come in and the nurse asked where she would be placed, the doctor pointed in silence to Nancy's bed with Nancy still in it. She was not feeling at all well, less like going back to crawl up and down long steps to the toilet than she had felt the day before. But the mill grinds them out in four days.

The December 3 *Tribune* was full of important items. There was a Roosevelt, Churchill, Chiang and Stalin meeting at Cairo and Teheran, full of import. Mme. Chiang represented as there also.[39]

The War Relief kits won't get here any too soon. We need to know, and not only to know but to see concretely for ourselves—with hands touching it—the proof that people at home are thinking and working for us, that somebody cares. There is so little to talk about except prices and scarce supplies.

December 7, 1943. Kata Kana characters are almost second nature now but I need much practice in Hira Gana. I translated two short tales from one into the other.

The Sergeant broke into the Committee meeting last night and asked when the war was going to be over. They said they didn't know and asked what he thought. He said he didn't know either but he wanted to go home and was getting mighty tired of it. The guardhouse and the barracks, the prisoners and the enemy feel alike. The radio has moved to the new guardhouse so the old one is dark tonight and no one watches us from there. No one went to hear the radio in new quarters but some diehards will soon go again.[40]

The *News* says, "Unable to purchase milk for 24 children for whom camp supplies the product because of their youngness, the kitchen has begun to manufacture soybean milk to supplement canned and milk from camp cows. The beans are cracked in a coffee grinder, skinned, winnowed, soaked two hours to eliminate the natural bitter taste, drained, strained, ground, strained (the pulp being re-ground and re-strained). The beans are boiled in a pressure cooker under 15 pounds pressure for half an hour, producing a palatable "milk" product. With the beans at P4 a kilo and extremely difficult to obtain, the milk is only given to babies; nevertheless, it represents considerable saving in cost." Also in the *News*: "Watch your belongings—high prices seem to be tempting the light-fingered."

December 8, 1943. The roaming cows are creating sleepless nights. They nose covers off of cans, tip over and eat garbage. They moo, not to say roar, at each other from opposite ends of the grounds and gambol around the barracks. Irate women throw rocks in the dark and hit Miss McKim's cottage by mistake with a loud thump, scaring and rousing them all thoroughly. Daphne returning from the toilet before dawn ran into a black bulk around a corner, raised her arms and went "shoo, shoo" at the cow—which turned into Father Barter in his wide black cape. Daphne, ever polite and resourceful, pretended she was exercising against the cold.

More signs of time and change: There is no more graft in waitressing. It is not even made easy any longer. Doris finds she can't do both typing at the office and waiting on table and cooking for her invalid so she is giving up waitressing, of all things. A year ago this wouldn't have happened. Quiet prodding, even dynamite, could not dislodge one of these loyal girls. If one quit or was pushed out, the kitchen staff would strike, we were told. And now one of the best is voluntarily departing. It is sensible and the thing for her to do, but it wouldn't have happened even six months ago. It means that waitressing is just another detail with no frills and no graft to speak of. Papaya is left over now and then, but on the whole it is all square and on the level. Most of them have two jobs now.

People discuss the Chef and his friends who have huge roasts, delicious whole meals, planned and cooked with the Chef's touch, often. Every other day, sometimes each day, there are lovely juicy cuts of meat, while the rest of us eat camp meatless diet, occasionally meat when we can get it. The Chef gets some "cumsha" [graft or tip] from market stall and gathers his friends around.

The Executive Committee in an effort to save wood, ruled that on 4 nights a week when the main stove is not in use for camp baking, it might be used until 8 for private cooking but after that hour the kitchen must be cleared. . . . The Sanitation head stated that as a sanitary and safety measure the General Committee should make every effort to fence the campgrounds so that cows could not come into camp. He suggested if wire for this purpose could be secured, the goat owners were willing to insert reeds through the fence so that goats, too, could not get into the grounds.

The *News*: "Faced with the necessity of extensive winnowing to remove large amounts of chaff contained in Thai rice now being supplied by control authorities to camp, the Rice Detail chief called in Jess Vickers. Result: a rice blower which mechanically does the work of two winnowers and aids the short-handed rice crew." Also, "A tin can is a rarity in the garbage now and veg peelings fail to fill more than one third of a 3 gallon tin container, as there is no soft rice in the kitchen slop or banana peels in Barracks 1 and 2; even the hospital can fails to make its two carriers stagger. This is prosperity index (or shall we say scarcity index)—by their garbage cans ye shall know them."

December 9, 1943. The grinding department will work overtime now that everyone is stocking up on peanuts. Our order for P10 worth came in from the Tong market stall this noon. Eggs are 70¢ each but none available says the store. We used to get two dozen for 80¢ in the provinces. This must be the "hard days at the last" which we have spoken about before. Everyone is stocking up on fat, beans, peanuts, bacon. With no meat and no eggs there are only the bean and nut proteins left to us. Milk is no more, except soy. Jerry is experimenting with some of our peanuts, trying to make peanut milk with help from the Soy group.

December 10, 1943. There was a meeting of all Americans in the dining room to say Yes or No on repatriation. We do have a choice[41] and we four said No because the voyage could be awful. After two years of it here, it should be easy to stick out the rest. Could it be worse than these last months? We are about to find out. There was no assurance of another ship whichever way the vote goes.

December 11, 1943. Christmas season is in the air. Jerry and Bedie are carving at the shop in spare and secret moments. Adults are busy with scraps and scissors, needles and what thread there is left—unraveling old sweaters and socks full of holes. Dolls with hand-sewn faces and silk scrap gowns peak out of hidden corners. Men are making carts and wood toys out of scrap wood—it really is down to scrap this year.

All is Christmas, good will, and politics and cooperation until after election. Political tickets or platforms are pruned down and nominations go up today. Two of the bachelors will no doubt stick with the hospital staff due to parties, cooking and girl friends. It is an amusing lineup, with switches if one changes girls or economic companionship.

December 12, 1943. When attack came, [one man] took much into his own hands when he was in the Army. He took a prominent Japanese who was a leader in the Nipponese community and who made no attempt to leave but gave himself up quietly—he took this Japanese as though he were a wild animal to a wired-in space like a cage, at the Moro Penal Colony, where all the Moros were called to gaze at him as though he were a wild beast and where they watched him beaten at this American's orders, beaten as we have watched a tougher type of American beaten here. He was kept there and ill-treated under the name of American patriotism, revenge for national treachery, hate and stupidity, sadism in a smart-aleck manner. This Japanese leader of the community was highly intelligent, sensitive, well-bred, educated far above average. He would be a fine figure of a man in any country. Where does it end—this circle? A flashy, unintelligent boy, full of patriotism and importance, leaps into a position of influence where he can control and abuse a man who is by far his superior in most ways—all because of force let loose by war. How far does this one act reach, this act committed in the early days of war? It travels far and fast as such stories do. Months later when the invader himself has the reins and the boy is dead, his evil lives after him, piling on and on. Father Griffiths in Northern Luzon mountains is tied around the neck with a rope, led about like a dancing bear and finally tied to a stake for all the mountain people to gaze at in his turn. This time it is not a prominent Chinese or a prominent Japanese businessman but a high-strung, sensitive Anglican priest whose only real crime is being an American. The prominent Japanese, free again from the horror, carries such loathesome hours and days in his memory forever, and is once more in a position of influence. War—the great psychosis.

December 13, 1943. If we do stay instead of repatriation, we may be letting our children in for a period of low food level but they will learn much, and life will be full of history and interest in the rebuilding. With so much behind us, we can't bear not to see it through at least to the Marines and the war's close.

Election results are most intriguing. We will never forget the election when the missionaries all united and even went on from there to a spontaneous coalition worked out by five different groups.

December 14, 1943. Every effort is being made to secure an increase in our daily allowance for the running of camp. Because of soaring prices, this has been No. 1 request in all contacts with the Japanese authorities since the date of our last increase. We now spend almost P1 per day per person, over and above the allowance given us by the Japanese. Relief and other funds have been authorized in this emergency in order to maintain for the camp a subsistence diet. They cannot be depended upon, however, as a permanent source of help.

December 15, 1943. Jim Thompson, our satirist, points to the garbage can and asks the carrier, "Where did you get that little dab?" and the answer is, "Back of Barracks 2." "What!" yells Jim, "Things must be low. We are down to bedrock if you can't get more garbage than that from the kitchen!" Dr. Welles looks wistfully into the hospital can for peels and gabi and things to feed the goats and pigs, but finds only a few cans, dust and scraps. Mike on the garbage crew says, "These goat getters and pig grubbers are cutting into our garbage. Between them and the times we don't get a load any more and won't be able to get gardenias."

Win is organizing a Christmas tableaux of Madonnas of many lands for Sunday Vespers. There are reservations for tables on Christmas Eve, from 6 to 18, adults and children together. Tables will be on the parade ground with bonfires or flares as light. We are to join with Scotts, the wood crew, and Littles. Everyone is organizing into holiday grouping. It is almost like the country club or the hotel reservations.

Hayakawa with a golf club and three guards in high army boots are creeping about out in the back, beating the bush—not on military or guerrilla maneuvers—but hunting for their strayed mother hen and 6 chicks which have left the guardhouse and moved to a new spot. This is food walking out the front door, the reason for heavy attack and surrounding.

Never is a long day and two years in Concentration is ages, but when a few hopes come true and some things begin to really work out, then it is worth it.

It was Carl's suggestion that the Chair be responsible for contacts with the Japanese authorities since such contacts now require one man's full time and thought if he is to do justice to his office. The Vice-Chair's work would be in conjunction with that of the Chair so that when the Chair is absent that work is carried on. The third member's work should be that of Work Details and such business that arises as a result of routine and emergency work and contact with internees in connection with such details. Denki became Vice-Chair.

Enid's Welfare report is worth chronicling. "The source of our materials has been loot and charity. Such items as curtains, mattresses, mattress covers, mosquito nets, bed and table linens, blankets, pillows, waiter's uniforms, chairback covers, costumes etc., came in from Camp John Hay, Baguio Country Club, Brent School and the Little Theatre. Boxes and bags of clothing, cloth, shoes, books, games, came from the Belgian Sisters and Brothers, Maryknoll Sisters, Sisters of St. Anne, Episcopal Mission Women's Auxilliary, Lutheran Mission, Presbyterian Mission, Monday Club, City Hall and Manila Red Cross. About 12 individuals donated also. Many clothes have been donated by camp members. In the beginning it was a matter of sharing their scant surplus of good clothes, but as time goes on it is cast-off garments we get, even so, greatly appreciated. Many that were given as scrubbing rags were patched into usefulness. As a matter of fact, this has been our chief source of supplies during the last six months because few things of any value have been given from outside. The number of garments given to camp members the last six months is far less than for any other six months because we did not have them to give. On the other hand, the patching and repairs are far more. This accounts for the many "remade" articles on the list. Garments listed as "sewed" are made from private materials. Unclaimed things from the Lost and Found and from the gutter are also a source of our supplies. When garments get beyond patching, they are classified for patching material, potholders, mops and various scrub rags, the lowest category being stuffing for dolls. It is fortunate that many people supply their own scrubbing rags as we could not supply all needed. The ten miles of strong thread used for community sewing on the two camp sewing machines during the last 11 months was donated by the Sisters of St. Anne. The hand-sewing has been done with abaca thread, stocking and other ravelings, and private thread. The darning has all been done with bits of raveled yarn—too short to be knitted into reclaimed sweaters.''

Echoes from the election. One man wrote a straight vegetable ticket such as ubi, gabi, kang kong, kondol etc. Another tacked up couplets about ''To the Styx with Mix.'' ''Don't vote for Denki, he's stinky.'' ''Dunne is done for,'' and so forth.

Today the Men's Committee has abolished the liaison end of their Committee, leaving it entirely to Miss McKim who does not dramatize it. Now the Chair will do it, with Miss McKim's excellent diplomacy.

December 16, 1943. There is a rumor we are in the Marianas,[42] and a marvelous story of Nelson and another mechanic at Tugeuguerao who were put to servicing a big transport plane. They hopped in and took off, knocking down the Japanese guard. They got away too. But how will they find a landing—with two fried eggs on the wings? What a daring try and predicament!

Things may come and things may go but Arthur still lives with his wife during the two years of nonconnubial bliss for camp as a whole!

All the adamant nonworkers for the community are now borne down in a tide of public opinion. The men in particular ''think the least of those that are idle.'' It is wonderful—practically a Camp Millennium. Coalition and compromise has worked out a number of items; groups amalgamating, willing to discuss, give in here and there to bring about good for the whole. A judiciary trial yesterday cleared up some private graft in the veg room. The accused admitted all charges. The penality is—no more work by the accused, in the veg room or the kitchen or with any food preparation. The accused is now assigned to toilet work far from the food preparation room. This is final to months of flagrant snitching. There was much bravado, shrugging of shoulders, in a dramatic trial.

December 17, 1943. Yesterday an Igorot woman was brought in on a litter from a nearby barrio. She gave premature birth. The infant was fed sugar water in a medicine dropper, but had little chance of life, particularly under its family conditions and war. Some of the older boys here dug a little grave on our hillside cemetary and Father Maquire read the services, attended by Miss McKim. A tiny Igorot child, resident of the New Philippine Republic, is now resting by the side of Americans in an internment cemetery.

When we asked for a tin of our own milk returned, we were given a flat, cold ''No.'' Jerry remarked that Daddy Harbog had figured up and discovered that his family and our family had turned in more supplies at the beginning than anyone in camp. And when Jerry tried to stop the graft and stealing then and *asked* for a couple of cans of his own milk—he was defeated in the elections, dropped from the first committee by those who wanted to stay in power and grab the privileges. It was bad enough to be hungry—but to see our own food taken and eaten by some of our own people before our eyes for weeks—that was torture indeed.

December 18, 1943. Husbands now visit upstairs with families discreetly. Cups of coffee together and Daddy "minding the baby." Now that fire-eating guards are gone we can relax. There is still the battle over animals—cats and dogs and chickens. It is tough on those who love pets but animals do get in the hair, in the way, and in the food.

One mother leaves diapers in a terrible condition in the laundry bag to be washed daily by another one who is detailed to do it. No wonder they all kick and quit. While others do this dirty work she cooks fancy things for her own tea parties, and is sick often.

Jerry made good sweet and sour rice at noon. Peanut gravy was good for supper. Afterward news went like wildfire that Tokyo admitted U.S. landing on New Britain December 15.

Carl received a permit from the Mayor to cut two trees only in Trinidad, which enabled him to see the man in charge of forest reservation to get permit to look it over for firewood possibilities. It is a mile, then another five miles walk in there and back. The cutters and sawers will have to take lunch and stay all day and it will be tough on shoes. Jerry has only one good pair so he has been weighing the pros and cons all day and decided to be put on some other detail. He became so run down on heavy work last year, that he can't do it this year, particularly with the addition of hiking. It is time he changed his detail, so when the trees on the hill above are finished Jerry will be through.

The childrens' three-act presentation of *The Bird's Christmas Carol* was perfect. All of us Ruggles in the audience saw ourselves and laughed until we cried over the washed and starched sassiety family looking "like prisoners," exclaiming over pictures pasted right on the plates (many of our kids haven't seen a dish with designs on it), the napkins marked in a corner so no one will nip them (just like our spoons and plates), the ill-assorted costumes, the interest in a good meal. All of it was close to home. All the grades sang Christmas carols and songs. Jerry's beans on muffins for us were the final touch.

December 19, 1943. We had special permit to go up the hill and out of bounds in order to bring down six logs to make into bakia. It is nearly a year since my last trip up, when Jerry strained his back. Bedie didn't want to go as he wanted to finish a Christmas knife for his girl. He was so cranky I felt I couldn't stand it, for he groused all the way up and back last time. I begged Jerry to leave him behind then went and told him to stay home for we didn't want him. He was dumbfounded and we started off as he went slowly back to the barracks. As we neared the top, Jerry turned to look back and pointed down. There, all by himself, a solitary, lonely-looking speck in the middle of the parade ground stood Bedie, trying not to watch us go. We waved and moved on. No sign from him. Jerry called down, "If you really want to go up, you may come and I will help you with the knife this afternoon." Slowly he moved toward the hill. Faster—in no time he was with us, breathless, smiling shyly. He put his arm around me, gave helping hands as we climbed. I told him that Jerry would be going on wood detail on the hill only one week more then it would be finished up there. That if bombings or attack started, trips would be cancelled and this might be our last chance to go up all together as a wood crew and we were glad he had come. He was happy and we were each happy. We were set free. The exhilaration of the day is inexpressible. The keen breeze swept the sky clear of clouds and the air shimmered with blue haze. The "purple mountain majesties" towered over yellow-green rice terraces filled with water. One terraceful quivered as it hung as though suspended over a ridge out into the valley. There were many shades of color, lovely shadows, the sea haze a softer blue than others. The leaves and earth gave forth a damp, rotting odor as we wound our way through tropic growth. Over the ridge, across meadows, a glimpse of limestone cathedral-like rocks, the first view of Baguio and the church in a year—far off, smoke drifting from the town's combined chimneys, all remote from our life.

We passed the goats' tin shack for wet weather, and the gray-bearded slant-eyes themselves who were grazing all over the other side of the range. Cows with wet noses gazed nervously at us, their soft melancholy eyes very appealing. We left the wood-crew cart far behind, pushed one of the wheel barrows along the trail made by it along the contour of the hill, stopping to look down both slots.

Bedie, as surefooted as a goat, made me dizzy as he stood with his sling out on some rocks. I couldn't watch him. Way up the ridge beyond sight of Baguio, Jerry cut across an old trail which led along limestone cliffs, to the damp spot where fresh cut logs lay. We looked up at moss-covered stalactites all along the way, with delicate fern leaf and fragile begonias nestling in moist spots. Bamboo shoots reared into the air, with feathery tufts at intervals on the branch of this climbing variety. We were wary of leeches but found none. Igorots had built a rock-dam below a small opening in the rock, possibly a dried-up spring. They had left long poles leaning against the cliff, whether to pry for birds' nests or honey or what else we could not guess. All was mystery and everything seemed important, even the exquisite red spores on the back of dark green leaves. Birds called or sang as we rested on the wet leaf bed laced with discarded branches. The view from this point was heavenly as we hung directly over the long barracks. We could see all of camp below, with the entire pile of Northern Luzon mountains beyond. We picked out Haight's place and Mt. Data on the skyline, as Christmas carols rose clearly from camp church in the sunken gardens. Through the trees which protected us from falling off sheer edge, we could see the congregation sitting on the terraced bank at service. The Christmas hymns were beautiful as they reached up and up.

Jerry and Bedie began to carry the logs to the first stage of the barrow while June and I gazed at the leaf-framed picture below us. The air shimmered with sun, moisture, specks drifting in the breeze. I could not bear to have it come to an end and hated to leave the cool wet spot under the cliffs, so quiet and secluded, our family a happy unit. But it was necessary to go back for waitress time, so they loaded me with sweaters, water bottle, a fungus growth resembling a flower cup on a branch, and later a spray of wild white roses, while they carried the six logs. We laughed, expanding in the warm sun. Jerry pushed the loaded barrow, June and Bedie pulling on the rope ahead. They made speed, puffed and worked hard, stopped for water, on again. We left the goats, meadow and cows behind. Soon we rolled the logs down the first slot, left the barrow and walked to the foot of the slide. The two boys rounded up the logs and we all rolled them by hand or foot to the final slot, reaching there just as waitress bell rang below.

As the *News* puts it—"Amazing were the results of a short announcement made by the Executive Committee stating 'If you are able-bodied enough for loading the trucks with Red Cross supplies at Damortis and would like a trip to the coast, please sign below.' Apparently able-bodied enough for the task were nearly 90 men who will be whittled down to 50 in a lottery. Never before has the camp seen such a rapid improvement in the health of its hitherto rather decrepit, ache and pain wracked manhood."

Christmas feeling permeated the audience that watched Winnie's beautifully conceived and executed living portraits of Madonnas of Many Lands in the evening. The Chinese set with soft red wall and dull-toned scroll, Ruth Zimmerman as mother with infant, clothed in white satin Chinese gown, holding adorable black-haired and solemn Betty Jo by the hand, was the most exquisite and perfect artistry. The Japanese set with Jane's delicate flower arrangement against the kakimono, a kneeling mother in dark kimono, casting strong black shadow on the wall, was extremely effective. It was somber, shadowed, the lullaby sad, the figure tragically submissive as is all Japanese womanhood. Mrs. Loddigs was Norwegian, Gerry Rasa a lovely Spanish mother, and Bunnie the American with Grace singing to her doll at her feet. At the end, all joined around Jo Florey who was the traditional Madonna beside the manger. If we don't catch the Christmas spirit on the 25th, we had it with us tonight, for all joined in the carols and the room was jammed. Bedie hugged close to Daddy on the counter.

December 20, 1943. Rumor says that the truck with Manilans will arrive at 3. Peg wound up a huge day by baking cookies and applesauce cake, space scrubbed like a mirror, ready for her Davao husband who *might* appear. She is all ready and keyed up to fever pitch. We are all a bit dithery over package prospects. The swapping and bargaining going on about the contents which have not even arrived is a riot.

Virginia was trying to explain to Della how we felt up here versus the hospital world. We can't iron at night and why should they? Are they any different strata from us? They are very close friends. I often think of Russia as I see the struggles among groups. The cook taking special care of his workers, the doctor looking after his staff, the shop after their interests, the garbage crew patriotic about their detail. Each advanced as far as the group, but not advanced enough to visualize camp as a whole, and so the scramble goes on.

A British woman commented on what fine fathers and husbands American men made, how good they were at caring for and playing with their children, how equally they shared the domestic burden with their wives. For British and Americans who had not known each other before, it has been a revealing exchange and acquaintance, good for both sides.

December 21, 1943. Just before dinner, I went up to see Peg and we were standing in her window when the truck from Manila drove in. Immediately, little girls and boys rushed toward it across the parade ground. There was a swish and thunder of feet in dorm as dozens rushed downstairs. All converged on the road, surrounding the bus. Clark tried to saunter casually and we could see his child lifted down. Porky streaked out to meet his little pint o' cider wife. Handsome, white-haired Al Bailey came back arm in arm with his wife. McGinnis embraced her daughter. All six were there, but Peg and Win and I strained forward looking for Peg's husband from Davao. We didn't speak, only gazed and searched, hoping for a glimpse of one figure in the milling crowd. For five minutes, silence and suspense. Suddenly Peg's hopes crashed and down went her head on her arms as her shoulders shook with sobs. It was sad but we did not speak for there was nothing to say. It was no use to hold out another thread of hope, as her son did as he trotted in wide-eyed saying, "Daddy isn't there but perhaps he will come with the packages."

A crowd of us, including myself, rescued cabbage leaves from the discard basket in the veg room, hovering over them like any poor Chinese peasant, cutting them small and cooking them into a tasty dish for lunch.

Many people are fussing about three heart cases who seem able to climb the steep hillside every week, and a fourth who signed up and drew the chance to lift cases at Bauang.

We had a marvelous roast beef for supper and shared it with Scotts. It is our first in months and months. Scott bought and cooked it for us. The delicious gravy straight from the pan almost dissolved me in tears. I wanted to concentrate forever on each tender, juicy mouthful, but the children couldn't wait to open Aunt Jemie's packages which finally came through from Manila with a note. We let them tear and cut and delve, exclaiming over three dresses, some slacks, a sweater, a pencil box for Bedie, string to make socks, 2 large bars of Primco Nippon Yusi soap (the ration kind we should be getting), 2 bars of toilet soap, 2 kinds of white buttons, needles, snaps and a wonderful roll of khaki thread, a bag of puffed rice, a bottle of cinnamon with embroidery thread tied around it. It was all exciting and Christmasy.

When babies were born in Manila camp after rules went in force, the fathers were jailed for six weeks. At one short period they had what was called an "affection tent."

December 22, 1943. I ran around giving out five of June's outgrown dresses for Christmas; one for Anne, two for Eloise. June pressed two and we tied them up to go out in the bag for Eppie and Felie [the Bacanis' daughters] for Christmas and we do hope they get them.

During the evening the lights of the first truck appeared. It wheezed up the road and finally balked entirely. One by one until there were eight, they came in to turn around and unload at the bodega, which is packed half full now and under guard. All but 55 of 631 cases arrived. The main food packages are actually all in camp tonight and we sit pinching ourselves, hardly able to believe that what we have been doubting could come true.

December 23, 1943. Muzzie sent us a package of tea with our 1941 family view on Christmas card dated December 20. June says Daddy looks surprisingly young and handsome in it and has a nice smile! It is as though she saw him as an outsider for the first time, not just "Daddy." He was secretly pleased and amused.

Young Butch who is now attending Sunday School overhead his aunt say "Darn" in the kitchen. Plaintively he asked, "Do you have to swear? I wish you wouldn't when I'm trying so hard to be a Christian."

Heather up in the window had a long word-battle with Robert two stories below. He said he had a big knife to cut her eyes out then gradually he subsided and wandered off. She called after him, "Oh Robert, come back and fight some more."

It was a 15,000 mile trip [for the Red Cross supplies] from the United States via South Africa, India and Manila. Our men brought back with them 437 pomolos and 50 coconuts purchased in the lowlands. The Red Cross cases total nearly 18 tons.

"The Commandant, Mr. Tomibe, emphasizes that no relief supplies in any amount are to be sent outside camp. Strict compliance of this rule is enjoined. The supplies are in paper cartons in new clean-smelling pine boxes. The 520 food parcels weigh 24,440 pounds. The instruments, surgical dressings and first-aid kits in 34 cases are worth a fortune in real money these days. Many are unobtainable at any price. Over 4,000 pounds of miscella-

neous apparel and toiletries are in 27 cases. There are 880 pounds of sheets and 300 pounds of men's heavy clothing. You are advised to save contents of food parcels for a rainy day. Kept in a cool dry place, the whole kit can be left just about as it is, except a few items like prunes (likely to mildew) and the high power chocolate bars should be kept dry.'' From the Camp Holmes *News*.

Japanese words taken from English: They use "speedo" for anything fast, not any word of their own. "Derucato" (delicate) is used for an embarrassing situation. Many such words are taken straight from English with only one syllable added to balance it for the Japanese intonation. "Jeepu" is another.

December 24, 1943. There is a big poster made by Daphne Bird with reindeer drawing Santa and toy bag in sleigh; in the lower corner watching him sail across the sky are concentrees at a table holding steaming cups near a blazing fire, all framed in holly and barbed wire. In the center is printed the menu for Christmas day.

Breakfast	Lunch	Dinner
Fruits	Peanut butter sandwich	Fruit cocktail
Rice	Fruit	Beef loaf
Beef and onion gravy		Rice
Hotcakes		Green pea gravy
Cocoa syrup		Minted Baguio potatoes
Coffee		Smothered string beans
		Sliced tomatoes
		Coffee

After dinner dessert and coffee with entertainment indoors

Last year was good but it was all our own and Baguio—no city or home contacts. This year the Outside has arrived across thousands of miles. It is exhilarating! Every one is hacking or dragging pine fragrance, red and tinsel streamers, silver ornaments, arranging and trying out this, surveying that. All are busy until the camp hums, echoes, resounds with Christmas morale. There is no rice for tonight, no coffee for breakfast, but no one dwells on it.

This is why the Old Golds were removed from the boxes: "*Freedom. Our heritage has always been freedom—we cannot afford to relinquish it—our armed forces will safeguard that heritage, if we, too, do our share to preserve it.*" It was printed on each one. We will get the cigarettes minus the encouragement.[43]

The tree is trimmed, the pine screen nearly finished. The dining room has *real* curtains made of precious sheets held back by ties. We shoot the works on torn ones now that crisp new Red Cross sheets are in the bodega. The dining room is a completely different place, quaint and puritanical in curtains. On each table are candles in bamboo sticks, a center tree with icicles of cellophane paper giving a frosty touch. There are pine cones around each tree, a holly spray at each candle. The mantel with "Learn to Labor and to Wait" is covered with holly sprays, red flannel stockings hanging in front of the brick fireplace with logs ready. A clock in the center of the mantelpiece points at 5 to 12. The curtain ties are colored cellophane.

The Kiosko in town sent a 5 gallon ice cream freezer full of coconut ice cream so that all the Special Diets (about 75) were served after their rice tonight. They even had seconds, with squeals of joy. It was pure Babel for a waitress and such a hustle. But it was fun and the dining room servers received a ladle full of the frozen cream too. I put mine in a cup and divided it with June, Bedie and Jerry—just a spoonful taste. I went from mop pants into my red-checked Christmas dress and put on makeup.

We talked with Evelyn and Father Sheridan who both expect bombing any time and say that the people everywhere act terrified of the food shortage. All along the way [from Manila camp], silence—and waiting. No one on the roads; only two trucks passed in the whole trip up. No pigs, cows, chickens or anything alive on the roads. They said it was a terrible experience—the feeling of terror, want and waiting.

Evelyn says we are far less crowded here than in Manila and that we do far more cooking. She prefers it up here in every way. Both said that the Kitchen Gang down there held the power and couldn't be put out. The food was awful, badly prepared, and even the children's diets poorly prepared, nothing as well done as ours.

This pageant was not as elaborate, simpler than the Easter pageant, but quite beautiful because of this. The choir was screened so that no light bothered the silent congregation gathered on terraces just above the sunken gardens. Over all was the soft evening fog which drifted slowly away, revealing a spangled sky above dark pines along a mountain skyline. Crickets hummed and chirped in the wet grass and shrubbery which sent up a cool wet-earth smell, relaxing to tired humans who had been handling heavy cases or digging post holes or cooking all day. Into the quietness, after carols sung by the choir, moved four scenes already waiting in the dark, needing only light directed on them. First—No room at the Inn, with Joseph knocking at the door and being turned away, Mary kneeling in shadows as her time had come. As Dirks' splendid voice died away on "No room, no room, at the Inn"—the light fell on a higher level where the Three Wise Men stood before Herod clothed in rich purples and wine reds. They asked for the new King and were pointed the way by those who asked that He be delivered to Herod when they found Him. Again the light traveled to a piece of hilly ground-pasture surrounded by bushes where shepherds stood in long cloaks guarding their flocks which were two camp goats tended with rough staves. To us this was the most real and the most picturesque for it was like the meadows and goat-tenders on our own hill above camp. Ann was thrilled to see Bedie in a sack-loincloth, bare from the waist up, holding his crook steady. The angel, in white robe and shining star crown, came from somber trees bearing glad tidings of a newborn Savior. As the light died, a group of children crept forward to sing in young clear voices before the dark was illumined again on the fourth and last scene—a manger under green pine boughs for roof. Ruth Zimmerman was a serene, gentle Madonna who sang "Away in a Manger" to her infant son on the straw bed, she the only one to make a sound outside of the choir. The Wise Men came, bearing gold and frankincense and myrrh for sadness, followed by the shepherds with goats, the black one bleating and struggling in Bedie's arms. The little animal called loudly, nearly escaping, but Bedie held on tight till the light went out. Ann loved it all, in spite of her worry that Jesus would be killed. I assured her that did not happen at Christmas time for that was when He was born. We found Jerry and June and all went home together on the night before Christmas, delivering Ann safe to her mother.

We four then sat in the festive dining room with pine and holly wreaths in windows, lighted tree outside, as we drank Herm's cocoa with Nida's sugar and fresh-milked coconut cream. What was left of the cream became luscious thick cheese by morning. The children did not seem as homesick as last year for other memories are fading and we are all more used to communal living.

December 25, 1943. I thought June was walking in her sleep when she crawled out of bed at five muttering about carols. In spite of sniffles she had Katie wake her and they quickly dressed and joined the carol singers. It was delightful to lie there half asleep in the dark, listening to the chorus of old and young voices singing, "It Came upon the Midnight Clear"—"O Little Town of Bethlehem"—"Hark, the Herald Angels Sing"—"Joy to the World"—and "Silent Night." Starting far off at the flagpole, they grouped next at the schoolhouse then moved down to the hospital where they were warmed with steaming coffee. From there they went to sing a song or two at the guardhouse. Jerry brought coffee and bananas to a bench in front of the barracks where we opened our family gifts. He had made me a polished box from a chopping block, with a fitted cover, and inside were two yellow candlesticks for small candles which set into holes made at each corner of the box. A mirror could be set between, or a vase of flowers. June finished socks for me and Bedie made an art design and had good marks from school. Jerry gave me a woven straw purse in blue and green with a can of talcum inside. He gave Bedie six eggs and a can of jam. I gave Bedie a notebook and three pencils. Jerry gave June a white wool blouse and I gave her a blue lace blouse. Bedie scraped and polished in one day the coconut from which we drank our cream and cheese. Jerry helped him put on the hinge cover. They worked like Trojans to complete this gift for sister June. Bedie spent much time on a bone ring for Annie and a yellow-handled knife for his girl. I presented Jerry with Peg's pigtail sketch of me prefaced by an I.O.U. from the author and artist. "Happy Christmas for Jerry, and an I.O.U. of one personal chronicle of Camps Hay and Holmes, days of two years, for which this is the Frontispiece—or should it be the Finispiece! With love from the author assisted by the artist Peg." It is the radical slant—to the left; the pigtail and tie a sign of freedom, the New England head and Camp Holmes heels!

Then I hurried to waitress, a busy time with oranges, hotcakes, syrup and juice. We worked fast. There followed our own breakfast together as a family in the crowded dining room. Beside coffee, hotcakes and syrup, there was a huge pomolo each from Bauang, and even rice again! We went to church in the sunken gardens at 10. Immediately after church, Santa came with gifts at the tree. Charlie Fothergill looked very natural in his own beard and no mask. This time he came down the chimney in the dining room. The dolls with yellow wool braids and silk scrap dresses, adorable stuffed animals, were made by many loving hands; carts of all sizes showed us how some babies had grown into boys; all sorts of wooden toys from the shop were there to delight the children. There were books from Manila with the Japanese chop-mark of "passed inspection" inside, for the older boys and girls. June and Bedie had these. They will be interesting mementos.

In the bag from Nida was a whole roast chicken! Soap, sugar, cigarettes, and a pomolo. Mrs. Leung Nang sent us a box of candy. There was peanut brittle from Lilian Lim, and a wonderful package from Miss Ramos saying she had been gone a year, only just returned. In her box were 12 diamond-shaped cakes with curly frosting and strawberry jam in the center of each; also sugar, coffee, 2 boxes of matches, two bars of soap and some cigarettes. This was a real surprise after the year of silence. It made us happy to hear from her when times are so hard and we know that such a gift is a sacrifice.

Then it was time to dress in the red outfit, get the peanut sandwiches, an orange and some candy from camp chow, take plates, spoons, water for lemonade, and our precious fried chicken down to the gardens to picnic together on the grass. We wallowed in chicken for the first time in many moons. I shall never forget the complete joy of eating such flavor of home-cooked meat.

When we finished our picnic we decided to try to join the large group of relatives and friends from Outside who were picnicking with internees around the new guardhouse. The Intelligence was out trotting about with guns but on the whole far more lenient than last year. Three big bombers flew over at high speed going south. We heard three versions of Ismael's imprisonment and Nida being searched and questioned. P300 was taken from

her. What stories Nida and Ismael will have to tell us. He was working at
the mines and was taken in a group of four to jail over looting of acid. One
version said it was his third offense, another denied this. Nida had transferred
our cases to the lower garage where they were looted, clothes and files
scattered, a Chinese picture burned. All the things we had thought saved are
now scattered worse than ever, looted, searched, burned, spreading wider
and farther. The past and the Indusco period and records are sinking into an
ever-deepening and ever-widening circle of war, terror and destruction. Ismael
was given a six weeks' sentence this time and is said to have been sent to
that hellhole of Fort Santiago but Nida is not sure. Poor Nida. Marie said
she looked prosperous and well dressed. She always did look that way when
she made her own clothes. I wonder why people resent others coming up in
the world. And I wonder if she is a friend of the Filipinos or the Japanese
these days. It is hard to tell in the pressures of this strange world. In spite
of being upset and anxious, we can't help being proud of them both. Our
house is the only one intact and is now being lived in by Japanese Navy
officers. There is still some furniture there apparently. Looters set it on fire
one night and Ismael discovered it and put the fire out. Lallie and Fuzzy are
still alive. Nida's brother is a guerrilla somewhere. Jaime and the sister are
living with her, also turkeys, ducks and hens. They sell rice and other produce
so are getting along all right.

Roosevelt had made a speech telling us to have great courage, for a human
typhoon was gathering in the Pacific and would soon break upon us and we
must be ready. There was also news that Rabaul, the hardest nut to crack,
was taken, and Tarawa in the Gilberts another hard nut. Truk in the Carolines
is the scene of a Navy affair.[44]

Muzzie was there too and said she had been hearing great things about
me and thought it was swell. I said I was nothing but a mopper and a waitress.

I rushed down to see Helen at the hospital who completely bowled me
over for the day. When everything had been swept away, then into my hands
were placed beautiful matched turquoise and a pendant from Peking, with
a story about it and praise for June who is to have it. I said I hoped to take
a book out of here. She gave me an Emerson quotation which we talked
about. I was speechless over the glorious color I held in my lap. As I came
away with loveliness in my hands, I discovered the package trek had begun.

Like spiders crawling in every direction from the center of a web, all of
the 450 internees were coming from the bodega with carts, sacks, poles,
ropes—anything that would help carry 47 pounds or more [for the Red Cross
packages]. If only the people at home could have seen it! Morale soared so
high that people went out of reach—"exceeded grasp." Before Jerry even
knew the line had started, Bedie had been down and carried his own case of
47 pounds, stopping only three times to rest between the bodega at the foot
of the road and our space where he deposited it. Dr. Shaffer and others carried
stretchers loaded with cases. Sacks, poles, wheelbarrows large and small,

Christmas carts on wheels precarious for such weight—everyone smiling and sprinting back for the next one or to help others who had no strong arm. As fast as men put them from the bodega onto the counter out front, they were checked off as each was trundled away joyously. One man sat right down in the bodega and opened his box, stuck a cigarette in his face, took a slice of cheese in one hand, a slice of Spam in the other, then came striding up the hill with the heavy box on his shoulder, his mouth busy three ways and a wide grin beside puffs and chews.

Then the fun began. Fathers joined families and all commingling rules were off as cases were shunted about, opened and spread out in piles, stacks and rows. Counting and sorting occupied the next 48 hours. Inventory was taken as each can and box was lovingly handled, felt and gazed upon, exclaimed over. Exhilaration is not the word! Now we know that America is thinking of us, working for us. There are V's for Victory framing printed directions, a slogan here and there in picture form, which have escaped the all-seeing eye which peers into every private corner here.

The box breathed American efficiency, even to the little brown envelopes with can openers. Nothing was forgotten and the contents were concentrated essence of all we lacked for two years, all we need for now and perhaps three months to come. The care, thought, research, long development and planning that went into it oozed out of every corner. We could imagine every soldier and civilian prisoner in every occupied country opening one just as we were, singing with relief and bounding spirits. Each can is a meal in itself, perfectly balanced. Pride in America stretched out as we realized it was covering the world. No longer are we haunted by fear of famine. The cases stand for *Security*. Shoulders lifted, backs straightened, eyes lit up from within—the body and mind together rejuvenated as everyone worked beyond expected capacity, duties doubled cheerfully and eagerly. It was a great day, a never-to-be forgotten feeling after the depths and defeat of last year.

Best of all—everyone was equal. Each package was even as to weight and contents, some slight differences but no discrimination, no special privilege! All were alike and what is more, everyone was satisfied. Father and baby each had the same—one to satisfy labor hunger, the other to feed growth. Cash on hand no longer needs to go to stock up for future fears. Now it can buy eggs and fresh fruit for each day. If attack comes and transport ceases, and rice stops coming for days or weeks until the struggle is over and the enemy dispersed when the Islands are retaken by the human typhoon—we can take it, for the packages are here! Some of it will be eaten now in order to build up, but much will be held over for the expected interim weeks when the country will be paralyzed during battle. We are not forgotten. We are remembered. So must every man and woman feel who is lifted from poverty, fear and hopelessness, from despair and darkness into the light of security, equality and trust, able to face the future in confidence. We did not forget the Filipina women and children Outside who had none, no Uncle Sam to hand out to them. They will have it yet for it can be done. Last year when the first relief money came I said, "This is the first only. There will be more." Many scoffed and doubted. But it is only the beginning of what will happen in the world. I remember reading Red Cross plans for feeding starving people on a world scale after the war. [Then], if the American Red Cross could send just one case to every undernourished mother, child and young person in Japan and other defeated countries what a powerful piece of persuasion it could be, propaganda to show our high intent. If the defeated can be given even half the feeding that we had on Christmas Day 1943, they will sense gratitude instead of hate. They will look toward us instead of away from us during their defeat which will be more final and black than was ours. The sickening depression of mind, the nosedives of morale over Corregidor, the horror when all is lost and must be faced—these things that we knew, they will know and more. They have been undernourished longer and will need more than we do.

From boxes we turned to trimming the table for dinner, with shining sharp holly caves and red flower clusters brought by Don from the hill. Two brilliant poinsettias were added by the Hinds. Dinner was a triumph, starting with fruit salad containing a quarter slice of pineapple and one luscious strawberry; through the savory meat loaf, Baguio potatoes of which I ate till I couldn't eat more, smothered green beans and sliced tomatoes. Gravy mixed with peas made both go farther and added flavor. Then coffee, cookies and Camp Holmes pound cake.

We sat out under the stars all evening where Jerry and I talked over what we had heard from the Outside—Ismael, Nida, loss of Indusco files, the Japanese Navy, looting, smuggling, suffering—always the huge kaleidoscope of war around us. Everyone is saying they will give gladly to the Red Cross next time an appeal comes. No crabbers after this! Whatever its shortcomings, it achieves greatness.

Jerry says he never had a better Christmas, and he never expects to. He was surprised that I took the loss of my [Indusco] files so equably, but it is like caring for a child. You do all you can to protect and shield and spare it. If it goes, there is nothing to be done.

December 26, 1943. It is such fun to handle the cans and read the contents of each mixture. There is repacking in various systems—some emergency, some to save, some for immediate consumption, some for quick-get-away!

Bedie wanted to smoke his first cigarette so I lighted one and said come on. We sat in the dining room but he was too shy and thrilled, hid behind the door. It did not bother him, nor really please him much. He did feel a bit older, bigger, and chuckled shyly over it all evening. Several pals gathered in admiration, asking about it. So that is over. I told him to smoke with us whenever he felt the urge, not out back with the gang. June is having fun at bridge.

December 27, 1943. Back to mops, cans and regular routine. Jerry is up hill with the wood crew. June is cutting veg. The high school girls are invaluable as many women are shirking. It is the morning after, with every one out of routine. One day holiday wrecks the groove.

After lunch Jerry and I repacked the kits, putting all of each kind together instead of split up. We had the fun of handling it again, seeing new points, and talking about it endlessly. Many others were doing it for the third time, in trying a new combination, or just for fun! Never was anything so welcomed and enjoyed!

There was a furor over strawberries at the store. 50 baskets at 50¢, a sign up that they would be for sale at the store, not more than 3 per person. When the window opened, all baskets were sold. What a howl went up.

The children's party at 2:30 was a grand one. Two long tables were covered with cellophane. Each child received an orange, a piece of fudge, cookies, taffy, 2 camp-manufactured lollipops, peanut brittle and Japanese Army candy. The young ones received a toy gift apiece. There was hot tea for all. Parsons performed with cards and other tricks, there was a treasure hunt, and races and games. Such squeals and howls of enjoyment. Internment children fared much better than any children Outside in occupied districts. Chicay, the meat man, gave camp a heifer, and Tong's market stall gave us two pigs.

Bulletin Board: "By order of Camp Commandant, it is strictly forbidden to send any part or parcel of Red Cross Comfort and Food Kits out of camp. We also wish to call attention to the International Regulation prohibiting sale of any Red Cross supplies. . . . The Executive Committee considers it a duty to urge all internees to conserve their Red Cross kits, after removing perishable articles, for their possible future emergency needs."

There were 34 cases of medical supplies, with the worst breakage so far only among bottles of vitamin pills. *No lipsticks,* but 200 shoes for women, 100 for children, 84 for men. Tek toothbrushes and Squibb's powder (in wartime cardboard containers), cleaning tissue, cold cream, dresses, shorts, sunsuits, socks, wool, soap, bath towels, sewing kits, shoe repair, underwear and nightgowns.

Camp is back to normal, cranky in spots from the letdown and being on extra details.

December 28, 1943. It is said that a Lutheran and a Seventh Day Adventist were in the strawberry deal. People always like to point out missionaries because they are supposed to be less subject to human frailty. It is a crime now to buy before the store opens, without taking turn in line. The Manila people who came up here are still astounded at the fine spirit in this camp, of working for camp and not for pay. It all goes back to that first committee when the ruling was made of no charge for services either from doctors or dentists or at the shop. It has made a special government here, and has set a high standard. In Manila, no one will carry a bag, help anyone with moving; they just refer you to a gang who does it, for pay. They won't even lift a bed at one end, except for cash.

No resentment is apparent in the Sergeant as he walks about watching us open boxes, curious, interested, smiling.

We finished up the pâté and cheese in Jerry's bread which is one of his best loaves. We had a cup of hot bouillon each, which is simply marvelous! It comes in small waxed envelopes. Bedie cheered up over it and June was ravenous when she came in tired out. Everyone is able to enjoy each bite because all have the same and we do not feel guilty in eating it. It is a different world without envy or greed or resentment. What a relief! We know at last from experience what the Socialist means. We are lucky to have Tomibe.

December 29, 1943. There are very few parties because all being equal there is no point in splurging.

I am down to 89 pounds, the lowest I have ever reached.

December 31, 1943. We ate supper on the grass and it was fun sitting around the bonfire watching the young and strenuous Virginia Reel which many entered into, with June in flaming cheeks loving it. Finally Art and Al danced Igorot style, with Cam joining in. Lewis and David beat ganza tin pans and Rachael was the Igorot woman with hands and thumbs upheld as in a frieze of primitive tribes. Art gets the sway, the shuffle, the rippling effect of muscle, the leap, control and surge forward and up, perfectly. There was a circle of watchers close around them. It was a splendid windup to the folk-dancing and outdoor celebration of New Year's Eve. Peg Wilson and Mrs. Griffiths did an amusing hula in calapias which gave us much laughter. The Sergeant and the guards stood by watching, smiling. The Sergeant is friendly and says 70% of the women here are all right, do their proper work according to Japanese idea and custom. Woman submissive!

We wound up with modern dancing in the dining room, with tea served on a side table, at ten. Three took turns at the piano and the Sergeant leaned against the counter watching the modern clutch and steps, interested but sleepy. He is from the country and never saw such celebrating before though he admitted that the folk dancing resembled some in Japan. Jerry danced with June. My leg ached from a fall in the ditch and I was too tired and in no mood to dance. Someday I shall want to dance again and love it but now the spirit is lacking and I cannot enter into it.

We took our children to bed about midnight though Jerry had wanted to drag them away before. I told him he might as well start 1944 by realizing that his daughter would be staying up late from now on, reluctant to leave and needing chaperonage. He made a wry, sleepy face and stayed on.

1944

January 1, 1944. It still burns me up that we have no letters, no message of any kind from America as we enter the third year of confinement. They came but have not been given to us. Food is vital of course and comes first, but they could have given us letters for the spirit too. It was in their power.

After lunch, Bedie brought back his Red Cross distribution for a boy of 12—1 bath towel, 2 handkerchiefs, 1 bar laundry soap, 1 brown shoe polish, 1 black comb, 1 Tek toothbrush, a pencil, 1 bottle of 100 capsules of multiple vitamins—a total of 9 items.

Later June and I went down and stood at the end of a long line until it began to pour rain and we all rushed under the eaves. We received the same things plus a large box of cleansing tissue, Tampax, a roll of toilet paper, a pink seersucker nightgown with blue at the neck, similar in style to the angel gowns on which we had sewed (they can be made into blouses, shirts, children's dresses or undies), panties, bras in pink and a playsuit with a skirt, in lavender or ecru. There were pinks, greens, turquoise and several shades of lavender. Immediately, the feminine contingent blossomed out in soft pastel shades, trotting about the campus like Girl Scouts all in one style of suits. Some say we look like orphans or prisoners, institutional. But to me they look pretty, gay, new, with fresh color and cut, something to talk about and trade or swap or work on. Each woman wears hers "with a difference."

On the first day of the third year, I asked Peg to get someone else for can-carrying and am turning over the porch-scrubbing on Tuesday to June who will get two hours' credit a week for it. The heavy work is too much for me now. I will wash and hang out the mops, place them out in the morning and wash the aisle, but the tough part is finished.

January 2, 1944. On the way down on our walk we heard a call, "Hi, Crouter" from the old guardhouse and there was Nakamura with a wide smile and a friendly hand stretched out in greeting. He said his family was all right but food was hard to get outside. He is in lumber work in Tayabas and looks rounder, fatter in the face. He always comes out to camp whenever he returns. When he went off in the car, he waved and grinned till out of sight.

Everyone has fallen hard for the gay colors and playsuits. We slept in "the cool kindliness of sheets" instead of "the rough male kiss of blankets," as Rupert Brooke phrased it. We have had roughness at our throat and neck for over two years, no sheets. How smooth, comfortable and restful sheets are.

January 3, 1944. The dentist is now a member of [the wood crew], so with all his skill he won't do more than an hour at dentistry. Everyone needs it but he prefers woodcutting, getting out to town, or most anything else. It is not only the Japanese who have postponed our teeth. Perhaps he hopes to make a cleanup afterwards.

We hear that all the dental supplies, lipstick and rouge in the Red Cross shipment went to Shanghai [internment camp].

Everyone is making up lists, talking about the Fair Division Lottery [for extra Red Cross supplies].

January 4, 1944. In the evening the large room was turned over to the lottery. Children were drawn first, then men, and women last. It was all in public, according to strict rule, and no complaints have been registered as to cheating, fraud, preference or privilege. It is clever of the Committee to draw it out over several weeks, bringing in the fun of chance as well as equality, prolonging the boost of Red Cross supplies into weeks. My possessive and acquisitive instinct has receded to such an extent after losing twenty-five years of accumulation that I cannot raise any steam at all but I am glad to see others do it for their own benefit. I shall be content with a pair of shoes and anything else I may receive. With some it assumes large and serious proportions and with others the old horse-trading trait is coming to the fore. Some try to be fair in swapping, others try to be smart and slick even with the Sisters and their cigarettes, but in the end it all depends on what one wants and if he or she is satisfied. Jerry gave half a package of his American-brand cigarettes to Nakamura because he was pleased to see him and knows he likes our brand.

January 5, 1944. June was among the first 75 to have her shoes fitted and came back happy with moccasin toe and Cuban heel. I was in the next 75 with different style and lower heel. It was a treat to see everyone coming back with new brown shoes and a broad smile. All toes are built out square and the part which is laced is fancy, in-and-out design on the leather, apparently the style at home but new to us. Each woman who needed or wanted a pair had one by three P.M. By four all the children were fitted. Only half the men can be supplied tomorrow, but for the rest of us Camp Holmes is no longer down at the heel.

The kits may cost $20 in the U.S.A. but here in inflation and scarcity they are worth not 1941 pesos which would be 40, but at the very least

P1,500 each. About U.S. $700. Oh, the toilet paper after months of dual-purpose *Tribune,* white bath towel (not brown or streaked with gray), a comb of one's own (June and I were using one between us and Bedie had none when he went to the hospital); vitamins in bottles, a drink of milk in the morning, even the coffee filled with Dextrose and Maltose nourishment—the result is incalculable, inestimable, boundless. The whole camp has taken on new life, a verve and dash. All morning the question as one passed another—"Do you have your shoes yet?"—faces lighting up, smiles spreading from one to another.

The *News* account of the great piano mystery is as follows: "Sometime between December 27 and 31 a person sneaked into the dining room, cut all the leather strips attaching the keys to hammers on the community piano. Although competently done with a knife, the vandal's job of destruction has been reeemedied to some extent by patient repair (with string knots), using makeshift arrangements. Who did it?" Jerry and Fabian think it was a mouse or a rat, others say it was a fanatical missionary who didn't want dancing on New Year's and considered it an "instrument of the devil" (various comments and stories are quoted about New Year dancing in this connection, including one who refused to loan her violin for such a wicked purpose as square dances). I am inclined to think that a member of the waggish, smart, tough-guy gang in the kitchen might have done it, being thoroughly fed up with some monotonous practice and compelled to work and listen right next to it day after day. Everyone speculates on which one might be demoniacal enough to do it; this is as good as any murder mystery though it makes the entire camp indignant.

Some of the Committee and Woody were invited to sukiyaki dinner, sake, and beer at the guardhouse. They say it was very good but too much alcohol mixture. Most of them got high and sick, due to Nipponese custom and persistence and the Sergeant following them home in high fettle to serve more in Ray's cottage, insisting that all of them come and partake.

January 6, 1944. Nida sent us bananas, a pomolo, cigarettes, red radishes and 4 baskets of big red strawberries which we hulled and washed on the spot, eating them with sugar and milk, recklessly. I felt better after lunch than for weeks. Being better, I felt angry and wanted to go home and turn the Japanese out of my house. I hate to think of their Navy taking a bath in my tub, sitting before my fireplace and hate them for intruding. I hate them thoroughly tonight. I wonder if Nida has had to move to Vida's wretched house nearby.

January 7, 1944. Beginning at 7 the men could be seen trailing in from all angles with Red Cross Carton on each shoulder in direction of [the] bodega. These were empty cartons to be filled with stacks which were waiting. At noon they brought the cartons back full, with wide grins of satisfaction over shoes, suits, undershirts, blue and white shirts. There were shouts over the husky balbriggan underwear and immediate trading began in size or kind.

Knots of people gather, all gazing down—not depressed, nor praying, just looking at swanky new shining brown Oxfords. Soon new shirts, olive drab shorts by the dozen, coveralls, turtleneck sweaters, rich brown wool sweaters, all kinds of combinations of outfits burst forth all over camp. Such fun—men are like kids. Jerry is tickled with a beautiful brown suit owned by a big man. His pile included much needed cotton undershirts; three pairs of fine olive drab shorts; two pairs of warm balbriggan drawers in which he can sleep on cold nights; gray wool socks; cotton socks; tooth powder; a neat army sewing kit with buttons, 10 yards of 8 colors of thread, 2 needles, 2 safety pins and smart little scissors. There were six packages of Burley tobacco accompanied by 2 packages of cigarette papers; 2 jars of brushless shave cream and a pair of shoe laces. Jerry is overjoyed with all of it and has been fussing over the pile all afternoon. He looks and feels like a million.

About 6, a sharp earthquake rocked us. For once I sat still but I was scared. The building rocked and creaked, bottles rattled, cupboards danced. It kept on and on until we thought, "Isn't it ever going to stop!" Several women screamed, children began to cry, everyone poured out of the buildings. June said she suddenly felt dizzy and seasick, could hardly walk.

Scott is run down again, beginning infections on his thumb. He and Isobel arranged for a day on the hill after he took his mother to the hospital where she will rest and be built up. The children are left with Duke and Martha, while parents in wide straw hats, an Igorot basket full of food strapped on backs, in shorts, carrying pots and pans, went blithely climbing. They came back in midafternoon with eyes shining, cleared minds, tired and sunburnt, but radiant. They said they ate all day. They built a fire and cooked about every hour. Breakfast, brunch and lunch. The hill always works miracles for everyone.

Jerry is wondering who was the man last inside his brown suit, whether he still lives and where. One large button is gone on the front and there are a number of burns on the coat.

January 8, 1944. There are many infections now—thumbs, feet, boils in many areas. Lack of some vitamins is causing trouble with vision for a few who cannot see to read at night even under electric lights. Others cannot see distant objects. Many of the worst cases are getting vitamin shots. Clara has a mouth full of cankers and cannot wear her plate. Her tongue is like mine was and she has to rest a lot. I went to Dr. Shaffer about my weight and lassitude. He wants a stool check; due to recent discoveries he wants a check for hookworm. He said my eyes showed a still low hemoglobin. He prescribed 50 iron tablets, to take 3 a day. He said I needed a vacation and I said that, like my mother, it was the one thing I didn't want.

Many have gas pressure on the bladder. Some get up 7 times in the night because of this. Others have little control. It is instantaneous when a certain stage is reached and is much more advanced than a year ago when Dr. Hall mentioned it in class in connection with starch diet. The food money is not half enough. It is not called "adequate" any more.

I notice that if my meal is delayed by even five minutes I become petulant, irritable and could dissolve into tears.

In the last Minutes an egg a day is promised all children from 2½ to 8½—75 total—to be handed out and checked off by one person at noon, with the egg raw, to be cooked by parents for the child's evening meal which has been only rice without even sugar or bananas. This egg comes out of a special allotment and is to be bought through the store. Our kids are always beyond the age limit for everything. They get adult chow but their teeth and general growth suffer for it.

The Women's Committee asked through the General Committee that the dentist give more time to patients, fewer hours to wood crew. There is a solid block of public opinion behind that.

Father Sheridan told of knowing about 1,000 of the 3,500 at Santo Tomas. He said there were several millionaires who don't know there is a war as far as diet goes. One pays 50¢ a day to have his bag carried from the gate into his shack. A Negro cook prepares his excellent noon meal outside for him. One of the men who earns money by carrier service has a Filipino family outside, destitute, so he sends all he can earn out to them and is glad to pick up anything he can. There are at least 30 men with families destitute like this. The food provided by Manila camp must be awful—always beans, black beans, at noon, no attempt to make them appetizing, no variation in the monotony for months on end. Hundreds of poor devils have to eat it without any extras, for no one cares. A freighter steward is in charge, with a similar type as cook. It is bad enough to be at the mercy of the enemy, without being helpless, exploited and robbed by our own American people.

Father Sheridan was eloquent about our climate here and he praised the Chef for his food preparation. [He] was asked to tell about Work Details in Manila. He smiled, said of course it was nothing like here for the spirit was entirely different. There, one paid for everything—wood for cooking, food in shack restaurants, laundry paid for, even the Red Cross packages were not carried to space by their owners but were paid P1 for transport up. This caused a scornful laugh from our crowd as we remembered the fun, each not only carrying his own but helping others less strong and able. He looked at us all, still smiling, and said, "I like it here. I like your spirit. You are all cooperative, really communal. I am grateful to Carl who helped in my transfer for I would rather be up here."

He is a likeable, sincere Irishman, with wit and a genius for understatement which added to his talk. He is informal and in a simple way rather eloquent. After his talk Blanche played on the reconstructed piano.

January 9, 1944. I disagreed with Jerry as usual. I refuse to look on some Japanese as animals to be exterminated—their culture or ours. To me, they are all human beings, not animals, struggling in their way as we struggle in ours, both complex, mixed with right and wrong. Though force had to be met with force, still I loathe flamethrowers and the horrible death they bring about. I hate to use terrible Axis weapons which make us little better than they. Whether it be German, Japanese, French, Chinese or Russian, I have no wish to undernourish or make them suffer, even to go through what I have felt in here. I would not ask it for anyone, except perhaps punishment for those responsible for cruelty. Certainly not the women and children. It is being like one's enemy if one does so.

January 11, 1944. Yesterday the four Military Police left and were replaced by 14 Regular Army. In town also the Military Police have gone, the Army is in charge. "Charlie," the Sergeant who prolonged the sukiyaki party, came around to say good-bye, left the parting word "Watcho!" He is right, for the new guards are everywhere, poking about curiously, on guard in every direction with gun and bayonet, standing in helmets with gun over shoulder in the market truck when it returns. A company of Filipino Constabulary marched on the road below us. Trucks loaded with soldiers go up and down the trail. Two bombers cruised around for some time.

Excerpts from the *News*: "All tin cans should be saved to use at the shop. . . . There is a dearth of articles in the store. . . . Sulfa drugs, just coming into their own in the late thirties, have apparently taken forward strides, judging by the large quantity in the Red Cross shipment. Sulfadiazine is a drug new to most doctors here so far as actual experience in its use is concerned, although described in prewar medical journals. Two varieties, sufanilamide and sulfaguanadine, were also sent in powdered form for direct antiseptic application to wounds, boils etc. They are being tried here with much interest.

"Dr. Manalo assisted by Dr. Shaffer removed 100 small gallstones from Mrs. Weinstein at town hospital this week. Her husband was allowed to go to town to be present . . . . Lower temperatures can be expected. Blankets, sweaters, and wool gloves are distributed just in time we say . . . . The Day's Theme: 'I didn't get everything I wanted but I wanted everything I got.' "

Sign on the Board: "Do you want clean rice? The only solution to this problem at present is *more Rice Pickers*! The present force of regulars is unable to take care of palay and dirt found in the rice, even though they are trying hard to do so. We appeal to both men and women to volunteer to help at rice tables, especially during this emergency."

Walter was given a transfusion after an operation for carbuncles on toe and leg. Perhaps they used the new gadget for transfusion on a battlefield. It is compact, with plasma in one container, sterile water in another and plain directions on the can how to mix and give right on the field. Plasma means it does not have to be typed. This is one of the biggest advances in science and the slickest item contained in the [Red Cross] shipment. The doctors are keenly interested in it though they say there was more sent here than we can ever use. Of course they do not know that we might see plenty right at the back door and have a really crowded hospital some day, caring for wounded or first-aid cases, which would push out the social whirl.

In these days of sore mouth and lassitude, I think often of poverty and the thousands of women who endure it all their lives, feeling worse than I do, yet going to work long hours every day in factories, doing their own washing and cooking and bringing up their children in hardship.

At four Bedie proudly brought our Red Cross boxes full of the distribution from the bodega where the Distribution Committee has labored for 9 days. I am delighted beyond words with what we received. More than expected came our way. We each received a second pair of shoes. June is thrilled with a black wool dress. I have a jade playsuit, June one in rose. I have another huge pink crepe nightgown, 4 pieces of dress material which is just what we wanted, a khaki mosquito net which Jerry helped us arrange, tooth powder, Tampax, and a size 40 bra which would fit an elephant better than me. In the military sewing kit for which I had yearned were good scissors, needles, buttons, pins and thread. It was Christmas again and such fun, the barracks a riot of coming and going, chatter, laughter, swap and barter. June said with shining eyes, "Oh, Mummie, now we know how poor people feel, don't we?" and I answer, "Yes, and don't ever forget it either." Now we know the thrill of receiving when we were down to holes and patches and rags. We who no longer care for the latest style are very content. Jerry came over to see our things as excited as we were. No one has ever thought of the word "charity," yet three years ago we would all have been unreasonably high hat about taking things.

In talking about work details, we agreed it was good for women to have experience at serving, waitressing and other work, with all the points of view and the irritations of each. It is real socialism for each to have comprehensive experience. And not only the women—many times a man sawing, chopping, or cutting, rolling logs, after slim food has remarked, "Well, I'll never blame a Filipino for being lazy again. I know now how he can't get along on a poor diet!"

January 12, 1944. Camp *News*: "So long as our financial condition is precarious, *no Relief Funds will be distributed to individuals*. The General Committee feels that Relief Funds can at present be put to no better purpose than for the purchase of a rice supply and other food items necessary to our diet which cannot be kept at a subsistence level on our present allowance. All internees benefit from their appropriation for this purpose. The Executive Committee realizes the importance of getting high school started at the earliest possible date, and every effort is being made to secure building materials necessary for the work.''

Camp is chuckling at Dr. Benedetti, who took his blood pressure etc. then sent himself to the hospital with jaundice. Within two hours he left there, blowing up about how he couldn't stay in a noisy place like that. He sounded off well about the social center, a doctor finding out at last that the hospital has been run more for the staff than for the patients. Benedetti's small son told someone, "My Dad came home because it was too noisy at the hospital. And it wasn't the patients either. It was the husbands." They have [parties] not only in the lab but in the various rooms and the garage, sometimes five or six going on at once and bridge games until very late.

January 13, 1944. Young Rae did up a gift basket of berries in the new toilet paper and when her mother remonstrated she answered, "But Mother, it is the best paper we have!"

January 14, 1944. I made June stay in bed all day; Jerry brought her breakfast. Dr. Mather finally gave us some Ergot for her this afternoon. She has been ill almost two weeks.[1]

January 15, 1944. A sign on the Board accompanied by drawing of pins, spool, scissors and dresses: "Will be glad to help YOU cut out any garment, by appointment." It was signed by Dorothy Sims and followed by days and dates for signature. This is really communal spirit, inspired by the Red Cross material. The children are flowering into blues covered with rosebuds or carnations. There are ruffles and sashes on all sorts of ready-made dresses, and many new ones made from the cloth. The pajamas are wooly and warm and so gay that they delight their new owners. The Board is also covered with propositions to swap or trade.

With Jerry I visited Eric's vinegar factory out in back of the shop. I saw the thick tough mother [of vinegar], like hide, which keeps it working. Fabian was deep in the throes of trying to evolve a separator for rice and palay, experimenting on the gold panning line, with a table on incline and strips of boards at intervals to hold the heavy grain, let the chaff by.

News items: "Sports took on new lease of life as result of a gift of equipment American prisoners of war recently received from the Red Cross. Sid is lining up three prospective teams for softball, and a volley court already laid out in front of the hospital. (The young fry are rejuvenated, show vast enthusiasm.) Included are 3 base-, 1 softball bats, 2 pair of 10-ounce boxing gloves, a badminton net, 3 soccer balls, 2 volleyballs, 3 softballs, 3 regular hard balls, a set each of chess, flint, pick-up sticks, a football inflator and a violin! . . . Priority list is out to repair 160 shoes from the new repair kit. Preference is given to outdoor crews, second to men who did not get shoes. Included are leather, thread, heel pads, rubber heels, brushes, hammers, knives, nippers, pincers, tack pullers, rasps, heel removers, shoe nails, tacks, rubber cement, wax, pegs, lasts and stands. . . .

The children say, "Oh what a pretty dress. Did the Red Cross send you that?" Even the youngest know a new meaning for the scarlet symbol, for it is on every shelf, under every bed, in every space, with cartons stamped with it.

January 16, 1944. Jerry cooked eggs in bouillon juice which was good on rice for breakfast. Bedie had a chill in the night and Jerry got into bed with him to hold and warm him. He is better but June is just the same in spite of the bitter medicine. They are both in bed, with me traveling in between. My hands are in water washing something all day long. Sunday is like every other day. June is white and weak. I feel desperate.

January 17, 1944. Sy hears that the Russians are 100 miles into Poland, revolts beginning in Bulgaria, Rumania and other occupied countries. France expects invastion of Allies from the North any time.[2]

January 18, 1944. Ola and Phyllis waited two hours for the dentist, with holes where inlays had fallen out. But the dentist played ball after wood crew and didn't show up. His hands on wood crew will be calloused and tough when it comes to more scientific work. He is willfull. If he can't be on the Committee, the hell with teeth.

January 19, 1944. June was very ill during breakfast time and we went for the doctor. Ruth gave me a can so we could stop the long trek to the toilet and for the first time I was able to see that it was hemorrhage condition. My heart sank. It is clear now why she is in pain and weeps and writhes. Her blood count was taken and at ten the doctor said to get her down to the hospital. We gathered the net and other articles together, first marked with her name. Jerry carried her in his arms.

At Japanese class Miss McKim told of the Sergeant "Charlie" coming back, homesick to see his friends. She and he sang a popular song together before he departed, about the beautiful cliffs!

Bridge with Scotts and we made a Grand Slam. About nine, I could not keep the tears down any longer so we stopped and Jerry and I sat together on a bench outside in the dark. I wept my heart out on his tweed shoulder, pouring out my worry over June. The two weeks have been a nightmare of helping her up and down long stairs, washing and sore hands, which seemed to get nowhere after all the hard work. Jerry held me tight. He is terribly upset himself. There is a great bond between them and he has forgotten he ever wanted a son first.

January 20, 1944. Dr. Mather went to town and found some Antuitrin for

June and two books to read up on glands and hormones. Control is lacking because of lack of Vitamin K, they think. He hopes to establish balance.

January 21, 1944. Thanks to the Red Cross, June was given a plasma transfusion in the evening. She is the third one who has had it. I spent visiting hour with her and we laughed, she was so full of stories. June does not realize how ill she is.

January 22, 1944. They had taken June's blood count in the morning and found it very low as she lost much of it after the plasma. Dr. Mather came to take June's blood for typing and again he sweated trying to get into the vein. Her count has dropped so low that the veins have collapsed. Jerry went off and sat in another room while I stood by with her. At last the doctor got enough to type.

At the program, Jim Halsema read an imaginary letter from home telling of all the two-year developments in aviation, movies, rationing, production and other ways which he had culled from papers (some of which came from the States in Red Cross packing). It was an excellent compilation and broadcasting is one of his fortes.

I ached all over from weariness and anxiety repression. Bedie came over for muffin with strawberry sauce and I sent some back to Jerry. Then I went to bed where I lay quietly feeling like weeping but knowing that I must gather all my force into strength for June. Jerry was so cast down because he could not give his blood (not her type). God be thanked for the Red Cross and American packages which brought food kits and medicine and plasma. None of it came a day too soon.

January 23, 1944. Up at 7. Dr. Mather had said they would give the transfusion early and be finished about 9:30 and I could go down then. I started down to June with Emergency chocolate, cheese and vitamin capsules. Carl stopped me by the door and said they had only just finished taking the blood from Dr. Shaffer. Dr. Shaffer went past me on his way to town with Ola and I took his hand and thanked him without words. He was shy and embarrassed. Carl said it would take a long time to give the transfusion and I had better go home for a while. Well, I didn't want to go back to space so I stopped to tell Jerry it was delayed. Then I went to see Peg.

After a while I went down to the hospital again and from the bottom of the stairs could see the white gowns of the doctor and nurse at work. I stood for a time watching them then went out to sit on a chair on the point back of Baby House trying to draw courage and strength from the blue pile of Philippine mountains. I lifted up my eyes to the hills and drank silently from the air and sun, then went back. They were still at it. I went to sit on the bench in the hospital garden and I lived a thousand years in three hours of waiting there.

Helen came down and sat with me. She said she couldn't stand staying in her bed next to June's, watching them work over her, any more, but that June was standing it marvelously and wasn't even whimpering. I could see Ina, the nurse, holding the can of blood and the red tube. After an hour I saw the can still nearly full and I said to Helen, "My God, haven't they put in any at all yet?" and I guess they hadn't, for she was so low that the veins had no pressure and were collapsed. It was nearly two hours of working over her before they even started the transfusion. Suddenly I couldn't sit there and walked "home" to get the two custards for the hospital ice box. When I sat down again in the garden below that window, Ina called down, "Soon be through." Ten minutes later they were no longer bending over the bed and I went to the foot of the stairs. They called me up and there she was, smiling, against the pillow, starting at once to pour the story out to me. She talked fast, chuckling over various items and saying they call her "bedpan Jane." "See all that red on the bath towel? That is good Dr. Shaffer blood," says she. "They gave me 400 cc. and when they couldn't get into the vein in my arms or legs, Dr. Mather said well, here goes and he put it straight into my neck with a strong jab. It spurted out and then he began to let it in and it wasn't bad after that, felt like water running through my throat. My, but I'm sure glad he didn't have to put it into my jugular vein!" Later I repeated her remark to Dr. Mather and he shot a look at me and said, "But that's just what I did do," and I wasn't surprised. Anyway, I answered, *she* doesn't know it. When I told Jerry at supper, he said, "My God, but that took guts. That man has nerve as well as skill." I heard a doctor say he had never known it to be done before. June told me proudly that she and Dr. Mather made history today for he told her so, but she doesn't know why. Dr. Mather told me that only once before had he ever given it in the neck in an entirely different case and never in all his experience had he given such a difficult transfusion. He said June was perfectly marvelous and that Bea and Ina were battling over who was to make up her bed afterward. When I told this to Jerry, he broke down, but it was a relief for him. I guess I am like the Duchess in Alice in Wonderland who always cried *before* she pricked her finger. I am always shedding my tears ahead of time before there appears to be much to cry about. What drama has taken place in that homely, top-heavy building down on the point, with beauty spread so lavishly in the valley below it. June has a lot to do in the world, something for the future, and she must pull through. I could bear it for her, but it seems she must learn to bear it for herself and she has.

This afternoon when I went back to see her, she told me, "Mama, you were right. It was better for me not to have you here till afterward. With you near I might have cried, but with strangers I had to be brave and I was. I didn't cry once and I'm proud of it." And well she might be. The whole staff adores her. When Ina felt hurt because she lost out on the bed-making, June reminded her that she couldn't have done without her for whenever she felt like crying Ina would wink and then June had to laugh and this helped her. This delighted wry Ina. June is being fed all she can take but she may have to have another transfusion, though the veins may improve from this one. Tonight the doctor is encouraged about her general condition.

The Court has sat on two cases—suspended sentences on plate stealing—and a forfeit of all cigarettes from Nick who sent out a package in his bag with a concealed note saying he would send more from time to time. Camp is very sore at him!

January 24, 1944. Dr. Mather says June is far better than she was three days ago. He calls her the Princess of Patients. Jerry told Dr. Shaffer that June was talkative, and he kidded Jerry, asking him if [he] was implying it was the good Shaffer blood. She inherits two talkative strains as well.

June is learning in one terrible swoop what women go through. She adored Daddy's eggnog chilled in a bottle in the icebox so that it was like ice cream. Betty sent her a luscious prune bar. Bedie finally went to see her and she said disdainfully, "Hello, Squirt," hurt because he hadn't come sooner but not letting him see it. They batted each other like a couple of puppies biffing affectionately with paws.

After Japanese class Jerry made a soluble coffee and we had strawberry jam on muffins. I was dead tired and lame from letdown. Harry came and sat with us, telling the news of our landing in Italy thirty miles behind the lines and close to Rome; of evacuation of Japanese troops from New Guinea to New Britain and New Ireland.[3]

January 25, 1944. Jerry says if we tried to thank all those who have offered for transfusion we would have to entertain a big crowd. Everyone is being kind, generous and helpful. After my work I gave Bedie some banana with milk, with a muffin buttered thick. He loved it all. Jerry is keeping his leg up though it is better since he burnt out three boil cores with carbolic in the dispensary yesterday. It ruined his appetite and he feels rotten.

June is by the window in the sun and light which gives her mental pep and her condition is definitely curbed. If I spread half a muffin thick with butter she will eat it. While I was there, Carol rushed up breathlessly saying, "Dr. Benedetti, we are going to have a baby," and behind him came four Igorot men carrying an improvised stretcher made of rough-cut tree saplings with a straw mat over them. On this was a small Igorot woman in labor. June was glad to have something to watch. The poor soul had been in labor two days and the doctor could do nothing here because he had no instruments. He found several things wrong and said there must be an operation in town. She lay in the operating room from 11 till 2:30 without making a sound of pain in all that time. During this event, a second Igorot woman was brought in with gallbladder attack, slung in a cloth on her husband's back in the manner of carrying a baby. She too waited with never a sound.

There are two new rulings for us—the *Daily News* is to be censored and is bearing its first Japanese chop this evening. Another note on the Board says, ''The following instructions have been issued today from the Commandant's office. Effective at once, all notes, packages, bags and money addressed to internees of Camp Holmes, are to be *delivered to the Commandant's home* where they will be inspected and delivered to camp. Kindly advise market stalls and friends Outside, so they may comply with this new rule.

January 26, 1944. Lees *gave* us the bones for marrow yesterday and Dr. Shaffer has ordered them to sell us these bones and liver every time they have it so we will get precedence through medical order while June needs it. He had given orders about her diet at the hospital and she can have 4 or 5 eggs a day in various forms and hot calamansit juice which she craves. Under this setup she has more than one doctor attending, they are all co-operating and everything is being done for her. It is a long slow pull but she will make it. It is better than three months ago for it is not just one doctor now but all working together, the food kits and new medicine as well. I wrote Nida telling of the new rule about packages and asking her to send calamansits and a few carrots every week.

Peg made June a chocolate custard for supper and she laps up Jerry's eggnog before she sleeps. He mixed it on the front porch. She hadn't touched her cheese or emergency chocolate and I scolded her. I took it out and cut it in four slices and squares. When I went down later she was pleased with herself after eating all four slices. She is getting plenty to eat and we painted pictures of liver, bone marrow and steak, for her appetite is poor due to the anemia. She feels a letdown today but is better generally. We came so near to losing her that I still shake all over when I think of it. I cannot put my mind on anything but June, find it impossible to concentrate on Nippongo and these notes seem incoherent, with many gaps and omissions.

Bridge with Scotts after Japanese class but I was horribly nervous all evening and must get hold of myself. I didn't break down as I did a week ago but my mind is in turmoil, turning and revolving around June. I want to push and hurry her improvement and it cannot be. Lost possessions have faded entirely. The preciousness of June is an obsession and I must adjust myself for it will not be good for her or me or any member of the family. It is not wise to concentrate on one thing and worry about it. Bedie is ravenous, his appetite returning in leaps. We must satisfy it somehow. He ate four bananas after supper. We will buy baking bananas as they are filling.

January 27, 1944. As we came out of the hospital we heard why there was so much running back and forth. After doing a huge stack of ironing, Mrs. Morris went back to her space and sat down on her bed. She gasped, clutched her throat for breath and fell over on the bed. As quickly as that she was gone, beyond all help from the nurse who was near and came at once, of Father Maquire who knelt to pray beside her, and the doctors who arrived breathless with hypo and stethoscope. Worried over her husband who was taken away to the military camp, a chain smoker who refused all medical advice to cut down on smoking, she was a bundle of nerves, winding tighter and tighter like a spinning top. It was release for a tortured soul, but is tragic for her two year old son and her five year old daughter. Dolly had never adjusted to camp. She had never balanced time and her small amount of strength to caring for the children. She never got hold of herself but tried to forget her anxiety in study classes, with foolish energy spent on ironing, cooking fancy cakes and cookies for parties. All this extra work took strength needed for plain duties, simply living requirements for the children. I would break down too if I ironed or kept up with fancy cooking. No one notices un-ironed clothes in here. This sudden attack could happen to any one of us—all of camp felt this and became serious, panicky.

No bag from Nida as I feared so I hated and cursed the invaders. It is not enough that they take all possessions but they must kill all friendly gestures and contacts. That weekly bag was like a letter from home. It meant they were still carrying on, able to buy and deliver. Will they adjust to new, stern rules? I feel I would like to squeeze some of them in the same way—this enemy—would like to smother them with infinite detail and the breaths of war and hate. At this minute I would have no mercy and would return in kind. I needed that contact after three weeks of piling up misery, and they have stopped contact. How I wish for relief for Nida, freedom for Ismael, help for her home, her brother, her country, soon! Yet I know that this is war and everywhere it is like this, for war is a psychosis for everyone concerned.

January 28, 1944. Jerry is keeping his swollen ankle in the air so to speak so he could not be pallbearer. I told him to stay flat for I would go to the service. It was most impressive, the Episcopalian service sounded majestic as it reminded us that the Lord sent us into this world with nothing and took us out of it the same way.

When the men took up the spades, we turned to leave but the voice of a Japanese was heard, loud and staccato, the clipped accent of words from Nippon. Hayakawa, Saito and Tomibe stood near the grave, and turning, I saw Tomibe facing all of us. He looked fine, so straightforward, as his voice boomed into the hushed group. Miss McKim stood beside him, her hands placed palms together in the submissive pose of all Japanese women—a sort of folding in of the body, drooping shoulders, fallen eyes, complete subjection and humility. She translated for him, adding her own sincerity and simple expression to what he said. It was more than impressive. I shall never forget him standing there. He wished us all to know how sorry he was about what had happened and wished that he could do more than he could. He understood that we were very upset. The Japanese had telephoned to the father but it was not possible now to bring him here and they wished that he and we would remember that there were two little children to care for and bring up. Would every one of us please do what we could to help them? Again he wanted to say how sorry he was. He seemed to sense the feeling of panic, the knowledge that it could have happened to any one of us who felt more shut in and far away than ever before, helpless to reach out for contacts we wanted. His was an honest, brief little speech, with the best advice any one could have given us. We took it away down the hill with us, for no matter what is done or destroyed, there are always the children who are the future.

Denny, the little girl, went right back to her space and threw her arms around Ruth Zimmerman's neck. Don came with supper and they all ate together in the security and stability of a family, the gap in the childrens' lives closing as the circle rounded out as gently as possible. The happiness of the young couple shines like a star and must affect the children. If only their father could know how blessed they are. Father Barter has volunteered to do the stack of laundry for the children.

June's blood count has gone from 43 to 56 and even the doctor looks encouraged. We are feeding her about 4 eggs a day, two slices of steak.

In the evening at coffee, Dr. Benedetti sat next to us correcting his MS., and it seemed like other days. Men come in to spend time with their families now. Scott keeps saying what a difference it makes having coffee with his wife upstairs while she is putting the children in bed. Formerly this separated them after supper. Now the children can talk and play with Daddy. It is cosy, casual family life.

I was awake hours in the night with a bitter feeling in my stomach. It feels like my mouth, full of blisters and canker sores. Pre-sprue mouth they call it. Others have had it for months too.

Notes from Men's Minutes of January 25: "Starting February 1, we will get our food from the Japanese Army. We will not handle the cash involved. Food will be obtained on a ration basis as follows:

Rice	400 grams per person per day.					
Vegetables	200	"	"	"	"	"
Meat or fish	100	"	"	"	"	"
Sugar	20	"	"	"	"	"
Salt	25	"	"	"	"	"
Lard or Purico	20	"	"	"	"	"
Tea	1	"	"	"	"	"

"All persons over ten years of age will receive the above ration. Those under ten will receive half of this amount. People who do heavy or hard work will receive an extra 100 grams per day and an extra 20 grams of lard."

January 29, 1944. After three and a half weeks of illness, June is over the hump and we are breathing again.

I talked to Dr. Shaffer about my diet and his face fell when I told him about my burning stomach. He says our whole diet is acid so there is really nothing I could leave out. I should go onto an alkaline diet but he has none to give me. He says liverbraun would help but it is more important to keep it for June right now and that I was right to do so.

At noon a bag from Nida made us happy. There was a list in her own writing. Four baskets of berries which I prepared and made into a sauce on Peg's stove, a whole kilo of carrots (at P6!) but just the sight of them was cheering. I divided them into a mess a day for June and me for three days. We cooked them whole without even scraping them. The strong earthy taste was wonderful. I almost wept over them at supper. We put butter on them too. June's were supplemented with some from camp. I drank a lot of juice and it answered months of craving, and seemed to soothe my stomach. Nida also sent bananas, a head of fresh green lettuce of which we ate the heart leaves and cooked the outside ones. There were two large cookies apiece also. It was a tonic to receive the bag and to know she had received our message about the carrots.

Tokyo has told of 15,000 tons of bombs dropped on Berlin in 20 minutes. There was another raid the next day. The Berlin we know is no more, wiped off like beautiful Hamburg and London. Oh man, when will you learn to build without destruction? Perhaps like birth which has labor pains, it cannot be done without suffering.

The *News* says, "Resourceful papas and crowded conditions are rapidly boosting baby-house youngsters skyward. One crib is equipped with pulleys for day storage under the ceiling. Premium on floor space has its reflection in other camp buildings also. A walk through any dorm discloses not only beds, but clothes, food kits, suitcases, drying laundry, sacks of peanuts, bucaco, beans and other commodities suspended from the rafters."

January 31, 1944. It is John Hay's second birthday so we gave him an egg.

June is frightened about getting sick again but I tell her they will look after it in the beginning this time now that they know the condition.

The Medical Committee discussed sore mouths of which there are at least ten and some unreported. Dr. Mather came by to look at mine and to tell me that I am going to be the guinea pig for ascorbic acid shots for it. If my tract responds, others will get the treatment. I am worn out with the nerves and the irritation it causes. I simply can't face camp hot pepper stews any more, nor gabi or camotes. They make my mouth smart.

Everyone is gloomy about the Japanese taking over our food supply on the first. No fruit, one half the amount of veg, more rice. They also want to cut our market and other contacts.

February 1, 1944. My family seems to be on the upgrade while I am on the downgrade! Jerry went back to wood chopping and Bedie is well and ravenous. June is walking about slowly but says it is all she can do to get up one step on the stair. The procession which wound up the hill to the grave the other day was very typical of camp. Most of us were in our working clothes—I came from the mop pail in old brown slacks and a sweater. Some wore new Red Cross clothes, the Sisters were in black gowns and white headpieces as always; the ever-present, inscrutable Japanese face was there like a scroll weaving in and out of the main design. This time they seemed as understanding and as humanly sympathetic as they have ever been.

February 2, 1944. Jerry gives me an egg and pâté for breakfast. He is very concerned about my sore mouth which may be scurvy.

At bridge, Church told us about the squeeze in the chow line—how they shortchanged us, giving us 30 [kilos] of meat, instead of 50, when it was weighed here. The Filipino started to put it on the scale before loading it but the Japanese officer waved him away, saying no. A good reason why. There is the same shortchange in every direction, including the Relief Fund of P100,000 coming through Tokyo which was less than that in pesos by the time we received it. The old Army game—graft and chiseling the world over.

February 3, 1944. While I was at the wash table, Jerry came with a surprise pan of fudge. He said I was to eat all I wanted and it was not to be paired out or saved on our 17th anniversary today! The day brought memories of jade in Peking, bouquet of chrysanthemum in Tientsin, a chaplain and a consul, and white satin. I fried a can of corned beef at noon and made toasted cheese on the camp bread.

Our food from the Japanese is rice in abundance, fish each time (with me allergic to it), excellent tea for breakfast and sugar for it and the rice. Jerry is giving me an egg then too. Camp meals, however, are dull. Rice, camote gravy and cabbage; rice, fish chowder and Wong bok. No more fruit or eggs in camp chow unless relief money comes. My mouth is still sore and I'm dead tired every night but it is heaven to have June gaining steadily.

Bedie and pals have had their heads shaved, thinking it was fun to put it over on me. It made me heartsick. He knew only too well how I felt. That awful, blue-veined, gray look of a prison head. It makes me ill to see it, but his thoughtless, smart-aleck stage is worse. He is inconsiderate, bluffs his way out of dishwashing, prevaricating continually. He just doesn't develop or grow up at all. I suppose suddenly he will, some day.

General Committee Meeting: "We recommend the following for February:

1. Budgeting P125 per day
   (for purchase of fruit and seasonings)
2. Of necessity we must eliminate the egg ration of both Baby House and children's diet.

3. The Dietician is authorized to see that the children receive an equal share, with the adults, of the proteins that come on the present ration basis.

4. Wood crew—Since we cannot supply the extra food ration on the same basis as formerly we recommend the formation of two complete crews to work on alternate days.

"At a recent conference with the Commandant, we were advised that the treatment of American nationals in internment camps is to be on an equal basis with treatment of Japanese nationals interned in America. Therefore, any regulations put into effect here, will be the same regulations that apply to Japanese nationals in America. . . . The Commandant expects to make arrangements for use of some land where a camp garden may be grown. . . . When censorship has been completed we may expect to receive some of the 80,000 letters in Manila from the U.S. . . . International Red Cross messages received today for two camp members and 7 Catholic nuns on the outside. They were sent in February and April *1943*, on office forms in English."

February 6, 1944. At noon I had the 5th ascorbic intravenous shot and felt the reaction of less acidity. The experiment is tough but interesting.

Jerry says Bedie's growing up was delayed because we lived so far from people that he did not have enough companions.

The Sergeant came with all his huge teeth in a delighted grin at our Japanese class. He is very pleased that we learn it and he wants to learn English.

February 7, 1944. My sixth shot today seems to be taking hold. I feel shaky and my stomach feels as though I had been crying but it is not twisted, squeezed and tortured feeling any more. It is more neutral and soft. Even the perspiration is no longer acid. I am resting every afternoon, and I have arranged to have a week off from waitressing if Dido can return Wednesday. This means I can stay in bed later in the morning, no set time to be anywhere, only a bit of mopping and cans. Jerry wants me to do it, says he will give me eggnogs if only I won't pour my energy out again. I can sunbathe too.

June's hemoglobin is 72 tonight. Jerry whooped to the full moon when I told him.

The Sergeant asked Miss McKim to get six or eight people to write their impressions of Japanese treatment of internees and she refused.

February 8, 1944. From the *News*: "Placed in operation today was the camp's first power-driven rice separator, a Rube Goldbergish contraption of pulleys, wheels, cams, a motor and a shaking table with serrated baffles constructed at the shop by Fabian and Jess out of salvaged materials, including part of a Red Cross box. It separates rice from *palay* (the unhulled grain) by utilizing the difference in bounce and friction between the two on the same principle as the winnowing baskets formerly used.

"More than halfway through the task of resoling the shoes of those who did not receive new ones from relief supplies are the hard working cobblers. . . . Our library is one of the most important facets in the costume ' jewel we have built up out of largely ersatz material to resemble the life we used to lead . . . . Home gardens flourish here and there in every nook and cranny. Rain has helped, but bugs destroy. . . . A wash shed is now under construction to replace the tent which has seen its best days (and typhoons)."

June is restless and the nurse couldn't let her go home without a written order. I went to the goat pen on a hunt for the doctor and saw ten of the 25 or 30 goats that have been born within the last few weeks. Pure white ones, soft all-brown ones, white and black, brown and white—all standing about on spindle legs, bleating or running up to wise-looking Mama Goat who chewed placidly and answered the little bleat now and then. Two of the babies were only three hours old, still moist, with hair curling on their heads in wet strands just as they were born.

In bed later June purred like a happy kitten to be home, while I breathed a thankful sigh at having my little foot warmer back. It is thanks to many working together that she is home again. The list is long—two doctors, one who gave his own blood and one who administered it, while both were responsible for her care; several nurses who assisted during the three hours and were among others who made bed, gave baths, answered bells and carried out orders; the staff cooks who fried eggs or meat, brought trays; Gibby who washed the sheets, towels and nightgowns; the wood gang who chop for the sterilizing stove; the pathologist who watched the rise in count every day or two after the critical fall and crisis was over; the pharmacist; people who generously offered their blood for transfusion; visitors who brought eggs, muffins and custards, and we parents who shot our wad on beef, bones, eggs, carrots, trotting back and forth to help build her up in any way that offered. It was a perfect cooperative, functioning through skilled and unskilled brains and hands. And it worked so well, with wonderful results.

February 10, 1944. The dentist's technique is not improved, perhaps from too little use and hard work at woodcutting. His hands are rough. Whatever it is, I lost confidence and do not care to go to him again. He just doesn't give a damn and hates us all. Peg had had a similar experience for he had scratched across the front of her gums in a line which is still sore and she was exhausted afterward, though hot coffee pulled her together. Ruth had one filling and did not get over it for nearly a week. She said it was so rough it was like a horse doctor going after a horse's teeth. So I guess I did not dream my experience. I was all in but I went to Japanese class. My mouth was sore from instruments and my whole head felt as though pounded with an ax. But I was glad to be alive just the same.

At siesta time the Outside came in again to us. Doreen came with P100 folded in a small paper packet from John Co, the loan we so badly needed after shooting our wad of several hundred down to 25 after June's illness. It was wonderful to receive it from [this] Chinese friend. It was like bread upon the waters, on the day before Bedie's birthday.

February 11, 1944. Bedie enters his teens!

I took my last Vitamin C shot and asked Dr. Mather what he thought I had. He wouldn't name it, said all those pernicious anemias were allied, had similar symptoms of sore mouth and tongue, stomach and intenstinal disorders, lassitude etc. It was deficiency, more than one vitamin perhaps, not simple at all. C was obviously lacking and the ascorbic intravenous helped at once. My stomach has cleared up and I hope the mouth will follow.

At 7 Bedie made his party ready for his two cavalier pals and the three girls who are all pretty blondes. The boys all have shaved heads. The tablecloth was two new Red Cross white bath towels with Pat's sweet peas in a pickle jar for centerpiece. Bedie borrowed Peg's dishes on which Jerry put muffins with strawberry sauce, served with cocoa and Emergency chocolate.

Everyone is deficient and it takes many forms—a fine test tube we are! Everyone feels tired and can work only half as much as last year.

February 13, 1944. The sign was put up on the Board: "*Important notice*: Effective Sunday February 20, 1944, no more bags will be permitted to come in to camp by order of Camp Commandant. Signed, the Chairman." By the side of the radio notice it makes a combination of bad news. We cannot listen at the guardhouse anymore.

The latest rule, in the evening *News*, is that the garbage wagon and crew can go out no more, must dump all garbage in the dirt pits at the end of camp. So everything is shut down except the *Tribune* and the store and we all pray that the latter keeps going.

February 15, 1944. Damn the enemy. Even Germany permits bags and letters from home. I don't want these officers killed, I want them isolated and incommunicado in a camp for months on end; no bags, no word from home, just plugging along without any toilet paper, living on rice and cabbage.

February 17, 1944. Nida sent a wonderful bag and we had a great time stowing it away. 8½ dozen new green limes as precious as gold to us, two kilos of white sugar, a bag of white potatoes, little orange cookies, lots of kidney beans, shelled peanuts, bananas and four baskets of beautiful strawberries.

Internees will be allowed to send 1 special postcard per month to either the Philippine Islands or other countries, but not to both.

Other items are that we mustn't use braille or invisible ink when writing

Natalie Stark and Jerry Crouter celebrate their engagement in Peking, January 1927.

Natalie and Jerry Crouter, 1931.

Igorot tribesmen, Baguio, 1928.

The Crouters' prewar home in Baguio.

Natalie, Jerry, June and Bedie Crouter in Baguio, 1935.

Nida and Ismael Bacani with their daughter Eppie, 1936.

Bayview Hotel, Manila, August 1940.

June, Natalie, Jerry and Bedie Crouter, Christmas 1940.

Above, a group of Japanese soldiers with (top row) Carl Eschbach, second from right; (bottom row) Nellie McKim, second from left; Rokuro Tomibe, third from left. *Below*, Bilibid Prison, Manila.

The Crouter family in Bilibid after their release, February 1945.

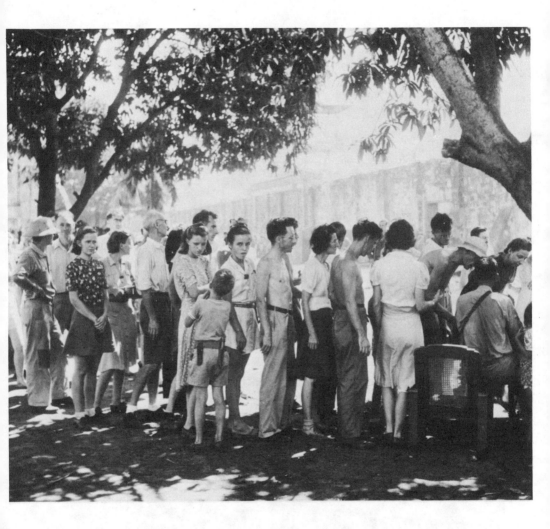

Bilibid after liberation, February 1945. *Top left*, children enjoy a ride with soldiers. *Bottom left*, fresh bread is delivered. *Above*, mail call.

Devastation following the Battle of Manila. *Top left*, Legislative Building. *Bottom left*, Finance Building. *Above*, City Hall.

Bedie, Natalie, June, Jerry. Hotel Sir Francis Drake, San Francisco, April 24, 1945.

Nida Bacani with daughters Felie, left, and Eppie. Baguio, 1947.

Cleveland Heights, 1950. Jerry and Natalie Crouter with Natalie's sister Marguerite Bellamy.

June and Fred (Bedie) Crouter, February 1951.

Reunion of Camp Holmes internees, San Francisco, February 1977. *From right*: June Crouter Wortman, Natalie Crouter, Glen Wortman (June's son), Rokuro Tomibe.

letters; that people over 70, lepers, and those in serious condition or insane may stay outside of camp. There will be equal suffrage (Imagine getting it after all from the Japanese!) and one of the vice-chairmen must be able to speak Japanese (which tells us to vote for Miss McKim which delights us!). As to food, Tomibe answers that we were getting better than the Japanese Army.

Mr. Tomibe said we would be allowed to have medicines, clothes and toilet articles and money sent in.

"In the Health Department, Dr. Skerl presented the problem of privately purchased milk for babies that will result from discontinuance of the food bags. He was asked to make a list of those now receiving milk from Outside. This list and a letter stating the problem will be submitted to the Commandant. . . . In Finance, a report stated that the store has been reasonably successful in supplying a greater variety of veg for sale. . . . A system has been set up for handling meat sales as a camp project. It will be workable as soon as attempts to purchase beef or pork are successful. . . . On our present diet, the demand for foodstuffs has greatly increased."

To Camp Commandant:
Attention, Mr. Tomibe.   February 14.
Dear Sir:

Mail and Communication with U.S. and England:
We have been interned under the Imperial Japanese Army for a period of more than two years and during this time we have been permitted to send one letter only to our relatives in U.S. or England. This is certainly wholly inadequate and unsatisfactory, and is undoubtedly not in accord with the general treatment of civilian prisoners of war. . . . We have received from the U.S. a very limited number of messages (17). The majority of these messages have been over one year on the way. We bring these facts to your attention and for your consideration. Naturally, we are anxious for a closer contact with our families in U.S. and England, and anything you can do to rectify these discrepancies will be appreciated. Yours very truly, The Chairman, Executive Committee.

Copy of Another Letter

Same Heading:
The present ration system for supply of our daily food allowance has been in effect two weeks, or ½ the present month of February, and we wish to make a report on its operation to date. . . . The medical authorities of the camp are of the unanimous opinion that the present food allowance is totally inadequate for our requirements, and unless some definite improvements are planned for the immediate future, the health of the camp will suffer considerably. The doctors repeat that they cannot be held responsible for the health

of the camp on the present diet allowances, and hence we register this official protest with you, Mr. Tomibe, as the representative of the Imperial Japanese Army, which is accountable for our welfare. A considerable quantity of the fish and shrimp were rotten when received and not fit for our use. . . . The vegetable ration has been filled to date, but it has consisted almost entirely of cabbage. We cannot live on cabbage alone. Living as we do in a section of the country noted for its variety of vegetables, is it not possible for us to obtain a greater variety of this vital commodity for our use? We know you are interested in maintaining the health of the camp and we make these suggestions in the spirit of cooperation and as evidence of the desire on our part to continue the health record of the camp. Very truly yours, The Chairman, Executive Committee.

February 18, 1944. There will be no more Women's Committee—it will merge with the General Committee and we all vote for the one.

The dentist is making a plaster of paris mold and is affably filling teeth. He hasn't been this way since the last election when he started his gay dark little plan of "No committee position, no dental work."

Poor humble Tanabe fell off his bicycle and cut his knee, then fainted. They took him to the hospital on a stretcher. The Japanese staff roared with laughter at the accident for he has lost face still further. He has wrecked two cars (the last one being the Lincoln in the sunken gardens), and now he can't even coordinate on two wheels. With more roars as they stand around him on the operating table, they say he will have to walk from now on. Hayakawa tells him cheerfully he may even die of the wound. Of course the injury is not serious.

February 19, 1944. It is our last day of freedom and bags from town. We had two fat and bursting ones from Nida. Wonderful girl, she thought of everything and then some. I wrote only for a large package of bijon [fine rice noodle], and she sent three kilos of it which ought to last for the duration unless the Marines take another year on the way. It is a protein product. There were two gantas of coffee beans (a gold mine in these times), real Benguet coffee, 1 ganta of black beans tied in a cloth, two kilos of light brown centrifugal sugar (where does she get it?), more calamansits totaling 150. Jerry thinks [their juice] helps his back. In the bags also were 3 kilos of white potatoes, 2 pounds of "family" carrots, about 3 kilos of camotes, 11 gabi, 3 papaya, two bunches of bananas and 4 baskets of berries which we ate on fresh baked muffins.

I have been too weary to take notes since June was sick, and notice a big difference in my ability to do things since a year ago. Then I took notes in two courses and typed them afterward. Now I take no notes, do little typing and scarcely find energy or time to study Japanese. I attend classes but that is about all. It is all we can do to keep well, do the work and cooking required. I mopped and picked rice.

February 20, 1944. Today is our entrance into complete isolation; no bags, no Japanese radio, no market, nothing but medical trips to town, no news or rumors (that's what they think). Many rumors are around however. Truk is being heavily attacked. Another tale says that Guam and Wake are now ours and that on one of these not a living thing was found—all wiped out by bombings. We had some landings in the Marianas. Good reason for jitters if this is all true.[4]

February 22, 1944. The Japanese have sprung a mean and ominous one. They want us to sign a paper that we won't try to escape no mater what the conditions. The Committee discussed it at length, put it back in their laps where it now is. The Committee said we had not been asked to sign this two years ago and had shown no intention of escaping since then, and they couldn't see why we should be asked to sign anything like that now. They asked to talk with someone who knew international law for they felt that now we would sign only under duress which would make it invalid and not worth the paper it was written on. If men were outside on duty with a permit, and they were fired at by jittery guard, they could say the men were escaping after signing that they would not. It sounds like a cover for more devilment. Meanwhile they talk of taking our books to censor them; they pop into school at any hour, trying to catch "dangerous thoughts" or "anti" teaching. They are in a fine state of mind again. Back to the old days.

February 23, 1944. "The Commandant stated that the order had come from the Japanese Army and that the oaths must be signed by all individuals over ten years of age and by the parents of children under ten. He explained that should a group of internees refuse to sign the oath, he would have to report them to Manila and the assumption would be that they would not obey the orders of the Japanese Military Authorities and that they planned to escape. Motion carried, that when the signed copies of these oaths are turned over to the Commandant, they will be accompanied by a covering letter to state that they have been signed under protest."

Jerry sent out his watch to sell to raise money for eggs for me and meat for the kids. We have so few possessions left that it hurt me to have him do it but Shikataganai. (There is no help for it—nothing can be done.)

Rules and Regulations issued by Commandant's Office
Japanese Army Internment Camp No. 3

"Since the Japanese Army has assumed control over the management of internment camps, they are now issuing the following regulations to be observed. The Army will enforce these regulations which are to be the same for the three camps in the Philippines—Santo Tomas, Los Baños and Baguio. 1. Internees must obey all official commands given by members of the Japanese staff and guards. 2. Internees wishing to go outside fence for any reason must obtain permission from Camp Commandant. (This fence will be constructed by authorities, boundaries to be defined later.) 3. There must be no communication with people living outside the camp. Special cases may secure permission from the Commandant. 4. There must be no political meetings held in camp. 5. No private food packages are allowed to come into camp. Money, clothing and toilet articles may be sent into camp. 6. The Commandant approves the present social relationships between men and women but cautions against unseemly conduct by the young people. 7. Visitors from the outside will be allowed only on the following days (include only parents, wives, children): January 1. February 11. April 29. November 3. December 25. 8. There must be no construction or building in camp without permission of the Commandant. 9. All books and magazines are subject to censorship. 10. Conduct by internees prejudicial to good order and camp discipline will be subject to punishment as defined by the Commandant. 11. Releases. Internees suffering from incurable diseases, mentally deranged, afflicted with leprosy or 70 years of age, will be released. Other requests for release which merit special attention will be referred to Manila for decision. 12. A daily time sheet of all hours spent on Camp Work must be recorded for the Commandant's office. 13. The Camp Store will be continued. Orders for merchandise will be handled by the Commandant's staff who will arrange for buyers in Baguio. 14. Classes must be held in school buildings, and elsewhere only with permission of the Commandant. The subjects of the present war and Japan must not be taught. Permission for the adult language classes must be obtained from Commandant. 15. Cases of hospitalization, X-ray or dental treatment must be submitted to Commandant by Chief Medical Officer. 16. The Camp Medical Officer will submit in advance, monthly, the requirements of the Camp for medical supplies which are not available from our present stocks. These will be obtained by the Commandant's office either from supplies held in Manila or from Nipponese Army Authorities. 17. Permission must be obtained from Commandant for special entertainment such as plays, pageants, or dances. 18. Internees will be allowed to send one letter each per month, either in the Philippine Islands or to the homeland. No guarantee is given as to their delivery. It is forbidden to mention affairs of a political, military, industrial or economic nature; to criticize treatment of internees; to mention Japanese affairs; to use code, secret words, invisible ink, braille or any other secret means of communication; to use other than English, Tagalog or Japanese language for letters in the Philippine Islands, and English or Japanese in letters to the homeland. . . . The Commandant has issued the following order for reorganization of the Camp Committee. . . . All internees must be treated equally, impartially and without special privilege to anyone. The Committee will act as liaison between the internees and the Commandant's office. It will be known as "The Internee Camp Committee," composed of the following persons to be elected by the camp, subject to approval of the Commandant. Chairman, Vice-Chairman, a Japanese-speaking Second Vice-Chairman, Heads of the following departments: 1. Internal Affairs. 2. Finance. 3. Utilities. 4. Work Details. 5. Education, and Religion. 6. Health. An election will be held on March 1 and those elected will hold office for a period of six months. The electorate will be composed of all adults over 20 years old. Membership on the Committee is open to both men and women."

At any rate the Nipponese have handed suffrage to the women and the right of serving on the Committee.

February 24, 1944. Mela gave a baby shower for Ray's wife who delivers in May. There were twenty guests, a crib basket and layette. It is best summed up in Mrs. Greer's verse with her gift.

> Roses are red, violets blue,
> It can't happen here
> But it happened to you!

Hayakawa's open mouth of surprise and his subsequent grin was priceless when Carl informed him of the coming event.

On Ash Wednesday, all the Sisters were crosses of gray ash on their foreheads after service.

February 25, 1944. No more *Tribune* for camp subscribers, alas.

February 26, 1944. Carl went to his house for the first time in many months. He is broke, and so are Fabians and Peg and many others. Yesterday in the kitchen, the huge roasts, meat loafs, hamburgers, stews on the stove nearly finished me. We could buy none and the sight and flavor was overpowering. We shared Nida's pineapple and coffee in Peg's cubbyhole cubicle.

Over the dishpan, Miss McKim's talk with Tomibe was related. It was a highlight on these last months and reveals many changes and possibilities between Japan and America. He talked very seriously, told her he had brought up the subject of dancing on his last trip to Manila. The Commandant had growled his disapproval but Tomibe had answered, "It is American custom. They like it. I say let them have it," and Baguio has a permit at any rate.

He told her he thought language and customs were a great barrier to peoples getting together, the cause of great misunderstandings. It troubled him. He told her of a Filipino-Japanese misunderstanding which he had been called in to clear up, on the Outside. The Filipino had grunted in assent "Mm huh" as we say it also, and this particular sound made in the mouth and throat is equivalent to a Japanese word meaning, "I am looking down on you. You are way beneath." At the sound, the Japanese struck the Filipino fiercely, and the battle of complete misunderstanding was on. Tomibe was called in to unravel it, thereby learning a great deal of the difference in language and custom and the damage that can result from it. One can easily imagine the bewilderment followed by fury in the Filipino's mind, after he had assented to orders.

Tomibe also told of his great embarrassment over another matter to which he had given much thought. He wanted to know how the women got along without certain things that must be necessary to them [sanitary supplies]. He said that being a man he had given it no thought until a Filipina woman doctor had come to him, inquiring anxiously if he couldn't supply certain necessities. Miss McKim told him we had had many difficulties and outlined some of the makeshifts. He said he would do everything he could to help.

He wants to learn English and begged Miss McKim to teach him to which she finally consented. Tarumizu, the peasant, was studying with Peter Saleeby. Like me, studying Nippongo, they wish to learn and understand the enemy. Tomibe, who has never been out of Japan before, with the possible exception of Korea, has shown more comprehension and desire to be considerate than anyone connected with our administration. He wants to know Americans and their customs, apparently admires many aspects of us. The Japanese *people* as a whole will make a good democracy—like any other people under the right leaders who give them a chance to learn and express their interests and desires.

February 28, 1944. Miss McKim told of complaining of the rice to Tomibe San and he asked if he could eat our breakfast. He arrived at the end of the last line and John dished out the lumpy, poorly cooked rice, with hot tea. No sugar for that morning. Tomibe ate a little of the rice, enjoyed the tea. He asked if there wasn't soup or sugar or something to go on the rice and the answer was negative. He shook his head, said, "Sa!" looking as though he agreed with Miss McKim—and went off to think some more.

February 29, 1944. Mary says Marie sold some clothes for her, sent in over P200. She says velvets are popular (to make into evening slippers) and asks what about Natalie's. . . . I shall send out word to "use" red, purple and wine colored but not the black. I am sentimental about that Singapore dress. Maybe we will eat my clothes yet. We need the cash and there is no word about the watch.

Wilma and Carol are to have a camp wedding on March 23d. The announcement on the Board was signed by the Chairman and Hayakawa. "February 29. To Whom It May Concern: By written permission from the Commandant, persons wishing to marry in the internment camp may do so."

Camp is all aflutter over romance and nuptials. Betty has sent out for her white satin and maid-of-honor gowns.

After two years, thanks to Tomibe, we can commingle at mealtimes in the dining room. The Chair and Miss McKim deserve thanks too. It is hoped to reserve the last table for men only.

March 2, 1944. *Next year* I suppose our mops will have lavender, pink and green playsuit rags in them, very colorful.

After rice and tea breakfast, Tomibe asked Miss McKim what we would have had at this meal in normal times. She told him fruit, cereal with milk and sugar, eggs and bacon, or ham, or hotcakes, or toast and butter, coffee with milk and sugar. He said nothing, went away in deep thought.

The wood crew still exchanges rice or something for fruit for the children's diet. The expert sawyers, Clark and Mac, have been ordered to cut 300 fence posts so many feet long and thick. We are about to go behind barbed wire. They are taking their time however.

Life is always like this. We will soon be living off a gold watch and velvet gowns. All is no longer vanity. The red and purple gowns from Ethel on my birthday will bring a lot more than she paid for them. They have traveled far, from parties to steak and carrots.

Whenever I go up the hill, I am impressed each time with the magnificent imperturbability of the mountains, how little effect any national invasion has had upon them whether it was Spanish, American or Nipponese. Even the manmade rice terraces go on unchanged and beautiful, producing food in the fresh green shoots pushing through the water. Only the people are disturbed, not much else in the nature of the Islands.

March 3, 1944. We learn we are to have roll call twice a day. It is like being back in the old days.

March 4, 1944. I took a long walk beyond the goat pens with Peg and her children. It was great fun trying out trails through the brush, seeing wild roses and Sampagrita [tropical flower]. We heard the roar of planes over the coast. There were many lovely views from under small pines and in clearings. We enjoyed pushing through dewy weeds and bushes which were cool and delightful with uncurling fern fronds, delicate fresh green ground-pine tendrils. We heard the wood crew tree fall on the opposite hill and saw them sawing. We could see the market crowd at Trinidad.

Committee again: "The Chair stated our supply of rice and cabbage is sufficient, but we do not have salt, sugar and fat. We need more of these staple articles, eggs, and a variety of vegetables and fruits. . . . Mr. Tomibe stated that he did not think that their ration, which was set up by the Army, could be increased, but that we might prepare a request giving reasons for such an increase, and he would take the matter up on his next trip to Manila.

He felt quite sure, however, that any additional food would have to be purchased individually through the camp store. . . . Sergeant Sato stated that our present ration was based on Japanese Army medical opinion and that from a medical point of view it was adequate for the caloric requirements of working people. . . . Dr. Shaffer said that if everybody was in perfect physical condition the ration might be adequate, but that the civilian internees in our camp were not selected as they were in the Army, because of physical fitness. Many of them were not well when they were interned. In the past we have had camotes and other foods that could be pureed, but we now have no veg or fruits suitable for those who have intestinal disorders. They cannot digest cabbage. Many of these people are now living entirely from their Red Cross kits. When that supply is exhausted, Dr. Shaffer anticipates a great deal of digestive trouble unless a more suitable diet is supplied for the general camp diet, for children and those in poor health. . . . The Chair stated that one third of our food intake had previously come from our Japanese allowance, and that purchases from the store and food bags from the outside had represented two thirds of the food consumed by camp. Sgt. Sato said he would try to get camotes as a part of our regular diet, and that he would do all he could to secure a good variety of foods for sale through the camp store. . . . The members then raised the question of obtaining money for such extra food purchases. Could we establish regular channels for loans? The Command thought that this would not be possible, but intimated that individuals might continue to receive money from friends on the outside. The need for Relief Funds for those unable to borrow money was stressed. Mr. Tomibe will take the matter up with Manila. The Chair asked whether or not it would be possible to use money received for cloth etc., for the purchase of camp food. Mr. Hayakawa stated that white material and thread amounting to about P750 had been ordered for the camp and that if we did not want the material we might use the money for food, but that since no further cloth would likely be available to us, we might prefer the cloth. The Chair asked for time to consider this. Skerl called attention to the need for using our most able-bodied men to secure wood for cooking camp food. The Command felt a plan for raising additional food was more important than the money with which to buy it. The Japanese Army has a plan to purchase chickens and pigs, but we will have to care for and feed them. The growing of food and the raising of livestock are the real answers to our need for additional rations.''

Jerry said grimly that *now* we are going to eat a bit off the watch. If he feels like two eggs he's going to have 'em. It is no end of relief to me for it was no fun for June and me to eat eggs while Jerry's face grew gaunt with a self-denial which he denied to us. Now we will all have eggs and beef and carrots as long as the bracelet, hour and minute hands, and watch case last.

March 5, 1944. Jerry told me about the new project for letting families live together. Jim Thompson is making a complete map of camp, and the Committee is to ascertain the sentiments of camp and discuss it in meeting.

March 7, 1944. Such pros and cons, such violence against the Family Unit Plan. It is the first normal thing that has been put up to us and we can't take it! In the rice room, in the kitchen, the battle rages. Some thinking only of sex and modesty are scandalized, horrified, aghast. The comments are amazing. After two years of Nipponese oppression in sex matters, we seem to have developed a large crop of inhibitions. I mention that thousands live this way—with birth, death and sex crowded into small space all their lives—and I am told with raised eyebrows that we hope we are above that level. Well, we aren't, in here. I'm for it—the Family Unit. In case of emergency and panic, it is better to be together. And for young couples who want companionship and home life, with or without children, even including sex experience—let them have it. Those that don't want it can go on as usual. Why should they keep normal, married experience from others? The horrified looks, the snickers, disgusted leers and all the rest are not normal. Betty said she expected to see all married couples rush into each other's arms—she would if she were married, but no, they don't. Mae and Mrs. Donadio say it is Animalism, just pure Animalism. Laura looks rapt, opens her arms and says, "It's wonderful!"—and there are the two extremes!—with the range in between. Talk about Sex Complexes—they are rampant in here. Most of them just can't face it. You are gazed at as immoral if you want to live with your husband. The Great Sex Battle—what two years has accomplished! Or were many of them this way before the war?

Some who stand against it are terrified of having more children. Others who are not happily married become apparent; still others who are not happily married but don't know it. This one does not *want* to see any more of her husband than she does and she says so loudly. Another one says they can't even get half through a meal without quarreling, so why ask for more of it. The single men and women naturally do not want to be disturbed, moved out of quarters, upset again, for it does not concern them—except the friction. Mac said he thought everyone had gone crazy. If we had settled down in family groups two years ago at Camp Hay, we would have become used to it quicker that we have single life—but now, after passage of time, it is horrifying. Some of the men aren't too anxious to take more care of babies, to be routed up at night or during siesta. The old bachelor instinct is just as strong as the spinster! Over bridge and muffins and coffee with Scotts, we discussed modesty and men being more modest than women. Dr. Benedetti says it is biological. I say it is parental training and temperament.

March 8, 1944. It is a good solution to have a *survey* instead of a vote, and *both* signing. Those who aren't interested don't enter into it and those who want to live together can probably have it arranged. Those who don't like much sex are obvious. To some, Concentration has been surcease, a relief from all this and its connected worries. The chief point against has been the great chance of pregnancies in time of war and scarcity. However, it is no different from Outside and there will be the same means, and ways of getting around difficulties or prohibitions will be worked out. Some think the camp wedding and permit has started all this. Ray's wife thinks her prospects in May have started it. I think it is normal and healthy and should have been started long ago. Tomibe seems human about such things. Jerry says that many feel a distaste for close living, dressing, bathing etc. This also is true. Men can stand it among men, women among women, but not mixed. It is the way one feels in a Pullman car, stuffy and messy and at one's worst—which is what we may embark upon. However, too much emphasis is put on the sex end of it, none on the companionship and help that a father can give. Some need a lot, so let them have it. Others do not so they can let it ride. No one *has* to have it. Jerry thinks the friction and bitterness involved might not be worth the result *in the short time left*!

Mrs. Luzon says it has reached the point where if you want family life you are immoral, and if you don't want it you don't love your husband! Della at the hospital sees her husband at all hours, opposes family project for the rest of us. She needs a week without those privileges which she does not realize she has, a taste of single-women regulations. Then she would change. Arthur remarks it is a little late in the game to change things now. He'd better keep shut too, or we'll ask for his removal from family quarters. God deliver me from privileged people and smug mid-Victorians, uncongenial marriages and some who don't even know what the score is. The family unit has been the basis for thousands of years and those who want to live in a unit should be able to do so regardless of bachelor opinions or comforts.

March 9, 1944. I came from rice picking to hear the cry of "Letters! Letters! The letters from home! They are out! Art is taking a bunch to the hospital and Cleo has 20. Did you get a letter? Did you hear from home?" Like a wave it swept over camp and excitement mounted. I hardly dared to hope, having heard no mention of one for us. Jerry called from the doorway, "Pete, have you any letter yet?" No, no letter. I went off to wash dishes, looking at groups crouched with smiles over sheets of paper, laughter and squeals of joy in every direction. When I returned, Jerry came up the front steps from a trip back to his space, with hand behind him, a wide grin. He asked which hand I wanted. I couldn't bear it—if he was only teasing me and had nothing. I pointed to the left—and out it came—Mother's firm big black writing in letters as strong as ever. It was postmarked August 1943. *Mother still going strong at 88* after the long silence; still alive and keeping track of ships like the *Gripsholm* to send mail, writing, "What a joy it would be to have one little message from you all. We keep well. John and Molly transferred from

Washington to Cincinnati. They wanted a lawyer there. (Molly? We never heard of Molly before. John[5] in government legal department? What is going on in Cincinnati?) A baby is expected in December. (So Molly is John's wife—oh boy, how wonderful to hear he is married.) Ethel with Marguerite two weeks, I remained six weeks. Everyone sends love. God bless you all. Mother.'' There is such restraint here, yet telling much if one reads between the lines. What a difference that single sheet of paper makes to us—Contact! At the top of the letter is the telephone number they have had for 20 years. ''Columbia 0603''—there is Boston and stability for us! They are still going on in the same grooves, with only a few changes due to war and romance connected with it. How difficult it will be to tell them all we have been through. Their sheltered life is a quiet backstream in comparison. We read the letter over and over during pot roast on the front porch. We try to draw more news out of it, wondering about Dick and Peter[6] and their families. Though we said little, we all knew that Jerry felt very low because of no word from his mother. We were braced for any kind of news. It is such relief to know that Mums is carrying on and must have our letter by now. A letter and a new cooking pot give us independence again.

The *News* says only 35 couples signed up for family life!

March 10, 1944. A most devastating analysis of marriage could be conducted with this survey. After reviling the Nipponese for two years for not allowing family life—we turn it down ourselves when the chance comes! No one wants to move an inch of cubicle or shelves—oh no, not for a little thing like companionship and family life. They don't want to legalize sex and married life. They prefer it furtive and hidden in the bushes or back rooms. We are informed that we are the oldest couple who signed up for it. There is nothing like being abnormal among the mid-Victorians. This survey and the result is even funnier than the votes for women which the Japanese finally gave us and we took quietly without fuss. They must be aghast to find we don't *want* family grouping after all. One lady tells her husband who wants family grouping that he isn't patriotic. Patriotic—can you beat that.

I saw red this morning and snapped at Rita that I was tired of hearing about the soldiers and the sailors. Did she suppose that everyone in the U.S. was foregoing matrimony and eating and living together, just because the soldiers and sailors weren't having it? Patriotism—what sins are committed in thy name!

Jerry at the woodpile also went off the deep end after listening to two men talk for another's benefit. He said he had about come to the conclusion the Nipponese were right when they said we were degenerate and gone soft—when *only 30 missionaries and 8 other couples wanted to live together in family group* out of a total of about 100 couples. As for himself, he was proud not to be too old to want to live as married people with children should live, together. At this point the other man remarked that it was so inconvenient. Whereupon Jerry said it was a lot more convenient being together than running back and forth separate in everything as we were now. The man agreed. Furthermore, said Jerry, I'm mighty tired of seeing people look down their noses, saying nasty-nice things as though we were immoral or oversexed to want to be all together. He mentioned Enid's and Arthur's cosy place and said he thought no remarks at all should come from that quarter, nor from Ray's either with an offspring in prospect. There was silence to this. As for immodesty, dressing in front of each other where there were two couples to a space, he didn't see why a curtain couldn't be arranged or one time for the men to dress, another time for the women. At night when one couple went off to play bridge, the other pair could spend the evening in the cubicle, with arrangements made beforehand. It could all be settled quite sensibly and reasonably, and it would quiet down once it was adjusted. Again, the indifference is worse than violent negation, more serious. If it were for only two days, we would rather be together, especially in time of crisis where much can happen from the skies or the valley below. In the face of all this, 60% quibble and look snooty. It makes me feel like committing a chapter à la Hemingway, "the grass pressed down by two molding into one," and all such like. Except that I loathe being furtive.

A report to the Commandant of a trip made by four members to inspect the new camp garden site was read. It was found that the soil, having lain idle for a long time, was extremely hard and would be difficult to prepare for planting this season, unless specified equipment including a tractor, pump, fencing materials etc. could be furnished by Japanese authorities. No answer has been given to this request. Even if the plot is worked to the fullest extent, it is not large enough to make the camp independent of other sources of vegetables, but will supplement in a small way the veg diet.

In here, Bedie goes back and forth between us much as a child does between divorced parents. It splits the discipline, and he is jealous of June's close association with me, the fun we have together. He hates to miss anything and tries to be two places at once.

March 11, 1944. According to Camp Holmes "patriotism" standards, everyone at home is being very unpatriotic, for all the letters tell of marriages and babies, babies, babies. In time of war and separation, people seek more than ever for ties that bind and what little affection they can grab from the maelstrom. Most of the couples here have cabbage juice in their veins instead of red blood, are too tired to move in order to be normal. Dr. Bruce says it is the diet and he is partly right.

For supper we opened two pork and carrots, and Jerry made a tomato, onion, raw carrot and green pepper salad. But my mouth has begun to kick up again and my tongue is so sore from sliced tomato on camp bread sandwich at lunch that it is torture to eat it. In the night I had another stomach attack, the old squeezed-dry acid feeling. It is a week since our limes gave out and we don't get much fruit. Camp vegetables are cooked beyond the juice stage or too peppery for me. We have a fruit cocktail about once a week. I will have to talk with the doctor. Whatever it is, it is back again, and when it is acute it is all through my system. Poor Jerry is discouraged. He says I can't be normal or the vitamin tablets, food and other medicines he buys and that camp gives me would have fixed me up. I agree but the facts are there and have to be faced. I guess I am one of those who would never have survived in slum conditions, who need extra care due to a poor physical start.

The evening program was a spontaneous affair with a scene from O. Henry's story of the man who forgot he was married and proposed to his wife at the office again in the morning; there was also a burlesque of Shakespeare, with Cam a riot as Cleopatra dying from the bite of an asp (a light brown fur piece), and Jack as Antony whose Roman toga fell off at the close of the scene to reveal olive-drab Red Cross shorts. The high school kids did Romeo and Juliet songs from a balcony, after the Pattons had portrayed it beautifully, with Paul and Gene giving a modern slang version (very bawdy) to the right of the scene, playing alternately together. Prof. Harry, with white eyebrows, mustache and beard which kept coming off to the delight of the children, was excellent in his takeoff of the serious intellectual introducing the "drayma." Phyllis sang and Art read, while Tanabe and several guards trooped in noisily to watch the fun. Our family had cake together afterward. Bedie walked home with me, sounding very homesick. He wished this moving was over and we could all sleep in the same place. "I mean I wish we could be together all the time, not just sleeping," he added wistfully. Poor kid, he wanted to stay on and I had to send him back to the other barracks for roll call. It made me see even more clearly the necessity for family grouping, not only for Emergency but for everyday living.

March 12, 1944. Rumor says the *Tribune* headlines were "Keep Calm. The Japanese Army will handle any emergency." This is a fanciful oasis in a long dry desert of no news.

It is not wise to borrow and endanger others outside who may be accused of pro-American sympathizers with guerrillas and all the other reasons for jailing anyone who might lead or help, during invasion. Mañana is coming nearer and nearer. Anyway, we have the oath returned to us and it is stowed away. Under duress, it wasn't worth much to them.

Yesterday one who has been very offensive about family group[ing] asked me if I ever went up the hill. I wondered just what the sequence was but said that the last time we went up was just after Miss Lucy's funeral. We had a permit to take the kids, and it was about six months since we had been up before that. I told her it was worthwhile, for up there one found perspective and came to realize that only people were troubled, not the mountains at all! She went off saying, "Hmm. Maybe you are right." This morning I hear that she and her husband went up the hill yesterday and when they came down she signed up for family grouping. It is a camp joke now, with the family side having its innings. Maybe the mountains told her something after all. It is possible to pull a lot from blue haze, distance, and piled up earth.

March 13, 1944. In the month of January 126 cases of beri-beri and 54 cases of scurvy were compiled.

Many of the palings have been taken out of the stairways—every other paling in fact—and replaced with a long horizontal strip of bamboo to keep the kids from falling through. Palings are now used for table legs with the top from Red Cross packing cases. Library shelves [are] made from the same cases. The carpenters are also going to remove the long boards from under the eaves when they need more. At talk of doing this for family group partitions, they instantly figured many reasons why it could not be done with eaves boards. In many ways like this we keep on finding more boards and nails.

Leora came hurrying for Peg and they went out to meet husky Walter—''the missionary who looks like a miner'' as the children call him. Son Curt, shy and emotional, ran away to hide out beyond the pig pens so that his dad had to go hunt for him. He had told his mother he was going to do this. It was wonderful to see them all united after two and a half years—wife with husband, children with father, irrepressibly smiling from ear to ear, the whole face radiant. The entire camp was made happy by their happiness.

After Nippongo, I joined the four—Jerry, Carl, Walter, and Peg. Over coffee and muffins drowned in chocolate sauce and cream, we listened fascinated to Walter's saga of Davao and Manila. All over the islands it was the same debacle of the American Army. It became very plain that the U.S. was unprepared here and had been attacked ahead of time, so had ordered all forces to pull out as far as possible. There was no defense at all, which demoralized officers and men, making a very poor appearance and record. It became very disorganized. They knew no help was coming, felt trapped, let down and hopeless. They could only dash from one island to another, or into the hills and back in the end, left unsupported, unspeakably disillusioned for over two years. They have hung on as best they could, in hills, caves or jungles—or captured, imprisoned, tortured or starved to death.

Walter said that on the boat to Manila the rats were dreadful. There were no portholes in the sleeping quarters where they were crowded in down below. Later, in Manila, many had fever which reached high temperature and severe illness: typhus from rat fleas. In Manila the first blackout has taken place; a switch turns all lights off except for blue ones in the toilets. One building was left on by mistake, glaring, bright in the blackness. All hot plates, irons and even electric bulbs have been taken from everyone. Wow! We hope not here. It was an evening crammed full of dark and light mosaic; exciting, tragic, sad and happy stories.

March 14, 1944. I have been to both doctors about getting on the raw vegetable list so I can cook my own and drink the juice, as I cannot eat the peppery stews of camp with my present mouth and alimentary canal. Jerry is buying me green peppers which I scald and eat raw. It has been a bad day for me, with headache, sore mouth and throat and stomach. I mopped half the porch and did the usual rice and mop routine.

Peg showed me the pail which Walter had salvaged from the funeral parlors where they were first interned. He had to clean the embalming wax out of it. Now Peg is using it to wash her clothes.

Betty gave a grand party for the bride, using her embroidered cloth, pink candlesticks and a low pewter bowl with Jane's exquisite flower arrangement. She shot the works on extra special food.

March 15, 1944. The pros and cons of family life are going again, with couples buzzing and knots of disturbed single women and grumpy single men grouping to complain, grouse or sound off in horror. One woman said, very high hat, "It is neither the time nor the place to ask such a thing."

Jo and Bev sent Antuitrin for June [to prevent hemorrhage], with 3 skirts and a blouse which delighted her. The truck from Manila was loaded with barbed wire for our fence, Walter's baggage, office supplies, lime, buckets, 5 sacks of mail (about 45 packages and 3 letters), 3 boxes of Red Cross medicine, mostly vitamins, and a box of recreational equipment. Relief Funds from three sources total P9,270.

The garden plot at Trinidad is being ploughed by one carabao, 2 hoes, and a ten-man detail. Camotes are to be planted on it. Meat ration is to be 3 pounds only per person. There is a long line waiting for it, with almost a riot over some who tried to sign for five others.

In Japanese class we enjoyed Miss McKim's description in Nipponese English of Tomibe's studying of our language. He told of the difficulties of a car trip out from Baguio, the chief trouble being no gasoline. Every time he reached a certain point in the telling, he would say, "And when we reached there we got some!" He related an argument with Lt. Harada on how to treat the internee visitors at Christmas. Harada was very officious, herding them together, making them stand in line over here or over there, pushing their lunches around. Tomibe said it was no way to do it. Pointing to Harada's shoulder insignia, he said emphatically, "If you are of that opinion, you had better take off the insignia of rank and go back to Japan!" Whereupon, Harada shouted back at him, "And if you are of that opinion, you had better take off your insignia of rank and go back to Japan!" Tomibe has a fine head, well set on his shoulders, with a thick shock of hair. He is honest and forthright. He says his Baguio friends chaff him about being too lenient, tell him perhaps he will receive a medal from the American government after the war. He tells them No, for the Executive Committee does not think him lenient. Miss McKim says that Tomibe San is by far the best man we have had on the job. He is making a real attempt to understand and adjust problems, with a wider scope, vision and comprehension than others before him.

March 16, 1944. Daisy called in the window, "Were you expecting some things from outside? The truck brought a lot of bags, boxes and a trunk for you." Astonished, I rushed out to the bag table and there were two of our suitcases and other things. The soldier told me it would have to be examined. I tore out to the woodshed to beckon Jerry to come. He wanted to split another log, but I urged, "Our things have come in—our bag of silver and the ivories." His jaw dropped and with a whoop he lifted the sledge, letting it fall on the steel wedge with a terrific wallop. Two guards helped to go through the black trunk full of clothes, two suitcases, the bag of silver, a wooden jewel box and a cardboard box of ivories. The ivories and silver have moved five times since they left our house. They went to DeBoers' who have moved twice, to Carl's, then here. With moving, looting, and Emergency prospects, DeBoers did not want further responsibility as the end nears, and I don't blame them. Carl described how Nida and Ismael and Jaime had carried and carted the clothes over, four miles across town on many trips.

Every bit of silver, every piece of ivory was there except the carved ball which was left on the table. The silver is just as I packed it before leaving, and the ivories as I packed them away four Christmas times ago when we trimmed the tree on that table and every time I thought of taking them out after that I would think, "Oh the war is coming. I'd better leave them packed." Now here they are in Concentration after long journey roundabout, through several hands and homes and an underground note sent nearly two years ago with advice about their disposal. There is not only the silver I packed, but all the loose pieces which were left in the drawer and gathered up by Nida, with the three silver bowls, the meat platter and the Tiffany dish whose flannel covering came in [months ago] filled with marbles so that I was sure it had gone too. There is the crimson-lined kimono, the gay cerise costume of cotton cloth (but not the Black Forest shawl to complete it, alas), the two fawn brocade Chinese coats copied from Peg's and Jo's, my black velvet evening coat, the jade-lined haori coat[7] which I love, about 8 furoshikis, about 3 dozen crepe de chine or satin nightgowns, the orange wool sweater to match the sash which came in over a year ago and which I had nearly given away several times. The big leather suitcase was full of clothes as was the gray army suitcase—dresses, sweaters, stockings, underwear, orange embroidered Chinese pajamas, the black satin embroidered ones, wool suits and pants of Jerry's, Oriental silks and colors tumbling into the drabness of Concentration pell-mell. We went through each case, covering the bed with rainbow shades. My jewelry, except for the empty boxes which showed that the most valuable pieces were in the safety deposit box in the bank, was there—two small opals, Peking glass beads and rings. Will I ever see the jade, the opals, pearl and diamonds again? If these had been left in the box would they have come in safe through the guards? The guards helped to examine and were much interested. It is almost a burden but exciting, stimulating to have these ghosts from the past coming into my mind which has been detached and made into a new mold. June's dresses when held up before her are too young and outgrown. I see she has become a young lady now, if I had not realized it before. There are only six of her dresses anyway as the rest were looted, so I take three to Ann and three to Peg's girls, presenting the silver pusher and baby spoon to John Hay, a curved spoon to Susan and a straight-handled spoon to Ann. I give some Red Cross bath towels to Ruth and Jane, also a large pair of black sateen trousers which were a costume of Jerry's at some club party. The material can be made into a skirt. I feel that I want to share what has come in without effort on my part, almost undeserved. We pack and repack and store the cases under the bed.

March 17, 1944. Jerry and I dove into the trunk on the porch, finding the second box of ivories. We had waves of gratefulness for our faithful servants, the risks they took which showed in the candle wax on many fabrics, dangers of being caught and charged with looting.

Executive Committee Minutes: "Father Sheridan presented a plan drawn up by three members interested in the Family Unit Project. According to this plan, families would not live together in the hospital, No. 1 barracks and annex, the Sisters' cottages or No. 2 cottage. The plan proposes that No. 2 barracks upstairs be divided by a partition, allowing fathers to join their families in one part of the barracks, the other part to remain as at present. Secondly, for the south end of upper No. 3 barracks, another partition would be made. In this southern part, married people without children would live. Baby House and Fathers' cottage were included in this plan with slight changes only, resulting. The plan was discussed at some length. Some members felt that a vote of the electorate should decide whether or not the project should proceed. The practice of handling this survey in a confidential manner was questioned on the grounds that the members of camp had a right to know the details of the survey and the names of those interested in such a plan. Out of an eligible 105 couples, 43 couples had signed for space.

"Dr. Skerl outlined the work to date at Trinidad garden site and stated that little could be done until seeds, fertilizer, water and a number of other items necessary to such an agricultural project are supplied. Preliminary preparation of soil is being carried on in one section of the plot.

"Dr. Skerl explained the inventory of Red Cross articles just received and suggested the following plan for their distribution: That a public lottery draw be held for men, women and boys March 18 in the dining room. On Monday the distribution will take place. Men will line up in order of draw to receive a cap, a choice of sweater jacket or turtleneck sweater or a heavy undershirt, plus a pair of long drawers. The reverse order of the men will then have a choice of either an undershirt or long drawers, and finally the original order of approximately 36 men will have a similar choice of remaining items. Then women will line up in order of draw to receive a choice of either a pair of brown cotton stockings or panties or vest. Then the reverse order will have a choice from the remainder of these items (approximately 50) or a cap (approximately 80). This plan was adopted.''

Fifty Irish had a celebration in the veg room, singing songs and being bright.

March 18, 1944. Walter spoke on how the war came to Davao. He hit straight and pulled no punches, giving a firm, all-round picture which reminded me of Hemingway's *Bell Tolls* with first one side in the saddle being nasty, then the other side reigning and taking revenge, *all just people*. It is so clear that nationalities, races, groups, are all the same when it comes to basic moves—fear, revenge, disorganization, looting, hunger. His description of families fleeing across rivers to the mountains, some drowning in the current; the return of 10,000 starved Japanese internees to Davao where they left no store or house untouched in an orgy of loot in memory and revenge of what had been done to them—all was very vivid. They invade, drop bombs, and kill, pour in in hordes, bringing about fury, panic, natural resistance. Then it begins again on the other side. Everywhere is personal conflict, he noticed—even here, though he said we had far more community feeling than the other camps and he was glad to be here. It is noteworthy that all three camps have protested signing under duress and have won out either by the oaths being returned or backing down. Davao camp was asked to sign that they worked voluntarily after they had helped to rebuild roads, but they would only sign by dating *after* a certain date in July which satisfied the Captain. Manila and Baguio separately refused the oath except under protest of duress. Also, both did not turn in any names of specialists or trades. Ray's name was the only Diesel man turned in and he was willing as they knew it anyway. He is independent and cocky with them for he knows he is invaluable on the internals of trucks. They need him and both know it.

March 20, 1944. The wedding march is in the throes of practice in the dining room and the strains drifting out stir up everybody. One who is against the family project says severely, ''It is this affair at the hospital, this wedding business which has suggested family life to others. They think they want it, if one couple is going to have it.'' As if any normal married couple needed any suggestion since the days of Adam!

A doctor says that hot pepper in the camp food is used to cover up the lack of salt.

March 21, 1944. After lunch my name was posted as having a note from Baguio so I went to the office to receive P220 in Japanese government bills—for dresses sold.[8] First we ate gold, now it is velvet, taffeta and felt.

One of the pigs developed hog cholera and within three days 4 have died. Brown, the veterinarian, came out and one which was dying was killed for autopsy, showing the spotted organ. Brown rushed off for vaccine, came back after dark to administer it, but fears we will have to kill them all as have many owners before us to their sorrow. It is tragic in these times especially. It is too bad the Japanese didn't isolate that [new] livestock for a few days. It would have saved others.

We all received a box of matches from the States in the draw.

Monday we had a change of guards and those departing always go about the night before, chatting with friends for the last time, giving out candy to their favorite children. We undermine the common soldier. He likes us, and we feel friendly toward him. They have to be changed every so often before they become too soft. One guard, watching the wood crew, remarked apropos of nothing, "Japanese government not good." This was received in silence. The guards have been avidly interested in every detail of the Red Cross shipment, looking over all the sweaters, suits, food, medicines, and think it is wonderful that the U.S. government sends all that to mere civilians. They all want to go to America after the war ends. One even remarked that after war here, Nipponese, Americans and Filipinos get along together.

March 22, 1944. Four cables were received from the States, and they mention receiving letters.

One man has announced that he never expects to pay what he has borrowed from the Outside while he was in here—he prefers to go bankrupt instead. What an attitude to take! We will be only too glad to pay every cent even if it takes several years. It was the difference between life and death for June, health or wretchedness for the four of us and can never be fully repaid for all it did to sustain us mentally and physically.

March 23, 1944. The Wedding Day for Wilma and Carol and Camp! The piano has been moved down to the church garden and the screen is covered with ferns and pine branches. Tomibe was married seven years ago at the beginning of the China War. He went to China, to Manchukuo, then to the Philippines. He has had only two years out of the seven in Japan. They have two children, a boy and a girl, aged four and six. He is a graduate of Kyoto University. According to another conversation he has held no other position though he is trained in the legal profession. He is obviously from the moneyed class, well educated, with a fine background. Of his [own] marriage he said, "I what you call in love." He is much interested in this wedding and just before the ceremony he drove in from town with a vivid bouquet of pink dahlias and calla lilies, a bottle of sake and a bottle of whiskey for the bride and groom. He was all dressed up, watching the ceremony closely, and afterward congratulated the couple assisted by Miss McKim. He signed the guest book and mingled with the 500 guests.

blue Park ~
Carroll Dickey wedding
23 March 1944.

Sheets were laid in a narrow aisle from the hospital to the fern trimmed bower in the church garden. Each peg holding the white strip down was decorated with pine spray, the green at intervals being very effective. Mary sang "Because" and "O Promise Me," then to the slow, stately strains of "Here Comes the Bride," the procession came down the slope toward Carl and Don who joined in performing the service. The two Ruths who were the attendants looked like clouds floating in gently through the slight mist. Their gowns were powder blue, with bouquets of pink and white sweet peas, surrounded by old fashioned frilled paper. Betty's white satin gown from Saks was lovely on Wilma, who lifted the tulle veil from her face as she reached the altar. Young Ann and Grace were flower girls, Ward an intent and concentrated ring bearer for the double ring ceremony. The thin mist came and went in wisps and streamers, the green outdoors made a happy setting. It was so peaceful. Many wore evening gowns or coats, and everyone dressed up if only a little. Along the upper bank in a row sat a number of spectators including small children deeply absorbed in the wedding ceremony. They have heard wedding, wedding, wedding, for weeks. Below the bank, goats were grazing near several guards who sat in the grass to watch. On a bench at the guardhouse were ranged another row of guards with six or eight Igorot children whose eyes were glued on the garden. Having no evening gown, I wore my brocade Chinese coat, the Genoa pink corals, jade engagement ring and Grandmother's diamond for the first time in two and a half years. When the original service by Don and the old, old marriage lines by Carl were completed, the bride fairly jazzed up the aisle, then ran down the slope with her new husband. It is always over so quickly, after the endless preparations taking weeks. There was a long receiving line of good wishes, then to sign the guest book. We took our cake over to the front porch and made coffee to go with it. Afterward we went back to a less crowded room. The four-layer wedding cake was surrounded by Wyllie-Crouter silver on a beautiful embroidered cloth. There were white curtains in the windows; ferns were banked and lights shaded. Tomibe gave us all permission to dance till 9:25, and for the first time in two years I felt like dancing both mentally and physically. We waltzed, one-stepped, two-stepped and fox-trotted, throwing in a few other slides for good measure. In my Chinese coat, I felt like Cinderella leaving her mops behind, and received a number of compliments. Bedie and June danced together. June danced with her Dad and learned to follow. Thanks to ascorbic acid and a letter from home I could enjoy the evening.

Walter drove the bridal pair around the parade ground then down to the hospital in the Lincoln car, with clattering tin cans tied by Larry on the back. Fern and Cleo gave up their big front room for the couple and just before lights out some of their closest friends serenaded them with tin cans. Ruthie, who was the only unmarried attendant, caught the bride's bouquet. It was a happy occasion but everyone felt let down the next day, tired after all the hard extra work, gaity and keyed-up excitement. Will there be another wedding from sheer contagion?

March 24, 1944. Among the wedding gifts were a handmade wooden tray, a silver cream pitcher, a coffeepot made at the shop. It still appalls me that good white sheets, so scarce and hard to wash with soap lacking, should be used on the ground as an aisle to walk upon, but we survived it and are none the worse. Somebody has to wash it all now.

Somebody made a poignant remark in connection with comments about the bride being able to get a job at nursing in case her husband was out of work. This person said that in all her years of marriage, this was the first time she was free enough from child and family cares to be able to pursue her profession as a nurse. Family ties do begin at once, so that independence is lost. Many really enjoy the life in here—it is very "bachelor" and there is a strong desire to keep to it. A good number have hours of leisure now after years of overwork outside. Others are able to express their ability in various ways due to camp details taking care of home duties like cooking, child care, veg preparation etc., giving them free time which they never had. Some have companionship, friendship, which they never had time for in the past. While we all live as single, life is essentially shared. It is unique. If families join, then some men think they will have to help more, read less. Wives worry over connubial complications. On the other hand, much time and energy expended in running about would be saved.

Tex has killed 12,595 flies from February 20 to March 20.

March 25, 1944. This place is marvelous! So irritating, so amusing, so instructive, so maddening! Fifty percent who are single-minded, set, stubborn souls in a deep rut, will probably keep the rest of us who want a normal, married, family unit after two years without it—still without it! Yet we have gone a long way in some respects in two years.

Stunt Night by the new Entertainment Committee was a howling success. There was a takeoff on the hospital, and particularly an operation with Dr. Mather and Bruce as surgeons, Mather handling knife, saw, auger, and chisel; Bruce striking a gong for the patient's head in ancient Egyptian anesthesia. Harry was perfect as he dusted, swept and took down cobwebs during the operation. Gerry was nurse leading in Jim Halsema with his mouth open and body swinging from side to side like a pendulum, which was diagnosed as watching rice machine too long. "the Rickeys' Honeymoon" was a big laugh, with husky, determined Frances as bride in a wide hat held by scarf under chin and a duster coat. Mary Kizer was a slender, dapper groom, nimbly leaping in and out to change tires or spark plugs. The wheels were taken by four persons who wailed during rehearsals "I'm only a wheel!" They humped up and down, trembled and shook realistically, as the Model T got under way. Margaret as the spare tire was finally pulled off with a vigorous tug of the bride's after the dapper groom collapsed. The bride being carsick brought a yell of laughter, as did another stop for the bride to make a trip into the bushes. The car finally collided and collapsed, the bride getting out to walk, leaving a dejected groom behind the wheel. There were many jokes at Wilma's and Carol's expense, the best one being a reference to "all my worldly goods"—whereat someone remarked, "Oh, now she'll get his wash bucket!"—This being the prized possession of all of us nowadays, irreplaceable and clung to like glue, more precious than silver, ivories and linen at this stage of our life. The show was good for us, a lifesaver of laughter. Some of us can still take it at any rate.

Peg Whit's scene of arrival [after the war] at San Francisco custom house, called "Exposed," showed Edna in a sheet, Fred strung with pots and pans and a Red Cross muffin tin set, Peg in plus fours and a wool cap (with Phil reported as being in his fundoshi), brought down the house. The arrivals were interviewed by Tex, a smart reporter in short skirts and my silver fox fur hauled out of the bath towel where it has been sewed up and is still untouched by moths. The arrivals chattered of Camp Holmes, odd recipes, people being hung (swung)[9] and desperately maladjusted to States living. This released more energy in the form of laughter from the audience. We all need to move, for even battling over the family project is better than a nervous breakdown if it doesn't go on too long.

March 26, 1944. We had our hot cakes and duck eggs in the sooty cook house. Charles joined us and we discussed how many of us will really miss camp life, the companionship and jokes, when it is all over and we have gone our separate ways, flung apart to far corners of the world. If only we had a balanced diet we could enjoy this experience more. When we leave this life, many will be maladjusted, cranky and unhappy, and we won't know why. It will be a form of homesickness for the days, the months, the years, that we tried to work together and didn't do so badly, managed to live with people we never dreamed we could get along with, and had fun doing it too, thanks to rice machines, peanut machines, banana machines, lines and numbers.

I went down to see Wilma's wedding gifts. Some had given her personal silver spoons, forks, ladle. As she said, one could tell who had things rescued or sent in. Another table had bamboo salt jars with bark covers, bamboo spoons and forks, a copper hand-beaten coffeepot and small dish beautifully hammered out by Jess, six Café cans set on a long board in two rows of three each marked Sugar, Salt, etc., all detachable, cleverly made by Junkin. Another table contained all Red Cross items—sheets, embroidered with her initials, bath and hand towels initialed, handkerchiefs and pink step-ins all cleverly made into wedding gifts. About one third of the camp, her most intimate friends, gave presents.

March 27, 1944. Camp is preparing for General Kwo[10] in every direction. Wooden squares are painted "Store," "No. 1 Dorm," "Dentist," "Dispensary," with Japanese characters over each English word which *may* stop questions and pointing. Tomibe bowed to me and pointed to building near stove trough, asking politely "What building used for?" I answer that it is bathroom toilets. "Ah, sank you," he says, bowing again and writing it on a blank square. Name bands are also being made by Verna in a hurry. After they were sewed, black characters were painted on them, designating Committee members, doctors, nurses. We all want a job now that carries an armband! Carl even kidded Tomibe, telling him the wood crew was on strike because they had no armband! He took it seriously at first.

The Committee gathered around the office, looking like the laying of a cornerstone. But it had to do with making a sidewalk into the building—how long would it take cement to set? A week, says the Chairman. "Oh," says Tomibe, "it must be ready tomorrow." One of his staff says, "We might lay down a sheet," whereupon they all laugh uproariously. The wedding gave them humorous ideas, and the sheets evidently impressed them as much as they did me.

The Japanese came to look at the fish situation, couldn't see that it was rotten. They were shown green gills and the inside smelling to high heaven. Tomibe said, "But you get better than we do. We Army have only cabbage and rice." "All right," answered Carl, "We will let you have these which our expert cleaner says to discard. We will cut off heads, clean and send to guardhouse so you may have." "Oh no," was the general chorus from staff, with no more protest. Just then Smitty arrived wailing about two pigs dying of fish poisoning. "Not mine, not mine, are they?" jumps up Mr. Sato. In the hog cholera deaths, three belonged to camp and three were Sato's pigs. Too bad, too bad, for both. We all feel the pinch.

March 28, 1944. General [Kwo] made the rounds with about eight officers. He looked at the shop, the pigs, nipa hut, Mont's shack, shoe shop, private kitchens, dorms and cottages. He is long-faced, elderly, benign-looking.

Camp gave us good rice and pâté, then movies down in the church garden were great fun. The Marx Brothers in *Go West* and two comics of Pig and Panda, and an old Raft picture—all creaking with age but it was exciting to hear music and see the rhumba again.[11] There was much trouble with the projector and the Raft reels were all mixed up, voices shaky at times. A big sheet was stretched on bamboo for a screen. Two guards and a young Filipino sweated over the projector and sound effects. There was a beautiful crescent moon setting in the west. The audience which spread all over the slope, kept sliding down hill, drank coffee, muffins and cookies and peanuts just like circus days. The kids had a grand time. June was disgusted with all the movie actors, thought them terrible smoothies, hated the kissing and "mush." She shows all the signs of the Concentration complex—no affection, no loving, nor Holy Matrimony. All Taboo! It shows a little of what can be done in molding of the young.

March 29, 1944. I went a week without an [ascorbic acid] shot, then the first canker appeared. There are many sore mouths being treated with Vitamin C now. There are two bad cases of beriberi, with legs swollen to the thighs, swollen face, etc. I have a prescription of multiple capsules for June and thirty Vitamin C pills at one a day for me. There is much athlete's foot in camp too.

Jerry and I drank double coffee. He was dying for it but put the temptation away from him. I said if we ever have two cups in a day, now is the best time for it. So grinning, we did. He made a fried rice for supper.

Outside contacts are very dangerous—hill, bird calls, Igorots over and down the other side. It is time to lay low.

Miss McKim says Hayakawa admires Ruth Ream most of any woman in camp. He says she is all that a Japanese woman is expected to be. He tells her that we do not know it but they know a great deal about us all, who they like or don't like etc. Same to you, boys! He sees Ruth going to the shop every day at noon with a tray of food for her husband, then returning with the empty tray. She looks self-contained, enfolded, quiet, submissive. (This last she is not!)

March 30, 1944. The dentist moved from the dispensary to the lab where he will set up his office furniture and can lock it every night. The dentist says a hole will have to be bored into the cement in order to attach to the water tank. And anyway, says Vinnie, he won't be able to do much more dentist work than up here as none of his materials came in. I reminded her that they had been moved elsewhere and she admitted they were cached but the Japanese are not supposed to know this. [The dentist's] attitude is the same and I don't believe he has the slightest intention of bringing materials in, neither his own private stock nor those from the Army Post which he knows about.[12] He says he didn't want to go and get his equipment but the Japanese wanted him to and made him bring it in and set it up.

Miss McKim told us a delightful version of the special Committee meeting; of Suda calling us all one big family and why can't we act more friendly when he comes around. She replied that there was a time when we were slapped by guards and perhaps we remembered it. This was received in silence. A number of people remember Suda heckling at Brent while we struggled with baggage and other difficulties. Tomibe said that if some escaped and were promptly caught, they would be put in jail which would not be pleasant. Carl said solemnly, "No, it would not be pleasant," and Art said, "No, it would not be pleasant." They have both had the experience.

Once or twice the Japanese lapsed into English which confused and embarrassed them. Their orders are to speak always in Nippongo.

March 31, 1944. "The question of living quarters and the request of some families that they be allowed to live together, was taken up with Gen Kwo. He stated that they could not construct new buildings for this purpose but that if something could be arranged in the present buildings, he would not be opposed to it.

"In connection with more strict supervision of all internment camps, the Command stated that unfortunately rule-breaking on the part of one individual causes inconveniences and even penalties not only to the members of the camp where he is interned, but to all of the internment camps. Some internees in Santo Tomas for instance, were reported to be leaving the camp and later returning. Because of this, internees in that camp have had to get out of bed for unannounced roll calls at 2 A.M. The order for our fence came as a result of such rule-breaking by internees in Santo Tomas. Mr. Tomibe stated that he did not wish to have to call roll at inconvenient hours and he made a personal request to the internees of this camp that they do everything in their power to keep the rules and not cause trouble so that the whole camp will not be forced to suffer for the indiscretions of a few. He said that if the Military Police made any complaint in connection with the personnel of this camp, he would receive all of the blame and would have to shoulder all of the responsibility for allowing such an infraction of rules, should the person be found guilty. The Commandant asked that the members of the various work crews who must pass the sentry each day, pay him the courtesy of saying, "Good morning," or "How do you do." Mr. Suda stated that when he or the soldiers must go to the woodshed or into the dorm in connection with their work, that people are sometimes not polite. He said that the young and very old people are almost always courteous, but that some of the others show open resentment at their presence. . . . It was explained by one of the members, that the civilians interned here had for the most part never experienced military discipline, and that if they go about their work without seeming to acknowledge the presence of a soldier or a member of the Japanese staff, that they are not conscious of giving any offense."

While Outside [on camp business], Carl heard that Nida had had word from Ismael that he was in *Davao* in the *labor battalion*, probably helping to make an airfield. He was offered release from Fort Santiago and glad to get it, by enlisting in this battalion.

April 1, 1944. Jerry bought papayas, bananas, mulberries and strawberries and everything he could at the store. He shot the works for we need fruit dreadfully. I should be having it three times a day, but we were two days without any. Bananas have been fit only to make yeast.

A python on the hill is getting some of the chickens, the young ones. Shafe wants to burn the grass and get rid of it.

April 2, 1944. About ten pigs have died in spite of serum shots. This is a tragic burial of relief money for all of us.

April 4, 1944. Esther celebrated what was to have been her wedding day today, gardenia in her hair and friends gathered for a party. Her fiancé is now in India, she here—waiting till they can join each other.

The children in school are making small posters to go at the sinks and tank faucets. Their ideas are very good on the subject of pails, faucets pouring water, leaks etc, with pictures captioned "Save water"—"Don't waste water." It is an attempt to teach them to leave faucets alone but they still dribble much over bubble cups, mud pie pails and pretend-medicine.

April 5, 1944. At a more strict roll call late in the evening, we heard for the first time that Ritchie and Wick had not been reported and were not found. Both had a pass for the hill today. We did not see them all evening and cannot remember seeing them during the day. This will be tough on us—no more hill picnics and tightening up in every way. It is fatal for them, if caught. It all seems rather futile for them to escape anyway, but perhaps it isn't. Here's hoping they had real contact and know what they are doing and that it is not too soon. They have plenty of strength and nothing to hold them back.

Minutes: "The following recommendations presented by the Safety Committee were approved: that an effort be made to secure permission and materials from the authorities for painting large red crosses on the hospital and Baby House buildings, 'Internment Camp' to be painted on roofs of all main buildings, in white; that the question of providing air-raid protection be discussed with the authorities and an effort be made to get them to help us construct suitable shelters; that the camp be urged to prepare emergency packs containing certain food supplies and clothing articles to be recommended by the Safety Committee. They would also arrange for instructions to all individuals on the matter of arranging and preparing the carrying packs. Such packs are highly desirable to have on hand in readiness in case of fire or other emergency; that volunteer classes be organized (probably under supervision of the hospital staff) for first-aid instruction and training; that the entire personnel of the camp be grouped into six companies, each company to have 4 platoons and each platoon 2 squads, and that the organization personnel be organized by Safety Committee to facilitate handling the camp in case of fire or other emergency."

I didn't sleep much. The [Commandant's] car came about 11 and Tomibe checked all the men himself. There was much coming and going, and Carl was up nearly all night. Well, our one and only guerrilla has gone. He worked "isshokenmei ni" [doing his best] to the last in camp, always cheerful, smiling, willing to lift a screen or a piano or a huge piece of chocolate cake. His appetite was insatiable and it is well he stocked up while he could. His great energy and strength will be perfect for guerrilla activity. He wanted to go out when the time came so perhaps it is getting near. He was an interesting figure of solid worth. While some doubt the value of the heroics, we hope it will be worth all we have to go through on account of the escape. At least he knew what he wanted and took it without any fanfare. I suppose the risks for them and the train of consequences for 450 of us are details in a larger picture which has one single purpose.

April 6, 1944. The men were called to a meeting at ten and were in the dining room nearly two hours. No wood crew was allowed out. Tomibe spoke loud and firm with Miss McKim translating. The women were called in at twelve for the same talk. Dorms were searched for radio meanwhile, though they said it would be baggage. Tomibe said internment was made for two reasons: "to prevent liberty of action and for protection of those interned." He realized internment had meant much discomfort to us as an altogether different way of living than that to which we had been accustomed before war. Because of the escape "our internment from now on would be much more difficult than it has been," he said (so said the General), since he was holding internees responsible for not having prevented it. The new rules are: 1. No more picnics on the hill. 2. The Commandant will take over

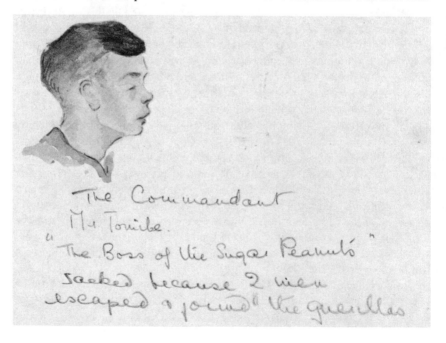

The Commandant
Mr Tomibe.
"The Boss of the Sugar Peanuts"
Sacked because 2 men
escaped & joined the guerillas

roll calls. 3. All internees must see that no repetition of the incident is made and for that reason watchmen should be stationed by barracks at night. 4. No one may cross the fence. On the whole it is mild punishment, at this point.

The Family Unit Report: "Tuesday evening the General Committee requested three members to prepare a detailed report of the Family Unit proposal. The previous survey had been exploratory: 45 couples out of 97 on the camp roster signed up for the plan. Including children, 154 would be affected. . . . The ironing room has been reserved Saturday and Sunday and Monday evenings from 6:30 to 9:30 for a public display of a tentative layout which will list names, locations and areas of floor space; dislocation is to be kept to a minimum."

When Tomibe first talked [in the meeting] he shouted in loud angry voice which could reach the ears of the two Intelligence men from town outside the door, but Miss McKim could not always make it out and he gave a modified quiet version which she translated. With the finest Japanese courtesy and manner, he apologized for the upset and inconvenience, said he was sorry as we were over all the trouble. Still he expected our discomfort to be worse for he holds us responsible and was disappointed that his trust in us had been betrayed. (That is all very well, but as you say yourself, Mr. Tomibe—these are war times.) He asked who had seen either man on Tuesday evening. Everyone had seen Wick in the dining room till 9:30 and Tex had offered coffee to Ritchie which he had declined. Ruth had seen him at Mrs. Patterson's window about 9:30. Mrs. Patterson had already been questioned twice at the guardhouse, was naturally let down and upset, and she knew nothing. When man goes to war, woman doesn't count. It is a separate brain compartment. Neither did these men take into account what might happen to some of their best friends after their escape. Tomibe then asked who had seen either man on Wednesday. No one had except Ty who said Wick had called in at the kitchen door that the Chef was not to prepare breakfast for him as he and Ritchie were going to a hill hotcake party. It was the day off for both and no one thought twice about another hill picnic. This was just after roll call at 7. On the side, one heard that small Helen Watson had seen them both out by the pig pen not long after seven with packs on their backs bound for the hill. It makes sense that they would not leave at night to risk being missed at 7 roll call, but leave just after it with a valid reason for absence which would give them a whole day's start and part of the evening unnoticed. No one missed them till supper time and substitute cooks had to be found. Wick had been asked to the Chef's dinner party at 6 for which Helen had prepared ice cream, so they too were dumbfounded at his nonappearance because he did love to eat.

Each man had several women knitting socks for him, but these knitters did not get together on it until afterward. Ritchie, the gay and foolish one, had given out wool to about 7 different women, urging that they be finished by Tuesday as a surprise birthday gift. All were knitting like mad, making 1 sock in a day—he had six pair at the Tuesday finish, it seems. June had one sock half done, full of knots where each machine thread was tied, but he didn't care, for he said it was to wear over other socks. I told her that this was a good lesson to get things done quickly, without procrastinating, for it often made all the difference in the world. Now it is too late to help the guerrilla! Both were bachelors, without ties, bored and thirsting for action and adventure. Yet who isn't—and here we are, suffering for their freedom. Tomibe asked further if any of us knew any reason why they might want to go. Father Sheridan said that they did not like the food—and there was a stir of smiles, laughter. Even Tomibe and Hayakawa smiled widely, perhaps in Japanese embarrassment. Walter stood up and spoke of two and a half years of inactivity and confinement. He said he thought "they flew the coop because they just couldn't stand being fenced in any longer." When Miss McKim translated this, Tomibe nodded and answered that he thought this most reasonable, a very sound idea. A number of us women had noses pressed against the screen all through the men's session. I wouldn't have missed it for anything. Tomibe has imagination which gives him comparison and comprehension. Hayakawa is said to have remarked that the two men had gone too soon—he could tell them when to go if they had waited! But the garrison is coming, and that makes all the difference and probably speeded up plans.[13]

In the afternoon, things blew up in the Committee's face. They called a meeting right after lunch and Tomibe announced he was moving out from town with all his staff and he would need the whole camp office building to live in. The safe went out one door, the desk out another, and in no time it was all piled up in the hall at the hospital where all the dentist equipment was piled last week and was moved just in time. A truck arrived with Tomibe's effects. It was finally decided to take the large corner room in the hospital, moving the four girls out! We first heard that *all* the girls would have to move out of the hospital, and Jerry simply whooped when he heard that the Nipponese had accomplished in one quick swoop what angels and many moons and administrations had failed to do.

Jerry made a beef-bone stew, adding bijon, and we fell on every little scrap of meat.

Meanwhile, the fat one and another member of the Intelligence questioned Tony, Crocker, Gene, Scotty, Lofsted, Jess and Byron at the office. They were all very polite and courteous. Miss McKim was surprised at the general lack of fury and indignation. Jerry told her he thought that taking away the *Tribune* and all subjects of conversation had added to the unrest, bottled us up too much. She agreed and said she would tell Tomibe. They have screwed the cap on too tight, but they don't care if we do blow up. They will have an answer to that.

Russia is said to be in Hungary, through Poland, Czecho-Slovakia and

Rumania. There is a supposition that Germany is asking British and American forces to occupy in case of peace—not Russia.

April 7, 1944. Gene and Lofsted were taken to town for questioning. Lofsted was brought back at noon, Gene still there at nighttime. It is Mary's turn to sweat now. She sits on the grass, waiting, then ironing in the afternoon—anything to keep busy and hold down the jitters. We all wonder if Gene will get the heat put on or just be forgotten for two days, two weeks, two months, on rice and water, very little water. The Intelligence wants to know the contacts and where the two men were going. Tomibe said in the meeting that he was sure it was long planned, carefully worked out, and with news contacts. They are probably right, but if the two men were wise they told no one—not in this camp!

Camp gave us good roast pork for supper. There was a cantata in the evening, of the Crucifixion. A three-hour service at noon. Amid all the Lenten, Maundy Thursday, Good Friday services and Easter plans—work goes on and Gene is still in town, leaving the *rest* of us worrying and wondering.

April 8, 1944. Several are now remembering that Wick cheered them up when they were depressed and wondering if the Marines would ever come, by saying, "I haven't gone yet. When I go, you can know it is not far off." These things are only significant afterward.

It is said that dozens of Filipinos are held in Baguio for questioning—any who were friends of Ritchie and his former girl friend. The ripples from this escape, like ripples from a stone, reach out and out, covered by the long arm of the Intelligence whose business it is to put two and two together, making whole facts out of little pieces.

At noon Bill Moule was taken to town for questioning.

While Wick was in here, he learned a few things—how to play bridge, how to dance smoothly, and a few more things about women generally. He seemed to leave as fancy-free as when he came in. We feel that with his state of mind he should have been in a military camp, not a civilian one, but that being here where he wanted to be he should have abided by our rules and code, not by the code of a military group composed entirely of men. He owed us something after all since his lot was cast among women and children. Now we all come under the punishment for his escape—the tense days, waiting and imagining what is happening in the town jail.

The Japanese have wiped the smiles off our faces. There are few wisecracks now. Double-time work at the bodega and no Easter holiday feeling. There will be no fiesta like last year with special menus. Two friends are now hostage for these men and we are back in the old days of terror. Work and guarding is part punishment, says Tomibe. Guerrillas must ignore all feelings, I suppose.

Lucy Vernardo brought me three dresses which made three aprons and some swell mop rags. Bart found 16 small cockroaches in Jane's clock and wondered why they went in there. She suggested maybe they wanted privacy and he retorted, "Maybe they have the cubicle unit idea!"

Under a full moon, the guard quietly made the rounds with gun and bayonet. They mind their own business, seem restrained compared to the pushy ones of the past.

The Cubicle Plan was on a chart in the ironing room, with two members on hand to explain or accept suggestions. Walter tried to tell Peg how harmful it would be to the camp, against all the best interests etc. He recommended that people take to the bushes, sneeringly putting emphasis on that phase of it, and ending with the real reason which seldom gets through the various smoke screens—"if one member of my family has to move one inch, there will be hell to pay." Harry goes off the deep end, gets up a petition against it. Most of the men will sign it, worrying about women seeing them with only a bath towel wrapped around their loins etc. They are a bunch of old hens, worse than women when their bachelor instincts become set. It is a new low in morale, with even Serré who is one of the most intellectual men in camp, deciding against family unit because both would have to move and he wouldn't be able to study Greek which he has just started. This outweighs the need of being together to help with the child.

Suddenly word comes up from the hospital that Sam Weinstein has died. We feel so badly for poor Gert, his wife, who was devoted to him. His blood pressure had been growing higher and higher. Yesterday he was taken to the hospital on a stretcher with phlebitis.

Even the Japanese tell us to be ready for any eventuality, which admits something. There are many signs of unbelief, cynicism, despair, depression from diet deficiency, tense nerves because of the escape and two men taken to town and held there.

April 9, 1944. This camp has certainly been led to vote wrong, at first, on everything from woman suffrage to Family Living as Unit—and has been handed each in turn by the Japanese, themselves. As for me, the General says we can have any or all of it if we can arrange without building materials, so if our own Americans turn the project down and I can't move, I shall break the rules of singleness and have Jerry come in whenever I like, to eat or talk or get plates. Mrs. Mills said, "I saw your new place on the cubicle sheet," and I replied, "Yes, I'm getting ready to live in sin." Her husband chuckled. Later, she signed up for the project though she had been in favor of it all the time.

The Episcopalians woke us at six with Easter hymns and the chant of litany. June, Bedie and I went to the Easter sunrise service at hospital point where the scripture was read and Easter songs floated out over the beautiful valley. As we finished, the sun burst bright over a heap of gray cloud.

Back to breakfast of boiled eggs, bucaco and milk on rice, coffee, fresh muffins and guava jelly. We were through just in time for roll call.

At 10 there was another full service in the garden, with Carl preaching on Doubting Thomas and those who must see in order to believe; how one must have faith without seeing and cling now to those things which are eternal and of real value, a value which everyone can know. The Masons attended the service in a body, with a sprig of evergreen in each lapel, sitting in the front three rows on spread blankets. Don made a fine prayer for all in trouble or anxiety, mentioning particularly the two men who were "detained needlessly," asking return and comfort for their wives. It was a solemn, very serious gathering, quiet and attentive, with all thinking of three wives, two living men and one just gone beyond human ken. We wondered also about two others who had escaped and brought all the present troubles upon us. Tomibe, seeing the men march down in a body for the first time (we are being forced together in some ways if not in others), came and sat on the bank above us to look down. Near him sat Meg and Mary, drawing what help they could gain from the service. Tomibe moved off, came down to sit close, heard all the prayer and the sermon. It was one of Carl's best, all embracing, containing elements for a Japanese or American defeat or victory. Tomibe sat quietly taking it all in.

Jerry looked very handsome in his new green coat of rough materials. Bedie was much impressed with his father's looks as he sat with us during coffee. June who sang in the choir was thrilled over the magnificent "Hallelujah Chorus" in which she took part.

We had cold meat with small boiled potatoes for lunch, with jelly. Bedie is not too well, his appetite picky. He is starting to have a sore mouth, upset internally. It worries me.

He has no girl at the moment, has drifted apart from his two pals on account of girl trouble and seeing the boys too often. He has lost Wick and Bill Moule and is worried about them. He feels the atmosphere and tells Meg he wants to help her any way he can with the children. In church I could be only too thankful that June was safe with us, Jerry not in jail, Bedie standing beside me, myself able to walk, thanks to the Red Cross.

At two there was a church service for Sam Weinstein, then the procession wound slowly behind the heavy flower-covered box to another grave on the lowest hilltop. It was a sad Easter, a tragic one, with hard labor for the men who dug the grave, prepared the coffin, completed the bodega for the garrison in double time. There is no spring feeling, no fiesta spirit, hope tries hard to even flutter. We are all weary of waiting, waiting, keeping the flag flying while knowing little, having only faith to go by. We look back on coconuts at 45¢, fresh-made butter and the peace of dullness with a wistful feeling, praying for quick release. The Masons conduct the service at the grave, drop in the evergreen spring. The Catholic service for an Orthodox Jew made the bereaved wife happy. In here we are used to [diverse] ways and many forms of religion. Anything that can help is welcome, often rites being combined. Many are the paths to heaven, say the Chinese. The garrison has arrived. Thirty khaki figures line up for a long harangue by Major Tomibe, now in uniform.

Later—when I go out, people are talking in knots, groups, as though there was news. While we fight to keep husbands and wives from living together with their children—Bulgaria surrenders and Rumania collapses. This came in last night from KG[14]—how no one knows.

April 10, 1944. We decided at lunch that if the [Family] Project couldn't be put over we would play bridge in our space, come and go as we felt like in cubicle, since the General is willing. Some who hear this will get the jitters but we might as well live like the Arthurs and the hospital married couples.

Letter to the Bunshiyocho (Commandant):

"Dear Sir:

"In order to clarify the question of the need for night watchmen, we wish to make the following suggestions: 1. In regard to fire, earthquake, flood or other emergencies, we recognize the need for watchmen to prevent such calamities if possible or to control the confusion that might result from them. Regarding the escape of internees, we must insist that this is not our responsibility. . . . We believe that making internees responsible for the escape of other internees, is contrary to international laws governing civilian internment camps. . . . While we will cooperate to the best of our ability to have the camp as a whole obey the rules and regulations of the Japanese Army, it is obvious that we have no control over personal views of individuals, nor have we any means of forestalling or preventing any drastic action that individuals might take without our knowledge." Signed by Carl and Denki.

Camp office is now in the hospital. Office and bedroom for three nurses all in one, a lovely mélange and epitomizing camp as it gets crazier and crazier. The most prevalent neurosis is "space-itis" whose symptoms make moving of a body and its appurtenances or possessions almost impossible. The jaw becomes set, the eye takes on a glare, the patient repeats continually "not one inch!" The head of the hospital doesn't seem to be able to relieve the disease even among his own staff, where it has taken the most virulent form from the beginning.

At supper time Jim Halsema was given fifteen minutes to prepare his blanket roll for a trip to jail.

Three men out now and the atmosphere is charged. The strain is almost unbearable. Everyone is upset, thoughts scattered and all coming back to one point—the jail. It is surmised that Gene's diary was found, a possible mention of listening to Jim's *News* which may have brought about his being called. Jim will have to explain how he adds two and two from the *Tribune* and the

Nippon Times.[15] Probably they won't believe it. I am now going to "bury" these notes and start a new series.

April 11, 1944. Tomibe says the men are all right, may not be beaten up much (!) but will be gone for a while.

April 12, 1944. It appears now that all but three (Cleo, Fern and the new-lyweds) signed the petition at the hospital against the Family Unit. En masse, and they live in a glass house.

Arthur and Enid signed the petition against family unit, the heels.

Jerry was able to get a pound of liver through the Japanese who, hearing it was for someone not very well, said, "No charge." Jerry cooked it in the men's kitchen and I ate it remotely and quietly for it would create a furor. He wants to see what a dose of liver will do for my mouth and will try to get it every week. I drank a whole glass of milk which really helped.

April 13, 1944. Word went around that Bill Moule and Jim were coming home on the truck but Mary was told that Gene would not be coming. At noon the truck appeared, with only the Chef and the guard, but finally the other two were seen walking up from the guardhouse, to the office.

The stories began to drift about. Gene has taken a terrible beating and is in the hospital with a broken rib and no one knows what else. Bill was hung up by his thumbs, his hands a dreadful sight. His face is hollow, haggard and white, even after he shaved the beard growth. He says he never knew anything so terrible and he wanted to commit suicide more than once but he hung on. He wishes they had taken him first instead of Gene because Gene lied and this is when they torture. Bill told the truth and he says if anyone else goes out they must tell it straight at once and not go through what Gene did. Tomibe has gone in to see what can be done and if Gene can be brought to this hospital here. Sadists always choose Gene's type. He is fresh, quick-tempered, cocky and young. But he had to give in at last.

The Commandant stated he was sorry for the difficulties we were at present undergoing in camp but they had been a direct result of the escape of two internees. He said that their escape had also inconvenienced a great many persons outside of camp. Should anyone else escape, it will mean further restrictions for the whole camp and our lives will be even more difficult than they are at present.

April 14, 1944. *Special Section* on Bill, Gene and Jim in jail.

Bill was strung up by his thumbs 4 times in 4 hours. They tied his hands behind him, then tied the thumbs and pulled him up with arms behind him. He could touch the ground with his toes which helped a little, but the back was bent over and the head down, lasting for about 20 minutes each time. They hit him from underneath, in the face; they beat him with sticks, kicked

him in the ribs. Once he told them that Americans wouldn't treat a dog like that and they beat him unmercifully. The 4th time they strung him up they ordered him to get up on a chair and he wouldn't. Five of them jumped him at once, and he ended standing on the chair where they handcuffed his hands behind him and strung him by the thumbs again. He said he kept hoping he would faint but he is too powerful and could not, so he kept striking his head against the door, trying to knock himself out. They beat him for this too. He said he was not conscious of making a sound until he saw a Filipino crowd gathering outside to find out what was going on, then the Japanese put a gag in his mouth and he dimly realized he must have been yelling. Twice his shoulder was pulled out of the socket and they took him down to put it back in. He had a huge black spot on one leg, another on one arm. He says the Filipinos fed him afterward and he ate like a horse for four days yet he is 12 pounds less than when he left here even after all the food. He sweated so that he stood in a pool of water. What they wanted to know was *where* the men went, who took them and what way they went, how we got the news and who got it. Much of this he could not answer—which made it only worse. At last he lost track and doesn't remember much. He could only give them a vague idea of the destination anyway. After it was all over they told him they had all the information they wanted anyway after torturing Chicay, the meat seller, and two others, one of whom they caught with a [type] script of news from K. P., a guerrilla.

It is as I surmised. They *were* trying to trace the type and thought it came from in here. They are sure we have an organization ready to rush when news and orders come and that someone in here is at the head of it. There will be no more news under stones or trees or wherever it was. No one knew who got it, perhaps it was the two who escaped. News was just talked around, starting nowhere. Bill was given by far the worst because he was the strongest and stood firm. How he hated them when they told him they had all the dope anyway and just wanted confirmation. They showed him a sheaf of records gouged from the two Filipinos. He did not read it so they may have lied, but it is Intelligence business to put two and two together. Tomibe asked Bill to come into the office and tell just what they did to him. He told him all, showing him the wounds like deep burns in his thumbs. Tomibe said, "No, No, they didn't do that!" in several places. He begged Bill not to tell it around camp but Bill said he was going to tell the whole story so that no one else would try to escape, and later on it would all be settled up.

Tomibe went into town in the car this morning and brought Gene back alive. He was taken right down to camp hospital, able to walk by himself. At the top of the steps stood little Terry and Kim. Terry shouted, "Daddy" and ran to him. Gene bent over and Terry grabbed him around the neck and would not let go. Gene patted his little rear softly, saying his name over and over. Gene is bruised and took a tough beating because he really did not know a lot of the answers, but he passed out into unconsciousness and they had to cut him down and take him to the military hospital. Before he left jail he says the Filipinos rubbed his thumbs and hands and arms back to life or he feels he might have been worse off. All their thumbs were badly cut.

Jim was put in with a bunch of Filipinos and not touched the first night. They advised him to tell anything he knew. Next morning they strung him up at once, before asking any questions. His thumb became infected. He speaks of how wonderful the Filipinos are—Dixson in jail for the fourth time, accused of sending money to guerrillas; Jo in on the same charge but let out now. Konrad is in for listening to his radio. There are only two kinds of prisoners, those in on Buy and Sell, and those sending money to guerrillas. Jim says they are marvelous and keep right on going in spite of jail and beatings. Blanche saw a fellow brought into the town hospital so emaciated he couldn't hold his mouth together and it was held by a strap under his chin. His stomach curved in until it touched his backbone. He was a horrible sight, barely alive, mumbling half out of his mind, scarcely human. Blanche says he was probably a victim of water cure. The Japanese seem to know where guerrillas are gathered and other things. Can they *do* anything about it?[16]

Gene went straight to the hospital and stayed there, with dysentery. Bill should have gone there too, for too many talked to him and he was keyed up anyway and finally gave out nervously. He couldn't eat and was nauseated. They gave him drugs to make him sleep. He is lucky to be still sane, but it will be months before he is normal and he will never forget the horror of it.

Jo and Win asked us for lunch to celebrate Jerry's birthday of the 11th. Win's cooking and Jo's garden combined into a work of art that was like something from heaven. There was a huge flat dish of crisp, dewy, vivid green lettuce leaves with slices of huge red tomatoes piled in the center, a frosty pink luster on each one. On another plate were firm green peppers stuffed with Red Cross beef, some celery and onions. The Celadon green reminded us of ancient pottery at home. There was tea with real-honest-to-goodness ice in it, covering the white cups with delicious sweat. Nearby was a gently browned coconut pie, rich and creamy, with delectable aroma. Camp bread was toasted in strips to make rusks. First of all was cream of onion soup with mashed brown beans to make it thick—all from Jo's garden. What a feast and how much it did for the stomach and the mind!

April 15, 1944. At noon Jerry comes to tell me that with an upswing of the sledge he has torn the ligaments in his back again. My heart hits bottom for this means running back and forth between barracks and even possibly the hospital for two or three weeks, many lonely evenings such as I had before. I could sit down and weep, but I shut my teeth together, for what is the use of weeping. We had a bone and bijon stew for supper and Jerry came over to eat with us but was in misery.

Father Sheridan has promised to tell me my minimum and maximum space. Mrs. Sproul came in to talk to me about the measurements. I said I was going to move my bed around, occupy my full space and put up curtains for privacy. I said I had never taken my full share of space in two years because I didn't think it mattered, but now it did. Mrs. Sproul calmed down and told me my share was 35 square feet each—70 in all for June and me. Jerry and Walter measured it. We discussed the whole business and I finally decided to move the bed with Walter's help on Monday, since it was too late now. He put up the sheet so I wouldn't have to look at Garsons anymore and with this sign of a state of mind I felt better. While the confab was going on, the two families in the room were staring avidly and it was quite evident they had believed the rumor that Jerry was going "to move in," taking it literally. If it hadn't been sad, I could have shrieked with laughter at their anxious, scandalized faces, worried over what might go on behind the hanging sheets! They must have been sweating all day over it for I've caught Vinnie watching me several times.

April 16, 1944. The Petition Against Family Units: "We, the undersigned members of camp, wish to present to the General Committee our protest against the plan to set up joint quarters for married people in this camp. The scheme will result inevitably in pregnancies, at a time when preventive measures cannot be taken and when such pregnancies would be inopportune. Our rations are already inadequate for the maintenance of health, yet we shall be called upon to draw on our meager stores for the care of expectant mothers. How, without demanding unwarranted sacrifices from every man, woman and child, can we make provision for more? Naturally we have no objection to couples living together under normal conditions. Times are not normal. Can any man in this camp talk of his right to family life at a time when it will prejudice the safety and health of his wife, and impose unfair responsibilities and privations on those around him? Is he privileged to subject his neighbors to an intimacy of contact which offers untold possibilities of friction and embarrassment? Furthermore, when a half dozen necessary important projects wait to be accomplished, is it sensible to turn upside down the housing arrangements of the camp and to pull men from their usual details to undo and reconstruct much of the work at which carpenters have been busy for months? Finally, we object to the procedure by which this scheme has been pushed. By regrouping people in a manner inconvenient, ill-adjusted, offensive to standards of propriety and even of decency, [Family Units] threaten an unlimited prospect of further bitterness and of quarrelling."

Father Sheridan's letter about the Family Unit: "It is more than a month since this family unit plan was first suggested. Today, I hope we shall settle the issue. There can be no question that serious people in camp realize the acuteness of conditions prevailing in the Orient, the Islands and even the environs of Camp Holmes. The mere suggestion of air-raid shelters, platoons to keep families united, packs to be prepared for marching orders or even worse disorder, these are simple warnings that, to be mild, all is not well even with our own little world. . . . It is further evident that fire is ever a treacherous hazard, in the middle barracks especially, where women and children are ready holocausts should a conflagration cause panic among these defenseless dwellers who are imprisoned in these structures so tempting to the demon of flames. Now briefly to state certain facts. Of 97 married couples, 50 have asked to be included in the Cubicle Plan. Of about 350 potential votes, 159 signed the petitions, and this represents as clear cut a vote as one might ask because it was taken up under ideal conditions for the three petitions. I see no reason for voting a second time, or a third or fourth. Two thirds of the children would be favorably affected by bringing their fathers permanently even into such a home as cubicles can make.

"Some of us witnessed yesterday the reunion of Bill with his wife and children. I saw strong men swallow lumps in their throats as these two and their children were gathered together again. As the story of tortuous trial was unveiled, I was touched and impressed as seldom in my life with the ideal of what married life can mean to such people; it is their right to be together in normal times but especially in these days when the sword of disaster hangs over the heads of all of us. I stayed with this group part of the afternoon and evening, and as Bill and Marj cried and laughed in anguish and joy, I had a vision of how deeply they must still be in love. And I thought of the economics of babies, reputed plan to confiscate food supplies of other internees for possibly pregnant mothers, the insinuations that sexual passion is the basis for this plan—and I took courage for whatever difficulties might be ahead as I looked into the reddened and wet eyes of a crying hulk of a man and a mother who knew how close she had come to being a widow or wife of a deranged spouse; and I thought of the nobility, the purity, the sanctity of their affection, and how we as a committee have been asked to permit them to enjoy not a privilege but an alarming necessity and right. And celibate priest that I am, I vowed through sobs that I'll pay any price to bring such families together, not only for their mutual companionship but especially for the mutual protection they can afford in the days as yet unborn when we shall perhaps be penniless, hungry, and obsessed with fears of what may befall the Islands, this camp and our individual selves. . . . I believe that we as a committee can do our small part to give some measure of joy to distracted mothers and endangered children, and for whatever span of years God may appoint us, may we generously hold aloft the ideal of family life, and in union with our fellow internees of Manila, Los Baños and recently Davao, permit married people to share one another's joys and sorrows and be together should dread disaster in any of its appalling forms invade this camp."

Comments by Dr. Skerl: "I have the following remarks to make about the petition signed by 63 subscribers. 1. It is full of gross exaggerations such as "pregnancies are inevitable and preventative methods cannot be taken here in camp." The absence of pregnancies in the Davao camp when the families lived together for 16 months is a sufficient reply to the statement. 2. The fact that 3 out of 4 of our doctors in camp are heartily in favor of the plan is surely sufficient evidence that there are no real objections on health grounds. 3. The plan calls for segregating the families and any possible conflicts and embarrassments will arise more likely from the presence of obstinate people hostile to the plan who say that they intend to stay where they are regardless of the families who move in around them. 4. There is no reason why anybody need be excused from their work detail because of the moving involved in the plan. 5. The accusation that the subcommittee has campaigned for the plan is completely groundless and a misrepresentation of the fact.

"As to the last sentence of the petition, all we have to say is that 'Mrs. Grundy' is always present in any group of people such as ours. . . . A few weeks ago a marriage was celebrated in this camp and practically everyone partook of the wedding supper, thus giving their tacit approval. However, 164 persons were persuaded to sign these petitions which in effect would make the marriage a mockery. Many of these people, however, signed because they had been misled into believing that they would be personally inconvenienced. The General Committee is now putting into effect a detailed safety plan in which families form the ultimate unit. The working of this safety plan would be greatly accelerated if the families are already living together. Again the women and children in the Baby House are too isolated from their menfolk if a sudden emergency should arise so that the presence of men would be desirable. The married people who have asked for this plan strongly resent any suggestion that the camp as a whole is entitled to have any say in their family relations. . . ."

It is a tough time, food is low, Jerry is sick, my condition always teetery. I took my 28th shot so am in balance at the monent. I put P50 cash in the store. There is enough for three more weeks and that is all.

April 18, 1944. At breakfast there were three cartoons on the Board, put up by the Opposition to the Family Unit. One showed many cans of milk, saying "Save Milk!" Another had a drawing of two swing beds with a baby in between, also swung, and under this the caption "For Greater East Asia." A third was a drawing of the Bulletin Board on which was hanging a paper entitled, "Father Sheridan's tearjerker," with babies all around the base of it. It was all the same theme and implication and it made me sick. It is lies and no joke to me anymore. I want to get us all together before anything happens personally or generally. Bedie sees and hears all these things and he wanted to know what it was all about, especially the smutty stuff. I didn't know where to begin. I have managed June as I went along but Bedie is here, there and everywhere. What to tell him about the whole mess and how? I didn't feel equal to it. The room was full of sniggers and giggles over it. Harry was laughing very superior laughs. When I saw Wayne Miller in the little cottage helping with the lunch and dishes, talking it all over at 11 o'clock, when I can't have Jerry in my place until five to seven, something exploded inside of me. I wrote and pinned up a sign on the edge of one of the others, "Lost—the Holy State of Matrimony, for better, for worse. Finder please return to the Episcopalians."

Tom was back with Father Maquire, meeting Carl and Miss McKim on the way. They all went into a huddle around the Board and took *all* down promptly which suited me fine. I marched out into the field with Bedie who had been with me and we walked up and down talking out the whole problem. I told him never to let anyone tell him that mating was the only reason people wanted to live together, that companionship and being with someone you loved and wanting to tell the world about it was what counted most. I told him Carol felt that way about Wilma so they had the wedding, and that he must not pay any attention to dirty minds and the ways in which they tried to distort it. I said that millions of families lived in one room, close to others; that while it wasn't ideal at all, they got along all their lives that way and we could too. He said, "You can be real happy in a little bit of space too, can't you?" I answered, "You sure can." We talked about mating and how some were made so that they needed it more often than others and some less. We talked clear and straight, no beating about the bush. I told him he would probably fall in love a number of times before he found the girl he wanted to marry, but I hoped he would try to keep himself clean and decent for her, not getting common or cheap trying to find out what it was all about. I don't know how clear it all was to him for I must have been incoherent and torrential at times, but we grew closer together and he heard some facts that will stick by him or come back strongly someday. We had to stop when the school bell rang but he seemed more settled and had something normal to chew on.

Dr. Mather came to me later, told me he was gunning for me, ashamed of me for putting up that piece. I told him I knew such things were cheap but I didn't care at all this time, I was proud of it, for I hated the whole crowd that signed that petition; for half of them lived where they could have men in to help them often and they did have them come in while I couldn't have even my own husband in but a short time every day; that I didn't feel too well most of the time and just about managed to keep going. I didn't give a whoop any more what anyone thought or said. I was past caring. Then I walked off, saying I would look after myself. Bedie heard both my tirades today and he said, "Mother, you almost cried both times!" I agreed and said that I was angry, very angry, and tired of people snickering over what wasn't funny. I felt like crying, but didn't, couldn't, just as hard as nails. I'm certainly learning what lots of people go through in the world.

When I went under the barracks with Marie Thompson to see the cubicle Jim had built as a real home to get away from some hateful people, almost I did weep. We crept along with bent backs, and even then I hit my head on a rafter and Marie exclaimed, "Look out, this is the Underworld!" With odd pieces of tin and board and logs, picked up from the discard heaps, in three days Jim has built a very smart little room with 3 tiny windows on as many sides, and with canvas squares to pull down over them. Marie has a low stool in one corner with a napkin and a vase of flowers on it. They have fixed up a couch, goodness knows how, but it looked attractive. The room was a refreshing miniature love nest worthy of any Depression flats or shantytown. It is pitiful that they have to do it this way but it is home and they are happy there, as Bedie says. They are grim and radiant at the same time.

Tomibe is very human. When he heard the children call the dog Tojo, he says they can call the dog Roosevelt!

Two things seem to stand out from the jail experience; one that there is a "pipeline" to the guardhouse, some means of information, perhaps even more than one means. I still think that in large part it is our own weaknesses—volubility and desire to show that one is in the know, etc. In any case, they seem to know just about everything that goes on, which is their business after all. Second, it appears they have a conviction that we have some kind of organization in here which gets word out to keep up the morale of the Filipinos. This is very encouraging. They can't understand why the Filipinos resist, hold out, for they are the only occupied country and people who do. The Japanese can't see that the very fact of our being here at all, shut off from contacts, raises the morale to heights all by itself. Perhaps they do see, for they wanted to exchange us desperately for a while. They know what thoughts can do without even being expressed. Thoughts can't be killed, either.

April 19, 1944. Our friend Sergeant Murata was one of those who kicked and beat Bill the worst in jail. 7½ ounces of water a day is what hurt Bill the most for he sweated so terribly that he was badly dehydrated. He will have to go slow and watch his heart for a while.

Two others have Underworld Cubicles. A complaint was lodged about the new cubicles (they all guess it was from 606 under whose august feet they are so cosy), so the Committee came on a tour of inspection. They can't do anything about it and probably secretly think it is one solution to the Green Barracks problem. Jim and Marie are happier than they have been in here and wish they had built the place months ago. Tomibe gave Jim a table drawer out of which he made a table. Tomibe also inspected the Underworld, with another Japanese. They asked how many in all and were told 10. They nodded, said "Sa, very good, very good." Walter made a tour of inspection and got a big kick out of the ingenuity displayed. Vinsons have made their cubicle of runo [reed] sticks. All huts are made from scrap, but they spell quiet, privacy and happiness.

April 20, 1944. Bedie came in with 15 june bugs in a pencil box. He said half were David's and they caught them in study hall light, which made me doubt his studiousness. He wanted a box to make a cubicle for the bugs, for he was going to watch and see how many babies they had. He said they were going to draw a line and put the bugs on it. Those that went this way were pro-cubicle, and those that went in the other direction were anti-cubicle. "Just like camp," said he. He has been absorbed in them ever since. I found a box and told him to give them light, air, water and food. He watches them curl up, chewing pink hibiscus flowers and leaves which are sprinkled with water. The bugs are interesting to all of us. The box has holes for air and we see that their prime interest is food, second is propagation of the species. I took Bedie to see two cubicles and he was entranced and wants one for us.

April 23, 1944. Bob Dyer came back safe from jail looking tired and wan. He is forbidden to talk under serious penalty and signed a paper to this effect.

April 25, 1944. I washed, cooked, and mopped mud. Then I went for a blood count. I thought the color looked better than in November. At noon the doctor called me in to say that my white and red cells were both much too low. My count has dropped a third. I heard later that it was 2 million 700 thousand. Normal is 4,500,000 or more. He gave me two prescriptions, one for ten more ascorbic shots and one for a series of green iron pills. He said he would take it up with the Medical Committee about liver shots. They have only 15 of these left.

The Commandant stated that there were some changes which should be made in upstairs No. 2 Barracks before the family units could move in. He feels that the married couples should be in one section, and that no women who are not living with their husbands should be interspersed between. The work will be supervised by the Japanese Army contractor, with aid of camp labor. There are to be four [new] buildings; a school building composed of 10 rooms and 1 large room for use of the General Committee office, which will be erected on site of second nipa shack; a building to be erected on the corner now occupied by the barber shop. This will be occupied by the camp store, library, barber shop, shoe shop and bodega. On the site of the present veg shed, a building will be constructed for housing the vegetable bodega and meat house. An addition to the present shop building will house carpenter and blacksmith shops.

April 26, 1944. We four went down to sign the oath at six. Here it is:
"To His Excellency, the Commandant of Military Internment Camps of the Philippine Islands. I, the undersigned, hereby solemnly pledge myself that I will not, under any circumstances, attempt to escape or conspire directly or indirectly against the Japanese Military Authorities as long as I am in their custody. Name. Date (April 20)". Is this milder than the other?[17]

April 27, 1944. Two years ago today, 800 of us, including Chinese, moved over to Camp Holmes. That awful crowding—how did we ever live through it. Now again there is to be moving, for Tomibe has approved the plan and given his okay to move in all around. There are meetings to discuss space, with explosions here and there, and the Opposition meeting out front and back, trying to stem the tide. We have named our little sheet enclosure The Dog House for we certainly are in it these days.

There is talk of the outer fence being electrified—300 volts. Also a rumor that France is already invaded.[18]

Tomibe came to Japanese class and talked to us for an hour. It was most interesting—all in Nippongo, with his eyes shut tight in thought sometimes, his hands and arms in use, his thick black hair tossed now and then. Miss McKim translates beautifully, subtle in catching the shades and nuances of both languages. The two together were fascinating and it was an absorbing hour. He asked each of us about our home mail first, then told us a story of a woman of the Samurai. It was moving, impressive for one felt he was deeply stirred. He said by study of the language we could perhaps gain a little insight into the Japanese spirit and character. He is imbued with the Samurai spirit, said his father taught him the hara-kiri ceremony. With a quick strong thrust, he showed us the dagger going in, the pull around and up, then back again and out—the raised hand signifying the victim wishes his head cut off by the sword to end the agony. Tomibe is living with this idea and may do it, as he said he must after he turns camp over. This code seems dreadful to us—it makes no use of defeat, only pride, and no humility of learning. They cannot bear to lose face, to bow to disaster.

It is plain to see Tomibe's mind working and turning around his training. Is he modern enough to break away, to learn from defeat what he could never learn from victory, as we have for two years? Will he help his children to carry forward a new Japan—or will he take the old way of annihilation? Will we see him use old methods or the new ones of knife or bullet which he says is often done now, after he has turned camp over to his enemy? We stayed on listening to the short, clipped accents, the strange burr of Nippongo, alternating with the clarity and beauty of the translation. Miss McKim interjected exclamations of horror which increased at the end as he described ancient methods of torture—prisoners buried up to their necks, sitting on spiked bamboos, the guards jabbing their faces and necks with bamboo spears. He noted that this was Oriental, Chinese as well as Japanese. We might add that primitive Europe did such things too. He said it was not done anymore. We told him we all expected to have bad dreams and dispersed laughing, but it is a weighty and serious matter to him. They see the end and the number of their days if they follow the old way. We hope he decides to survive.

April 28, 1944. I woke at 1 A.M. with poor respiration and my sight cloudy. I felt very queer and ill. After breakfast I went to Peg and told her I was resigning all my jobs for a week or month's rest. I am sorry to give up the char work but I will do rice when able. I did it all as long as I could. Now I must conserve what strength I have for the family. There won't be much and they may have to look after me a bit. I talked to the doctor and he said it was my condition, to take life easy and not to worry for they would take care of me.

Camp started to move for the Family Unit Plan and the whirlpools raged around my quiet cubicle. Baby House moved up, and others moved in. The same in lower dorm. The missionary men turned to with a will, helping everyone who needed it. It was good to see them, carrying trunks, bags, mats, blanket rolls, shelves, tins, beds, boards, all kinds of dunnage, rusty and otherwise—some of it on backs or shoulders, some in arms, some pulled on the garbage wagon, some pushed in carts. The move was on and it looked like a hive or an anthill! It has done a lot for morale. The air crackles. Changes in space and neighbors are all to the good. Ladders and pieces of ladders, swung beds pulled apart, it was moving day with a vengeance. Pounding, hammering, beds swung up, everyone busy except the sour ones who oppose. These might be termed those who fiddled while Rome burned. It has half stopped the moral crusade which was trying to keep us apart. I am not the only one who is ill and needs help. There are many others.

For a couple of weeks I have been having lapse of memory, just going blank on things, not coordinating at all. I left Jerry on the porch in order to get a cup for him, completely forgot he was there and all about the cup until he whooped for it and even then I did not click.

April 29, 1944. Moving and hammering all this day too which surged around couples who refused to move. They remain obturate islands, but Tomibe said to go by them.

Jerry went with Bergie to get four boards for his bed. The guard asked what he wanted it for (in perfect English, a graduate of Imperial University in Tokyo, now wearing blue denim and digging post holes.) He let him have the boards from a pile. This will help Jerry's back, which still bothers him.

April 30, 1944. Mac came for coffee with us. His wife took a trip to Manila where people are either leaving to return to the provinces because they are broke, or pouring in there trying to make a cleanup. Only a few trains are running and it took her four days to get back. All the trains are mobbed as in Russia or China. It takes several days to get passage for Tarlac then one is stalled there several days. Conditions are awful, with only two meals a day for almost everyone outside. They cannot buy more, so they get used to going without breakfast. People make a living any way they can, clean or otherwise, buying, selling old clothes. A worn coat brought P70. Present money is valueless and those who have it, blow it. People go to old American movies and try to forget their troubles.

We went to pay a birthday call on Peg, then visited in all the new cubicles, looking at creative and constructive ways of swinging beds, economizing on space, storing possessions, tucking away the baby, etc. It was good to see it, inspiring to watch husbands and wives working it out together. We then went down to Baby House where 16 people have done wonders and are settling down happily. Morale is high for some, very curdled for others. Thank God the moves are made this far—for they can't be undone.

May 1, 1944. Practice for Maypole dancing, rope wreaths made of evergreen, monotonous piano tunes tinkling for days—will soon be ended after today's program.

At quarter to six there was a May program of dances with long chains of green and flowers, colored dresses, curled or flying hair, extremely pretty young and older girls. Three were dressed as Folly in red, green and yellow wigs, cutting antics and capers as they waved long red, green and yellow fingernails while leaping into the air, tossing heads. Mrs. Griego says she *never* wants to play *any* of those tinkling tunes again, and *I* never want to hear them. But the whole springlike affair was pretty, from the crowning of Barbara in white filmy gown among her maidens in waiting, to the last chain-flower dance around the queen. Gene sat close by, his head still with that beaten, battered look, swollen here, sunken there, and eyes tragically not normal.

We visited No. 2 barracks cubicles again where sheet partitions are going up until it looks like a combination Pullman car and trailer. They are having such fun. It is the happiest place in camp, a hive of activity and release, while the other dorms stew in their own sour juice and become more and more ingrowing. Fildeys have the trickiest place, with a tiny kitchenette curtained with red check napkins cut up, used wisely and well. Compactness is the keynote, with vast ingenuity displayed. The ex–Fathers' House, now Family Unit, is said to be a good exhibit too. None of them have time to worry about rumors or lack of rumors. They are too healthy and busy with creative ideas budding on every branch of activity.

May 2, 1944. Another rumor says that the Japanese have named 8 open cities in Japan and Roosevelt had reported ''we will not bomb Tokyo but—we give you 45 days to get the women and children out of the other seven.'' The 45 days are up on the 4th of May.[19] Perhaps this is the reason for jitters, nerves and tightening up. We wait like the blind and the deaf.

May 3, 1944. The dentist has brought in the panels from his office which, with other boards, he is making into a paneled apartment for his wife, taking plenty of space. Perhaps they will move the daughter over, solving a space problem in this barracks too. They will go out as they came in, insulated, learning little but bitterness, taking all they can get and giving as little as possible.

I wondered if I could get P30 for my shoes that I have in here. Carl said if they could be sent out they would bring in P170 and he would keep them in mind. He told us that jewelry would go better and Jerry answered that all we had was the diamond bracelet which would bring more cash than we would want. He took this up quickly, saying that if I were willing to part with it and the Japanese assented to its going out, we could have enough for ourselves and to divide among the various mission groups whose boards would stand behind them in repayment. If the bank jewels are gone, I only have three pieces left with me, but I am so on the ragged edge that parting with one more "thing" does not matter. From my own case, I know to the full how much other people may be in need. Jerry's mind always clicks instantly and he was all for it at once. He has few sentimental attachments for things. Carl told me to think it over a bit. After ten minutes, I asked Jerry, "Do you want it now? Come and I will give it to you." It no longer bothers me to think about it. One wrench and it was gone—the sign and symbol of our gains from the Gold Boom, a gift from Jerry, one more item to put on my list of things bought for one purpose and used for quite another. It satisfies me that it goes not only for our family but for many groups of people in need. No strings attached.

Minutes of the Special Meeting called by the Commandant: "All members present, (including Mr. Green and not Fabian). Mr. Tomibe said that the meeting had been called to discuss the resignation of Mr. Green as Head of Finance. He said he was unable to understand the reasons for his resignation. . . . Mr. Tomibe said that the desire on the part of any member to resign should first have been submitted to him and he criticized the Committee in going ahead with an election before consulting him.[20] . . . The Chairman stated he realized the Committee did not follow the proper procedure in the resignation of Mr. Green and in holding a new election, but that they had followed the precedent in this matter. The Command stated that he would give his decision in the matter on Thursday morning. That morning the Committee was again called before the Command. He stated that the Committee had worked hard and with difficulty, that he was pleased with their work. He appreciated the difficulties but that since the Family Unit Plan was started there had been bitterness and dissension to a serious degree in camp. This must not be and so it was his desire to dissolve the present Committee and have a new election. He asked their opinion of this plan and whether or not they would be willing to serve if reelected. Most of the members said they would not serve. Several said they would serve if elected since they felt it their duty to do so. Some felt that this problem was not serious enough to warrant a new election, and they felt that any ill will or bitterness would pass. . . . After a long discussion, the Command finally announced that the present Committee would continue in office and he asked Mr. Green if he would be willing to continue in office as Head of Finance. He said that he would."

This is Mr. Green's punishment and a great lesson for all. Mr. Tomibe is a fine administrator. If there were more like him in both countries, neither would be at war. The enemy tried to be fair and impartial. He looks at it straight and balances it well. At one point, Mr. Tomibe turned to Mr. Green asking him why he took so much interest and effort in the Family Unit plan since it was out of his department and in the province of Father Sheridan. Even to the end he tried to force Tomibe to his way—saying he would withdraw his resignation if cubicle moves would stop where they were. Tomibe smiled and said they would—until more materials were obtained, then it could continue. So they lost.

Jerry cleaned the diamond bracelet today and I held it and looked at it in the sun. We chuckled over the day he gave it to me.

Our rice ration has been cut 25% since Christmas.

May 5, 1944. We had a casual conversation with Father Barter last night in which we told him of Bedie digging under the house. He said he had watched him out by the bank. I kidded him that we would allow him one third interest in our Underground (Curt being a third) if he would help on the project. I never dreamed he would take it seriously, but to Bedie's and Curt's delight he came to use a pick and shovel for them for awhile at noon. We may have some fun over this yet.

Jo loaned Jerry P100. It seems like the hand of the Lord!

On the Board: "Hours 9 to 12 A.M. 2 to 4 P.M. By appointment. The dentist wishes to announce the reopening of his dental office in its new location at the hospital on May 6, 1944. The hours above are on Tuesday, Thursday and Saturday. Please *make appointments at the office,* to avoid emissions or duplications. . . . The dentist wishes to express his gratitude to the Commandant and his staff for their helpfulness in bringing in the equipment to camp. . . . In order to correct any misunderstanding which may exist in the minds of the camp members regarding dental service, I wish to make the following announcement. This service is not a camp project but is a part of the personal services which have been rendered to the camp. With the exception of the limited supplies purchased with the Red Cross Relief Funds, the materials and the equipment are the personal property of the undersigned and as such may be bestowed at the discretion of the donor as are other charitable donations. Signed by Wormrath."

"Bestowed"! With all his former flourish and suavity, as though the opening were prewar and social. Many do not know what to make of it and ask what he is driving at. Some ask if he is broke, leading up to charging for services at a time when no one can pay. Others ask, "Do you vote the right ticket in order to get an appointment?" A number who heard Dean's fight with him, over a year ago [actually, two years], when Dean wanted him to go out and get the cached materials from the Army Post before the Japanese came in, remember that these cached dental supplies were taken as were all the medical and hospital supplies by Dean at the same time. But

鯉
幟

May 5ᵗᵇ 1944   Boys Festival

Dean turned the others over to the camp hospital which the dentist did not. In this he was far ahead of the dentist who has only now produced it as personal property, reminding the camp that this is the case.

Things are happening almost too fast. The gardeners who thrive on their own fresh veg, and the sun and air and quietness which comes with digging and growing things—the gardeners who have been encouraged are now being disheartened. There is a new ruling and all gardeners are called to a meeting to hear it. There are 30 odd gardens but only 10 gardeners may receive passes to go outside the fence to cultivate, water and pick the green things. There is despair among some who count heavily on their gardens.

The Opposition have seen all the cosy, attractive cubicles, with curtains and kitchenettes and dressing corners, happy families in each, children gathered around a home center, stability—no longer roaring and rolling up and down the centre aisle, screaming, colliding, fighting. Father is now a permanent part of the picture, his deep voice and firm hand quietly taking over when Mother's frayed nerves turn her voice shrill. Many circles are complete. Children's bad dreams and talk in sleep will grow less as stability creeps over the circle, from quiet evenings as father reads and smokes, and mother sews, all together—no longer hunting for each other or for a place in the crowded dining room where there is no room for family life. No longer will children tear about the parade ground or around the building long after dark until bedtime, overstimulated and keyed-up from dawn till dark. Communal life combined with Family Unit is a vital arrangement. They are all like new people. If only we had it too.[21] Bedie is so disappointed and has a lame back from digging under the house. Cubicle or Bust is his slogan.

May 6, 1944. After breakfast I went over to Peg's to lie down as Elizabeth was having her bed swung to make table space and dressing corner curtained beneath the bed. My head couldn't take the hammering. At Peg's I began to get cold, hands and feet, poor circulation all over. Peg made me an eggnog and she and June managed to find two hot water bags. I drank gallons of water. I did not feel like fainting at all, just stopped as in shock. It was merely very low vitality. Afterward, June said, "Mummie, you look lots better." I said, "Why, how did I look before?" and she answered like an adult, no longer my little girl, "You were pinched and drawn, lines in your face and head, your eyes looked bad, your mouth pulled and strained." She saw all that fight for control when balance is slipping and one holds on by a thread. I began to come back just as Jerry came with coffee and an anxious face. Before noon, I came "home" quietly and we reveled in pot roast with gravy on the rice, a flavor to it that we haven't tasted in months, making me want to weep again. The doctor came and said I must go slow, that I *did* need meat and a lot else.

The dentist says every doctor in here should be paid for his services after the war. How about waitresses, moppers, dishwashers and ditch cleaners?

May 7, 1944. Shelters, arbors, roofed gardens, shacks and cubbyholes are going up in wide variety, ingenuity and attractiveness.

Camp Bulletin: "The Consensus of opinion [is] that available relief funds appropriated for purchase of additional meat for the whole camp would be a wiser expenditure than would be the distribution of such funds for personal relief. No meat has been furnished the camp by Japanese authorities for some time. Whenever beef or pork has formed the main part of the menu, it has been purchased with these relief funds. . . . With the closing of the camp office in town a new ruling came into effect . . . that relatives can bring clothes and toilet articles but no food, once a week on Sunday mornings to the guardhouse."

The dentist is going to charge. The dentist says he has seen lots of missionaries buy many times more than he is able to buy at the store every week and he figures they can pay him for dental work. The small daughter of the dentist is now wearing a white embroidered coat given by someone in gratefulness for having her tooth fixed. The first payoff, taken without scruple.

May 9, 1944. Little Walter got up at four to do guard duty with his Dad. The family are proud of him and it was an excellent idea. Sheba has *another* new sweater with a big-needle weave of yellow and brown mixed this time. Last week it was bright yellow. June says that Sheba will go mad if she runs out of wool, for she sits up in the dark knitting by the outside light until nearly midnight. When I cannot sleep, I often hear her needles clicking and she goes outside and back again sometimes. But there is no sound of tumbrils! I think that she will just unravel and re-knit when her skeins run out. Today she laughs her light superior laughter as she listens to a row over space outside the door. Then she says, "And there is a war going on! Who would think it? That is about space too—isn't it a coincidence!"

May 11, 1944. At Japanese class Miss McKim related Cinderella in Nippongo.

May 12, 1944. Camp pictures—the wood crew walking in after lunch in all kinds of caps and clothes, battered and patched, torn and dusty, motley but picturesque; Dr. Mather and Johnson carrying goat garbage can between them on shoulder pole.

The bank-side shacks are so amusing, with roofs of canvas, cogon grass, rusty tin or woven branches. Some are very disheveled, awry, rakish and blown looking; others are neat, with tight-packed earth terraced in, flowers growing already in prim but scant border. They are odd pictures, with their owners sitting at tea on log benches, a dirt terraced couch, a plank settee, or chairs created with no two pieces of wood alike.

The night I was sick I literally cut myself out of my girdle which is so completely patched that it has no more elasticity and is molded on to hold up my socks and hold in my scar. My stockings are now finished except one pair in which to be rescued so I have taken off the museum piece girdle and it is a sight to show the family at home.

May 13, 1944. Those who are caught with shortwave sets are now shot, no more bother with jail terms.

May 14, 1944. A sound sleep and a good day. Jerry was busy in the cubicle building underground. He talks about building the West Wall as though it were the Hindenburg Line. He bought a large tan moth-proof bag from Edna and when I said I had managed to get along two years without one, he answered, "Well, I figured in that case we could use it in our cubicle." It is now cut down one side and forms the mahogany panel East Wall, with a gay blue furoshiki as decoration. The orange, reds, purple, birds and characters that once hung upon Vigan old Spanish walls are now suspended against rusted tin walls in a dugout Bohemian quarter under the floor of a building, with rafters over our heads. There is canvas at the window and door, pine logs for props, and Mansells looted tin full of holes on the North Wall, with charming runo sticks held together by woven string on the South Wall which was built by the four girls in their cosy room next door. The Underground is a help-each-other community; it has the spirit of the trenches and dugouts, of the bomb proof caves in North China. We share shovel, pickax, hammer, ax, walls, nails, and everything else which is scarce, picked up in every direction, all salvage, nothing new—bent, rusty, bedraggled, worn, but it turns into a miniature Greenwich Village. The stalls, cellars, attic tearooms have nothing on us. They aren't nearly as smart as the new Underground cubicle town which is even being wired for electricity! Cubicles are now the thing, socially. Cubicle fever has proved to be the most contagious in camp. And Family Unit, like a forest fire, has swept beyond stopping.

Jim Thompson says that all the children growing up in here know nothing about privacy. They think nothing of bursting into any room, corner or gathering, and will have to be re-educated. With adults, however, privacy is more than ever a commodity—to be bought and sold and sought for!

May 15, 1944. I am now trying to enjoy Sheba as a study in psychology. June and I are timing her shampoos during a week. She is always washing her hair, having it done up by expert hands more and more often. In the morning she wears a crystal choker with a lacy-string sweater and slacks. She can keep dressed up all day because someone in the family does all the hard work and food preparation for her. If Sheba becomes ill she does not need the care of her husband because this same person looks after her and the family meals as well. As Jerry says, it can be done if one has a servant. She has a complex beyond doubt. Having plenty of money, with people kowtowing, has built it up in this particular setup.

Our cubicle will be an excellent spot in which to lie low in case bullets or shrapnel fly during retreat or battle. It is a real shelter dug down into the ground. We could stow away together, with water and food there, if we had to for a few days of uncertainty.

May 16, 1944. Afternoon rains are here. It is our third wet season. There was quite a gale last evening. Jerry carried our table into the dugout and I hemmed and hung the rest of the furoshikis—six on the wall and one as a tablecloth. With nipa covering the tin on the outside, it is not unattractive. There is a board on one side as settee and Jerry has put my steamer rug on top of canvas and nipa which makes a comfortable springy couch terraced out of earth. The gay colored Japanese squares and the reed sticks will give it a strong Nipponese look.

May 17, 1944. We had all our meals in the dugout and I spent the whole day there, resting and reading. A box is our cupboard and Dr. Hall's wooden tray makes a good buffet, with the silver Spanish candlestick and two chromium plates catching highlights. The two hand-carved trays are against the dirt wall on a ledge; silver, agate and tin cups hang in the rafters. It is compact, casual, a real home. Jerry likes to putter about in it, putting in small additions, but for me it is finished. I can relax and catch up a little.

Saban barrio people (the banana gate on the mountain trail) were all taken down to San Fernando for questioning, so there are no banana pickers or sellers. The enemy kills the goose that lays the golden egg by picking on laborers and peasants.

We are to have 100 guards. It seems odd, for our possiblities of action are not worth that much. The two who escaped certainly poked up a hornet's nest for us.

The new Mr. Yamato is an entertaining character. He has a tip-tilted expression, precise little mouth, is very short, and extremely correct in manner. His sayings as reported by Miss McKim in class are delightful. Upon arriving, he pronounced, "I hope to cooperate and be kind and true." He was "pleased to find everything serene and calm." He said the office building was "simperu but beautiful." He must have been looking at the painted front. As to roll call, he said it must be more "strict" which he explained to mean "regular." Carl suggested to him that we had always been more free than Manila camp, and Mr. Yamato nodded, "Yes, we will be strict but free."

Tanabe went out with ten of our men to bring in more Presbyterian cottages.[22] He asks, "When will the Americans come?" Tomibe answers, "They will never come. They are not coming." Denki says, "You know blankety blank well that's not true. They will come!'' ''Yes, but you must not say so,'' Tomibe says.

This dugout is heaven—to get out of that room, hear no more opinions or sour critics. I am out of the stream where I need to be right now, gathering strength, after two weeks of sleepless nights, months of sore mouth and going downhill. Thank God for liver shots sent by the Red Cross.

Scotts came over for coffee and quiet bridge. They purred over the dugout, loved it. Izzy took her shoes off and curled up on the couch. Church as always liked such a casual place. We had a good time. The children came in to study near us, with Bedie's eyes shining. Scotts admit that everyone is pleased over Family Unit now that it is accomplished. Each one is visiting other cubicles, bridge foursomes are taking place, there is interest and curiosity in seeing each cubicle arrangement. It is the same in the Underground. Various ones come calling and no two dugouts are alike. Mansells' is huge, has a window with two panes of glass, a door, curtains, couch, chair, all on a grand scale. Phil's and Peg's is like the saloon of a ship, with curtains at porthole windows, settees at a table with one leg in the middle of it, a white sheet tacked up on the wall into an effect of white paint, drawings of sailboats on it, a sloping ceiling like a cabin.

May 18, 1944. Jerry woke me at 6:30 and I dressed quickly. With a cup of coffee in hand and a bun, we sauntered to hospital point to watch the sun rise over a soft blanket of clouds on one ridge. It was a tender beauty, delicate dawn colors; there was only strength in the great mass of earth, none in the colors except the green which stood out vividly against pastel shades. The sea was vague and far away. The sentry was alert on the ''path.'' Behind us, the Episcopalians chanted early Mass of Ascension Day.

Roll call on the playground was finally arranged in a U by Mr. Tomibe who made a short speech with the help of Miss McKim. He opened with a bellow of attention which impressed his staff at least. The order to follow each day was then given to us. First, in Japanese, ''We will take roll call now.'' Then they say, ''Ohayo'' to which we reply, ''Good morning.'' After that when the check is finished they say, ''Go kuro sama desu'' which literally means I am sorry to make you suffer but figuratively means they are sorry to have troubled us. This is also dismissal. Miss McKim assures them that we are literally suffering. All this came after Tanabe and Yamato had gone down the line to 22 groups, with Yamato standing stiff and precise, making a quick bow with his good morning to each group as soon as it was checked. He is so diminutive, so passionately serious, that it is impossible to explain how laughable it is or why. It is the contrasts which are ludicrous. Carl could not keep from smiling all the way and even Tomibe's face showed humor. After watching all this laborious process, Tomibe quickly swept it into a compact order for future assemblies. He told Miss McKim that he would never have a nervous breakdown because he said right out what he thought, kept nothing piling up underneath, but that Mr. Yamato took everything very seriously, was conscientious and sensitive in the extreme and therefore Miss McKim must not tease him too much! He shows an understanding of Miss McKim as well as of his countryman.

The diamond bracelet proposition is too big to handle—the sum is too large to get in right now, so I dug up my gold Igorot earring drop and turned it over to Jerry for weighing. It is within a fraction of half an ounce and should bring in P200 which will carry us about four weeks at present prices.

Japanese class was great fun with Miss McKim laughing until she put her head on the table, about Bob's account of Dean pushing a bottle of pungent gin under the nose of a searching guard and yelling "Misu" (water) at him over and over until the guard stopped shaking his head and went away defeated in his search for gin. We also laughed over Yamato saying, "Please count off now" to the Baby House group of six mothers and 15 infants who couldn't count to save their little pink skins, with Denki desperately patient, explaining all this to Tanabe and Yamato—"But don't you see, they can't count!" Roll Call is a gay spot in our lives, holding our dumbest and most addled moments. Tomibe told Miss McKim that all human reactions and emotions are the same whether it is a Japanese or an American fondness for children, that we are all alike in those things. Tomibe has a keen understanding of people. He *looks* intelligent from head to foot as he stands alone on the field, silently watching his staff and us. Then he makes a decisive move, after thinking it out first from watching the errors and the bungling. He speaks of his beautiful weapon handed down in the family as "my sword is too precious to be stained with the blood of people." There is continuity of life, generation and spirit as the sword passes from one to another. He feels it is a spiritual matter, as he does about roll call. These people are heavy with symbolism and history. One cannot discard the past entirely, for the good and fine in it can be used.

All my time is spent in the dugout. It delights me out of all proportion to what has been put into it. For the children, it is home, real home. They come to it as a focus now. It is a warm, quiet, colorful gathering place. Bunches of onions and a frying pan are suspended from the rafters in one corner. Our electric wire was handed down from Kink to Dr. Hall to Bill Moule who traded it to us for a mattress cover. Water bottles, chromium, green pepper and pink tomatoes give highlights and cheer. Everything is simple. We have only to reach out a hand for spoon, plate or cup. No effort, yet Paradise enough.

May 19, 1944. Dr. Bruce came in and was also impressed. He said that in our dugout he could see the continuity of Culture! I said, "Yes, we have gone back to the earth again," and he answered, "And made a boudoir out of it!" We asked him in for coffee later and he sank back on the couch as though he would never leave it, actually purring. All who come in here love it, collapse on the couch, take their hair down and their shoes literally off. We have all suffered for quiet and privacy. When we get it, we let go the whole way. I lie here for hours doing nothing, just recuperating. *It feels like disintegrating, to come together again.* It is odd to watch it happen to others, even the tough ones. The home touch, warmth and color, melt them at once.

Father Sheridan came for coffee and a long chat on the past of our camp. He is organizing Beautification Week for the Catacombs, as he calls the Underground. He plans to have the Japanese staff visit to see how much we have done with nothing.

New word for looting, "He's a good accumulator." One also speaks of whether a person wishes to be Cubicle-ized or not.

May 20, 1944. Jim saw Marie Outside and told her to go ahead on selling clothes for us. Tonight Bea tells us that she has sold things and will send money in soon.

Peg and Walter and Carl came for coffee and talk in the dugout. Then we went to the program, with Walter Neal speaking on Mexico, and an amusing drama skit, with Blackie, Johnnie and Carol as three cowboys singing ranch songs. They were so good that the children stamped, whistled, banged and begged for more. Bedie was homesick afterward. He says the dugout is better but not enough. The songs made him think of Nida and Ismael who used to sing Kay Yippy Yippy. He wept on my shoulder.

Sevastopol fell five days ago.[23]

May 21, 1944. John Rasmussen, hearing we were out of money, asked Jerry if he could use P20 which Jerry clutched like a drowning man. He was able to buy a dozen eggs, bananas for our yeast, and some tomatoes. It was sweet of the old soldier to tide us over. One does not ask for loans in these times when many are at bedrock.

May 22, 1944. I went to answer the three questions at the office where I received over P200 in Marie's name. It is the felt and taffeta which will feed us eggs. We repaid John first.

"By Order of the Command, no more outdoor shacks of any kind are to be constructed within the camp as of today." This applies to Will's cave which has been tamped down with great labor, but cannot be used. Mr. Tomibe says the digging will undermine and wash away the bank, that the outdoor shacks will be destroyed by steady rains and winds and that furthermore they look like beggars' shacks and he does not care for them. Of course, the shacks also overlook the guards and the view, and the guards cannot see what goes on inside so they do not like them either. The Japanese approve of the Underground homes.

May 23, 1944. We heard early that the Japanese had decided the Family Unit for 22 more who signed up for it could go through—that the men's lower barracks would be cleared for it, with the men moving upstairs, and any family overflow could move into the schoolhouse. This will start howls from below. If the Opposition had not thrown it into the lap of the Japanese it might never have gone this far. Only the Japanese could order it, not the Committee.

The black dog attended roll call, standing stiff and straight in the front row.

May 25, 1944. From the Minutes of May 23. "No word that cannot be found in the dictionary may be used on monthly correspondence cards. . . . The shortage of rice amounted to 731 kilos. The Sergeant promised to supply us with 400 kilos, which would allow the camp to go on half rations for the balance of this month. He was urged to make up the entire shortage and to check weights at the bodega so that this shortage would not occur again. Attention was called to the fact that in spite of decreased rations, rice is still being wasted by some individuals, while others have to be satisfied with small portions. Owing to shortage of waste food for the pigs, members are requested not to throw suitable livestock feed in regular garbage cans, but to put it in special pails or the "pig buckets." All waste garbage in camp is needed for camp livestock. Three camp-raised roosters were recently supplied for use of special and childrens' diets. Six more are available for that purpose. Another pig died, leaving 12 in the camp-owned herd. . . . Food prices have soared so markedly in the past few weeks that the camp store is now attempting to limit stock items to simple staples."

Miss McKim arranged for Mr. Tomibe to tell us in Nippongo the story of the Forty-seven Rōnin in class held in our dugout. I asked Jane to make the ikebana (flower arrangement) on the tokonoma (alcove). She made a lovely one of green pine branches, tall and short, with the lower cluster of red-orange nasturtiums, their round green leaves and rock ferns in Jane's charming, low, oval bowl with turquoise glaze inside, gray outside. It was perfect on the dried palm fronds below the furoshiki with birds, flowers on blue and orange hanging against the runo wall which is very Japanese. Ten of us crowded into the little space. I sat in the doorway. Mr. Tomibe was late for he would not come without his bath. He looked very spick and span indeed. I had finally memorized a greeting of "Kon ban wa. Irasshaimase! Ohairi kudasai!" (Good evening. You are welcome. Please come in.) I forgot all the "dōzo" (please) in between which is politeness in greasing the wheels, but it did not matter. Jerry said I should pass American cigarettes to him so I had some Camels ready and Miss McKim's second phrase ready, "Tabaco—ikaga desu ka?" (Do you wish tobacco?) Mr. Tomibe looked much surprised, smiled, bowed, and took a cigarette from the package. Then I passed the matches. We gave him the seat of honor with his back against the tokonoma, Miss McKim sitting next to him as translator. He spoke of the pleasure and honor it was to come, then gave a brief description of the setting for the story which was 240 years ago with the rich, picturesque costumes of the men in those days.

After he finished, he turned around to look closely at the bamboo wall construction, the decorations, the flower arrangement. He said that most of the furoshikis were used for special occasions—the one with a character in red would be a wrapping for a bride present. I said I had not known the character then, had bought it because I liked the color. He pronounced it all "Nihon rashii" (like Japan), a very nice "home" indeed. I wonder what he really thought at seeing furoshikis used for wall hangings for the first time. Did it shock him a little, or merely give pleasure.

May 27, 1944. The servers are now under fire, accused of being mean because they stick strictly to the ration; Mothers accuse them of starving their children.

Jerry is now Fish Cleaner and is about to go on Dishwashing.

May 30, 1944. We ate our own bucaco with milk and sugar at noon, and that was all for lunch. Camp gave us bread only, no rice. We baked camotes for supper and put half a can of corned beef in soup. We had the first half for breakfast. Jerry keeps his yeast alive on sugar.

With Japanese Army food, Red Cross Relief Fund and our own cash feeding us, we still starve due to inflation, no confidence in currency, scarcity, and hoarding what is available. Higher and higher go prices. Eggs are really golden.

May 31, 1944. A letter from the Internment Camp Committee to the Bunshiyocho on May 31: "Dear Sir, on February 14, 1944, we wrote you a letter calling attention to the inadequacy of our daily food allowance. A copy is attached. At that time our medical authorities stated that the health of our camp would deteriorate if that system of food rationing were followed. Today in consultation with Dr. Shaffer, the head of the Health Department, he emphasized that whereas in February 15% of the camp population was suffering from food deficiency, at the present time over 50% of the camp is suffering from undernourishment or malnutrition, resulting in marked increase in medical treatment for anemia and stomach disorders. You will readily see that the health of the camp is the most serious problem which confronts us. We wish to point out the following: the Red Cross supplies have helped to maintain the health of the camp to the present time. However, these are practically exhausted. [We need] 1. More fresh vegetables. 2. A definite increase in the amount of protein foods such as meat, eggs, beans, peanuts . . . "

Kaito of Taiwan asked today for the masticator. Miss McKim looked very blank, discovered it was the meat grinder he wanted. Someone asked

Kaito why such different questions were asked of camp members and he answered, "Oh, to let Mr. Yamato practice his English."

June 2, 1944. I went to see Bedie move up to 8th grade. One more year, then high school. Sometimes there are only three study books to a class.

Church Scott feels low. He said he couldn't see anything funny about the Japanese anymore, couldn't even laugh over the masticator story. He is so equable, with such balanced humor, that times are bad indeed when he is low. Everyone is hungry all the time. Meals are less and less. No vegetable for my bag for three days, only enough to put in stews for camp. Many are losing their sense of humor and out of funds which should be here. June wakes up ravenous.

Helga hemorrhaged for 20 days, terrible headache, low blood count and is taken to the hospital. But in spite of low morale and hunger the open house under the house was a success. It showed how something can be made from nothing. Some said they had no materials. Well, neither did we, for our neighbors built two of our walls from runo and old tin. For the first time we are in the "smart" class with a smart dugout, cosy and colorful for bridge games and coffee parties, if one is able to hold them. We have arrived, in practically the last word in Concentration style, with artistic den or studio or whatever Bohemia wants to call it. A Shangri-la in the earth literally! It saved my health and sanity that first week, smart or not.

Meanwhile the Japanese turn nasty. They had heard the children call them Japs and complained to Carl. Now the Chef, asked where some supplies came from, replies that the Japs brought it in. He is overheard by the buyer and reported. It grows into a major incident. The Chef is called to the guardhouse, given a tongue lashing, nearly half a day tries to explain it is a slang term, but to no avail. He is threatened with three days in the jail room at guardhouse (two or three recently built), finally made to write an apology. The Committee was called to a meeting about it and about our attitude of fading out when a General comes, etc. They complain that we don't like them. What do they expect after poor treatment. Denki told them bluntly that as we grow more hungry and tired, ill and nervous, we would grow more disagreeable, blame them, blame the Committee, for no food, no housing etc. Evidently the General gave *them* a raking over and being nervy and jittery anyway they pass it on to us as they have done before. This happens to all people.

June 3, 1944. Sign on the Board: "Since the term 'Jap' is considered an insult, the Command requests that in conversation when you refer to the Japanese the term 'Japanese' and not 'Jap' be used."

The Safety Committee is doing a good job. They have put up a large iron bar with a gong-ringer above it, hung out in front where even a woman can reach it in the night in case of fire. They plan to gather the small boys into a Junior Safety Committee to see that the littlest boys don't get into danger spots.

Tomibe thinks as long as we cut our own wood we can have hot plates, which we ourselves supply. He is between the devil and the deep sea, with the Committee and General. The Japanese want to make us feel what their country is going through in blockade, privation, etc. Miss McKim remarked during the long session that she often said good morning to them and received no answer at the office, whereupon Tomibe lit into all his staff about rudeness. He put it down on the line that there must always be politeness. Saito could see the point about the "Jap" being an abbreviation but Tomibe was very tense, oppressively silent in long spells, refusing to admit that it was anything but an insult.

The evening show was a huge success. It was "Cabin in the Pines" with Cleo and Jo stealing the show as Mammy and Pappy. The scenic effects of the kitchen were perfect, with the men's old stove covered with pots stirred by Cleo. The second scene of a Broadway tryout of voices showed Cam as Carmen Miranda, Harry as a flashy promoter of various girl singers. It was the Hillbillies who really brought down the house. The crowd roared, had the best laugh of the year, which was much needed. Five high school boys in short skirts, band-waists which they held their breath to keep on, flashy necklaces and bracelets, waving colored handkerchiefs, switching hips, skirts and shoulders, were a riot.

June 4, 1944. We have 2 eggs apiece these days, while we have the cash and they can be bought. We are storing up internally.

June and I were sitting on a bench taking sun bath when along came Bunshiyocho Tomibe, as he likes to be called. He came up from the hospital with Saito san, passing us. I said, "Ohayō gozaimasu" (Good morning) to which he bowed and replied, "Ikaga desu ka?" (How are you?) I answered, "Genki desu, arigatō gozaimasu" (well, thank you). He said something which I did not catch and Saito pointed to the sky. Finally I caught that it was sun-bath and said, "Hai" (yes). He bowed as he did at each gozaimasu, for politeness always delights the Japanese especially when it is their own variety, which they understand. Then they beam. He turned to June and I told him "musume" (daughter). He looked at her, then back at me, then her again and exploded with, "Sa! Sō desu ka!" He asked, "Ikutsu desu ka?" I thought he was asking her age but I guess he wanted to know how many children I had. However, I broke down into English. Suddenly he raised his head, tense, asking in a clipped voice, "What are those children calling out over there?" We watched a line of them tramping along waving one arm up and down, shouting what sounded like "chop, chop, chop" to me. They were very young ones and I explained they were playing a game called "Follow the Leader" where the first one raised his arm and everyone else did the same; leader climbed a small hill, every one followed. He seemed to understand and calmed down at once. It was not until later that I realized he probably thought they were saying, "Jap, Jap, Jap." We were on the verge of an international incident! It appears that the Sunday School teacher, in dramatizing Ruth and Naomi, had given the children small cardboard scythes with which they were going "chop, chop, chop." Carlos, our Italian, says all Americans use nicknames, never full titles and he hates it—being a Wop or a Dago. Anyhow, I like the Bunshiyocho. He is a fine person and I never think of him as Japanese or myself as American when we speak to each other.

At the end of camp there is a mud-ball battle between small boys. Three months of vacation and the boys are tearing all over the place, yelling, taking prisoners and tying them up—as though being captured were not enough. What instincts we have for imprisoning one another—even at the age of five!

After lunch my name was on the Board. At the office I received P200 from the gold "blob," and P480 from N. Baloli which is Marie—or is it Nida again? Twice they have saved us from despair. We have now about 800 on hand, enough for two months.

June 6, 1944. We had rice three times today, and for supper camote, and coconut milk gravy. And that is all. We each had a fried egg for breakfast, and one for lunch, thanks to shoe sale. We fried tomato, peppers and onions for a sauce with our rice.

Rumor hath it that the *Tribune* says Nimitz says that our new major offensive front line is New Guinea-Palau. We have received no papers at all, though they come to Baguio.

June 8, 1944. Most conversation now is exchange of symptoms and cures for deficiencies. The phase of emergency packs is long past.

June 10, 1944. We watched the dancing. I had one waltz with Jerry and he danced many with his daughter who is learning fast and adores dance-night. Bedie learns fast but painfully. He wore his long trousers made to fit his welfare coat, and plugged away at dancing. He finally took the plunge and asked Eloise for two dances, which grew to four by morning in his estimation.

June 11, 1944. Ten of us including our two families and Carl filled our dugout, eating until we couldn't sit up, to celebrate June's 15th birthday, with Peg's wonderful cooking and Crouter contributions.

At roll call Bernie whispered to me, "If you hear any good news I think you can believe it this time." Later I heard of a Cherbourg landing of our forces. The New Guinea advance is carrying them 400 miles ahead. Still later we heard the *Tribune* of June 7 had admitted landings all the way from Le

Havre to Cherbourg. At last, at last, the invasion of France from England—so many times rumored too soon.[24]

June 12, 1944. Jerry talked to Dr. Mather and they discussed feeding me Red Cross meat, with liver shots. If I eat so much of the canned meat, Dr. Mather asked how about the rest of the family if the pinch finally comes and Jerry replied that we would just have to take a chance. He said Pete needs to get that blood count up. I argued with him at breakfast, finally compromised on a two weeks trial, not a month. Two ounces a day for two weeks would use three cans. Later I talked to the doctor and told him we were having a big argument over it. He laughed and said he knew I would have something to say about it. Jerry and I sat over coffee in the sun and argued some more. I maintain that I have lived over half my life and the children need the meat to carry on the torch for us. He growled and scolded me. I told him it was settled at two weeks and he said it was nothing of the sort and that he was the best judge and it was going to be his way. Back and forth we went. We will be glad to have the Army come in and settle the race with time against anemia. These basic, ethical decisions are difficult and desperate, now. It is more difficult to fight one's own battles than those of another. I have given the children about all I can to help guide them. Their formative years are nearly over, at least the basic ones, though growth should never stop. They have learned about life, people and working together in here in two and a half years which they would not have learned in college or in easier, softer conditions, and I shall love watching them use it if I come through.

June 14, 1944. The great pork graft is really the major topic. Schultz, who used to get kitchen squeeze but is now out on account of illness, squealed that the kitchen staff got 8 or 9 fat juicy pork chops *the day after* we all had pork. Carl went on a tour of investigation and found several still warming in the oven. Henri had picked out 8 or 9 of the biggest and best, passed them to the Chef to cook and divide among the elect. It all happened just in time to be presented to Committee Meeting. The pork was worth P2100 at present prices—the stolen chops worth about 65 or 70 pesos. As Jerry says, it has reached the point now where a man might get killed over a pork chop.

No newspapers will be allowed to enter camp. "We are not to be concerned with social occurrences outside," Mr. Yamato said. He feels that we can lead a more peaceful life by ourselves. He again stated that he wishes this to be "an exemplary camp."

The *Tribune* tells of landings all along Brittany—40 thousand by sea, 60 thousand by paratroops and gliders after them. Previous to this, 11 thousand planes bombarded. The sea was rough holding up landings which were finally sent by air. Transport planes landed tanks and a big tank battle was in progress. The first phase was completed, the second about to begin. Gen.

Dwight Eisenhower was in command *on French soil,* Rommel commanding Germans on French soil. The two great antagonists meet again, after Africa. Rome declared an Open City and evacuated "to spare its art treasures," according to the *Tribune.* The front is now 40 miles north in Italy.

Father Gowan was asked to attend the meeting on June 13 to explain to the General Committee his reasons for wishing to retain the grade school building. Following is a summary of his statement: In the high school there are 25 classes comprising 15 regular and 3 graduate students. Elementary school is divided into two sections. The upper grades meet in the grade school building. In the lower section the classes are held inside and outside of grade school building, in hospital arbor, in nipa shack, in dining room and on veranda. Some of the grades are so large that they had to be divided into 2 sections, making a total of 14 classes in the elementary school. This does not include the preprimer and kindergarten classes which meet wherever they can find room. Father Gowan called attention to the difficulties under which the school had worked from the beginning of internment, the necessity because of students' widely varying backgrounds and educational training, for makeup courses in order to meet college entrance requirements. They have endeavored to keep the graduate students who hope to go on to college in academic training. Reorganization of adult classes, discontinued in many cases because of inadequate space, was advised as a stimulating interest to the adult group in camp. Aside from these special educational considerations, the need concerns some 90 students, not including the kindergarten. Father Gowan pointed out the difficulties that would occur if the new school building were used for several purposes. Lab work should be done over weekends to make up for the work which has been lost in recent months. Religious services would be interrupted if students were passing back and forth. If the rooms are to be used for religious purposes, partitions, desks, tables, etc., would have to be moved daily. . . . In addition to the school's need for the building, it was pointed out that during the rainy season last year, supervized play for the children was arranged in the grade school building. . . . Father Gowan said that at the end of this term the teachers were worn out because of the undesirable conditions under which they have been forced to work. The teachers have had to maintain discipline and interest from their own nervous strength and intellectual resources. He said that he had been assured two months ago that members of the Committee were very definitely opposed to the plan of using the grade school building for other purposes, and he felt that the situation had not changed. The standards should be maintained in order that the children shall not lose by these years of confinement.

Denki stated that he felt the first problem that confronted the camp was food, and the second was living conditions. It was his opinion that it was a great deal more important to the camp to try to relieve the crowded conditions by making use of the facilities we have with the new school building and using the grade school building for family living quarters. Dr. Skerl suggested that the rooms in the new high school building might be divided to make room for the classes. Denki made a motion that in order to help relieve the crowded conditions in the barracks, the grade school building be used for Family Units when the new school building is turned over to us, and is ready for occupancy. Carried. Five members voted in favor of the motion, Miss McKim, Dr. Skerl, Gowan, and Art casting opposing votes.

We have that terribly cut-off feeling again. It is horrible until one gets used to it. No wife can write to or hear from a husband at Cabanatuan or Hong Kong prison camp. No Chairman can contact another Chairman. No problems or needs can be exchanged or met. But we hope it means nearness to the end.

June 15, 1944. A *Tribune* comes in now and then, no one knows how. The Chinese cook for the Japanese staff had one on his head when he carried sheet iron to the shop. The guard grabbed it and tore off the front sheet quickly before our men could see it. The Chinese said he was using it to measure by. One guard who is beginning to think for himself says they don't get enough to eat. He says that before this they could pound the posts in fast, now they go very slow and are tired. They and we get less and less, tired all the time. He said more about maybe we would win and be out in a year. If he was wounded, he would get paid P24 and go home, no food for him or family. If he dies his family get only a little. There is little to look forward to, no way to turn.

Without Jerry's constant thought and effort, I would never have survived by my own strength which has worn slowly down, nor am I practical enough. It takes combinations of all sorts to survive this situation.

June 16, 1944. Supplies and clothing received from the Neutral Welfare Committee of the International Y: Peanuts, soap, coffee, tea, sugar, salt, cigars, margarine, powdered milk, 6 tampipis of used clothing, 5 pair of bakia and a box of sewing materials for Welfare Committee action. The sewing materials were divided by "drawing" number and choice in order of this among women. Men's coats the same way among men.

June 17, 1944. At 10 A.M. the new school building was dedicated, turned over to the Committee, students and teachers by the Commandant and his staff.

Mr. Tomibe in uniform made a brief speech translated by Miss McKim, presenting the new building in which he hoped we would find a little happiness though it lacked perfection due to difficulty of supply and other obstacles. Carl accepted the building in the name of all who will use it, thanked the Command (after thanking the Imperial Army), expressed appreciation of the difficulties and problems of getting the materials together in times like these, most of all appreciating the cooperation of British and Americans who had started the building with the Command's consent, followed by the Japanese contractors and Filipino laborers who put up the sides and roof and finished the edifice. (His unwritten speech could have described American foundations strong and well laid, but with every other joist removed by the contractor as soon as the Army came in on it, the walls and roof becoming weaker as they reached upward, with possibility of its being blown away by the first typhoon, the edifice returning to the foundation laid by the Americans.) However, Mr. Tomibe did the best he could for us against great odds, opposition, and [poor] transport.

At the evening entertainment Mr. Suda asked for the front row of the audience to move back, clearing a wide space for his three acts of sword dances. Mr. Yamato read a description of the first two in English which we all found difficult due to his accent. One of the staff sang in a strong Oriental manner while the last two acts were performed. Dressed in short, old-style skirt and blouse effect, with a wide band around his hair and Mr. Tomibe's precious sword in hand, Mr. Suda became transformed into a dramatic actor, stamping his feet, uttering strong strange cries, with gleaming eyes and tightened muscles and strained features. He leaped about, flashing and thrusting his sword in every direction including into the audience. This was too much for some of the small children. Susan wailed first, then clambered over benches headed for home-space and mother. Several others whimpered and followed, with more during the second act. The majority stayed looking

dubious but with curiosity winning out. Miss McKim translated the third, about the warrior who was tired, seeing a big snake crawl before him, thrusting his sword in to kill—only to find it the shadow of a pine branch! Mr. Suda's new role has added to his stature, invested him with theatrical glamor.

June 18, 1944. The kitchen has been investigated. Times are hard. We are back to the hungry days of Camp Hay with the same group doing the same grab. We want them out, completely out is the cry.

June 19, 1944. The kitchen staff special group had a meeting today and demand that police put guards on kitchen doors to keep people out! The same old answer—cut down the number who get special privilege, make it more select and don't let people see. Right now this is the wrong answer. A howl of derision goes up from us mob!

Bedie will never forget what it is like to be hungry, not to have enough day after day, as we all plan together to stretch out the Red Cross supplies and what we are able to buy. He weeps over a bad potato. Coconut milk is too rich, beans are too gas-producing and peanuts he doesn't chew enough. All these upset him in any quantity and he doesn't like fish which makes his diet difficult.

June 20, 1944. From Ashford's "Soldier in Science": "Pre-sprue is a *condition,* not a disease. . . . People who ate excessive quantities of foods destined only to be burned up as fuel for the machine and who secured an insufficient amount of those fragments of protein necessary to build into the tiny elements that replace worn out vital organs, were people who soon showed their organic deficiencies in function: indigestion came about, loss in weight; there followed an *excessively acid reaction inimical to health and irritating to the mucous membranes.* Hence the sore tongue, the sore rectum, the burning in the pit of the stomach. . . . Sprue is essentially a *wasting* disease."

June 21, 1944. Miss McKim says she is sorry for Mr. Yamato. He is so homesick that he is ill, his hair going white and he has beriberi. Tomibe asked if she didn't feel sorry for him too and for Mr. Saito. Both would like to see their families. But she answered Tomibe, "No, you can take it." And he can, for he is direct, adaptable, as the other serious little man is not.

What relief to know that Nida, alone with her two small children, needing help, had contacted Marie who could give her cash from my dresses and shoes, returning when she most needed it some of what had been loaned to us so generously when we needed it. What complex interchange of all this help—they stand by and rescue our things, keep them from being looted until Carl has them under his wing. They send us other help and later, from the clothes they saved which we left outside, both of us are supported from the sale through that staunch standby, Marie, who has been a cornerstone in our lives since we came to Baguio almost ten years ago. *We are able to give aid even in prison.*

June 22, 1944. Bedie's early specimen looked bad. We feel despair over prospects of dysentery for him, with no bananas to mash, no eggs to buy and prices soaring in any case. I covered him with a blanket in the dugout and he wept at the thought of salts and starvation diet for three days and staying a week at the hospital. He gets so homesick. It will be his third dysentery. He weeps again when the doctor says to take the mattress down. I gather towels and all the rest together, hunt for Jerry to carry the heavy part. We get two library books and some juice for him to take. He is very forlorn but cheers up when two carnations come from his girl friend and when Jerry reports he will buy potatoes to give him mashed with butter as soon as he can eat. We sent some Y tea along with him. It is discouraging but it might be worse.

The Committee not only leaves the Chef in but condones, backs up his strong-arm requests. The kitchen, like the hospital, goes on forever. There will be mutter and murmur but no action.

June 23, 1944. Sellers are afraid to come into town with veg and fruits and the Japanese blame it on the guerrillas.

June 27, 1944. The Episcopalians give 10% of any group sum that comes in to people who have no money and need it.

Jerry, June and I weighed. He was 212 and is now 184. June was 75 and is now 103. I was 98 and am now 92.

June 28, 1944. The big news is all over the place. Paris and Warsaw are rumored taken and another European landing talked about.[25] Miss McKim asked Tomibe why more people couldn't go to the hospital in town. He threw out his arms and said, "But you don't know what it's like Outside!" (then very quickly) "I didn't say that. It is nothing!"

June 29, 1944. Committee Report: "Dr. Shaffer reported the most severe dysentery epidemic in 9 months and explained the difficulties of treating these cases with the shortage of nourishing food. As a precautionary measure the serving of raw veg through the kitchen will be discontinued. Dr. Mather is formulating plans for recording physical exams data in connection with a cross-section health report of 10% of camp members. . . . Parents are requested to keep children quiet morning and afternoon when first-aid classes are being held. At times the noise has made it impossible for those who attend the classes to hear what the instructor is saying."

June 30, 1944. I typed a card to Mums, saying "Had to quit Work Details, resting which don't enjoy as you know, Mums. Jerry keeps busy, children school, rains beginning. 4 loves to 3 families." I underlined *poor* as to health. So much for the 25 words allowed.

Tomibe will not make any announcement about it yet, not until Monday or Tuesday he tells the Chairman. But he says it is his idea of the Family Unit Plan which he is taking into his own hands because there has been so much fuss and trouble over it.

July 1, 1944. Four, then six, planes roared over us. Two then one, then three pursuits. Seven more bombers went over the coast, four came back. All going north. By noon 36 had passed by. Excitement.

Arthur was upset over his trip to town because trees have been cut everywhere, even the mighty ones in Forbes Park stacked for firewood. What does he expect—there is no big company cutting and bringing it in from selected far districts because of no transportation. In fact there is no other fuel to heat food except wood. The war will set the Philippines back years in more ways than this one. He says Session Road is dirty, unpainted, neglected—just waiting, for 2½ years. The present administration takes, not gives. Houses everywhere are minus tin roof, plumbing and electric wiring. Stevenson house had been already stripped of all this and they completed the demolishing. The apitong [hardwood] floors go to the administrative building addition, we get the pine slabs. Truckloads have come in all day with material and more rice.

Dr. Skerl talked on mountaineering and his ascent of the Matterhorn from Zermatt with a guide, down the Italian side and around by glaciers back to Zermatt again. It was thrilling to hear about it. He told all the elements of scaling heights, his manner of understatement and modesty very appealing in such a talk.

July 2, 1944. Bob D. told Bedie he was released to go home. Bedie shot out the door and up the hill in his pajamas, not even a coat. He now *loves* fish!

From the *News:* "Dentist report for June: 25 days in office, total 98 hours. Treating 210 patients or nearly half camp population. 139 fillings, 45 treatments, 33 extractions, 28 exams, 9 X-rays and 18 miscellaneous jobs." At last he has begun to make up for the past year.

We talked about war, and the future. No one felt real bitterness of the Japanese, except for those responsible for the horrible treatment after Bataan and at the prison camps. The deliberate neglect and starvation must be accounted for by those responsible.

Saipan is ours, also Cherbourg and a hundred mile line around it.

July 4, 1944. Our men laid off work, allowed to celebrate the holiday of July 4th, putting the extra energy into a ball game.

July 5, 1944. Tomibe is leaving. At Japanese class we learn that both new men are lieutenants, Oura and Isshikawa. The Command is 42, releasing Tomibe who is younger, for battle. Tomibe is glad to go on active service for this has been "muzukashii" (difficult)! Almost everyone likes him, feels sorry that his equable regime is at an end. Many have said, "Here's wishing him luck." At the last both he and Nakamura gave us something—the latter, Mrs. Quezon's wardrobe "clothes for the women" and Tomibe, housing for school and Family Unit. My first feeling of real regret at his leaving, for he has been very just, was mixed with relief that now nothing would happen to him here where we would see all the horror of it on him who had tried to be fair to us. We will not have to see heroic hara-kiri by himself or a savage, slashing revenge by primitive mountain people who have many reasons for hate for the invaders. Tomibe has done great service for his country, though his small-minded, narrow and prejudiced countrymen will never appreciate it. There have been only a few like him who have imagination, comprehension of other people's difficulties, understanding of general problems. He is a good interpreter, a fine ambassador for Japan and if 500 of us have sympathy and liking left for his land and his people, it is because of Tomibe's qualities which he translated into effort and action. He too has learned from us. I hope he is spared to do much for Japan's future. They seem to be taking the retired younger men, sending the older ones into noncombat positions like this. It is said that Sugano, the new sergeant, hates all Americans and does not hide it in word or action.

July 6, 1944. Nothing very eventful until we were called by bell at three to be introduced to Lt. Oura. Many were asleep, had to dress in a rush and go without makeup! The men went to the schoolhouse, the women to the dining room. During his talk to the men, six planes roared over *very* high and with a new *sound,* in a new diamond-shape formation. Or as one man said, "The double V," which was recently begun by the U.S. and is not used by the Japanese so far as we know. It was a sight and a sound and for once we felt it might really be ours.

News account of the Oura talk is brief, probably taken from Miss McKim's interpretation. "The substance of Lt. Oura's remarks was that he knew that before the war we were living more comfortably than at present, but because of the present war we were in internment camp. 'Two days ago,' he said, 'I visited the camp in Manila.' He believes that internees there receive as much food as the people of Japan. The Philippine Islands having been a colony did not produce all its needs. It will be necessary to work in order to produce food. He deplored the recent escape of two members of camp and said he hoped no more of us would attempt to escape because such actions would result in further restrictions in our lives."

The new high school was occupied by classes on June 26.

July 7, 1944. There is still no offer to fill the mop and can job. It takes three to do what I worked at alone for two years. The job has been split into 2 on the porch, 1 to fill cans, 1 to clean and hang mops. It was a good job while I could carry it. I've done the whole porch in one swoop on several occasions.

Miss Spencer tells me adorable stories about the two small boys in her cottage while we wash dishes side by side. Robert, grandson of the Admiral, tells his mother, "When I grow up I will stand in store line for you!" He and Derek discuss continually what Work Detail they will join when they grow up. One favors the garbage wagon, another the wrecking crew, another the carpenter or shoe shop. But the point is they are going to join, they *want* to! None of these tasks are looked down upon by their young eyes. Robert tells his mother, "When I get bigger you will have to get me a larger bed so I can move over to the men's side." This endless future in here—he accepts it. There is no hurt pride, no looking back or forward, because he has no comparison.

July 8, 1944. All the guards are dead tired. They have long hours of work and guarding, little sleep, little food. They doze a good deal. On the wrecking detail, our men wake them when they hear a truck coming so that no one will be caught dozing. One even left his gun behind and Johnnie noticed, stopped the car and made him run back for it. It was a narrow escape for the guard and he was grateful.

July 9, 1944. Jerry added a wide board to our bed yesterday and it makes a great difference in sleeping.

Dr. Skerl says it isn't house or space that people hang on to, but the facilities—the stove, icebox, convenient toilet (with no long walk to it in rain or sickness).

July 10, 1944. I washed clothes in the morning and rested all afternoon. Rice and tea for breakfast, rice and cucumber for lunch—What a life. Beans for supper with sautéed cabbage. I can't get my mind off vegetables.

July 11, 1944. The *News* says, "There are a few new buildings and somewhat less crowding; food is less, prices more; clothes, except for the Red Cross, more worn out. Otherwise, few changes as time drags its weary way."

"All available land within our camp grounds must eventually be placed under *cultivation* in an effort to produce an increased share of our food supply," the new Command, Lt. Oura, told three of our members at a conference on garden problems. Every available person must share in this effort, he emphasized. A supply of cucumbers, pechay, and Swiss chard seed is on hand to be used when proper season arrives. A quantity of onion seed is being tested and will be used if germination takes place.

Tomibe had given his okay to move into the grade school and 8 couples were helping to put up supports and suwali [woven bamboo] for partitions. Added to this was the astounding rumor that Russia, Spain and Portugal had declared war on Japan.[26] If a big group of internees [should] come in, this is why Tomibe wanted to get Family Units into the schoolhouse before too late.

July 12, 1944. I'm not happy these days. My morale is at rock bottom for I can't do any work. The slightest exertion and I'm all in, whether it is laundry or rice picking. It infuriates me. I would give anything to be able to carry those 3 five-gallon cans every morning half full of water. Now there is no incentive. There is no reason to get up in the morning—only rice and tea for breakfast, rice and camotes for lunch. I am restless, irritable, sarcastic, sour, cranky, everything which can be included in a thoroughly nasty disposition, due to rotten diet and a low blood count. Every day is dull and boring because I would sell my soul for a good active day's work. It is loathsome to rest all day, wandering over to new cubicle units to watch other people cut doors, nail beams and suwali walls, while they chatter happily as they plan and execute like busy ants. Beds are either swung from beams or set high on stout stilts to make room for kitchen shelf or parlor underneath. Space is at a premium over there too, but they don't care because they are all together, congenial couples, out of the acid atmosphere of single minds in the Green Barracks. Their morale is soaring. We will probably end up in a cottage full of people who wanted Family Unit with "reservations"—if we move at all. This adds to my vinegar content!

I met small Bobby and Jane each with a can of polliwogs, he saying positively, "Spawn must be icky gooey. If it isn't icky gooey, it's no good."

July 13, 1944. Cocohonee [syrup made from sweetened coconut] for breakfast from camp—the reason for no sugar yesterday. The menu for tonight is rice, lima beans and camotes. Plenty of starch. This noon we had rice and cream of rice soup. So it goes, in a handicapped kitchen.

From Camp Holmes *News*: "Since establishment of the camp hospital in February 1942, [the seven] nurses have worked long hours, often as many as 12 and 14 a day, with few days off. Occasionally (during emergency), other registered nurses among the camp population volunteered to help, but recently, and especially since the establishment of an internee ward at town hospital has necessitated the detailing of at least two nurses for duty there, the need for a trained staff of assistants has been felt. Last month three girls began a course under Mrs. Morrison to fit them for work as Nurses' Aides. They were soon joined by seven more girls. Classes began June 19 and the aides began to work in the hospital a week later. Already they are taking much of the burden of routine care of sick from nurses. Working under the nurses' supervision, the aides will eventually have had most of the work of practical nurses, enabling them to undertake certain types of nursing care within the limitations of their study. At present they meet once a week for conference in which new techniques and methods are explained; work is criticized and questions are asked. The training will have special value to the students if they are requested to attend invalids and sick following their release, or as the first step in learning to be a nurse; besides helping both nurses and patients here and assuring the camp of the presence of a trained group of hospital helpers in event of necessity.''

July 14, 1944. Those moving into Grade School Unit who possessed Underground cubicles have turned the latter over to someone else.

July 15, 1944. Camp has given us a banana each for several days this week. The Japanese only give us rice and some fish, part of which is bad. They do not give us 10% of what they promised in the list the first of the year. They count on Relief Funds and our Red Cross food to feed us and even then do not buy enough with it, because of scarcity. Yet a top Filipino official gives a large party for the assemblymen, attended by Japanese officers and aides. He has made millions out of buying and selling looted goods.

In a quiz program I finally distinguished myself, knowing that the boniest fish to the square inch was shad, that the Pilgrims came before the Puritans and that Washington's wife was the Widow Custis.

July 16, 1944. I found a whole shiny green pepper on the road, probably dropped from the truck. We ate it with relish and doubtless others think we stole it.

July 17, 1944. My blood count is 3,200,000, hemoglobin up from 69 to 75. Iron helps. The doctor says my symptoms are Vitamin C and B-2 deficiency combined. He may give me a course of nicotinic acid. Don Zimmerman is down with dysentary again and there are two more suspects.

July 19, 1944. What must the poor be like outside, without any help from the Japanese on rice or the Red Cross.

July 20, 1944. The hospital and Baby House had a wild night. Many were sick in the latter and the light bulb went out during all the to and fro of emptyings. Dr. Bruce was up for hours and so busy that he did not even hear the frenzy in the hospital. As one says, ''The hospital is all organized except for someone to turn off the heat!'' The drying box scorched and scorched from the electric heat which was left on all day until 10:15 P.M. The sign that it was on was not put up and the one who turned it on forgot it. At that hour, Dr. Shaffer and two others playing chess in the kitchen smelled smoke and rushed into the operating room. The heat had charred through the box, releasing smoke and fanning the smoldering garments. When they opened the drier, the smoke poured forth—and out the windows when they threw the smoking piles of towels and surgical gowns and sterile gauze outside. They say they cannot operate for most of the operating material was ruined. We have not heard who forgot or who is responsible but the nurses and staff were all called together for a very serious talk by Dr. Shaffer.

Letter on the Board: "Office of Internment Committee to Office of Commandant, July 14. Re: Firewood used by the guards. Attention: Mr. Yamato. Dear Sir, May we call your attention to the practice of the guards taking wood from our wood bodega for their use at the soldiers' barracks. They are using wood which we must split at the woodshed and they are taking such quantities that our men cannot keep the supply up to date. We have repeatedly asked you to supply us with ax-handles and saw-oil that our men may have adequate tools with which to work but this request has not been fulfilled. . . . We therefore suggest that the soldiers be asked to cut their own small wood, down at their barracks. The supply of wood that is now down back of the garden can be used for this purpose. You will recall that we agreed several weeks ago that the soldiers could use this supply for their cooking. Yours truly, the Chairman." In pencil was scrawled beneath the typed letter, "Let them do as before. As the soldiers have not time to cut wood. We are going to give you oil (a bottle of gasoline) and you may make ax-handles by yourselves." This is the temper of the times—or is it just Yamato? He has beriberi, homesickness and *Bureaucrat Fever*.

We played bridge with Scotts and finally cheered up a bit. Izzy is panicky. She kept repeating over and over, "They might as well take the children out and shoot them as starve them slowly before our eyes." John Hay has been blown up with gas and not well for weeks.

July 21, 1944. I picked rice. It poured and blew, poured and blew. The third rainy season—which we were sure we would never have in here! And if there is to be a fourth, we will have to take that too, but a number of us won't last until it comes.

The dugout has begun to leak again. Tavie curled herself up there all evening alone, under our blanket, finishing her book and loving the quietness she said. Everyone goes to bed early now, with roll call at 7, and many sleep hours in the daytime. Incentive and energy are lost together. We know how the millions of underfed feel now, the three-fourths of the world population.

There was a rumor that Baguio was all agog today over rumor that Tojo and cabinet had resigned. It sounded authentic.

A shaving stick was sent in to R. Hind as the only thing left of his house in the provinces—nothing but the foundations.

There are no light bulbs.

In Committee, the Finance Officer emphasized that as for food purchase it is definitely not a case now of what we wish to get, but of what is obtainable. Mr. Furuya, the camp buyer, buys what he can find in the market.

All the Minutes tick off the facts and atmosphere of our days, the increasing tension and what it is like when a Yamato or Oura take charge and a good administration passes.

July 22, 1944. Jerry came in with a bamboo frame he had made at the shop to put on the dirt couch but it was far too wide. He stood there looking boyish, with the frame stuck halfway and no place to put it. I suppose I won't be able to use the place for two days while he digs out more dirt. Yesterday it was a "sump" he was digging to hold the leak. Then it was patching the wind holes. He is insatiable, but happy in working. At supper he and the children were talking about the bamboo frame and at the remembrance of his face I began to laugh. We all laughed till we rocked. It did us all good. Jerry says he hasn't heard me laugh like that for years.

Emil received a letter from the Elks Club in Seattle telling him he was posted for $15 dues and to please remit at once. Another letter said, "We were so glad to hear you were concentrated." They don't know the half of it!

July 23, 1944. Four couples, including us, surprised Peg and Walter with a housewarming. We took tea with mint, open sandwiches, cookies and pop corn balls. It was a jolly evening, with rain outside, but light, warmth and laughter inside. We looked at all the handsome coconut shell, pine and bamboo work by Walter and Carl. Then I slept all night, waking only once.

July 24, 1944. It is hard to write as my hands are numb.

Jo Florey brought an armful of camote tops and I boiled them. We had only rice at noon and June made a rice pudding. I am cold and would like to come alive and warm. I am a tottering ancient, weak as a cat after my sponge bath.

Four Nipponese cities being bombed every hour. Osaka a mass of ruins, Nagasaki also.[27]

July 25, 1944. Sugar which was 15¢ before the war is now P8 a pound. Eggs were 40¢ a dozen and are now 21.60 (40 times prewar). Sugar is nearly 100 times.

The last few months I have watched Jerry rubbing his hands and his legs as though to stir the circulation. Now I know why. My own hands ache, are numb and cold. We are all failing slowly. Panic is nearer the surface than it was.

July 26, 1944. Jerry dug more dirt and put a door-frame covered with khaki canvas in the dugout. It is a week I hope not to repeat. Half of it was spent in the dugout with no lights, cold wind blowing, alone for hours, but the quiet and privacy was a boon.

After we had tried to dislodge them for two years, the Japanese have ordered the hospital staff to move out into the new seven-room tin building on the volley court!

Church says of all the small signs indicating nearness of attack, the strongest is the wild flight of currency and tightness of supplies.

July 27, 1944. From Peg's I watched the agitated inspection of the new building by the feminine contingent of the hospital staff. I hear they all turned on Carl because he backed up the Japanese when they first proposed it. When Dr. Shaffer started at once to say there was no room for the town patients at the hospital here, he was immediately told by the Commandant that all the staff would move out before Friday.

Most of the staff resigned (but reconsidered), showing their noble sacrifice was for the comforts and freedom obtained, which, when lopped off, changed the whole picture. Now they will have to put lights out at 10, go to an outside toilet, walk somewhere to bathe, walk to use the icebox, just like the rest of us in dorm life.

Yamato said at roll call tonight that he was very sorry but the other patients were returning and the staff must move out tomorrow. They have been saying "only at the point of a bayonet" and it begins to look as though the Japanese would have to use the point.

Jerry had a conversation with Yamato in the cook house, about Kyoto where he lives, how beautiful it is here; how bad times are outside and how hard it is to see people hungry. He asked how we liked the simple life of Thoreau's *Walden* and Jerry said that the nearest he had got to the birds and wildflowers and quiet nature was when he worked hard cutting trees on the hill. They discussed how America probably had plenty to eat, as it always raised enough for more than home needs and was able to buy Argentine beef. Yamato discussed how unpleasant it is to have beriberi, for he too has it. When he started to leave he acted as though he wanted to shake hands but was afraid of being turned down. Jerry stuck out his huge paw and the little teacher of middle school grabbed it and hung on in a long shake, loath to let go. They are hungry, homesick, lonely, with their own homes being battered at last. Their country is on the down side and they know it down deep.

July 28, 1944. *Executive Committee Notes*: "Dr. Bruce submitted the following figures on basis of the 80% weighed: Average weight loss—9.4%. Average underweight—8.2%. It was agreed that for the present time an attempt would be made to have one meat meal every 8 or 9 days based on a consumption schedule worked out by the kitchen Department. 40 pounds of pork was received yesterday from the Japanese for camp. It was agreed that the next meat butchered for camp would be one of 2 big pigs in order to relieve the acute shortage of pig food. . . . A cloth ration has been received from the Japanese for which we paid P1,328. This consists of 144 men's undershirts of assorted colors; 80 yards of blue shirting material and 500 yards of prints. Motion carried that any of this material not needed for camp and welfare purposes to be sold at cost price to internees. The two cones of thread will be used for camp purposes.''

It is the tenth day since I started nicotinic and what a week. After misery being doubled and trebled, my head has finally cleared, stomach is settled and appetite returned. I feel weak, bleak, but ashore at last. Today they began digging, pounding, renovating next door in the dugout. Camp is no place to be sick for there is no quiet or peace anywhere for long.

A priceless note from Mr. Yamato, ''Oh dear Mr. Chairman and Mr. Denki—In this scientific age of ours we must make things all indistinct, not obscure. The little fences which we have just made yonder is the boundary of the Japanese soldiers and you. They do not go beyond without special

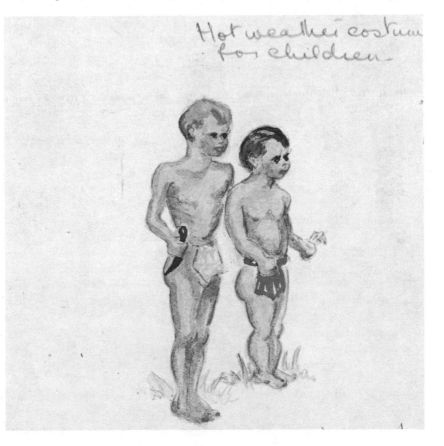

Hot weather costume for children.

business, and you must not cross also. We do not stop the children, but when they played against it and had it broken, please mend it by yourselves. That is the order. S. Yamato."

I feel sorry for the Japanese of the rank and file. They have known hunger and desperate insecurity. For the sadists there is no excuse but many others are caught in the net of economic pressure and the drive for power. As in our camp, very few, if any, can throw the first stone.

July 31, 1944. My onions are growing beautifully in the coconut shells. I feel like starting some lettuce. We had yeast for supper. Jane brings me a few little lettuce leaves every day, a gold mine of green vitamins.

The Japanese have ordered Jo to get more men onto the garden work as the Army is demanding and taking more and more and they cannot give us many vegetables. They give him spinach seed and beans, but it takes six months to grow veg. They only say get on, get on, grow more, labor more, add more men. Jane has given me some lettuce seed and Jerry is making bamboo joints in which to put earth to grow it. Then we can all have two leaves a day. It grows fast.

Jerry comes in looking discouraged. He rubs his hands as though they hurt, sits with his head in his hands, saying nothing. He has heard about no more vegetables but he wasn't going to tell me. He goes to siesta right after lunch and acts all in, both as to strength and morale. He has been denying himself, but trying to keep going.

Are there many additional soldiers in the islands or are they taking the produce to the lowlands to sell at high price? Many here are very depressed but it is low vitality as much as anything for we have never been nearer our hopes than now. No wonder poverty, malnutrition, produce dirt, sores, sickness. There is no energy, only dull minds and slow bodies.

Bedie has brought me some small nasturtium leaves, knowing my hunger for green. He hides them and is almost in tears at finding something for me. I make him promise to pick no more leaves of any kind unless he is sure they belong to no one for they are green gold now and one might be deprived who has raised it and needs it desperately. Every leaf counts in desperate days. Those taste so good chopped into my pâté. Both children are inspired over our bamboo and coconut shell gardens. They bring fresh dirt, plant new sprouts. They have seen a nasturtium in the grass and rush to dig it for our garden. Our days are composed of tiny items like this.

Japanese class again. Miss McKim told delightful stories. Kaito has learned new expressions for his English. "Take it easy" is his favorite and "on the job" and "asleep at the switch" which he just took on from Miss McKim. When asked how things were, Tomibe answered, "Do you know Cervantes? Or better still, Cyrano? Yes? Then you remember his last message to Rosamund—when I died, I died." This evidently applies to his own status about which he is very sad. He was demoted because of the two escapes. He had no fence, no guards, and did all he could in every way, but there were two escapes. He lost face and this is unforgivable. He said, "It is the first time I have ever been told my work was no good."

Miss McKim remonstrated, said we thought him a good administrator, but he shook his head. He says he has nothing to do—an office, a desk, but only to sit at it. At any rate it will not last long for he would be leaving to fight, he hoped. Miss McKim expressed regret and he brightened a little, asking, "Will you sing 'Auld Lang Syne' for me?" (His language has a version to the same tune which a Sergeant long ago wrote on paper while humming it for me.) Miss McKim said, "Of course we will." Cheerfully he rejoined, "And let's all go on a picunicu (picnic)!" Then his face fell—"Oh dear, it is because I say things like that, that the Army says I am no good!" He is educated, a liberal, a misfit in an army group or any group with hidebound minds. He sees ahead, is progressive, imaginative. The Filipinos were against him because he had no time for their parties of dancing and sake drinking. He does not like the type that plays the Japanese game in order to keep in or get preference, dislikes hypocrisy and showed that he did. So he is a lonely wanderer like any of us in any country who feel the same and won't conform.

Miss McKim says that all Committee meetings with Oura are merely nodding and "Yes," while with Tomibe they discussed and worked out problems together. She told him he was missed and how boring were Yes meetings. Next day she was talking with Oura, saying Yes over and over and bowing, when she caught Tomibe's eye watching the pantomime with a wide grin. She was just about to wink when she saw Sakashita observing them and stopped just in time. Miss McKim has a good time with her delightful sense of humor and Tomibe has one too.

August 1, 1944. Jerry brought two lengths of hollow bamboo for lettuce gardens. Bedie's camote vines are sprouting.

The kitchen was full of men chattering over the news that we are each allowed only P50 a month to spend, beginning August 2, effective at once. All other cash is to go on deposit in the Taiwan Bank to be handled by them henceforth. Aside from having no confidence in the bank, it is not a bad idea. There is little to buy; it will equalize buying, putting all on the same level and ending the three-layer cakes. Rumor says 20,000 Marines have landed at Guam.

August 2, 1944. Many small lettuce and onion gardens are dotted about in corners beside a wall, in coconut shell, boxes or bamboo like ours. It is the thing to be a Cubicle Owner now, either directly or indirectly, or to have a close friend who will invite one. Even the rabid Opposition has secret yearnings. Many who signed petitions against, now eat in them. It is amusing to watch the adjustments, shifts, and new combinations of the hospital group.

Mrs. Macy made the classic desperate cry, "But I *must* have privacy, a place to myself!" But we haven't had it and you have! You are still lucky to get a suwali walled room in the tin house instead of the noisy barracks.

August 4, 1944. Minutes: "Following our custom of requesting that certain patients of the doctors and the dentist be allowed to go out to town hospital for treatment or X-ray, we submitted a list of such patients on the 1st of August and the requests were all refused. Mr. Yamato informed us that the order concerning such requests is now that only the most serious emergency cases will be allowed to go to town. Poultry for July showed a total of 298 eggs from camp chickens. We now have 47 hens, 12 roosters, 16 chicks, totalling 75. There are 5 ducklings. . . . The head of Work Details was requested by the Japanese to submit a detailed report showing working time of every man in camp—hours and detail, at the same time classifying the men into various groups, as follows: 148 men; 58% (74) of these fully able-bodied, and under 50; 34 over 50 years old, but doing camp work; 30 men under 50 years old, but incapacitated, and doing some camp work; 10 who are not able to work at all. The Command reviewed the garden project as a whole and was emphatic on the points of more work done and more food raised. He also inspected garden tools, took a list, and said he would try to supplement our supply of both tools and seeds and would try to get some fertilizer. Permission has been given to include the site of the old pig pens for garden. . . . The rice ration for first ten days of August has been reduced to approximately 100 kilos per day—1,114 kilos having been received for a period of 11 days. Camotes, cassava or potatoes may be received to make up the balance of weight ration. There has been an increase in green veg received lately, but until after the 20th of this month there is no hope of receiving any eggs for special diets. . . . The Chair reports that Mr. Hayakawa has donated the two drakes for children's diets. . . . Dr. Bruce is now ready to proceed with physical exams of 10% of camp personnel. Part of the roof of new building on tennis court has been repaired and will be finished soon. . . . The devising of wooden lids for the rice-cooking vessels to provide for better steaming of the hard rice was referred to Utilities."

Jerry is sleeping better with an added blanket but he is hungry and is trying not to show it, denying himself for us. June is all right but Bedie is constantly hungry, has never caught up since dysentery and still weighs 80.

August 5, 1944. Jerry comes in with a grin asking, "Have you heard the latest?" It seems the monitors are going to ask us to list all knives, bolos, scissors, for the Japanese. We may lose our nail files and scissors again and we're getting darn sick of such restrictions.

Lucy's *Hamlet* was a parody superior to *Othello*, which was good. Mary Dyer was the stuff-full-bosomed Queen; Gene a bibulous king with a tin can cut into points for crown and his bathrobe costume stopping the show in order to repair it when it parted showing the bulging pillows which Gene clutched in vain. This brought down not only the house but Lucy who rushed out with pins, and the Queen laughed till she cried. Ruth Zimmerman was a lovely Ophelia, playing the mad scene with a delicate balance of humor and not a little pathos. Jack Vinson in white shirt with ruffled jabot, a round tin shield (cover) tied above his olive drab shorts, and a wooden sword, was Hamlet. Pat was the ghost. Jo Smith was the suave introducer who had to stop them from singing *Othello,* remind and guide them into *Hamlet* again. Even Yamato thought it wonderful, putting his appreciation into writing.

August 6, 1944. Bedie asked his rival to play bridge with him and two girls on Friday. A truce, a truce! They had a good time. June enjoyed bridge too.

August 7, 1944. Poor Bedie is so hungry. I told him to come to me when he couldn't stand it and we would talk but not to ask Daddy for it drives him crazy to be able to do nothing and we just haven't enough to keep giving extras. I told him Daddy was a big man who needed a lot, that he was hungrier than Bedie all the time because he denies himself for us constantly. I suggested that Bedie try to keep busy to forget hunger, but not to run it off. He understood and almost wept but said he would be a soldier. I told him the last few weeks would be the hardest but with planes and a knife list it began to look near so he must tighten his belt another notch.

Yamato's critique is simply priceless. He gave it to Jim to publish in the *News.* "Seeing the Camp *Hamlet* on Sat. Eve. Many years have passed since I was interested in Shakespear's *Hamlet* or Goethe's *Faust.* This eve. (Sat) I had the chance unexpectedly to see Camp *Hamlet*—'the tragedic-comedy *Hamlet.*' I have not yet acquaintance though I must, with those persons who acted the roles or the writer of the opera or the musician. Though I had already some 'ahnung' that it was changed *Hamlet* from the old drama, I went to see it, from curiosity and ennui, with Mr. Smith, the Camp Engineer. And lo! there the *Hamlet* was played! Within such limited dining room with little clothing (except those female persons) and, to make the matters worse, with no curtains or back-scene, it must need the most skillful actors or actresses to play it's performance. And then, it was played well, admiringly well, with profound humor. I like best the Gost's monology, those musical melodies. And when all persons sang together in comical yet mournful chorus, tears involuntarily spread from my eyes. It is 'Humor' in psychological terminology. All persons' roles were performed very well, each actor or actress having individuality and charmingness. The Queen's garments were very beautiful as well as the nice gesture of Ophilia, King's comicality and Hamlet's 'Voice.' It took somewhat longer hours, and it made the play more interesting, and all passed smoothly without a hitch, except the carrying of Ophilia and doctor's treatment. All combined, Camp *Hamlet,* the masterpiece was born. To conclude, you are very artistic, musical, profound in aesthetics and serene in this living. That is what I cannot help admiring you. God bless you! Good night. S. Yamato.''

At a small quiet prayer gathering last night near us we heard supplication for as peaceful a transition as possible, as little violence and bloodshed as possible. Everywhere is the feeling that the time is drawing near. Even the Chinese are saying the Americans will really come *this* August.

August 8, 1944. Derek had everyone agog in the kitchen as he fried four eggs at once, for himself. He said he had been saving them up to eat the whole bunch in a good mess. This is typically male, for Jerry says that one small one is no good. He says if he can't have six he doesn't want any.

Our men feel that something is doing that the Japanese know but we do not know. It may change their attitude. I think, too, that they have found we can take it. They have been told we couldn't—that our soldiers were soft fighters, that our women did no work, in short—we were sissies and parasites. They have seen that it was not all truth. They have fought against our soldiers, have seen the women wash, mop, cut veg, teach and make homes out of nothing. They have seen us all hungry even as they are the last months, yet we carry on without too much rebellion. Experience, suffering, and hunger bring all kinds together in a common understanding. Thinking that they hated us, they have really admired and have wanted the things we have attained. We could get along, adapt to each other under different conditions.

We hear that Denki said to Yamato, ''What really happened was that the U.S. granted an allowance of $50 a month to adults and $25 to children for spending money, so you take *our* own money and give it back to us to spend at the rate of 50 and 25 *pesos* which at the present rate buys almost nothing—isn't that it?'' Yamato answers, ''Maybe, maybe.''

August 9, 1944. *I would like to eat many potato skins with dirt on them.*

Jerry says it is funny that three of us should get B-2 deficiency when he hasn't had it yet. I tell him he has had the other kind, B-1, for longer than we have had ours. I don't talk about a lot of things but I know them. He looked at me and didn't say a word for he had just been examining his swollen ankles, rubbing his aching hands.

June and Bedie were still empty when they finished lunch, though the beef broth was good and sautéed radish better than it sounds with Jerry's pickled onions. What would we do without Jerry's versatility, his constantly sprouting ideas and practical efforts? I can do nothing but conserve the little strength I have, on a dirt couch, reading Durant on all the Chinese philosophers. I am hungry to read radical writings on poverty and hunger and struggle for social betterment through the ages. One forgets appetite and emptiness for awhile in [reading about] the suffering and struggle of others.

We heard that our men objected to mending the guardhouse roof, for they said that was not their ''pidgin.'' Yamato told this to Oura who replied,

"They are prisoners." Yamato said, "But not Military prisoners." Oura retorted, "Did they surrender voluntarily or were they captured?" (A good many did the first.) Yamato mumbled, "Well, they are civilian internees." To which Oura replied, "Are we the Internees or are they the Internees? They will do the roof or perhaps some day when they ask for rice or other things, they may not get it."

August 10, 1944. In Japanese class Helen Mann told a good story of Kaito trying to learn English. He calls on Ray frequently to practice and when he came last night Ray's wife told him that Ray was taking a shower but would soon be back. "Well, I guess I'll park my ass here," said Kaito in his most polite manner and English learned from Ray himself.

Again we hear that all transport, all movement between places has stopped. The attack has begun. But now it is said that Vigan and Cavite were *bombed*. The *Tribune* admits bombings of Yap and Palau, warns the Philippine Islands to be ready for blackouts and bombing at any time.[28] All roads out of Baguio are closed.

Oura revealed that the care of civilian internees costs the Japanese Army twice the sum spent on war prisoners (God help them, say we!).

Continued and persistent stories, even from the Japanese buyer for our store, tell of refugees along the roads coming in to Baguio—whether Nipponese or Filipinos or both and where from or why, there is no telling. The trek seems to have begun again, that restless fear which drives people on, anywhere, to get away from they know not what, going in all directions with bundles of pitiful belongings, as many going to the place that others are leaving.

August 12, 1944. I feel old and wonder if I will ever be able to go to a dance again, twirl about all evening, dancing every dance until two or three A.M. then on to talk somewhere till nearly dawn. I hate this lying about, no strength for anything except a bamboo garden, just holding [on] by the eye teeth, slipping ever so little backward, jerked forward now and then by pills or two ounces of meat. I have no stamina for dancing even one dance with Jerry and no incentive to even dress up for it. I stayed on the dugout couch waiting for the children to come bounding in [from a dance], giggling full of joy over their progress in learning steps.

August 14, 1944. We have *all* found how impossible it is to do real work, good work, on low food, too small wage. Oura says the garden is *the* most vital work and that we are going to have even less than now and be far hungrier.

August 15, 1944. Jerry strained his back again in trying to help the garbage crew move materials up from the court. He crawled into the dugout looking gray in the face and discouraged, wanting hot coffee. I filled a hot water bag for his back, boiled up the bijon with bouillon and fried onions—we'll eat while we can! I haven't scurried around so much in weeks.

The Command has let us come of age and into the secret—that transport has broken down, supplies there are none, soon everything will be impossible. Wood crew and Furuya may not go out, prices have blown wide open and they don't know where to turn or what to do. This should make it perfect for invasion.

From 3 hour Committee Meeting, August 14: "The Command opened the discussion by asking whether we had completed the collection of private money in camp. Upon [it] being requested that we be allowed to hold these funds in the safe instead of depositing them in the Bank of Taiwan, he agreed at least for the time being. The Command stated that food is extremely scarce and that it is now up to us to raise more of our own food. We mentioned the need of more tools. He said first we must get more people out to work the land, then he will secure more implements for us. He pointed out that food will become more scarce and also mentioned that in addition to limiting the spending of private funds we might also be limited in spending community funds. The Commandant: 'Work in the general shop, blacksmith shop and carpenter shop must now be curtailed, not only because of the scarcity of materials but also to make more men available for farming. In the future, permission must be obtained from this office for any work to be carried out, even small repair jobs, etc.' [He] stated that we have too many cooks on our work sheet for the kitchen and that some of these who are not doing heavy work should be released for farming, and be replaced by women; that in his opinion the kitchen department should not employ altogether more than 10 men. He then again emphasized the seriousness of the food shortage in the Philippine Islands, stating that in Manila all supplementary vegetables to rice must be grown by individuals. He said the time is coming when those who do not produce will not be able to eat. We pointed out that a large part of our population are ill and many too old to do farm work. Again we promised to get a larger farming crew on the job. To emphasize the importance of raising our own food, he said that at a later date Mr. Furuya would perhaps be stopped from bringing in supplies. We pointed out that farming would not ease our immediate urgent food problems and suggested the possibility of the American Red Cross making another shipment of supplies to us. The Commandant laughed and said, 'Impossible, there are no exchange ships contemplated; both countries need all available ships for war purposes.' The Commandant next stated that all persons are ordered to work longer hours, stressing again agricultural work and curtailing other types of work. He then ordered that private cooking must be stopped except for the ill and for children, in order to allow more time for people to farm. He then said that the private stoves at the hospital and the women's barracks may continue in operation. He then ordered that we collect all private tools such as hammers, saws etc., allot some for community use and put the balance in the storeroom to be drawn out for private work only by permission of his office. This will also include all farming implements. Only community hot plates may be left in service. . . . Lt. Sakashita mentioned that prices are now getting entirely out of hand. He said that his entire salary would be only enough to buy 3 bananas per day, or one cup of coffee per day.''

The response [to the Command's orders] is instantaneous, wholehearted. Far underneath is fear, anxiety, hope, speculation but no waver of intention to support Carl and the Committee and Commandant. Now that we all face facts and a crisis, the tension has begun to ease. Women have begun to make flour into crackers to stow away for hard times when there is no stove. Bedie helps a crippled Jerry make hardtack. June said she felt a lot older after the meeting. Bless them, they are learning in a hurry the hard way, growing up fast. They will never forget the storm and stress, the hunger and worry over security, with only a hope that the Marines will come in time, which is more than the Nipponese have right now. They can only see defeat and death in all directions. Feeling their black depression which was once ours, I find no hate within me, only a strange sympathy and a recent understanding, a sadness that we all had to meet in the great psychosis of war.

Dr. Shaffer says he has treated all the staff and half the garrison in the last two weeks. They are deficient, have intestinal upsets, beriberi pains, sleeplessness. Yamato asks why and the doctor replies that it is the poor diet, adding "the war has been going on for a long time." Yamato grasps this like someone sinking—yes, it is true, the war has been going on too long. Many are rushing about trying to loan the money coming in to people who haven't had any for months or only a little.

August 16, 1944. During the meeting, Lt. Sakashita kept saying to Yamato in Japanese, "It's no use telling them that if they can't understand the underlying principles, the spirit of it." Yamato tried to convey it in English to us, "You must overturn your brain. You must not forever stand still in the status quo ante!"

When Yamato went to the hospital at 4 A.M. one morning, sick and in pain, someone heard him in the hall moaning in a small weak voice, "Somebody, somebody, please wake up!" He has beriberi and very bad nights. We are all in the same boat at last—hungry, sick and miserable, homesick, and fed up with war. Dr. Skerl said he wanted to tell them they were all scared too but he didn't. Miss McKim says Yamato is really pathetic, he tries so hard to interpret and explain each to the other. They are almost desperate because we do not see how very important it is to work together for our own good in a great Emergency. Of course they have kept us in cotton wool and Yamato told them that we had not been allowed to read the *Tribune* and to know how bad it was.

Tomibe was singing in their fashion one day and Miss McKim said to

Daphne, "Mr. Tomibe always sings at his work!" "What's that?" he asked gruffly, then answered, "Yes, but out of tune." "Oh no," she protested. "But yes, out of tune," he insisted. "With the music or surroundings?" asked she. And he affirmed the latter. "Oh, so am I!" was her quick rejoinder at which they all chortled.

One says it is a scandal that Dr. Shaffer is giving hypos to some of the officers and guards who come to the hospital—he should give only sterile hypos of clear water. This type of thought infuriates me, not only from the humane standpoint, but from the immediate practical once. We are still in their hands, depend for food and life upon them and their whim. If they should get wind of such a thought, they could refuse to give us any more medicines and take away all that we have. While we depend on the Japanese, and are in their power, we certainly cannot turn them away even though supplies are dwindling. Perhaps it won't be long. Another side of the story is Marion, whose husband met death in jail at their hands. She feels sorry for the guards who are sick, hungry, panicky. She wishes she could hide them away in a box and spare them what is ahead.

August 17, 1944. I went to the Sisters' kindergarten and primer classes graduation this morning. There were about 25 children, hair slicked down, in best clothes, with frills and bows; shiny, serious and thrilled. Mr. Yamato was there looking pathetically eager, sitting beside the Command, whose face is very dark because of heavy beard growth. He looks like the peasant type, ponderously serious because of a hard life, with little ease or pleasure in it and many difficulties. He enjoyed the songs and pantomime, the enthusiastic rhythm band which the children are so intense about. The Sister was a program all by herself. She bent low down to conduct, with her habit trailing out behind her in black waves, her hand impatiently pushing it back when it interfered. She had done fine work and the children love it. Heather was all on tiptoe, Aileen wistful and absorbed, in dainty green frills. Oura remarked to Miss McKim that children everywhere are the same, which she took as comparing favorably in his mind with Japanese children. Sakashita was there, amused and smiling, after an inspection of the garden crew digging. Sakashita is solid, husky, with round plump face, rather rosy-cheeked. Miss McKim told Yamato that Sakashita looked so well fed that he seemed hardly the proper person to tell us that we must cut down on food. She certainly tells them, and they take it.

Miss McKim agrees with me that camp feeling or spirit is lacking for we are extremely individualistic.

Skerl remarked that when men found jobs they liked or at which they were clever, they worked well—exactly as in industry. They also like a steady job. What was difficult was finding men to do the odd jobs.

August 18, 1944. Mr. Tomibe said he felt that there are some people in camp who have all the money and all the food, and that those who did not have money did not get their share. By cutting out private cooking, all would share alike. Also by controlling and limiting the spending of money, he felt that all would share alike, and there would be no more "rich" and "poor." He says Lt. Sakashita feels that we spend far too much time on private cooking, and not enough on working for the community.

We received 5 new American-made shovels, 12 Philippine-made shovels, 3 picks and 3 hoes from the Japanese. We have received a supply of news-papers for use as toilet paper.

"The Command has notified the Executive Committee that as long as the entire camp population demonstrates satisfactorily its spirit of cooperation in the garden project we will be permitted to do private cooking. S. Yamato."

It was pleasant to see Tomibe out and around again—part of Miss McKim's diplomacy, bringing him back into the picture, into use and out of the background where he had been thrust in Oriental discipline. This draws him out of his own despondency.

The truck came in with all it could buy at Dagupan market-day—one ton or 31 sacks of corn—P10,000 worth! We will have that for a few days at least. Chicken cost P25 each so they did not buy. Realizing that there is only corn at Dagupan market gives us a graphic picture of the Outside.

I picked 15 minutes rice, the first labor in a couple of months.

August 19, 1944. Rumor news says the Russians are in Warsaw, the U.S. troops have reached Rouen. Goebbels is in charge of Germany due to Hitler and others injured in raids. No more English print news for the Philippines. The *Tribune* is to become defunct. The Japanese tried to retake the big prize Saipan, were caught in a big naval battle and socked, tried to get the remainder of ships back home, were driven south and struck at Davao under a rain of bombs. The Chinese are giving them a licking and Japan is being bombed.[29] Various wild rumors embroidered all this. Some people even packed their bags, the news was considered so hot.

August 20, 1944. The [hospital] patients like the new regime. They say the regular nurses are in evidence very little, only for medication, and the attitude of the aides who do all the work is cheerful, eager, willing and glad to do anything they are asked.

Jerry is going onto garden project and I wonder if he will be able to stand it.

August 21, 1944. Sign on the Board: "The Command has advised us that from time to time, without warning, the soldiers may have rifle practice or other maneuvers around the camp. The internees are not to be alarmed at such maneuvers as they will not in any way interfere with their normal life in the camp. Signed, Executive Committee''

In any case, the long sequence of tea parties, cake parties, is a thing of the past. The recent epidemic of corn-flour cookies is also ended. Due to cooperation on our part, the Command feels relaxed and the General has ordered less severity. He says we are to be treated as civilian, not military, prisoners and must not go hungry.

For the first time a conference was held at the Command's residence. Minutes: ''Carl stated that the spirit of this camp is different from that of the other large camps in that the needs of those who have not had enough have been taken care of by those with plenty. . . . Then he expressed appreciation on behalf of the camp for these informal discussions which promote a better understanding between the camp and the Commandant and his Staff. . . . We then explained to the Command the system of camp elections, pointing out that the present Committee's term of office expires on August 31st, and requested that we be allowed to hold an election for a new Committee. He agreed. . . . [There was] a discussion as to the advisability of marking the hospital roof with a large 'Red Cross' and of marking our living quarters so as to be identified as such from the air. The Command said that there was no objection to this but there was no paint available. There was then a long discussion on possible developments in the Philippines affecting our camp. The Command assured us that every precaution would be taken for our safety and that if at a later date developments were such that the internees would feel more comfortable with some identification from the air, we might display an American flag. . . .'' Sakashita admitted they expect attack, first Mindanao, then Manila, and Baguio will be the last, about Christmastime probably.

While reading in the dugout in the evening, Jerry and I talked of how valuable this experience has been for the children, far more impressive than a life of ease at home without us. Jerry says with a grin that we will have a hold over them when they think they must have certain things—we need only remind them of how little they were able to get along on and without at Camp Holmes. Further, it will give them a feeling and imagination for other people's sufferings and lacks. They will understand slums, poverty, malnutrition with allied sickness and mental states, more than they ever could by reading it. We have no regrets at keeping them with us even though their teeth, eyes, and bones may need a lot of rebuilding. There is no gain without some loss and they have other gains which cannot be taken away from them. So with their parents.

August 22, 1944. Miss McKim asked Kaito just how he thought it would all end and he replied that he did not like to think about it.

Many men in here have an awful series of boils and carbuncles, rashes on the face so they cannot shave. The women are having period troubles, either hemorrhages or terrific cramps that cause fainting spells. There is increasing glandular imbalance.

August 23, 1944. We have a "lovely" Hira Gana chart made with brush for us by Mr. Saito.

August 25, 1944. Camp Holmes *News* says, "Garden work hours on P.M. shift are from 1 to 3:30 . . . 55 broad hoes, 3 spade forks, 3 rakes, and one large plow of carabao-pulled type are to develop land outside camp for us. Seeds are talinum, radish, pechay, green pepper, cucumber. Sakashita inspects the garden every day. All hillsides must be done by hand . . . 1,191 packages of cigarettes (local) at 1.44 per package, 48 pounds of soap and 148 boxes of matches arrived."

There are 300 grams of camote given to those who work on the garden project. This sounds big but it is only one large camote or two at the most. It is a great sight to see the gardeners going out or trailing back in all sorts of disreputable hats or forage caps, old shirts and coats, ragged shorts and varied high and low boots or shoes, with many different types of shovels, picks and forks over the shoulder. The sun won't hurt them, the air and wind are good, and they can exercise according to strength and ability when out in the field. The best part is the joking and camaraderie. I wish I could join them, but I'm only just able to stand on my feet.

After lunch I had chills and internal upset which discouraged me horribly and almost broke my morale but I figured it might be too much underdone hominy and tried to cheer up, for Jerry gets frantic and there is nowhere for him to turn.

We dashed to the office for mail. More than 475 received letters this time, a wider spread than before. Some were as recent as March '44. Some people received five or ten. One snapshot of a modern hat like a flat dish nearly slayed the entire camp. Jerry's hopes [of a letter from his mother] were dashed and I hated to see the depths of his disappointment.

We took our letters[30] up to Izzy's. She had nothing from her family, only a Christmas card from an old friend of her mother's, with delicate handmade pink and blue tatting enclosed, presumably for the "new" baby—John Hay who is now sloshing in and out of mud puddles and gutters. If only they could see him beside this dainty tatting! It brought home to us how long we had been buried Rip Van Winkles, how little they realize our position, our life, our lacks.

August 26, 1944. Orange juice for all for breakfast, and how heavenly it tasted. I wanted to roll in it like catnip. We had a papaya too and a little milk. I had rice crust ground into cereal while the others ate cracked corn and rice which my teeth can't take, nor my insides. It was a good meal though

I could hardly get up for it. Each day it is harder to keep going and one must speak less and less of symptoms for many have more or less, and no one is much interested any more in anyone's. We just think the other fellow is neurotic!

The latest chuckle is that three mission women who were strongly against Family Unit have inherited an Underground cubicle and three of the men who were most vociferous against it are wielding shovels today to dig it deeper. They are all conquered by the idea and there are not nearly enough plots to go round.

The Russian girl visiting in one cubicle calmly explains Communism. In reply to every horror point they brought out, she countered in broken English, "Oh, killing, dat's Russian. My sister she writes it is good now. Instead of ten, maybe twenty, getting things, like before, now thousands get it, ten thousands, everybody. No luxuries, not yet, time not ready—maybe later when necessities are better divided."

August 27, 1944. I woke with diarrhea and then had bad chills, one after another. My hands and upper lip were numb, ears filled and cracking. I crawled into the dugout with my blanket and pillow, unable to eat the poorly cooked rice, feeling as though part of me had stopped working, wanting only to close my eyes and rest forever. The family hovered anxiously, asking questions I was too weak to answer. I lay exhausted in measureless weakness, calm and peaceful as though suspended, not caring about anything, whether they had food to give me or not. Poor Jerry looked sunk with worry but I was too weary to care. I did not go to roll call. Dr. Mather came, asked what I wanted or could suggest. He admitted the Special Diet was not much more than rice, corn and fish, and that what I needed was food they did not have. He said the corn was too rough for my condition. I told him how little I was getting to eat due to fish allergy, that Jerry had only corn flour left and that we had had bananas and papaya but now our limit was reached at the store until September 1st. He shook his head, admitted that many were like this and that nearly everyone had symptoms of one sort or another. He finally left saying if I did not improve I could go to the hospital, and he would try some thiamin in addition to nicotinic, also special diet if I wished. He says, regretfully, that the iron pills from the Red Cross have given out, that Gene will make some ferrous powder next week.

The tripe soup was marvelous and I never dreamed I could eat so much as my appetite is gone. Jerry is sore and desperate, says he doesn't give a damn how he gets the tripe. There is a little for tomorrow and we get beef and fried rice for supper. The menu says, "Onion tops for lunch; onion bottoms for supper."

Rumors jumped from one about Russia being 150 miles from Berlin at noon, to capture of it last night. It is dubious as only Warsaw, 300 miles away, is certain. Paris does seem to be recovered, and to the French this is the symbol of all France.[31]

At times I write a little, read, but mostly I relax, thinking of cherry blossoms outside Mother's window at home, of liquid notes of robins and orioles in the elm trees, of the hectic active days of Indusco work.

Jerry's resourcefulness knows no bounds. He continually pokes into year-books, dictionaries, and all sorts of directions for information and a way out of problems. He never stops talking until someone listens and acts on it.

August 28, 1944. Jerry is cooking his earned camote for tomorrow when the menu says we will have rice and tea for breakfast, rice and onion for lunch, rice only for supper.

I nearly had hysterics watching the garden workers. One man was in ragged rolled-up pants, sloppy white slouch-hat, all-over-face beard, in bare feet which were warily and tenderly wending their way homeward, his shoes and socks in hand. The carabao hadn't pulled a plough for ages and whenever he became tired, which was frequently, he lay down in the furrow and wouldn't go on until he was ready. The plough was a poor one, very difficult to manage, so that Alan and Florey fell into the furrows behind it. The Command, Suda, Hayakawa and other Nipponese tried a hand at it, gave advice from the sidelines about Japanese methods, until Douglas yelled in exasperation "But this isn't Japan. It's the Philippines!" Still they are desperate and the work must go on even if little is gained from it. They are panicky, frantic, over the complete breakdown of supply and distribution in the Islands which no one knows better than they, who see outside what is hidden (partially) from us.

Win says that she and Jo will never be any nearer divorce than right now. She has only a store of camotes to give him extra and he is working on his nerve at terrific tension, with the Japanese behind him. He is in constant conference with them at the guardhouse in his overalls which smell horribly of the compost pits, but he says why should he spare them any of it! It is his job to oversee, check and coordinate all the workers, the planting, the irrigating. When he is dog-tired at night then he has all the work-hour sheets to collect and write up for Sakashita. She says she can't even speak to him he is so driven, irritable and jumpy. He is doing a wonderful job with a very swinging, free stride, head high, but he can't help taking it seriously and is increasingly unable to throw off the tension. And someone has to wash the clothes that smell of compost!

August 29, 1944. Jerry refused to go to garden work, said he was the carabao laying down in the furrow—wasn't going to let an animal be smarter than he. He baked corn bread and we ate it with tea at 10. We had his hard-earned camote boiled, sliced and fried at noon. He was very proud of it, like a first salary. There was only rice from camp but Jerry heated up Scotts' hominy which they won't eat and gave to us. Jane gave me a last bunch of lettuce from her garden.

August 30, 1944. Oura said at a meeting that we could expect to see American planes at any hour now.

Oura simply says there is no more food to be had, that the Army gives us all it can. He says we had many cans from the U.S. (they can't get over this one) and that we are still living too high while people are starving in the lowlands. He is frantic for more garden produce, no matter how temporary and shallow the planting. (It must be ready for the next General *to see* and there must be enough planted to absorb the few rainy weeks left.) (American subs are really around the islands, air bases and carriers are almost ready to attack.) He says he cannot give any more food; that those who cannot stand it will have to go to the hospital and he cannot give patients any other diet either.

August 31, 1944. In the elections we enjoyed Skerl's landslide win. Carl doubled Guiness, making his third win. About 294 voted.

Jim says Jo Smith should have a sign hung on him "First white man to be loved by a carabao." The carabao does seem very attached, trails him about with lumbering affection.

At Japanese class there was much discussion as to whether we smell like Americans any more now that we live on Oriental rather than white man's diet. Helen gave us a laugh by quoting a Filipina who said that white people have an odor like Jacob's Crackers, sort of semisweet. I have heard similar descriptions before. If we do smell different now, it might eliminate some race prejudice!

Jo sprays the carabao with a hose after its work and it is blissful with joy.

60 children will be in the reopened school next week, kindergarten through 4th grade. First grade will meet on the green porch; 2nd, 3d, and 4th in the school building.

September 1, 1944. Executive Meeting: "Carl explained about our former sources of extra food, how more than half of it used to come through the bags, and then when that was stopped people had to depend on the store. The share and share alike would still be accomplished if all were allowed to spend more at the store as everyone has an account. The Command said that it would be impossible to get more food, even by purchasing it through the store, as that would be taking it away from the Japanese Army which is in the Philippines and which must now buy all its food in the Islands. Oura says we have not fundamentally changed our ways—our spirit has not changed. There are still too many people working in the kitchen and the hospital. . . . We asked for his suggestions on the garden project, but he only said, 'You must review your manner of life—must rebuild your manner of life, and put more labor into the farm. You are still very luxurious in your living. If you want more food you will have to work to get it—produce it yourselves.' ''

Bill and Marj came over in the evening to the dugout and talked of their life in the hills. Marj lived five days in the open in a riverbed, alone with three small children, while Bill trekked to the lowlands for food. They told how their mattresses were ripped open by the Japanese and how three different caches of food were found when the Japanese cut the cogon grass in a wide swath, everything laid flat for yards around. The Moules climbed up and down mountains, carrying children and goods, with no food in their stomachs. Once Bill tried to catch a cow and failed. His second attempt succeeded for he roped the horns and cut the jugular vein, waited for the animal to bleed to death. Then he dragged the carcass over ridges and down gulleys, his pockets filled with liver and bloody entrails. He carved the carcass later with a dull bolo, a penknife and the seven-inch blade of another knife. How they ate meat and drank the soup from this kill! Bill was graphic with hunger, breathless climbs and descents, fears, terrors, nights and weeks in the open, sounds of rifle shots, people wailing, soldiers shouting. Many were tortured uselessly for information they did not possess. It was the same in Baguio jail where there was constant weeping, moaning, crying out, yells of pain. He said Jim Halsema passed out after they strung him up and later they found a hole in Jim's sock where the Japanese had held a burning match to see if it was a genuine faint. It was a vivid last evening together in our small Underground before I was to go to the hospital in the morning.

Dr. Mather came to talk with me and said the corner downstairs room was ready for patients. Poor Jerry was sunk and said, "Oh hell, hell, hell." He hates to have me go and has worked so hard to stall it off. He said they would eat in the dining room from now on but I begged him to keep the home nucleus going here. He can't bear to face it there without me but he didn't say so, just said he would try. At least I will get an egg or two now and then, and be there for the daily medical round.

September 2, 1944. Jo is a picture in the garden—his head high, eyes looking far ahead—all giving him a joyous, free look, even if he is dead tired. His patience with the carabao is inexhaustible. The animal turns slowly, casting a rolling eye back hopefully, but Jo shakes the rope a little, signifying, "Go on, pick up that hoof," and reluctantly the beast takes three steps then stops to repeat the process all over.

Saito stood at the door watching the plates of rice as they came from the serving counter. He asked David how many his plate was for and was told three. Saito turned to Tanabe saying, "It is not enough for one."

Jerry asks what assurance we have that the Japanese won't use all our garden effort, as they took our pigs prisoner.

At noon I walked slowly down the steps to the hospital with Jerry and June. It is another little world, a sick world, but with the same rumors.

Explaining what he meant by our failure to adjust our lives to present conditions, Mr. Yamato said that the war has been one of exceptional severity, causing suffering and hardship to people in many parts of the world. When he arrived here from Japan, this camp seemed to him a pleasant mountain resort, but he found the internees complaining. He says we are much better off than Santo Tomas where weather is hot and living space crowded. In Baguio, he said, by way of illustration, many hungry people can be seen around the market these days. The soldiers often get only camotes for breakfast. Now that we have a garden (a privilege which cannot be enjoyed in Japan owing to crowded land) we must strive to raise more of our own food and "and to make our lives serene."

September 4, 1944. Grade school opens today which will tie down Bedie. June has enrolled in third year French and first year Spanish, Geometry, History, English. Father Gowan complimented her on her talent for compositions and appreciation of literature.

September 6, 1944. Dave Foreman has lost an ace of hearts—a sad loss in these times of no more packs of cards.

Bedie came in to see me with slicked hair, full of a safety bulletin about laying flat on the face in case of bombings, not to run out or shout because the guards will be busy and might shoot; not to run out to pick up leaflets and if on parade ground to work toward the first floor of some barracks.

The Japanese Ambassador says the Americans intend to land on Japanese soil but every man, woman and child would kill themselves before permitting it.

Sister came in all aglow with the rumors and we sat beaming at each other, thinking of food, friends and outside contacts. I'm going to put half a bouillon paper in hot water to celebrate.

September 7, 1944. We are all kidding each other about our synapses, the nerve ends that Skerl says don't meet or fit together like the fingers of each hand as they should, because of malnutrition—so we all forget, cannot remember very well.

September 8, 1944. June copies the Minutes for me since I came to the hospital. "The Japanese authorities have repeatedly urged us to refrain from any enthusiastic display if the U.S. planes should fly over the camp. . . . Skerl submitted a summary of hours worked in August: men working, 138; men unable to work 13; women working 138; women unable to work 29. The total working hours of men was an average of 29 hours per man per week; of women the working hours were an average of 12 hours per woman per week."

I listened to Mrs. Baker tell of how she watched the Japanese burn all her chests full of clothes, linen, silver, all of her daughter's wedding things—through binoculars from their hiding place. In this way they saw Igorots tortured for information, homes burned, villages badly treated. Afterward, her daughter found a brass lock and glass handles in the ashes—all that was left.

September 9, 1944. Miss McKim tells of the Committee giving a farewell coffee and cookies party for Tomibe. He is going to be head of Trade and Commerce (former position). They are severe with him over the two escapes. He told them that whenever an American made up his mind to get away, no fence or guards or guns can circumvent it. For this he was severely reprimanded.

September 11, 1944. June came straight from the garden with a muddy rear where the hoe had let her slip twice into the ditch. She looked adorable in a tan short sunsuit, a huge rolled Mexican hat with cord under the chin, borrowed tan gloves to avoid blisters, and black rubber boots, with cheeks flaming under dark hair curling with dampness of perspiration. She was tired and awfully empty. She says she cannot work nearly so well after a lunch of nothing but hominy.

September 13, 1944. The wood crew say that some Filipinos going by grinning, asked *sotto voce* "Why do you work so hard? It won't be long now." Others from the back of a Japanese truck hold their hands out with fingers in V, grinning.

Three cheers for the gardeners—we had our own camp camote tops for lunch.

One small child took all the cookies offered at a party but "saved them for when we are really hungry." Children are playing First Aid.

September 14, 1944. I asked Miss McKim to please say "Auld Lang Syne" to Tomibe San for me and to tell him I will long remember the two evenings when he conveyed to us the spirit of Japan, and that if each person is, in a sense, an ambassador from his native land, then he has done his country a great service in here. In a way it is a relief to have him go before hostilities for guerrilla revenge will make no discrimination, no concession. All Japanese will be alike to them. In Manila he may escape death at the hands of Americans, but not among the mountain people, and I would not want to see it.

Sister tells us that once in a discussion with Miss McKim about the cause and start of the war, Hayakawa said, "We had to strike first or America would have." He was educated in Japan but born in the Philippines. Nakamura who knew Americans from close association in the Philippines, "We had to strike then or never strike at all," knowing that his country had reached a height of strength. The visiting General said, "When Japan strikes, she strikes." Here speaks Japan without outside influences, self-contained in an age-old spirit of conviction and inner belief. It was inevitable growth under present world economics. All three answers are part of the whole reason for war.

Jerry is sorry about two things in our three years—one, that it was the *Japanese* who finally gave us Family Unit and cleared out the hospital to make it what it should be and not ourselves who cleared it up; second, that they had to order us to make a garden for our own good. Both we should have done ourselves willingly, but so many opposed that our Committee couldn't put it across.

Summary of weight reports for Committee: The average adult lost 15.2 pounds compared to prewar weight, as of August 15. The average loss between July 1 and August 15 was 1.3 pounds. There are 144 men and 176 women. Children, including 139 between the ages of 1 and 20, gained .2 pounds in [a] six-week period.

September 15, 1944. I could hear Mr. Tomibe's military bellow voice from here at 7:30 as he made his farewell speech to roll call assembly. He said we had become friends under difficult conditions of war and he hoped that after peace we could be friends again under better conditions. He was now transferred to Manila to another position and must say good-bye. The entire group of Americans spontaneously clapped his speech.

Five pounds of bulk tea has been set aside for the garden crew. Tea will be served them every working day at 10 o'clock.

Skerl was interested to hear about what the yeast did for me. He thinks that several vitamins do their proper work only in a yeast medium.

Health rating for the 10% cross-section, chosen to represent all ages and conditions, shows 6.5% excellent, 56.5% good, 26% fair, 8.7% poor and 2.2% very poor. Noted are "the great preponderance of deficiency diseases among all classes of internees."

The dentist wants any spare false teeth. He is experimenting on replacing a few single missing ones.

Mont is surrounded by a sheet wall, with orderly and nurse in surgical gowns taking all precautions. They don't know what it is. What they fear, they don't say, but it is evidently typhoid. He is a sick man and everything is turned upside down over it.

Without me, the family almost never use the dugout. There is no focal point and Bedie is running wild. June and Jerry scatter in the evening. Jerry is lonely and won't go to the dugout alone. He doesn't even keep up the Scott [bridge] date. He never liked the dugout as much as I did and without me there is no reason to go there. I wish I could go up and gather them all together.

September 16, 1944. Junkins gave me some lettuce leaves. With so much rest I do not get so empty because I do nothing to dissipate strength. My poor family is ravenous, working hard, never filled up, *really* half starved most of the time. I save camote skins filled with rice and the children love it. They say it fills them up.

This is 82% of the cross section of 46 persons recently examined by the camp doctors as a check on group health. Of the 18 women, 19 men and 9 children, 8 had dental caries, 7 were diagnosed as malnutrition, 7 had chronic enterocolitis, 6 had errors of optic refraction, 5 were suffering from nutritional malaise, 4 had avitaminic stomatitis (caused by lack of vitamins), 4 had hypersensitive heart disease, 3 nutritional myalgia, 3 nervous irritability, 3 post-dysentery colitis, 3 allergic rhinitis.

Oura said there must be no more about health in the *News*, for it would make us "cowardly." In truth, it might!

September 17, 1944. Razor blades that are sharp are at a premium.

Miss McKim came down to give me a special message from Tomibe.

She liked my note so much that she read all of it to him and he was terribly pleased and sent his very best wishes and thanks and "o dai ji ni" (please take care of yourself!).

Jim Halsema asked Tomibe to write in his autograph book and Miss McKim told him to make it verse, which he did. It was so fine and so like him. She has promised to send me a copy in Japanese with the translation beside it. She said Tomibe was very sad about leaving and she felt sad herself for he had been very helpful in understanding our many problems. Miss McKim says one never knew what he would do or say next. He was dynamic and very young, with great strength in a powerful build, yet withal charming and attractive, and *so* alert!

September 18, 1944. Oura asked what anemia was, said he was only a farmer, but he had never heard of it in Japan—they didn't have any there.

The Safety Committee advises no more formal dances on Saturday night since Tomibe's departure. So the young people are to retire again for a while.

Mont has paratyphoid. Where did he and the dentist get it? There will be checking of water, flies, etc.

September 19, 1944. June tells me she is trying to make her Dad eat more. She says he fibs and denies himself for them, and two can play at that game. When I tell him this, his face is a study. He was caught cold but smiled, deeply touched.

June doesn't like the dugout any more, says it is shameful that we have to crawl under the house to be together and she hates the people who prevented our being together. Only I made the dugout enjoyable apparently. I liked it and made them like it. Now it is a dead thing, with no life or happiness left in it, and she is being undermined by those in our [barracks] room [who oppose family units].

Loan money[32] is pouring in here and no one wants it. It is worthless when one cannot buy.

September 21, 1944. Jerry came with maps, almost incoherent with excitement and belief, so full of real news he couldn't get it out fast enough; about a big Task Force off Luzon bombing the southern part, perhaps even landing on Polillo, the island off Atimonan. Mindanao and other central southern islands bombed daily. Morotai in the Moluccas was captured in 80 minutes and Gen. MacArthur himself is on it, about to regain his lost islands and prestige, to reach a pinnacle of fame forever.[33]

We are diving into the Saar at Metz, Nancy and Strasbourg; we are 60 miles into Germany in another drive at Aix-la-Chapelle; and north of France (which is *all* free) they have gone *around* the Siegfried line, and still further north in Holland have driven another prong into Germany. All ways at once, as they promised, the same out here. Transport planes land hundreds of tanks and parachute troops in one of the biggest invasions yet, pouring in a flood by land and air. It shouldn't last long now. I was so confused I couldn't grasp it all.

On September 16, London turned on its lights for the first time in five years—no more blackouts.[34]

The wood crew say they heard bombs twice. They report that the Filipinos rushed out into the streets and the Military Police tried to drive them into shelters but they said, "We want to see it. We want to see it."

The choir and other groups are practicing "The Star Spangled Banner" so they will be all brushed up for the Marines and the Army. The secret flag is being shaken out of its folds.

September 22, 1944. About 28 planes went north over the coast and we heard booms. Patients began pouring out of the hospital or leaning out of windows, coats flung over nightgowns. Internees began to troop down the steps and the bank was lined with figures. We heard the planes distinctly, then loud bombs followed by constant staccato of either anti-aircraft or machine gun. It continued for half an hour, with camp exhilarated into chatter, laughter and ecstatic joy. The guards were blowing whistles and wigwagging signals with flags from the ridge above and the staff was popping into its recently dug foxholes. It was a sure-enough raid within clear sound, a roar far more exciting than any movie, on our *1,000th day of internment.*

About 11:15 we heard several big sounds like explosions and every one began to figure it might be the oil tanks at Poro. This conclusion led to the high plane of yesterday which went over in a direct line from there, no doubt after photographing it. All doubts were now dispelled about its being an American plane. Not long after this, smoke was seen by those on the hill, and we could even smell it. The Japanese buyer returned from town, saying "Poro—no more!"

Jerry came at 12 with coffee, muffins and a can of grape jelly. He was gruff, could hardly talk. When we began to sip the brew "strong enough to knock your can off," he finally said, "Whew, what a reaction I had after it was over. I listened calmly, without feeling at all; we could hear it plainly from the garden. Then I decided to come back to see how the bread was getting along and when I saw June coming toward me smiling, I began to go all to pieces inside and wanted to cry like a woman. My knees got all weak and it all seemed wonderful. Whew, how it hit me!" He has been hungry so long, losing ground, working so desperately to keep the three of us going, worried over dwindling supplies, afraid to believe any news, almost hopeless. And suddenly it came, into his own ears, so that he could believe with every inch of him. It was truly wonderful sitting together under the tree, all three of us smiling with hope at last. To anyone else, Jerry pretended he wasn't impressed; he was scoffing and gruff. The relief was so overwhelming he did not dare let go.

At four Tavie was sitting up in bed singing the second verse of "The Star Spangled Banner" for Bedie and I was chiming in, when Bedie put out his hand a little and said, "Sh" softly. Tavie stopped, looked up and shut the book. There stood Yamato in a rain cape in the doorway. We all smiled foolishly and he asked how we were. Tavie bobbed her head and said, "We are getting on very well, thank you." He bowed himself out, telling us to get well.

Ruth Culpepper is teaching "The Star Spangled Banner" to her young class who have never heard it or seen the Stars and Stripes.

September 23, 1944. Jerry brought a marvelous soup he had spent all morning cooking. He had wanted to warm it up in the Green Barracks kitchen but the three in charge said that wasn't for them to do. He answered, "Shall I have June bring it to you?" They took it. He carries wood for that kitchen as our share, does hard garden work and has two children to keep going which none of the three in the kitchen have to worry about. He was furious.

September 25, 1944. After siesta, local news came in that after October 1 there would be no more private cooking. The wood stoves would be taken out. No mention was made of hot plates.

Igorots are stopped on the road, kept from going into Baguio. There is panic as there was three years ago. Filipinos and Americans are cheerful, waiting for freedom and food, but for the enemy it is death. They no doubt picture torture, hunger, all the things they visited upon our men. Some of us would not like to see anything happen to dignified, quiet Mr. Saito, to amusing lanky Kaito who tries so anxiously to learn English and has never done any actual harm to any of us; or to Suda who performed the sword dance; Furuya who has done his best at buying; poor Yamato who strives mightily according to his own lights.

September 26, 1944. At noon, Carl called the whole camp to a meeting. He told them that many had dropped out of garden work, some only going once a week, and we were not keeping up the hoped-for schedule, let alone any added hours. He pleaded with every individual to do his share—not those who were sick and not enough to make oneself sick, but as much as one could do to help cooperate. Carl said he wanted to tell three things the Commandant had said yesterday. First, he said, "You know as well as I do what is going on." Carl answered, "Won't you tell us what is happening, please?" but Oura answered, "I cannot tell you anything." Second, he said that they would not leave, they would stay, to the end. And third, he said, that at first it seemed Japan would be completely victorious but now it looked as though she might not be victorious. Oura's mind is narrow like his experience but he is no coward.

September 27, 1944. Bedie did his first garden work and the meals were awfully thin. 300 pounds of cucumbers, 200 pounds of onions and three fourths of a pig is all for today for 460 people.

"Our driver" brought in the news that the Japanese families are concentrating. He doesn't know where, but he saw them pushing carts full of goods, of possessions and food. The Japanese Bazaar is having a "Selling Out" sale. It is reported that many are trying to get rid of things looted from American homes so they won't get caught with the goods.

One guard says *he* does not want to commit hara-kiri. The ferment is beginning to work; they are beginning to question and to talk among themselves, seeing approaching defeat, morale crumbling, doubt entering the mind about all the propaganda they have learned.

September 28, 1944. As usual, a whole pig was brought in and the garrison hacked off two thirds of it. The hind end and one forequarter, only the head and a foreleg left for 460 of us, while 45 of them get the rest. Denki is furious and the Committee is trying to get word into town that we are not getting the whole pig that is sent to us. This noon there was only one cup of rice to divide between the two children. June was beside herself. Bedie had a terrible grouch and Jerry didn't say how he felt—but he opened a precious can of corned beef and brought me a fourth of it for supper.

The dining room is blacked out so the rule is no smoking until better ventilation, but the [bridge] tournament is on. High school graduation is to be held on Sunday so that it will not interfere with gardening activities. Three graduates will get the unique ball and chain diploma.

Work Detail Supervisor Skerl's figures now show 129 persons put in 294 hours [in the garden] yesterday, including 64 men (216 hours), 43 women (66 hours), and 12 children (12 hours). Quick-growing beans were planted. Today's meals were cornmeal mush, and tea, for breakfast; rice for lunch; rice, cassava gravy and camote for supper.

Kaito is keen to go to America. They all admire our success and efficiency, our land of plenty and our customs.

September 29, 1944. It seems there are two pregnancies in camp, one Family Unit and one not Family Unit, so that ought to shut all mouths. One pair are anxious to have another while they can and are now fearful of losing it. It is a ghastly time to start an infant but that is their business.

September 30, 1944. At the Medical Meeting with Miss McKim, Oura yelled, banged on the table and roared. Dr. Skerl said that all he got out of the meeting was that Japan had just been bombed for three days. Poor Oura, he sounds beside himself, desperate. He is afraid of what might be happening to his country, his family; worried about imminent invasion; worried that he may be demoted again if he isn't strict enough or there is some escape. I can't help feeling sorry for him. He typifies Japan right now.

October 1, 1944. Dr. Mather came in and tried to explain in simple terms what was wrong with my digestion. It is somewhat allied to shock, neuro-circulatory, low tone of blood not enough for proper distribution and when it rushes to help digestion it becomes low in other places, the balance upset. There is occasional heart flutter but no heart trouble, nothing to worry about that diet and the Marines cannot cure. He suggested spacing my meals, eating less at one time and eating more often which sounds all right to me. It is horribly wearing when the spells come three days in a row. Also I feel very confused and not like myself. I click part of the time and then my mind doesn't feel like me. It gives me a wild picture of my blood dashing from one end of the system to the other, running a race with the Marines.

Postponement of the opening of the high school classes for another month was approved, and the date of opening set for October 30, so that the students can cooperate on the Garden Project. It was pointed out that the Command is most anxious to see the high school group do several hours work in the garden a day, and that at the present time this would be too much for them, in addition to regular school work. Grade school children are putting in an hour, five afternoons a week, in a separate garden of their own in [the] sunken garden, under supervision of teachers.

October 2, 1944. Dr. Mather said if we had one more bottle of liverbraun to save it for any acute anemia. Jerry and June came in with a box full of selected emergency food for me from our storage, looking grim and determined. They said they had held an indignation meeting and I was to eat any of these things whenever I felt like it. There was the last of the wild honey, some Emergency chocolate, ground rice and the malted milk tablets among other things. This had all been carefully saved for some last terrible week of Emergency, though they try to deny it, the darlings. They are trying to tempt me to eat when my capacity is getting less every day.

October 3, 1944. I had thin milk several times in the morning and held it down. Water bags help. I trickled tears on Jerry's hand and he was all upset. He started making soup and trying to get it fixed up for me. He has been wonderful—resourceful, steady, strong and loving. If I don't pull through I hope he will keep the children close to him and not turn them over to relatives or other people, and that he will be specially patient with sensitive Bedie who acts tough but isn't and who takes subtle handling. Jerry has lost 5 pounds in two weeks, as have many others.

October 4, 1944. Moved upstairs in a hurry, Jerry carrying me. They gave me saline tablets. Ellen bathed me. Three trench mortar shots nearby. Very loud. It is evening. They think I had pâté meat poisoning on top of everything else, my meat kept too long in back of hospital icebox. Jerry broke down tonight over me and the kids. Toxic all day. Double dose of saline tablets. My throat closed and I could hardly swallow so much salt. Slept from 11 at night till 5 in the morning, then asked for bouillon.

October 5, 1944. It is now October 5. I'm very weak and mixed up on the days. I started feeding myself at supper time. Had first egg for breakfast and tea—good. The attendant said chicken for lunch and I said Real Chicken? It was part of the two Canton ducks and were they good with camote and rice.

I shall always remember Jerry coming in the morning when I was in complete collapse, saying, "Here I am, Honey, coming to take you to a good bed upstairs where they will look after you. The doctor is very much on the job for you." He engulfed me in his arms and carried me limp as a rag upstairs. I couldn't even hold my head up. When he had come in early I had pointed out my bag of notes for him to take care of. He took one look at me and went after the doctor who came down and started things moving fast. He raised the roof with the staff and they did much for me that I don't remember.

Ray says that people in Santo Tomas ran about collecting souvenirs of shrapnel as it dropped from antiaircraft firing. One plane dived over camp and saluted by "flapping its wings." The people all yelled and went crazy and sang "The Star Spangled Banner." It must have been a thrill.

October 6, 1944. Jerry has uncovered a couple of rackets—the pig bones which boiled way down made heaps of fat as well as soup, this after lots of camp chow had been made from them. Second, the hospital kitchen was getting *all* the rice left after patients had their first serving. Sometimes there was none left but often there should have been seconds given out.

Dr. Mather says I had protein poisoning, similar to my sieges with fish. The first night I was *afraid* I would die. The second night I *hoped* I would.

October 7, 1944. Jerry has bought beans and a kilo of sugar. He is going to trade the hidden cocoa for 2 pounds of muscovado sugar so we will be set till invasion. So he feels easier. I am taking the "hidden" vitamins. Maybe my bad memory was Providence.[35] The kids have given up all their Red Cross meat and camp sugar for me. Jerry is ghastly thin. All camp is losing fast and morale is very low but the Red Cross supply division will help. The Committee voted 5 to 4 on giving it out. Jerry is going to put all our food in Carl's trunk and lock it, there is so much pilfering. There is terrible hunger, fear and anxiety. All the serious patients are getting better, however.

When I moved here they put the empty Kiddie Koop at the foot of my bed to get it out of the way. When Bedie saw it, his face lighted up and he turned to me saying, "Oh, Mama! Are you—?" I hated to tell him it was just stowed there, for he really hoped. This has become the big laugh of the week.

I have had a wonderful experience in here. When I was so sick in the night, afraid of death, I found some kind of a stream of life to rest upon. It was in far and deep but it was there and I found it at last and relaxed as in coming "home." It taught me what Tolstoy and others mean by "The Kingdom of God is Within You." Once I thought I had to go up the hill now and then to look "toward the hills," then gradually I found that I didn't even need to go to the hospital point to find peace—it was all inside. Since then I have been deeper in and found it to be buoyant, sustaining, a regular rush of life.

October 8, 1944. Rumor says there was a tipoff from some Japanese that we'd better distribute the Red Cross supplies.

It is said that Dr. Skerl has done a wonderful job on the Red Cross emergency supply distribution. His mathematical, scientific mind, and keen sense of integrity have been a boon to camp, great help to Carl and the Committee.

October 9, 1944. Sakashita's boils are syphillis and the doctor told him so when he asked what they were. He was furious and hasn't been near the hospital or the doctors since. This may be back of all the tirade against doctors and other difficulties.

Oura said that American planes covered the Philippines, that there are 100 [aircraft] carriers off the islands (our most optimistic guess and hope was 20).[36] Whether this is true or some propaganda that the U.S. put out, the point is that the Japanese believe it. He hints at withdrawal from Baguio mountaintops by asking that we do not "interfere" if they start to move away. They might "melt away" in the night after all and we would see little violence. Some had feared they would move, taking us as hostage with them. This fear has been laid to rest. It had not entered my head. Oura said we might be cut off from food and could do three things—1. Start to lay in all we could stock; 2. Cut down ration and conserve (Oh God!) 3. Rely on our garden.

Cleo told me she didn't often cry but she felt like it when she saw my two kids dividing up a pan of something so justly.

Jerry and the kids got hold of a Sears catalogue and figured up how much it would cost to equip a kitchen—including a set of dishes in golden yellow, or sea blue or terra cotta. A thousand pesos (five hundred dollars)[37] will do it and I think I may have that in the bank at home after three years. We figure we have mattresses here and all we need is a kitchen outfit! They had such a good time poring over the pages.

October 10, 1944. I can sit up twice a day in a chair, have visitors and normal diet.

"Report of a Conference with the Command and Mr. Yamato, Carl, Miss McKim and Skerl. October 9, 1944. Among other things, the Command said, 'If one or two million soldiers come to the Philippines that does not mean Japan will be defeated, nor will the American Navy be easy to defeat.' What he tried to emphasize in the talk about the war was the fact that it will take time for war to end, so we must make preparation for food shortage. The Chairman asked about the shooting on Saturday evening. The Command replied that the guards thought someone was trying to enter camp. He stated again that the guards would shoot at anyone trying to enter or leave camp. They are soldiers and this is their business."

But they are finally able to get together with the Committee to work all problems out. It is strange how each nation thinks the other is insincere, "saying one thing, thinking another in the heart."

Minutes: "The 387 eggs produced by camp chickens during September were an all-time high. There are now 52 hens, 15 roosters, 5 chicks (as of 1st of month), 5 ducks—a total of 72 in camp poultry flock. The two drakes contributed by Mr. Hayakawa are to be used in children's diets tomorrow. 4 chickens were used for the children last month and 3 chickens died from unknown causes. We have four pigs and 7 piglets; one cow and 2 calves. . . . For this last 10-day period, we have totaled 1,828 hours in the garden, according to Skerl's report."

Masaki is a fine person, the son of a General. He sees no sense in blackouts unless an air raid sounds, so order was given at roll call by Hayakawa that there will be no more blackout. The camp let out a whoop and in one second was a blaze of light from one end of barracks down to the hospital. General jubilee. There was a complete change of atmosphere in one night. It may be only the difference between Masaki and Sakashita.

October 11, 1944. Jerry earns camotes which help the family meals. He seems to like the garden and has his second wind like Bedie. I have mine and wish June would get hers.

I sat up reading pages of my toilet paper—*Women in Love*. There are many pages of majestic writing.

Internally I feel normal for the first time since February. My feet are still ice but my mind is functioning almost too well.

I was up in a chair when my family came down to visit, Jerry and Bedie with spring in their hands; the exquisite fragrance and waxy petals of pomolo flower, with dark green leaves below the fresh yellow green of new shoots. It was most heavenly to sniff and gaze upon. Bedie found it in a tree for me. June brought fresh-picked lettuce from the box garden and I buried my nose in the crisp green which was still wet from being washed. We all chewed a leaf, like rabbits. It makes my heart sing to see Bedie snuggle up to Jerry with a shy smile. Jerry tries to cover up his pleasure at the demonstration. He says the big scandal in camp now is one white rooster missing from the hen yard. Those in charge and on the Committee went to the pig pen where they found it cooking in a pot hidden away. Shorty takes full blame, brags about similar snitchings over a period, but they suspect others in it with him whom he shields. Since eggs dropped in number they have been watching the hen yard, suspecting "foul play."

Sugano fished a tall can of Nestlé evaporated milk out of his pocket, asked Denki to ask the doctor if it was any good, and if so he could give him twelve more for hospital use. Another miracle.

June was depressed and weepy, so I sent Bedie off and talked it out with her. She is lonely, does not belong to the various cliques of the young as she has no one with which to pair off. Low vitality makes her feel there is no help for anything, no way out. She can see no future, feels she will never pull through this and live to grow up. I know so well this low-vitamin state of mind that I could take hold of it and pull her up, though her youthful despair twisted my heart. She wept with homesickness, misses my companionship and needs more young people to draw upon. I told her to ask three to play in our cubicle some night, to make a definite date. She promised she would and left a little more cheerful.

Dr. Mather said I must be sure to eat some chicken for lunch. It is *the* rooster which was snitched, plus three other small chickens. The sick get the benefit of Stolen Fruits and the planned party did not come off. About four of the young people were in on it. It was a gay lark that they could brag about, without thought of the sick who depended on the eggs from the camp flock. The prize rooster was killed and cleverly hidden in a pot, boiling *under camotes* and something else. There is an open trial tomorrow and a lesson for all.

October 12, 1944. Jerry, Charles Bary, and Clark are the Investigating Jury. Eighteen chickens and many eggs have been missing since February. It goes back months, so that it involves more than this one white rooster. No one wants to tell or be a witness, each tries to avoid a share in clearing it up. No one wishes to place blame in these hard times, yet it must be done or there will be chaos in camp.

McKim San gave me Tomibe's poem in Japanese, with her translation and one by Yamato which is equally interesting.

Miss McKim's translation: Poem to Jim, by Rokuro Tomibe

You are a young man bearing upon your shoulders
Your fatherland. I am like you.
We have become friends here, but if the fate
Of our countries demands it, I am sure that

We will confront each other bravely.
However, into the dawn of peace, our friendship
Will be deeper than before.

Yamato San's translation: Poem to Jim.

You are, also, the Youth who is shouldering
Your country, and so am I. I made friends
With you here, but I expect, if emergency comes,
I must confront you gallantly; but when
Great peace comes brilliantly, of course, I am
Sure, to foster much more deep friendship between us.

October 13, 1944. I have walked quite a bit today.

No visitors will be allowed on November 3 which is Meiji-Setsu holiday. This is because of "difficult and dangerous conditions," says Mr. Yamato who has become a permanent member of the early garden crew, the shovel and hoe gang, and who tells Jo Smith he used to be "that brown" too when he worked in garden in Japan.

The Department of Education is preparing a record card for each high school student, showing marks and academic credits to date, *for the student to take with him*. Instructors' names and academic experience, addresses, etc. are included on the card.

Since coming into Concentration and during my recent illness I seem to have become more "aware." I can put myself into people's minds and into their troubled hearts better than before. I can appreciate beauty more too, whether it is the mountain, a baby goat or a sensitive spirit. Appreciation has been growing, ripening, into more clear-cut understanding of everything, no matter how sad or disturbing. I have come through to another side, and though it is only like a beginning, I feel very much alive.

I only hope Marie keeps on looking after Nida. Rice is P5,000 a sack, sugar is 1,000—which used to be 25¢. Eggs are P10 a piece, P120 a dozen. Poor, poor people outside! What vast suffering there must be. But the Japanese admit planes over Luzon. Everyone is hungry. Hunger colors every move, every conversation.

October 15, 1944. Jerry has been given special permit by the doctor to have coffee up here with me at 10 on Sunday mornings. His spice cake is delicious and Benguet coffee was an aromatic treat. Once a week I permit myself the indulgence of coffee.

Peg and Jerry talked about camp and democracy and how at last it seemed it might survive.

The doctor gave me bathroom privileges at noon so I have graduated. It makes quite a day in the life of a convalescent. My face in a mirror looks awful, wraithlike, still puffy and lined around the mouth, eyes very sharp. Jerry says, if it is any comfort to me, that my face is a great improvement over last week when my cheeks were swollen, eyes and nose bad and lip paralyzed, not to mention the drawn look around the eyes. So I have hopes for next week! He says over 20 thousand camote roots have been planted and we are about to eat the first harvest which will give more incentive and zest, a less futile feeling about gardening. The old spirit of "we'll soon be out and won't ever benefit" has finally begun to die. It has been a drag on community spirit, a prop for the lazy and the grouches.

October 16, 1944. Out of deep sleep, I found Jerry sitting on my bed trying to explain to my befuddled brain why he wanted my watch and silver filigree bracelet, the result of two past anniversaries. He is trading it out sub rosa, hoping for exchange in food—peanuts or sugar instead of money. Then he can trade these in camp in exchange for milk or Spam or beef. Without even a look or qualm, I took it off and handed it to him. He oozed relief. Food is a terrible problem for the three of them. There was so little rice this noon that they simply had to open a can of beef and his mind began to figure new ways out of the dilemma. Again we will eat diamonds, platinum and silver, to keep our bodies going. Jerry said he was all in after pushing the wagon up the hill. June was weary after doing a large washing. I made her fix up a glass of calamansit juice for them all. Bedie's grades average 81 which is an improvement. I told them about the three aides who almost fainted because of hunger and dehydration. So we live from day to day, waiting, weaker and weaker, for the Americans.

October 17, 1944. Onions planted in July are now being harvested. Several kilos were cut for the first time.

June's blood count is 4 million but her hemoglobin is low. She needs iron, the doctor says, and there is no more. He is going to put all three of them down for B-1 tablets. The poor doctors hardly know which way to turn when starvation creeps closer and closer.

We hear one Japanese brought in a big lot of unbilled food supplies in his own cash, unknown to the Command. He told the store to disburse it in a hurry and keep it very down-under, for if the Command hears, the purchaser will be transferred to Manila. Furuya is trying to bring all he can before the Americans come in, for then he says the people will hide away and not bring anything to sell and we will suffer. He tacitly admits the last weeks are here. Outside of my quiet room there is a desperate feeling in camp. Jerry seems near the end of his rope.

Jerry said the Investigating Jury turned in their verbal report to the Executive Committee on the Chicken Case. They said it bore rather heavily on them because they had let too many past demeanors go unpunished and this was just one more, which made it difficult. It is hard to begin now to clear it up because each culprit points backward—"He did it."—"Everyone was doing it." There was complete moral and ethical breakdown for some who only regret that old maxim "It isn't what you do, it's what you get caught doing." They are only annoyed at being caught, not ashamed of it or of the act itself.

Some people don't seem to have a straight bone in their body. Thank goodness, most of the people in here are decent, kindly, neighborly, and considerate.

There is conflict between the Japanese who like us and those who don't. Some expect to die but others hope to live on and it becomes acute with both.

October 19, 1944. Little Ronnie took the mouse in a trap to the cat, opened the trap, released the little mouse upon which the cat pounced, then Ronnie ate the bait which was a peanut.

Oura, dark and anxious, sat in the arbor yesterday looking out toward the blue range and overseeing the garden workers. Miss McKim says he knows none of the polite Japanese language at all, only the strange guttural peasant tongue of his section which few of them here understand. I keep feeling interested in him, such a lonely figure, misunderstood even by his own countrymen, in a position beyond his powers, trying not to fail by desperate effort, somewhat controlled by the big brute army type, Sakashita, watched by Masaki for his reported failures. He is tired of a hard life, tired of waiting for death which is the only release he can see ahead out toward the mountains. He feels hate and dislike all around him. Oura has all the making of revolution in him. Every line of him tells of eating bitterness. He should not be fighting Filipino farmers at all. I think about him, adding each bit of information to the mosaic of his character. I would like to talk with him, hear his story in simple peasant words, then have it translated simply. It would have a tragic power, I am sure. Peg and Jerry cannot see this—they detest Oura's mean, narrow provincialism. No one sees what is behind it.

October 20, 1944. It is like a squirrel cage [here], round and round, getting nowhere except every day a slight slipping backward, that losing feeling. How many millions go through life with it—hideous insecurity and malnutrition which makes only half a person.

There were distinct changes of attitude toward Americans among the Japanese who stayed here any time at all. Tomibe, Kaito, Saito—they liked us, wanted to understand us even as we wanted to know them. But the sterner characters among them call this cowardly, feel it undermines the will to fight (as it does), so had them transferred, removed from danger and subversive thoughts, from too friendly attitudes.

Shorty came to tell his sister "good-bye" for five days as this is his sentence in the Chicken Case. In comparison to the others involved, he showed stamina. The small closet room which used to house the Red Cross supplies is now the jail, with a double bunk and window which looks out onto a red dirt bank. A hind quarter seems to have been filched from one camp-killed cow, cooked in one delectable roast for the Kitchen. Only now has Jerry heard of it, when all the rats and roaches are coming out of holes into the light in order to play down present guilt. This roast and the Pork Chop Case when no one could be found who would testify are the chief highlights of kitchen graft uncovered by the Chicken Case. I think the peasant class would have had a cleaner, straighter record than some of our intelligentsia.

October 21, 1944. Last night Jerry kept telling me over and over about the 800 pounds of peanuts brought in for sale or for camp consumption, by Furuya. He was almost babbling with relief of the supplies coming in, repeating the 800 pounds over and over like a grooved record.

Fabian has manufactured a Ouija Board out of cigar boxes, and the Green Barracks inmates and all the young fry have gone wild over it. Miss Lucy and Mrs. Morris have sent messages. When asked how are two escapees were they said all right. Asked where they were, the pencil made large question mark with circles around it. Every war revives this attempt to contact the departed, to peer into the future, soothing bereaved and suffering minds. It does no harm, seems to give a lift to some, and adds to conversation where news is barren. It starts lovely new rumors out of the ether and is great fun for badgered and beaten camp members.

The doctors don't call any illness by names any more—just refer to it as low nutrition.

October 22, 1944. I talked with Jerry about June and his own slow decline and how I wished they could quit corn. He said, simply, "I know, Pete, but nothing can be done about it. We must eat corn when there is nothing else from camp. I haven't the energy nor the supplies to correct it." It was the first time we admitted aloud what each of us had faced and knew full well—the gradual but more and more accelerating decline of each individual making up camp as a whole. The symptoms seem to come in cycles, more pronounced each time, then a brief respite before the next one. There are spells of actual cheer. The children are all right tonight but Jerry is miserable; sleepy, exhausted, with a swollen hand and a temperature from his boil, internally churning from infection, pain and low vitality. He had not been to the garden all week.

Suda performed "Kenbu," the sword dance, and Betty talked on her travels. Miss McKim translated for Suda. He sent Liz a bunch of bananas by Carl, "so sorry" she was sick and could not see the dance in which she had expressed interest. Mac and Jerry sat on their heels, by now an accustomed posture in this era of no chairs or comforts.

The garden spots were full of coffee parties. Suda was taking pictures of some of the young people. Then he and Oura talked, squatting on the ground, drawing plans in dirt with sticks.

Gibbie's tiny black kitten, clean but mangy from deficiencies, crept into my lap and cuddled off to sleep. It is a small derelict that dragged itself into camp. Jerry said it made him feel homesick for it looked so much like our darling Pippy who died in my hands just before bombs fell. He said he never felt about any kitten as he did that one for it was so joyous. I remember trying to warm it as it grew cold, not able to believe that in two short hours such leaping life could be stilled. I wept over it until Jerry said I mustn't and we went out to bury it together. I felt then it was only the beginning of what we were to see and it was true. We buried our past gay life in the little grave with Pippy. Shortly afterward everything was lost or changed and we became one of many families pushed about, terrorized, helpless.

I wonder how Nida is feeding her little girls with her husband in a labor battalion.

Father Sheridan has asked Jerry to serve on a sort of District Attorney investigating committee. Jerry agreed. Another case is developing around two who take community food. This has to be tracked down, watched, and wild rumors verified or discarded. They laugh about the Ouija and say they will have to use it in court. Jerry seems interested and is not taking it too heavily. It is odd that he should get into law again through internment conflicts. The police department is to work with them. Jerry says he is really doing it to take some of the load off Carl's and the Committee's shoulders for they have more than they can handle, with such petty details.

October 24, 1944. About 7:30 six planes roared over from east to west over the mountain backbone. The last two tore ahead of the middle two, zooming, dipping and soaring. Yamato asked Denki later, after the camp had lined the bank to watch, "What did you think of the planes?" Denki said, "I think they were American and naturally I am glad to see them." Yamato answered, "I see you believe in telling the truth." Denki said he thought most Americans did. When Carl came along Yamato asked, "Were you glad to see American planes?" and Carl said yes, he was. He asked for it and he got it.

Later, in the garden, with Jerry pouring some good soup and serving bread to June and me, two planes went over our own hill, high and cavorting in and out like the others. The two hill guards signaled with flags, all the others dropped into foxholes and our men working in the garden were ordered home for the morning. An Igorot girl and a man on the road, and several Filipino children, all ducked out of sight. Only the Americans stand and look while planes soar fast overhead, toward the airport. We heard no booms however.

June has bad cramps and Jerry says they are going off hominy onto corn flour. He and Scotts will combine this and soft rice together, making six or eight steam breads a week for each family.

Rumor said that Yamato had remarked there was no need to extend the garden further as we would probably be out by the 15th of next month.

It is wonderful to feel so much better. Jerry says it is longer than a year since I have felt well.

October 25, 1944. I can see that Jerry too has traveled a long journey in here through books, deep experience and mental turbulence. In agonizing worry over the children and me during the last two months of hunger, decline and desperate illness, he has touched some unfathomable moments. He shows change and growth too, and has plumbed some universal feelings as I have. We know what thousands of people have suffered. He says he never could express the relief it is to see me well and in balance again (as if he had despaired more than once).

We heard that Carl had been asked if he would be responsible for any who tried to escape and he said no, he would not.

Jerry gave me back my watch and I was glad to see it.

An aide said that Hayakawa's father had given us our pork for supper and that Masaki had given us 750 bananas, more than one apiece for breakfast. The first Red Cross funds since August have been allowed to come through—P25,000. This makes all the difference between life and decline for us.

An American now has charge of roll call and bowing. Things are changing fast. Carl as our representative bows, and the Japanese in charge bows to him as symbol of us all.

Some brief Minutes of the 18 of October: "In an effort to put a stop to the increasing amount of food stealing in the camp, the Committee has issued this statement: It is the duty of every internee to report at once to the Chief of Police the name of any other internee whom he may see in the act of stealing. Only by the full cooperation of the personnel of this camp can we protect individual property. The hospital acknowledged receipt of 24 tall cans of Alpine milk from the Japanese, a gift to camp. . . . Dr. Skerl reported that a steady decrease has been noted during the past week in the number of people reporting for garden detail, and in the number of hours worked in the garden. . . . Many were collecting driftwood! . . . Three camp pigs were butchered today. . . . A pen, like a duck pond, has been constructed for the ducklings. . . . A request for the preparation of additional chicken food from camote peelings to overcome a decrease in the camp egg production was referred to Dr. Mather.

"His Excellency, Highest Commander of the Philippine Islands. Your Excellency: We the undersigned, members of Camp Holmes Civilian Internment Camp No. 3, respectfully submit this urgent appeal to you for assistance in obtaining enough food to keep us alive. . . . At present we are not receiving the essential foods in sufficient quantity to sustain life; anemia and other illnesses resulting from malnutrition are increasing at such an alarming rate our doctors state that unless immediate steps are taken to obtain more food the damage to our health will not only be irreparable, but deaths will follow. . . . We submit this personal appeal to you through our Commandant. . . . We appreciate the difficulties confronting the authorities but we believe it is not the desire of the Japanese people to have such a situation continue and we turn to you gratefully for relief. Respectfully submitted, Civilian Internees of Internment Camp No. 3.''

October 26, 1944. Dr. Shaffer came in looking very young and cheerful. He asked how we all were and said, beaming, "Well, it won't be much longer! If we were in Leyte now, we'd all be free! They've landed! There is even a rumor that there is landing in Aparri but we aren't sure of this."

Jerry says that MacArthur and 250 thousand troops landed on Leyte. Four landings on Mindanao and one on Luzon says another rumor. So the General has come back after three years.[38]

October 27, 1944. There is fish today, pork tonight, and camote tops! Meals have improved the last fortnight. 100 eggs came in and are to be used for general diet, scrambled in fried rice tomorrow.

Jerry says Yamato talks to him by the hour at the tool shed and is obsessed with food. He has beriberi and perhaps sprue as well, feels wretched. *Their diet is as poor as ours.* He asked Jerry what he used to eat on the outside so Jerry told him an average day. He told Jerry about a P7 meal at the Pines Hotel now; a little soup, a chunk of pork, a little potato and small vegetable. I wish I could listen to the two of them—big and little in size—commiserating with each other. Jerry feels sorry for the sad little man. He tries so desperately, with his limitations, to do what is right.

October 28, 1944. Masaki says Gen. Kwo is not interested in anything but gates and fences. It is all he sees, not people at all. He says the Philippine camps are the worst of all, Shanghai the best with many advantages.[39]

Miss McKim told of how hipped Yamato is on roll call etiquette and when Carl tried to get a permit for two men to go up to the spring to look into its condition, Yamato kept saying, "It all depends on roll call conditions tomorrow." Carl exclaimed, "But what does roll call have to do with?" Eventually it was discovered that it was not roll call but the Japanese pronunciation of "local" which is "rocal." They have trouble with *l*'s. So goeth language, a great stumbling block between peoples, even between Oura and his countrymen. How pitifully difficult life is, even between those who try to "work together."

The whole camp, especially the young ones, are agog over the costume party tonight. Sheba and daughter tried to rule that those under 14 could not attend. It nearly precipitated a riot. June has dug up my green earrings, my turquoise chain and ring, my costume bracelets to wear with the cerise and

Black Forest costume of country club days. She will wear the black apron and black bridge square over her shoulders since the purple shawl with cerise roses did not come in. I only hope Nida has it.

Someone said, "Don't quote me but the news is a great naval battle between Formosa and the Marianas in the China Sea north of the Philippine Islands. The deciding battle, it is said." Already the Japanese admit losing two battleships and a cruiser, say that they sank 11 carriers and much else of ours.[40]

Mom says that what they have lost in possessions here is nothing compared to the clean sweep that the peacetime depression gave them. It wiped out the savings of years that they had put away for old age. They had to start all over again at the beginning. "But," says Mom, "what are these losses—they are nothing compared to the mothers who have lost sons. We shouldn't utter a word of complaint."

October 29, 1944. Doctor and the nurse said that many people who are never upset were sick last night. It must have been the fat in the fried camotes—we just can't take fat in any quantity—for nearly everyone was trotting in the night.

Over coffee, Jerry told about Anne's lovely costume as a Chinese girl at the party, of Reamo as Cupid, Ricky as a Red Cross box, cowboys, and many simple but ingenious getups out of nothing. He said the children's parade was great fun and it was hard to judge the best. Yamato attended and is still in a daze over it all, transported with delight.

At midnight I woke suddenly, hearing planes. I sat up but thought I was dreaming it. But it was a plane overhead, very low and roaring loud. The Green Barracks was a riot, with people in all sorts of dress and undress, which, after the roar faded into the sea, subsided into the long trek to toilets which is always humorous. Supposition says it was a Japanese plane getting out to Japan but nobody really knows. Some slept all the way through the racket but most of us will not forget the excitement and noise in the dead silence of night—the first time it ever happened in the dark.

October 30, 1944. Camp gave us French fried camotes and gravy, then Jerry and the kids came down with luscious fried rice, still hot in the pan, sliced Spam on fresh green lettuce on a chromium plate, for my birthday. Afterward we had scrumptious ice cream made by Peg and covered with a spoonful of Emergency chocolate, melted into sauce. She made the ice cream with half a can of butter, rice crust grounds as thickener after a futile attempt to find something else, with maple flavor and of course sugar. It was marvelous. We ate outside on the rustic table and bench. It was a rushing time as June did not come from school till 12:45 and Jerry had to return to the tool shed at one. It was grand being together even if hurried. Bedie has grown tall. I miss June's morning visits now that school has begun.

We were full of appetizing food and my feet became warm and I slept over an hour.

At teatime Peg came down with her hair done up very chic, in her best blue dress and party air. June with pink cheeks brought the cake and chocolate sauce for it, with some of Lim Sian Tek's rare China tea (we wonder if he is still alive). Peg loaned us her rice pattern cups and plates. We put calamansit concentrate in the tea to enhance it, and all gathered around the dilapidated rustic table. Walter carried the tray, looking thin and very young in slicked hair. The cake was made of bucaco flour, soft rice, a bit of cassava, sugar, a little fat. It was light and fluffy which most of our cakes in here are not. So good with chocolate sauce—and forks to eat it. *It is three years since we have used any forks.* It was a feast, eaten slowly from blue china which was another treat. No tin plates, no butter-tin cups or tin spoons. All borrowed finery.

October 31, 1944. Prices jumped high in three days. Peanuts were 80 a pound, jumped to 120, 240, and today are P400 a pound. Rumor says the Japanese admit Marinduque, Mindoro landings, and that the sea battle is over, in our favor.[41]

Our friend Helen has slipped away and again we wonder who will be next. It is better not to know. A day at a time has helped us through three years. I told June tonight who gave her the turquoise and of that other gift which Helen hoped she would carry on through the years—the wonderful foundation of music which her teacher gave her.

November 3, 1944. The guards turned out to a ceremony or drill on the road, guided by bellows from Sakashita. Then they went out the gate at various paces until finally they were into the goose step, which is always incongruous when transferred from Germans to Japanese.

Several outside families waited at the gate with bags of food hoping that Meiji-setsu holiday would get them by but it did not. Minus bags which were finally taken in, due to pleading of Miss McKim, the families waved forlornly to three husbands who were straining their eyes from a point behind Baby House. The mountains were beautiful, blue and distant and unmoved by human longing and disappointment.

November 4, 1944. Local rumor—the guards get no more *Tribune* and civilians can make only special permit trips to town after today. Also the guardhouse radio has been ripped out and taken to town forever. The news must be good, the rumors true.

Sylvia's garden seat, the rustic arbor and all other seats were torn up for firewood on the Command's order. It is a wonder they don't come down and take the rickety garden benches at the hospital too. They have never wanted us to have chairs or places to sit down. Of course they do not have any in Japan, but this keeps them superior, to have us standing. We must work, not sit. People who have worked all their lives and never have had time to sit probably always feel this way when they get in the saddle. The Japanese always sit on the floor.

We spend hours talking of food as it seems to assuage hunger. Gingerbread with whipped cream or hard sauce, apple sauce, whole wheat bread with gobs of butter—endless lines of dishes parade in our talks, each talker going the other one better. Then we laugh about it. Clara copies British cookbook recipes all day and reads them out to us.

November 5, 1944. Jerry and Charles and I talked of Oura's bellowing rampage at roll call, making Kaito lose face. It goes back to yesterday when Yamato told Carl he wasn't doing roll call right—he was walking too far ahead of Yamato which was an insult. Carl asked him how he wanted it done and they talked around and around, getting nowhere. Yamato said Carl must be responsible and yet do it such and such a way. Carl finally said if the Command wasn't satisfied with the way he was doing it, he was only too happy to have the Command come out and take it himself. Yamato, who wants all sorts of bowing and scraping, misinterpreted as usual and this morning the Command showed the results of it. He stormed and raged all over the parade ground, went into the barracks to see if any were hiding out, stomped about in there, then out to the Administration building where he raked Masaki over the coals. But it is not really Oura, it is little snake-in-the-grass Yamato who is fairly bursting with his own importance.

Jerry has made inventory of all our supplies, taking the kids into his confidence, mapping out how it must be used, how long it must last etc.

The doctors have a two thousand peso fund to spend for certain sick ones. They can allow P25 or even P200 a month to some if they feel it necessary. This is one glimmer of concession and light. Two malnutrition deaths[42] may have scared the Japanese, if anything could. June is very listless; Bedie goes to bed early, Jerry says. They are all so hungry. In answer to Jerry's message sent out sub rosa, Marie sent in Benguet coffee beans which will make about 2 pounds of ground coffee. We can drink it or trade it for peanuts.

Jerry says he will work to earn those two camotes a day as long as he is able and they continue to pay it. He wonders how much longer he can keep going some days. We go on from day to day as unemotionally as possible, as unfeeling as we can keep.

November 6, 1944. "From the town hospital was received fifteen 60 c. bottles of triple vaccine (cholera, typhoid and dysentery). The first of three shots are to be given tomorrow and motion carried that the taking of these shots is to be compulsory for all internees, except those excused by the

Medical Committee for very exceptional reasons. . . . High school opened Monday October 30th for the new term, with an enrollment of 15 high school students and 4 graduate students.''

Jerry came down, so very tired. With all his worry over extras for me, keeping the children fed and himself going at garden-garbage-tool and fish cleaning, with five hours a day for camp, he will collapse when he can let down the load. The only way I can help is by being in the hospital.

November 7, 1944. I shall never be able to express how I have widened my mind and horizon in the confinement of this prison camp, not only through the beauty of the mountain range and cloud-filled valley; from deep personal experiences; but also from contact with an infinite variety of people, their troubles, problems and casual stories from their lives—their happiness, sorrows and struggles.

November 8, 1944. We hear that a limit of 1 pound each of peanuts has been imposed so that patients or healthy camp members cannot corner the market.

Everyone is seen with bunches of onions given out by camp. They are fresh green bouquets tucked under arms.

Jerry is so strained that he cannot bear an interruption—his voice shakes. We all lose track of thought if interrupted. These last weeks are ragged, with nerves raw.

June says, "Mummie, Dad and I see that Bedie gets more than we do. He is growing and needs it." Dear June, she too is still growing at age fifteen. Poor Jerry, how awful to cope with all this. He has lived through years in these last months.

The returning buyer brought nothing from Manila except soldiers and helmets, with the cold comfort that we are better off than people at Santo Tomas. He did bring soap and undershirts. He says Santo Tomas has used their reserve rice and eaten all their Red Cross supplies. We dare not let ourselves think about them, being too near the edge ourselves.

June and Jerry came down with a mixture of sub-coffee and burnt peanuts. Jerry's conversation with Yamato at the tool shed is most entertaining. He asked June's age and said his daughter was the same age and he had dreamed about her last night—dreamed that she had a special permit to come to the Philippines to see him. Poor Yamato, he is lonely, homesick and isolated, speaking as one father to another. Jerry said, slowly, "Somehow I don't think the Philippines is a very good place to be right now." Disconsolately, Yamato agreed that it probably wasn't. Jerry then embarked on a long persuasion to let us have news—why couldn't we hear about the U.S. election and such topics, even if they didn't find it feasible to let us know about the Pacific? Yamato said we must not worry or disturb ourselves, must keep peaceful and serene. Jerry assured him that having no news disturbed us because being in a vacuum was very bad when we had only poor food to talk about. He told Yamato we might forget food, work better in the garden and be more cooperative if we had a little news. Yamato said, "But if it were bad news?" Jerry replied, "Even bad news was better than nothing at all. If we could listen to Tokyo—" "But would you believe that news?" asked Yamato. Jerry said we would discount it, believe what we liked even as the Japanese did with our radio news. He told Yamato that if he had been interned three years without hearing news of his country he would not like it either, and Yamato allowed as how this might be true. He argued that the Japanese were not allowed radios in the U.S. and Jerry stoutly denied it, said he was sure they could listen to Tokyo or U.S. news as desired. Jerry outlined a suggestion that some Japanese staff member prepare a weekly news summary for us to post on our Board. Jerry said he was sure that one of our two Japanese-speaking ladies would be glad to translate it and suggested Miss Spencer. Yamato thought it worth thinking about.

Adults are said to be giving up food for the very young and the very old. The ethics of this is debatable, for the older ones do not do heavy work and others must carry on the labor. Such questions and weighing as this fill our days and become increasingly delicate—which should survive?

November 9, 1944. We overheard Skerl and the doctors discussing the hens and the decreasing eggs. Now that camp does not peel the camotes [it] means that the hens get no skins to eat, so that there is almost no food for them, the sow or the piglets. Dr. Mather says, "Well, shall be go back to giving them the peelings?" and Skerl answers, "It all depends on what you want. If the hospital can get along on six eggs, never mind feeding the hens. We can kill some of the poorer layers." Then they thrashed over whether to kill and eat, and how to feed them if they didn't kill. It is one of the endless problems.

I wind up by telling June to get the teacher to arrange her geometry for another hour as she has to help her Dad at noon. God knows, if one is crazy enough to want geometry, heaven and earth should be moved to give it to her! This made her happy.

Then followed a night in which all the devils in hell were loose. It is what we have feared and not really had in three years—a typhoon of most violent nearness. Sometime in the night the center must have come close to us and stuck there for outside our window a wind roared as if through a long endless funnel. The roar was steady, with no letup at all, with a drawn sound as though compressed into definite confined space. The velocity was terrifying and we moved about in total darkness trying to close windows, as the electricity was off. In the dentist's office a window blew open, but only he had the key so no one could go in to stop it. It crashed and banged back and forth, with breaking glass panes added to the din of the night. Such precious panes being destroyed! The tin roof crashed off the water tank, windows shook and rattled, branches tore past. Upstairs the aides mopped the operating room, sopped up 13 bucketsful in [one] place alone; went up and down stairs in dim light or blackness, answering calls. About one, Betty burst in out of the storm, calling, ''Bob! We want men and a light—the Baby House roof is blowing off.'' She sounded desperate but the men answered, ''You'll have to get man-help from topside. We've been up all night here too and can't spare anyone.'' But the doctor went over as his wife and son were there. He found them without lights, no hammers or nails, holding down the roof by tying a rope to the rafters. Fortunately it worked but they were frantic for a while. Always there was the long steady roar and draw of wind between the two buildings, like a huge mass of animals in stampede or a primeval force unleashed. There is no sound like it. Once heard it stays in the mind forever. As though man had not been unkind enough, war not cruel enough, nature added to our terror and misery by striking with sudden and overwhelming fury. No one went into the flooded toilet except in great extremity. Wet beds and blankets and corners flooded. The kitchen upstairs was a sight, flooded, and the workers there were barefoot with slacks up to the knees. Operating tables were all pulled into the center of the room, blackout curtains dripping black over everything sterile. The dentist came down with his key, waded in to take sofa cushions out to dry, fasten the windows and pound a covering over the broken panes.

November 10, 1944. Bedie came down full of tales and eager to hear more. We patients read in bed with hot bricks. Others were busy toiling, mopping up pail after pailful of water, scooping up dustpansful of water. Hot soup at 10 was most welcome, and big boiled camotes with camote stew and boiled cabbage tasted marvelous at noon. Rain deluged all day, far worse than in the night. It started to let up a little and the sky lightened about three but it still poured. Jerry came down with a pot of hot tea, looking cheerful. He told of stoves lighted in the veg room to make plenty of hot water and to dry clothes of those who had to work outside. He said the guards sounded forlorn and cold and wet all night. He felt sorry for them. June popped in bright-eyed, busy mopping all day after the dispensary window blew in and flooded our space but no damage to bags. We saw the Command out early in raincoat and hood, sword banging against his legs. The roof had blown off the hen coop and the hens didn't lay. All day the roar, the rain and floods of water. Small differences melt away in the torrents which nature pours upon us.

Rising and dying as though in spirals, gradually the storm was gone.

During the mop-up in our space in Green Barracks, the problems all came to a head. So we are stuck and today's blowup made it apparent that I will have to stay on in the hospital for I could not stand up in a room that has grown worse. I would like to go back to topside but I can see it is not possible.[43]

November 11, 1944. Armistice Day, but a mockery now. There was heavy fog which cleared suddenly and revealed glorious blue sky with soft clouds, golden sun, air as heady as wine, the mountains unmoved by all the beating of elements—etched sharp and clear in blue line against the sky, terraces washed clean showing green sprouts still growing, the ridges lovely in gray and purple shadow contrast, clouds drifting lazily in a middle strata. There is a roar like the sea from the river far down in the valley with all the draining brooks pouring into it. We hear the children outdoors again, twittering like birds rejoicing in the passing storm. People stream out all over camp, meeting as though separated for two weeks, with broad smiles, ready to face hunger, shortage, anything, after the terrors and darkness of nature. We walk about to see the damage, chiefly at Baby House where the rafters are lashed down with heavy rope, the center beam broken like a match box. The laundry shed next to Baby House lies in a pile of twisted tin and broken beams, far from its moorings.

The storm is over, and the luxuriousness of stillness, the joy of quiet, the beauty of peace permeates us. We comprehend Yamato's yearning for Serenity! Mattresses, bed quilts, thick down-puffs, clothes of all sorts hang dripping from wire and bamboo lines.

If I have learned nothing else, I have learned to stand alone in here as well as to stand in a multitude. Now more than ever, it seems to me not individuals who are at fault but Society, the training and attitude in which the whole population is reared.

Jerry came down in the evening and we had a quiet talk, nearer than for some days because he did not try to conceal anything or treat me as ill.

November 12, 1944. The Committee ruled that camote water is community property and can no longer be boiled down into syrup exclusively for the kitchen staff.

Jerry says it is an important point that the garbage from the guardhouse kitchen for forty guards has fattened their sow and six piglets, while the leftovers from garbage of 460 internees is not enough to feed the camp sow and six piglets who run around the pen mad for food, with their sides like slats and outstanding ribs. It is no use hating Oura and Yamato. They are placed there by Manila heads with orders to do just what they are doing. It is no use to say they will pay for it because those responsible will die by the sword as we come back to the Islands and it avails us nothing to wreak vengeance on innocent ones who are left.

After a supper of luscious ground beef and tender young green beans, with rice—good servings for all—everyone felt better.

The electricity was on all day but at 7 it was turned off. Every night now the switch is pulled in town. Not only camp but Baguio is in complete blackout from 7 to 7.

I enjoy my new milk—one tablespoon of powdered milk mixed with one teaspoon of pressed butter, giving it a creamy effect, prolonging my remaining half can of milk into a month instead of two weeks. Jerry has given up trying to trade for milk. It is prohibitive.

We hear that permit is granted for us to sing patriotic songs on Thanksgiving Day and now from topside comes the practice. In complete blackout, with a brilliant dome of stars, we listen to the piano and lusty voices in distant accord singing "The Star Spangled Banner," "God Save the King," "God Bless America." It is moving, how moving, tremendously impressive even though it is faint, as we drift off to early sleep.

The children come down and ask me, "Mummy, did Daddy tell you—we have a couple of handsful of extra rice in case we need it!" Yes, he had told me, during a moment of exhaustion, yet shaky with relief, how he had helped in the bodega and after all the sacks were stored in piles, he garnered bit by bit little grains of spilled rice from the cracks in the floor, a small pile of dirty, moldly, discarded rice which would be swept up for the chickens as was done with the rest that has been left there. But he gathered a couple of handsful, even as I have watched Chinese gather it grain by grain from cracks of a godown at Hong Kong or Shanghai, watched them with a shudder in realizing that every single grain is so important as they pick it out carefully, close to that narrow margin between life and death. Now we know how they think and feel. Like the old sow, we are running around madly in circles, turning, twisting, trying to find enough grains to keep going. This time *we* are the 500, not the 40 who have enough.

Now we know this too—that hungry ones were hemmed in, helpless, prisoners in another sense than ours but still prisoners, even as we are now. We must work five hours for a camote. We get 300 grams while our conquerors get 600. We watch their pig grow fat while we and our pig grow lean and weak, yet we are surrounded by little Formosans in tin shelters and tin hats, with bullets and bayonets which gleam even in the total darkness. A telephone could call more soldiers to kill any revolt. And besides all this, there is a growing languor, dizziness, shakiness, heaviness, lassitude. Not all of us feel it yet, but more do each week, even with tablet vitamins. Hemmed in by those who feel superior to us, with growing famine even on the outside of our fence, we know that it is hopeless to move or rebel. There is only one way—to take it. Help can come only from beyond, out where there is strength and no hunger, out where there is growing force to fight the captors. Even as an observer's thinking may be changed for life after watching such a condition, turning him toward a desire to help from then on such hopeless, helpless people, so should our thoughts change direction from now on, to devote our lives toward solving the great complex world problem of distribution, so that nowhere can 500 starve while 40 become fat. Revolution does not need to be revenge or complete turnover of class, but a basic change toward equal distribution, a turning over to a new standard and attitude.

November 13, 1944. The mountains are beautiful. Nature quickly covers all ravage of the storm. Yellow green terraces nestle in blue canyons. The sun pours down.

Trinidad and other gardens are washed out and nothing coming in.

Only ten minutes of visiting hour was left when Jerry came down so tired that he couldn't connect his thoughts or keep up a sustained conversation. He can't bear to hear about any hospital cases which is about all I see, hear or know, and he went around and around on his cooking details—how many peanuts he had, how much he took for this, how much value in that, the little groove of our days over and over (he used to call it counting diapers when I was that tired), until I could scream. We stop each other, irritable, snappy, until it became a wretched brief visit for which I had waited all day to no avail or pleasure. He goes back to the warm kitchen which is lighted by new storm lights and full of buzz and friendly chaff of men, while I come in to undress while I can still see, then crawl into bed to lie in the dark.

November 14, 1944. Last night the guards all gathered on the road without any fear of traffic, below the high bank at the hospital. Here under a sort of cheerleader they shouted and roared rhythmic calls or cheers across the wide valley. It sounded like many voices, echoing and reechoing. They kept it up for half an hour in great variety of cheers, between rest periods. Someone said they heard that the soldiers did it in New Guinea to frighten the Americans. Perhaps it is like Gideon's trumpet blasts against the Walls of Jericho—to frighten the guerrillas and Igorots in the mountains, making them think they are many and only waiting, warming up. More probably it is only to cheer themselves up, a sort of pep talk before the fray, a boost to morale, after cold, wind, rain and boredom. They brought a bucket of meat up to our kitchen to have it ground, and gave enough meat in payment to make a large hamburger for the one who ground it.

Jerry was up at five to make muffins and says he can't give up, he has to keep going. June came down and whispered, giggling, "Mums, I must tell you something funny. I asked Daddy what was in that marvelous soup he made for this noon and he said, "My dear, that was pure, concentrated essence of garbage!"

June looks well and is happy again.

November 15, 1944. Rumor says that Yamato has admitted that Roosevelt is elected.

Don was working in the garden near the road when several Filipino boys passed by and one threw over his shoulder, "The Marines have landed, Sir." Whether he meant Leyte or Luzon, we do not know, but they all know it, think we should too.

I told Jerry no more special Red Cross meat for me—I would share only with the family now because we are getting down to bedrock.

November 16, 1944. I went topside for the first time in two months and a half. It seemed strange and I was greeted like Rip Van Winkle.

While I was walking, for the first time in three years I saw the red, white and blue! A plane came suddenly over the hill, passing over us quite low so that I caught sight of it through the thin veiling cloud against brilliant blue—all combining to make aluminum paint hard to see. There was a red circle on the left wing and I thought "Oh, a fried egg." Then my heart did a flip-flop as my eyes spotted on the right wing a dark blue and red stripe with dim white. At the same time I saw a dark star-outline within the circle. "That looks like the Navy insignia," I said out loud.

One of the Japanese staff came to ask for a blood count and says he wants an operation of some kind—anything to put him into retirement *for the next three weeks.* He doesn't want to go into the Army. They all have to fight, civilian or not, and they want to stay here. We have undermined all except Yamato and Oura. Even Yamato finds us interesting. Only Oura withstands. Only he does not like us. But into the maw they all go.

November 17, 1944. Minutes, with the Commandant, November 14: Mr. Yamato also present, but Miss McKim interpreting. "The Command asked us to proceed with the matters we had for discussion. First, we asked whether he had approved of the trip which we requested for two patients and two doctors to town hospital for X-rays. He said, 'Yes, they can go—if they walk both ways and make the trip during one day. There is no available transportation for them.' We replied, 'This is impossible, but possibly they would be able to walk from the market to the hospital if they could go with the truck when it goes to market.' He said that our doctors should be able to get along without X-ray; we have much better equipment than the military prison camps; that in his homeland they get along without X-ray for such cases. He said there was no fuel for the truck, and that if they went with it on one of its trips to the market, there would be no way for them to return. We explained the importance of these patients being X-rayed, and that we did not come to him with minor cases, but made such requests only when our doctors felt that it was absolutely necessary, and a case of life or death. He replied, 'No matter. It cannot be done.' . . . We told him we did not think we were getting a fair ration—that people are actually starving, and that according to international law he is responsible to see that people in the camp, under his direct control, do not starve. He replied that his responsibility ended when more food was being supplied than people Outside were getting. . . . We asked if our petition had been forwarded to the Highest Commander. He said, 'No, it would only anger him if he received it.' . . . The head of the Work Details would like to make the following statement to the women concerning the request for more helpers in the veg room: 'Out of 189 women, there are now 45 from whom we can expect little or no camp work, owing to sickness. To take care of the sick we now have 35 women, and consequently an increasing burden has been thrown onto the rest of the women to keep going such essential services as vegetable and rice preparation, and education. The schedule of women's work hours set up some time ago is now inadequate and a number of women are already giving much more of their time to the community. In the vegetable room, more workers are needed the first thing in the morning so that our vegetables, particularly camotes nowadays, are well cooked by lunchtime. Perhaps some can do their gardening in the afternoon and prepare vegetables in the morning. Please do not feel that you are being "picked on" or censored if you are asked to help. Also do not criticize other women for not "doing their bit," because the odds are that they are handicapped by sickness of which you are ignorant.' In the garden, the average number of hours dropped to 200 per day, with 70 people, for the first two weeks in November (excluding the days of the typhoon)."

I think how often poverty and ignorance breed obstinacy. Tomibe and Oura—two sides of the face of Japan. One was educated in a cultured background; the other in poverty and bitterness, not understanding polite Japanese conversation. There is a world between, yet both are Japan, just as wealth and poverty, culture and ignorance live side by side in America.

I told Jerry if he couldn't give me an hour a day from six to seven that I would come home sick or well and he could look after me. June and Bedie finally popped in after two days' absence.

November 19, 1944. As usual, Sakashita was barking drill orders in what is known in camp parlance as the Daily Puke.

One of the English girls has taken to pipe smoking as there are no more cigarettes or paper, only strong leaf tabaccy which has to be tempered with guava leaf. Most smokers will do anything for a smoke. All of them are groveling slaves to a stimulant.

Notice to Hospital Patients and Visitors: *"Those caring for the sick are underfed and may be actually ill sometimes themselves. . . .* The hospital is crowded far beyond convenience; repeated efforts to obtain other supplies and facilities (light bulbs, for example) have met with little success; the supply of some of our most valuable medicines is becoming depleted; nevertheless the policy that all internees too ill to care for themselves should be hospitalized is being maintained, so try to overlook the inefficiencies of an inadequate staff with very limited facilities and demand as little personal service as you can. Signed by the Medical Committee." This rubbed us all the wrong way thoroughly.

From a distant black line of planes like wild geese we heard the sound of bombs. Over the blue range 12 bombers crossed in a straight line. After them four others very high and directly over camp, each glistening white in the sun. One very fast plane dashed aside, showing a circle on it—then a stage whisper from the onlookers, "A star in the circle and 3 stripes on the other wing!"

Jerry and the kids had a meal outside with me, bringing a plate of cool green lettuce from the "hako niwa" (box garden), with a masterpiece made by Jerry—a meat pie of camotes, pork loaf and soup stock, with a crust of cassava flour. We reveled in it and enjoyed being together after seeing our own Americans fly overhead. At last, they came like many birds.

Yamato asked Bedie if he knew Wick and the other one who escaped. Bedie said of course he did. Yamato counseled, "You must not try to escape as they did, for we will stay to protect you, even with our lives."

There was a thrill, happiness, radiance and hope all over camp. It will be harder to wait than ever, now. Jerry's cheeks and throat look awful—sagging and full of hollows.

November 21, 1944. Poor Jerry, he will collapse when it is over and he can let down the strain. He says when he has a pain there, he doesn't know whether it is his back or his stomach. Up topside, they have all been on starvation diet for weeks. The Formosans asked the wood crew today why they didn't bring their rice out with them to eat at noon and the wood crew replied they hadn't had any noon rice for months, only a camote. The Formosans looked surprised (none of the guards like camotes) and asked why they didn't use some of their money to buy rice to which they replied they did not have any money—it was put in the bank and they weren't allowed to spend. This stopped them. Now the termite process will begin—the guards will feel sorry and help them buy with jewelry in exchange. Maybe I'll lose my earrings after all.

November 22, 1944. Jerry says there are two guns and a trench mortar near us, and a mountain howitzer near the point. Rupe is worried about my diary but I said Yamato was going to be too busy to search that deep. The trail is reported blown in 5 places.

November 24, 1944. I spent most of the day walking in sun and wind, enjoying the green and blue steeps of mountains, watching the Formosans plant onions and handfuls of seeds on the small terraces they have made back of the hospital. The onions send up a strong springlike odor from their warm hands. On the opposite rocky hill with a backdrop of radiant gradations of blue, I watched the Igorot woman make holes with a pointed hatchet wherein she planted camote vine. The husband, son and daughter younger than June and Bedie have hacked and dug and prepared the ground for days, working from the road right up the steep slope where black earth nestles in rocky cradles. Now it is beautiful—row after row of plants evenly set up to the point, then curving beyond and out of sight. They have worked hard, with bent backs and heaving arms, strained muscles. It is something to look at, already a reward, as is camp garden opposite. Ours is not so patiently dug, I am afraid. Jo has been an admirable garden leader, with monumental patience and effort accomplishing much with recalcitrant mortals and slow carabao, not to mention pricking and prodding commands constantly interfering. But the garden is there, growing, with a few actually enjoying the making of it.

Jerry came down at six about sunk after a day of starvation. They had camotes which were only half cooked for lunch, green beans which are not bulk enough. For supper, after all day on nothing, they had no camotes, only a little meat gravy, cabbages and soft rice because so many took hard rice that there was not enough to go round. Soft rice does not stay by one. Jerry could not keep his eyes open, his head up, or his speech and thoughts connected. He brought the *American Woman's Cookbook* but I could not bear to look at the colored pictures of roast chicken and fruit salad. I feel like clawing the air for fruit. It is two months since we had any. I felt bad about Jerry and worried over his condition long afterward.

November 25, 1944. Announcement of marriage of Kaye and Charlie on Thanksgiving Day is posted on the Bulletin Board. It is to be in church, by invitation only. It is the logical outcome to a camp romance though there are many pros and cons and ideas as usual.

Jerry says we just knocked the pants off the enemy in Leyte. The Japanese soldiers had only rifles, nothing else. How awful to pour in those young kids with nothing to fight with. Yet is is We or They, Our turn now. If only they would give in, instead of national hara-kiri. The wood crew struck, without any noon meal of rice, so Suda persuaded Oura to exchange camotes for rice for them. It is less in weight but all to their advantage. They watched the guards eat rice and meat right in front of them at noon and could not stand it anymore. The Formosans are losing their gaunt look with good chow here. Our men cut wood for them.

November 26, 1944. Jerry brought my Port Said pale topaz earrings and bracelet, asking if I minded exchanging them for food. I said no. I was giving them to June anyway and when I told her, she said she would rather eat them. Jerry said huskily he would make it up to her later but she won't need jewels any more than I will after being in here.

Jerry brought coffee and we went out to sit on the big beams used by the outdoor choir when church meets in the garden. The gray and green of pines in the sun, a white lamb with flopping ears nibbling near its mother by the bank, the deep dome of sky covering the blue bowl of our mountain valley; warmth, earth, and grass fragrance—it was a lovely spot and we talked long, ranging wide, smiling at some things. Jerry grinned awkwardly and his voice broke as he told me he had dropped from 212 to 159.

I tried to make Bedie connect his history book with his own life here and his personal experience—what men have been moved by, how and why they act, in the light of his own thoughts and actions.

On Saturday night topside, there was an introduction to a Japanese Nō play, with another one of Saki's, full of gay lines, which brought forth many laughs. The teenage group performed well and haori coats were the costumes.

November 27, 1944. Oura had a row with Carl yesterday, telling Carl this was Japanese soil and Carl retorted, "No, it isn't—it's American soil and if you wait long enough you'll find out."

I appreciate close contact with June and Bedie now, watching them grow up and learn for the future. Soon they will be adult and away. These days together are too precious to handle, lest they vanish at a touch, in spite of hunger. We will look back on them as wonderful some day, tough, but wonderful. At least we have not been separated. We will talk the same language after this common experience, not a gulf between us as there would have been if the children had gone to America. Now we have all been through it.

November 28, 1944. This camp with its American lack of, or obliviousness to, class feeling is an eye-opener to some of the British.

November 29, 1944. All the guards are out digging foundations and sawing fence posts to keep us off our lovely point. I had my last steep in the sun there yesterday.

There was a trade bazaar today in the dining room. An ivory carved ring in exchange for 2 pounds of peanuts; bath towels, sheets, for coffee. Most people crave food, not goods, but there will be some exchanges. Alan of the Co-op Exchange is in charge, with Edna, Harriet and others helping in different departments such as jewelry, stationery, towels, etc.

November 30, 1944. Thanksgiving Day: breakfast was late by about an hour, but there was a beautiful yellow banana by each bowl of rice and in the cups was steaming coffee, and on the rice was a spoonful of sugar!

Father Gowan, Carl, Art, and others took part in the Thanksgiving prayers and service. Bedie looked handsome in his sweater made from the long drawers, and his long trousers; June was lovely in my white dress with gold belt, red ribbon in her dark hair. She sang in the choir. From our bench we could hear Mary's rich voice singing "God Bless America." Then everyone stood up and we three stood too while they all sang "The Star Spangled Banner" for the first time in three years. Even the birds seemed silent, listening. It swelled out into the green bowl of the garden, up into the blue sky, deep and more full of meaning than it had ever been before. I preferred listening to it, not singing, for this way we had the full effect. We stood quietly, listening and singing in our hearts. I think Jerry was afraid to attend for fear of being too deeply moved. "God Save the King" followed the

"Stars and Stripes," so everyone sang what was deepest in him, his home-land.

After "The Star Spangled Banner" was sung, Jerry looked at me as though asking, "Are you all right? I am" very firmly. It was beautiful, the way we heard it.

Jerry made a good meat loaf from my half of breakfast rice, some corned beef and part of their corn meal and some curry. It was one of his best. We ate in the garden down here and [the family] shared their camp lettuce with a dressing of peanut butter mixed with vinegar which was made from camote water. Special Diets had camote, squash and tripe gravy for lunch. It took Jerry two hours of hard work to clean the tripe for this diet. He is one of the few who knows how to clean it and the only one willing to do it without a rake-off.

We ate leisurely, enjoying being together.

Supper was late, the line long, and Jerry brought my food—hamburgers from a camp cow, good candied camotes, our own private box lettuce, with sub-coffee from camp.

It is really something to be able to say that Carl has kept aloof from graft, with no breath of scandal or suspicions, in his position. It is an integrity which no other chairman has achieved in here. Some of them kept in position through those they shared with, in fact. The constant reelection of Carl is our great claim to democracy.

Kaye and her beloved Charlie were married at a small wedding by Carl at 4 P.M. today. The bride wore Daphne's lovely white organdy print. There were about 16 guests at a dinner afterward, including a wedding cake. It was in two cubicles in the Ark. The Dawsons gave up their cubicle for one night honeymoon quarters. The aides all attended the ceremony and Kaye is happy, cannot imagine herself married to anyone else. So all is serene and the couple settled for life, maybe. Young people have had a hard time in here—cramped, limited, suppressed. But not any more than the married ones at that. We have all been repressed beyond endurance, with all natural inclinations damned up for three years either by the enemy or our own fanatics.

It rained hard during the ceremony and clouds drifted low about us, like wide white ribbons through camp. Finally a dim moon showed and Joanne decided to have her dance exhibit. Oura enjoyed it thoroughly from the front row between Skerl's dark beard and Miss McKim's cheerful countenance. The girls were all barefoot, in short white gowns, with flowing hair which was most effective as they swayed, leaped or went weaving in and out, arms expressive. The real charm was in the peace and stillness, the soft footfalls and gentle running. Sakashita came in a Napoleonic swirling cape, with Yamato, to observe. A guard walked right through the path in the middle of the graceful white figures, his bayonet gleaming in the light, a contrast to the tranquility. His guttural sharp obeisance to Sakashita in the shadows behind us startled me as much as the swirl of dancers made him falter. The watery moon and the hospital spotlight gave illumination. Mary's voice in "Barcarolle" and others who sang could be fully appreciated in the outdoor space, and the young people closed the day joyously.

December 1, 1944. A crucial month. Camp runs out of vitamins sometime during the month, I run out of milk, the Marines come or not, and we have a good or a bad Christmas!

Kaye and Charlie have moved into the small space vacated by Skerls in the barracks when they moved to the Ark, so that settles the turbulent young romance which can now proceed normally, with sanctions of the guardhouse as well as the church and society.

The young art students of Mrs. Angeny's class made Future Rooms, which were on exhibit at school and later brought to the hospital. Bedie had brilliant red curtains in his room, a bookcase at the head of his bed and a radio beside it, convenient to reach. Lazy boy! All the girls put in mirrors. One boy had a fireplace, a big desk with drawers, and a bed—all very severe and business-like. Another had no place for clothes, insisting he was going to keep all his things under the bed in boxes. Sally's room was simply crammed with furniture, all jammed in together. Each showed the result of Concentration up-bringing, traits of character, desire for mirrors, frills and beauty. Bedie sold his later for three sheets of heavy white paper for me to write on! He said each sheet should last a week as I could write on all sides.

December 2, 1944. Dr. Mather told Jerry that the Medical Committee had allowed me P50 extra spending. This means two pounds more peanuts!

Bedie announced that he wished to be called Fred or Frederick, not Bedie, any more. I volunteered to start it. He *is* growing up.

December 3, 1944. Our morning coffee was a stormy period as I tried to urge Jerry to speak out strongly for any place that is vacated in a move or moves. I must get June into a new atmosphere, for tears come into her eyes often these days. She wants to move so badly. Jerry and Bedie like where they are, so Jerry cannot see it as I do because he is satisfied. He has lost more for his size than any one in camp. He looks dreadful and feels it. It has driven me almost crazy this past month. It is three months since I entered the hospital, a long time to be under sick rules when one is nearly normal at least two thirds of the time.

December 4, 1944. Wilma was taken out for questioning after she came back from town. Yamato could not believe she did not ask people outside about "news." He finally said, "Have you no curiosity?" Thinking very fast all through the interview, she maintained that she had no curiosity, she only wanted to get her husband on his feet before the Americans came in and this she had been able to do by nursing him. She told some people that all Filipinos looked alike to her and she did not dare ask any of them, never knowing when it might be a stool pigeon; and anyhow, "one was way up or way down whatever one heard so we just kept going on an even keel" she told Yamato which finally convinced him though he shook a puzzled head, as every one else is ravenous for news! He just can't figure it. They were smart and figured it out ahead, gave out no news when they first came in. Later they let some seep out gradually.

Notice on the Board: "At our meeting with the Commandant he again warned us that our American type of friendly greeting with just a nod of the head does not meet with his approval and that if anyone should happen to be within speaking distance when he passes they must bow in accordance with the approved custom of his own country, thus showing proper respect to his position over us. The Executive Committee."

[Clara Bergamini says] "We have a horse and they have cut the wagon in half for the horse to take it to market for our supplies—because there isn't any more gasoline, no fuel to run the truck!" There is no more alcohol. Either the Army is taking it or our own planes destroyed the supply and there isn't any. Therefore we acquire a horse, cut something in two to make a cart. The children will be entranced with a constantly present live horse. There will be manure and the millions of flies that it brings. The garbage crew won't have to pull the cart to market, thanks to the horse. That is progress of a sort. What will the horse eat is the next topic and question. Probably the grass that belongs to the cows and goats.

December 5, 1944. Marie sent in word that one sheet is worth P1,100 on the outside. Mom just traded her sheet in here for a small can of coffee and says it will be the most expensive coffee she ever drank.

The wood crew saw little signs along the road saying, "Soon. Very soon."

The horse is to have more roomy quarters than any of us. The building proceeds amid chatter and laughter of the Formosans.

The Command told the Committee they must only come at certain hours to ask or talk over problems, and they must come to his office. They said they did not think this was the way to have friendly relations—that he should feel free to come to the Committee office at any time and the same with our taking problems to him. He retorted that we were not friends, we were enemies.

December 6, 1944. Today the hot plates are turned in and those who owned and used them constantly feel tragic about it. We who have known only what it was like to be without them feel no loss at all—very much like the underprivileged feel everywhere. It is nothing to us when a privilege we did not have is denied to others. The only way we notice it is by the overcrowding at the small stoves which are left.

Three different plumes of smoke rise from three different areas. The season is still too wet for grass fires or brush. The smoke is too thick, too heavy, for anything but a village and all its supplies. Conjecture begins to fly about and even Church comes down from the kitchen to watch Kapangan burn. Those who have been there say it must be there—one smoke the church area, another smoke the Chinese store area. At first every one said oh, the guerrillas are burning Japanese storage and supplies. But it is more likely the other side of the war picture—that the Japanese have finally gone in near some of the guerrilla strongholds to burn these villages which are "sympathetic." A heavy dark smoke cloud spreads all along the valley, out along the seacoast. It is a pall, a portent of what is about to commence, of fierce action, suffering and killing of thousands before the island of Luzon is lost and won again.

All morning we watch the puffs of white smoke spring up, turning into dense black columns. It is being systematically carried out, we can tell, as the torch moves on to the next place. The flames are high at times, easy to see even from this distance. We only hope the Igorots had warning and left their homes in the night, were not caught and held in the burning buildings as so often happens. Will every habitation go this way as the Japanese begin to relinquish? Tomorrow will the cloud rise the other way, toward Baguio, with nothing but ashes left when Armageddon ends and the last Japanese is dead, only a Phoenix left to rise from the smouldering ruins of habitations? We are about to find out, as villages burn on ridge and in valley.

With glasses at the hospital window, Gene watched huts and houses burn. It is tragedy for those people who are desolate enough in these times of no rice and food scarcity. What little they have left is taken away in a night and day, but they will survive, many of them, to kill and hate and take revenge. The barrios are near guerrilla areas so it is elimination. Loss of stores and gardens may affect our food supply.

When I suggested we walk a bit, Jerry admitted he was having chills, whether from the boil, the vaccine, too much sun this morning or the flu, he did not know. I am frantic to get up there, for us to be together to look after each other. Perhaps he will have to come to the hospital, then the kids will have to look after themselves and bring chow down here to eat in the garden. It is no use to worry but I can't help it right now. I feel desperate tonight. The food is so bad and they get so little. It could be as poor as this for weeks. Jerry is worried about January but I said not to think as far as that, we might all be dead by then and he said perhaps. Anything can happen to us in the hands of desperate people, but I think we will survive. If only Jerry would let go and rest. His mind is in a bad state as a result of fatigue, undernourishment, with loss of weight. He is even worried about himself as well he might be, for his hunger has been frightful for weeks, his weight loss alarming.

I was hours getting to sleep. The horse was homesick, whinnied all night off and on, in his palatial quarters.

December 7, 1944. Minutes: "A salt issue cannot be made to each internee because no ration has been received this month. The salting down of camp pork consumed an unusual amount. . . . Garden attendance for last month shows a 35% decrease in persons, 30% decrease in hours, from the October figures. . . . We now have 49 hens, 7 roosters, 11 chicks, 12 ducks, 6 ducklings, 3 cows (1 on hill), 1 yearling cow, 2 calves; 1 pig, 7 piglets" (the Japanese will not allow us to list the "interned pig and 5 piglets" imprisoned by the guards), "20 goats and 9 kids."

Dr. Mather came in to tell us what Sugano had answered when pressed as to why no food or camotes. He said the Igorots were not bringing in any camotes for a few days because the Japanese had had to burn all their villages from which the camotes came, because of so much guerrilla activity. They had wiped out their stronghold and food supply. So they admit it. The ten Constabulary were shot as an example. It is just building up more hate for shapened bolos in the end. The guerrillas have gone into action, the Japanese react to it, and we cannot expect otherwise now. It is hard to remember the inevitable, the two sides of every question, when one feels sorry for the Igorots. It is their country, after all, and it is not the first time history has intruded to change that direction. First the Spanish, then the Americans, now the Japanese.

December 8, 1944. A load of camote greens came in, thank heaven. We start on our 4th year tomorrow.

Nearly 300 Baguio Japanese are being impressed into service. All these sons and fathers are forced to take part in a thing they did not start or want, caught in the whirlpool, the desire for a new order contolled by the Rising Sun. Even though they perish, they have played a part in the future of the Philippines.

Dear Junie said, "Daddy has been so cross and snappy and irritable. I used to cry and get upset over it, but today I could see he was sick. His eyes looked terrible and his impatience didn't hurt me any more. I began to treat him as though he were my little boy and it seemed so funny, Mama. He was just like a sick little boy." I told her to always remember that men and women were just grown-up children.

We all discuss the latest "orders." In the office Carl shouted to Yamato that he could go tell the Command he was crazy—that the hospital could not be moved. Yamato said he could not tell him that because he was afraid of him. Once before Denki sent the same message and Yamato answered, "I know. I have known it for a long time." This time Carl told him to go to

Manila and tell Gen. Kwo that we were being run by a crazy man. But several groups of officers have been here with maps, paying special attention to the hospital, looking toward the burned area.[44] As their hour nears and guerrilla action increases in fury against their reaction, the Japanese think less and less of what happens to us. They not only do not care, but they simply cannot think of us in their complete absorption in war and survival. We are all down to the bitter dregs and the draught has more poison for them than for us. If the Generals and Colonels decide to take over the hospital building for their own observation glasses and points of vantage and protection against what may surge to the very road below—they will do it and in a hurry.

December 9, 1944. The head nurse had a birthday party in Baby House garden for all the nurses and aides at 10. Trays full of cakes—cupcakes, in these days of few stoves! Parties should stop. Even eggless cakes take wood for fire and the Command has cut the wood ration. Eggless gingerbread is good too, they say. No one ever knows when to stop in here whether it is rum (steak) running, note passing or cooking in the hospital kitchen. They always overdo it, until it is cut off from all of us.

Jerry's voice shook, he was so relieved to find that we have 2 pounds of beans which had been used to bury my notes.

Jerry is better. His temperature broke in the night. Bedie has been faithful about visiting me. I asked him if he thought he had learned anything in here. He shrugged, replied, "Not much, except I've learned what it is to be hungry." I told him if he had learned that, he had learned much, for then he would understand one of the things that made revolutions—because hunger and seeing their children hungry drove many men to desperate measures. He looked surprised and had never thought that hunger could be a motive. He does not remember much of life before Concentration, only the general outlines of the house and the servants etc. It constantly amazes me what details he has forgotten.

June came along glowing from choir practice—dewey-eyed and dreamy. She certainly loves music—a heritage from Helen perhaps. She talked of the Christmas music they had practiced—beautiful, beautiful! I told her we would not have any gifts this year, not even Daddy's lovely carvings, perhaps not a great deal to eat. She scarcely noticed what I said, brushing it aside, "Oh Mummie, the first Christmas in here I lay in bed and *listened* to the carolers in the early dark-dawn. The second Christmas I joined them, went about singing with the group. This Christmas, the third, I can do it again. I love it!" She has the real spirit of it, not caring about gifts or a big meal, but possessing a singing heart. When I told Jerry what she said he replied, "I don't think either of them care that there are no gifts, no big splurge celebration. All Bedie talks and thinks about is ships and Marines coming in droves and of a Family Unit for us." This last he wants passionately and perhaps he will get it. June talks and plans all the time for the future—how

Daddy has promised her some [eye]glasses with only a gold rim at the top so they won't show like her present ones all patched with aluminum; how we will visit Gaga [her maternal grandmother] in New England and Aunt Bunnie in Shangri-La (Virginia) and Grandma Crouter who will make a crisp flaky crust on an apple pie for us like she used to do; of visiting Aunt Margy and seeing all the Bellamys; and of eating, eating, eating, everywhere, until we become balanced again but never forgetting what it is like to be hungry and not have enough from one meal to another, always a corner of our minds haunted by prison camp and millions who never get away from such conditions. All this will sharpen our appreciation of whatever we see in America. First we want to join with and look after Nida and her family—Ismael perhaps returning even before we do. We cannot go away from these islands and leave them unprovided for, because whatever we may have left of material goods and health is due to their loyalty and courage in standing by. How I pray that nothing happens to them during these last weeks and that we may get together and show our gratitude for their steady faithfulness.

December 10, 1944. If only I can make Bedie relate history to actual living, give him a new slant, take it out of the printed page and give it life. I asked him if he knew he was actually living history in here and he said yes, quite simply; no more, but he was stirred by our conversation.

Clara gave her steamed ground watercress to Bob who thanked her politely saying, "If I hadn't seen it beforehand I would have thought you had chewed it," which sums up the watercress perfectly.

December 11, 1944. Jerry told about his talk with Yamato, telling him how hard it would be on the undernourished men to move. Yamato asked why he did not go to the hospital and he answered that too many felt as sick as he did and those taking care of the sick didn't feel too well themselves, that nearly everyone was sick including Yamato himself. Yamato says Oura worries a lot. Jerry says he almost likes Yamato at times; he tries to be so friendly and is just another father, feeling under the weather himself. If Jerry could talk with Oura he would discover the same. Language is an immense barrier.

There apparently was a commando raid on Northern Luzon, which then withdrew.

December 13, 1944. The Commandant was walking about watching the soldiers work. He passed behind our bench and I was afraid not to speak even though he did not pass our way, so without rising I called out, "Ohayo, gozaimasu, Bunshiyocho!" He turned with a surprised look and bowed deeply, pleased. Then I went in to look up the last word to be sure it was right!

Carl surprised us with a visit which was chiefly to ask if June would join the Union Church a week from Sunday. We were both willing to leave it to her. She listened to his outline of what it meant to join—fellowship with those believing in God and Christ who forgives all sin. She hesitated, then asked if she could think it over. He was not at all insistent. Carl was not at all sympathetic with my going home or a Family Unit for us.

December 14, 1944. Jerry came down with tea, quite excited over the activity, especially about all the planes coming from the north as though from a field established there and not from an east coast carrier. As we sat on the bank, six planes flew north again and afterward four circled around over Baguio and camp and Trinidad. A boom sounded over near Santo Tomas Mountain. There was constant dashing about camp, straining of eyes, and general excitement. Bedie jumped out of the school window twice to see planes.

The horse—oh the horse—came galloping home with a bareback rider, with six soldiers pulling the cart far behind him. It was loaded with grass for his fodder! It seems there is no harness, so it is being made. Now we can see him hitched to it, experimentally, being urged up the hill from the gate with our vegetables, but he does not like and is saying No. A wild cow, a wild horse, a wild bunch in here, including the Command.

December 15, 1944. Committee Minutes: "After last week's meeting, a written request was sent to the Command that families of internees be allowed to visit the camp on Christmas Day. Mr. Yamato replied that this would be impossible. Owing to the dangerous conditions Outside, we may not expect visitors. A second request made at the same time was that Christmas packages of food, clothing, toys and other gifts be allowed to come into camp from friends and relatives Outside during Christmas week. The reply was that 'the Command will take care.' However, packages will be allowed in on the 17th, next Sunday, which is the regular day for money and packages to come in. While there is no way to get word out to interested people on the outside, it is felt that they will take advantage of the opportunity to send things in on that day. Salt was received but no tea is available. A soya sauce issue will be made to individuals before Christmas, also an issue of salt. . . . For the first time specific medicines as requested by us have been received from the Japanese. . . . Attention is called to the lack of care being taken by some men in the fulfillment of their night watch duties. It was pointed out that this shift comes to each individual at long intervals, yet many men are not reporting when it comes their turn. This was brought sharply to notice last night when an emergency case occurred in No. 2 barracks and there was no watch on duty to help out. An appeal is made to the men to take their responsibility in this matter more seriously. . . . It has been reported that some of the camotes in the camp garden are nearing maturity, and that in another six weeks the garden should be contributing to our diet, perhaps one meal a day. . . . It was the opinion of the Committee that the camp as a whole should have some demonstration of celebration of Christmas, and Father

Gowan was asked to appoint a Committee to take care of the decorations for a tree etc. The Japanese have been asked to provide something 'special' for that occasion, if possible. . . . A Christmas pageant will be held Christmas Eve in the sunken garden under the direction of Winnie. Other plans will be announced later when it is seen what can be worked out. There will be a program next Saturday evening of music by the Male Chorus.''

800 pounds of camotes came in, with a little cabbage. . . . We were informed that the hospital and Baby House are to be vacated immediately, and the Command asked how soon we would be able to accomplish this. We replied ten days or more, and he said it must be completed by the 23d. We said we would try. We must leave the two wood stoves at the hospital and Baby House, and electric hot plates would have to be used at the new location.

Dr. Mather said to me, "You want to cubiclize, don't you?" I answered, "Yes, if you think I can leave the hospital." He said I could and Bedie began turning handsprings and doing leaps. The doctor laughed and said, "Whoa, it's not settled yet." But Bedie was off in a cloud of Family Unit dust. The family came down with Peg and we made plans. The doctor gave me permit to hear the Men's Chorus tonight.

December 16, 1944. During the complete quiet of roll call we all heard a long sustained salvo of guns, heavy guns, also planes and the rip of bombs. Kaito who was lounging through roll call as usual, suddenly called out, "Dismissed" and the entire 450 camp members burst into a din of joy, whoop and Oh Boy, chatter and laughter, as they flocked to the edge of the bank or down the steps to Baby House point. We rush out of the hospital to listen to the sound of battle which is plain. All past sounds pale before this, which to our ears could be naval guns for landing forces. The spotters on the hill whistle off and on and later blow the all clear. These signals are phoned to town, it is said, even as we did it three years ago. We are almost worn out already, dashing in and out full of thrill.

One of the most interesting features of the present Big Move is the number of people who want Family Units—to be together as crisis nears, to take care of each other when sick or run down.

June is making a potholder for Dad's Christmas—"He uses such a black one now. I want to give him something." She is fully cognizant of how much her father has gone through, how hard he has worked to keep them going and how much he has denied himself and suffered. Each one of them tries to make up to the other one, now, and in future plans.

We all went with Peg to the fine concert of the Men's Chorus. It was my first appearance in three months and I enjoyed being back in the smoke, din, the mob. The program was made to suit all tastes—"Old Virginny," "Old Kent Road," "Home," "Swannee River," and other popular ones. Then there was a stunning modern one of Tchaikowsky's "On the Desert," and a final tremendous chorus "By Babylon's Ways." This was applauded until it was repeated and it sent shivers of delight up our spines. Several quartette numbers were well done, by Carl, Vinson, Gene and Dirks. They all smiled and enjoyed singing so lustily. Father Gowan then came to the front of the stage, reminding us that this was the last program due to the room being used for other purposes ''and because we are also busy being entertained by outside activities.'' He recalled the first program in June 27, 1942, when Nick Kaminsky spoke on astronomical matters and it was our first commingling, because it was during this period that we could speak only 1 hour a day to our husbands and wives, with barbed wire between and a whistle calling us home on the dot. At first, programs were on Wednesday and Saturday, then after four months they were on Saturday only, for two years. He spoke of the various talents which were generously given, and the amount of labor put into programs which was never recorded on the work sheet but which lifted our morale and held it high. He closed with special gratitude to Marvin Dirks who had trained so many choruses, quartettes and other singing groups and who so fittingly closes the entertainments with this splendid men's program. After thunderous applause, we left the dining room, as a dining room, for the last time. Plates and cutlery have been given out and people henceforth eat in their cubicles, wash their own dishes. There is no more Common Room in which to eat or sing or play. Single women will live in the dining room, Family Units in the men's lower barracks.

December 17, 1944. Elizabeth started the day's rumor by telling of Yamato saying that we must be happy as we would be free by Christmas or at least soon after. She treated the statement as though he were joking but he assured her he was not.

We watched many relatives coming to see their families in the morning.

Bedie comes down all aglow and begs me to come outside quickly. He has a package—from Miss Ramos outside! Perhaps she heard and hurriedly sent it in, for they had not been told that we could receive food. We waited for Jerry to come before we opened it and then found three kilos of coffee beans, two cakes of Lux toilet soap (in great demand on our Barter Board), three cakes of laundry soap. Jerry was deeply moved at this expression of thought from his office girl, when we need it so badly. He may even trade some of the coffee for flour and the soap helps to replace what we traded for my milk. If camp gives us sugar we can carry on another month.

The noon serving was good and a full helping so that Jerry and the kids were almost satisfied for the first time in weeks.

I drank my fill of the view which was glorious today. There are such beautiful blues and grays and snowy clouds resting on them like frozen peaks. The terraces are clearly defined on levels like children's building blocks; some yellow, some full of mirror-like water, some emerald green.

One of the Formosans said to young Vere, "You are English. I liked the English, and the Americans too, at Cabanatuan. Maybe I can get you some Christmas.'' Then he added, ''But I probably will be dead by then.''

The children say Jerry is wroth over our cubicle space—it is on the dark east side, and a damp dark place, due to a family of six needing the larger space. We who had always worked for it and waived our rights more than once could be given no preference at all. But it is settled and we will be together which is all that matters.

December 18, 1944. Conference December 18, Command with Carl, Miss McKim and Jo Smith. ''The Command first said he would talk about the food problem. The food coming into the camp for the internees will decrease in the future. After one month we will probably receive one half of the present vegetable ration. The corn and rice ration will remain the same. However, Sergeant Sugano will try to get more vegetables from the Army. That is just a friendly act—he has no authority to draw from Army supplies, [so] we cannot expect to get very many vegetables from the Army. We must think about the future in regard to the garden. One thing is very certain—that the vegetables received will get less and less so it is up to us internees if we want to increase the garden activity or not. . . . We may think in light of recent activity that the war will soon be over, but the Command does not believe it will be over soon. It may last for ten years. . . . Mr. Smith reported that they are ready right now for 1,500 camote cuttings, and the Command agreed to secure these day after tomorrow. The Command again suggested that now is the time to prepare for the next planting season, and if it is our opinion that we want to make further plans for the garden, he will tell us *where to plant both inside and outside the fence.''

There is housecleaning everywhere and big dumpings in the waste cans. The barracks are chaos. Camp is on the move! It is one of those irritable, devastating times, yet with exhilaration too. Spring cleaning, pioneering, new plans, new neighbors, new outlook. Consternation among hospital staff who now have to get their chow in line like the rest of us, by act of Committee. Frantic last baking on the hospital stove. All plants in hospital garden are being transplanted into boxes to take topside.

· Typhoon, the calf, fell in the ditch and broke its neck so had to be killed. We will have ''typhoon'' fried rice for supper.

December 19, 1944. Art thinks I'm crazy but I insist that to think like a Japanese one must throw out all preconceived ideas and start new as in learning Kata Kana, Hira Gana, Chinese characters or shorthand. There is no sense to it on the basis of our way of doing things, but it could be their way. I have tried to make a beginning of getting inside their thought process.

After going to Peg's I looked into the Green Barracks which was partly vacated and turned upside down. I peeked into our corner, the curtain down and our stuff piled on the bed and in the corner ready to move. The under-house cubicle looked as though a tornado had hit it. I should not have gone there, but kept the memory of its charm instead. Next I went to the dining room where partition was going up in the center, another one being taken down and about 8 or 10 posts and beds being swung in a clamor all at once. Men were carrying beds and trunks on their backs, and bags, boxes and lumber were going in all directions. Our space was bigger than I had pictured it. I sat there watching Jerry cut and carve notches, slashing himself with the knife and dripping red on the cement floor, using his bunk as a stepladder, with others sharing it and the tools as well. This is by far the most difficult and tiresome move, with limited time, materials and tools, and with everyone worn to a frazzle and at rope's end. This week I will leave the mountains' peace and go back to humanity.

When asked what he wanted to be when grown up, British Derek answered, "An American." What a blow to his parents!

I found a bunch of very tangled fence wire and Jerry was thrilled to have this discard of the guards. He dragged it home and started stringing it and sharing it with others.

June came down later to tell about a lost plate and some fat stolen from our cubicle. She was in tears over Jerry's scolding and said it was not her fault, but I told her that she was tired and he was groggy and that she must go home directly to bed. She dried her eyes and I hugged and patted her. Loss of even two teaspoons of fat is a calamity in these days when there is no more. I know how savage it makes Jerry feel and he just lets go.

Kaito asked Ray if he had any message for Hayakawa whom he expected to see in a couple of days. Ray said, "Tell him for God's sake to surrender."

December 20, 1944. I spent an hour up topside and didn't feel nearly so buzzy or shaky as yesterday. But everything up there looks so shabby, so dusty, cluttered and messy. I cannot get used to this. Can it be we all look as crummy as that? No doubt we do.

Another tragic animal loss for camp—the wild cow has not returned! Dirks has combed the hill all day but can find no trace of it. He thinks an Igorot has it branded. It is a dreadful loss in milk for us.

December 21, 1944. It is a big day in my life—leaving the hospital after four months and cubiclizing all at once. After three years of separate living quarters we four are together as a family. All afternoon I kept saying "Oh it's wonderful to be home. It's heavenly," until the children groaned. Kept apart by the enemy for two years—then by our own politics and some people—thanks to Tomibe, we are finally united, no longer running back and forth between barracks and underground and hospital. It will be a rest cure just to settle in one place. Jerry and the children can relax. I laughed in joy all through supper, it was such fun. Jerry looked at Bedie and said quietly, "Well, son, you've got your cubicle at last." and Bedie looked as though he were lighted from within. He has wanted it so long and needed us both. It is our Christmas present and we are happy.

After ten, the children lolled on the bed, hungry and listless, but at least we were together. June and Jerry took all the cans and bottles off the shelves, cleaned and rearranged them. On the other side I hung the gay colored furoshikis to brighten up the room. Moths and silver-snails have chewed holes in the squares but they still cover dingy tin and bamboo uprights. Our side wall is a white bedspread of Smiths, with the flamingos on orange square in its center. The other side is a battered sheet iron of Pat's, half dusty red, half rusty and peeling gray paint. Two colored squares help cover this and it is much like our dugout. The front wall is a Red Cross sheet and the cubicle canvas-door with our dresses hanging against the sheet. Shelves line the wall space, bags, boxes and trunk are under the bed. There is a table, three stools and a big box with improvised pillows to sit on under the windowsill where there is a freshly potted geranium sent up by Miss Elaine! One of the furoshikis screens the window from public gaze, for we keep the shutter pushed back to let in some light.

Oura is seen walking along the upper path, surveying the tireless coming and going of all of us, resembling an ant hill gone wild over some mysterious stir-up from within. As order comes out of chaos, our belongings do not seem to look shabby any more but take on the quiet content of home. Only the hospital remains to be moved, the most staggering job of all.

December 22, 1944. To think that in all the devious workings of camp life, I should have to bow thanks to Oura and those above him for my possession of a Family Unit, after all the attempts to get it otherwise.

Bedie is here reading or helping, June is sewing and chattering.

December 23, 1944. I slept well, and warm, even without a brick. June is a brick in herself!

Lt. Sakashita's fat little chow puppy died and they feared it was poison. He came with it cradled in his arms, saying, "It's my little sweetheart!" almost in tears over its death. They finally decided death might have come from a fish bone. A second pup died and a third was sick and the Japanese were greatly upset as they are much attached to the little dogs. They need to give and receive affection when they are lonely and homesick.

December 24, 1944. June sang in the choir and Bedie went to church with me to hear Walter's fine sermon when his daughter became a church member, with two other girls. The questions they had to answer on the Bible, God, Sin, and Repentance were far stronger, more orthodox than I had thought. I was just as content that June had not "felt the urge." It was the first time I had attended church in the school building. Three planes came overhead and wrote a smoky V in the sky for us during the service. The guards galloped past the open windows on the horse, the ducks quacked importantly underneath the church floor, chickens cheeped and pecked in our view, while Walter reminded us that before long we will be going out—to freedom *and* community obligations; to a life where *rights* should be less important than *duties*.

After lunch Jerry cleaned the tripe for special diets. It came from the young bull which was brought in on the hoof and presented to us by the Commandant for Christmas dinner, with the request that the guardhouse be given a front quarter. Pauli slaughtered it as well as the young heifer whose wild mother has not returned, so we will have hamburgers and plenty of gravy tomorrow. Sugano also brought in a big order of sugar, peanuts and bucayo, and Santa is to give these out in rations to families tomorrow. Skerl is certainly relieved to have something come in that Santa can give out. Several men were allowed to go on the hill yesterday to cut Christmas trees and these have been decorated with paper chains, borrowed tinsel and ornaments, set up out near the schoolhouse.

As I lie on the bed and look up at the bamboo uprights and the tin wall, I feel as though we live in a scaffolding. It is the vague outline and beginning of a future which will be more bare, less gracious, but more vital and interesting than the past.

In the pageant, Bedie was a shepherd kneeling before the manger, and June sang in the choir, so my Godchild Anne and I sat on the bank together as we did last year, listening to the music made by voices and violin. It was much simpler than last year but most impressive for adults if too somber for children. Down in the garden, next to the paddock, the crowds "walked in darkness" as Jo Smith read to us—walked in tribulation, sorrow and despair, until the Watchman called "What of the night?" and was answered from the hill. Then the Angel appeared to Mary who sang her joy and the final manger scene was a gem against the bank. Nipa fronds covered the roof and the Wise Men and Shepherds came to worship. Baby goats added a realistic touch with their bleating, until they ran away even before their appearance and were caught by their owner at the top of the bank. Through the living pine boughs shone the star Venus with that steady, clear, unshimmering light of a planet. It was a perfect Star of Bethlehem. Don Zimmerman read the preface which compared our present darkness with that one in the past, looking toward the light of deliverance. Around us were sounds of war—the laughter of Formosans in the lighted windows overlooking the garden; the click of cleats on the boots of a changing guard; the rumble of trucks on the trail. But we sat for a little while in the cool darkness, listening to "Joy to the World" and hopes of Peace.

December 25, 1944. June was up at 5:45 to sing with the carolers.

We each had a present—June's doodad potholder for her father; Betty's puzzle for Fred and a headband for June; my pink pillow with an N on it from Peg with a card-poem about Cute Curtains for the Crouter Cubicle for Christmas. Izzy sent June a lovely chain with rose quartz and a pair of matching earrings. It thrilled her. We took three small panties, a pajama, a little bottle and a gold finger ring up to the Scott children after dark last night, where we saw their small tree with paper chains, cotton snow and handmade decorations, around it piled two light green painted doll beds, a green cart, a hobby horse, some stuffed pandas and refurbished dolls. It gave us a Christmas feeling to see it, with three small stockings hanging beneath the tree. All gifts for the children were made from absolutely ultimate in scraps, dresses ripped up to make stuffed horses, clown dolls, teddy bears, and hobbyhorses which are the current youthful craze along with carts, wheelbarrows and kites which doting fathers like to fly. Izzy made six Red Cross bath towels into three bathrobes with initials in colors on each for Anne, Susan and John Hay. There was astounding ingenuity as usual—more, because of far less to do with.

Breakfast was double portion of rice, coffee for each, sugar and a banana apiece. Jerry made a luscious onion gravy with Vegex and suet cracklings for our rice. How we loved the small coating of grease it left on the roof of our mouths when we have had none for months. On our second helping we had a big spoonful of peanut butter and a big pour of syrup. At eight, we were given a peanut ration and some bucayo, still full from breakfast for the first time in months.

We called on Peg and Scotts to see their gifts. At ten, Charlie Fears' Santa in a red suit and long gray beard drove in, in the cart, behind a very refractory horse led by Lewis Robinson. Up the hill road they came and the children let out loud squeals when they saw it. Santa dispensed chewy candy from the Japanese, a ration of roasted peanuts, coconut candy and a banana. At Santa's elbow stood Dr. Mather with a list of children's names up to 18—so that this time there would be no duplication or omissions. Afterward the grown-ups lined up with cups for another drink of coffee. Jerry was on duty as K.P. from 9 to 12 but took time out to imbibe this with me.

We had signed up for raw hamburgers without onions, intending to cook it ourselves. Then we decided to eat it raw, making finely chopped raw onion sauce with a soy-ginger preparation spread over it. Was it marvelous? Oh! We made it last as long as we could, with lettuce from our box garden. Camp gave us corn mix and camotes but we did not eat them. We had some tripe-rice soup instead and it tasted like chicken! The family was staggering after this meal but we went to Peg's for coffee and the light cake Peg had made by pooling ingredients with Jerry. It was even frosted with our ration of sugar and an egg which came in Carl's bag from Maria. Such fluffy frosting! Carl was with our two families and we lingered over all of it. Then we needed a siesta.

Bedie's Christmas note to Daddy, "I want to tell you I appreciate all you have done for me this year and I'm glad I could help you with the tripe today.'' His card with an American flag on it was lost in the moving but I told him Dad would appreciate the message without it and I was right.

We had Jerry's tripe soup with camp rice, acres of onions which were mostly tough green tops, candied camotes in a syrup made from their own juice, gravy from hamburger drippings. We could not eat the onions so I put them all through a strainer to add with the gravy to the tripe soup. June filled the plates with heaping soft rice and Bedie wolfed his down as he has all of today's meals. I eat slowly and far less than they do.

When Fildey and Mrs. Greer played gay tunes for dancing, they were ready to have fun. Bedie is a good leader. June dances well and has plenty of partners. Bedie had a dance with Eloise and John didn't get one which just put the top on Bedie's day with that odd happiness that such things bring.

But the dancing and general excitement of the day, not to mention the pitiful overeating (if one can call it that) was too much for Bedie. As the last tune died away and he was sure he would not miss any more, he went tearing past us through the kitchen, sending word back by his sister that ''I lost it but don't tell Dad.'' I guessed it was the Christmas feast and went out to hunt for him, just in time to hold his head over a Socony laundry tin. Poor kid, I felt so sorry for him, losing all that good food. Weak and shaky, he was soon asleep with a hot brick against his tummy.

The three small trees glittered with lights again as on Christmas Eve, symbols of the shrinkage in size, manner and content of all our celebration this year. As for me, in my heart there was no lack, for my two wishes were given to us—health enough for me to leave the hospital after four months and a Family Unit cubicle in which we revel all day.

Jack and Ruth announced their betrothal—the third camp romance to reach a culmination.

December 26, 1944. Jerry's best gift was learning from Dr. Mather that his badly swollen feet and ankles are *not* kidney trouble as the test for it was all right. The doctor says it must be some vitamin deficiency.

Red Cross messages on the Board were cold comfort but here they are. Canadian message: ''To all Canadian prisoners of war and internees, The Canadian Red Cross sends warmest good wishes and transmits from all your next of kin affectionate greetings for Christmas and the New Year.'' Text of the year-end message from International Red Cross at Geneva to prisoners of war and civilian internees: ''Once more you are passing the festive season far away from your homes. The I.R.C. Committee addresses the following message to Prisoners of War and Civilian Internees of all nations and asks all camp leaders to post the text in their respective camps. To you prisoners, disseminated in a world of war, the IRCC brings an affectionate message of comfort on this last day of 1944. It does not ignore your grief and your anxieties. It also knows how increasingly painful the separation is the longer the days of your captivity drag on. It is with this knowledge at heart that the IRCC and its three thousand collaborators in Switzerland are doing everything in their power to bring you help and relief. To all of you and to all of those who are dear they send their sincerest wishes." Still, this is better than nothing at all!

A truck drove in full of guards singing, cheering and greeted noisily. The Committee was called into conference with the Commandant while the guards rushed with candles to make a place for the new soldiers *in the vacated buildings*.

I lapped my milk quietly in the kitchen, then Bedie and I took a walk. Suddenly one of the missionary girls said to us, "Oh, I do hope the latest rumor isn't true, don't you?" "What is it? We've heard nothing," we replied. She gasped, "Yamato rushed to the shoe shop wanting his shoes whether they were done or not for we were all going to Manila on Thursday or Friday he told Carl." Roxie dashed in with the "low-down." "Sixty percent of camp was going on Thursday the 28th and the other 40% on Friday. We all sat down and looked at each other, simply floored. Such news on top of the exhausting moving and holidays was the last straw. Jerry looked absolutely sunk. He slumped and groaned, "Oh God—oh no—not that, now!" But it was true.

Jerry sat down looking old, his swollen feet protesting every second at more standing. I started to take down the furoshikis and when he saw me do this, he believed, jumped up and began to tell me what I must discard, and throw away. Two suitcases each, a bed roll and *no* mattresses. Rumor says we are going to the hospital of Old Bilibid. That will be something—*a real* jail experience.

It was tough business eliminating our possessions. Lights were allowed till 12, and we packed and packed and packed. I never slept all night.

Four days of peaceful, homelike cubicle, after waiting a whole year for it—then it vanishes! All our work and scaffold is upset by war! Jerry said, "To think that yesterday I was worrying over losing a Cottora can, while today I am throwing away suits right and left."

December 27, 1944. All day there was packing, killing of chickens, cows, goats, giving out of rations of onions, garden camotes, grain rice, sugar, corn flour. Drugs were hurriedly packed again and rushed right off to Manila by Sakashita before the Military Police could take it, as they moved in and took possession of the dental office—promising a receipt for it. We worked all day but we did have good food. For supper huge pieces of stewed chicken, two apiece. It was the first taste in two years and how heavenly it was! There was lettuce from the garden and all the rice we could eat after starving for weeks. We could hardly believe it.

It is a tough trip ahead. One officer says it won't be long for us—maybe invasion within three weeks and then we will be in care of our own people.

Rumor says there is a landing at Mindoro and that an ultimatum tells the Japanese to put *all* Americans in one place in Manila Open City, gives them a certain period in which to do this. So we are torn up by the roots and rushed to the lowlands.

We think of three weeks in Bilibid without a mattress.

Many cars came down the trail, including blue buses which no doubt brought up troops and will take us on their return trip. We are to leave our blue mountains and view, our fun and our misery. Bedie says, "We'll see our friends!" and Jerry who is beat answers, "Who wants to, right now—and I bet they feel the same about us." Sakashita says they see our planes in Manila every day.

The Japanese came out from town to buy mattresses, paying P75, P100 and P150 for them. For shame—that is only the price of a cup of coffee now! They will make dozens of times that amount on each one we leave. It is the old game of the world—profiting by the misfortune and pressure on others. June sold one for P100 and was very proud. The bill looks like a freshly minted one and we may keep it for souvenir.

December 28, 1944. Up at 3 A.M. after sleeping a couple of hours. Last packing was frantic, of two big bedrolls and six pieces to carry on our laps. The children and I carried five Red Cross cartons over to the school building, addressed to Nida. It was pitch dark except for a glorious full moon and heavenly cool air which we gulped in large breaths before descending into the heat.

Roll call went on forever under Yamato and we were all dying to dash to the toilet. Standing, standing, standing by baggage on the parade ground, changes of whole groups to another place, confusion, shouting and mad rushing about in the dark. There was a raw rice ration, also a cooked one. Roll call was at 6 and we were supposed to leave at 6:30 but did not until 8. There were ten trucks full of people—open army trucks under the full glare of the sun. People sat on the bedrolls, baggage, pails and other dunnage which was piled in. The people who are left will have a terrible job cleaning up the grounds, for in back of the women's barracks there was a snowbank of paper waste thrown out the windows. A bonfire behind the men's building had burned their debris continuously.

Jerry had been a general baggage carrier, so at the end we were left for an overflow truck as ours was full in the scramble for good places and there was no room left when Jerry came from helping, to carry his own things at the end.

Out the gate we went finally, with me perched on top of Sheba's mattresses—"*for a sick lady*," [Jerry] said, and got away with it as usual.

Like an immigrant woman, my hair tied in a kerchief, sitting high on top of the mattress, surrounded by bags, pots, cans and boxes, I rode through Baguio with my family around my feet. Everywhere were Japanese, in Trinidad Valley, in town and on the trail. The Filipinos all looked surprised and interested in our cavalcade-departure, but very quickly we and they were yelled at by the guards if we waved, called out hello or even smiled. "No signals," they commanded. We saw many familiar faces turned our way—drivers, market people, amahs, store clerks. We went past the market, by Burnham Park with tall grass around it, by Baguio Hospital, out the Kennon Trail, looking at Chinese and Filipino friendly faces for the last time—for how long?

There were four soldiers, two in front, two in back, guarding each truck. Sakashita and Yamato were in front seats in two different trucks. We had no seats, no railing to keep us from falling over the side off our pile, no cover from sun or rain. My shoulders were heavily burned but I was glad I had a suit coat when rain fell on us near evening. The wetness, coolness, was blessed.

Flashes of sights on the trail: the road in bad condition all along, full of big holes; no tollgates to collect for repairs; almost immediately we began to pass staff cars which were camouflaged, as were all trucks, with palm fronds, banana leaves, dried and dusty after long journey; dozens of trucks in convoys with soldiers riding on top of sacks of rice, camotes, vegetables and war supplies. We saw at last why food was scarce and who *was* getting it. Everything for the Army until that big locust leaves—it will grab and consume all. The Filipinos transport rice and any other supplies from the lowlands by pushcarts which are slowly and laboriously shoved up the trail in stages. Igorots and lowlanders alike smiled in friendliness with eyes half veiled as we passed not waving. At nearly all curves and at each end of bridges were stone redoubts full of guards; often a soldier popped out of some hidden pillbox. In the lowlands, guards jumped out hung with vines from the top of the helmets down over the shoulders to the ground. It was picturesque and resembled a stage scene of Robin Hood or the Mikado. Bridge spans were out here and there, barrios looked shabby. As we neared Lingayen section, traffic increased enormously. We stopped once or twice only, held up by two of our own trucks with mechanical trouble necessitating their falling behind temporarily. Once we stopped so that people could "wee wee" when Sally became desperate and I tapped a guard on the back, pulling proudly out of the hat again another Japanese phrase, "Chiotto matte kuda sai" (please stop a little) while pointing to Sally, whose face was screwed up in agony. My phrase worked but they kept urging us "hurry, hurry."

About 11 we reached Binalonan and were told to get out of the trucks along the road by the side of the Plaza—that plaza where there was still an execution stand on which guerrillas had been shot as "examples," traitors, "troublemakers." We were told we could eat and we did, promptly. The ration meat had begun to smell high from the heat, but we ate it all, giving scraps to a starved dog. Those who tried to save some lost it, for it spoiled in the heat of the afternoon as did the cooked rice, which turned sour by evening, and corn bread which molded. We ate all our "splatters" (dropped rice cookies) and camote cahoy crackers en route.

After lunch we were told to take all our handbags off the trucks as the trucks were going back to Baguio. In the noon heat, the men slaved, dripping with sweat, to unload all the baggage. Sakashita and Yamato said we might be sitting by the roadside for some hours as they were negotiating for trucks, so we were to rest till three o'clock. The soldiers formed a ring around us, yelling at any Filipinos who came too near, shoving horses, carts and people roughly to another road. They certainly treat the people savagely, worse than cattle.

In the broiling sun, on our mat rolls, we lay surrounded by straw bags, cloth bags and jumbled possessions, a perspiring, tired, confused crowd. About two thirty, they announced that trucks would be coming soon, but not as many as before so the trunks and heavy bags must be left by the road under guard till next day. Of course our hearts sank and we thought it another shakedown, a chance to examine or take from us again. My notes were stowed in a large tin in the middle of the food sack, as Jerry said I could not carry them by hand this time. It was in utter despair that I saw them taken off to be left behind. However, I felt we might get it all right for Sakashita and Yamato seemed to be doing everything they could for our good, and they were upset and apologetic about all that was happening. Nearly all of us were sure we would never see any of our baggage again. We had had to leave over half behind us anyway and now felt that this would be looted by hungry Filipinos or stolen by guards.

I will always remember Kaito sitting on the stone steps of a house near us, watching different groups as they stretched out exhausted, and looking at me as I took down my streaming snarled hair, combed it out and wound it up again. He was inscrutable yet somehow sympathetic.

About three o'clock, the trucks came and we were allowed to take on bedrolls, the small bags with our food for meals and some lap bags. Instead of ten trucks there were nine, so that seven extra passengers were packed onto the 9th truck with all the others who had filled it up before. What a crush. They then called for men to carry the left-behind baggage into the municipal building and this made us feel better as it was not to be left exposed to weather and people and could be guarded easier. Jerry piled down from the truck and carried heavy stuff while June and I were outnumbered as usual by people who scrambled in first, held on to the best places and refused to move or help. June had a seat finally along the edge but Bedie and I ended up in the middle, on bundles on the floor where there was no air, it was stifling hot and we could not see a thing in the passing scene. The children were angels all the way or we could not have borne it. None cried or were sick. They were lulled by the wheels and swaying which slid most of the adults back and forth out of position so that someone was always snapping

Ride to Manila. 29th December 1944
23 hours for 120 miles.

at us for crushing them. Also the children were so busy looking at the panorama of war that it was an absorbing story for them.

When Jerry came back from his heavy lifting, the only place left for him was at the rear end of the truck, with his legs and poor swollen ankles hanging over the side all the way to Manila. Not one man offered to change about for a while with him.

At Binalonan, June had a bevy of females hiding her toilet act, in a ring around her. Not long after that, she would squat like any Oriental, in the middle of the grass plot with a guard near and other people close by. One ceases to be modest at such times. One is too tired and driven.

After Tarlac I couldn't stand the bottom of the car any longer. Two hours without sight or air was enough, so I switched to June's place on the side. I hated most of the people in this bus more than I ever detested any of our Japanese Commandants, and do not ever expect to see so much selfishness and inconsiderateness at one time again.

All afternoon and evening, we passed hundreds of loaded trucks, miles of calesas [carts] drawn by horses, miles of pull-carts drawn by six soldiers with faces strained and dripping with sweat under the heavy load. At Binalonan we saw an entire hospital contingent—nurses in blue blouses and long bloomer pants, carrying their bundles and packs from the school house where they had obviously spent only one night to another spot where they were congregating to move north again. Big trucks, little trucks, wagons, carts, tractors, and even tanks were going north. Before long, it was evident that a large troop movement was taking place, presumably evacuating Manila, not slowly but definitely "on the run" and in a rush. Hour after hour the army traffic flashed by—food, ammunition, officers and soldiers. All the way to Manila on the lowland road, in village after village were deserted (or commandeered) houses, taken over by the Army whose faces were in every window where we used to see Filipinos. It looked like Japan—not the Philippines. The children have seen two evacuations or retreats—one when the American troops left Baguio, disconsolate and hating it, with lowered heads; and today when the Japanese moved from Manila and environs on a big, fast scale. It was exciting to see it.

When evening fell they drove with dim lights or none at all and said that none of us were to smoke. We had several long waits by the roadside for no known reason except fear of planes. Many long convoys such as we had seen in daylight passed us silently in the dark, crowding us on the road, the pullers grunting and panting under the pressure. Our passing south was an infinitesimal matter in the stream of what was taking place before our eyes. We could tell that our own little pile of baggage was of no more importance than a drop of water. They had bigger problems, more pressing and desperate affairs than searching or looting us.

One of our trucks hit a calesa and knocked the horse into the stream, smashing the wagon shafts. We stopped while the animal was pulled out and the cart set on its wheels. The countryside looked drab, sad, waiting, waiting for life to come back to it. People looked thin, forced into silence, driven out in many places which we knew well from other journeys. School and municipal buildings were all taken over by the Army in every town. At Angeles, we saw the beams of four huge searchlights by the airport which was shrouded in darkness. These enormous fingers searching the sky thrilled the children endlessly. Planes began to fly overhead.

At one town, some internees bought hard-boiled eggs for P35 each. We spent the P100 obtained for our mattress for two thin packages of bucayo.

I shall never forget the agonized strained faces of the soldiers in the shafts of carts, like animals, nor their dreadful panting breath which sounded in the dark after our headlights' glow no longer dimly illumined their faces.

Toward the end of the trip my arms were stacked with bundles and bags as June was doubled up with gas pain. We tried to find malted milk tablets and other food in our sacks but could not locate it. Jerry and the children ate bucayo and rice with peanut butter at one of our stops but I could not eat.

Finally we reached the monument and crept into Manila by Avenida Rizal under a watery moon and with blackout lights. Bilibid walls loomed up. We turned left on Azcarraga and stopped in a long line in front of the old Spanish prison which had been condemned some years ago. We could see the wire along the top of the wall and the sentry towers on each corner where guards sit with guns. We waited awhile in hushed darkness, then the gates began to open, the trucks backed up and turned in, chugging slowly between gate after gate, groping in a file of nine cars until we stopped inside a third wall under trees in a yard. We were in prison—that historical, famous, infamous, Spanish prison which has been used by Spanish, American, Filipino and Japanese rulers.

Again we waited in cool darkness, while the soldiers jumped off and stood with guns and bayonets in a ring around us. After a while a small door in the wall opened and we were told to get down. We gathered up our bundles, and with aching bones and stiff heavy limbs jumped or were lifted down. I staggered, reeled and sank onto a stone bench—perhaps it was a large wooden beam but it felt like stone. Jerry carried my things in the little wooden door, the children helping him. The soldiers guarded the door and stood in the watchtowers at all corners.

At 1 A.M. we stood for twenty minutes by the wall, lined up for roll call which was taken. Then we were told there was no food to be had, no hot water, no fire, nothing but to unroll our mats and forget in sleep. Skerl told us this quietly from Mr. Yamato's translation.

Jerry lugged our bedrolls and lap bags up the stone stairs from a dark corridor, carried up three old bed frames and three old mattresses selected from a horrible pile beside the front door where there was a wild scramble for them. Then in the dark he dug out the dry baked camotes, opened a can of Spam, found the peanut butter and malted milk tablets. We chewed a tablet and June made a cup of cold milk for me. At the taste of the Spam I started to cry. How can anyone know how that first mouthful could taste after such a nightmare day and night—for it was nearly two. June said, "Mummie, do you remember how you cried at the first taste of fried meat two years ago at Camp Holmes?" I tried to say, "Yes, because I feel the same way now," then I laughed and cried together and the children said, "Why Mama!" They gobbled the camotes and Spam and peanut butter.

After untying the ropes on the bedrolls, Jerry went off. I got up from where I had flopped and helped June to find the sheets and mat covers. We covered the filthy mattresses with the latter then put down the sheets in order to cover ourselves from mosquitoes.

Just after we had arrived the Japanese had announced that lights would be put out completely in twenty minutes and while we were still making beds with all the speed we could muster in our exhaustion, the darkness descended. I managed to put up one net under which June and I slept on a narrow bed, steaming together in the tropic swelter which was new to us. She finished making up Jerry's bed as he staggered back on puffy legs, so tired that he could not walk. Before this Bedie had wept with nervousness and exhaustion when Jerry scolded him for eating some ground rice crust which Jerry had prepared for me only. He had misunderstood so I comforted him while June smoothed out Jerry's sheet and pillow on blankets covered with a mattress cover. When Jerry returned again, June whispered in the darkness, "Daddy, your bed is all ready. Just pull back the sheet and crawl in." We heard him say, "Oh God, how wonderful," pull the sheet, crawl in, and not another sound or move. We all hit the pillow and knew no more till seven the next morning, when daylight opened our eyes on thick cobwebs laden with black dust all over the walls of stripped Bilibid Hospital building.

Though we are now used to defeat, loss, moving, readjustment, how sick to death of it we are. Such a day and night brings out the worst and makes us horrible people.

December 29, 1944. Roll call at 9 and no food till afterward. The kitchen staff of Brown, Scott and Gray had to organize everything from hot water down. Only a small amount of wood came in for cooking.

We spent the day reorganizing our bags, trying to locate things and place them around. June had been devoured by bedbugs and we killed many. Some mattresses were alive with them and were thrown out the window. Because of this and contamination from dysentery stains (as well as blood), it was decided to throw them all out so we pulled off the covers, and Jerry and Bedie carried them down again. June and I shook every blanket carefully, every cover, every sheet, inspecting each spot for bugs and squashing them. We then piled up the bedding in towering stacks. Every person in the prison was doing the same things.

The rice is good, better than the moldy variety in Baguio, and we are introduced to our new diet of bean curd—the residue left from soybean grinding. Pechay tasted awfully good. Even smelly ground salted fish tasted good to my husband and children.

There were bombs, planes droning and zooming all night and all day. The children out exploring, made their way to the third-floor structure which is mainly stumps of cement columns, parts of window frames, standing like ghosts left from bombing, fire or a dismantling process when prisoners were removed from here out to Muntinglupa by the Filipinos. It may have been stripped for scrap iron by the Japanese. All the plumbing is gone and many of the pipes. Those who went upstairs, looked down into the next yard of the prison, over walls, upon a group of American soldiers in chow line. They were *really* thin, says Bedie, but they looked happy to see us and put up two fingers in V. In another section could be seen Filipino Army prisoners.

Later we looked at a long row of cement cells, open sides with bars enclosing. On the cement walls there were many signatures, dates, and some writing. [One] said, "The Japanese are a perverted race; we have been broken physically, mentally and spiritually by them and leave it to you who come after us to wreak vengeance. Look out especially for barbers!" Another one wrote, "God Damn the Marines and soldiers—where are they—why don't they come!" How often we too have cried this in our hearts. A chalked calendar marked the bombing days by American planes several months ago; also noted was November 23 as the day that 700 were removed to Japan and December 23 when about 70 were moved from this building to the other side of the wall where we saw them.

Partly dismantled — no plumbing inside
2 elec lights on each floor
loaded with bed-bugs + filthy — red things are
Bilahid. beyond
g.l. sheets to keep
our rain —
Trustees cells in foreground
dishwasher

Almost immediately we were forbidden to go onto the third floor or on the front balcony where we could see over the wall to other walled yards and across the city.

Jerry built a little grass fire of wood chips, and made coffee on four tiles put together, out in the yard under the trees near the cells. He also opened a dented can of pâté and cooked it in our rice with soy sauce so that we had a tasty meal which did a lot toward reviving us.

Except for what we produced for ourselves on the tile campfire there was no food until one in the afternoon when our kitchen was finally organized.

Bedie developed an explosive diarrhea suddenly after 4 P.M. and after a dose of sulfaguanadine he went to bed, refusing all food at supper time except a glass of milk. When I told him he need not eat but could sleep for two days if he wanted to, he went to sleep and never moved until 8 the next morning, worn out nervously and physically.

The toilets are the lowest we have had yet—long troughs with beams to stand on down each side, a mechanical flush running water through the trough every few minutes. It is all surrounded by a small fence as it is out in the open yard beside the prison wall. There are two showers in another place nearby, similarly enclosed, but neither with any roof. Two faucets on a long wooden shelf arrangement are all the washing facilities for 460 people to wash hands, face and dishes. Later three more faucets were repaired by our own crew. There are open drains all around the wall breeding mosquitoes and huge bluebottle flies which hang in humming swarms over the yard. The trough was slippery, my unsteady feet let me down and I fell in the first thing. We are all unsteady from fatigue, nerve strain, emptiness and the swaying of the truck from 8 one morning till 1 the next morning.

There are two or three royal palms and a number of big old mango trees in the yard to give us shade and coolness. This is the one touch of beauty and nature left to us, except the burning blue sky and a faint, gentle breeze now and then.

The hospital and dispensary are now set up in one block of cells with iron bars. There is an unspeakable toilet in each section. Some families have moved into the other block opposite, about six cells to a block. At least they are open and cool and somewhat isolated, but just as filthy as every other place.

During one raid, shrapnel fell on the roof and in the yard and two internees were grazed by pieces of it. We were ordered to stay in the building during all raids and to observe strict blackout or the lights would be turned completely off.

All day Sakashita was apologizing for conditions here, admitting it was no place to bring women and children. However, we made the best of it, borrowing brooms from those who brought them along, sweeping up the filth again and again, bringing order out of chaos gradually, as women do the world over. Once more we could be proud of ourselves for standing up under long strain and bad conditions.

About 11 [P.M.] I went up to try to sleep in the steam bath of our section. The second group from Baguio, with about 100 people, had not arrived even then. There were air raids all night and Japanese planes flying low over us to various airfields close by. At 4 A.M. Skerl called Jerry to come help on guard duty as Yamato and Sakashita had gone through the yard saying loudly that the trucks were coming. I got up too and we stood by the gate from 4 until 8 when the ten trucks finally arrived. They were 24 hours on the way and were as exhausted as we had been. Loddigs passed out and was carried to the hospital on a stretcher. Hot water, tea and coffee were ready, poured out by many friends. I took Peg's wash cloth and brought water for all the sooty faces of the children. The adults washed themselves. We had rolled into bed without this comfort and cleanliness so we knew what would feel best. Jerry brought them coffee and they fixed their own rice and peanut butter and had bananas which were given them en route by a sympathetic guard. They too had eaten at Binalonan, had been told they could take only emergency food and bed rolls which they could carry. They started to walk with these—were told they might have to walk to Tarlac. This shakedown of baggage is the usual Japanese process of elimination and wearing people down. They carried these things for about three blocks, then found that the trucks were there, ready all the time.

Masaki appeared, serene and smiling as usual. He told the Committee that due to present conditions we could expect no help from the Army, none at all. We asked for pails, mops, brooms and disinfectants as prime needs. The dentist, who always rises to an emergency, was made head of a Bull Gang to carry baggage, to take away the condemned mattresses, to do any heavy work or emergency act when called upon. This is the dentist's element and like a young boy he is back in the fray again, in the spotlight, attending Committee meetings and given permission to contact the Japanese direct as do the three Executive Committee and the Finance Officer. He is efficient when he wants to be and if he is interested, so it should be all to the good as many of the men will rally around him. If only he will keep his head size down and politics under. Arthur is also swimming in his element again, with his whistle, making announcements and calling for workers all day in great importance.

Bedie is better after the long sleep but Jerry developed bad diarrhea and has started treatment. He is wretched from this and the swollen legs. In the night his kidneys troubled him and he had to go down in the dark six times, falling over Mrs. David's trunk and waking her to utter feeble martryr cries, knocking down Lottie's net when she was dreaming of bombs and thought one had fallen on her so she yelped. He promised to help fix it up when he got back but all was settled then, so he crawled in to sleep. He is passing blood in his urine. The trip on the tailboard of the truck did him great harm. June and I had mosquitoes under our net. It was streaming hot; then it rained and drip-drip began on our bags so I got up to move them away from the window. June and I finally broke down into giggles over all the absurd happenings, but it actually was a hideous, hot and never-ending night.

December 31, 1944. All night there was roar of traffic out Rizal Avenue—car horns, sirens, train whistles on top of raid booming and plane roaring.

We suddenly decided to move downstairs, not to climb stairs any longer or be hemmed in by all the families around us so that we barked our shins or knocked into their boxes, bags or beds whenever we made a dash for the toilet. We are now in the center of the building, on the corridor not far from the door and the stairs, where there is a noisy trek and much talk, but it is cool, near a window, and we don't care.

The Committe on Housing met and thrashed out a plan and map, but when it was posted with locations and a key diagram, there was a furor and whole sections sat down and refused to move. All places seem equal to me, alike as two peas, but the usual barnacle attachment has begun and people are too tired to think of moving. They just squat and defy.

Masaki says that Oura and Yamato are leaving and we will have a new Commandant of higher rank, a Major who is sympathetic to Americans and who talks English. Tanabe has arrived and so have the sassy pups belonging to Lt. Sakashita. Masaki reports that Los Baños have been very badly off and Dean was so thin he did not recognize him. They were all moved into Nipa barracks to make room for the Army.

The last day of 1944—what a year! It went out in turmoil and complaint which is typical of war days. Kaito is still with us, looking most unhappy and sorry for us. My back hurts horribly as it used to in Camp Hay when we slept on the floor, only then I had a mattress and now it is only blankets on boards. I can't turn over or breathe well—it hurts like pleurisy and toothache. I groaned and Jerry came over to rub my back in the night. June rubbed it this morning. I go to bed so tired I can't stand up, and wake so lame from boards that I can't sit.

1945

January 1, 1945. There is nothing dainty and childlike about this New Year, such as magazine covers depict. We have swept and swept this new space and Jerry has widened our bed with boards so the two of us can sleep with more room to move. Everything we have tried to do or touch, some member of the Committee has leaped on us and criticized us or attempted to stop us. I am tired of helping others, holding back and being left out in the end. In this gang there is so little community feeling that after the ride on the truck we have decided to stand pat and see that we are not left behind or on the tailboard any more. I am completely fed up—since the trip down. I have decided I am not sick any more. I've traveled about this prison and worked like a horse since we landed. I am just plain sore and out to see that we get at least some equality for a change.

The children have a new song—"I'm Going to Alabama with a Benjo on My Knee" (benjo is Japanese for toilet).

January 2, 1945. The Committee held another housing meeting; then each head talked with his group as to the placing. Each one knew his space so when Yamato brought the order at 3 P.M. that we were to be moved and our places clean and orderly by next morning at 9:30 in time for the visit of the new Commandant—we all started moving. Our goods looked shabby again. People seemed to be carrying the weirdest collection of wood and twisted iron. Others moved stuff into our corridor space even before ours was moved out. But thanks to our morning consolidation, and our previous move downstairs, we were complete within an hour, busily settling into our third space in four days.

Yamato assures us that all will come to us. He pulled another classic—that if we were not taken over by the U.S. within six weeks, we would all be shipped to Australia. Of course we look forward to another move. How I hope Nida can save the Celadon somehow, and my two Chinese coats, Black Forest shawl and wedding gown.

January 3, 1945. We sit on bags and use half of Jerry's bed as a table to eat on in our space.

In the double row of crosses in back of the prison yard, there are 113 graves.

In one cell block where we think they may have put psychopathic cases were scrawled messages, one of which is—"Words cannot fully express, nor can the mind conceive the trials, hardships and tortures we have endured at the hands of the Japanese as prisoners of war . . . "

Here is the new Command's announcement. "It has suddenly occurred that we transferred you to Manila, by order of the Japanese Military Authorities. I think you were vexed much by so sudden a removal. . . . This building you are to live in is coarse in construction without complete equipment, and very probably caused you dissatisfaction and inconveniences. I am very sorry on that point. Of course I am intent on supplying you with various conveniences but, to my regret, owing to the shortage of materials in Manila, everything cannot be done as I wish to do. As to food, it is also my regret to say I cannot supply as much as I wish. . . . At present every belligerent country is suffering from shortage of food and material. And I hear that even your native country is also among the rest. Not only you alone but also I and my subordinates are all living in this place and are taking (almost) the same food as you. Now I am obliged to tell you to be patient. Someday peace will come to all of us. Observe the orders of the Japanese Army, and taking good care of yourselve, wait for the coming of peace in quiet perseverance. Signed, Major Ebiko, Commandant, of Japanese Army Internment Camp No. 3."

One truck came through with our baggage, leaving three truckloads still to come. Anyhow, it is still there.

At Bilibid we are like Camp John Hay again—many sleeping on the floor on mattresses or without, others on wooden bed frames mostly without mattresses. There is no privacy—all is out in the open and even the most violent anti-cubiclers are living in Family Units in full public view. Husbands and wives take siesta side by side on beds, with children sleeping all around them, like any crowded tenement anywhere. Lines strung with towels, clothes and washing, mark our space boundaries. Even tobacco leaves are hung out to dry across one apartment.

December 30th, 1st Bilibid Camp Minutes of Special Meeting. "Carl still in Baguio. Denki in the Chair. He stated the meeting had been called for the purpose of discussing and making decisions on vital matters. One thing, he pointed out, was self-evident after discussions with members of the Japanese staff—that due to the urgent problems of the prosecution of the war itself, we could expect little or nothing in the way of assistance from the Japanese administrators. We must therefore be prepared to attack at once the three most important issues—Food, Housing and Health. Denki suggested that definite rulings and suggestions be drawn up about these matters by the Committee at this meeting. General Proposals Formulated and Approved. 1. An absolute necessity for health of camp is to give the internees a chance to catch up on their rest. For this reason, a quiet hour from 12 noon to 2 P.M.

Fronyard
Bilibid Prison Manila. Toilets. Shower
Arrived 6 am

Spanish
Wall
18th century

and also after 9 P.M. must be observed. All internees are asked to cooperate fully. 2. Family Units may be observed in housing arrangements. Internees are requested, too, to be as prompt as possible in presenting their requests, if they have special preference as to location, to Father Sheridan who is head of housing arrangements. 3. All materials of any kind on the property when we came to this camp are community property and may not be used by individuals for private purposes. 4. An emergency squad will be organized immediately to act in any and every emergency. 5. Two lists of materials needed were drawn up for Mr. Masaki and Lt. Sakashita, the *most urgently needed,* and a secondary list of vital needs. On the former, the following were itemized: Toilet equipment, for making two or three extra toilets; insecticide; cleaning equipment—brooms, mops, buckets, brushes etc.; faucets, shower heads, plumbing fixtures. Also garbage cans; ice—there is a large icebox in the kitchen; a wheeled cart of some sort. . . . On the secondary list were: extra light bulbs, benches, seats etc. . . . Permission has been obtained to use G.I. and other materials from pig pens etc. on the property, for community construction. Permission will be requested for use of the prison shop and tools by the Utilities Department. On motion carried, all prison mattresses must be taken out of the building for health reasons. The following resolution was passed; on principle, because the first contingent of internees moving from Camp Holmes to Bilibid were informed that they could not take with them their own mattresses, while the second contingent was instructed to bring theirs, all personal mattresses will be considered community property; they will be collected and issued to the sick, the aged, and then to women and children: in the meantime, they will be kept under lock and key until such distribution can be made. At the discretion of the doctors, these mattresses may be confiscated for hospital use. (Denki pointed out that the Committee was explicitly informed by the Japanese authorities in Baguio that we would find complete equipment, including mattresses and beds and kitchen utensils, already here.) Denki stated that the last group of trucks brought none of the community equipment, but that Carl and Willis remained in Baguio and will probably be able to bring all the personal baggage left there, as well as the community baggage, and they were expected to arrive here tonight. . . . For the present, two meals a day will be served—one at 9 A.M. and one at 4 P.M. The food situation at present is still uncertain as it is necessary to await the arrival of Sergeant Sugano from Baguio before definite information can be obtained about our rations for the future.

"By order of the Japanese, there must be no private fires built. . . . Because so few of the internees were able to bring their wash buckets, owners of buckets will be informed of the number of people with whom they must share. . . . Floor space per person will be about 40 square feet. . . . Each member of the Housing Committee has been allocated a certain group of internees whom he will be responsible for re-housing. Every effort is being made to form the personnel into congenial groups of 21, with four groups to a section. . . . There can be no hot water furnished for anything but tea and coffee. With our limited cooking facilities, it is impossible to furnish hot water for dishwashing or laundry. . . . Jess has been looking over plumbing facilities and found many of the sewerage lines are plugged and fittings broken. Some of the garbage is being buried and some being taken out of the gate to pigs.''

January 4, 1945. I mopped the cement floor on my knees with a hand rag like Camp Hay days. It does keep the dust down. We are asked to mop often to lay germs and dust. We are settled. Jerry has put flat pink tiles on four square ones to act as shelves and a buffet for serving. It gets things off the floor during mopping and prevents so much bending. In this particular phase, space and privileges are very much equal. It gives a better feeling and atmosphere.

June washed her accumulation of clothes, Jerry has done his, now Bedie and I must do ours. I have mended much, slowly and casually sitting in the center of bedlam but not hearing it.

With a broom wound with Bobby's old bathrobe on the end of a long pole, we all wiped our share of Bilibid's ceiling, corners and walls clear of cobwebs filled with black dust. It seemed lighter immediately and is greatly improved in looks. This old Bilibid never had such a cleaning! It is the third building we have cleaned out for ourselves and the enemy. Pounding is less, nervous crying is less, voices toning down.

Jerry is making a small stool on which to sit or eat from. The top is removable for tray purposes. He is happy and likes this place better than any we have had so far. There is far more space than at any time. It is 40 square feet. Our last cubicle was only 33 per person, and here we are all together, not split into sections. We have settled in, quietly and contentedly, both of us feeling better, Jerry's feet less swollen, the boil at his throat come to a head and cleared of pus, our food more than in Baguio. Jerry gets all the rice he can eat; I get camote greens, and the bean curd helps a lot in bulk even if most of the nourishment has been crushed out before we get it. The children are swell, eating well and helping wonderfully. Our appetites are never satisfied but we do not seem as starving and desperate as we were in October and November. We will make the grade if it keeps on like this. Also we like tropic Manila for a change. June would like to sleep, eat and stand under a shower all day, but she keeps busy.

Peg is very depressed and doesn't sleep well. The mosquitoes are bad and they have no baggage yet, nor do Scotts. Griffith's blankets were soaked from the rain; Bill Moule and the Sisters lost their corn flour, rice, ground rice and other supplies which were removed from their bags. This is like losing money only worse, for they bought these things when they could get them. It is constant loss all along the line. One never knows what to buy or sell or what to leave behind; the only thing is you can't win in this kind of situation. It is always loss over and over again.

Meals are all alike as there are no longer Special Diet facilities. The hospital is a very poor place now, in the cell block. There are no privileges left. We are all on the floor, so to speak, and take what comes out of the few cooking pots.

Two trucks arrived bringing [to] Peg and her family, Carl and the Scotts their things. One truck remaining has broken down on the road.

We had rice, camotes, bean curd, camote tops and soft rice with salt pork as gravy for supper—five things and good for empty stomachs. We slept at 8 as usual, a hot night, and two big booms heard. We split our rice into three meals and slept after lunch.

January 6, 1945. Beginning early, there was a heavy raid by American planes over Grace Park, Nichols Field and Camp Murphy. We watched the dive-bombers open the way, zooming down, leveling out, shooting up again. Then came the B-24's—48 of them in groups of 8 or 12. There were about 60 planes in all and did they paste the land! The anti-aircraft sent up black and white rosettes to no avail, either ahead or a little behind, so that the big bombers kept steadily on. There were at least six raids that we could hear during the day. Zoom, zoom, bang, all day. Our metal triangle kept ringing signals of alert, raid and all clear. We dash to the toilet in between raids. It is a front seat in the theater of war, yet we are protected by concrete walls and we think we are in a safe area. Santo Tomas is nearer to it than we are. We stand in the windows peering out under the wide tin shutters to watch the soaring planes, diving planes, aircraft puffs, our ears filled with the sound of heavy bombs and ammunition dump explosions as well as the sound of anti-aircraft guns and machine-gun fire. We are spectators, yet in the middle of it, watching the circumference being destroyed. Everyone crowds the doors and windows, and the guards move about with bayonets to see that we keep inside. They wear their tin hats and look thoroughly warlike. The Formosans are still with us.

We took our showers under one of the guard towers about 5:30 after supper. The fireflies are charming, flitting in and out among the mango trees' dark foliage and resting on them like Christmas tree lights.

January 7, 1945. Notice: "Many internees are disregarding the air raid protection rules. We point out the following: 1. These rules are for your own safety. 2. Many pieces of shrapnel from the anti-aircraft fire fell within camp limits this morning. These could cause severe injuries. 3. We do not have hospital facilities for removing shrapnel splinters and bomb fragments. We have no operating equipment to do this work. 4. Please cooperate with air wardens by going into building promptly when alarm is sounded, and by staying away from open doors and windows. We cannot stress too strongly the necessity for obeying the air wardens. Remain under cover until all clear sounds. The Executive Committee.''

We sat on the front steps in the dusk awhile after walking in the yard under cool mango trees. Just before we settled down for the night there was a big display of searchlights. When all were on from points in every direction there were about twelve. It was a fairy scene from the door—the gray walls, the corner tiled-turrets, the sky spangled with stars across which streamed long beams of light at many angles, and through the dark leaves of one mango tree shone brilliant Venus surrounded by dozens of fluttering, shimmering fireflies. There were four kinds of light—stars, planet, insects and electric.

The Safety Committee put up a notice in the evening. ''The continued bombing of the past two days emphasizes again the seriousness of our water situation. If a bomb should destroy the water main to the north of us, we would be in serious difficulty. All internees are urged to keep every available container filled with water at all times. Pans, basins, bottles, jars, cans, should all be used to supplement water reserves. We have no community water tanks.'' All evening, people were seen carrying water in all kinds of jugs.

There was great activity around Bilibid all night. Trucks, men shouting. We learned that Sakashita had departed, coming to say good-bye to Denki and Ray. The whole city was a hum of traffic until almost dawn. It was not only Sakashita who pulled out.

January 8, 1945. The guards who left sent in a huge kettle of cooked rice that they could not eat so we are drying it for grinding.

The rats in Bilibid are very annoying at night, reminding us of prison tales we have read. They squeak loudly and scamper along the bags and tile shelves, knocking over bottles, rattling cups and poking into tin and paper. We have to cover all food and soap.

Tarlac and Baguio were both bombed before they could get the rest of the Americans out.[1]

We went up to Peg's space and sat out on the half destroyed porch watching the bright lights on planes getting ready to land. They looked like big glow worms coming near, as they turned past the four rather battered royal palms on the street outside the wall. The stars were myriad over our heads. The fried eggs only come out at dusk and at night now, hidden under brush all day while our planes are abroad bombing. Two searchlights were taken away from the corner turrets on our walls during the night and day. Another convoy left. There was no roll call.

January 9, 1945. Jerry finally gave in and went to bed. He had a chill at breakfast which lasted for an hour. As I watched him shake with it, I could not believe my eyes. I am the one who has had such things before. He has smoked his last cigarette and has no more tobacco, no book to read, and how he hates it all. His temperature was 103 at noon.

Hayakawa is reported to have said that the Japanese would be all out of Manila in about two days; therefore, Mrs. Patton could make her own choice of hospital for confinement.

Hoshino brought in both Japanese and American drug assortment, with forceps, other instruments, small size rubber gloves etc. to replace what they took from us in Baguio and give what we asked for.

Jerry has a bad infection which has settled in the bladder and the doctor is moving him to the hospital onto a bed with mattress this afternoon.

About ten, as I was groping down the steps, a plane went over without any lights. Just beyond the prison, a flash of machine-gun tracer went after it and two sounds like bombs went off. I didn't see the fire afterward which others tell about. The plane came over again very low as before, on the other side, and nearer and louder were two more big booms. We don't know whether it was an American plane after an ack-ack or machine-gun nest, or a Japanese plane on demolition. There were rifle and machine-gun shots and various demolition booms all night, making it a poor one to sleep. The plane circled around till dawn, now near, now distant.

January 10, 1945. Yamato is reported to have said that inside these walls is safer than the streets of Manila right now. Demolition booms all afternoon but no big raids today.

The doctors are still trying to locate drugs in the big boxes. We've had no vitamins for a week.

Some people go all agog over the bombing, but I can't say that I like the awful drone of so many planes, nor the pound of bombs. I am relieved that America is coming in but I cannot get the thrill out of war that some do. The planes are so high and white and steely looking that they seem unreal. Their precision is awesome as they soar over, then keep straight on out of sight when their job is done, regardless of the titanic destruction below.

A child picked up a leaflet dropped by some plane. It was about MacArthur, with five pictures of him landing in various spots and being received by the inhabitants. It told how he had left Corregidor on the President's order but had promised to come back and now he was here, in the Philippines, and would be in Luzon before long. He would advise by radio and pamphlets how we could help to further their plans. It all seemed too much about MacArthur, not the American Army. Of course he has to show a real comeback but it seemed spread on too thick.

We think the new [hospital] setup is excellent. It takes care of the acutely sick and the brief emergency and dysentery cases. The chronic cases will have to depend on families and friends. The whole new regime gets rid of a lot of graft and racket and spreads such things very thin. With Dr. Shaffer sick, the only two left on the Medical Committee can cut loose and tear through, trying out new methods. Dr. Shaffer has dysentery and he is now moved into isolation cell in the first block. He is the second case and it is a severe type.

January 11, 1945. The Minutes say *we are a "protected city" not an "open city."*[2]

We saw two low planes approaching and one man said, "Look—they have no gear down to land on!" When the planes swung around right over our heads we saw beyond any argument a star on blue circle, with blue and white stripes near—oh boy! The Navy is here!

What a mess. Open trough toilets, a million bluebottle flies and other kinds hovering in between the sluicing of the toilets, and in Manila a type of acute dysentery. There is a rice supply within the prison of about two weeks.

"Excelsior is available for anyone who wishes to make himself a pad or a mattress. . . . All religious groups are now having their regular services mostly around the No. 5 cell. Times have been rearranged slightly for a satisfactory schedule. . . . People have been asked to bring books to Father Gowan to form a small library, but thus far there have been no results. . . . A supply of recreational equipment has been brought into camp—some musical instruments, and athletic supplies of all kinds. . . . It was suggested that informal group sings be held from time to time and the Committee approved the idea. . . . Father Gowan expressed his opinion that actually there had been no recreation problem here as yet, as people have been either too tired or too busy, or not in the mood for organizing activities."

January 12, 1945. News came in that the Americans had landed a big force at Lingayen, with four thousand ton landing barges from which tanks rolled onto the beach of San Fabian spouting flame. The brave Japanese defenders stood their ground, fighting—and the tanks went right over them. This landing was on the 6th and the bridgehead was effective on the 9th—a three-day battle. They are now pushing south toward Binalonan, and north in a spearhead toward Baguio, trying to cut the Army in two and block Japanese retreat to the Cagayan, make the fight on the plain of Lingayen. All that section where we saw them piling in, every barrio which was full of them and their activity, is now the center. They saw where we might go and we struck them at their strongest point and may indeed finish it right there.

At 10 after we were all under nets and June was asleep, the guards began poking about with lights, and soon our Monitor said, "All stand by your beds for an emergency roll call! The guards say that someone has been trying to go over the wall." Disgusted, irritated, we tumbled out to stand in the pitch dark with mosquitoes buzzing around our ears and other bare spots. We waited and waited, until finally Denki, Carl and Kaito whose hair was disheveled, his eyes drooping with sleep and illness, came to check us off, seeing each one in the new units. We went back under the nets again, but lights were going around out in the yard as they checked all the cell families and the hospital, and carefully examined the wall. The guards talked loud and we heard rifle shots outside off and on. They are all jittery beyond words. We thought the electric current was off and that this made them fear an attempt at escape—but there were lights on in town and it became known that the alarm had gone off through some contact with the wall wire. It went off again at 6 A.M. It may be a rat, or someone hitting it with a stone or a stick. Or it may be an attempt from outside to get news over the wall to us somehow. Then the toilet trek began, and rats tore about fighting over camotes.

January 13, 1945. Skerl, Doug, and others are digging for water in the yard. They found it sooner and easier than they expected and say that there is no more to fear on that score if the main is bombed. They have dug two wells and we can boil the water and flush the toilets from these if needed.

We opened some Prem and ate half of it for supper. It was so good. The kids and Jerry are very hungry, but I'm skating along. Bedie snitched his first mouthful of rice. I told him he ought to be ashamed for we all felt like doing it. He admitted it was the first time, so I said, "Well, make it your last, and I don't mean maybe." We did not say any more about it after that, for after all we *are* hungry and he is growing and it's *only* rice! But he will have to stick it with the rest of us. It won't be much longer.

Our cash account was returned—P40—and our Taiwan [bank] account of P380, so now we possess 420 worthless Japanese government notes for the future. The Committee has paid in full.

After six, the choir gathered back of our building and sang, chiefly for the benefit of the boys over the wall who were seen listening. The choir sang "Pain" and "The River," "Cargo," "Sea Fever," "Go Down Moses," "The Old Ark's A-movering," and "Tannhäuser," also "A Gypsy Life." It sounded wonderfully well, the choir at its best due to the inspiration of those boys over the wall. They plan to sing every day.

We ate some extra rice and sugar with Jerry in his hospital cell in the evening then went back under the net in the dark, away from mosquitoes. About 10, there was a huge fire, with continued explosions, over by Tutuban station direction. I routed the children out to see it and we watched it flare, die and flare again in billows of black smoke. We could hear the roar of flames. It was something to see and remember. We figure it was demolition of two or three oil refineries in Tondo.

January 14, 1945. The electric current is on and men are shaving with a buzz razor. The favorite sport is a huge poker game with the remaining no-good Japanese government bills.

We had fun together under the net last evening. Bedie stuck around of his own free will and when I said, "I like this place and space better than any we have had," he said, "So do I." We agreed we were happy, and decided it was because we were all together in one cubicle. Having a new assortment of neighbors is a big help. There is nothing like a change from a rut, especially a deep and old one.

Sid and Sally moved in on the talinum plants with huge pans, so the rest of us decided if we wanted a taste we'd better get on the job too. There followed a scene known as the Talinum Pickers; bent figures, jackknife double, rear-end up or Filipino squat were used. It was quite a sight. June and Bedie gathered a small can full for us. It is smooth, very tender and somewhat tart like a mild vinegar taste. We added the Scott-Jerry soy mixtures and it was delectable, a vegetable known at home as pigweed. When one has had no vegetable or fruit for weeks, months—try it. We are definitely down to cowpeas and pigweed and such, and we like it. Compared to three years ago, we adjust like lightning.

January 15, 1945. Skerl had a gang out putting up the long iron grills with the green nets stretched over them and placed over the women's toilets. Now it is going up over the men's. There is that much done against flies and epidemic.

Dr. Skerl made the following statement: "We have been here over two weeks and thus far have not actively pushed adequate measures to ameliorate the dysentery-producing conditions here. This time we already have 2 cases of virulent type. No doubt many of the crosses at the back of this camp are mute witnesses of the ravages of such a type. It is within the realm of possibility that the destruction in this city will be so extensive that the only place for us to live will be right here even when a relief force has reached us. . . . I therefore ask the Committee to proclaim a state of emergency and put a vigorous anti-dysentery campaign into effect."

The man of science is still with us. He has been invaluable in big and small ways—one of the finest, most useful members of camp, with never any deviation in integrity, no reaching toward any exception or privilege.

Rumor says Sakashita came back in last night and said the Japanese Army had left for good yesterday, taking all the rice with them, so no more from that source for us. Kaito, Masaki and Sugano have walked the streets today, hunting food for us, resulting in many sacks of corn. They are smiling as though a miracle had been produced.

January 16, 1945. June's huge reading group of children almost stumped her today. They began to trail her early, and when there was a raid and the alert sounded and bombs boomed, they all scattered like chickens, ending in a noisy mob in our space.

Father Sheridan gave out the athletic equipment. Now balls of all sizes and weight fly at one from every direction. Life is not safe—what with balls, bullets and shrapnel.

Bedie heard me say that the fireflies in the tree were a great source of pleasure and comfort to me, so he caught and brought two of them in and put them on the net above our heads. They glowed and dimmed, one finally taking flight, the other one dying there. I told him that beauty could not be taken captive for it lost half of its loveliness when removed from its element or the surrounding atmosphere.

January 17, 1945. We have 100 nicotinic tablets and our B-1's now, plus some traded multiples which will give us a little ascorbic.

Today the head of the garrison has ordered the north porches boarded up, and the north windows boarded up halfway. This will shut out air and light for all the second floor. It is partly protection against stray bullets which clattered on the shutters in the night, and partly to keep us from seeing traffic and other things.

How many months ago was it that Kaito told Miss McKim he "did not like to think about the end"? and now it is upon them and us. There is nothing in their education with which to meet defeat except hara-kiri. They have seen the planes, the bombings, heard of the landing with tanks and many men, and they feel overwhelmed. They can only stand rooted until the tanks roll over them, or hide in the hills even as others have done before them to no avail. Surrender is unthinkable. It does take a certain kind, a different kind, of courage to stay, to go on living in defeat. Masaki may stay, but most of them have been taught otherwise, trained for Victory not Defeat.

I think continually of Nida and her family. When and how will we see them again, and how will they fare now, and how can we help them? We wonder where Tomibe is "gallantly confronting us" and will we ever see him with his family.

Oura cut the clothes lines and says if we don't bow he will hit us on the head or put us in jail. June asks, "But where are we already?"

January 18, 1945. The Staff have told the Committee they will leave very abruptly, suddenly, but will tell them just as they are leaving.

January 19, 1945. "Dr. Skerl reports that the toilets have been screened; posters to call the need for hygienic precautions have been posted; buckets of disinfectant water provided for washing hands in each bathroom; and nets provided for hospital toilets. Internees are urged to continue to observe every care; to swat flies; and to watch particularly that hands are washed and food covered.

"The mango trees and the garden are community property and permission to pick the greens or fruit must be obtained from the head of work details. . . .

Winnie has arranged a daily story hour for the younger children, probably between the hours of 10:30 to 11:30 A.M. with various women assisting.''

Milk is selling for $50 a can on the Cooperative Trading Board. Three cans of beef for $50. This is based on trades of three beef for one can of milk. Alan offered one lady P50 for a can of milk and she laughed and asked, ''Where's the other half of the price?'' The exchange and barter is as crazy, as excessive as the currency which is worth nothing. Everyone wants food and will give anything for it.

After I wash dishes and the floor, by 11 A.M. I am all in for the rest of the day. There is such gnawing emptiness and fatigue.

Bedie works hard to find some salvage in the camote scraps but he achieves only a handful and comes back worn out and sick at heart because he cannot help us. The vegetable parers are cutting closer and closer, and some few women move in on the discard so that there is no residue for Bedie's great effort. I tell him it is not worth the energy even if he is trying to help get some extra for Daddy. He throws himself on the bed while June dishes out the ugly mush. I go over to him and rub his back, saying nothing. He nods that it helps and is surprised, because I have never done it before. His pillow is wet with tears of discouragement but neither of us mentions it and after a while he relaxes and is normal again. He is so anxious to help and there is no way to turn. Even the green mangoes are denied him, by Committee order.

There were many potshots in the night, with guards running about as bullets pinged on our walls.

Thievery is increasing. Petri was looking in his duffel bag at his tin goods, zipped and locked it to go see an air raid. When he returned, someone had slit his bag and taken out three beef tins. They must have been watching him. He has had so much extra meat that he does not get much sympathy.

January 20, 1945. One huge bomb shook the whole building. Afterward, from the east, many big planes roared over us, hidden by the low ceiling.

How much longer will we have to stagger on, eating corn mush and tough green stalks? There is no doubt that it is heroic for a Japanese to get supplies at all in these times.

Clark found a bottle in the dungeon underneath our room. It is a damp place where a man cannot stand upright. In the bottle was a message telling of 20 thousand American prisoners made to build the airports all around Manila. It said that 50% had died of execution and starvation. It was a tragic and dramatic find, such as one reads about in ancient tales. The Japanese worked them to death too. There is nothing so cheap as human labor and soldiers in the Orient and Germany.

The children carried Jerry's bed home after lunch and we are together again. He ate rice and coconut lunch with us. After he moved out of the hospital, I swept his space there for the last time. He must stay quiet for some time but he is better. He is getting B-1 shots for his swollen ankles.

The Church service cell is also an emergency dental cell for tooth extractions, with three forceps brought in for pulling. It is also an emergency operation room where Marj's baby will be born if we are still in here. Camp Bilibid baby No. 1. Church, surgery and dentist are all equal in one cell, no precedence, except in emergency.

Oura came around with the two other Japanese after Yamato's inspection, and said that the toilet nets were the property of the Japanese Army and they must be given back at once. Carl said, "But we needed them for dysentery precautions." "Never mind," Oura answered.

January 21, 1945. We hear there are 800 Americans in the compound next to us.

Sugano says that five American boys have died of dysentery since our arrival here, so our cases come over the wall with flies, no doubt.

January 22, 1945. We *can* keep the green nets over the toilets, though the shower net is taken down.

June made a good camote—gingerbread with Jerry's help. We ate it all at noon, thanks to Bedie's camote salvage. We are still hungry and very tired.

January 23, 1945. Conference with Major Ebiko, Lt. Oura and S. Yamato and the Executive Committee, January 22: "We suggested, that possibly, the supply sergeant could let us have more brooms, buckets, some lime or other disinfectant, plumbing fittings for improving the toilet and shower facilities. We told him this was important to us because of our fear of a real dysentery epidemic, pointing out that we now have 11 dysentery patients ill in the hospital, including 6 children. He asked whether we allowed the people to drink fresh water, and said he thought it would be wise to drink only boiled water. We informed him that this was desirable, but we get only a very limited supply of firewood, not sufficient to boil water for the entire camp. . . . We said our next most important problem was that of obtaining suitable food; that we now have nothing but corn and a tiny bit of rice every third day. We told him we realized that food was difficult to get and transportation even more difficult, and suggested that possibly he might allow us to contact the Red Cross representative in the city, or some other neutral, or even Filipino suppliers, for obtaining money and food. We said we had no Red Cross money on hand with which to buy food and asked whether more would be sent in to us. He was sorry about the situation, but that Santo Tomas was also in the same position. It was necessary to obey orders from higher up, and this prevented any special contacts for getting supplies. He said food of all kinds is extremely scarce in Manila. . . . He said it was better that we do not know all that is going on, lest people might get too excited. We secured no information of any importance to camp.'' All was bowing, politeness and serenity, but the answer was always No. It is not Oura, but H.Q. as I've always thought, at the top. As for rice, we have already seen that going north in handcarts and calesas.

January 24, 1945. It is four weeks tomorrow since we entered real prison walls and started to put up with dark nights, toilet troughs, bluebottle flies, mosquitoes and the last two weeks of corn fodder cattle diet.

Walter is disgusted over a discovery that there were plenty of A and D vitamins which no one knew was in stock in Baguio. The doctors thought it was all gone. The Hospital Committee must have done some poor checking but it is typical of Concentration memories and slipups.

There are no books to read during lassitude and enforced idleness. There is only my N.E.T. checkbook,[3] *Thorndike's Dictionary* and Muzzy's *History of the American People* which all four of us are reading!

How many unfortunates have suffered worse than we have inside these very walls, not only under Japanese domination but under Spanish tyrants and others. There must be many ghosts of prisoners haunting these buildings and yards. Prisons will some day belong only to the past and will be looked upon as barbarous as dungeons are now to us. There will be only hospitals and homes to care for the abnormal, the socially sick and maladjusted ones who are deformed by our own social defects.

Miss McKim says that this sauce we get, called ''o-misu,'' is an inferior brand of what can be a most delicious thick flavoring sauce, with a consistency of mustard and made from soy.

Dr. Mather operated at 4 with Bruce assisting, Tavie giving the ether, and Bun the surgical nurse. The green net covered ceiling and walls. Over the ceiling were six white sheets sewed together by Enid, and these were also halfway up around the walls. The cell must have been stifling with the ether fumes. The diagnosis seemed to have been correct, as the whole area was inflamed from the appendix. The patient was later carried on a stretcher to the men's acute ward cell at 5:30.[4]

January 25, 1945. Sugano is back. He has some gasoline and may get corn and camotes for us but says no chance of rice, except for hospital patients, because 600 sick men next door to us get the rice. *They have 600 dysentery cases.* Only the sick soldiers were left in the Philippines. All the healthy ones were taken to Japan and Formosa.

Walter says Yamato told Carl that *he* did not know any news but if we knew it we would be very happy!

Peg Whit having read in a book about some old women in South America making beer by chewing cassava (the enzymes in saliva being the active principle) has chewed some cassava, added water to it, and now has a very active vinegar (or beer—she isn't sure which, but it is bubbling swell!). She doesn't dare tell her husband how she made it!

Sugano returned with soap and toilet paper for camp. We asked for food and we get paper! But it is all needed.

There were planes in the night, and a lovely moon.

January 26, 1945. Everyone is making Modernage-type chairs out of the twisted scrap iron in Bilibid. They bend the rods into shape and then slip a cover over it made of straw sack, gunny sack, canvas, hammered tin, strands of rope, sections of wire netting or anything else that will let the weary human form relax in a chair. Our forms haven't had a chair for over three years. How wonderful not to have to sit on a bench, a stool or a bed!

We picked out dry charcoal like any other street urchins and put it away in a paper sack. Jerry is going to make a big round cocoa tin into a charcoal brazier with some screen wire as a grate. These are also the Bilibid rage.

Sugano brought in 500 coconuts as balance on our orders. He finally got them in the market as he could not get them from Nacoco at half price as he hoped. He brings them all in looking triumphant.

Minutes: "A few individuals have volunteered to take care of some of the talinum beds, and they ask the cooperation of other internees in the observance of the ruling laid down by the Committee that any produce from the camp garden is for the community as a whole and not to be picked by individuals. Dr. Skerl reports that he needs volunteers to swat flies, to further the anti-dysentery campaign. He also urges everyone to swat flies in his vicinity. Fly swatters have been liberally distributed, and we are requested to use them often. Great difficulty is being experienced still in getting workers. There are actually very few details now, but many internees have apparently given up all community work. Women are requested to come early to vegetable detail, in order to get the vegetables prepared before it gets too hot. It has been proposed that a large net be placed over the vegetable preparation table to cut down the annoyance and danger of flies. It was moved and carried after Committee discussion of the matter, that internees will not be allowed to pick over the rejects of vegetables such as camotes, until all the vegetable preparation has been completed. At that time, the reject containers will be set out where people can get at them."

The moonlight on the walls, the guard towers, roofs, shutters and trees was glamorous, making it look like a street scene in Seville. The old prison windows, hacked out irregularly, make a lovely frame in the darkness against the light.

January 27, 1945. Jerry and Ted made a charcoal stove out of a large round can, piece of wire and a wire net. Jerry fanned the coals while resting on Bedie's bed, cooking cornmeal cakes, rice and corn flour cake for me, then

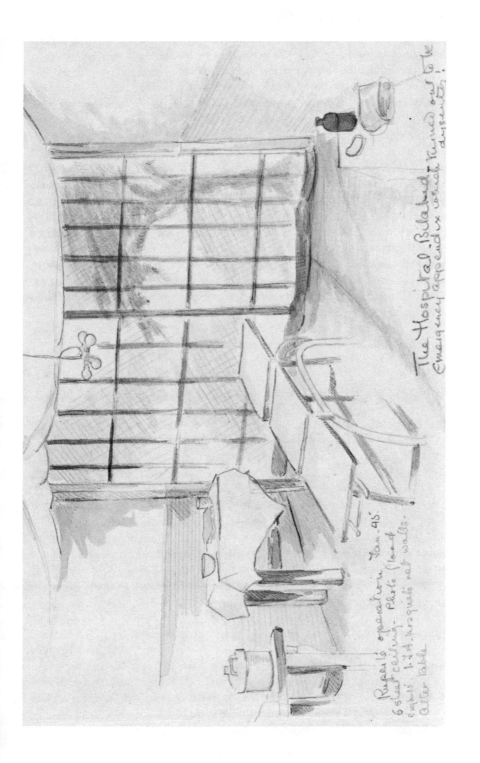

winding up by boiling coffee. The children helped and watched, and no one thought of being hungry or where the Americans were for two hours.

Gene thinks the last explosion might be Jones Bridge. The bridges may be blown at the very last. Some say that by Monday—two days more—the American boys will come in! When asked where the Americans are now, Yamato replied, "They are everywhere. They are very potent."

Tentative Proposed Rules for Camp upon Our Release. "There is absolutely no indication as to the imminence of our release by the Japanese, but we all know that this day is not too far off. It will probably be abruptly announced some day or night and we feel that for the good of all of us some advance plans should be made looking toward the safety and protection of all individuals. . . . The Red Cross or whatever organization takes over our camp will necessarily want to have every individual of this camp available for any instructions or information they will have for us. . . . In view of the above, we propose that as far as possible the camp continue to hold together as a unit until such time as we receive instructions from our government. This will mean keeping a daily record of the movements of individuals who may make trips into the city for supplies or to contact friends or relatives. Passes somewhat along the following lines would probably be used to advantage by those wishing to leave camp:

PASS FOR MANILA CITY

The bearer————is an *American Internee* of Civilian Internee Camp No. 3 of Bilibid Prison, and has permission of the Camp Authorities to proceed into Manila City for purpose of *Procuring Food Supplies* until 6 P.M. today February 1 '45. Signed by Chairman of General Committee, I.C. No. 3, Bilibid Prison.

"The camp has a limited supply of soybeans and cracked rice, together with our regular corn ration for the month of February. . . . It is suggested that it would be very wise for people to continue living where we are. The Japanese have told us that they have prepared a document outlining terms and conditions of our release which will be presented to us immediately our release is announced. People are urged *to be careful about demonstrations when our release is announced. Premature celebrations might provoke an incident,* endangering the safety of the camp."

January 28, 1945. Bedie came in at 7 almost speechless with delight because the guard had picked out 7, including him, to give some leftovers of their breakfast pot. Thanks to a Formosan we have had a delicious Japanese meal—rice, fried rice, gravy with chopped egg, greens and soybean. We divided this one helping into four and felt well fed, as well as enjoying the taste. They eat appetizing chow and have plenty of it.

Sugano to the Executive Committee says there are only a few soldiers left in Manila. Some of the guards cleaned out their kits yesterday and received field rations. We are accustomed to their smiling, friendly faces, their jaunty walk, well-knit figures, slim but solid build. There are among them some stolid types, others attractive youths with a lively interest in all we do. They all desire to go home to Formosa and have no strong belligerent spirit.

Some of our men have been watching a plane-spotter group of Japanese on a nearby building. Today they saw them take down their aerial, dismantle and leave. Is this indicative?

A Japanese medical officer was insistent that Roosevelt, being so eminent, must have many wives. Miss McKim said no, he had only one. "Oh, he must have many—men in Japan as eminent as that always have many!" Miss McKim said it was no use denying for she could not make it stick.

Oh to be able to sit on a real toilet! My polio leg and hip are not adapted to squatting on a trough.

January 29, 1945. I saw a huge rat come in our window last night.

Yamato brought in a piano, of all things, and it stands by the front gate. It is a big help to the children's rhythm band. Yamato asked Mrs. Greer to play him the "Moonlight Sonata" under the moon tonight, and she retorted, "I told you I didn't want a piano. You go trade it for a carabao and bring us some meat." He is quoted as saying, "The Americans will come soon and you will be free. They go slowly because they save men and protect their behind." What a wonderful little man, so homesick and pathetic, wanting a piano in the middle of all this. Something has happened to his glasses and he can scarcely see without them. He has very poor eyes, squints them much. I shall almost miss this odd little man.

January 30, 1945. We have become accustomed to nearby rifle shots and pistols, demolition, grenade and bombing booms. It will seem a tame life when such noises die away, and planes, smoke billows, no longer dot the horizon. There is a gray smoke pall all around Manila.

The soybeans made the best breakfast we have had in ages. At noon, we had rice-cornflour hotcakes fried in cold cream! It was the guard's gift to Bedie and we do not recommend it for frying. It was not bad, but scented! As Jerry says, it is the ultimate low in cooking grease.

Jerry says it is a good thing we rid ourselves of a lot of false modesty at Camp Holmes by seeing the wood crew in fundoshis. It is true, for all those shrinking attitudes, niceties, prejudices and opinions have gone by the board here, where we live on the aisle and the floor, four to six in one space, with no suwali or sheets or tin; only mosquito nets and blankets to hide the dress and undress process, with mother and father sleeping side by side on one mattress, with all the intimate scenes of tenement life. Some people's "standards" have taken a long fall. Culture is often shed in a hurry.

We go about silently, the mind not a blank, but thoughts quiet, the effort to talk too much, a state of suspension, reserving all comments and action within oneself.

Corregidor and Cavite were bombed today. One crash was followed by the sound of a building collapsing, long drawn out. This must be demolition.

Sugano wanted to go to big buildings which were being demolished, so that he could salvage soybeans and other stores for us which are going to be destroyed, but Oura said No and the permit will not come from H.Q.

I don't sleep well on account of "empty" spells. The children say they wake up from this too.

January 31, 1945. It was John Hay's third birthday. We gave him a U.S. button and a minute glass [timer]. His parents gave them milk and tea and opened the last can of jelly. Celebrations are slim these days but the children are pleased with little.

We lie on the bed or sit on Daddy's while he draws plans for our ideal house in Baguio or Shenandoah Valley. There is no food to prepare, no books to read, no strength for anything, so we all plan various futures, talk about the future and the past in order to forget hunger and food and the monotony of living from day to day, waiting—.

Toilets are cleaned every morning, and talinum beds are tended by the husky British girls who hoe with much energy trying to keep weight down due to the effect of heavy starch diet.

Bedie wants to talk about food all the time—how he will raid the icebox. Bread and butter—oh! says he—with chicken or ham or cheese on it! When we get under the net I let them talk food for an hour every night, then they must not mention it again. I can only stand it that long every day.

Father Sheridan announced that if anyone had any Japanese money and wanted to buy anything they must turn it over tonight for it was the last chance. Well—!

February 2, 1945. Church brought about 4 pounds of real brown sugar from a deal he and Jerry made. We ate a spoonful at once with grated coconut on breakfast mush. The kids were thrilled pink. So we are swallowing topaz earrings and bracelet from a world trip at Port Said.

Jerry's toe is less painful and his ankle swelling down. The Medical Committee calls it Protein Starvation.

February 3, 1945. Our 18th wedding anniversary in Tientsin 1927. And here we are in Bilibid listening to planes tearing the Nipponese limb from limb. Heavy raids all day. Ten planes came over northeast, bombing four times in three hours, while 10 others bombed in the south over Cavite way. They were pasting the east toward Antipolo all morning. Death is pouring down continually on human beings—the only way to get it over and done with quickly, and they must have it to the last man they say.

Committee Report, January 31: "Dr. Skerl stated that many people are covering their food and dishes with small pieces of netting, but unfortunately, this is not sufficient protection, as to the flies' feet, and also their droppings, which can still come into contact with the food or dishes through the meshes. Dr. Skerl urges the use of cloth, therefore, rather than netting. . . . Drinking water, chlorinated, is now available at the front of the building on the main wash tables. Internees are warned that a possible strong source of infection might be the food that some internees are receiving from Japanese guards. This food is carried into this camp in open containers, and no efforts are made to protect it from flies or other contamination. It is prepared near the soldiers' quarters, and many of the soldiers have dysentery. If internees persist in taking this offered food, the least precaution that certainly must be observed is the re-boiling before eating.

"Father Gowan said that the first consideration should be the actual physical safety of the internees in case of hostilities approaching this vicinity, or in the event of vindictiveness being displayed by retreating or other Japanese. He felt that there was need for an organization within the camp for the sole purpose of keeping a rigid check on excitable or incautious members; that our own guards should be kept in every section of the building, to maintain caution and order; and that the occupants of the second floor of the building should have arrangements made whereby they could evacuate in orderly and expeditious manner to the first floor if firing or bombing should suddenly begin near this prison. He also mentioned that while our building is fireproof, blazing fragments might set fire to mosquito nets and bedding, and that therefore a fire crew, equipped for any emergency, was a necessity."

Jerry traded a pound of sugar for four coconuts as we need the fat in them. We have had no meat in over a month from the Japanese, since leaving Baguio. No fruit for six or eight months except a small banana at Christmas. The fat in the soy and the coconuts gave Bedie diarrhea.

At supper we opened a can of Spam and had two thin slices each, saving a fourth for breakfast. Bedie came back absolutely thrilled with seconds in everything in chow, even misu, and bean curd. We decided to eat all of it, not save any, to celebrate our anniversary. The Spam was our next to last can—the last one we are saving for Bedie's birthday in a week.

As we were finishing our extras, Peg and Walter and Carl came with a big pot of steaming tea and it was a regular charivari. Peg's syrup which was a little "high" added a gay fillip to it all. Scotts came for coffee with us and the seven of us had fun. It revived and cheered us no end, after the day of exhaustion. I said to Izzy, "Two surprises—first the sugar and second Peg's party. I wonder if there will be a third." There was—the vanguard of the American Army!

As I came out of the new tunnel toilet, there were shots outside the wall. I ran to the building and was going to stop at the Board and read the evening news bulletin when Bedie grabbed me. With a suppressed thrill in his voice, he said, "Mummie, you must come. Don't stop to read. There's a heavy humming noise getting nearer in the north and people think it is tanks coming in." We ran up to Peg's balcony and found a gang there peering out, trying to see. Filipinos were running up the street, peeking cautiously out of doors and windows, all looking in one direction. The view was limited so I suggested we go to Betty's porch at the other end. As we passed a window, Bedie looked out and came back nearly bursting. He insisted he had seen a tank going by and that it was American, like the Clark Field tanks, this one number 73. He acted very nervous and said we had better not go to Betty's for it would be dangerous and we ought to go downstairs. He begged me so insistently that I turned back and we started down. Halfway down, all hell broke loose and there has been no peace since.

At first some people said it was Japanese tanks for they thought they saw Japanese characters on it. I timidly told Denki that Bedie had just seen an American tank. Denki was at our space trying to fix the burning electric wire before nightfall, so that they could turn on the current before dark. Like so many of us, Denki could not believe the Americans had come. His lip curled in doubt as he said, "Nonsense! There are lots of Japanese tanks in Manila. This may be some in retreat from somewhere. It can't be an American one." He turned back to his wire and I did not try to convince him. I wasn't sure Bedie was right myself.

Rifles, machine guns and bigger guns began ripping all around us and we could hear the grind of more than one tank. The Committee ordered everyone inside and people poured into the building.

Kaito had returned from the hospital a little while before and was telling Miss McKim that the Americans were in Tarlac, and that when they reached Caloocan all our Japanese staff would leave and we would be given our release. While he was telling this, bedlam broke loose and Kaito went out the door like a shot. He returned shortly, looking very sick and sad, to say good-bye as he would probably not see us again. The whine of bullets, the ping and sing of shot of all kinds was in the air and we were ordered to *stay* in the building. Very soon all families on the second floor were ordered downstairs for the night. A trek of mattresses and nets began.

At dusk, we saw a silent line of Japanese in blue shirts creep from the gate to the front door. They went through the long hall, upstairs and out on the roof—of all places—with machine gun and bullets, grenades and gasoline. This made us extremely nervous, to put it mildly.

A flamethrower tore through the building next to the men's barracks just outside the wall and the building was a seething mass of flame immediately. It made me sick to see how quickly it happened and to wonder if any people might be inside. Fires began to rage in all directions. The sky was ablaze all night. The oil gray pall has hung over us ever since, some of it a greasy brown color. At sunset, the sun was a copper disk in the sky, as it is during forest-fire time at home.

We learned later that it was the Japanese who ordered everyone down from the upper floor, and not the Committee who ruled it. The Japanese soldiers were up there all night.

Everyone went around talking about whether it was or wasn't the American Army. It wasn't very long before we were sure. Some of the usual nervy, hardy camp members went up on the roof to see what was going on and when the tank went by outside one of our walls it stopped and they heard a southern voice drawl, "Okay, Harvey, let's turn around and go back down this street again." Another pair of tanks was heard "God damning" each other in the dark. There was no mistake about this language—it was distinctly American soldiers! The Marines and Army were here! And they had caught the Japanese "with their pants down." There couldn't have been good communication or the Japanese would have had time to leave.

Yamato told the Committee members that he would go to get our release papers. He left poor Tanabe sitting in charge on the front steps for hours, half the night, with his sword in his lap. Miss McKim talked with him now and then.

A fire broke out just behind us to the north and the flames piled high and bamboo crackled and popped like pistols. I was so excited all night that I almost burst. I would doze off, waken with a jump at some enormous detonation. Win and Jo and little Freddie came down to our cement floor-space for the night. I was up most of the night, going from one end of the building to the other to watch new fires that leapt into the sky. Jerry, who was tied to crutches [legs swollen with beriberi] and to his bed, scolded me—"You darn fool, go to bed. You'll be dead tomorrow if you don't stop running around." He was right but I didn't care and just answered, "I don't care if I am. This is the biggest night of my life and I'm not going to miss any of it."

Jo went out to do guard duty at 1 A.M. and I was dashing back and forth to see fires and pillars of smoke and all the rest of the racket. Later Jo lit a candle and opened a can of Spam and a coconut and we sat on the floor and ate it on our corn crust which tasted heavenly with red glare shining in the windows on it and all the fiends of war making a din outside. Bedie was everywhere at once, missing nothing and reporting each new item like an old hand.

Miss McKim tried to persuade Ebiko to move his men off the roof but he evaded and they stayed. Once in the night, they came down to roll an empty gasoline drum to the back gate near our door, where they put gasoline and fixed a fuse in order to blow up a tank if it tried to come in that way. The young Formosans were still guarding around the inside walls and corners, loaded down with equipment. Strands of wire were being switched around on the roof as though they were mining it.

When Yamato had had his sore hand fixed by Dr. Mather, he had asked how soon it would be well and the doctor replied, "in about a week."

Yesterday the hand was worse and Yamato asked the question again and the doctor said "two weeks." Poor Yamato looked sunk and said, "Oh you will have to give me some medicine to take with me in case we have to leave." The doctor told him he would.

February 4, 1945. The eight Japanese were still on the roof and the Formosans were still guarding us when daylight came.

Carl took Yamato to the doctor to have his hand dressed and he was given a package of sulfa to take with him. Later he said good-bye to a number of people and told them he was going "to meet my destiny." He had not returned during the evening, which left Tanabe sitting dumb and mournful with sword on his lap on the front steps. There were fires and flames as near as the fighting as the tanks went around and around outside our walls all day. A dead soldier lay in the square where roads crossed just beyond the corner wall. Filipinos looted his pockets, took off his belt, then his outer pants, kicking the body over and leaving it there clad only in underpants. It might even be Kaito or Sugano who helped us so much—but it is now only another symbol, this time representing Change, the dying New Order in East Asia.

About 10, we saw Carl go out the gate to join Major Wilson in receiving orders and release from Major Ebiko and Yamato, who at last satisfied his correct soul by turning us over with all the proper formality. About noon Carl came back and we were all called into the main corridor. We crowded

about the small office space, then someone said, "Gangway." We all pressed over to one side as the clank of hobnails and sound of heavy feet came from the stairs. The eight soldiers had received their orders to come down from the roof. This was the most dramatic and exciting moment of all. It pictured our release more vividly than anything could. They had been persuaded to withdraw so that our danger would be less. They were giving in that much and were leaving Bilibid. They filed through the narrow lane we left, they and we silent, their faces looking sunk and trapped. The corporal's fat face was sullen and defeated. One short, beady-eyed pleasant fellow looked at us with a timid friendly grin—a good sport to the end. With machine-gun bullets and grenades in their hands, they trooped out the door, joining the still jaunty Formosans at the gate. They all went out without a backward look and the gate stood open behind them. We were alone—and turned toward Carl who read the Release. He emphasized the change of [release] dates on it and described the meeting in Ebiko's quarters. We cheered and then Carl took the hand-sewn Baguio American flag out of the drawer and held it up high. The crowd broke up and began to move away singing "The Star Spangled Banner" and "God Bless America." I went out the front door and around in our door at the side where June was trying to tell Jerry who had his face in his hands, his head bowed. I put my arm around his shoulders and the three of us sat there with tears running down our cheeks for quite a long while, not saying anything.

Ebiko, Oura, Yamato, Kaito, Tanabe, Sugano—all the good and the bad went out the front gate and locked us in with double barricade.

I began to feel horribly sick in my soul as I watched war hour after hour—snipers picking off men; men cornering snipers, creeping down alleys; hunting; cornering; killing. There was plenty to watch, hour after hour, our own men and the enemy.

This is the Release.

February 4
~~January 7th~~, 1945

Message

Commandant Major Ebiko: 1. The Japanese Army is now going to release all the prisoners of war and internees here on its own accord. 2. We are assigned to another duty and shall be here no more. 3. You are at liberty to act and live as free persons, but you must be aware of probable dangers if you go out. 4. We shall leave here foodstuffs, medicines and other necessities of which you may avail yourselves for the time being. 5. We have arranged to put up signboard at the front gate, bearing the following contex:—Lawfully released Prisoners of War and Internees are quartered here. Please do not molest them unless they make positive resistance."

February 5, 1945. I was awakened by feminine shrieks of delight and men's cries of "Hooray!" Little Walter came rushing in calling to his mother, "Mummie, Come, Come! Do you want to see a real live Marine? They are here!" I was too worn down to go out and join the crowd, so I just rested there letting the tears run down and listening to the American boys' voices—Southern, Western, Eastern accents—with bursts of laughter from our internees—laughter free and joyous with a note in it not heard in three years. I drifted into peaceful oblivion, wakening later amid mosquitoes and perspiration to listen to the rat-a-tat-tats, booms, clatter of shrapnel, explosions of ammunition dumps, seeing scarlet glare in every direction. There is battle all around us right up to the walls; two great armies locked in death grip. Today we watched flames leap and roar over at the Far Eastern University building just two blocks away. It is the Japanese Intelligence and Military Police Headquarters. The building was peppered with bullet holes Sunday morning and a dead soldier is slumped out half across one windowsill of an open window.

While outside washing clothes, I heard a big strapping fellow say to Marty Walker, "I've seen you before but can't recall your name. Mine is George Wood." I waited till they finished talking, then went over to him and said, "Would you mind coming in to say Hello to Jerry Crouter? He has a bad foot and cannot walk, but it would do him good to see you." He said, surprised, "Jerry Crouter! Sure I'll come see him! I've been in his house in

Baguio." He did not recognize me and I am sure I resembled a tired old lavandera dragging my pile of wet-wrung clothes and old tin wash bucket as I led him in to Jerry who was too thrilled to speak. Seeing George was like ten liver shots for him. He gave Jerry some cigarettes and from then on there was no more saving of stubs, for the boys showered their rations on us. George gave us three K-type ration boxes and four C or No. 2 type, containing crackers, a tin of cheese with bacon, a candy bar, four cigarettes in a small box, a piece of gum and four packages of powdered citrus juice. Oh boy, Oh boy, Oh boy, was all we could say over and over.

George had come up from Guadalcanal, Bougainville, Munda, and tore down with the first group from Lingayen. Three groups were converging, all trying to get to Manila first, in terrific rivalry! They didn't expect to find us alive and were racing with time to catch us before anything happened. The officers knew that we internees and the American soldiers were in Bilibid but the enlisted men did not. They were just looking for a place to spend the night when they started breaking down the barricade at our front gate. Major Wilson and Carl and some others began to hack it down from inside and when the soldiers heard this they thought it was Nipponese inside and put their hands on their rifles all ready to mow down. They called out, "We order you to surrender!" and our men cried out, "We can't. We are American prisoners of war in here." The answer from the outside was, "The Hell you are! Not now—we're here!" And they broke the door barricade and came in laughing with relief at finding us alive and not having to shoot their way through a nest of Japanese. There were not many dry eyes among our men, who were laughing with relief too. Some of them said that Tokyo had said over the radio that they would take us out and shoot us and this started their rush to Manila for a quick rescue. It worked, for they came through ahead of expectation or communication.

Our old friend George was only the first—for we have seen thousands now; huge, husky men, almost overpowering in their health and energy. They have such an American look; above all, secure and well fed.

After hunger, saving, scrimping, worrying, no news, the only kindness shown us required to be hidden from those high up; to emerge into all kinds of news, boys heaping kindness and attention on us, food in every direction, new avenues of life opening every hour—the mental and spiritual chaos is beyond expression. Like a rush of waves, a mighty sea breaks in and we swallow huge gulps of efficiency and freedom which leave us breathless and gasping on a new shore.

Fire began to burn on Echague and we saw the Great Eastern and Marco Polo hotels burst into flame, burn fiercely and spread, spread, spread. Our forces, which by now were coming in faster, began to dynamite buildings in an effort to stem the conflagration. It kept coming nearer and nearer.

Notices which tell a little of today's happenings. "The Red Cross will be here this afternoon and take Personal Messages. Please *print* your message clearly and hand to camp office as soon as possible. Please make them brief.'' Mine to Mums: "Transferred Bilibid Manila December 28 Released February 4, well, being cared for with American efficiency, need nothing yet, don't worry. Notify Jerry's family from whom no word in three years, anxious.''

Some advice given to us on the 4th: "Members of camp are strongly advised to stay indoors except when absolutely necessary to go out. The soldiers next door have sent in this advice from their own more militarily experienced judgment. That it is really dangerous to get out from under cover while shelling and machine gun firing is going on is amply evidenced by the piece of shrapnel now suspended from the bulletin board, which flew into our yard today from one of the explosions. At the present time, no reason for occupants of second floor to move down for night, but please observe this precaution—*sleep below level of windows*. If situation appears dangerous, be ready to evacuate when called. The Safety Committee.''

Another notice: February 5. "Colonel E. M. Grimm of U.S. Army has been put in charge of Civilian Camps. Col. Grimm ordered that no one is to leave this compound until permission is granted. He stated it is extremely dangerous on the streets now. Carl and Denki have just left to accompany the Colonel to Santo Tomas.''

Stop Press. "February 5. Gen. Fellers and Col. Soriano came to see us this afternoon at the request of Gen. MacArthur to give us his very best wishes and to obtain a general idea of our circumstances. Gen. Fellers is struck by our healthy looks as compared to Santo Tomas Internees, but he agreed that the Baguio climate would be responsible for this. He stated that a supply train of foodstuffs and medicines for us will arrive in Manila soon. The Red Cross is organizing to take care of us and anyone who wishes to go home will be given that opportunity. 550 men from Cabanatuan are now in proper hospitals and our own very sick will also be so taken care of. Gen. Fellers expressed his great admiration for the way in which MacArthur has conducted operations. Three divisions have landed in Lingayen, Zambales, and Batangas respectively. They have all converged on Manila, arriving within 18 hours of each other. But for MacArthur's insistence, the present campaign in the Philippines would have been delayed for another year. He expresses regret that he is three days behind schedule. We briefly thanked Gen. Fellers for his visit and gave him the information that he required which included the camp roster. Signed, A. C. Skerl.''

About 7 as dark closed over us, we groped about our cement space and got ready for bed, to rest after talking with anti-tank gunners, machine-gunners and infantry boys, watching sparks fly upwards all around us in the battle din and exploding munition dumps. Word crept around for us to be packed and ready to leave on a moment's notice with bedroll and handbag only. Our weary minds staggered but we filled the zipper bag, the duffle bag and two straw bags with change of clothes, some food cans, several coconuts, the precious sugar bought with topaz, and some other stupid enclosures. In less than half an hour, we were told we were to be moved outside the city at once. We piled our three airplane luggage suitcases, two leather ones, two big straw sacks and the typewriter into the middle of the space against the cement wall (to keep the heat from reaching it!), left all the loose things hanging on lines, hooks, and sitting on shelves as they were and walked out into the dark lit by sparks and flames. I held onto my bag with notes and three pieces of jewelry—one thing always packed and portable—and we walked off without a qualm or backward look at ivories, silver, brocades and other possessions we had saved for three years (worth about four thousand dollars). Jerry hobbled out on crutches and the children carried some things out with him, saying they would come back for me who stayed with what remained to be carried. It seemed ages that I waited and it was. Suddenly I realized it was silent, that there was no hum of humanity. I went outside calling June and Bedie and there was not a soul left in the prison yard. It was the loneliest, most terrifying feeling I have ever known. A young American soldier who was left to guard heard me and came looking very anxious about my still being there. Just then the children arrived and loaded themselves down. The soldier took another bundle of bedding and we were led out through the grassy compound where we had driven in weeks ago, then through other long, walled-in compounds and buildings full of junk and cobwebs and dust, out to a street next to Rizal Avenue. We sat on our rolls and bags under the eaves of Filipino huts which had been evacuated, and the fire crept nearer and nearer, until it was only two blocks away. Army trucks and jeeps roared up, people and bags piled in and the vehicles roared off around a corner. We were all cheering and the Filipinos were calling "Mabuhay" and good-bye. We were among the last as usual to pile into a light, fast ¼ ton truck and off down Rizal Avenue. The heat and glare and flame increased behind us, and we had a full view of the avenue of fire which was approaching. Nobody was nervous or upset or hysterical. The soldiers could not get over how calm we were, but it was just one more thing to most of us, and for the children it was adventure out in the wide world. All of the kids were very quiet or else cheering the soldier boys who simply adored them and lavished affection on each one. The children hung onto soldiers' hands and hero-worshipped day and night.

I had been called out to the gate in the dusk to see a man who wanted to talk to someone from Boston—huge, husky, bronze and beaming Cornelius J. O'Leary, from Worcester, Massachusetts. He asked would I please get in touch with his wife and tell her how I talked to him at the gate of Bilibid prison; that he was fine and now a Major and was thrilled over the letters and pictures from the three children, and the picture of the fourth baby, two years old, born since he left home. He talked and talked and we listened avidly—about his wife, children and home; about Guadalcanal, Bougainville and Munda, and how they wondered, as they pushed through the jungles, in those places, what it was all about and for. "And now, Mrs. Crouter, I can tell you that when we came in here and found you people prisoners in these walls—found you women and children—then we knew what it was all for and that it was worth it all!'' Many of them said this in their different ways to all of us. They had not seen any white people for two years and they now hang around just to look at us and talk, talk, talk, mostly about home and mothers, wives and sweethearts there. The wives in the pictures look so glamorous to our eyes!

We went through dark streets during our flight from the wall of flame, in trucks and jeeps. Filipinos were grouped everywhere, cheering us and waving. Outside the city we went faster, leaving the black pillar of smoke behind us and only the red glow over us still. They said there were snipers everywhere but we did not think about it or even realize it so we were not afraid. All we could take in was that we were free. Along shell-torn and unrepaired streets, in and out we went, looking at buildings blown up in partial destruction, windows smashed everywhere, ruins in silhouette surrounding us. We finally pulled in at the model shoe factory of Ang Tibay.

The shoe factory was Division Headquarters and was going full tilt.

In the entrance hall, radio men and telephone operators were working every second. How could they hear or send anything in that madhouse of noise! The stairs were crowded with men in olive drab going up and down, up and down.

We set our rolls and pitifully small hand-sacks on the balcony floor and plunked ourselves down on them. Now there was no need to hurry or set up another space. We were just perched on another edge waiting to take off again. As we leaned over the rail of the balcony, we could see downstairs the 800 prisoners who lived on the other side of our wall. They had been taken out of Bilibid first and we had watched the never-ending line stream from their compound through ours to the back gate. First had come the stretcher cases, then those who could walk, many helping each other. It was a slow procession of sick, exhausted men, in ragged clothes, touseled hair, many unshaven faces with sores. I shall never forget that line of military prisoners wavering through the dark yard, with the glare in the sky pitilessly showing up their condition.

As we looked down from the balcony, we could see that some were not so badly off and were walking around, but many were actually skin and bone. Collarbones stood out like shelves. Eyes were gaunt and hollow. Faces were drawn tight with nerves. Elbows were bony knobs. Arms and legs were literally pipe-stems. *There* was starvation and we felt that our troubles were nothing. Yet we were told that they had worried when our children cried, that they had loved the little rhythm band and the singing. There was one tall fellow who haunts my memory. He must have had a magnificent physique and handsome features once, but his ribs and all other bones stood out like a skeleton without flesh and he could not even sit up on his pallet. He just lay there with a slight smile on his face. I looked down at him many times, praying that they would bring him back to health.

Beyond, in another section, were emaciated, staring-eyed mental cases, terror on their faces, unstrung nerves jangling openly. June said it made her really sick to look at them all—she couldn't bear it.

Between the two balconies was an office in beautiful paneled wood where Generals and Colonels conferred, coming and going constantly. We will never see so many "stars" at once again probably. I think it is Generals Sutherland and Willoughby whose faces and strapping figures I can recall the best. Opposite them G-2 had set up their desk and apparatus. Further on was the department dealing with Japanese prisoners and translation, to which was attached American-Japanese U.S. citizens, that Major O'Leary called "Nisei"—second generation Japanese.

Bedie stayed up all night though we had spread our blankets on the balcony floor. We only saw him once or twice and then he was off again. He says he made "fifteen friends"—one a Don Bell from Ohio. We let him run, for it is once in a lifetime. He was shown the inside of tanks, amphibian trucks known as Alligators or Water Buffalo or Ducks, and all sorts of new, compact marvels of American invention and efficiency in this war.

I watched the tanks and trucks roaring past Headquarters on the road toward Manila, and looked at all the thousands of trucks and jeeps and new kinds of equipment. In part of my brain flickered two pieces from the past—a shadowy voice saying, "We had the best time of our lives in here—sorry to leave." And again the sight of primitive carts at night flashing by on a dark road, drawn by six men with Oriental faces straining in fatigue, pulling these carts to meet—tanks flashing by— Where am I? In the past? In the future? In the present? We are where the past and future meet in combat and who will survive?

February 6, 1945. The Army gave us breakfast of powdered eggs, grain cereal with milk and sugar, and coffee. But earlier we had been given a cup of cocoa with milk in it and I cried and cried right into the cup. Some soldiers gave us a big can of apricots that they could not eat and we simply wallowed in it—our first in three years. Another lad gave us a big tin of beer which was most relaxing!

In another section we looked down on piles of airplane parts left by the Japanese who had used the building as assembly plant and did not have time to remove or destroy.

Bedie came to look for me, swinging his shoulders like half a dozen American doughboys and chewing gum like another half dozen—shifting shoulders and gum with that tough cocky cheerfulness which was surrounding us. I sat down beside him and laughed and hugged him.

We began to have all sorts of marvels in canned and dehydrated food. Potato and onion, corned beef stew, which tasted like heaven.

In the late morning Carl came out and called us all together to tell of his thrilling trip to Santo Tomas. He said they had to remain there until next day and then heard that we had been moved out. He went in a jeep to Bilibid after he left here and somehow sent back a message to us at the shoe factory that all our possessions were gone, looted by Filipinos. The guards had left the prison for a while because of the intense heat and looters rush in where angels will not tread. I felt numb by this time.

June and I stood hours in line at the pump in the front yard, waiting to wash dishes. Latrines had been dug in a hurry for us the night before when we came in, by soldiers who had not slept for three nights. There were many flies and it was difficult not only for us but for the Army.

In the afternoon, Santiago, our Filipino friend of many years, came to hunt for us. We wrung each other's hands and he cried over and over, "Oh Mrs. Crouter, Mrs. Crouter, Mrs. Crouter!" How good it was to see him again and to know he had come through the occupation safely. He took our coffee to a nearby house and brewed it for us, sending a big bunch of flowers back with it by his two daughters. We gave him some of our brown sugar as he had had none for ages, also a No. 2 box with sugar, crackers and candy. He said he would try to see us in Bilibid.

About 7 P.M. they decided to move us back to Bilibid because Japanese mortars were shelling too near Headquarters, and anyhow we were most appallingly in the way of the general staff who were planning siege on a vast scale. Nearly all of the 800 soldiers were taken back and half of the internees had gone when we started out. We had not gone far when we heard ack-ack explosions and saw the rosettes over a fork in the road where an American soldier was waving frantically for us to stop and go back. Our driver turned around on a nickel and tore back over the bumbs and holes while we crouched down in the truck so we wouldn't be jounced off. No one made any fuss or seemed afraid but it was a wild ride. All the other trucks tore back behind us and we lined the road into Ang Tibay where other trucks were loading to leave. In about fifteen minutes, we started again, with escort in front and behind us, and this time we saw a big column of black smoke. It was a dump that our planes had hit and the ack shells were going off all over the place. We passed into town through deserted streets without any further incident, arriving at Bilibid wall where we had left the night before—but how much had happened! We poked through the dark buildings back to our original space as we were told to do—to find every single possession gone and the most indescribable mess of cans, filth and all kinds of discarded stuff jumbled into piles by the looters. It was even dirtier than the night we arrived in December, and was wet beside. The entire building and hospital cells had been completely looted.

It was dark and we had no lights which added to the misery. Jerry put his hand into one of our bags and exclaimed, "Why did you put a sharp knife in there, Pete!" I said I did not. It was the sugar bottle which had smashed on the trip in and glass was mixed with sugar so we had to throw it all out. Jerry had cut his finger very badly on the glass and it bled horribly. I desperately hunted for gauze and adhesive which I knew was in the emergency bag. It seemed a thousand years until I found it and Jerry soaked three different gauze bandages until the bleeding finally stopped. It was one more wretchedness, one more loss, which scarcely registered. I stormed at the Army and the Committee and heaven because we could not see. We lighted some papers to try to locate our things and the firing began as though trying to get our range so the Committee ordered no more light of any kind. It was a hideous night. June and I finally made up the three beds, with nets half arranged. The heat and mosquitoes were dreadful and we listened to long range guns all night. It was battle again and we were in the front line. There was glare in the sky from gun fire and conflagration. I slept a little but my bones cracked on the boards whenever I turned. It was somehow comforting to get back to a settled known space even though the irony of losing all we had left, under American protection, after we had dragged it through three years of Nipponese trials, hit us a ghastly wallop. We didn't blame anyone—we know the heat was terrific because we saw where the fire burned up to the wall at the front gate and that there was fighting everywhere as well. We know how the Filipinos have suffered from hunger and want.

February 7, 1945 It was a day of trying to reorganize again, without anything to do it with. I wanted to wash clothes in order to have a change into fresh ones, but there was no bucket—even our leaky one had been looted. Everything was gone except the rolls and handbags we took with us, and the wooden beds which were still there.

Toilets had been bad before but now they had to be pail-flushed by hand, for the Japanese destroyed the water-pressure pumps. We dipped into Skerl's wells to advantage. All water must be boiled and even dishes must be rinsed in hot or purified water. The kitchen was hopelessly disorganized, storeroom looted as well as hospital drugs and supplies. Even the grinders were gone. But the soybeans left cooking the night before when we fled were still there in the pressure cookers though electricity was off!

Six letters were brought to us from America, written in December, a feast of home.

About ten, there were big cheers in the hall and someone said it was General MacArthur and his staff. I was too dull and weary to go to look and not much interested. Still trying to function mentally as well as physically, I was standing in our space by the double bunk when MacArthur came through the door at the far end of the room. I stepped back and my mind registered disjointedly, "Here comes another Commandant, down the long aisle just like Oura did—was it last week? I wonder if I should bow from the waist down." I felt hopelessly mixed up. When the General passed the bunk he turned and looked into my face directly. He grabbed my hand and shook it, over and over, up and down. I was utterly dumb. I felt and looked more miserable and wretched every second. I could not say a word and just looked back at him speechless as we pumped our arms up and down, up and down. All of the last three years was in my mind and face, and at this actual, concrete moment of release, this biggest moment of my life, I felt no joy or relief, only deep sadness which could not come into words. The General did not say anything either. We just stood there pumping our arms up and down, looking at each other searchingly. Then he went on out the door. I was the only one he stopped to speak to in this long room, and there was no reason for it—it wasn't recognition of anyone he knew or thought was familiar. He felt deeply moved and there was inarticulate expression of it in the strong, speechless handshake. Neither of us could have expressed any of our thoughts. It was unexpected for me. I wasn't prepared for any personal recognition and would have been silent in any case. What is there to say when social amenities are overboard? In a brief mental flash, I was impressed that he had lost that soft, spoiled look, was solid brawn—steady, heavy, fined-down like the rest of the Army. There was nothing political in the handshake or the look. He was sincerely comprehending of my strained face which showed what all of us had suffered. He must have sensed that no active spark of any kind existed in me. The lights had almost gone out. He was deeply shocked and sorry for all of us, and looked it without trying to say so. For this I was grateful. He is very handsome and looked young again, not jaded like the last glimpse I had in the Manila Hotel lobby long ago. The penthouse look had gone. Perhaps he too has learned a lot through defeat.

All day long boys hungry for affection came to sit with us, talk with us—to talk of home, of mothers, brothers, fathers, sisters, wives, and sweethearts. They love being asked where they came from, how many children or brothers they had. They crowded in, talking with internees all over the building, coming back after another round of duty, looking at us as though we had been friends forever. They wanted to hear about all our experiences, reluctantly told of theirs when we plied them with questions. They were shy, modest, but ready to open up.

Handsome young Spencer, age thirty, was with us every free moment, answering my questions about the scar on his face where a bullet went through which knocked out two teeth and raised havoc with his jaw bone but now it is well and his looks not impaired. He has that wonderfully fit look—solid, chunky, eager. All the boys pulled Bedie's hair as though they couldn't bear to let him go. Spence, like all the others, marveled at our morale, said they never saw or imagined anything like it—the way we drove out on that road after dark with fire at our heels and snipers with bullets and grenades ready on every side; bumping over shell holes, yet never a whimper from one child, not one case of hysterics or weeping or nerves. Then, they said, we came back here to a looted, filthy building after dark and stood up under an all-night bombardment of the enemy with return by our own guns. Only a few of our Committee men knew how serious Wednesday night was for us and the city. The Japanese exploded ack-ack shells directly over Bilibid and two fragments fell right into the compound. The tin roof of the men's barracks was no protection and a huge piece of shrapnel went through the door, stopped by the hinge from doing any real damage—the hinge was twisted to pieces. A smoking iron piece fell on Patton's bed. Then all the men moved out in a hurry. My bones cracking on boards whenever I moved kept me awake more than the awful muzzle blast of trench mortars five miles away. The big guns began about two, solid, long blasts, and we could hear the prolonged whine and whistle of shells as they passed over our heads. I didn't mind these at all—only the nasty trench mortars. I went out the length of the yard to the toilet twice in between bombardments.

The night that we returned here fifteen men were wounded (five died) and several Filipinos—one a small girl who was horribly torn—were killed by trench mortars near the front gate of Bilibid, the very spot where we came in. We have been right in the middle of the front line since Sunday.

Major O'Leary wanted to give us something—food, clothes—anything! I told him we were getting all we could eat but that I would like some paper to write on and two good pencils. He said it was as good as done. Next morning in came two swell American pencils and six student's notebooks. Oh Boy, am I writing big after three years of cramped notes!

We heard that Santo Tomas was badly hit by shells—five killed, among them Rev. Walter Foley, instantly, Anne Davis, and Monica Robb; 70 badly wounded and some of them dying from shock. The Japanese got the range from Santo Tomas tower and shelled it and the whole district including Bilibid.

February 8, 1945. The looting mess is cleared away a bit and all of us are getting used to the trench mortar. A good thing too, for about 5 P.M. our own olive-drab soldiers set up six or eight sticks on the grass just behind Bilibid and the sticks turned out to be those damn trench mortars! We had salvos of these regularly all night and got so we could even sleep through it.

Spence came to say good-bye about 4 and just hated to go. He said, "We are moving up to the next front line on short notice." We felt we had known these boys for ages and there was a close bond between us. After they all went out the front gate, silence fell, and we missed them terribly. They were dear boys, from every state, all sorts of small towns, and from every walk of life. June kept Spence doubled up over her ambition to eat in an Automat, etc. She was dying to wash our plates in his tin hat, so I asked him if she could and he said Sure. What fun!

The family still kids me over how I cried while drinking our first cup of cocoa with milk out at H.Q. The 7th we had our first real flour bread, which was simply marvelous! The American Red Cross trucks came. PCAU (Philippine Civil Aid Unit) came with Filipino boys to take over all the cooking and serving of food. Other kits are rationed out by our Committee. We had a heavenly potato stew, and the following night another one with tomatoes and peas and beef. What they turn out of cans and big dehydrated bulk staggers our imagination and delights our palate. All we had tried to tell the children about America and what the boys would bring in pales before what is given us every day. I don't cry over good food now as I did, but I hear an item like, "They are going to level Tokyo and blast Japan off the map," then I break down and weep, crying, "Oh, I can't bear to have those women and children over there go through it too. They are helpless and not to blame."

Dave Griffin, an old friend who came into Manila taking war pictures, might go up to Baguio so we told him all Nida and Ismael had done for us and wrote down her name. We broke down at this point—even Jerry who turned his head away and covered his face with his hands. Griff said he would find her, give her money and help if she needed it, go right to our place to see if the house was gone. He told of friction with the British, of our working together with Russia which he says is not nearly so radical as it was. Endlessly we talked. Then he said he would come back again. We must have been a sight in his eyes. My hair was literally down, in a braid tied with green ribbon, as I had lost all my hairpins here the night we moved out in half an hour. I caught a glimpse of myself in a mirror and wondered who it was—face pinched, lined, drawn, huge eyes. Jerry is thin, on the verge of collapse.

February 9, 1945. Dave blew in with a paper bag holding three of Ann's dresses for us and two children's sunsuits that she and Hannah had made. June looked stunning in a black crepe with rainbow colors at the belt and in stripes on the blouse. I have a canary yellow and black print. If I only had "looks" to put inside of it, I would feel grand! June is radiantly happy as she has been dying for clothes. The soldiers have been very appreciative of her simplicity and spontaneous manner. They flocked about and came back again and again. She is talking her arm off.

We received small air copies of *Time*, the *Saturday Evening Post, Readers' Digest, Liberty*. We hear that Roosevelt's electoral votes were 431 to Dewey's 91. All these soldiers are for Roosevelt, not MacArthur. Also, Truman is Vice-President, not Paul McNutt. We asked, "Who is Truman?"

A Shipping Board man took Jerry's name and said he could have a job with them any time. This did Jerry more good than any food or pill or injection. The man took our home address and application to sail—he urged us to go back to the States and build ourselves up—and he promised to help Nida too. He wrote it all down in a book.

We hear that rehabilitation of the Philippines began at once—that each town from Lingayen down is being rebuilt, all the people being hired at a peso a day, put to work at once, fed and looked after. This thrilled me as it showed vision and is along the lines of a new future. They say that everyone between the ages of 18 and 25 in the States must work at some useful occupation, women and girls included.

It was a terrible night for me, not on account of the violent bombardment which went on crashing, booming, whistling and singing overhead all night, but because of my sore back and hips from lying on boards. I am black and green from the truck ride anyway, and it is agony trying to find a soft spot. The night seemed very long but at least one could listen to the various kinds of whines of bullets and shells passing over.

Tank boys coming in from the front told of big losses that day—1 in every 20 in their company, they said. They ran into pillboxes and a heavy concentration of Japanese.

About ten of our soldiers scaled the wall, sitting on top in a row, yelling, "We want to see Americans. We want to talk to Americans." June says it is easy to talk to them now, and we find her surrounded by all types, all kinds of grammar and colloquialisms. One boy said he would be back on the wall tomorrow night with a bunch of bananas for her. They ask her ambitions and tell her she must not be a nurse! The slang we hear, the cocky, fresh expressions are simply wonderful.

February 10, 1945. I slept half an hour on Jerry's bed and felt renewed. Trench mortar shells are going the wrong way over us this morning and there is thick firing from both sides all around us. We were told that they were our guns and all was under control   but we must stay inside and not congregate in groups but spread out in our spaces!

8 tanks and 700 men held the city for the Americans that first night we saw them come in, until reinforcements came the next day.

We had marvelous spaghetti and cheese with tomato sauce for supper! Tomato we have wanted for over a year. And we had grapefuit juice to drink! Eating these, I find I have a sore mouth, very sore. Bacon this morning with cereal and applesauce—milk, butter, jams, candy rolls—we cannot take in mentally all that pours in. Canned asparagus this noon with creamed salmon! We take Vims three times a day, plus 5 milligrams of B-1.

We hear there has been a spy among our own ranks, signaling information somehow. Each time a place was shelled and the people moved to another spot, this spot was shelled next, happening several times. They think they know now who is giving the information.

February 11, 1945. O'Leary gave Jerry two pairs of socks and two under-drawers, which he needed badly. The Major says the Geneva regulations are strict on the care of U.S.–Japanese internees, and the U.S. follows the rules even if the Japanese did not. He had asked how we felt about the way prisoners should be treated and we said we had no hate and begged him to be particularly good to the women and children for we did not want anyone to go through what we had endured. He asked if we knew where the food had been going and why they did not feed us. I said Yes—the Japanese Army was taking it, for we saw this all the way south. He said also that our boats were sinking tons of supplies and this made the other reason, which was Scarcity, which we knew of course. Still there was malice too on the part of some high up.

There was an early rumor that Oura and Yamato had committed hara-kiri, but today a rumor says that Yamato is prisoner here in Bilibid. Suda and Kaito were said to be dead, carried in feet first, at the gate. Miss McKim said one of Sugano's men is a prisoner in here. Most of our Formosan guards are prisoners here.

Griff celebrated Bedie's 14th birthday with us. He took flashlight [photos] (the first pop scaring the whole room with its burst of light) of us sitting on beds, my hair down, dirty bare feet and all, but smiling at each other as we ate pork and sauerkraut from the Red Cross with a can of corn from Griff which Jerry fried in bacon.

The fraternizing scenes all around camp are marvelous. Yanks are walking along with tiny fingers of children curled in their big hands. Groups crouch together talking of home states and towns. Australian coppers and silver Dutch New Guinea coins, all sorts of paper currency are being given to the kids for souvenirs.

Shells are still being fired from the post office where the Japanese are heavily entrenched and it is MacArthur's policy to spare Filipino lives and buildings as far as possible.

We are living in a world of such big men and such strong action that it will be hard to go home to quiet times and a manless world—or is it? The children say, "Mummie, what are Americans—a race of giants?" The contrast between them and the short Filipino and Japanese we have seen for three years makes Americans look stupendous.

We just can't eat all that is given us. Even the children are stumped. There is more in one day than in a whole week, a whole month before.

Piles of dead bodies of Japanese are now cleared from the street beside the prison walls. The battle of Manila is fierce, nasty, sharp.

Today I put on my jade engagement ring and Grandmother's diamond for the first time in over three years—untying them from a handkerchief corner.

We heard a building blow up and collapse, planks and pieces of wood dropping in an enormous shower. It was another one of those nights.

February 12, 1945. Jim Halsema, our newsman who put out the Camp Holmes *News*, is released and is now a member of the Associated Press. Phil says the moral tone at Santo Tomas is horrible—not just the morale. He says it is like animals and dog eat dog. They stole everything he had with him when he moved out of range of the shelling, but a Press man found his case of pictures hidden in a cupboard. He says we were united and cooperative compared to that group and had a wonderful spirit. He says we were divided into two factions only, while they were individual entities. The majority had nothing extra, some had plenty, and this made for breakdown and terror. He says it was better that we were all alike in spending money, and all made equal the last year. Shades of Oura! This is almost the end of our lesson.

Poor Yamato's piano out by the gate with the front board gone looks very dilapidated and forlorn. It was his last gesture of kindness when we wanted meat which he could not supply. Gibby bangs out jazz on the keys for the soldiers.

Water-car fills our Lister bag several times a day, then there is a rush by everybody to fill cans and bottles.

The first shot at Santo Tomas was a direct hit on the hospital there, fired from a gun in San Sebastian Church. There are big guns also in the Philippine General Hospital. All churches, schools and hospitals were stored full of munitions and many had big guns.

Griff said I looked better yesterday than I did two days ago. Jerry now walks everywhere and is washing sheets. He has no more sore joint or swelling, his face is filling out and losing that strained look. I still feel "old, most old" and have 102 temperature.

The rivalry between 1st Cavalry Regiment of Tanks, the 37th Infantry and the 11th Airborne Division is just like the play *What Price Glory*.

We saw Frances and Rachael in odd nightclothes, with hair streaming, and didn't know them, they were such a sight. Frances, who is large and not in as bad shape as some others, said to one husky Yank, "We don't look so bad, do we?" He looked her straight in the eyes and answered, "Lady, you look God-awful to us."

There was singing and dancing in the street outside of our wall last night, much laughter and cheering. It was the tank boys getting ready to go into the Walled City[5] to fight—and die. Losses were big all day and they knew it, but they must have fun in between.

February 13, 1945. June now writes down what I tell her. My back ached so I didn't sleep much. The shells were nothing to the pain. I developed diarrhea and had to use a can with a sharp edge, in pitch darkness.

I have had three bed baths by Philippine nurses and two alcohol rubs—imagine it! A fresh egg from the U.S. and an alcohol rub in this Bilibid space where we would have starved but for Sugano's soybeans.

My high fever gave me all kinds of sensations all night. I seemed to be hanging in space and kept forgetting who I was. I felt if I could only remember my name I would be all right. In the immensity I would lose my identity, and then for a few minutes would grasp it again. The three years' experience, the last two weeks and the guns, the surging of fire, the wave of looters clearing away everything like locusts, make one feel infinitely small.

February 14, 1945. I am doubled up with pain; I have dysentery and get sulfa guanadine-diazene.

I heard the clock strike six as I was dozing. Then I heard a quiet plane sail overhead. After it went beyond, there was an explosion, then the low hum of the plane returning. As it reached our end of the building there was a tremendous detonation and burst of light almost at the door, followed by immediate concussion. The building shook, the tin windows rattled shut, everything—even our brains—staggered. After a second of thick silence, people began calling to each other—"Daddy, are you all right?"—"Son, are you all right?" No one in the building was hurt though the bomb fell just outside the gate near our door, between two tanks parked there for the night. It mangled the Captain in Command who had become the friend of many in here, and killed three other boys who were sleeping in their hammocks. People on the wall side were covered with cement, dirt and stones as they flew in the windows. Immediately everyone started pouring out to the toilets through our room, and there was release of emotions in chatter out in the yard, no one knowing till later of the deaths outside the wall.

February 15, 1945. Our wall is bulged way in and cracked from the concussion. The fronts of two houses on the corner are blown out so that the rooms look like stage settings which have been deserted.

There are several stories about Baguio by a Marine flyer who helped to level it. They bombed all Session Road and the two hospitals, then took a look around, saw one building still left and knocked that off too. So far as Baguio City goes, we had our last look at it the day we went through. I wonder how many Chinese and Filipino friends were killed there, unless they were warned by guerrillas to get out.

February 16, 1945. I was completely exhausted and wept. I can't take it anymore. I never could imagine such violent sickness—such pain, such unimaginable inconvenience and agonizing discomforts all in the darkness. After a very bad day for me, late in the afternoon, six Filipino boys lifted my bed and carried me on it over to the cell hospital behind bars. It was none too soon for all of us. Jerry's feet were swelling and the children were tired out. My head was about to blow off with pain, no sleep, odors of food and families all around getting chow, dividing chow, eating chow, Santo Tomas visitors, endless confusion. The hospital was heavenly quiet by comparison and a breeze blew through the bars during a night of terrible pain, continued inconvenience and unending discomforts. Guns all night. During sleep I had "involuntaries," staying in the resulting mess until something could be done about it in the morning. I was woozy with fever and weakness after no real food for six days and whatever I ate rushing through.

February 18, 1945. June and Jerry walked to Santo Tomas and Jerry passed any number of old friends without stopping to speak for he felt so heartsick over their looks. There are dozens like ghosts, he says. Dr. Hall is in good shape and full of pep! They did have a reunion with 2 families.

Miss Velasco and Miss Santos are two dainty little Filipina nurses bristling with efficiency. I will never forget those two girls that first night in this cell, putting up the nets for me where there were no nails, nothing to do with. One went off and came back with a spool of fine copper wire. They strung a strand of it. It would not hold any weight, broke. They said nothing. Silently they pulled out two long strands of wire, twirled them together to make a stronger strand and strung it between the bars at each end. With two lines like this, the use of one nail stuck on a door, and we were all ready for the night, after serene, silent activity. They are so sweet, so gentle, so truly eager to serve. Oh the blessed relief of this after three years! It is a lesson for some who are grudging in their service.

It is a miracle to see Filipino faces moving about freely and all of us able to smile and talk to each other.

The Army medicos seem to use plasma for everything, no other kind of transfusion at all. They are giving it to Filipino starvation cases—babies and children who were dying of malnutrition are brought back by plasma.

February 19, 1945. My cramps abate gradually, the flame dying down. Maj. Olmstead, a huge doctor from Indiana, strides in and out on cheerful rounds all day. Our own doctors are worn out. The Major said I was so woozy when he took over my case that I could not answer any questions he asked about my condition. My head is almost clear and the Major says I need food now for my trouble was partly starvation.

Jerry and Pop Crandon obtained passes and went outside all through the burned area. Jerry was full of it when he returned but he should not walk so far with swollen ankles. He is so restless, says he will take Bedie out tomorrow.

Mr. Yu and Mr. Chen came to see me and just stood and beamed and beamed. We were all glad to be alive.

Peg made me a pillow case out of a piece of sheet. My pillow is a stuffed flour sack, but I have a new fresh smelling sheet marked Santa Catalina Hospital (so I can't loot it!).

Every one who can walk today is up watching the American dive bombing into the Walled City which is *still* holding out, all cheerful Headquarters reports to the contrary. Post office, city hall and other big buildings are strongly holding out also. Manila Hotel is still intact but a stronghold of Japanese. MacArthur hopes to use it for H.Q. eventually, it is said. He reported capture of Manila a little prematurely.

It is reported that 300 Filipinos and Spanish a day manage to escape from the Walled City, creeping up over the wall, rolling off it and away until they are safe. Many were living in the aquarium under the sod bank. We wonder what happened to the fishes, water, and big green water eels and snakes.

February 20, 1945. I feel almost human and myself again, with a fine bath, violently scrubbed teeth, my hair combed by Edna, sucking a Root Beer Life Saver!

There is a great tale of Pete Saleeby being rescued. A nurse pushed him from the hospital in a wheelchair across a plank bridge, found herself in the front lines, was rescued by two soldiers in a jeep, and her hands are still shaking. Pete is shell-shocked.

I lay here thinking how desperately homesick I am going to be for mango trees like the one I am gazing at through the iron bars, and for all the Philippine things I love so deeply. Even if we are away only six or eight months, I will be miserably homesick for my islands. I know it already. I do not want to leave.

I heard the Major say that formerly each cell contained from 30 to 50 men.

Brief item from news sheet from H.Q. February 7. "5,000 prisoners released. The latest group was freed when Americans drove into filthy Bilibid Prison."

The yard is still being swept. June says it is exciting to have soap issue and plenty of it. It helps keep down dysentery. Real toilet paper rolls came in just as our Sugano paper napkins reached an end.

February 21, 1945. A tank broke through one gate of Walled City and about 7,000 Filipinos poured through the breach. Saved! What stories, what stories, about how dreadful they looked and what they endured.

A Red Cross worker in khaki uniform sat and talked with me for a while. She drew her head in whenever the big shells went whining over. Like everyone else who visits me, she asked, "Wasn't that one rather near?" When I said, "Oh no, they go over like that all the time, night and day," she looked floored and replied, "You must be right in line of fire."

I had a long interesting talk with a Filipino boy who was sweeping the cell. He said the Japanese could have done almost anything with the poor people if they had been even half way decent to them. But they were not. They were only cruel. He said, "We do not ask for much and if we get it we are grateful. But they did not give." His simplicity was very moving. How stupid conquerers are, and how quickly man loses contact when he grasps power!

I slept a good deal in spite of huge shells whistling in the air path overhead and slamming down against the Walled City as though in the next yard. Zowie. Zam. Wham. What pasting they gave it. It certainly was a lullaby—to sink off to sleep under the sound of pounds of shell traveling through the air. There was something soothing about its monotony!

February 22, 1945. All camp is agog over the drawing for the first 20 to fly to Leyte. We are out of it until I can get medical permit to leave. I must be cleared of dysentery and get on my feet. My feet have no feeling yet—I tried them out.

The truck pulled out at 4 with the first 19 going to Leyte. Leaving tomorrow are 9 men without families, and four couples including three children. Charles and Carl are among them. It will fill up a troop transport with only limited space above deck for women and children.

February 23, 1945. I stagger round my cell like a drunken sailor. It is a good thing that my sheltered, gently-reared New England mother and sister cannot see me now. My delicate background must have buried a narrow tough fiber in me somewhere to pull me along, for my troubles increased after American invasion rather than lessened. Of course the food and the Army medical care and supplies make all the difference between life and death. I still get two teaspoons of sulfaguanadine four times a day.

Jerry says that someone reports seeing Yamato cooking for his fellow-internees in the Nipponese compound before they were transferred elsewhere. He still had his glasses.

One officer said that when MacArthur starts publicizing victory and reports the battle won, then the rest of them know their real work and fighting is about to begin, the mopping up only started. They admire his tactical brilliance, but not his political leanings.

The Major saw me tottering around my cell and said not to overdo! Dr. Mather did a wonderful job but was worn out when the Major took over.

Marj Patton has given birth to a son and they are all right now, after a Caesarian.

How could I forget to put down the luscious mound of creamed canned turkey and the three large red tender beets I ate for supper last night! I had prayed for beets all day—and they came! This noon a beautiful golden fried egg which I ate to the last crumb.

Walter chortles as he tells me our troops held the first floor of Manila Hotel, with the Japanese holding the mezzanine on up to the penthouse. We picture our tough Yanks tossing grenades up into MacArthur's penthouse, clearing out Nipponese. Whenever there is a floor cleared in a building, the looters swarm in right behind the fighting, fearing nothing, thinking only of gain.

June and Jerry are doing a big wash. Still no water pipes—only dirty well-water. Army cars still bring our drinking water, using water purifier. Everyone is busy tearing around with washing, rations or talk. I spend hours alone in this jail cell.

I read in the *New Philippines* paper that Senator Quirino's wife and two daughters were machine-gunned during the burning by the Japanese and he has lost all in the fire. "His face had a lost expression," wrote Felipe Buencamino III. That must be the way I looked at MacArthur. Rich and poor alike were shot, burned out, looted. All of us together have only our lives and lucky to have those.

Bedie came home with a bulging stomach after a marvelous day at the battery of "105" guns which have sung over our head bombarding the Walled City. He was McKimmey's shadow and was shown everything. He rode in an army truck in khaki hat and shirt, his legs hidden by a gasoline can. He ate Spam and gravy, potato with cheese, peas, corn, peaches and cherries, bread with cheese-spread and a big can of coffee with milk for supper. No wonder he swelled up. He returned with a can of beer, a Japanese book and some gun souvenirs. It was a supreme day for him. McKimmey is a nice lad to do so much for a small boy who is utterly happy, swaggering like ten Yanks rolled into one.

A big American soldier came up to Millicent and stuck out his hand and said, "Congratulate me, lady—you are the first American woman I've spoken to in three years," beaming with pleasure. She turned her lovely sullen face upon him, drew up to her most frigid pinnacle of ice and answered, before turning on her heel and walking off without a handshake, "That is the greatest insult you could give me. I am not an American. I am British." She is not too proud to gobble down good American food.

February 24, 1945. Two Filipino boys carried my bed home about 4 and I tottered home slowly on my own steam. Space looked small and crowded after the big jail cell, and it seemed very dirty and dusty. It was a shock to see the Lloyds from Santo Tomas but Jerry says I was a shock to them too, and I could see that I was.

February 25, 1945. I saw myself in the long mirror set up in the corridor—drawn, twisted and lined in the face—a ghastly sight. My eyes looked pulled taut at the corners, sharp with suffering. But everyone says I look better than I did!

All my pages of Japanese language notes from class are gone in the looting—two years' work. My silver baby-cup and spoons, tiny gold baby-dress buttons, Jerry's hand-carved tray and bowl—all irreplacable and no money can pay for them. When I think of the agony of our Baguio all-night packing, straining every nerve to get the last piece in—saying good-bye to it all on Binalonan Plaza, only to have it guarded and arrive safe—then the irony of being looted by our own allies, the Filipinos, after American occupation and efficiency had come in—there is no sense, no reason in anything. Everything has gone to the locusts in the flash of an eye. We have as much to complain of now that the Americans and Filipinos are looking after us as we had from the Japanese. It is a mad, insane world—only chaos and every man for himself.

Jerry says the tray does not count, only the fact that he had the fun of making it, that he created it. Perhaps he is right—that things do not matter, only the spirit. But beauty—what of beauty? Is it not important? The tray was beautiful hand-work, satin finish on lovely old wood from the hill. It had the exquisite grain of years of growth.

Bedie's big pal said our troops had to use flamethrowers to finish up the fight in the basement of the post office building. My mind refuses to dwell on flamethrowers since the sight of it that first night. They are horrible, horrible methods. What a hideous war. What man can think up to do to man.

February 26, 1945. When Herm came in he told of 20 Spanish and British people in one compound being bayoneted and machine-gunned to death where they were eating together. We knew them all. The entire American, Spanish and foreign residential section beyond the stadium and around the American School was the Japanese front-line defense sector. They had mined and prepared many houses for it.

Several months ago a Japanese officer asked a foreign girl at a large dinner if she would be glad when the Americans came back. She answered Yes and he asked why and she told him. He said, "They will come back but you will not be here to see them." This is exactly what was said in the poor districts, as the little nurse reported. They intended to kill everyone they could, to take as many with them as they could when their world crashed. They did take many, *almost* all of us. We are fortunate to have been brought down from Baguio, fortunate that our men were not machine-gunned, or the women used as hostages between them and American tanks. Anyone left alive today is lucky. Things do not count, as the Chinese said—we are alive and we have food.

No passes in or out of Santo Tomas today because of strict checkup and roll call as there are too many on the food line! Also there were so many out running around sight-seeing that those who were listed to leave on the plane could not be found!

Los Baños people had been told they would all be shot the next day. Instead they went wild when the Airbornes, tanks and guerrillas came in to rescue them.

Two years' food supply was found in the Walled City, including the last shipment of Red Cross food and comfort kits which never came our way.

At dusk after supper there was a scene we never expected to see within Bilibid walls. An American Army band of about 50 tanned khaki-clad men, seated in a semicircle, fanwise from the main door, with instruments from the biggest brass horn down to the reedy piccolo, played about an hour to us. It was stunning music—the kind we haven't heard for three years. We loved a piece called "Deep Purple" which had a Gershwin sound to it. They closed with "The Star Spangled Banner" and "Philippines, My Philippines"—the first sound of it in three years. I stood with tears steaming down my cheeks. It was just too much, something we had hardly dared to dream. The ghosts of the past two months mingled with the olive-drab uniforms squatting or lying around the yard listening in groups with our pretty girls. Kaito, Saito (who must have been killed at Los Baños). Yamato in his thick glasses and with bandaged hand, dour dark-faced Oura, seemed to hover in the atmosphere. Now in solid substance it is Bill Haskins who is homesick for America, MacLane, Red, Bawkin, Campbell, McKimmey, who are hungry to talk to Americans after 18 months in New Guinea and the Solomons. Japanese, Formosan and American soldier shadows stirred against each other in the night enclosed by old Spanish walls. Jerry and I sat on a little bench under a mango tree. Flares lighted the soft tropic sky, hung in the heavens like Halloween lanterns, showing up snipers, tanks, romantic couples listening to a band beside ancient grey and moss-covered wall of a prison. Above us on the grass mound sat Major Olmstead who made a powerful outline, just up from bed with a high fever like some of his patients. The trumpets and saxes blared cheerfully, the drums tolled genially, and the music filtered into our starved souls and broke down all our defenses. I shall always be carried back there when I hear "The Star Spangled Banner."

MacLane says the only way to stop a pillbox in action is by the flame-thrower, where human beings are burnt to a crisp in chemical fire. It becomes so hot that the one holding the container cannot keep it on very long. We are thinking up worse instruments than our ancestors ever did.

Camp flashes: Trucks being loaded with corrugated iron scrap from our dump piles, including the bent iron rods from which we made Modernage chairs when we first came—ages ago; Chinese and Filipinos working together in PCAU groups, cleaning up; the slow tropic gait of the Filipino who swept the hospital floor with soft grass broom, gently brushing the dust forward with all the time in the world. It soothed my nerves no end—his peaceful, simple face. I talked with him about his five children, his wife big with another child when he could not feed the five already here he told me, chuckling at the irony of it. He gets rice and a small portion of meat from PCAU for his own meal, his wages nothing in the face of profiteering in spite of pegged prices.

We have had a lucky star over Baguio. No casualties, only one death from torture.

February 27, 1945. There are hideous wounds among innocent civilians. It is a nightmare peopled with those we used to know, every name familiar. Total war spares no one, crushes all. One cannot win in war.

February 28, 1945. Peggy is weeping over the loss of a hand-brush which was probably poured down the drain in wash water by her son. She is writhing over its loss. It has no value but is irreplaceable, she moans. We all go to pieces over little things. Actually it is her mother who is lost. There is no trace of her and she was with the Nissens at the German Club. Hope has been given up for all of them. This is a terrible thing to face—so one breaks down over the loss of a scrub brush instead. Every day hideous stories beat against our minds.

Jerry came back from a market forage trip with eggs for Sylvia and me—and an exquisite bouquet of lavender butterfly orchids! How it took me back to parties, evening gowns and the gay past. He looked like his old self, with the handful of color and beauty held out to me. What amazing things happen in here. He said the market was a bedlam, full of American canned goods traded by soldiers. Chinese shops are being set up in the ruins. Lucy found her silver bowl in a shop on Avenida Rizal.

March 1, 1945. Stories almost too horrible to put down come from officers who entered the Walled City. One looked around a room in which there was nothing but a woman with her head blown off. She was sitting in a corner with a bundle on her lap. As he was about to leave the room there was a wail from the corner. Unwrapped, the bundle was found to be a starved, dehydrated baby. Fed plasma, it revived and will live. For what, I ask.

March 2, 1945. MacArthur has turned over Manila government to Osmeña, at Malacañan. He evidently hopes to engender confidence in the new setup and to coalesce the various chaotic factors, to control prices etc. It may be only a gesture and there will be chaos and destruction and destitution for months to come. Martial law is a necessity right now. They want to close us off from the growing collection of enemy prisoners filling the rest of Bilibid. There are Germans, Japanese, Formosans, recalcitrant Army, looters, "cooperators," collaborationists and various "criminals."

Dalton and Mrs. Chen and Mrs. Yu came to see me. They looked so cool, serene and neat that it was a joy to gaze at them in this hectic, shabby, dusty, noisy place. They presented me with a dozen chicken eggs!

There are pitiful ads in the brief newspaper. "Dr. Carmelo Reyes 1039 Bilibid Viejo, wishes to contact any person who may have information about his children, Carmelo Jr. 21, and Consuelo, 18, and Felipe. They were last seen with Pedro Morales' family." It is a tragic one of many.

"The Japanese threw three counterattacks against cavalrymen last night in the vicinity of Antipolo and all were thrown back. A Japanese officer with drawn sabre led a Banzai charge against a troop perimeter and after 9 were killed they turned and fled." "19 cave entrances were blasted and sealed on Hill 500." "Mopping up enemy remnants in caves and ravines. . . . Destruction of Japanese on Corregidor is practically completed. 4,200 dead Japanese counted on the island and many more sealed in a mass of tunnels. Our losses 675 killed and wounded." "Many Japanese sealed in tunnels were buried alive or blown to bits. Several hundred were killed attempting to swim away or leave by barge. 18 enemy prisoners were taken." This has a familiar ring. We are *not* taking prisoners. Too many have surrendered, only to pull out hand grenades. Human life is the least in value—when bulldozers scoop up ruins and bodies by the yard and *estimate* the bodies contained therein.

I try a few sweeps with a big new American broom, and get another thrill. It pushes all before it so quickly, like a bulldozer, after the wisps and shreds of brooms we have borrowed. Again I am weary and go back to bed.

Tiny baby Patton squeaked his new cry in the night and is sucking with strong sound this morning. It was wonderful to hear it, after no babies for so long.

March 3, 1945. Captain Wilson, after a cup of coffee, took Jerry and *me* on a long jeep tour. We saw miles and miles of tangled wires, ruins, shell craters, dozens of Japanese planes either bombed or strafed by dive-bombers. They took us way out to what they call the Quezon Strip and we came back on Calle España. Army, Army, everywhere—so much and so many that I was dizzy. We saw water being drawn up and purified by big water-tank units; gasoline tank units passed by; trucks, jeeps, pushers and carriers of every description. We went past engineer encampments, officers in tents looking very insignificant. When I remarked that little places sheltered important things, the Captain laughed and replied, "No *one* of us is important—because all of us are important in this Army!" How true it is, in a democratic Army. Everything counts and coordinates on a vast scale. We pass an evacuation hospital; long lines of tents in the hot sun; men swathed in bandages, legs bound in white up to the thigh; one fellow stumbling along on one leg, dragging the other behind him in obvious pain, others helping him; cot beds close together and partly in the sun. Our own space inside concrete walls looked cool by comparison. I realized again that my discomforts paled before such scenes. On the road-strip waited two huge planes, ready to fly the wounded to base hospitals in Leyte, then home. Near by were at least 40 destroyed Japanese planes, hit in the body by strafing and explosion, wings blown off not far away. All the cars passing were Army cars and from every one came grins of delight and surprise at seeing me—a feminine face! No matter how awful I look, I am an American woman! We passed huge gatherings of carryalls; six or eight tanks clattering like ten elephants, the boys on top with tired, strained faces covered with dust as we ourselves soon were. They were coming in from fighting at the front line and how they waved and called out when they saw me—a woman. Trees were uprooted, palms burnt, bamboos split and bent over, but many mangoes, palms and bamboos were as cool and picturesque as ever. A large college building was only a shell with one side standing, like pictures of the Rome Coliseum. There was a totally wrecked plane right beside a nipa house which was untouched, unharmed.

I am still in the shallow waters of Concentration Camp. It was a tremendous event for me to walk out our back gate and climb into a jeep to be shown the world—such a world, after three years' close confinement. The Captain and the driver who conducted us can never know what it opened up and meant to me who had been confined still further by illness and weakness.

We passed PCAU food lines; Red Cross and Army first aid stations; Filipino vendors setting up business in rickety stalls beside or in the middle of ruins; Chinese stores being cleaned out and rebuilt; Chinese guerrilla headquarters; Philippine guerrilla headquarters—all the relief and political forces at work in war or reconstruction. We went by Santo Tomas, with shell holes in the buildings; saw shantytown houses where Family Units lived; banana groves—they ate banana root boiled for vegetable the last weeks.

The Great Eastern Hotel was a shell with elevator shaft standing naked and empty up one wall. The Marco Polo Hotel was a twisted wreck inside. There was block after block of charred, collapsed wood, cement and iron. The whole district was unrecognizable. At Goiti, each building looked down at one with blind eyes—pitted walls, cracked and scarred, the sky inside each window. All the new theaters, modern, streamlined, air-cooled and luxurious had become ghosts, the wall surrounding empty interiors haunted by spirits of good times and gay enjoyment of the old Manila which is destroyed and exists no more. We recall sitting at jai alai with Bill, watching the hectic gaiety of games, gambling and betting, hot dancing to hot music—"waiting for Rome to burn," we said. And it did. Manila as we knew it for 18 years is no more.

Across the bridge, they pointed out to me the recently finished modern post office—black with shell fire, torn by shells, a grim picture of the citadel struggle of the Japanese last stand, where flamethrowers burned them in the basement to bring it all to an end. As Win says, the burning in Nanking was nothing to Manila. The destructive horror let loose here is unbelievable, yet China and Europe are full of it. I had no conception of it, could not picture it, until I saw it.

We passed the low buildings where we sat on our bedrolls waiting for jeeps to take us away from the sheet of advancing flame, turned into a side street and there was our wall, our gate, our prison. It looked different to me when I came back, smaller, shrunken, in a new perspective and proportion, after seeing the American Army spread out everywhere, rolling in from everywhere, planes taking off from wide roads, bulldozers quartered by the dozen. My head was whirling. I flopped onto the bed and asked for lemonade. Then I took a shower to remove some of the army color. What an hour—what a trip—what a world! Today's Manila is a third world—skeletal and dolorous, tragic, gasping for breath, with all its inhabitants intent on relief of wounds and food. The past is dead. Many tangible landmarks are gone as well as people we knew, never to return.

At Quezon Hospital, Mrs. Marat, who had been a lovely quiet blonde who we met once in Baguio, was strapped to the bed to keep her from murdering people, shrieking all night the most obscene language, bloodthirsty, wanting only to kill; she was found one night on top of a woman who had a frightful wound of the abdomen—the whole surface shot away—yet still living; Mrs. Marat was found on top of this heap of bandage trying to kill the woman. She had been thought cured once before, but the battle sent her off again, completely mad, so she is strapped still shrieking, "Get out of my bed, you S.O.B." She had been taken out for questioning. Her husband is dead but she does not know it.

I asked the Army doctor what made my lips seem paralyzed and he sat up quickly and replied, "Come in tomorrow and we will give you an intravenous ascorbic injection, next day a liver shot; these on alternate days for six days." They certainly know every sign and symptom. They do not give ascorbic until dysentery is over with.

No officers or men are allowed outside after 8 P.M. We internees must be in by 6:30. Reason: It is still dangerous. 300 Japanese were found in the Hong Kong Bank building, right where we passed in the jeep yesterday.

March 4, 1945. I still can hardly believe that all of us were to be shot—the orders were supposed to have been found on a desk at Santo Tomas—for they were not carried out, and there was time—at least 24 hours when it could have been done. However, since last spring I have felt there was a slow, systematic starvation. One, or at most two, months more would have finished many of us. It does not bear thinking about. We were close to being like the 800 soldiers over the wall.

I went up on the roof for the first time. The ghost city stretched crumbling walls toward heaven in a blind gesture that seemed almost human. Sanborne, Barnes and the good-looking Navy flyer were up on the roof, well relaxed from a bottle of rum. We tried to give Sanborne a cake of Lux toilet soap as he had said that toilet soap was the one scarce item with them, but after he had gone we found it on our table. They are all like this—give away their shirts but won't take anything.

One Japanese prisoner hanged himself in Bilibid the other day—poor tragic soul.

We had spaghetti and cheese at noon; potatoes, asparagus and cold luncheon meat for supper. I wound up with bad cramps and Major Olson gave me paregoric. Bedie was nauseated three times in the night. It was nothing but water, but all on the floor, so poor Jerry had to light a candle and mop. Bedie had diarrhea and his temperature jumped up. I did not sleep till after two—a wretched night. The new baby cried with colic.

March 5, 1945. Committee Minutes, March 5: "Captain Dahlstrom does not wish this Committee to disband until the actual breaking up of camp. He pointed out it will be only a short time until that event occurs, and it would not be feasible to hold an election at this time. (Carl has returned to his family in the States.) A few matters had come up on which he desired action by personnel of the camp. 1. The *Fly Problem*. Members of camp have become very careless on the subject of garbage, dishwater and wash water disposal. It is still vitally important that any waste water which might contain particles of food or grease must be completely disposed of. 2. *Visitor Control.* Until we began using the back gate, the visitors into this camp were controlled by the Provost Marshal in the outer compound, by the simple method of allowing no one into camp who was not vouched for by a member of camp. Captain Dahlstrom said we would continue to use this method ourselves. 3. A number of children have been given whistles to play with. Parents will please collect and keep away from the children all whistles. Whistles are a military means of communication and cannot be considered toys during wartime. 4. Everyone in camp is required to take the physical examination. Captain Dahlstrom said he understood we would also undergo complete physical examinations when we arrive home; however, he said that if this is not done, he would suggest that everyone have such an examination on his own initiative. He felt that it was of utmost important that this be done, for the detection of possible dysentery carriers, etc. 5. Please *report* if you have lost your passport. A record will be made and turned into the State Department as soon as possible, so that such passports can be ascertained if they are being used by any other person with malicious intent. Captain Dahlstrom recommends that a person be selected to be head of Men's Dorm, for purpose of dealing with Filipino laborers. He pointed out that at present many men are issuing orders, scolding and ordering these laborers around, making for inefficiency and also making it very difficult to keep laborers. These men are hired for the purpose of doing camp labor—not personal services."

Communication to Adjutant General of 6th Army: "All internees were told that their property left in Bilibid would be safe under guard and that they would probably be returned to those quarters the following day. . . . The following morning about 10 A.M. Mr. Denki arrived at Bilibid from Santo Tomas to find the living quarters overrun with looters, mainly Filipinos. They were immediately driven out of the compound and guards placed at the gates to prevent further looting. No guards were left the previous night to protect our quarters and looters began pouring into the compound some time during the night. By morning they had done a very thorough job of cleaning us out of all our worldly possessions. We were moved back to Bilibid on the afternoon of the 6th. . . . Most of our camp personnel had saved some of their valuables, including irreplacable records and good clothing throughout the three years of internment and are now entirely destitute. We do not know what machinery, if any, has been set up to take care of reimbursement of such losses, but shall greatly appreciate anything you can do for us. Signed by Acting Chairman of Bilibid Civilian Camp."

March 6, 1945. Jerry brought June and me two pairs of silk panties and how she squealed. We need almost everything.

March 7, 1945. It was suggested that we clean up because General MacArthur would visit at 2. I swept or mopped the space as a concession to the relief of having an American general. Then it turned out to be Mrs. Jean MacArthur, with her hair enclosed in a red net, red shoes and a bag to match, and no longer thin in features but on the plump side. She arrived yesterday, probably by plane, and the general reaction was, "Well, she looks as though she had had her feet up in front of a fireplace for three years, keeping nice and warm." Many resented her coming. No one else is allowed to have a wife out here. She moved about smiling and saying, "How are you?" when we are positively not so hot and don't feel in the least like putting on social manners, in fact quite the contrary. We are in a wretched, picky mood, only interested in talking to the men who are really *doing* things. In fact we like to be near them for we understand each other, and we do not want to go home to rest, away from it all. We are very difficult and contrary. Perhaps we should not judge Mrs. MacArthur. It may be a good thing for her to see our condition, the devastation, get a taste and smell and touch of it, closely.

In the night when the wind is from a certain direction over the Walled City, the air is laden with smell of charred wood, wet cement, gun powder, pungent chemicals, and over all that sickish sweetish odor which is rotting flesh and blood. Once in the nostrils, it is never forgotten.

June and Bedie were up on the roof with some of the boys but none of them dance much though the radio played and the roof had been swept for dancing. Too many preferred petting parties and Bedie is disgusted at such frank kissing. Internment has made him quite a Puritan. One of the girls says she is engaged, and all of them are besieged with hungry admirers.

March 8, 1945. Jerry and I took a calesa for a sight-see trip. It could not cross the river so we got out. I took one look at the Bailey bridge and my knees and ankles began to buckle. I just could not cross on it. Jerry was awfully disappointed as he was wild to go across. A car stopped and a young officer with "War Correspondent" on his collar asked if we'd like a lift. We said we were just poking around, but we came off the pontoon bridge with alacrity and jumped into the car. In no time we were over the bridge across the Pasig, passing the scarred and blackened post office building where such desperate fighting occurred, past the desolate Metropolitan Theater with all specialty shops empty and its tower cut in half; on the left the utterly horrible ruins of the Walled City, with the mass of sandy cement that was Fort Santiago; those battered, crumpled walls and desolate ruins inside, which point bony fingers to heaven in a supplication that was never answered, gave me a feeling of sickening depression such as nothing had so far. It was the result of three weeks pounding and whistling of big guns and looking at it one half imagined the unthinkable suffering of the thousands encased in those walls. It is said that in one building, the Filipinos and Japanese soldiers are piled six deep, becoming a mass of jelly-like substance under the tropic sun of hot Hot Season. The bulldozer will take care of these in mass burial.

We reached the beautiful many-columned legislative building, but only the front of it is standing—there is no longer beauty or colonnades—for these are staggering, black and beaten, the back of the building nothing but one floor crashed upon another, a vast pile of slag. There was the city hall, the new finance building—all three of these buildings are blasted by weeks of hand-to-hand fighting from room to room. Often our troops held half the building, the Japanese the other half. Encased in these shells, once busily occupied like an anthill, there had been fury, hate, primitive and bitter battle, exhaustion and sobbing breath before extinction. I am appalled and feel beaten by all I have seen. I listened all those weeks to the guns. Now I *see* what they did. Everyone should see it and learn one lesson forever.

We passed the skeleton Bureau of Science with all records of the past destroyed; past hundreds of handsome residences charred and crumbled—the grave of many families burned or machine-gunned as they tried to escape flames; past poorer sections where wooden and nipa huts had been leveled into flat acres; past a burned tank blown into a churchyard by a land mine; high and low, all are brought down in the great sieve of war. Back across the bridge, leaving the shuddering, sickening Walled City behind, we found the calesa still standing where we had left it, the driver filling his straw hat full of tomato and cheese spaghetti from a canteen which was sharing its extra rations in Plaza Coiti. Poor little waifs stood by, with longing, hungry eyes, as bigger men scrambled for a share and pushed the children aside. Caps, cans, cupped hands, everything was used to catch precious food. Some tough fellows had spaghetti in their hair after a tussle for it.

March 9, 1945. McKimmey took Bedie off for the day at Grace Park where he ate lunch, swam in a Spanish pool and saw dozens of wrecked Japanese planes until he was so thrilled and happy he could hardly contain himself. He came back with pieces of wing fusilage and electric meters as souvenirs. We will be weighed down when we leave.

June was not in bed by 11 P.M. and I began to worry and imagine. I finally made Jerry get up to look for her. He found her on the roof, the only strictly sober one in the group of G.I's and some girls. She was listening raptly, enjoying it all.

March 10, 1945. 282 of the 800 soldiers over the wall from us were greeted with wild acclaim when they arrived in San Francisco this week. Griff had told us that we did not know how famous we were—what enormous publicity we had had.

March 11, 1945. At one o'clock, Stanley and Lanier arrived with a "peep" [a type of jeep]. "I was the one" to chaperone June and Ann on a two-hour tour of the city ruins. What a ride.

Stanley said how about crossing the river and I said we were not supposed to. Soon we came to the latest thing in pontoon bridge and were so interested in looking it over that we did not notice he had taken us across—especially Mama!

In and out, around sharp corners, bumping into holes and through puddles, ducking wires and piles of rubble. Suddenly, we were in the middle of that utterly flattened and black district of Paco. Thousands of homes were squashed and families made homeless here. Many of the families were to be seen pushing the remainder of household goods in small carts to another pitiful location. How great the loss and suffering in those acres—each one important to the individual whether he had much or little.

March 12, 1945. Alice Bacarro stopped to see me. Her mother had died of cerebral hemorrhage in the spring of '43 but had written before that, that her traveling companion, Jerry's mother, had died in the spring of '42. I had to tell Jerry when he returned and though he had expected it, it was a wallop. He let out one groan as if he had been hit in the stomach, then just sat with his head in his hands.

MacArthur is pushing his veteran fighters too hard, keeping them too long at it. They need a rest but maybe he can't give it, for Europe is nearing the critical stage and the tempo out here is increasing in ferocity. They strike hard blows in order to make it shorter. They admit there will be long lists like Iwo Jima and we must be prepared for it. The Japanese want to make our bloodshed as near equal to theirs as possible.

March 14, 1945. I started packing.

Peggy had spent the day at the ruins of the German and British clubs looking for remains of her mother. She heard the story of one survivor and knows at last there is no hope of finding even charred remains. All the time I was packing she was trying to tell me the dreadful things she had seen and heard, almost as though it had happened to someone else, not herself. Such tragedy in the confusion and uproar. It is unbearable, so we are stoic. No wonder she feels like forgetting, at a party, in the evening, with three soldiers who come in. It made our space sound gay, casual, informal, for the last night together in Bilibid. The soldiers need to forget too.

March 15, 1945. Up at five finishing last things. Early breakfast, then we hung around the yard sitting on our baggage until 9:30 when the trucks finally came. Bilibid was really breaking up. It gave us a certain nostalgia. We had found a brotherhood in these years.

We all piled into six trucks and looked around for the last time on gray prison walls and green mango trees.

We drove down Calle Herran past the ghastly wreck of the Cathedral, by the shattered Manila Hotel which made us sick at heart, saw the Army and Elks clubs' floors fallen in, the High Commissioner's residence looking as if the top half had been sliced off. All the apartment houses on the boulevard were wrecked—almost nothing was spared. There were Japanese guns all along the boulevard and nearly every building was burned or blown. The beautiful sawali and nipsa Polo Club was only a flat mass of ashes, with lines of tanks covering the Polo Field. Everywhere was army equipment. We passed the black ruins of Liang's house—no wonder her eyes are sad.

We reached Nichols Field where the crashed hangars of our own forces in 1941 still stand. Wrecked Japanese planes were piled up all over the place, with piles of salvaged motors. There were land mines so we did not walk far. We sat over an hour in trucks until groups were "processed." Finally three planes took off with internees.

Captain Holder appeared, smiling and diplomatic. Our truck would be taken next. It was so hot on the field that we were wilting by the minute. Jo Smith came with the Red Cross truck to give out Coca-Cola, apples and chocolate, and to say a last good-bye to Win who was flying home while he stayed on.

I began to get horribly nervous. When we were given the Mae West life belts to hang over our heads, were shown how to pull the rope to inflate it, and if it failed—then how to blow it up with our mouths, and the heavy yellow contraption weighed us down, made us hotter than ever—then I was almost in a panic. I knew I would never remember it in emergency. Tired, dripping and jittery, I climbed into the plane after the kids.

We sat on the very uncomfortable side compartments, with a ridge hitting in the middle of our backs (I believe they call it a bucket job), fastened on our heavy safety belts (another load!) the door slammed shut and the plane moved slowly onto the main strip. We taxied around. Jerry opened the tiny round window to let in a breath of air. The motors roared and the children looked thrilled. The plane gathered speed down the strip. The feeling of life—we were off the ground. I began to weep as we sailed up and away from our "home" island. Oh Philippines, My Philippines! Bedie wept too, longer than I did. We are alike. June and Jerry never seem to mind leaving anything behind. They adapt instantly. It is a fine faculty, but perhaps they miss something by it. The kids were not actively sick, but squeamish all the way. We flew all over the ruins of Manila and suburbs—the officers wanted to see it too. We looked down on our prison walls with the buildings radiating from the center and saw the skeleton roof of our own living quarters as we passed close over it. We looked at all the port area and Pier 7 looking like the bones of a picked whale. Over the Walled City and Manila Hotel, along the boulevard, over Cavite and Sangley Point. It was a mass of rubble. In Ermita and Malate all the landmarks were obliterated. Yet we hated to leave the desolation, for it was home.

We passed high over bleak Corregidor. No sign of life in that grave of two armies. Next we passed over Romblon, recently taken by our troops. We looked down at narrow beaches with white fringes of surf and turquoise or jade shallows beyond. They were like lovely jewels. We looked down on piles of mountains, shadowed ravines, ribbon roads or winding riverbeds like string resting on earth. Interiors of jungles, cane fields—mile after mile looked untouched, unperturbed by battle, yet thousands may have died or be starving in just such quiet-looking places. The Philippines are not destroyed. By far the greater part is standing.

We went above clouds, the green or black earth fell away, the sea with small white caps became hidden. There were only limitless banks of snow; billow upon billow of whipped cream; soft, gentle, slowly moving, changing pillows of white, the stuff of our dreams. We scarcely moved it seemed. Then a rent in the white blanket—a glimpse of trees, a mountain ridge—gone again as veils swung together in misty union.

After two hours the snow bank changed to thick pea soup; gray, pale green, no longer gentle but evil looking. Rain drove past the wings, beaten by wind that roared on the side of the plane. We felt buffetted, a sense of pushing through and against storm. The plane rolled, rocked. I slept half an hour, probably a form of airsickness. June slept most of the way. Bedie kept his head on his knees. When I woke, the wind and rain were stronger, the roar was very loud.

We banked, looked down upon a long wire strip near a beach and point of palms. We flew past it to another strip. I had said to the children, "Remember those transport planes we used to talk about a year or two ago? Well, this is it—we're in it!" And here we were now, coming down on one of those miraculous wire strips we'd heard about inside barbed wire. We had thought they were dreams, mirage. Wisps of cloud flew past like veils. After prayers deep inside during the roar of wind, there was a wide enough lift and opening in the clouds to let us slip through, thankfully. The gear touched and we raced along the strip, safely grounded, guided by the skillful pilot with silver wings on his lapel. I began to unbuckle the belt, wondering if my knees would hold me. I was reeling and so glad to get out of the storm. The ground rocked for hours afterward.

We were told the men and boys would be taken to one camp, the women and girls to another—an evacuation hospital. June and I were helped into an army truck, the zipper bag and blue duffel stowed up forward—where it and all the contents became thoroughly soaked in driving rain during the two hours ride of 20 miles which followed. We rode through the thick mud and deep wet sand of Leyte for ages—trucks roaring and zooming ahead and behind us, loaded with engineers and every other branch of this great army. They waved and cheered, and we returned it. Tired and bedraggled as we were, it was fun. One jeep with two G.I.'s followed close to our tailboard for miles, talking at the top of their lungs about home States, home towns, and wishing they could date us. Many are homesick and war-weary, sure there is a bullet ahead for them in this wretched, strafing, total war.

We pass miles of shattered palms, all kinds of destroyed and new equipment—machines, trucks; the varied, multiple, endless panoply of armies and war. Signs with numbers of engineering outfits, signs saying "Red Beach," "White Beach." There has been battle here. All of it rolled past us as on a moving screen. If only there had been captions!

We stopped at Convalescent Hospital No. 1 mess hall and enjoyed a rich meal, then turned another corner and were ushered into a tent where a nervous Red Cross nurse herded us into a corner, while she kept asking whose protesting baby was lying on her desk. When Marj Patton finally claimed the infant, things began to pick up. We were taken to tents, with electric lights, cement floor, cots without mattresses but with clean crisp sheets, army blankets and nets. Before long we were on cots, dropping into oblivion.

March 16, 1945. We have awfully good meals in the big mess hall. Fresh roast pork chops, veal, apple pie with delicious flaky crust, milk or cocoa, and always the wonderful G.I. bread.

Last night a plane roared over the tent in the wind and rain. It was signaled not to land on the strip but to circle round. It crashed into the hill just beyond us and burst into flames. We watched it burn, feeling sick at heart. No information is ever given out about such crashes—was it a transport plane with 25 wounded brought from Quezon strip or was it the plane that left just behind us, with 25 boys starting home on furloughs?

We will never forget coming out onto the beach the first time at Leyte when the horde of khaki figures closed in from all sides to get acquainted. We did not know there were so many men in the world! June swam twice in the morning and again in the afternoon, surrounded by boys hungry to look and talk and laugh with a girl. She is radiant, happy as youth should be. Her cheeks get pinker every minute. I found her up the beach with four G.I.'s around her.

In the evening we went to an open air movie show of Judy Garland in *Meet Me in St. Louis*. Color pictures are greatly improved. Overhead a crescent moon, brilliant stars, and fireflies shimmering in and out among the palm fronds. It was tropic romance—but it only makes the boys homesick! The sea and beach and palms are worth a million dollars—but the beach had memories of a certain landing and strafing, they are sick of dying and went to go home. For us it was something special to sit in that atmosphere—an audience of a thousand men wounded and convalescent. They groaned when the heroine wasn't kissed quickly enough to suit them, then cheered and chuckled when she *was* kissed. There was constant whistling, cheering, jeering, catcalling, and hilarious comments.

March 17, 1945. In the morning we were all "processed" as they call it. It makes one feel like freight or supplies. Jerry had to sign a promise to pay passage of $275 for each of us which made every internee seethe with rage. There is nothing like being milked really dry, mortgaging the future. I signed a promise not to talk about our Concentration or release experiences—until "released" by the government—probably when we land, we are assured suavely in order to get us to sign. We are asked to tell the C.I.C.[6] anything we know about cooperators, even rumors, anything that might help the Armed Forces advance. I feel others will know and tell far more than I can who only knows by hearsay. I admit freely to having notes and am told they must be taken up and looked over. They can do this in my presence but they will be taken away over my dead body, I mutter to myself. I have lost too many things this way and notes are all I have left. We're being badgered by friends instead of the enemy.

March 18, 1945. I heard Jerry's voice "Hi, Pete" and there he was, unrecognizable in a G.I. outfit, cap and all.

Jerry and Bedie caught an early truck ride back. I left the girls with their dates for half an hour on the beach.

March 19, 1945. There seems to be a vast gulf between G.I.s and officers, more from below than above, I think. Combat area is more democratic than noncombat area where it slowly gathers conventionality, formality, rules, disciplines and salutes.

There are many badly wounded men, with foot, legs or arms encased in plaster casts, walking on iron-braced heel or crutches, or arms bound to the body. Some have shaking hands from combat fatigue and look haunted in the eyes.

Some of them have not found any real purpose in the fight, and doubt whether democracy will come from it. I understand their complicated feelings. They do not trust the slogans this time because it has happened all over again.

One reason for the gap between men and officers is the censoring of letters. The boys feel that their innermost thoughts and emotions are pried upon and made fun of. Many officers do this, some officers admit. They kid about letters openly afterward, so the men freeze and have no outlet even in mail home to those who love and understand.

One lad spent P10 buying two boxes of fancy crackers, 12 Hershey bars and 6 charms for June and Betsy. June's natural manner, simplicity, and lack of make-up interest a wide variety of admirers which amazes me.

March 20, 1945. June has no appetite at breakfast. She has nightmares of battle and is upset by many things. It is a big dose for age sixteen. All these kids are having to take too much too young.

Gene says I should not wear my diamond bracelet—it is dangerous—may be taken from me.

The nurse says that everyone in Tent 15 wants to move. She doesn't know why. The officer asks what camp they come from and she replies that a woman told her they are all from Santo Tomas. They all want to get away from each other—Internitis! When we sail, we will all have it.

Three truckloads of Australian and British internees arrived to be processed. There was a delicious breeze. Planes soared over the beach and sea; odd craft ploughed through the water; jeeps, Red Cross trucks and carryalls rushed about on special tasks; everywhere G.I.s walked or sprawled or swam or sat talking around a pretty girl, or leaned against a palm trunk listening. Internee husbands came and went, looking plump from good food. But Santo Tomas people still shock me with their drawn and harrassed looks.

March 22, 1945. We spent all morning on the sand with Gene and his pal from New Bedford. After lunch, June washed out a bunch of her clothes, with a little assistance from me. We hung them dripping on the line. I dusted and packed our shoes and some other pieces, just in case. A good thing too, for while we were standing at the ropes talking with our three friends, the Red Cross headquarters girl came calling our name, saying we were on the list to go this afternoon.

We were given a month's supply of Atabrine which we were told to start taking at once and will soon be yellow kids or army color [from the medicine]. So we must be headed for New Guinea, into the real South Pacific.

June came in weeping. I could not comfort her for I was ready to weep myself. We don't want to leave the palms, the sea, the long sand, the boys, the tents and combat area where there is so much fellowship and so much going on.

About 3:30 the trucks roared off. The road had been asphalted, cutting our driving time in half. With June, my heart was crying, "Oh, I don't want to go. I don't want to go!" And the [G.I.] boys would give anything to be in our place! The truck was badly crowded. Soon we passed the airstrip where the overturned plane had been cleared away long ago and there was no sign of accident, only dozens and dozens of Army and Navy planes of all types and insignia, fascinating for us to look at. We passed mile after mile of activity—Navy, Air, Engineers, Army, Supply—such confusion yet all coordinated, moving forward at a pace beyond belief. We passed nipa huts, nipa swamps, the entire place amazingly clean, constantly policed and picked up.

We are still in that stream of humanity—a mass of refugees, homeless, under the care of the Red Cross, the Army and the American Government—and a blessed care it is, too. We see a whole building, with its columns *not* shattered by bomb or shells. Beyond it are the newly raised docks, with all kinds of ships, barges, landing craft close to the shores or chugging about the bay which is fringed with tropic-island beach, surf and turquoise color. We even drive right onto the dock which seems to be fitted iron plates set on fitted cement blocks. Soon we climbed a gangway right off the dock up the ship's side onto the deck.

Those with children under age twelve had been assigned to lovely state-rooms with gleaming oval mirrors, dressing tables, shaded lights, shining faucets in white enamel bowls. There are 8 or 10 in a room, but it is still luxurious. June and I were put in the dorm, dark quarters set up in what was formerly the Verandah Café, with two squares of rows of three-tiered bunks—about thirty in all.

The dining saloon seemed marvelous, with china plates, many forks, spoons, knives, ice water, iced butter, cinnamon rolls, and sweet pickles! It was all bewildering for the little kids who went around pushing buttons and pulling off doorknobs. Plump Dutch officers and husky American officers laughed at the children's wide-eyed interest in the commonest things. The contrast from nothing to luxury is overwhelming. Delicious chicken, tomato soup, hamburg steak with gravy to pour over mealy potatoes, green peas, cake with whipped cream curled into frosting. We sit around in deeply comfortable plush chairs, walk about exploring, turn in early on a soft mattress and good pillow at last, a sheet under us and blanket over us. We feel closer to the Indian mess boys than to the Dutch officers who are so well-fed and assured. The Indians know better what we have been through. This augurs badly for our adaptation to well-fed Americans! We are going to be difficult and will only get along with the slums for a while!

March 23, 1945. We were up at 6:45 and had breakfast at 7:30—fruit, and two fried eggs with bacon. We were told there would be two meals a day, but at noon we would fix sandwiches from delicious slices of round sausage, slices of cheese. Hot coffee would be served also. It came to pass at noon and was very good. Everything is being done for us. Their concern seems lavish after the last three years. The ship shines in glass, brass and wood as only Dutch service (or the Army) could make it shine. It is paradise, fairyland, heaven, after what we have come from. But on the other hand it seems to pamper us, and we feel conventions closing in, formality stifling us. How much more will we feel it in cities and in homes, far from insecurity, privation and want. We are as unreasonable as the poor. We are storm-tossed still, between two worlds. I felt horribly depressed all morning, on the verge of flying to pieces, weeping inside.

Then, after lunch, the blow fell. The Intelligence or Counterintelligence came on board and took all my notes. I turned them in, hating it. It was the final squeeze, the last straw. "It is only paper," said the young officer, and I answered, "Yes, it is only paper to you and this is why I hate to turn it over. It means nothing to you, everything to me, for it is all I've saved. It is three years of suffering and experience, and I want to keep it for my children's children." I begged him to let me take it to San Francisco and turn it over there, to get it that far at least, but he was adamant—said they needed it out there. He said it would be returned to me—"Don't you trust the Army, the Government?" Passionately I retorted, "No! I don't trust anybody! I've had things stolen from me, been looted and squeezed even by our own people and this is the last shakedown of all I have left!" I spilled one of the envelopes on the floor, getting the numbered sheets all mixed up, but that is up to them to straighten out now. He asked why I didn't save silver or valuables instead of these paper notes. I said I could not carry it and it was scattered all through our bags when we were given only half an hour to get ready; that my husband was on crutches, and we were not allowed to take more anyway—big bags were ruled out. Besides I can buy silver and I can never buy this record of three years' experience. The young Filipino Intelligence boy with the officer nodded his head. He understood. We talked the same language. People at home just cannot grasp what we feel or try to express. They are too secure and have lost nothing. Poor young man, I gave him a bad twenty minutes. And my old blue bag with large tin box full of three years' notes went off down the stairs in cold blood!

I had looked forward to buying a new typewriter to replace the new machine which had been looted from me, then to spending a year sorting out all the notes and typing them into coherence and clarity. It would be something to do in America to bridge the gap and push off the awful homesickness for the Philippines. That night I stayed awake for hours, my stomach feeling full of rocks. I felt sick and beaten and empty. I don't care what they find in it for I will stand by anything I have been through or learned, but I did want it with me, for no other hands will take care of it. *If* they read it they can piece a good deal from it, knowing how the mind works in that connection. But most of it they will have picked up from other sources and mine will only be confirmation or slight addition. There is nothing like being taken to the cleaners by one's own people. If they don't return it, I'll do a lot of real howling and they can put me back behind walls or barbed wire and see if I care!

Even a chocolate éclair in all its rich beauty didn't cheer me at supper time. It was June's first éclair and she was much interested but she is as homesick and unsettled, uprooted as I am. We sat on the hall lounge with tears rolling down our cheeks, while everyone who passed stared at us as though we were crazy. Perhaps we were, a little. We are sick of being badgered and pushed around, made to sign this and that, promising not to talk about our experiences, turning over this and that to authorities, separated from each other, questioned and cautioned on what we say about the last three years. After being repressed for three years, we come out to what? Freedom? Hell, no. Now we are back in the Army, back to lines, ration points, strict censorship and regulations.

March 24, 1945. We looked from the deck down on our own men who had been on the dock since 2 or 3 A.M. They stayed there too, with all the medics, rotation and furlough troops, in the broiling sun until 11:30 when the ship was pronounced "unloaded." They were tired out, sunburned, and told us this was called "sweating it out." Rotten coordination, I call it, getting them out at that time. Bedie slept on his duffel bag on the dock just like the other G.I.s in slack, exhausted positions, draped all over the dock. We hung over the rail, exchanging comments and news. We handed some Coca-Colas to Bedie at the gangway and watched the milling about. Finally a Colonel came over from Convalescent Hospital about 11 and ordered that the men be embarked. Within half an hour it started. A few magic words and Jerry and Bedie slung bags over their backs. In their outfit they looked like all the other G.I.s trooping aboard. Orders are being shouted continuously over the loud-speaker to internees, troops, officers, permanent personnel, medicos, cooks, butchers etc. It is too loud and difficult to hear the words. It sounds muffled, so one must listen constantly for fear of missing important orders. It begins about 5 to wake the cooks, and is calling for Sergeant So and So or Pfc. Blank until long after we drop asleep. We are tired of its noise and monotony already, though we should be used to it because we had the same at Convalescent Hospital. It's the Voice of the Army. The voice of our rescuer, America! We will get used to it like all the other rationing and restriction because we are concentrees and used to far worse.

Jerry came up at two for the 2-hour visiting period allowed internees, but he was so tired and sleepy he only stayed an hour. There is no bar opened for cold drinks until 5 P.M. and we are supposed to stay out on deck, either standing two hours or sitting on the floor as there are no chairs. We all break this rule and sit on the soft stuffed chairs in the saloon. The Japanese may make us sit or stand on the floor, but we'll be darned if we'll do it for the Dutch or the Americans. We see the officers (Army and ship) sitting about in the saloon and smoking room and we know *exactly* how the G.I. feels over privilege. We resent and fume and glower.

As soon as the hatches are made fast, embarkation finished, preparations are made to cast off and steam out into the bay. Tugs nose at the bow and stern, puffing, churning. We leave the dock, become grounded a little way out. The tugs combine at the bow, push mightily. About one o'clock we are under our own steam, out in the center of the charming harbor of Tacloban, the new capital of the Philippines until Manila was taken. The provincial capital is intact, a contrast to Manila.

The ship swings about and soon we are lying off our beach, Leyte Beach, far out! We stand at the rail looking at the lights there, remembering how lovely it was and how free and happy the week there as we slowly relaxed from barbed wire and walls and strain.

We were given lifebelts or jackets, adjusted them to us and were told to carry them with canteens and head covering with us at *all* times. It is a job dragging them about but they give a strong feeling of security, and are better than the old round preservers. There is blackout about 6:45 and it is hard getting around, in and out the blocked entrances and exits which seem like the crazy maze in roller-coaster parks. The saloon is hot and stuffy with occasional relief from the air system. In the night I awake feeling stifled, going from one perspiration to another. It is only 11:30 I discover, and wake again at 3.

March 25, 1945. Bedie has grown inches and is very independent, not a little boy any longer. It is grand to see Jerry and Bedie again, to hear about all the craft they inspected during their full free week.

About 8, during [lifeboat] drill, we sail, and the Philippine Islands melt into a mist of rain and memories. When will we see them again? How long? I still do not want to leave. We recall that we have not seen many Filipinos since we boarded. Everywhere Americans do the work.

From one small craft, off blockhouse point, a tall, round, smiling Filipino stands up to wave farewell. He is a symbol of everything we are leaving and remains before us a long time.

Someone tells me that Carl talked with a Baguio Filipino just before he left Manila and learned that all Americans were taken out (who were willing to go) by guerrillas. Also all the loyal Filipinos who would go. Our mind travels back over three years. We hear that Hale and Mike Rozas are dead. Was there a bad skirmish? And what of Daddy Halsema and Marie? Another one tells me of Helen M.'s terrible experience, being raped every time the guard changed. Also of Jim N. who was tortured over and over before execution finally at Fort Santiago. Doctors attended him after torture. We remember his last stop at our house with his wife, before they took to the hills. She is safe at Santo Tomas. Mrs. Bergamini and I discuss personal problems and decide there is no more private or individual life. We all belong to the government, the Army, the war effort, which may turn into a similar effort in peace. The trend is that way and it is all right with me.

There are more than 30 ships in this convoy. All kinds, sizes and loads. There is one off either side of the bow, turning back and forth, sweeping the sea lane clear for us. We are not going very fast it seems, though the speed may be deceptive.

June and I walk the deck in fresh air to get our sea legs. We hear a story that we internees were nearly taken to Japan with all the other military prisoners, and how guerrilla information, a few timely planes and placed bombs sank ships that were to take us. We are still in war zone and will be near danger for another three weeks or month. But there is no more use in imagining what could happen or in worrying about it than there was at Bilibid in the front line or at Camp Holmes under enemy surveillance. Now we are surrounded by protection. If something breaks through—well, it breaks through.

To the far port side along the horizon we sight a huge convoy and figure it contains 200 ships—an invasion convoy, going where?

March 26, 1945. When I had my arm treated the three doctors were discussing "these people who lived on rice and corn seem to develop deficiency symptoms *after* several weeks of good food." From further talk, I gathered that the sore on my arm is from a deficiency source rather than impetigo type.

March 27, 1945. After lunch I was examining a swollen ankle and telling June I felt shaky. As we talked, the alarm squawked once. We looked up, thinking maybe they were sounding off for 1 P.M. The squawk repeated once or twice. We began to put on our life jackets, with a growing feeling of tension. The crew began to run, not walk, to positions. Officers and Indians hurried us off the decks, inside, to our bunks. Many of the seasick people did not put on jackets. We heard the crew dashing about and then the Indians ran in and shut all the front port holes *and* the door. It was dark and airless, not a pleasant sensation being shut up inside if something is going to happen. I would rather be on an open deck below as we are during dawn and dusk, but this time we were ordered inside. I suggested to Wilma that she'd better put on her jacket and Kay began to get into hers. Mary said, "That was the Air Alert." We all stood quietly in the stifling air. I closed my eyes and rested until the shaky feeling stopped. After fifteen minutes there were three squawks—all clear. All except the seasick ones made a dash for air. Doors and windows opened, tension relaxed. On deck, during Jerry's guard duty, I said to a young officer, "So it was the real thing—not a drill, this time." He laughed and replied, "Oh, they meant business that time all right. Until the radar signals in, they don't know which plane it might be."

I went down for arm treatment. The treatment this time was penicillin, the famous new discovery against infection and other things. Only the Army has it and it is scarce because it only lasts a certain time then has to be made up fresh.

The young officer we talk with says they all hope and pray to get on this ship—the *Klipfontein,* for the trip home—it is *the* liner to travel on now. All the others are converted to troops, no dining saloons or smoking room or drawing room or oval mirrors or beautiful glass over indirect lighting. It is the only luxury liner left and even its Verandah Café is no more.

Mrs. Kraus thought the Filipinos were very insolent at Santo Tomas. She says they lost all respect for us after seeing us in prison so long. I disagreed heartily and said we kept their morale high all the time we were jailed, and that Santo Tomas attitudes must be responsible for any insolence as we had no trouble in Bilibid food serving, handling its distribution ourselves and they worked with us without any trouble. She has a typical old Colonial outlook. There is going to be less and less servile attitude. Natives are learning to stand on their own feet everywhere, and are tired of being looked down on, treated as the The White Man's Burden. No one should return to the Philippines unless he realizes this, for the high and mighty overlord types make poor ambassadors from an America which preaches democracy and freedom.

March 29, 1945. The *Klipfontein* is still on its maiden voyage and the Dutch officers haven't been home for six years.

March 30, 1945. News on the Bulletin Board is very impressive. 950 bombers continually over Berlin and Hanover, and the German radio is asking for sympathy for the German people who are not as bad as they've been painted and who would like to have the war end as much as any Allied soldier.

I was awake hours, from one sweat bath to another. It simply cannot be called perspiration. The Equator zone is one long Turkish bath.

March 31, 1945. I had just gone to sleep when G.Q. [General Quarters] was called. There was a low strip of land on each side—New Guinea and Shoten Island. The convoy ships steamed slowly. We watched first one side then the other, our faces glistening and dripping. We saw a porpoise wheeling in and out of the water in its rhythmic loop. We steamed faster, leaving most of the convoy behind, except two large Dutch ships. One long spot of shore has completely blasted trees, stripped stark of foliage. It is where there must have been landing and battle. The ship anchors off a long strip of encampment, with airstrips in sight, docks with tankers and gray ships alongside. This is Biak [New Guinea]!

There is a missionary couple on board with a tiny thin boy whom they carry onto deck for air now and then. The child has hysterics and three doctors worked over him to stop his cries. One night they finally took him into another cabin. This family has had the toughest three years of any married pair we have heard of yet. They had lived for years in Japan and for some reason the Japanese wanted to capture them and put a price on their head. They moved continually from place to place, always hunted and eluding. The baby was born, then they had to run again, leaving the baby with Filipinos. After eight months, they saw the child, then had to hide again for a year and a half. No wonder the child is delicate after such insecurity and undernourishment. The mother still looks hunted, her face strained and harried.

It took hours to move in to the dock alongside another ship which was loading large shells. We saw several native dugouts with side rigger and a row of New Guineans with orange painted designs on otherwise drab paddles. One small boy sat on the outrigger quite naked. We felt satisfied after seeing some real inhabitants in native boats. They are brown with thick kinky hair, features and build not unlike Filipinos—lips and nose thicker, perhaps. They wore white drawers or patched khaki pants and an undershirt—mission influence.

Jerry feels rotten with chills and aching. He hopes it is flu instead of malaria. Jerry and the other men all moved up into more crowded quarters to make room for those who are coming aboard. There are 50 "psychos," 50 wounded, and others on rotation. Lots of Airborne, some of the 11th who helped to take Los Baños. There are all sorts of bandages; hands with jungle rot, splinted arms, bound feet. Air activity is constant.

April 1, 1945. Easter Sunday. Jerry came up with a towel and sugar sack full of his toilet articles en route to the hospital, still feeling rotten.

April 2, 1945. I read a lot and have a book ready for Jerry to read. I visited him at 2 and his swollen ankles are back to normal after sulfadiazine and soda. He is very happy in his comfortable cool bunk, with fever down from 102-1/2 to 99, but he says Oh no, he won't be well enough to leave by tomorrow!

April 3, 1945. We passed a mountain-cloud-topped island rising from the sea. Then the New Guinea coast again and very strange towering mountains. About six we neared Finschhafen or Finch as the men call it. It is hot but the shore looks like the Suez Canal, and on one side, the square piles of boxes looked like Arab huts, especially in the dusk. It seemed marvelous to have the ports all open and lights ablaze aboard as well as on shore.

The Counterintelligence Corps called all our men in to sign again and to ask questions, so now we are all sealed up again. We finally found out what they *don't* want us to talk about—the complaints of the *Gripsholm* passengers brought down restrictions on the heads of all of us internees and they want us to key down on any experiences so as not to bring hardship on remaining prisoners in Japan and China. If we minimize or even faintly praise the better things that were done to us, it makes far better feeling and treatment from the Japanese. This is not difficult to do if one has tried to keep a balanced point of view. Before, I wasn't sure they weren't after atrocity stories in order to whoop up fighting morale at home, and among the troops. I have no real atrocity stories at first hand to relate.

April 5, 1945. About ten we pulled away from dock and left the orderly, neat little port and palms behind. No more land for about 17 days—then the Land of the Free. Brave, yes, but not free, muzzled while war exigencies bind it.

Also at ten the Voice blared forth all the new restrictions. All the internees are herded together on starboard. We have to talk to internees only, all the way home! So again we are pushed around, segregated, told who we can or cannot talk to, hedged in and restricted. Don't ever tell me it is the Nipponese who think up all the cute restrictions or who bring them about. Every time the Voice blares now it is a new restriction, making us feel like the visits of Lt. Mukibo who was always bad news.

In reading over these notes, I find I have mentioned that every one has great concern for us. At the moment there is definitely too much concern. Every breath, thought, look, is watched! The guards with wooden clubs are posted at each end of the center passage and in the middle as well as on stairways. It looks as though we women were poison! We don't dare look or speak to a member of the Armed Forces—officers or men! The kids are all limited to aft and promenade deck, so it is bedlam again and all of us are cramped in together. June weeps and is homesick for Leyte and Bilibid! I try to cheer her by singing, "I want to Go Back to Bilibid" but she cannot be comforted. It was another hot night and I am going to try sleeping on deck.

April 7, 1945. Jerry came up on deck smiling, out of the hospital to our great relief. He and I slept on deck aft and it is the best sleep I have had for days even though the deck is hard. The wounded, guards, and internees were sleeping all around us. In the dark, I touched a mound looking like life jackets, but it moved so I apologized. One lady tried to lift her life jacket from the deck in the dark and a plaintive voice said, "Lady, it's not a jacket. It's me!"

April 10, 1945. The tension is gradually relaxing all around. Both officers and men are being friendly, and the guards take no notice. But Army rules still stand and there is no relenting except superficially. Guards still watch near certain staterooms at night.

April 11, 1945. I celebrated Jerry's 54th birthday at beer with the Quartermaster and several Dutch officers in their cabin.

April 12, 1945. Just before dinner time the Voice called out the sudden death of President Roosevelt and we were all struck silent. How tragic!

April 13, 1945. The G.I.s are making wonderful planes and windmills for the kids. Boxwood, cardboard and bits of metal grow into toys to occupy the lively youngsters who never seem to run down.

Doyle has been begging me to go to the dentist so I went and had six fillings on the upper right side alone. I was in the chair over an hour and what a relief it was to catch all the cavities so near the nerve. The Captain-dentist said they were all in very bad condition so this may save some of them. It was such a joy after the lack of the last three years. I feel like a new person already and will be able to eat properly again.

We had reveille, with the officers and men all standing at salute while the flag was lowered to half mast. In the evening, "The Star Spangled Banner" was played, with all standing at salute. There have been some fine broadcasts on Roosevelt's passing. He was appreciated by so many, especially the G.I.s.

April 14, 1945. At ten an impressive service for President Roosevelt. All the servicemen, the Dutch officers in dark blue uniforms, and the internees crowded the forward decks. The Chaplain read the service after the Dutch and American flags were unfurled on each side, and the Army Major and Ship's Captain and other staff sat behind. The Chaplain mentioned Roosevelt's Dutch grandparents which brought out the significance of the two flags.

April 15, 1945. Jerry inquired and found that I could still sleep on deck with my husband! The dorm is still very stuffy and most of the women are at each other's throats with noisy children complications, trying to straighten out turns at ironing, and personality conflicts, all of three years' duration. I'm one of the few enjoying the sea and the trip, in spite of rules and people. Apparently I have missed seeing some things by sleeping too soundly, but it's all right with me. There is strong wind and spray, the air cool and good for sleeping.

April 16, 1945. I like the Army on the whole and don't mind being a part of it even when it seems absurd. After the informal, unconventional Orient, I can see that the United States are going to seem too conventional and provincial at times.

The Captain did four more fillings in my front teeth, one which was just a shell. A beautiful job (21 total in 4 days!). My teeth are clean and white instead of black holes resembling the ruins of Manila. It makes me look human and normal again, after three years. I have almost a flashing smile.

April 17, 1945. June says that one of the lads told her that he and another guy were discussing who would make the best wife of all the women on board, including the married ones, and they both voted June was "it." This tickled her no end.

The Voice is telling of the Army rolling into Germany, of nearness to Berlin, and of some diversion of supplies already to the Orient. The boys all say this is what they have been waiting to hear, and I said I had been waiting to hear of the capture of Baguio—when the Voice called out its capture, with the rescue of 7 thousand Filipinos, some Americans and British and other nationals. The Lieutenant gave us a swallow of cherry brandy to celebrate. We won't forget this chilly but warming evening.

April 19, 1945. Everyone is bundled up and very cold. Tonight we may see the lights of America for the first time in 18 years. For June and Bedie it is their first glimpse.

April 20, 1945. There is to be no "catcalling" or whistling to those on the dock! They are pleased to have brought us this far, to the homeland, and want the arrival dignified. Everyone acts restless, detached, as one does nearing the end of a voyage.

April 21, 1945. Bedie and Jerry were up at 3 with the G.I.s who had to roll out their gear so that the holds could be cleaned out before landing. It was beastly cold, windy and very rough, all night. Up forward many G.I.s were sick.

The officers ate at 7 and we women at 8. Almost at once they began taking the Army off. At about 7 we left the cold green choppy sea and entered smooth waters with soft rolling green hills on either side. Ahead of us was the Golden Gate Bridge. We stood up on the forward deck in the icy wind with officers and G.I.s, watching our ship approach the bridge. A sleek, dangerous-looking submarine passed us—cold and efficient and deadly. Planes passed overhead, one with four motors. We gazed at all the changes at the Presidio and the marina and San Francisco skyline. Ahead looking cruelly bleak Alcatraz loomed up. The G.I.s began to yell to the Dutch officers, kidding them that the crow's nest was going to hit the bridge and they'd better lower it quick. We stood watching it, breathless, hunched down into our collars, hands pulled up into the sleeves of field jackets which felt very good indeed over WAC suits. Nearer, nearer—a roar burst from 1,500 throats as we sailed under the beautiful bridge which was shining under early sun. We will never forget that cheer and the grinning Sergeant beside us who said hoarsely, "I been waitin' tree years for dis!" We were home—all the foxholes far behind! Here was what the fellows had fought for. They were going to step onto that shore again about which they had thought in steaming jungles or on tortured beachheads. They don't know it but they will soon find out that somehow they have changed and are different. Landing will be heaven, but unsettling too. With us, they are between two worlds.

The CIC presented a long questionnaire which Jerry filled out. We were processed again by the CIC, given our landing slip, ration books and home mail! We have everything but the Diary!

We watch Buster and Gadget and other G.I. friends troop off the ship, gear on their shoulders, as the band plays down below on the dock. The officers all cheer the band. No one else can be seen on the dock.

Our family is among the first internees through with processing and off the ship, shaking hands with the two smiling Quartermasters as we come down the gangplank. Husky Negroes carry our duffel bags. Waiting relatives are fenced off, but as the travelers come down and there is a rush to hug amid tears, reporters take flashlight pictures of these moving reunions. There is a customs chalk on our gear in no time. At the Red Cross booth we enjoy hot coffee and cookies. The children drink milk. Here they direct Jerry where to pick up hotel reservations which have been made for all of us. They show us through a streamlined waiting room at the end of the pier, usher us into a snazzy Red Cross Motor Corps car driven by a competent girl in snappy uniform. We are impressed with the spotless cleanliness of San Francisco streets, the handsome new buildings. Everything seems to shine. They cannot imagine how it shines after Manila devastation. They laugh and say they do not think it is very clean but they have tried to spruce up for the U.N. conference.[7]

We land at the Cartwright Hotel and Jerry goes off in the same station wagon to the Red Cross Center to arrange for cash orders for clothes, continental passage etc. June and Bedie take their long-promised hot bath, sitting for hours in the tub, soaking the whole room with the shower. We have a suite, two rooms with connecting bath, three closets. My bath follows theirs, then we go downstairs to sit looking out the big wide windows, watching the people and the passing traffic. There are so many shining cars, sliding smoothly. We are homesick, uprooted, in a town of strange faces. And so we start to crab. We criticize and make fun of the hats which are crazier, wilder than ever. I'll be damned if I will wear one or buy one. June asks, "Are all people in America rich, Mama?" Bedie says, "They look as though they were all going to a wedding!" It is spring hats with flowers and pastel shades that look so gay. The hairdo is long bob curled under. Everyone seems to have permanent waves and everyone slathers on lipstick and rouge. There is a distinct undercurrent of sadness and longing in America. Many homes have heartbreaking losses, and every week ships sail overseas loaded with men.

We go to Hale's Department Store with our Red Cross order. $150 for Jerry, $125 for June and me each, $95 for a boy 14. Miss Dyson, an expert shopper, takes us around so that we acquire a coat, a dress, slips, panties, a nightgown (very smooth and sleek), pocketbook, suitcase, bobby socks and shoes. Jerry has a new suit, overcoat, gray-blue hat, swanky beige trousers and a brown coat. Bedie is the last word in brown pants, a brown and white sport jacket and brown and tan shirt. We now "belong."

The stores, restaurants, food, clothes, people, streets, buildings are fabulous to our eyes. There are so many cars, so much food. The contrast with the Philippines is too great. We continually rush to the window or street corner to see the fire chief and ladders tear by with shrieking sirens.

April 22, 1945. We had a leisurely breakfast, then I made a date with old friends. Again I missed out on being able to appreciate a big event in my life—talking transcontinental telephone with Ethel, as Mums was at church.

Later we went to DiMaggio's club, with an old friend, at Fisherman's Wharf and saw our first floor show. Some of the program and the jokes, mostly on homosexual lines, were nauseating to me. I could only think of guy crouching in foxholes or advancing on Baguio. It seemed horribly futile and only the war was real. We talked about the Philippines and the South Pacific. I was very weary and sunk when we landed back to sleep.

April 23, 1945. Lovely golden tulips in a tall white vase with "welcome home" were telegraphed across the continent from Ruth and George. It was like a burst of sunlight, so cheering that we felt we had arrived after all.

At dinner with friends, we talked and swapped stories till after 11. When I was telling about Nida, I broke down and could not go on.

April 24, 1945. An air mail letter from Mums and we went to Western Union for a cash Telegraphic Transfer. The girl asked who I expected it was from and I said my mother or my sister. Then she asked how much I expected and I said I had requested fifty. She laughed and said it was for one hundred. Then she asked for identification and I didn't have a thing. Jerry said he was my husband, and he pulled out a pass signed by Captain Dahlstrom to let us out of Bilibid! It was sufficient, but we had to laugh to think that a jail pass helped identify us.

At Paul Co's, an elderly friend came to join us and we somehow got on to Poland and politics. He called Roosevelt "that Communist S.O.B." and I could see Jerry's hair rising fast and stiff, as well as my own. We tried to explain what it was like to starve and to want more equal distribution, security. It was no use. Jerry stood up and said we must be going, so we left before any explosion took place. We get emotionally upset about things that touch us close and deep.

We found Bedie home at last from his spree—he sat through the movie twice! Then we went to the Sir Francis Drake for dinner and the floor show. Our picture was taken by flash. It came out rather well, with the four of us sitting in clothes bought by the government, eating a luxurious dinner at the Sir Francis, without a penny or possession left and not giving a damn about anything. We looked it, fresh and green and detached, with eyes that have seen other things. This is another world, a world of luxury which everyone takes as a matter of course, a necessity.

April 25, 1945. We boarded the Tourist Pullman at the long Chicago train at Santa Fe Mission Station. Soon we were on our way across the continent—two travelers coming home after eighteen years, two seeing America for the first time and with new eyes.

We rolled past lovely vineyards, miles of grapes, fruit trees, weigela, alfalfa, beautiful rows of furrowed black loam, soft waving fields of grain. Suddenly these reminded me of "America, the Beautiful," and all the times we had heard it during the war. I looked at the "spacious skies, the amber waves of grain, the purple mountain majesties beyond the fruited plain" and I began to weep. Jerry and the kids looked astounded as they always do and June said, "Oh, Mama's off again." We passed airstrips, army camps, acres of freight cars loaded with trucks, jeeps, Ducks, cars—all army color. Everything is defense and war effort. We are tremendously impressed and moved by the huge scale of it.

Towards evening we saw enormous smooth-rolling mountains, softer green and gray valleys. We climbed over the grade and through the many tunnels of Tehachipi Pass, with blankets of blue lupin on the hillsides. Gay fields of poppies were like sheets of sunlight. After sunset, the twilight was beautiful. Climbing, we left the fertile valleys behind, reached more arid ground with round rock formations, tumbleweed blown against fences, acres of sagebrush.

April 26, 1945. Mostly desert country all day, climbing up the Arizona Divide and down again, past Williams, Flagstaff and a glimpse of Devil's Canyon. In the night during the crossing of Tehachipi I looked out the window and could see enormous smelters glowing in the distance where there was never any industry before. It was mysterious. Like these glowing settlements in the distance, all around was waste and desert which isolated the teeming energy from prying eyes.

The children see their first snow on nearby hills and covering the towering mountains of the Arizona Divide. I made them get up early to see huge mesas, long flat table lands with castle-like walls and formations of weathered rock. They saw their first American Indians at Winslow.

Women in overalls are working on the railroad at Seligman. At Gallup a woman serviced the water tanks with a big hose coupled on.

Everyone is getting acquainted. People come to talk and share cookies and salted nuts and chocolates with us. We are on the other side of the Great Divide. America in spring is lovely. The trees are coming into fresh green leaf which hangs like soft pale mist around the brown trunks and branches.

Continually we are running into prejudice. The Negro and anti-Semitic question and prejudice was among the troops and is now as we cross the continent. It seems to be chiefly economic—people afraid of losing jobs or sore because Negroes are making good money in defense work. Also Negroes have become more conscious of independence since taking part in the defense effort—they want their contribution to the effort and unity recognized. I find myself explaining all the time how we feel about it. The porter on this train is a wonderful character. We like to talk with him and when he asked if we saw "any of *our* boys" out there, we told him how useful they were and he beamed at us silently.

April 27, 1945. Up at 5 dressing and then out in the biting cold onto [the] La Junta [Colorado] platform where we met Jerry's brother and his wife and 18-year-old son just back from the Pacific on a Liberty Ship. It was so cold that we all piled into the little smoking room where they astounded us with gifts. A handsome belt for Bedic, a charm bracelet for June, a tie for Jerry and in a big box for me a shimmering luxurious silver fox fur marked with a beautiful black center line, from their ex-fox farm. I was simply bowled over, for I never expected to own a fur again after losing the one in Bilibid. I looked and felt like a millionairess. It was snug and warm over my WAC suit. They told us they pelted all their foxes and sold the farm because meat was so high and so hard to get that they operated at a loss. This was the last fox they had left. It was even more beautiful than the one from the same farm, looted during the burning of Manila. Replaced without even a lift of my finger! How fast we talked.

The porter suggested we move to the club car in the back which we did, except for George who left to drive the car to Lamar while Van and Margaret rode on the train for an hour. We heard about Mother Crouter who sat by the radio all day listening to news and worrying about us as war broke. She died of a heart attack within two months. She had never believed Japan would attack or fight and was shocked and heartbroken when it came, so she was unprepared to meet the strain.

All day we have gazed at the great plains of Kansas—wonderful smooth rolling country of soft grays, browns, and lavenders in the shadows. As far as one can see in every direction there is grain. Grazing farms are so huge that the horizon swallows them. All the starving people of Europe look toward this state and others like it which are filling the storage bins with surplus wheat. Compact farmhouses, round grain storage tanks, all clean and well painted, stand in the middle of endless acres.

We *should* win; we *should* fight for more just and equal distribution with all this in our laps. We can afford to be fair and generous. We have everything, and the spirit to go with it. The contrast between here and the Orient is stupendous. Every inch counts there, but here it is by the acre.

Emporia—made famous by William Allen White and his *Gazette*—streets lined with shiny cars like all the other Kansas towns; brick streets, grain elevators; spring-green elders, grassy parks, flourishing business blocks, a long concrete bridge; a soldier standing in the station with a service-record envelope; prosperous homes. Still grain and more grain farms. Brown furrows or green velvet—fertility everywhere. No scorched earth of war.

April 28, 1945. South Bend, then Elkhart where we stopped beside two hospital cars, loaded with wounded in pajamas. At the end window three of the patients began making signs to us to come over. We could not leave the car, so they put up a sign, "Manila—Klipfontein"—they were three boys from the boat. Then our train moved off. We all waved frantically for the last time. It was a tantalizing glimpse. June was wildly excited. They do look different in gray hospital pajamas. It seems odd that halfway across America we should meet the wounded, our old friends again. June promptly had a touch of combat-area homesickness. And so did I.

Then Cleveland and sister Margy, with many changes since we last saw each other. The weekend here without any notes, we were so busy catching up on the past and so tired of traveling and war. I cried at the drop of a hat and particularly when the capture of Baguio was confirmed.

May 28, 1945. Mother and Ethel and Cousin Edie met us at the train in Boston, the *first day of May*. Three weeks went very fast, seeing old friends and talking and trying to rest. Spring was beautiful in New England. Mother is simply wonderful and does not seem nearly ninety.

We went to one of the Settlement Houses about our health examination, under the Bureau of Public Health. When I told one of the men how many changes there seemed to be for the better in the slums nearby and in Social Security generally, he looked at me and said, "I wish I were looking at all this with your eyes, Mrs. Crouter. We are too close to it. We cannot see." This district in particular had had a whole section of houses demolished to widen the street. It was clean and light, not as I remembered it. The government housing projects interest me more than anything else in the United States. I would like to live in one.

On Monday, May 28th, I entered the Marine Hospital as a guest patient of the Bureau of Public Health for treatment of Endomiba Histolytica and Hiss-Russel Y dysentery—some information I picked up in conversation later!

In the hospital we have earphone radios, two lights by which to read, a library which is rolled in to us; gray ladies, blue ladies, green ladies, white nurses; chromium indirect lighting, also chromium curtain rods and chairs; all modern streamlined. There is a rolling bed tray and a grand bed. The push-bell puts on a red light. What a different kind of hospital! I am so glad to be in a ward rather than a private room. They said I would only be here a week or two. My clothes are all taken away to a locker elsewhere.

May 29, 1945. Dr. P., aged 27, came to write down my long history of ailments. When I said I thought I was emotionally unstable right now, he said not at all—that my nervous reactions were entirely normal and I was doing very well for one of my size.

June 2, 1945. Mums and Dee came with poppies and a rose, and Jim

Halsema's letter saying our Baguio home was intact. It was a vivid, firsthand account of poor, smashed Baguio, demolished by our own planes.

We all do many strange things when war comes. My part was to wait, to study Japanese language and character, to write a diary and become more international.

June 5, 1945. Jerry seems to have a slight cardiac difficulty and took the news very hard. It only shows up on electrocardiograph.

June 6, 1945. This is Normandy D-Day and the broadcasts on both radios have been thrilling. They tell of men dying in Normandy for real democracy, for working together with Russia and all countries who want freedom. In this rising surge against the old order I no longer feel that three years in Concentration were wasted.

June 9, 1945. Jerry came with letters from Washington and a Corporal in Baguio. Nida is doing his washing. She is alive and able to take care of herself, living in our house. It is the happiest, most peaceful night I have had in months.

Washington may send Jerry to the Philippines after a month's training, if he passes the physical exam.

June 14, 1945. Jerry comes to visit almost every day and it is a long grind for him.

June 15, 1945. The USO show was a honey. I saw my first real jitterbugging, heard swell boogie-woogie, which is savage, primitive, like an Igorot tribal beat.

June 20, 1945. Jerry came with news of going to Washington on Sunday so we will have no New York trip together. He said he broke down at the First Command office when they questioned him about my condition.

June 22, 1945. New England has even more race and class prejudice than the rest of the continent, but this hospital is a priceless experience in democracy. Such a wealth of personalities and types. Every day I eat it up! It is a fitting end to my three-year cycle of internment. A piquant little Polish girl who got out of that country in time came in to visit. She is in WAC uniform and thinks American food and government are simply marvelous. A girl patient from Iceland thinks the same.

June 23, 1945. Jerry's Washington letter says that if he goes to the Philippines his family cannot join him for a year, probably two years, and he must go with this understanding. So we ask, "How about Jean MacArthur and her son arriving in combat area!" I felt horribly low and wept quietly for a long time.

June 24, 1945. June and Bedie came over, kicking each other in the shins every five minutes. Bedie's eyes were shining when he told he he was going to a camp in Rhode Island.

June 25, 1945. Jerry came in with Mums. The doctor is giving him heavy dose of vitamins to counteract his difficulty. He hates to face the ravages of starvation, and so do I! I am so tired of having others arrange my life for me, of lying supine when I want to *do* something.

June 26, 1945. I feel as though I do not want many possessions ever again; it is so devastating to lose beautiful things, all the little insignificant items of home. But after one gets used to it, it is rather nice being shorn and simple.

June 29, 1945. Jerry brought a wonderful letter from Nida in her quaint English phrasing. I have read it over and over. She saved our Celadon and other Chinese vases, Jerry's colored wine glasses, the snapshots and baby books and pictures.

July 3, 1945. Suddenly in came Major O'Leary and his wife and son Bryan—all very handsome. We had a big time talking Bilibid. It was a big surprise and quite a thrill. He said they had moved the Japanese and Germans to Muntinglupa [a new prison outside of Manila].

July 5, 1945. Jerry and Mums came with a letter from Corporal Evans who enclosed a message from Nida. Nida says both Lallie, our dog, and Fuzzy, the Persian cat, died long ago. Nida has had pain. The doctor told her it was mild pleurisy. It is nothing serious she says. But it upsets me and my heart touches rock-bottom. I hold on for all I am worth.

July 6, 1945. Jerry brought over his Mother's last letters to us, showing her breakdown, pitiful in anxiety and sadness. She left silver and jewelry to us. He broke down when I said I was too low to read it today. He buried his head on the bed and I hung on to his wrist for there is nothing to say. We both feel worried over Nida, and we are so cut off and helpless.

July 11, 1945. I felt cold and had a chill, with queer feeling eyes and a shaky sensation. They took a blood count and smears from my ear blood drop. I have been perspiring terribly, with the chills. Two hot water bags made me react finally.

July 14, 1945. More twitches and chills and queer eyes. I finally pulled out of it but I am not reading much now as my eyes do not seem to focus properly.

July 26, 1945. I shot the works and told Dr. Wilson how I felt and what they did for me in camp. He listened very carefully. The other two doctors came in briefly. They left the file wagon in the middle of the room and all went into a huddle outside. Dr. Wilson came back and said they would fix me up.

The nurse gave me a thick yellow enema and told me I must retain every bit of it. She also gave me the same yellow stuff orally, ice cold. I wonder if it isn't penicillin.

July 27, 1945. Jerry and June came over, full of plans for the future, a farm or something, but I felt so sick that I did not seem to be included.

Crosby says he felt like crying when he first came back to this country too. All Philippine people have it. It is nervous shock and the contrasts. Patients always think they are coming in for just a week. I'm still here after two months.

The diary notes end here because I was so ill that I could not coordinate. I could not keep food down and refused to take the penicillin. Young Dr. Wilson came and said, "What is this I hear about you, refusing the penicillin?" I told him something was making me nauseated and he said he would stop all sulfa if I would take the other. I agreed. The nausea cleared up but I had continuous chills and sweats, with the kidneys working overtime to carry off whatever it was that upset me. The nurses brought double blankets so that I could pull them up whenever a chill started. The sleeping medicine they gave me paralyzed my hands so that was stopped.

The weekend that Jerry was gone to see Bedie was the worst. They kept on giving me the penicillin orally and rectally but I shall always think it was the effect of the sulfa over too long a period. On Sunday the Catholic Chaplain came in the room, looking around quickly at each bed. I just barely realized he was there and saw him blessing each patient in each bed. One girl said she was not a Catholic and he answered that it did not matter, for anyone could be blest, just as God looked after and blessed the trees and the bees. It is the only time this ever happened and the others wondered if it had some connection with my being so sick.

Sunday night a nurse came to tell me my family had telephoned to say they were thinking of me. It seemed to reach me from a long way off so that I pulled back. I asked them later how they knew it was my worst night and how they happened to send a message at just that time, as they had never phoned a message before, but they did not remember. They just wanted to get in touch with me.

When Jerry came on Monday to tell me about his trip, he found the doctors fixing me up for a vitamin infusion. It was a very large bottle, looking like nearly a gallon size, and they mixed liquid thiamin, riboflavin and niacinamide from smaller bottles. I do not know whether there was anything else with it but I did see the name on these bottles and it seems to me the color was pale yellow. It took some time for it to drip into the vein and Doctor Wilson came in from time to time to adjust the flow. He sat on the opposite bed watching and after a while I said, "I feel queer." He asked, "Just how do you feel queer?" and I replied, "Oh, I feel as though life were simply rushing back into me all over." He smiled and answered, "I guess that is exactly what is happening." The following day I think they gave me a second large bottle of infusion. From then on I began to pick up gradually. Almost immediately the corners of my mouth developed wide cracks and the doctor nodded when I said, "That's riboflavin deficiency, isn't it?" It is odd that one often does not develop certain symptoms of any deficiency until one begins to eat or get what one has lacked.

The next two weeks [consisted] of continued penicillin treatment for the intestinal parasites.

Some results in research were probably achieved through us during that period. They were still trying to find a way to get penicillin past the acid in the stomach, into the intestines, without destroying its value, when I was taking it orally.

There came a day when the doctors started the three-day specimen tests again which this time proved the penicillin had cured that most resistant parasite. "Did I have *Shiga* dysentery?" I asked, surprised. So it was, after all. Dr. Wilson had doubted it, had told me I probably would not be here if I had. Dr. Wilson said I was their favorite patient so I am sure they gleaned a little research from my three months stay in the hospital.

Always and everywhere was prejudice, class, color and race. It continued to astound me that there should be so much and that it was growing apace in America, of all countries. Reaction had begun to set in, openly at the San Francisco [U.N.] Conference, more pronounced since the passing of Roosevelt.

On August 8, Russia entered the Pacific War, and on August 15 the hospital patients and the whole world went wild over V-J day. Jerry phoned me the good news through a nurse that evening but he only did it out of exuberance because the radio and everyone proclaimed it. There had been atomic bombs but the implication of this discovery had not penetrated. On August 17 I left the Marine Hospital on very wobbly legs and a still low blood-count but with parasites definitely finished.

After two weeks in Boston at the Brick House, Jerry left for the war shipping position in Washington and Manila, and the children left with me on September 8, for school and a new life in Cleveland, Ohio, but all this is another story. We were yet to find out whether our lessons in democracy had just finished, or were only begun.

Epilogue: 1945–1980

ONE OF THE CRUELEST of life's ironies is expressed by the axiom that "survivors must suffer," as the vast literature of the Holocaust testifies so poignantly.[1] Suffering may be obvious or more subtle, steady or intermittent, immediate or delayed—and is sometimes dormant for months, years, or even decades. Time and therapy heal some wounds, but often the scar tissue remains, disfiguring and sensitive. Yet, paradoxically, suffering can strengthen as well as diminish its victim. Growth of character and understanding can be among the fruits of adversity, as Natalie Crouter was well aware, both while she was writing the *Diary* in internment camp and afterward.

For the Camp Holmes internees, release was understandably welcome but not without difficulties. For many, including the Crouters, some of the most important problems were financial. Philippines residents had lost their homes; had had their possessions confiscated, looted, or sold to pay for extra food in camp; and had been without income for three and a half years. The U.S. government even tried to bill each repatriate $275 for return passage to the States, although there was no place in the Philippines, still at war, where these American citizens could live. (This expense was later waived as the result of postwar legislation, sponsored by Senator Claude Pepper, that also awarded the internees reparation payments of about 20¢ on the dollar for property appropriated under Japanese rule.)

For those whose businesses had been destroyed, as had Jerry Crouter's, employment became the paramount problem, one compounded by advancing age and the ravages of malnutrition. At once, Jerry faced serious questions. Could he start again in business with no capital? In the United States or in the Philippines? Would it be better to train himself for a new career? If so, what new skills should he learn—and could he learn within a reasonable time?

These concerns had troubled Jerry throughout the war, and at its end he set about immediately to restore his health and strength so that he could look for a job. He longed for the Philippines—his home, free or captive, for nearly thirty years—and wanted to return there. Because of his business expertise and his knowledge of the area, within a few months of his release, Jerry was hired by the U.S. War Shipping Administration to work in the Philippines.

The Islands had been devastated by bombing, and the necessities of living were in such short supply that American government employees were prohibited from taking their families in with them for a minimum of a year. Natalie was too debilitated to leave the States in any case. Suffering from dysentery and pernicious anemia, she had been hospitalized for three months after their return to her relatives in Boston. Ironically, while Natalie was in the hospital and Jerry was job-hunting, Bedie had spent his first summer of freedom in a boys' summer camp.

After Jerry left for Manila, alone, in the fall of 1945, Natalie and the children went to live with Natalie's divorced sister, Marguerite Bellamy, in Cleveland Heights, Ohio. The large, comfortable house—where they were able to live rent-free—was reminiscent of Natalie's childhood home at Savin Hill, as was the tree-shaded, upper-middle-class neighborhood, a combination of spaciousness and tradition much welcomed after the lack of both in camp.

For a year and a half after Natalie's rescue, her wartime *Diary* was missing, having been confiscated—"without even a receipt," laments Natalie—by U.S. Army Intelligence for its possible strategic use or as future evidence for war crimes trials. After the Crouters' persistent search, which ranged from Boston to the Philippines to Australia and back to the United States, the *Diary* was rescued from a huge Army warehouse in Kansas City, the packets still sewed up as Natalie had left them.

Natalie then began the arduous, bittersweet process of transcribing the tiny, penciled notes into a five-thousand–page typescript—with the type frugally crowding the sheets. She attributes her wearing of glasses to the attendant eyestrain of her labor, which took more than two years, but she had accomplished some of the most important tasks of her life by writing the *Diary,* preserving it, and putting it into legible form. For the next twenty years the *Diary* lay dormant. Natalie believed, in her words, that "if the diary had value it continued to have it, so I ceased to worry about time."

Meanwhile, Natalie reared the children. Although the Crouters' finances were somewhat precarious, she managed on what Jerry sent from the Philippines, with concert and theater tickets and piano lessons for June generously provided by Marguerite. Natalie devoted much of her energy, still limited because of her anemia, to liberal political activities. She supported Henry Wallace's Progressive-party presidential campaign in 1948, and she firmly refused the FBI's invitation to become a political informer. In contradiction to their logic, apparently based on the belief that her political imprisonment throughout the war had automatically made her a superpatriot, Natalie devoted considerable time and effort to the pacifist Women's International League for Peace and Freedom—an appropriate organization for a victim of the hardships of war, but one considered by the FBI to be highly subversive, especially during its strong opposition to the Vietnam War in the 1960's.

Jerry Crouter had been in the Philippines for nearly two years when, in 1947, he suffered a cerebral hemmorhage and was forced to abandon his job and return to his family in Cleveland. His health had been permanently damaged as the result of wartime malnutrition, and his memory was impaired as a result of the hemmorhage. Recovery was slow and frustrating to a man accustomed to being in vigorous control of his own life and an ample provider for his family. During the last four years of his life, Jerry trained for several jobs—with the Veterans Administration and in private businesses—and worked at several for a short time each, only to have the companies move out of town or declare bankruptcy. In 1951 he died, at fifty-eight, of cirrhosis and cancer of the liver.

Although some of the problems of the internment camp's survivors were physical, for the Crouter children more of the difficulties seemed to be psychological, and, says June, although some of the manifestations were temporary, other effects persisted. Bedie, now firmly "Fred" to everyone but members of the family, reacted by developing stomach disorders. He also had violent nightmares, cried out in distress and jumped off the bed in his sleep. "We were afraid he'd jump out the window," June explains, "and although he can control his stomach disturbances, he still suffers from both problems to this day. He's lucky [now] to have such an understanding wife."[2]

June attributes many of her problems in her twenties, including a delayed adolescent rebellion, to the fact that "in internment camp I couldn't rebel. And I couldn't separate from my mother—literally as well as psychologically; we slept on the same three-quarter–size mattress throughout our stay at Camp Holmes. I lacked the confidence I needed to be independent."[3] June spent three years in psychotherapy in her late twenties, and she credits this treatment with her ability finally to deal with her ambivalent postwar relationship with her mother. Therapy also helped her, she says, to gain sufficient maturity to marry and rear children of her own.

As a result of their schooling in Camp Holmes, June and Fred had been able to enter American schools at the appropriate grade level. June, a model student throughout the war, remained so in Heights High School, from which she graduated in 1948, with a scholarship to Western Reserve University. She lived at home, graduated four years later with a degree in sociology ("it all made sense"), and in 1956 earned a master's degree in social administration from Western Reserve's School of Applied Social Science. For the next dozen years she was a caseworker and, later, a social-work supervisor in Cleveland agencies working with families and children. In 1967 she married Richard Wortman, a wise and witty child psychologist at Case Western Reserve University Hospitals, and is now the mother of Rebecca (b. 1968) and Glen (b. 1969).

The Wortmans' spacious, remodeled brick house in Cleveland Heights, only a few blocks from where the Crouters lived after the war, overflows with furniture, toys, Oriental jade and statuary, plants, and large supplies of food. Unlike Natalie, who has always been an indifferent cook, June cooks superbly, as her father did. The abundance of food is not only an internment fantasy fulfilled at last, but is also a postinternment manifestation of June's continual readiness for emergencies. "In camp we never went anywhere without our emergency food bag. I'm always the one who takes food—and lots of sweaters for the whole family—even on short trips. You have to think of what you might need if you get stuck somewhere, or if disaster strikes."⁴

June's personal warmth and her concern for other people are always evident. She maintains Natalie's tradition of social activism, and is a moving force in her community, much involved in struggles for neighborhood stability and improved social services. She credits much of her enthusiasm for these causes to her internment. "I will not be muzzled," she says with firmness, "even if the City Council gets tired of hearing what I have to say. Once you have the freedom to speak out on issues that matter, you never want to be repressed again."⁵

Fred grew up faster than Natalie would have wished. He married Louise Patterson, a student from an Ohio farming family, in 1953 while he was a history major at Hiram College. Upon graduation he enlisted in the Army, in preference to being drafted. After two years' service at Fort Knox, Kentucky, he became a teacher of American history in a public high school in Caldwell, New Jersey, where he still lives with his wife and three children, Jerrol (b. 1956), Jennifer (b. 1959), and Lenore (b. 1962). Fred, too, has upheld the family tradition of defending worthwhile causes, and as a consequence he has had his day in court—and in jail—as a labor negotiator for the striking teachers' union.

In a master's thesis (Montclair State College, 1967) based largely on Natalie's *Diary*, Fred analyzed the development of the political structure of the internment camp. The *Diary*'s effects on other family members have been more complicated. Although its existence fascinates her, to this day June has not wanted to cope with the emotional demands of reading her mother's manuscript, and even now Natalie cries when she scans portions of it.

When her children were grown and her health was somewhat improved, Natalie was able to travel. In the 1950s she toured the Soviet Union alone and loved it. She studied Russian beforehand, saw much of the country, and enjoyed meeting a variety of people—as she always did in her travels. She spent 1956 in Switzerland with Edgar Snow and his family. There she served as his secretary, typing his autobiography, *Journey to the Beginning*. In the 1960s she visited Yugoslavia, traveled by Russian luxury liner around the North Cape of Norway, visited a variety of West African countries, and returned to the Soviet Union.

One of Natalie's major goals during the 1970s was to visit mainland China, especially Peking, which she had last seen before her marriage in 1927. Through the good offices of Madame Sun Yat-sen and Edgar Snow's widow Lois, she accomplished this in 1973, as a member of one of the first groups of Americans allowed to visit the country since Communist rule began.

Another of Natalie's goals during the 1970s, also accomplished with gusto, was attending the reunion of former internees that was held in San Francisco on February 13, 1977, to commemorate the thirty-second anniversary of their liberation. Rokuro Tomibe was the guest of honor.

Natalie has returned to the Philippines on several occasions, particularly to visit Nida Bacani, for whom she felt *utang na loob*. Nida continued to live in Baguio throughout her life; her daughters married and lived near her until her death in the spring of 1979. Ismael had been a casualty of the war; in 1944 the Japanese had accused him of collaboration and taken him to Mindanao with a crew of Filipino laborers, whom they overworked and underfed. The American liberation troops found the emaciated corpses of these men; after the Japanese had fled to avoid capture, their hostages, too weak to seek food or safety, had starved to death. For years, Natalie willingly repaid her debt of personal gratitude to Nida, sending her a quarterly check as a token for the years of lifesaving sustenance during the Crouters' imprisonment.

In the Tokyo war-crimes trials early in 1946, Rokuro Tomibe, then an American prisoner, had been obliged to testify about Camp Holmes conditions at the trial of General Kwo, the Korean Army official whom the Japanese had placed in charge of all the prisoner-of-war camps in the Islands. Jim Halsema, who was covering the trial as a reporter for the Associated Press, recognized Tomibe, with pleasure and surprise; the internees had assumed that Tomibe had been killed when the Allies recaptured the Philippines. The prosecutors asked former prisoners, including Halsema, to specify the charges on which Tomibe could be prosecuted. They exonerated him completely, praising his exemplary leadership, and he was freed. He became a successful businessman in Tokyo, and today he occasionally plays gracious host to former internees.

Two hundred and twenty people, including 100 internees and their relatives, attended the 1977 Camp Holmes reunion; Tomibe reciprocated their honor with commemorative medals for each. In an emotional speech, he expressed his understanding of the two cultures and the appreciation for democracy that he had gained as an administrator of Camp Holmes:

Do you, especially those who were still little boys and girls at that time, remember one day in Camp Holmes? It was on April 29, 1944, the birthday of the Japanese Emperor. On that day I got some bananas at a market in Baguio out of my slender purse, and gave them to the children under thirteen years of age as my congratulatory present on that occasion.

At first I expected to be given thanks in Japanese way; that is, if it is in Japan, a leader of the children would let all the other children make a rank, and command them, "Attention! Bow to the Commander!" After that only the leader would express thanks on behalf of all the children, "Thank you very much Commander, for giving us bananas as your Japanese Emperor's birthday present."

To my surprise, there developed a quite different scene. After equally dividing the bananas among themselves, every child, even to a really young one, came forward to me with the bananas one after another, and asked me to shake hands, one by one, and said, "Thank you very much, Commander." I strained my eyes, and here I could understand the existence of the differences in thinking way and the purpose of education between American and Japan.

I'm now sixty-five years old, and I have become able to make independent decision. . . . I must confess that it was the children who were in the Baguio Camp thirty-three years ago and who attached so much importance to everyone's free will that gave me this lesson. I'm now longing for most earnestly to acquire the self-confidence to express what we believe to be right openly, and to establish the world to make it possible to do so.

Perhaps the last major goal of Natalie Crouter's life has been to have this *Diary* published. She is fortunate to have survived to a time when an interest in the lives of women is growing, and when their diaries and autobiographies are treated seriously as works of human, literary, and historical interest. Natalie Crouter's *Diary* is a living memorial to her personality, her values, her life. It is also a monument to the lives of women of Natalie's generation, and to the lives of all women who embody the paradoxes that have dominated women's existence in much of the twentieth century; as they, like Natalie, fulfill socially determined roles and go beyond them, they exhibit dependence and independence, conservatism and innovation, fragility—and great strength.

Notes

Initials indicate the supplier of information in the note, though the writing is mine, except when an asterisk (*) appears after the informant's initials. N. C. = Natalie Crouter; J. H. = James Halsema; M. O. = Martha Ozawa; G. T. = Gary Turner; J. W. = June Wortman. All notes without initials are mine, Lynn Bloom. Major Turner and I checked every item of military information in two or more of the following sources: R. Ernest Dupuy and Trevor N. Dupuy, *The Encyclopedia of Military History* (New York: Harper & Row, 1970); Dwight D. Eisenhower, *Crusade in Europe* (New York: Doubleday, 1948); *Facts on File Yearbooks 1941–45: Person's Index of World Events* (New York: Facts on File, Inc., published annually); Sir Basil Liddell Hart, *History of the Second World War* (New York: G. P. Putnam, 1971); Francis T. Miller, *et al.*, *The Complete History of World War II* (n.p., 1947); *New York Times Index*.

Introduction: Diarists, This Diarist, and Her Diary

1. "Individual and Mass Behavior in Extreme Situations," in *Readings in Social Psychology*, ed. Theodore M. Newcomb and Eugene L. Hartley *et al.*, 1st ed. (New York: Henry Holt, 1947), pp. 629, 631–32.

2. June Wortman to LZB, interview May 22, 1979.

3. Ibid.

4. Brent School served about a hundred children in the first through twelfth grades, including many boarders whose parents were living elsewhere in the Philippines or on neighboring islands. Many of the British residents of the Philippine Islands sent their children to boarding schools in England instead of to Brent.

5. Unlike other foreign occupiers of many other Pacific islands, the Americans were operating on the principle that the Filipinos would eventually assume responsibility for their own country, and must be educated to do so. So the native schools, some taught initially by Thomasites (similar to today's Peace Corps), although separate were not necessarily unequal. In addition to providing the three r's, they were devoted to perpetuating Filipino culture and government, unlike the American-oriented Brent School. J.H.

6. *Philippine Collaboration in World War II* (Ann Arbor: University of Michigan Press, 1967), p. 4.

7. Robert Shaplen, in "Letter from Manila," *The New Yorker* (March 26, 1979), 99, observes that "in an age of nuclear aircraft carriers and long range bombers and

cargo planes'' these Philippine bases remain convenient to promote such strategic objectives but are no longer as essential as they were at that time.

8. Quotations in this paragraph are from a letter from Francis B. Sayre, U.S. Department of State, to the Honorable Charles A. Wolverton, Chairman of the Committee on Interstate and Foreign Commerce, U.S. House of Representatives, 80th Congress, First Session, March 12, 1947, in response to the House Investigation of how to treat repatriated U.S. citizens. *Enemy Property Commission Report* (Washington, D.C.: Government Printing Office, 1947), p. 153.

9. The Camp Holmes guards were mostly Japanese or Formosan peasants who during their tours of duty grew to tolerate and even to like the prisoners, especially the children. Jim Halsema relates that sometimes when the wood crews or garbage detail went out of camp to work, the accompanying guard would show them how to dismantle his rifle and put it together. The Japanese Military Police (Kempetai) in Baguio manifested much more hatred and savagery. (Told to LZB, interview, April 27, 1979.)

10. Quoted by Richard Harwood, "Tales of the New Pacific," Part V, *Washington Post*, May 13, 1979, Sec. C, p. 4.

11. See p. 527.

12. Even with such minimum security, prisoners rarely tried to escape. One reason was ties to family members within the camp who would have been subject to beatings, torture, or death in reprisal for an escape. Moreover, there was no place where escapees could go undetected, except into hiding more arduous and far more dangerous than life in camp. White skins stood out conspicuously in the Orient; American guerrillas, such as the Cushing brothers to whom Natalie refers, were usually of mixed racial heritage and looked like Filipinos.

13. Jim Halsema to LZB, interview, April 28, 1979.

14. Ibid.

15. Jim Halsema explains that according to Japanese official policy, clergy were exempt from internment. As in the case of many comparable policies, its interpretation varied according to the local military commander. The large number of missionaries in this camp was the result of two factors: many of them had served in China, which made them automatically suspect to the Japanese; and it was easier for the Japanese to keep them under surveillance in camp than if they had been living on the outside. Even though there were few repatriation ships, the clergy could probably have been repatriated if the Japanese had been willing. (To LZB, interview, April 27, 1979.)

16. Jim Halsema to LZB, interview, April 28, 1979.

17. See note 19, p. 534.

18. From May 1942 (''just in time to hear about the battle of Midway,'' says Halsema) until about two years later, the internees had a shortwave radio, whose existence and hiding place were known to only a small group. To prevent detection, the listeners released news information gradually, deliberately distorting and falsifying some of it so that the Japanese wouldn't suspect its source. The Japanese occasionally allowed the prisoners to listen to the Tokyo and Manila propaganda stations on the guards' radio. These stations were often accurate about the war in Europe and Africa but intentionally less so about the war in the Pacific as the Axis began to lose. Sometimes, when the guards were unlikely to notice, the internees could ease the dial over to the fairly accurate broadcasts on the Singapore station. The listeners considered it part of their task to gradually break the bad news, as well as to convey the good,

to the internees to give them a realistic understanding of the war and to dispel the view held at its beginning that ''MacArthur is riding toward Apparri on a white horse and he will set us free.'' (Jim Halsema to LZB, interview, April 28, 1979.)

19. *Doctor Spock: Biography of a Conservative Radical* (New York: Bobbs-Merrill, 1972).

20. Unpublished; written and translated soon after the February 13, 1977, reunion with Camp Holmes internees. In this memoir, Tomibe emphasizes his intention while in camp of allowing the internees as much self-government as possible, ''to make [their lives] free with least interference,'' yet through ''human warmth'' to oblige them to obey the Japanese regulations. He takes obvious pleasure in recalling ''many beautiful stories about how Japanese soldiers and American workers worked together, in spite of their language barrier, to accomplish their same purpose.'' He is particularly proud of his effective securing of Red Cross materials: ''all relief goods except ten packs of cigarettes were distributed to the internees. . . . It was very rare that [such] goods were distributed without any damage, robbery, confiscation [or bribery].''

1941

1. At the beginning of World War II, one Philippine peso was equivalent to 50 cents in American money. Near the end of the war, inflation had rendered 1,000 Philippine pesos, issued under Japanese auspices and known informally as ''funny money'' or ''Mickey Mouse Money,'' virtually worthless. (J. H.)

2. See Introduction, p. xvi.

3. See Introduction, p. xvi.

4. Carlos P. Romulo was then the editor of the *Philippines Herald*. He had just returned from a trip to Southeast Asia, where he had found great uneasiness over the Japanese military buildup. His speech predicted war and revolution in Southeast Asia and a great change in the governments there. He may have intended to convince the Philippines that neutrality was in its best interests. During the war Romulo served on MacArthur's staff as one of his chief advisors on internal matters in the Philippines; he landed with him on Leyte. (J. H.)

5. A collective name for five mountain tribes of Northern Luzon, some of whom were formerly head-hunters. Many Igorots were employed as laborers in the nearby mines. (J. H.)

6. As indicated in the Introduction to this volume, and as will be apparent throughout, Nida Bacani and her husband, Ismael, were among the many Filipinos who remained loyal to their former American or British employers despite their ''liberation'' by the Japanese, because of *utang na loob* (gratitude) and personal affinity. Throughout the war such people refused to ally themselves with the Japanese, who nevertheless commandeered their services.

7. These were all American military bases on Luzon. The surprise Japanese raid on Clark Field, one of the most important military centers in the Pacific, destroyed or damaged nearly all the planes there. (See Louis Morton, *The War in the Pacific*, the official history prepared by the Office of the Chief of Military History, Department of the Army, Washington, D.C., 1953, p. 88.) (J. H.*)

8. On July 26, 1941, General Douglas MacArthur, who had retired as Chief of Staff of the U.S. Army to plan the defense of the Philippines, had assumed over-all

command of the U.S. Armed Forces Far East *(USAFFE)*. When the war began, the Philippines was defended by a motley collection of armed forces, including American and Filipino professional soldiers in the Regular Army, American National Guard reservists, American Marines and Navy personnel, and the larger—but ill-equipped and only partially-trained—Philippine Army. (J. H.)

9. The oil-storage tanks at San Fernando, La Union Province, from which Jerry's gas station had been supplied, had been blown up.

10. After initial reconaissance landings at the northern and southern extremities of Luzon, the Japanese sent their main forces ashore on the Lingayen Gulf, 120 miles north of Manila, on December 22. Two days later they began a pincer movement by landing another force at Atimonan, east of the capital.

As a rest area for American military in the Philippines, Camp John Hay, Baguio, was garrisoned only by two companies of American-led Philippine Scouts, and no effort was made to defend the city. The Lingayen Gulf landings were within sight and sound of Baguio, and some exhausted Filipino forces retreated through it during the night of December 22-23, after which road contact with Manila was cut off. The last American units left Baguio December 24 to walk across the mountains to the east. (Louis Morton, *The Fall of the Philippines* [Washington, D.C.: Department of the Army, Office of Military History, 1953], pp. 123–26). (J. H.)

11. An "open city" is one whose authorities have agreed not to defend it. Thus, enemies are obliged not to attack it.

1942

1. "Committee" refers to the men's Executive Committee (see Introduction, p. xx). At this point the Japanese were still not providing food from their own funds for the internees, who had to contribute their own money to a common pool for their food.

2. The initial Japanese force in Luzon had been decimated and by mid-February the Japanese were in despair; thus the assumption that they were leaving. The invaders had greatly underestimated the strength of Filipino-American ties and the extent of the resistance (Morton, pp. 349–50).

3. This group, the kitchen crew in charge of food preparation, saved communal supplies and cooked special delicacies for a select few, who ate them secretly. Other members of the camp had observed this, and had shamed the crew by reporting the news.

4. Natalie felt that the estimates were unfair because either the Women's Committee or the workers themselves under- or over-estimated the time spent in performing the tasks, depending on the political pull of the women involved. Jim Halsema takes partial issue with Natalie's interpretation, claiming that with about 5 percent exception, the duties were assigned as fairly as was feasible and were usually performed in good faith.

5. The Capital Bazaar was a Japanese general merchandise store on Session Road, Baguio's principal street.

6. This is typical of the rumors that were to circulate throughout internment. Characteristic of fantasies that sustain the spirit, they were based more on hope than on fact.

7. See Introduction, pp. xix–xx.

8. This was an exaggeration. The report evidently refers to the Battle of Macassar Strait, January 23–25, in which the Japanese sustained heavy losses of ships and men but still outnumbered the Americans (Miller, pp. 446–47). Although the carriers *Enterprise* and *Yorktown,* under the command of Vice-Admiral William Halsey, were sending out planes to attack Japanese bases on these islands, at this time the Japanese were winning.

9. This is an exaggeration, but it illustrates the fact that the children of many well-to-do residents of the Philippines were reared primarily by servants rather than by their parents.

10. The chef was a White Russian who before the war had been manager of the Pines Hotel, a leading resort in Baguio. After the war he became a chef at Trader Vic's restaurant in San Francisco, and later manager of Trader Vic's in Beverly Hills. (N. C. and J. H.)

11. An unwittingly ironic comment. Although the Americans had not surrendered, MacArthur had left for Australia on March 11.

12. An Authentic is a report of a news event that Natalie believed to be true. Sometimes Natalie distinguishes between *Authentics* and *rumors,* unreliable or unverified news reports; at other times she simply refers to news reports in general as *rumors.* Until May 1942, with the arrival of the secret radio, Jim didn't have access to authentic news. See note 18, p. 530.

13. This is a mixture of true and false information. During the January-February counteroffensive, the Soviets were making deep advances on the German front. Thailand was occupied by the Japanese and was their base of operations for the invasion of Burma; at this time British and Chinese forces were fighting the Japanese in Burma. On March 11 MacArthur had gone to Australia, which did not have air supremacy; nor did the U.S. Navy have the control over the seas or air that this rumor implies. The information about Davao, Wake, and Guam is largely true. The fighting on Cebu presaged its fall on April 10.

14. Claude L. Stewart, a Jamaica-born businessman, and his father, George, were the only blacks in prewar Baguio, and Claude was the only black in camp. For social purposes, these local blacks were considered "white"; the principal racial distinction was made between whites and Orientals. (J. H.)

15. Daphne A. R. Bird, whose illustrations appear in this volume, was married to Godfrey V. Bird, a distinguished English architect who was stationed in Hong Kong during the war. Of the several captive British women of high social status (including a first cousin of the future British Prime Minister Harold Macmillan and a second cousin of then queen consort Elizabeth), Daphne Bird had the reputation among American internees of being the most relaxed and democratic. Many *Diary* entries reveal Natalie's appreciation of Daphne's artistic contributions to the camp.

16. The Japanese were releasing some missionaries to live in town. Later the Japanese decided that they should be moved back into camp for greater ease of surveillance. See also note 50, below.

17. Natalie is wrong. The plane was Japanese, though at the time the Americans didn't believe that the Japanese had four-engined planes. Not until the thousandth day of their internment did the prisoners see any American planes. (J. H.)

18. Except for the item about Mindanao, the information in this resumé is essentially correct.

19. The reference is to the Bataan Death March, in which 700 Americans and 13,000 Filipinos died. They were forced to walk up to ninety miles, from Mariveles Air Field and elsewhere on Bataan, to San Fernando before being taken to Camp O'Donnell. Many more captives died afterward from effects of the ordeal. The march became the symbol of Japanese cruelty, and a rallying point for American and Filipino resistance.

20. This was not true. (See note 24, p. 543.)

21. Natalie was voluntarily doing more than her share, hoping that others would follow her example.

22. Natalie's unusual sophistication about nutrition was a result of her own reading and of her conversations with the doctors in camp, who were continually investigating the nutritional properties of native foods. Thus, they looked for sources of protein in native vegetables, fermented bananas to get Vitamin B, and even produced sweetening from boiled-down sweet-potato peelings. Some of their findings, such as the excellent protein content of tropical winged beans, are being rediscovered thirty-seven years later. (J. H.)

23. Dr. Lee's husband, Major Lee, was fighting with the American forces against the Japanese, who wanted to use her imprisonment as a lure to encourage him to surrender. He was later captured.

24. Leung Nang was the proprietor of the Baguio Bakery and a leader of the Chinese community in Baguio. He was questioned because the Japanese were trying to bring into Camp Holmes the Chinese who were hiding in the mountains, many of whom were old and infirm. These remained in camp only briefly; the Japanese officially considered Philippine Chinese "brother Orientals" and gradually released them.

Throughout the war Leung Nang was one of the principal suppliers of food to the camp; his efforts on behalf of the internees were acknowledged by the award of the American Medal of Freedom after the war. (J. H.)

25. A guarantor was responsible for the good behavior of internees released from camp into the Baguio vicinity. The Reverend Carl Eschbach had already been released (see note 16, above). He was reinterned on November 12, 1942.

26. The "paper" was a pledge that they wouldn't undermine the Japanese war effort.

27. At this time a few American internees, long-time residents of the Baguio vicinity whom the Japanese regarded as "safe," were released from internment and allowed to live in their homes under the equivalent of house arrest. These people had to have an Oriental resident sponsor them to guarantee that they wouldn't work against the Japanese. Former Baguio Mayor Halsema and his wife, Jim's parents, were released in this manner and lived in Baguio throughout the war. Ironically, the senior Halsema was killed on March 15, 1945, in an American Air Force raid to free Baguio. (J. H.)

28. This information is almost accurate; there were sixteen planes in the raid. It was extremely important for American morale and forced the Japanese to keep four army fighter groups at home to defend Tokyo and other cities instead of deploying them on attack in the South Pacific (Liddell Hart, p. 345).

29. The week before June's birth.

30. See February 25, 1942. The Japanese had confiscated the school textbooks and had forbidden the teaching of American history or anything to do with democracy.

The teachers nevertheless taught the subversive subjects secretly and switched to safe subjects when the Japanese guards came within earshot. Jim Halsema taught geography and drew maps carefully modeled after originals found in books and magazines around the camp. He concealed this atlas beneath an innocent-looking cover prepared by Daphne Bird, which was labeled *Jim's Book of Fairy Tales* to deceive Japanese who might have seen it. The homemade atlas proved an invaluable means of checking the progress of American forces in the latter part of the war. (J. H.*)

31. The Constabulary was a national Philippine police force begun by the Americans and later reestablished by the Japanese. During the war its members were widely regarded as Japanese collaborators and were not trusted by either the Japanese or the Filipinos. (J. H.)

32. The essence of this information is true. Liddell Hart estimates Japanese casualties at 12,000. Nevertheless, this is a small number in comparison with the American loss of 30,000 in the total Bataan-Corregidor campaign.

33. Dr. Hall was severely ill and required surgery, transfusions, and treatment for postsurgical infections. Although Natalie's *Diary* does not reveal the nature of his illness, Halsema's recollection is that Dr. Hall, a noted authority on bacillary dysenteries, was suffering from dysentery with complications due to his age (sixty-eight) and previous poor health. His life was saved by the skill of another doctor with whom he had been feuding over differences of opinion on ways of running the hospital.

34. Aurora Aragon de Quezon, wife of Manuel Quezon, President of the Philippines, 1935–44 (in exile 1942–44).

35. A commercial vegetable shortening made of coconut fat.

36. This information is true in essence, though some of the figures are inaccurate.

In the Battle of the Coral Sea, May 7–8, the United States lost the *Lexington*, one destroyer, one oiler, and seventy-four planes; the Japanese lost eighty planes but only a light carrier. Here the Americans thwarted the Japanese objective, capture of Port Moresby in New Guinea (Liddell Hart, pp. 347, 349).

The news about the Solomons puts a somewhat positive interpretation on events that were disastrous for the United States, partly by ignoring the Battle of Savo Island, August 7–8, in which five Allied cruisers were sunk or damaged, with no losses to the Japanese (Liddell Hart, p. 358). On the other hand, in the Battle of Midway, June 4, heavy Japanese losses (four carriers, one heavy cruiser, and 330 planes) outweighed the U.S. loss of the *Yorktown*, one destroyer, and 150 planes and marked the turning of the war in the Pacific in the Allies' favor.

37. Philippine language groups.

38. Rufus F. Grey, twenty-six, was an American Baptist missionary whom the Japanese had accused of being an American spy because he had served in China and spoke Chinese. Bitter enemies of China, the Japanese mistrusted anyone with a Chinese affiliation. See *Diary* entry for April 14, 1942.

39. An area south of Boston, not far from Savin Hill where Natalie had grown up.

40. On May 30 and June 1, the British Bomber Command attacked Cologne and Essen, respectively, in night raids using more than 1,000 massed bombers. Düsseldorf, located midway between these cities, is not mentioned as a target. In fact, no mention is made of Düsseldorf as a bombing target until the next year between March and July, when the British conducted forty-three raids in the Battle of the Ruhr (Liddell Hart, pp. 598, 600). (G. T.) See *Diary* entry for June 13, 1943.

41. The Japanese were looking for a guerrilla leader, Herman Kluge, who had been employed by Arthur in his lumber company before the war. Arthur's company had sawmills located at several points along the road from Baguio to Bontoc, and they made ideal bases for subversive activity. The Japanese had taken Arthur out of camp to try to determine what he knew of Kluge's activities and whether they were in collaboration. Kluge finally surrendered to the Japanese when they began to kill Igorot civilians in retaliation for his successful forays, and he was executed. His wife spent the war hidden by Ifugaos. (J. H.)

42. Woven fiber bags containing food and supplies from Filipinos and other friends of the internees in Baguio were collected by a camp-operated van from a central repository in the Baguio market and were brought to camp en masse. The donors did not usually bring them to camp in person; hence the alarm over this irregularity. Empty bags were returned to the market stall, claimed by their owners, and reused. (J. H.)

43. In the Women's Committee elections. See *Diary* entry for August 13, 1942.

44. Clare Boothe.

45. See *Diary* entry for July 29, 1942.

46. For illicit consumption by the hospital staff.

47. Dr. Dean had volunteered to be sent to Los Baños internment camp as their chief surgeon because they were short of doctors and Camp Holmes was well supplied. However, Dean did not actually leave until September 14, 1943.

48. These rumors are not true.

49. See below, note 64.

50. A number of missionaries and their children were briefly released from camp on September 14, 1942. Among them was Peg Tong, the wife of missionary Walter Tong, who was interned at Davao. He was allowed to rejoin his family on March 13, 1944. See *Diary* entry for November 12, 1942.

51. As the Crouters might have been if they had sent the children to Boston before the war broke out.

52. These had been siphoned off by grafters, not used as community supplies, and the Crouter family got nothing back.

53. This was a great exaggeration of Japanese casualties but is typical of the rumors that gave heart to the internees (see note 32, above).

54. Guerrilla activity early on October 15 slightly damaged Trinidad Bridge. This was the first direct military action the internees had experienced in ten months. (J. H.)

55. From an abscessed tooth.

56. Tom Poulson, the camp goatherd, had died after surgery for appendix adhesions, which were attached to a kidney. Natalie had evidently forgotten about Paul Thorson's funeral. See *Diary* entry for August 11, 1942.

57. The dentist was sick with a high fever.

58. This decline resulted from the release of a number of missionaries and a few Baguio citizens to "house arrest." A number of internees from Camp Holmes had been transferred to other internment camps in the Philippines, sometimes to join relatives already there.

59. The Germans still held positions at Stalingrad and were on the attack until the Russian counteroffensive of November 19, 1942 (see note 64, below).

60. Natalie is evidently referring to the Battle of El Alamein, October 23–November

4, in which 75,000 Axis troops were killed, wounded, or captured (Miller, p. 413). General Bernard Montgomery's Eighth Army forces originally numbered 230,000 against General Erwin Rommel's 80,000; the British also had a six-to-one fighting superiority in tanks. The battle was a significant rout of Rommel's German forces (Miller, p. 413; Liddell Hart pp. 296–301).

61. The Japanese had accused these men of giving aid to guerrillas and jailed them. On November 11 the men were released from jail and reinterned.

62. Kata Kana is straight-line, or "square," Japanese syllabic writing, as opposed to Hiri Gana, which is Japanese cursive syllabic writing. (M. O.)

63. The naval Battle of Guadalcanal, November 13–15, began when a small number of American planes, reinforced by American ships, attacked a Japanese fleet so swiftly that the Japanese began firing on their own ships in the dark. As they fled, American planes continued to chase them toward their northern bases. The Japanese lost twenty-eight ships, with heavy damage to ten more; the Americans lost two cruisers and seven destroyers.

64. The siege of Stalingrad, which began August 24, 1942, pitted Hitler's command of "No retreat" against Stalin's of "No surrender." The Russians counterattacked at Stalingrad, November 19–23, and surrounded 330,000 German troops. By January 31, 1943, the German forces had been decimated to 92,000 and finally surrendered, including twenty-four generals. The German Army never fully recovered from the effects of this diasaster on their morale (Liddell Hart, p. 479).

65. See Introduction, p. xix. When 104 newcomers had to be accommodated, Dr. Dean, as chairman of the settling in, broke up this unique family arrangement.

66. The Filipino spouses of American internees were not interned unless they requested it, and the Filipino wives and children of these men had not been interned. The Japanese treated people who considered themselves Filipino as Filipinos, and those Filipinos who identified themselves as Americans as Americans. Thus, Filipino spouses who wished to be regarded as American were interned. (J. H.)

67. Jorge B. Vargas (b. 1890), lawyer, businessman, and bureaucrat, was extremely powerful during the Commonwealth era of the Philippine government because of close connections to President Manuel Quezon, who appointed him head of the Office of President 1939–41 and Secretary of Justice in 1941. The Japanese appointed Vargas Chairman of the Executive Commission, the Japanese-dominated civil administration in the Philippines during the war. Vargas became increasingly anti-American and pro-Japanese, pliable to their interests. He proclaimed the fall of Bataan and Corregidor a vindication "of all Asiatic peoples" and a year later promised that the Filipinos would stand with Japan "in joy and in suffering, in peace and in war." In July 1947, he was indicted on 115 counts of treason and collaboration, but his case was dismissed under the Amnesty Proclamation of the first postwar Philippine president, Manuel Roxas. (J. H.; David J. Steinberg, *Philippine Collaboration in World War II* [Ann Arbor: University of Michigan Press, 1966], pp. 66–70, 160–62, 190–91.)

68. Leung Shank was a leading Chinese grocer in Baguio, not to be confused with Leung Nang (see note 24, above).

69. Bedie had dysentery; Natalie does not indicate what the "drastic treatment" was.

1943

1. Natalie rightly suspects the truth of this. Luce was not jailed; however, "The President detested both Luce and his wife, and the feeling was reciprocated. The Luce magazines were among the President's severest critics. . . . Late in 1942 [Luce] applied for war correspondent credentials because he wanted to visit Chunking. The papers were not forthcoming; he appealed . . . in a personal interview, to Roosevelt himself. . . . The President promised to look into the matter, but the credentials were never issued while Roosevelt lived. Luce was convinced that [the denial] was an act of spite." (Robert E. Elson, *The World of Time Inc.* [New York: Atheneum, 1973].)

2. June had flu symptoms, which by January 17 developed into dysentery so severe that she was hospitalized.

3. The rumor is false; Wake Island had not been recaptured.

4. Sy Stone, who had escaped from camp on July 17, 1942, had been captured. The Japanese had been holding him for some weeks in the Baguio jail and torturing him repeatedly, both for his escape and his guerrilla activities while Outside.

5. At Casablanca on January, 14–24, Roosevelt and Churchill conferred on war strategy. They planned a seaborne assault on Rangoon, decided to move against Sicily to clear sea passage through the Mediterranean and to divert German pressure from the Russian front, discussed North African invasions, agreed to wage an all-out war of "unconditional surrender" against the Nazis and to turn to throw all their strength against Japan once the Nazis were defeated (Liddell Hart, pp. 368, 438).

6. "Swords" is Natalie's metaphor for high-ranking Japanese officers. Alarmed by the outbreak of dysentery, these officers, some scientists among them, had come to inspect the camp sanitation, the hospital, and the medical treatment. Arthur is wrong.

7. The survivors of the Bataan Death March were taken to Camp O'Donnell near Capas in Tarlac Province. American prisoners of war were sent from there to Cabanatuan camp, and the Filipinos were released. Far more POWs died there than on the Bataan Death March. (J. H.)

8. Natalie is reflecting on the difficulties of Bedie's birth, which was complicated by the fact that Natalie was allergic to ether and the doctor was performing his first Caesarean by local anesthetic. Bedie was born with a heart murmur, which caused his family to consider him delicate, though he had outgrown the condition by this time. (J. W.)

9. Between January and May 1943, the American Fifth Air Force and Australian units battled the Japanese for air superiority at Rabaul and elsewhere, and accomplished their purpose by May. Rostov had been captured on July 23, 1942. On February 16, 1943, the Soviets recaptured Kharkov, which was retaken by the Germans on March 14. Soviet troops did not recapture Kiev until November 6, 1943.

10. Bado Dangwa, an Igorot educated as a boy at La Trinidad Farm School, had been taught by Arthur to drive a car and had started a jitney service to his home village. By the time the war began, he was the manager of Dangwa Tranco, a bus line whose open-sided vehicles ran to every mountain village accessible by road. Putting his buses at the disposal of the American Army to take troops to Bataan, he became a leading guerrilla under Colonel Russell R. Volckmann of the American Army. By war's end this force had become a full-fledged army division, helping to

bottle up remaining Japanese forces. Dangwa, a hero, became the first elected governor of Mountain Province. (J. H.)

11. The poll on women's suffrage had been conducted to silence those who had petitioned for it. That it was not held in good faith is evident from the fact that the Men's Committee, which had the principal power among the internees, disregarded the results of the poll for another two weeks (see Introduction, p. xx, and note 13, below).

12. One member of the Executive Committee was responsible for the management of each category—Finance, Health, and so on.

13. Throughout the text of the *Diary,* Natalie's discussions of camp politics are full of disguised names, initials, innuendoes, and allusions to personal and political alignments and underhanded behavior that she never specifies. Consequently it is difficult for an outside reader to sort out the issues and individuals, particularly since alignments are temporary and many points of contention are short-lived. Her interpretation of the Men's Committee's reasons for granting women the right to vote in general elections is that it wanted a broader electorate, which would vote some of the Committee favorites into power. However, since this occurred two weeks after the poll on women's suffrage, it may also be a slightly belated acknowledgment of the majority vote.

14. Natalie later observed that the noise may have been made to "cover up listening to a hidden radio." Jim Halsema explains that although the radio was indeed in the hospital, concealed in a cupboard behind a false set of supply shelves, the listeners always hid in the cupboard and wore earphones (made of an old telephone), so no noise escaped.

15. Martha Ozawa explains that the traditional Samurai definition of Ronin is "a masterless warrior," as in the story Natalie tells here. Over thirty-six years the usage has changed; currently someone refused admission to college because of poor test scores is called *Ronin*—a new type of "masterless wanderer."

16. The information in this booklet is essentially correct (see note 36, p. 535). The attack at Dutch Harbor occurred on June 3–4. On June 7 a small force of Japanese troops captured Kiska and Attu unopposed. Liddell Hart says that although this looked like an important strategic gain, the foggy, rocky islands were actually unsuitable for either air or naval bases (p. 352). The submarine attack off the Oregon coast in June 1942 shelled Fort Stevens.

17. See note 62, p. 537.

18. See Introduction, p. xv.

19. Rufus F. Grey, who had been tortured and killed by the Japanese military police in Baguio and had died on March 15, 1942, was the only war-related death among the internees throughout the war. See *Diary,* entry for July 29, 1942.

20. To find guerrillas in hiding.

21. Herbie Wick had been sent out to bring in other guerrillas and had not yet returned.

22. This is a reference to the letter "to Americans and British at large," signed by the Committee and used for propaganda purposes by the Japanese. See *Diary* entry for May 16.

23. It is true that the Solomons were not entirely in Allied control by that date. The attack on the Solomons was begun on August 7, 1942, when the Marines and

a Naval task force bombarded Guadalcanal and soon captured the airport (Henderson Field). It was completed in November 1943 with the capture of Bougainville.

24. From recently repaid loans and money sent in by Nida Bacani.

25. Much of this "news" appears to be fabrication. However, on July 9–10 the Allied invasion of Sicily began, involving an armada of 2,500 ships, with air cover, and initial landings of 80,000 British and American troops and 300 tanks under generals Montgomery and George S. Patton. Thirteen Allied divisions eventually defeated twelve Axis divisions, completing the conquest of the island with the capture of Messina on August 17.

The invasion of northern France that Natalie describes here sounds like D-Day, the invasion of Normandy, which did not occur until eleven months later, on June 6, 1944. (See note 24, p. 543.) There is no evidence for the rumors about troop movements in Australia and the United States.

26. This was Baguio's share of relief funds from the International Red Cross.

27. Rabaul, the principal town of New Britain, was an important Japanese military center. MacArthur's strategy was not to try to take the heavily defended base there, but to isolate it through air attacks and landings on other parts of the island. Rabaul did not fall until the end of the war, but it was isolated and useless to the Japanese from late 1943 on. (J. H.)

28. A disease caused by Vitamin B deficiency, characterized by fatty diarrhea and, often, anemia.

29. The names mean, in order: demon, monkey, dog, pheasant, young boy's name, aunt, uncle. (M. O.)

30. "Congratulations" (polite form). (M. O.)

31. This rumor is unconfirmed. (G. T.)

32. The Japanese had a short-wave radio in the guardhouse, which they allowed the internees to use to hear broadcasts from the Japanese-controlled station in Manila. At times when non-English-speaking guards were on duty, the internees would "accidentally" tune in a Soviet-controlled station in Shanghai, China. Without shortwave, only the Manila station could be received. (J. H.*)

33. This rumor is false. Kiev was not recaptured until November 7, 1943.

34. The Manila *Tribune* had continued throughout the war, now appropriated by the Japanese and printed in English. The Japanese were planning to grant "independence" to the Philippines on October 14, 1943. The United States had promised independence to the Philippines by 1946, and this was granted, on schedule, after the war.

35. The first Allied landing in Borneo was not made by the Australian 1st Corps until May 1, 1945. In late 1943 the Allied advance in the South Pacific had reached only as far as western New Guinea (Liddell Hart, p. 688). (G. T.)

36. See *Diary* enries for November 7–12, 1942.

37. The internees' Medical Committee had used communally pooled funds to buy sufficient serum for the entire camp to receive a series of injections for cholera, typhoid, and dysentery. Natalie had recenly been given the first of the series.

38. Negative accounts of life in the United States, by Japanese repatriated from confinement there, were being used in the Japanese-sponsored newspapers for propaganda purposes.

39. This refers to the conference at Cairo between Roosevelt, Churchill, and Chiang Kai-shek in November 1943, followed by a meeting in Tehran later that month

between Roosevelt, Churchill, and Stalin; separate meetings were necessary because the Soviet Union was not fighting Japan. "At these conferences it was determined that the cross-channel attack through Normandy would have priority, along with supplementary landings in the south of France." In Italy the aim was to capture Rome, but with no Balkan campaign at that time (Liddell Hart, pp. 523, 526).

40. See note 18, p. 530.

41. In exchange for Japanese internees who had been repatriated, a small number of American internees were being sent home, with priority given to nonresidents stranded in the islands and to newspapermen. Considering the size of Camp Holmes, between five and ten persons should have been released. In fact, due to never-explained machinations in Manila, only one Baguio internee, William M. Portrude, a General Electric Company salesman from Shanghai, was released; he reached home via the *Teia Maru* and *Gripsholm*. (See *Diary* entry for September 27, 1943.) He was allowed to take with him a photograph of the camp's babies and their mothers. With his arrival in New York on December 1, 1943, relatives of internees were provided some information on Camp Holmes, both directly from Portrude and through an organization, Relief for Americans in the Philippines, that distributed a newsletter. (J. H.)

42. Naval and sea skirmishes were taking place well in advance of the first Allied landing in the Marianas in June 1944. This rumor may or may not have corresponded to an actual landing.

43. In his memoir written after attending the 1977 reunion of Camp Holmes internees, former commandant Rokuro Tomibe explained with pride how he cleverly avoided bribing the Japanese police during delivery of Red Cross packages to the internees:

[the MPs] ordered us to throw out [the cigarettes in the relief shipment] because the watch word on the wrapping paper of Old Gold cigarettes was agitative. It seemed to me that foreign cigarettes were mouth-watering goods for the military policemen and they wanted to confiscate all cigarettes [so they could keep them for themselves]. . . . But I only threw away the wrapping papers and stubbornly did not let them confiscate the contents.

44. Rabaul (see note 27, above) was not captured, but it was contained and isolated after December 1943. Tawara was taken by the Allies November 20–24, with heavy losses. Truk, a Japanese naval base in the central Pacific that was considered impregnable, was not bombed heavily until February 17–18, 1944 (see note 4, p. 542). (G. T.)

1944

1. At the onset of her first menstrual period June had begun to hemorrhage because of malnutrition. At this point the hemorrhaging had lasted two weeks, and June had become severely anemic.

2. The Soviet Army entered Poland on January 11, 1944, but made no significant advances until March of that year. The invasion of France did not occur until the summer of 1944 (Liddell Hart, p. 568). (G. T.)

3. Anzio, Italy, about 60 miles behind the Cassino line, was not far from Rome,

though Allied troops did not enter Rome until June 1944. Victories in New Guinea and New Britain gave the Allies control of the straits between central and southern Pacific waters (see notes 27, 44, pp. 540–41).

4. Truk had indeed been bombed on February 17–18; the Japanese lost 275 planes and 200,000 tons of shipping. Guam and Wake were not taken until July–August, 1944.

5. John S. Bellamy, Marguerite's oldest son, a Harvard law student at the beginning of the war.

6. Richard K. Bellamy, Marguerite's second son, later a partner in a public relations firm; and his younger brother, Peter Bellamy, subsequently drama critic for the Cleveland *Plain Dealer*.

7. Short, thigh-length Japanese coat, often worn over a kimono. (M. O.)

8. Nida was selling the Crouters' possessions and either sending them the money or using it to buy necessary items for them.

9. This is internee jargon and refers to the practice of "swinging" the beds by raising them high so as to provide more living space in the cramped quarters.

10. Kwo was a Korean army official in charge of Philippines prisoner-of-war camps (see p. 527).

11. Tomibe had secured a projector and films from Camp John Hay for the internees' entertainment. (J. H.)

12. Natalie maintains that the dentist had been consistently uncooperative throughout the war. At its outset he had hidden some of his dental supplies so the Japanese would not confiscate them, and he was reluctant to contribute either his private stores or his dental skills to the community. He also wanted to charge fees for his services. At this point the Executive Committee was trying, with limited success, to coax him into doing dental work for the internees, but the dentist was stalling. See *Diary* entry for May 5, 1944.

13. The Japanese were increasing the number of guards at Camp Holmes, having previously maintained only a nominal force. More guards would have made it harder to escape, though not until the latter part of the war did the Japanese put a fence around the camp. (J. H.)

14. KGEI was the American short-wave radio station in San Francisco. The rumors, however, are false. Bulgaria did not surrender until September 8, 1944; Rumania was not conquered until August 20–September 14, 1944.

15. Gene did not have a diary, but under torture, after he had been questioned repeatedly as to the source of news in the camp, he named Jim Halsema. Fortunately, Jim was never asked about what he might know about the escapes and their sponsor, who was still in the camp, but only about his news sources, which he maintained were Japanese-sponsored, English-language newspapers. (J. H.*)

16. Jim Halsema has supplied additional information about the interrogation and torture. There were ten men to each 8-by-8-foot cell in the underground portion of the former Philippine Cold Stores building, commandeered by the Kempetai (military police) as their headquarters. The prisoners, who had to crawl in and out through a low doorway—a further humiliation—were taken upstairs for interrogation, where they were strung up by their thumbs for several hours in the so-called parrot's-beam treatment. Their thumbs and adjacent parts of their hands were so damaged that they could not be used for days afterward and might have become gangrenous had not the Filipinos incarcerated with them massaged thier hands to restore circulation. The

Filipino prisoners also fed the injured Americans, when their injuries prevented them from feeding themselves.

The Kempetai eventually killed some of the Filipino prisoners, but the Americans were returned to Camp Holmes, Tomibe insisting that they remain in his jurisdiction unless the Kempetai could prove they had aided the escapees. Tomibe sent a truck to return the prisoners to camp and formally apologized to Jim for his maltreatment with a symbolic dish of sweetened beans.

17. See also *Diary* entries for February 22 and March 18, 1944.

18. This was not true. The invasion of France began on June 6, 1944.

19. This is unlikely (see note 27, below).

20. Green had resigned as head of the Finance Committee to express his opposition to the Family Unit plan. The Executive Committee had accepted his resignation and had held a new election the day before, in which Fabian, head of the Shop, was elected on an "anti-cubicle ticket." The Japanese, particularly Tomibe, who supported cubicle living, consequently disapproved of the election, and are here exercising their ultimate authority.

21. The Crouters didn't have a family cubicle because both Natalie and Jerry were living in barracks that hadn't voted to "cubiclize," and a given building's arrangements had to be all or nothing—with the initial exception of Enid's and Arthur's private quarters.

22. The Presbyterian mission in the Philippines owned a group of vacation cottages in Baguio. These were now being torn down, and the materials were being brought into camp for building purposes. (J. H.)

23. Natalie's information is nearly correct. The Soviets attempted to recapture Sevastopol on the night of May 6, but the German force held on doggedly until May 10, when the garrison retreated into the Khersonese peninsula. The 30,000 Germans finally surrendered on May 13 (Liddell Hart, p. 576).

24. The D-Day invasion of the Normandy coast had been accomplished on June 6, involving large numbers of American, British, and Canadian troops.

25. These are false rumors. Paris was not liberated until August 25, 1944; Warsaw, on January 14, 1945.

26. This rumor is false. The Soviet Union eventually declared war on Japan on August 8, 1945 (following the dropping of the first atomic bomb on Hiroshima on August 6, and the day before the atomic bombing of Nagasaki) and immediately attacked Manchuria. The last-minute entry by the Soviets into a war that was nearly over was calculated to reinforce Stalin's demand to share in the occupation of Japan and other Eastern territories. Roosevelt and Churchill had reluctantly agreed to this plan at the Yalta Conference in February 1945 (Liddell Hart, pp. 607–98).

27. According to Liddell Hart (pp. 690–91), air strikes against Japan were merely diversionary at this point and had no serious impact until December 1944. Osaka is reported as having been devastated by incendiary bombs March 9–16, 1945, along with 16 square miles of Tokyo. (G. T.)

28. M. Hamlin Canon, in *Leyte: The Return to the Philippines* (Washington, D.C.: Office of the Chief of Military History, 1954), says:

The first aerial strikes since 1942 [on the Philippines] were made in the early fall of 1944. On 1 September B-24s from New Guinea bases initiated their first large-scale attack against airdromes in the Davao area. On 4 September the first aerial reconaissance flights were made over Leyte. During the period 9–14 September Admiral Mitscher launched a large-scale, carrier-based air assault against the Japanese air defenses in the Philippine Islands in order to protect the Palau and Morotai landings. . . . On 21 September Central Pacific carrier-based aircraft directed their attention to the Luzon area. . . . On 11 October the flyers struck at Luzon (pp. 42–43).

However, another source reports a Philippines bombing August 5–6, 1944: "A rather ineffectual single bomber strike on Sasa airdrome, six miles north of Davao," with continued harassment in this area throughout August (*The Army Air Forces in World War II*, ed. Wesley F. Craven and James L. Cate [Chicago: University of Chicago Press, 1948–58], vol. V).

29. Part of this information is true. Natalie is referring to the militarily decisive Battle of the Philippine Sea, June 19–21, with heavy air and sea losses for the Japanese. This effectively opened the way for the Allies to recapture the Philippines and the Marianas (Liddell Hart, pp. 617–19). At this time, military historians agree, the Soviets could have taken Warsaw but for reasons never fully explained did not do so; the Germans rallied, and the Soviets did not enter Warsaw until January 17, 1945. The reference to Goebbels is false.

30. The Crouters had received several encouraging letters from relatives, including Natalie's eighty-eight-year-old mother and Natalie's sister Ethel.

31. The rumors about the Soviets conquering Berlin and Warsaw at this time are both in error. Soviet troops had surrounded Berlin on April 25, 1944. Warsaw was not yet taken (see note 29, above). (Liddell Hart, pp. 663–65.) Paris had been recaptured from the Germans on August 25, 1944.

32. The money was from people in the Baguio area who wanted to use it before it lost more value. Inflation was escalating rapidly, and the currency was highly unstable.

33. MacArthur's forces did indeed land on Morotai on September 15, essentially unopposed, and MacArthur went ashore later the same day. However, remnants of some fighting Japanese units were not subdued for several months (*Facts on File Yearbook*, 1944, pp. 294–95). (G. T.)

34. Most of the information in the preceeding paragraph is correct. However, the London blackout was not lifted until V-E Day in May 1945. (J. H.)

35. Natalie had misplaced the vitamins among her possessions and had forgotten she had them. When she was hospitalized, her children had found them in her bag and brought them to her.

36. American planes were at this virtually "covering the Philippines," but the United States did not have a hundred aircraft carriers. (Liddell Hart, Chapter 34). The Japanese are exaggerating the strength of their adversaries at this point.

37. Natalie is thinking in prewar terms, when one peso equaled 50 U.S. cents. By this time, given inflation, the peso was virtually worthless, and most transactions were by barter.

38. MacArthur and 132,400 American troops had landed on Leyte on October 20–22. There were no landings on Mindanao or Luzon at this time. Liddell Hart observes: "At this stage of the war it might well have been possible for the United States forces to by-pass the Philippines, and move on in their next bound to Formosa,

or to Iwo Jima and Okinawa, as Fleet Admiral King and several other naval chiefs urged. But political considerations, and MacArthur's natural desire for a triumphant return to the Philippines, prevailed against such arguments for by-passing these great islands'' (p. 620).

39. *Shantung Compound: The Story of Men and Women Under Pressure* (New York: Harper and Row, 1966), an account by Langdon Gilkey, a civilian interned in Shanghai, bears out this assertion. See *Diary* entry for January 3, 1944.

40. This appears to be a reference to the Battle of Leyte Gulf, four separate actions on October 17–23, "the largest naval battle of all time," in which 282 ships and hundreds of planes were engaged. The Japanese lost four carriers, three battleships, six heavy cruisers, three light cruisers, and eight destroyers; the Americans lost only one light carrier, two escort carriers, and three destroyers (Liddell Hart, pp. 622–27).

41. The great American naval victory in the Battle of Leyte Gulf probably gave rise to the unfounded rumors of landings on Marinduque and Mindoro. Mindoro was not invaded until December 15. Many of these rumors undoubtedly were due to misperceptions by people who had difficulty understanding some of the radio broadcasts (never very good on short-wave) and mistook air-attack reports for landings. (J. H.)

42. No actual deaths from malnutrition occurred in Camp Holmes during the war. Helen's death on October 31, 1944, was the culmination of ten years of poor health due to heart trouble; however, chronic malnutrition may have exacerbated her health problems and those of others. Natalie is accurate on February 26, 1945, when she says "No casualties, only one death from torture."

43. For a considerable time Natalie had been at odds with the woman—identified only as R. in the *Diary*—whose space was next to hers in the Women's Barracks. Their differences of opinion included disputes over space allocation—33 inches for R., 30 for Natalie; over the fact that without consulting the whole room Natalie had curtained off her space, thus angering R; and she had further angered R. by insinuating that R's opposition to the Family Unit Plan stemmed from marital problems. R. vented some of her antagonism at June, who was unprotected while her mother was in the hospital (see *Diary* entry of September 19, 1944). The "blowup" mentioned here—a raging argument—finally occurred when Jerry defended both wife and daughter before R. and her husband.

44. This may have been either a burned-over area near camp or an area farther away that had been burned as a result of a Japanese search-and-destroy effort to smoke out guerrillas. (J. H.)

1945

1. According to Jim Halsema, there were no Americans in Tarlac at this time (see note 7, p. 538).

2. A "protected city" is a city under military "protection" by its captors, who will fight to defend it. In an "open city," those in control have agreed not to defend it and potential attackers are consequently obliged not to strike. Admiral Iwabachi, commanding the Manila naval base, refused to obey General Yamashita's order to make Manila an open city and "fanatically persevered in a house-to-house fight" that

continued nearly an additional month, until March 4, and destroyed the city. His 16,000 marines died almost to the last man; only a dozen were captured (Liddell Hart, p. 630).

3. New England Trust. This was Natalie's checkbook from her American bank account in Boston.

4. An emergency appendectomy was performed on Rupert M. Foley, Jim Halsema's brother-in-law. Too late the doctors discovered that the cause of his pains was dysentery, not appendicitis. He eventually recovered. (J. H.*)

5. The Walled City ("Intramuros") was a 1-by-1/2-mile portion of Manila on the Pasig River and Manila Bay and surrounded by a 16-foot-high wall and moat. Originally a fortress built by the Spanish (1571), Intramuros was the last stand of the Japanese marines in February–March 1945, when six days of heavy artillery firing destroyed the district. (J. H.)

6. Central Intelligence Commission, predecessor to the CIA.

7. The preparations were for the United Nations Conference on International Organization, which met at San Francisco from April 25 to June 26, 1945, and drafted the U.N. Charter.

Epilogue: 1945–1980

1. A case in point is Helen Epstein's moving *Children of the Holocaust: Conversations with Sons and Daughters of Survivors* (New York: G. P. Putnam's Sons, 1979).

2. June Wortman, conversation with LZB, May 21, 1979.

3. *Ibid.*

4. *Ibid.*

5. *Ibid.*